## BOOKS BY MORTON HUNT

THE MUGGING (1972)

THE AFFAIR (1969)

THE WORLD OF THE FORMERLY MARRIED (1966)

THE THINKING ANIMAL (1964)

THE INLAND SEA (1964)

THE TALKING CURE (1964)
WITH RENA CORMAN AND LOUIS ORMONT

MENTAL HOSPITAL (1962)

HER INFINITE VARIETY (1962)

THE NATURAL HISTORY OF LOVE (1959)

# THE MUGGING

# THE MUGGING

## MORTON HUNT

ATHENEUM  NEW YORK  **1972**

FOR **BERNICE**

*because somehow, without knowing, I knew*

# *Prologue*

Ask virtually any American city-dweller today what crime he most fears, and feels he is most apt to be the victim of some day; in all likelihood he will answer: a mugging.

Yet vaster and far more dreadful crimes exist all around him: the savage acts and relentless extortions of Mafia "families" seeking and maintaining control over businesses, unions, and even political clubs; the white-collar crimes, so destructive of the moral premises on which our society is built, that are daily practiced by businessmen, politicians, and office employees; the widespread trafficking in heroin by dealers and pushers, actively aided by some of the very police assigned to narcotics control; and the bombing, arson, sniping, and other revolutionary acts by means of which urban guerrillas are turning parts of our major cities into battlefields.

But despite the magnitude and seriousness of these forms of crime, what most alarms us and most gravely damages our faith in our society is the ever present threat of some sudden, unpredictable, savage assault upon our own body by a stranger—a faceless, nameless, fleet-footed figure who leaps from the shadows, strikes at us with his fists, an iron pipe, or a switchblade knife, and then vanishes into an alley with our wallet or purse, leaving us broken and bleeding on the sidewalk. Headlines are made by riots, rapes, dope-smuggling, embezzlement, and kidnapping, while the mugging—moronically simple in execution and trifling in yield—is relegated to inside pages or ignored altogether; yet it is this, rather than the more complex and newsworthy crimes, that is responsible for the flight of millions of Americans to the suburbs, the nightly self-imprisonment of other millions behind locked doors and barred windows, and the mounting attacks of law-

and-order advocates upon constitutionally guaranteed rights that are fundamental to our concept of democracy.

Crimes of violence against the person—homicide, rape, robbery, and aggravated assault—have grown steadily more common for the past several decades until they have changed much of the tenor and character of daily life in America. At a conservative estimate, such crimes are three times as common today, per 100,000 population, as they were thirty years ago; in consequence, our feelings about our fellow men have sadly deteriorated and our freedom to do what we wish and to go where we like has radically diminished. This is truest in our great cities, for there the growing cancer of violent crime has metastasized, spreading wildly throughout the vitals of the urban organism: in cities of over 250,000 persons, the rate of violent crime has more than tripled in just the last ten years, profoundly disorganizing the patterns of everyday living developed by generations of city-dwellers.

Muggings play a very large part in all this; there are, however, no separate statistics dealing with them, since the term "mugging" has no formal status in law or police work, such crimes being variously lumped in with aggravated assaults, unarmed robberies, armed robberies, and homicides. But whatever their actual number, and whatever the total cost in injuries and stolen property, their impact on our civilization has been enormous and devastating. For when unpredictable violent attacks upon one's person become an ever present and uncontrollable danger, the great mass of citizens lose their faith in the integrity and viability of their society; they cease seeing themselves as members of a cooperating community of fellow creatures and no longer come to each other's aid or band together to seek broad solutions to the problem, but look individually for some private *modus vivendi,* some form of survival through retreat or escape. With this loss of belief and this erosion of the spirit of communality goes society's only chance of survival. As Sir Gilbert Murray once observed, the fall of Rome was brought about not by the decline of Roman morals, but by the loss of Roman morale.

But what are we to do? Solutions are propounded by experts of every sort, and overlooked by the general public; valuable studies are made by distinguished commissions, and ignored by lawmakers; each outbreak of crime, each police scandal, each prison riot is dealt with by proclamations, the reshuffling of personnel, a token reform or two, the granting of some federal funds for additional police weapons, a handful of pilot-project therapy programs in a few prisons, and some tinkering with court procedures to save a little time. Meanwhile, violent crimes continue to multiply, the harried police manage to solve a smaller proportion of them than ever, the court calendars and prisons are choked and unmanageable, and great cities sink slowly into medieval savagery.

A major reason for our apathy and for the inadequacy of our actions concerning crime and the criminal justice system is the depth of our ignorance. The average middle-class citizen has had very little personal experience of the police, criminal courts, city jails, trials, or prisons. Very few of us know what muggers are like as human beings, how and where muggings are most likely to occur, what effects they have upon the people who experience them directly or even indirectly, and what impact the criminal justice system has upon both the guilty and the innocent people caught up in its ponderous machinery.

What follows is an account of a single mugging and its sequelae, a chronicle of one such crime from its fundamental causes to its ultimate effects upon all the persons connected with it. Throughout the narrative I step aside to treat each aspect of the crime and the judicial process in broad national terms, and to explore the fundamental questions of law and liberty involved; these comments, taken together, add up to an overall portrait of violent crime, its impact on American society, and the efforts of that society to deal with it. But I myself learned as much about the subject, in a different and more intense fashion, from the narrative presented here of one such crime and what happened over the ensuing years to the victim and his acquaintances, the muggers and their families, the detectives, prosecutor, defenders, judges, juries, and the people who lived in the neighborhood where the attack took place. For this one story is something like an anatomy class in which, dissecting one body, the student sees how all mankind is constructed.

Listen, then, to the tale of Alexander Helmer, an elderly man of no distinction but of immense importance (for any one of us could have been, or someday may be, in his place); of four ghetto-reared Puerto Rican youths whose names have never made headlines; and of a crime all but unknown outside of one small neighborhood in Bronx County, New York. It is an urban tragedy of minuscule dimensions and yet of vast significance, for it is an archetype of tragedies occurring epidemically throughout the land and a foreshadowing of the vast debacle that will surely overtake America if we fail to take massive and daring—but rational and humane—actions not only to remake our entire criminal justice system, but to rid our society of those grave inequities that do so much to breed criminal behavior.

M. H.

*East Hampton, N.Y.*
*January 1972*

# Contents

Prologue     vii

## Chapter 1   The Score

I   *Alexander Helmer: A Mini-Biography*     3
II   *A Note on Victimology*     6
III   *The Victimal Behavior of A. Helmer*     8
IV   *Melrose: The Street, the Area, the Syndrome*     9
V   *Helmer Walking Homeward*     12
VI   *Muggings, Defined and Counted*     16
VII   *Helmer at the Threshold of Safety*     23
VIII   *The High Cost of Fear*     27
IX   *Helmer Plays His Part in a Nefarious Symbiosis*     35

## Chapter 2   The Investigation

I   *The Four-Two Precinct Gets a Seemingly Routine Call*     38
II   *A Policeman's Lot Is Not a Happy One*     45
III   *We Know a Lot Already*     52
IV   *Suspectology*     61
V   *Get Your Coat*     68
VI   *No Good Cop Would Do That*     79
VII   *I Believe It Was Voluntarily*     84

## Chapter 3   The Interrogation

I   *Opening Up*     93
II   *Forcibly Obtained Truth: A Contradiction in Terms*     102

III    *Anything You Say May Be Used Against You*            109
   IV    *Truthful Confessions and the Doctrine of Fairness*      117
V    *I Don' Remember Nothin'*                             122
   VI    *The Dispensability of Confessions*                  128
VII    *Do You Want to Tell Me What Happened?*               132


## Chapter **4**    *Detention*

I    *Keep Your Mouth Shut*                               137
   II    *The Law's Delay*                                  145
III    *What's Happening? Anything Happening?*              154
   IV    *Defenders of the Faith*                           162
V    *Leave It to Me*                                     169
   VI    *A Matter of Convictions*                          178
VII    *I'm Proud of My Record*                             184
   VIII    *Justice Without Trial*                           192
IX    *Are You Ready?*                                    198


## Chapter **5**    *A Matter of Credibility*

I    *Voir Dire*                                          201
   II    *The Purposes of Trial by Jury*                    207
III    *The People's Case*                                 214
   IV    *Credibility*                                      230
V    *The Defense*                                        235
   VI    *The Jury on Trial*                                252
VII    *The Sole and Exclusive Judges of the Facts*         260


## Chapter **6**    *The Presumption of Innocence*

I    *Cast Changes*                                       273
   II    *The Sequelae of* Gideon                          281
III    *The Best Defense*                                  287
   IV    *The Presumption of Innocence*                     306
V    *The Defendants in This Case, Gentlemen, Failed to Take
the Stand*                                               311
   VI    *The Benefit of the Doubt*                         321
VII    *How Say You, Gentlemen of the Jury?*                325

## Chapter 7    Correction

I   Is There Any Legal Cause to Show Why Judgment Should
Not Be Pronounced Against You?                          336
II   The Dilemma of the Criminal Sanctions               343
III  Prognosis Is Guarded                                350
IV   Functions and Dysfunctions of the American Prison   360
V   A Classic Example of the Institutionalized           368
VI   The Purpose of Judicial Review                      378
VII  The Defendant Appeals from the Judgment of the Supreme
Court, Bronx County (Lyman, J.)                          383

## Epilogue

1  Two Stories Without Endings                           400
2  The Growth of Crime and the Decline of American Cities  402
3  Limited Successes of the Police Approach to Crime Control  409
4  The Fear of Crime and the State of American Democracy  414
5  The Growing Fairness of the American Criminal Justice
System                                                   421
6  The Declining Efficiency of the American Criminal Justice
System                                                   428
7  Three Alternative Attitudes Toward Crime Control and
Democracy                                                441

Acknowledgments   447

Notes on Sources   449

Bibliography   463

Index   469

# THE MUGGING

# Chapter 1 The Score

## I  Alexander Helmer: A Mini-Biography

NINE blocks each way is a long distance to walk for a few dollars' worth of groceries, but Alexander Helmer was a frugal man and the A&P just above 151st Street on Melrose Avenue, in the south Bronx, was a few cents cheaper on most things than the dingy little Puerto Rican *bodegas* and Italian grocery stores nearer his apartment at 160th and Melrose. Besides, the A&P was large, bright, and thronged with people, and a leisurely amble down there and back along Melrose, nodding to a few old-timers and shopkeepers, milling about with the crowd in the supermarket, and exchanging a little small-talk with the manager, added up to an hour's excursion for him and was the high point of his day. For Helmer was one of those men J. Alfred Prufrock had feared to become—"lonely men in shirt-sleeves, leaning out of windows"—a single, tight-fisted old pensioner, wearing his pants until the tops of the thighs and the seat were smooth and shiny as satin, eating all his meals alone with a newspaper in his kitchen, filling his days with unnecessary little errands. And therefore, even though the once neat, once quiet, lower-middle-class neighborhood of

3

Melrose in which he had lived for most of his life had become clamorous, garbage-strewn, decrepit, and dangerous, as impoverished Negroes from the South and newly arrived Puerto Ricans crowded into it, Helmer decided to walk all the way to the A&P for one quart of milk, a loaf of bread, and a few other small items, late in the morning of Friday, October 9th, 1964, a date of no particular significance in his life, as far as he knew.*

It was a mild, partly sunny day, the noon temperature nearing 60° and the breeze gentle, but Helmer, a small, shallow-chested man of seventy-two, gaunt faced and rather bald, took no chances: under his shirt and trousers he had readied himself with a full-length winter union suit, and before going out he added a plaid woolen shirt on top of the white one, zipped himself into a brown windbreaker, and put on a brown fedora. Last of all, he screwed a flesh-colored Zenith hearing aid into his right ear and turned up the volume; being thrifty, he always saved on batteries by not using it until he went out, which was sensible enough in view of the fact that he had been living alone, and virtually without visitors, the past ten years, ever since his ailing sister Emma, who had shared his four-room walk-up apartment, had died.

In his youth Helmer had been a clean-looking lad, with the typically lank, blond, shining hair of his north-German ancestors; in a desk drawer in his living-room there was still a faded picture of him, young and scrubbed and grinning amiably in some summer garden long ago, and another showing him straight and trim in sailor's uniform (he had been a cook aboard ship) during World War I. But aside from his stint of military service, he never lived away from home, something never developed within him as it should have, and somehow in the course of many years as a milkman for Sheffield Farms he slowly changed into a settled, crotchety, middle-aged bachelor, living with his mother and sister, and then later, after both of them had died and Sheffield had retired him, into an aging, hollow-eyed, tight-lipped solitary, whose habits and thoughts were all but unknown to the people who lived around him. Like most reclusive people, and especially those who are hard of hearing, he was suspicious of everyone who lived near him; for years he had passed his landlady by without a word or nod of greeting, and the four neighbors

* As will appear later, there has been strenuous disagreement as to the exact time of the events being narrated; the weight of the evidence convinces me, however, as it did the jury at the second trial, that Mr. Helmer went to the store about noontime, and I tell the story accordingly.

whose front doors shared the second-floor landing with his own knew so little about him that once, when he spent two weeks in a hospital having an operation, no one noticed his absence.

Away from 399 East 160th Street, however, he was considerably more genial and talkative with casual acquaintances—fellow oldsters he met in a nearby park, storekeepers, a filling-station manager he sometimes stopped to pass the time of day with. To such people he often dropped unsubtle hints that he was well fixed (and indeed he had accumulated nearly $22,000, which he had invested in stocks), that he had no heirs, and that he might just put his listener in his will. He used this same pathetic device to maintain a tenuous connection with two widows, neither of whom he had seen in a decade —one a former switchboard operator at Sheffield, the other a woman whose husband he had known since his youth—exchanging holiday greeting cards with both of them and including in his greetings to each his lawyer's business card and a scribbled note saying, "Keep this card. I'll remember you in my will."

For the present, however, he had no intention of bestowing largess on anyone ahead of time. Indeed, he had broken off all contact with his relatives except for his older brother, George, whom he had recently visited in a nursing home for the aged, and when the manager of the home told him that the senile, helpless patient was running out of funds and asked Helmer to contribute, he had curtly refused, left in a hurry, and not returned. Oddly enough, he sometimes carried hundreds of dollars in his wallet, and kept other hundreds in cash in his apartment, as if he were likely to spend it for something enjoyable; but the mere sight and feel of it may have been more enjoyable than anything he could have spent it for.

## II  *A Note on Victimology*

ALTHOUGH every city-dweller is potentially a mugging victim, some are far more predisposed to attack than others. Those who are on the sidewalks late at night are, according to one recent study, three times as likely to be victimized as those who stay indoors after dark. But at least people often have some control over this factor; over their age they have none, though this too is a predisposing trait, the elderly being too slow-moving to escape and too feeble to offer effective resistance or counterattack, and hence being selected as victims more often than the young. A related factor is the presence of impedimenta of one sort or another: the person carrying a large grocery bag home is, other things being equal, slower-moving, less able to look around, and less able to offer any defense than one carrying nothing, and thus more likely to be selected as a victim.

A fourth element is dress. Until recently, according to crime statistics, the largest number of victims of robberies have been poor people, primarily because they were the closest at hand to the robbers. Today, however, when urban decay is causing slum areas to grow up within, or to intrude upon, solidly working-class or middle-class neighborhoods, the pattern is changing; along and just within the borders of the healthy neighborhoods, the man or women whose clothing indicates that he or she has at least a modest income, and is therefore likely to be carrying a fair amount of cash, is particularly prone to attack. A fifth factor is race, which is, obviously, somewhat correlated to that of dress. Although most assaults and most homicides are committed by people of the same race as the victims—indeed, by relatives, friends, or acquaintances of the victims, in the course of family or personal fights—robberies are another matter: almost half of them are interracial, the victims being whites and the criminals Negroes (or, in some cities, Puerto Ricans) who are total strangers to them. Non-white muggers most often choose white strangers as their victims not only to avoid being recognized and caught, but because such people, by and large, are more likely than non-whites to have a fair amount of cash upon them—and also because many muggers undoubtedly derive special satisfaction from "making a hit" upon a representative of the hated oppressors.

Still another parameter of susceptibility concerns numbers. A person walking alone is far more apt to be a target than one walking with a companion, even when the latter is elderly and frail. Yet another is propinquity: mugging is unskilled and unprofessional work, the kind of crime committed chiefly by youthful novices—many of them drug-addicted—from racial ghettos; such criminals function at very low levels of efficiency, having neither the drive, the daring, the experience, nor the clarity of mind to forage more than a short distance from their usual haunts in search of victims. Many if not most muggings therefore occur along the interface between slums and middle-class neighborhoods, or in neighborhoods undergoing a turbulent mixing of classes and races, rather than deep within solidly white middle-class areas in which the muggers would look and feel obviously out of place and suspicious.

Customarily and automatically we think of the doer of a violent crime as guilty, and of the victim as innocent, and in the case of an ideal mugging victim this seems both obvious and indisputable, for who would blame anyone for being old, white, or alone? But in recent decades certain criminologists, having analyzed the characteristics of a variety of victims, have advanced the notion that a great many of them voluntarily perform acts of commission or omission which contribute to, induce, or incite the criminal deeds done to them. Sociologist Hans von Hentig argues that a "nefarious symbiosis" often exists between criminal and victim, with the latter being an "activating sufferer" who stimulates the criminal response toward himself in someone else. Benjamin Mendelsohn, a Rumanian-born lawyer and behavioral researcher, and the first proponent of a science of "victimology," develops the concept further by subdividing victims into six categories of culpability, only one of which—that represented by such victims as children and unconscious persons—is wholly innocent of complicity. The wholly guilty type, in contrast, would be exemplified by the attacker who is injured or killed by the one he has chosen to attack, while the median and most common degree of "victimal" culpability might be typified by the woman who acts wanton and seductive, but only up to a point, and thus is partly responsible for her own rape.

This much is easy to see; what is less apparent is the complicity of those who, without seeming to, contribute to their own victimization by passivity, negligence, or imprudence. As Mendelsohn and various others have recently pointed out, there is a very substantial degree of responsibility on the part of those seemingly innocent victims whose flagrant carelessness about their property or persons has attracted criminals toward them. An example might be the case of a man who leaves the ignition key in his car while he goes into a store, or who flashes a large roll of bills in a public place; another is that of a woman who wears costly furs and jewels at times and in places where she is conspicuous, alone, and defenseless; a third is that of a man who, by injudicious or boastful talk, advertises himself as a moneyed, isolated, and vulnerable target.

---

---

# III   *The Victimal Behavior of A. Helmer*

---

ON nearly all counts (aside from the time of day) Alexander Helmer was a more than ordinarily good candidate for a mugging that Friday noon; indeed, the fact that it was Friday partly balanced out the time element, since robbery or theft accompanied by violence is more common on weekdays than on Saturdays or Sundays. In most respects he was not at all to blame for his victimal tendencies, but in at least two ways he was distinctly complicitous, in von Hentig's and Mendelsohn's sense. First, due to vanity, he had imprudently heightened his visibility as a target, for, despite his paranoid secrecy where his landlady and neighbors were concerned, he had been something of a braggart and blabbermouth with casual acquaintances, boasting of his stock-market holdings to half a dozen or more neighborhood people he knew only slightly, and making it plain that he lived alone and had no heirs—information which, passed along as idle gossip, could considerably increase his chance of victimization. Second, he had continued to live and to wander around in an area where predators were coming to abound, and where his personal traits marked him out as potential prey. The Melrose neighborhood had become distinctly dangerous during the past five to ten years, particularly that part of it a few blocks to the south of his residence, but he stubbornly (or perhaps blindly) remained in the apartment he had been in for twenty-five years and, in search of his meager ration of social contact and his bargain groceries, kept taking long walks down Melrose Avenue, past the decaying side-streets, past groups of street-corner loungers, and past the dark, urinous doorways and vacated stores that were the hangouts of local pushers and junkies.

Which is precisely what he did on this day. At the A&P, by noontime or a little after, Helmer had collected the things he needed and wheeled his shopping cart up to a checkout line being handled by Miss Annette Odierno, a tiny, dark-haired woman in her late thirties who had been punching an A&P register for twenty years, and who, without looking up, swiftly and mechanically checked out Helmer's little purchases—a quart of milk, a pint of ice cream, a few tomatoes and a couple of apples, a loaf of bread, half a dozen eggs, and a few other things—ringing up a total of $4.20 and stowing his purchases neatly in a medium-sized bag. Helmer left, and turned north, up Melrose Avenue, walking leisurely toward an unsuspected rendezvous.

---

# I V   *Melrose: The Street, the Area, the Syndrome*

---

MELROSE Avenue is moderately broad and busy: buses run both ways on it, there is a good deal of automobile traffic, and all day long a fair number of people are walking or lounging on the sidewalks, a welcome sight for a man who spends most of his waking hours alone at home. It had never been a beautiful thoroughfare—it was lined on both sides by four- to six-story brick tenement buildings with little shops at the ground level and tangles of iron fire-escapes hanging overhead, and the sidewalks had been built without allowance for grass or trees at the curbside, or room for shrubbery in front of the buildings—but in Helmer's earlier years the avenue had at least been neat, orderly, busy, and interesting. It was one of the several main north-south thoroughfares of that part of the south Bronx known as Melrose—a lower-income residential district very much like those established in many large American cities half a century or more ago which, though until recently sound and peaceful, are now rapidly succumbing to physical and social decay and turning into festering slums.

Melrose had been chiefly farmland until the mid-nineteenth century, when it slowly changed into a suburb of a couple hundred scattered frame houses. But the Third Avenue El reached it just before the turn of the century, making it easily accessible to working-class immigrants seeking to escape from the lower East Side of Manhattan; as a result, the area soon was solidly covered by cheap brick tenement buildings and inhabited by tens of thousands of people—Germans and Irish at first, Italians and Jews a little later. Along with the tenements, stores of all sorts sprang up, along with banks, movies, repair shops, and small industrial plants. The Italians and Irish built themselves several big churches, including one cathedral; the Germans made their own little Broadway of shops and *Bierstuben* along Morris Avenue; the Jews had their synagogues and even Yiddish theaters nearby. Somewhat noisy, altogether citified, Melrose was nevertheless much like a small town in its heterogeneity and completeness; as a report by the New York Department of City Planning wistfully puts it, "A person could grow up, live, work, worship, find recreation, grow old and die without ever leaving Melrose." And if this was not an exciting prospect, it was at least a comfortable one for many people. Reminiscing sadly a short while ago, Helmer's German-born landlady, Mrs. Anna Ambos, told a visitor, "In that time you don't have to lock no door, don't have to be afraid from notting. You could live in the proper vay then, not like now." Basically, it was a stable, modestly comfortable, law-abiding community of first-generation Americans who were doing pretty well, for immigrants, and hoping to see their children do much better.

And their children did. Soon after World War II the young white families on their way upward economically and socially began to desert Melrose for the suburbs. Partly they were seeking a quieter and more gracious way of life; partly, however, they feared, and were fleeing from, the integrated housing projects then coming into existence, one of which, Melrose Houses, was right in the heart of the area. This emigration of the younger middle-class families, which has been occurring in the row-house and tenement-apartment neighborhoods of nearly every major American city, is a self-propelling process: as young whites move out, leaving the aging apartments vacant, more recent immigrants and poorer people—mostly black—move in, increasing the motivation of the remaining young whites to get out. By the mid-to-late 1960s Melrose was only half white, the other half roughly equal parts of blacks and Puerto Ricans.

The population shift has undoubtedly been accelerated and furthered by fair-housing laws and the growth of urban welfare programs, which have enabled Negroes and Puerto Ricans to rent apartments in areas they would formerly have been excluded from or which they would not have been able to afford. The goals of these laws and programs are admirable, but in practice, rather than leading to integration and an improved standard of living for the underprivileged, their main result has all too often been the creation of new ghettos no better than the old ones. Without a radical revision of the newcomers' social and economic position in American society, they had nothing to show for the move to Melrose except different quarters; they not only brought with them all the wretched and disabling problems they had had in Harlem, the South, or Puerto Rico, but fell prey to a crop of new ones, engendered by their having ripped themselves out of a known cultural milieu and relocated in the midst of one that was unfamiliar, alien, and hostile.

Melrose, which had already grown faded and shabby during the Depression and World War II, now deteriorated rapidly, both physically and socially. The welfare load soared until it included nearly half the area's young people; streets grew filthy as the new immigrants took to disposing of their garbage by "air mail" (throwing it out the windows); by 1960, according to the Bureau of the Census, 42 percent of the residential apartments were in deteriorated or dilapidated condition (today the figure is well above 50 percent); the unemployment and juvenile-delinquency rates were soaring in 1964, and since have gone on to rank with the highest in the city, as have the venereal-disease and infant-mortality rates; and homicides, assaults, rapes, and robberies grew year by year until during the 1960s the police began to regard Melrose as another "jungle," and today often refer to it, only half in jest, as "enemy territory."

In all this, Melrose is neither unusual nor the worst such neighborhood in the Bronx; similar rotten spots have infected many formerly sound and wholesome parts of the borough, which, though a part of sinful New York City, has much the same workaday, stay-at-home quality, much the same practical, uninspired concerns, as many a more ordinary American city. Indeed, in its size (a million and a half persons), its combination of slums and fine neighborhoods, parks and industrial wasteland, urban renewal and urban decay, it could almost be a Midwestern commercial or industrial city of no particular distinction, not even in the overall rate or character of the crimes committed within it. For comparable conditions can be found in Newark, Philadelphia, Washington, Detroit, Chicago, and many other places; the disease is not peculiar to Melrose, the Bronx, or New York City, but is endemic in the nation—a disease with which we were infected in the very beginning, when we failed to live by our most basic principle—that all men should have the same rights and opportunities—and which now, after hundreds of years of incubation, and treatment by many halfhearted remedies, is erupting in virulent form and yielding its long-delayed but catastrophic results throughout the tormented body of our society.

## V  *Helmer Walking Homeward*

BY October 9th, 1964, the deterioration of Melrose had gone pretty far, though not as far as it has since then. Alexander Helmer, walking home up the avenue, could doubtless remember how it had been in the days of his early manhood and even his middle age; but much as an elderly person has had a lifetime to grow used to the slow changes that time makes in his face, only now and then becoming momentarily aware, when catching unexpected sight of himself in a mirror, of the strange ruin he inhabits, so Helmer had seen Melrose Avenue changing year by year, knew it was no longer what it had been, and yet was used to it.

The street was busy, as always, buses roaring and hissing past, automobiles honking and weaving around them. The stores, however, had greatly changed since Helmer had first walked along this sidewalk: nearly all those he passed now served the poor, and had become drab and bleak, their unwashed windows decorated perhaps with a faded, crudely lettered sign, a pot of withered geraniums, a dozing cat. He went by a small, dark store heaped with denim workclothes; an auto-insurance office, barrenly furnished with two desks, a battered file cabinet, and a bleak overhead light; a musty shop with malodorous used clothing piled on tables; several tiny Puerto Rican barber shops for men and garishly painted hair-styling salons for women with Spanish music blaring forth from them onto the street; and a hodge-podge of shoeshine stands, cluttered candy-and-cigarette stores, old neighborhood bars, and little reeking pizzerias.

Here and there, where some old-time shopkeeper had given up and moved away, a store had remained vacant, and its windows had been smashed and boarded up with raw, blank plywood. Sometimes, even when such a dead store had come to life again as a Spanish social club or a Gospel tabernacle, the plywood front remained, the new identity being crudely lettered on it in paint that dribbled down from the bottoms of the letters. Elsewhere, one or two buildings had been burned out, or torn down to save taxes, leaving an empty lot covered with broken brick—raw, unhealing wounds on which nothing grew but mounds of trash. Among the cars parked by the curb or in the parking lots were the inevitable derelicts, stripped of their wheels and collapsed onto rusting hubs, their windows smashed and their hoods gaping open like the mouths of dead fish on the beach.

The very sidewalks had changed: there were spreading cracks and broken areas in the cement, out of which thick tufts of coarse graygreen grass, tough and scraggly, sprouted like the hair growing out of an old man's nose. In such broken places and along the curbside, shards of broken glass glittered, and cigarette butts and crumpled papers collected in soggy windrows, along with crusts of bread, bits of orange peel, and unidentifiable odds and ends of garbage discarded by children and dogs.

And of course the people were different. These days the relatively few white men and women Helmer passed on Melrose Avenue were mostly middle-aged or elderly, like himself, and walked somewhat stiffly and self-consciously, carefully looking neither to left nor to right, as if by seeming not to notice the feared newcomers they could conceal their fear and their weakness. The newcomers themselves— some of them Negroes but more Puerto Ricans—were, in contrast, wholly at ease, the men, zipper-jacketed and oiled of hair, arguing volubly and vociferously in the doorways of stores or the steps of apartment houses, the women, warmly wrapped up and pigeon-shaped, chattering to each other and shrieking cheerfully in simulated anger at the children they were invariably shepherding along. The sound of their speech and the many ill-executed signs in Spanish on store windows made Melrose Avenue now seem something like a street in a native quarter of some Caribbean city. "Carnes Frescas," it said on one shop; "Frutas Tropicales" on another; "Barberia Latina" and "Bodega Borinquen" on a third and fourth; and on the lower parts of brick walls were innumerable graffiti, sprayed on in various colors, seeking to establish the identity of the overlooked: "Pedro," "Pablo," "Yvette and Go-Go," "Tonito and Tina," "Fuckface," "Poppo," and occasionally one with a touch of larger significance: "Viva Fidel."

Halfway home, Helmer passed the intersection of 156th Street and Melrose Avenue, unaware of its particular significance in his life. Here the old Melrose seemed briefly to resist the incursions and changes: a few doors from the corner was a small branch of the New York Public Library, and on three of the four corners were the Shamrock Bar and Grille, Duffy's Bar and Grill, and the One-Hour Cleaners, only the fourth corner showing the new influence in the form of the Melrose Coffe (sic) Shop, whose window advertised "Comidas, Criollas, Heroes." There was nothing much to distinguish this corner or its immediate environs from the others he had passed: the nearby stores were of much the same type, the windows above them similarly decorated with inexpensive faded curtains, the side-street disfigured by the same cans and bags of garbage bursting on the sidewalks, the same dogs and shouting children at play, the same idle old men sitting on doorsteps.

The corner was, however, one of several in the neighborhood favored as hangouts by a number of Puerto Rican youths. They would meet, sometimes at one and sometimes at another, to socialize and pass the time as men do in the public squares and plazas of Mediterranean or Caribbean cities. Aimless, idle, they chattered together, laughed loudly now and again, sometimes playfully pretended to fight, sometimes jigged and jittered around to music from a nearby store, sometimes fell silent and staring. Often they seemed to be waiting for something to happen, though one could not say what, or stared up and down the street as if expecting something or someone to come their way. Sometimes one or more of them had the stupefied, bemused expression and limp stance that any policeman can recognize from a block away as the look of one who has just "gotten off" and is "on the nod"—that is, has injected a shot of heroin into his arm in some nearby stairway or cellar and lapsed into a state of cottony and semicomatose comfort. Just why the intersection of 156th Street and Melrose Avenue should have been one of these favorite hangouts could not have been apparent to Helmer, and was not clear even to the police; perhaps it was merely that this corner was particularly familiar territory—P.S. 29, halfway down 156th Street to the west, was the school many of the youths had gone to—or perhaps it was simply the nearest busy corner to the Melrose Houses, one block west at Courtlandt Avenue; or perhaps pushers had made this a regular place of business and thus given it a special cachet.

Whatever the reason, there was nearly always a band of teen-age boys and young men here smoking and talking hour after hour, drinking Coke, going on various errands and returning, making soft and lilting remarks to passing girls, and sometimes whispering together about the possibility of "pulling a score" against some likely passerby. For these were youths with little chance of any but the most menial employment, and little hope of bettering themselves; soon after starting grade school, all of them had learned how poor were their chances of ever achieving the way of life they saw on television and in the movies—the hated but infinitely desired life of the white American, the middle-class native, that smug, superior ruler of the country and possessor of all good things, including, most precious of all, a good opinion of himself.

That day, as Helmer passed by, several of the frequent loungers on that corner were not there. Instead, they were four blocks away, idling in front of a grocery store at 160th Street and Melrose Avenue directly across from the entrance to Helmer's building, and waiting for someone—for Alexander Helmer, in fact, whom they had decided a few minutes earlier to go looking for and to mug.

---

## VI  *Muggings, Defined and Counted*

THE youths themselves, however, did not use this term; in their words, they were out to "pull a score." Criminals, whether big-time or two-bit, professional or amateur, prefer to use their own argot, avoiding the vocabulary of the police and the middle-class Establishment. The slang term "mugging" had recently been so widely adopted by the press and the general public as to feel not particularly comfortable to muggers themselves. But although it had become respectable, it had not—and still has not—achieved any status in law or in crime reports because of its uncertain meaning. A decade or so ago, "mugging," like its synonym, "yoking," was informally used by police to signify an increasingly common crime committed chiefly by youths who were not professional criminals: namely, an unarmed assault from behind, in which the attacker locks a forearm around the victim's neck and throttles him while demanding his money or having a confederate empty his pockets. Police departments and the FBI (in its *Uniform Crime Reports*) assign reported muggings to the category "strong-arm robbery"—that is, robbery in which physical force, but no weapon, has been employed—a genre also including face-to-face attacks with the fists, running knock-downs, stompings, and others.

But as the term "mugging" became increasingly popular with the public, it lost its specialized meaning and came to refer to almost any form of strong-arm robbery and, more than that, to robberies in which the victim is threatened with—and even wounded by—a knife, club, or other simple weapon; beyond this, moreover, it is even occasionally employed to refer to robberies in which a gun is used; and, finally, it is sometimes applied to robberies which result in injuries serious enough to bring about the victim's death.

But while the term has lost something by becoming so diffuse, it has apparently filled a need, becoming the useful generic label for robberies with varied techniques but a single underlying behavioral style —one characterized by desperation, recklessness, impulsivity, a lack of criminal professionalism, and, especially, the use of physical contact often involving violence far in excess of what is needed to obtain the victim's money. Indeed, there is a sinister relationship between skin-to-skin contact and the tendency to use excess violence, for in unarmed robberies, where such contact is an essential part of the technique, physical injury to the victim occurs in one out of every three cases, or three times as often as it does in robberies where weapons are used.

Because of the imprecise meaning of the term "mugging" and its avoidance in crime reports, there are no official statistics on its incidence; nonetheless, from the existing data one can make some reasonable estimates. As the term is used by the lay public, muggings probably account for nearly all of the 36.7 percent of robberies which are classified as strong-arm in the FBI's *Uniform Crime Reports,* as well as most of the 23.4 percent which involve the use of a knife, club, or blunt weapon: in sum, therefore, more than half of all reported robberies. This is a conservative estimate, since the term "mugging" is also applied to that small but unknown fraction of the 330,000 reported aggravated assaults in which robbery was intended but not consummated, and to a fair number of felony murders (which make up more than one fifth of all homicides), in which the intended robbery led to an unintended death.

One can reasonably suppose, therefore, that there were about 60,000 muggings in 1964, the year with which this account begins, and something close to 175,000 in 1970. The average citizen's chance of being mugged in 1970 would therefore seem to have been only one in 1,200, but this is falsely reassuring, for three fourths of all such crimes occur in cities of over 250,000, where the rate—again figuring it on the basis of half of all robberies—is more like one in 340, and in cities of over 1,000,000 more like one in 260. If the city-dweller lives in or near high-crime slums, or travels through them, and if he has at least some of the traits of the likely victim, his present chances of being mugged in any given year must be several times greater than this—at a conservative guess, around one in 100.

Such estimates, however, are no better than the raw crime statistics on which they are based, and these, unfortunately, are filled with distortions. The rapid rise in the rate of crime, for instance, is partly the result of more complete reporting due to growing citizen unwillingness to put up with crime, the improvement of police record-keeping, and the development of better and swifter means of summoning the police; moreover, it may in part be a temporary effect of the present excess in our population of people in their upper teens and early twenties—the age group in which there is by far the most violent crime. Some criminologists even argue that the FBI data on the rising crime rate are nothing but self-serving propaganda and without any validity: Norval Morris and Gordon Hawkins, for instance, in *The Honest Politician's Guide to Crime Control,* assert that one can make no valid inferences whatever from the rate increases shown in the *Uniform Crime Reports,* and that the publication of these figures "can serve no purpose beyond alarming and frightening the public, and facilitating congressional acceptance of FBI budgetary requests."

But even if serious shortcomings in the data cause the FBI reports to exaggerate the rate at which crime is increasing, they also cause the reports to drastically understate the total amount of crime being committed, since they include only those crimes the police know about and choose to report. The Crime Commission* conducted a special survey of 10,000 households, asking whether the person questioned or any member of the household had been a victim of a crime during the past year, and whether such crime had been reported or not; the Commission found that many crimes go unreported because the victims do not want to get involved, or feel the police will do nothing anyway, and the Commission concluded that for all crimes taken together, the real rate is several times as great as the reported rate. The more serious the type of crime, the smaller the discrepancy; but even for robbery the true rate was 50 percent higher than the rate reported by the FBI, and for violent crimes in general, 100 percent greater.†

The Violence Commission,‡ for its part, felt that, whatever the deficiencies of the published crime data, there was no doubt that the

---

* Or, more formally, the President's Commission on Law Enforcement and Administration of Justice, which published its final report in 1967.

† At this point, one might amend the city-dweller's risk of being mugged (see above, p. 17) from one in 340 to about one in 225—or, for the choice victims in the largest cities, several times greater than this: at a guess, somewhere around one in 65.

‡ The National Commission on the Causes and Prevention of Violence, which published its final report in December 1969.

crime rate had been increasing very rapidly in recent years. After allowing for all the distortions and imperfections in the *Uniform Crime Reports,* the Commission concluded, "It is still clear that *significant and disturbing increases in the true rates of homicide, and especially of assault and robbery, have occurred over the last decade"* (the 1960s). Then, drawing upon such FBI data as it considered most reliable, the Commission suggested that the rate of violent crime had *tripled* since 1941, and was roughly twice as high in 1968 as it had been in the violent and criminal Depression year of 1933.

The contrast between the high rate of 1933 and the relatively low rate of 1941 would seem to suggest that economic woe is a major cause of violent crime. The explanation is sensible and convincing— but insufficient: poverty has been associated with a low crime rate in some societies, while affluence, as criminologist Leon Radzinowicz has shown, is often associated with a high rate. But, more to the point, the only adequate explanation of violent crime is multi-causal: even where there seems to be a clear correlation between one factor and the crime rate, it is almost always true that several other factors were necessary prerequisites or were simultaneously operative. To explain violent crime in our own society today, one has to take into account not only economic conditions in general, but those of the criminals in particular; the willingness or unwillingness of impoverished people in any given era to accept their lot; the loss of consensus in unstable slums, and hence of traditional social controls over behavior; the cultural conditioning of children in certain subgroups to use violence in dealing with everyday difficulties; the stirring up and misdirecting of aggressiveness by bad family conditions and a disordered social milieu; the presence or absence of heavy police surveillance; hormonal and chromosomal aberrations that overload the bloodstream with excess testosterone and cause violent behavior; diseases of the temporal lobe of the brain that cause compulsive acts of violence; and still other primary and contributory causes.

In the case of muggings, the medical and biological factors are of little or no relevance, but all the rest are. Nearly all muggers come from urban slums, where poverty, filth, and disease are prevalent, and where family life is often harsh and hostile. Sixty-five percent of all persons arrested for robbery are Negroes, most of whom have grown up in slums—and all of whom have grown up black in those slums, learning early in life that they were considered by the white majority outside to be inferior, contemptible, and unworthy of equal opportunities. To the bigoted white, the astoundingly high rate of Negro criminality seems proof of a racial tendency toward violent crime, but there is no scientific evidence whatever that criminal behavior is coded into the genetic material. There is ample evidence, however, that immigrants of many a nationality—Germans, Irish, Poles, and Italians, among others—had high rates of crime during their own slum periods, and that for each group the rate diminished as that people achieved acceptance and success in the society around them. Indeed, an intriguing proof that it is not Negro genes but the slum milieu that makes for Negro violence has been pointed out by sociologist Edwin Schur: the murder rate among Negroes in African tribes is apparently only a small fraction as large as that among Negroes in America and, indeed, is smaller than the overall American homicide rate.

A related area of causation is sharply pinpointed by a remarkable pair of statistics: three quarters of all persons arrested for robbery are juveniles, youths, or young adults under twenty-five, and 94 percent of all persons arrested for robbery are males. Slum life is worst—or most criminalizing—for the young males in it, who feel most intensely the need to be somebody or do something worthy of respect, but who have almost no social or emotional resources for achieving their goal through legitimate channels. In the eyes of white middle-class society —and in his own eyes—the Negro or Puerto Rican teen-ager growing up in a slum is scarcely a person, is not really somebody; and as Erik Erikson has said, such a youth, lacking identity, "would rather be nobody or somebody bad, or indeed, dead . . . than be not-quite somebody." The idea of becoming somebody bad, or risking death by violence, does not strike him as terrible or frightening; in the lowest socio-economic groups, especially in Negro slums, training in violence and badness begins in childhood, when physical punishment is freely used by many parents and so taught to children, who learn to respond in the same kind. Not only at home but outside it, such children daily experience violence as a common, natural, and not particularly horrifying way of expressing anger or gaining respect; as the Violence Commission put it: "The slum ghetto . . . produces a 'subculture' within the dominant American middle-class culture in which aggressive violence tends to be accepted as normal in everyday life, not necessarily illicit."

These abstract terms become very concrete when one listens to actual street criminals talking. Psychiatrist Robert Coles talked to several Negro boys who had attacked an eighty-five-year-old white man in a Boston slum, injuring him so badly that he died a few hours later. None of the boys was psychotic or brain-damaged, but all were bored, indifferent to the spectacle of violence, and chronically angry, and when the old man refused to give them money, they exploded into an unplanned assault. As one of the boys told Dr. Coles, "We didn't think 'he's white' and then go hit him for that. . . . Truth is I don't know why we did it. One minute he was there, and the next minute we told him we wanted his money, and he refused, so we jumped him. . . . I don't think we wanted to hurt him bad or kill him; he was slow in giving us anything, so we started hitting him . . . and I guess we lost our tempers."

The easily lost temper and the easily committed act of violence are not only part of an overall life-style, but an assertion of manhood and an effort to seem important. Melvin Rivers, the black president of the Fortune Society, an organization of ex-convicts, recalls his teens as follows:

> I wanted everybody to know that I was one of the baddest guys that walked that street, so I walked around with my zip gun exposed or my switchblade knife in my hand. Then I started hanging out with a bunch and we wanted to be *something,* because everybody else, they weren't really doing nothing, they really wasn't makin' that money. So we started mugging.

Claude Brown, author of *Manchild in the Promised Land,* links both crime and the use of hard drugs to the need to assert one's manhood in a milieu which allows little other chance of doing so:

> A black community is a sort of super-hip-ultramasculine community. You don't dare not be in the know, and you don't dare show any signs of masculine weakness. . . . [If] you are a growing boy entering teenage, you have to sort of get in the know of it, and you can't be afraid. . . . A junkie, an addict in a community, has a certain respect, because most people are afraid of him, because they know that if this guy's habit comes down on him "and he catches me in a dark hall, I am in trouble."

Washington, D.C., psychiatrist Harold Kaufman reports on a prison interview with a twenty-year-old Negro who had savagely beaten a man he was robbing:

In response to my questions, he coherently relates how he has committed a robbery and beaten his victim. . . . He then begins to recount details of his early life, of being one of eight children brought up in Washington by a drunken father and a martyred mother, of hungry nights and brutal beatings dating back to his earliest memories. . . . He tells me school was a "joke" . . . only "jerks" took it seriously. By the time he was thirteen, all the "groovy guys" were out on the street "hustling." . . . There was no percentage in working regularly: "You slaved all week and what was in it for you? Probably less bread than in one holdup on the street." . . . He is afraid of being ridiculed by his friends if he dresses poorly, associates with unattractive women, holds a regular job, or appears to lack guts. Committing crimes helps to prove he is no coward.

Out of such motives, Negro and Puerto Rican youths become muggers, preying in considerable part upon whites and thereby immensely exacerbating the hatreds presently distorting and poisoning American life. To be sure, most run-of-the-mill acts of violence by blacks or Puerto Ricans are, as we have already seen, directed at other blacks or Puerto Ricans; but robbery is the great exception. As the Violence Commission put it, "Robbery . . . is the one major violent crime in the city with a high inter-racial component; although about 38 percent of robberies in the Survey involve Negro offenders and victims, 45 percent involve Negroes robbing whites—very often young black males robbing somewhat older white males." * (Although the Commission did not give separate data for robberies of whites by Puerto Ricans, the addition of such cases, if one can estimate them from the *Uniform Crime Reports,* would bring the total of robberies of white persons by non-white attackers very close to 50 percent.)

Considering the intensity of the hatred felt by many Negroes and Puerto Ricans toward whites—and the openness and legitimacy this hatred has achieved in recent years—it is not surprising that many robberies, especially those in which there is physical contact, now involve physical injury to the victim. Though not all muggers want to hurt their victims, a substantial minority do, and the proportion is

* In the Bronx, by 1969, in one high-crime racially mixed area (Highbridge), three quarters of the victims were white, and more than four fifths of the criminals were Negroes or Puerto Ricans, according to a police study reported in *The New York Times* of December 24th, 1969.

growing. In one recent study, made in Philadelphia, a sociologist found that in those assaults made with knives, blunt instruments, or strong-arm methods, roughly half the victims were harmed and 30 percent required treatment or hospitalization. Some of these injuries are the result of resistance by the victim; far more of them are the result of anger, fear, and sadism. In many jurisdictions, police report that it is becoming increasingly common for unarmed muggers not only to snatch a woman's purse but to knock her down, not only to throttle an old man and take his wallet but to fell him with a rain of blows and kick him in the face, the stomach, and the kidneys. Armed muggers, similarly, even though getting the money they want, more and more often beat or stab their victims before running off. As Sheriff Frank Powell of Richland County, South Carolina, quivering with indignation, said to the House Select Committee on Crime in words that broke all previous records for bathos, "Sir, the hoodlum of today has no ethics."

# VII *Helmer at the Threshold of Safety*

THE nature of the new breed of hoodlums was not as clearly recognized seven years ago as it is now. Alexander Helmer, for one, paid little attention to the street-corner loungers he was passing, and must not have been especially fearful of being attacked by such people, for in his wallet that day he was carrying $189 for no particular reason except that he liked to. Even if the thought of robbery did occur to him from time to time, he had little personal reason to think of it as involving physical brutality, for years ago, in his rounds as a milkman, he had been robbed twice without being hurt. Whatever he thought of the dark and alien-looking newcomers to his neighborhood, he did not greatly fear them or worry about the increased amount of crime that had come with them into formerly safe and peaceful Melrose. Indeed,

despite their noisy music, their ungoverned children, and their garbage, they had brought a certain festival air to the avenue that it had
not previously had. Women of various hues ranging from white and
pale café-au-lait to dark brown leaned from open windows and called
down to children or friends in the street; here and there a couple of
men, some with wide, flat Carib faces and others with the slim, patri-
cian features sown among the Indians centuries ago by the Span-
iards, stood by the front doors of shops and addressed each other in
loud, cheerful, mock-hectoring tones; from a radio in Mary's Mod
Salon came blaring music and the tortured shouting of a male singer
bewailing the state of his *corazón*. The raucousness probably bothered
the half-deaf Helmer less than it did other old-time residents, but even
if it had disturbed him, he could hardly have seen most of these noisy
newcomers as dangerous criminals when they were obviously something else; for even in areas where crime has become common, most
of the inhabitants are plainly law-abiding family folk, seeking to care
for their children and to pursue such happiness as they can within
their limited way of life.

Even the youths idling in front of the Vega-Baja Self-Service Grocery on the south side of 160th Street, directly across from Helmer's
building, did not look particularly malevolent or vicious. Had anyone
been watching them, he would probably have noticed nothing particularly ominous about their behavior; even when Helmer, carrying his
bag of groceries, suddenly appeared at the corner, they did little more
than whisper to each other and assume a broad air of nonchalance.
They watched with no evident interest as the old man crossed the
street at the corner, turned west, and walked toward the front door of
his building; they made no move as he pushed open the heavy glass
door with its iron grillwork, mounted several steps inside the tiny
foyer, and fished a bunch of keys out of his pocket; they stayed where
they were as he unlocked the wooden inner door and pushed his way
in, letting it close slowly by itself as he disappeared, out of the sight of
the enemies he had not even noticed and into the safety of the building
that had been his home so many years.

That inner door had not always been locked. In the old days, when
Helmer first came here, no one thought of the apartment house as a
haven, a fastness surrounded by hostile brigands, but simply as a
home in a family neighborhood. It had been put up in 1915, and in its
early years was considered a very fine building for that area. Six

stories high, of tan brick, it had a central staircase leading to the upper landings, and five modest family-sized apartments on each floor—
a decent, bourgeois building of a type common in big-city residential
neighborhoods that were developed half a century ago. Like many
such buildings, it had a few perfunctory touches of exotic décor: a bit
of Romanesque flavor in the form of rounded arches over the first-
floor windows, a Byzantine tile pattern in the entrance foyer. In its
heyday there had even been a switchboard and house telephone in the
foyer—a high-class feature for Melrose—but the system had long
since ceased working and been replaced by two panels of buttons and
a buzzer on the lock of the inner door.

The building had been owned and managed for forty years by Mrs.
Anna Ambos, the wife of a German-born physician, widowed these
past twenty-five years. Once, long ago, she had been a buxom, powerful woman built along German peasant lines, but age had slowly withered her, and by 1964 she had become wizened, bent, and sharp-
nosed, a tart, crackling old woman of seventy-two, full of memories of
better days. "Oh, it vos a very fancy building in that time," she would
reminisce to friends or to her now-grown children, who came to visit
once in a long while. "Clean, new, all the peoples around here very
decent. Now look! Vot you see? Kids playing in the street until midnight. Men drinking beer unt dropping cans on the sidewalk. People
living like gypsies, throwing garbage in the gutter, until the rain don't
go down the sewers, but comes up in the street unt floods mine westi-
bule.

"Unt all the time now, muggings. The teen-age kids, they grab your
purse unt shove you down, don't care you break a bone. Nobody goes
out at night any more; they vouldn't take the chance. Years already, I
had to put in peepholes in the doors; it cost me a lot of money. Peepholes! In those days, ve never needed to look who it vos, before opening. Listen, I don't have notting against the blacks or the Spanish, but
ve got to do something for ourselves. *They* have leaders, they get
everything. *Ve* got to have a leader, so the police can do vot's right.
Ve need a *leader!*"

And still she stayed on, wedded to her building and to her past.
"Ven I complain to the police," she would say, "they tell me, 'Move!'
Vare should I move? Vot vould I do?" So she stayed, installed three
extra locks on her front door, kept the inner door of the building
locked, never went out at night, and waited for some deliverance to

come, though from what quarter she did not know.

Like Mrs. Ambos, it was chiefly the older white people who stayed on, lacking the courage and energy to seek and make a new life elsewhere, and in any case unable to afford the newer apartments in better parts of the city. Rentals in Melrose, on the other hand, had remained low: Helmer, for instance, was still paying Mrs. Ambos only $49.30 per month, under New York's rent-control law, for his four-room apartment, and he would have had no chance whatever of finding anything comparable even at two to three times that price in any good residential area of the city. Besides, his apartment was his long-time home; he intimately knew every inch of the walls that he was even now repainting, every board and tile in the floors that he himself had mopped these past ten years since his sister died, every piece of old furniture that still reassuringly stood just where it had for a third of his life. Even if he did hear stories of muggings and murders, even if he did see the alien faces crowding in on him, he still felt safe enough walking the streets by daylight—and surely supposed that within the walls of his own building he was in a sanctuary, safe from any possible harm.

But he was mistaken on both counts: though there are fewer muggings by day than by night, they are hardly rare, not even at high noon; and although muggings were and still are thought of primarily as street crimes, more and more of them—over half, in one recent sample—are taking place off the street in foyers, automatic elevators, and hallways, where there is less chance of being seen. Had anyone been watching Helmer and the youths across the street that day—no one was, in all likelihood, for 160th Street was relatively quiet much of the time, and almost deserted at that particular moment—he would have seen a pattern with which police have become all too familiar in recent years. As Helmer went through the inner door and disappeared, there was a moment or so of waiting and urgent whispering; then one youth darted across the street and through the front door into the foyer, where he punched a button at random on the panel in the right-hand wall. As soon as the buzzer sounded, unlocking the inner door, he pushed it open and held it ajar, turning and waving to the others across the street to come on; they came running, burst into the foyer and rushed through the door he was holding open, and bounded up the stairs Alexander Helmer had just climbed.

# VIII   *The High Cost of Fear*

NONE of the tenants of the building had seen them run in, and none saw them go rushing up the stairs, but this is not unusual; muggers pick their moment to strike and are rarely or only fleetingly observed. And even if anyone at 399 East 160th Street had seen them, he would neither have recognized them nor been able to give a useful description of them, for none of the invaders had ever been in the building before, and although they all lived nearby, people in a crowded tenement area can be total strangers to others who live only half a block away. Moreover, when the victim or witnesses are white and the attackers are black or Puerto Rican (whom whites are notoriously poor at perceiving and recognizing as individuals), there is little chance that any eyewitness report will be of much help to the police. Such reports almost always fit hundreds of persons within walking distance of the scene of the attack, a typical description reading something like this: "Negro, male, early twenties, medium height and build, dark-skinned, wearing gray windbreaker."

In many robberies, and especially in hit-and-run muggings, the situation is hopeless; there are no clues, no web of personal connections, no motives leading inexorably to one person who has been involved with the victim. No wonder, then, that one third of all robberies are never even reported to the police, that nearly three quarters of the reported robberies result in no arrests, that over two fifths of those that lead to arrests lack evidence enough to prosecute, and that only three fifths of the suspects who are actually prosecuted are convicted: in sum, less than 7 percent of all robberies result in convictions of any sort—and a fair number of those are for something less than the crime that was actually committed.

Thus muggings, in addition to their other dismaying and alarming characteristics, seem all but uncontrollable by the police and the courts. Victims of muggers—and virtually all who fear they might someday become victims—feel helpless, unprotected, and without any means of redress. (In contrast, almost nine tenths of murders are reported—dead bodies do not go unnoticed—and in 86 percent of the cases an arrest is made. In 1970, 44 percent of such arrests led to convictions for murder, and another 15 percent led to convictions for lesser crimes.)

It is for such reasons that robberies, and muggings in particular, have so powerfully corrosive an effect upon American life, for, over and above everything else they do to us, they cause a loss of faith in our society, and a pervasive and demoralizing fear. Other things which might be expected to cause far greater fear do not, and have no such demoralizing effect. Automobiles, to take but one example, killed 56,400 Americans and injured two million in 1969—roughly 20 times as many deaths, and 25 times as many injuries, as were caused by muggers. Yet in comparison to our fear of muggers, our fear of automobiles is almost non-existent. This does not mean that we are fools, but that we far better tolerate the thought that an accident may harm us than that another human being—a total stranger to whom we have done no wrong—may suddenly and viciously attack us.

The effects of our fear have been disastrous. Throughout the 1960s the quality of daily life in America's major cities, particularly for the scores of millions who live in or near high-crime areas, has grown ever more impoverished and barren. Out of fear of walking in the streets at night, such people have increasingly given up many of the activities that used to enrich and vary their lives. Each year during the decade, the nighttime use of public libraries in many large cities declined, attendance dwindled at PTA meetings, and parks and public recreation facilities were less used. Midway in the decade, a national survey made for the Crime Commission revealed that one third of all Americans felt unsafe walking alone at night in their own neighborhoods, the proportion being even higher in large cities and highest of all in the crime-ridden areas of those cities. Over half the people surveyed said that there were parts of their own cities they would not and did not venture into; four fifths always kept their doors locked at night, and one out of four always kept the door locked even in the daytime; and over one quarter had watchdogs, and over one third said they kept firearms in the home.

All this was so by the middle of the decade, but since then the rate of robbery has nearly tripled, and the impoverishment of daily life has correspondingly worsened. *Life* magazine collected reports from correspondents in fifteen cities in 1969, and had Louis Harris & Associates, the polling firm, conduct a survey: among their depressing findings was word that the manpower employed by private protective services had grown larger than that of all police forces in the nation combined, and that in every city the sale of firearms, tear-gas dispensers, ferocious dogs, locks, and window grilles was soaring. Focusing on Baltimore, whose crime rate, though high, was not much worse than those of most other cities of about the same size (900,000), *Life* found that 33 percent of the people used parks less than formerly, even by day; 41 percent went downtown to movies or restaurants less often; 29 percent had recently bought extra locks and protective devices; and Sunday-night services in many churches were disappearing because parishioners were afraid to be out after dark.

Not only in Baltimore but in every large city, many of the more vulnerable citizens—particularly in high-crime areas—lock themselves into their apartments at night and hardly ever venture out; the socializing that used to bring variety and warmth into their lives is now gone, and they have in its place only the analgesia and passivity of televiewing. Even to visit their friends within their own apartment development—and even in their own building—sometimes seems too risky; every hallway, every automatic elevator is a place of potential terror. For a few, it is a confinement without mitigation: at Red Hook Houses in Brooklyn, a public housing project where many aging persons are preyed upon by muggers, one eighty-three-year-old woman and her retarded daughter never set foot outside the front door, all their food being brought to them once a week by the old woman's son, who lives some distance away and who summed up the situation for a *Times* reporter in simple, dreadful terms: "She stays in, that's all. I tell her, don't go out, and don't answer the door for nobody."

The contagion of fear has spread from such places into the heart of many a major city, including—to the disgrace of us all—our own national capital. All during the 1960s, downtown Washington had become increasingly dangerous and increasingly empty, until by 1969 most of it was virtually deserted early in the evening. According to newsman James K. Batten, even in those areas where after-dark activity persisted, people seemed to be hurrying along rather than strolling and sightseeing. By a bitter irony, a number of members of the Violence Commission at work in downtown Washington were mugged, burglarized, and beaten during their stay. And in a still more bitter irony, Jayne Brumley, a *Newsweek* correspondent, was walking along Pennsylvania Avenue at 6:15 p.m. on a winter evening when a man approached and scolded her, saying, "Lady, you must be out of your mind to be out alone after dark in a neighborhood like this"; at the moment Mrs. Brumley was practically outside the White House.

To a great extent, Americans were losing faith in their society and withdrawing, hiding, seeking private solutions, whatever the cost in the impoverishment of daily life, whatever the loss in human values. It was during the Sixties that we all became familiar with a new phenomenon—the Bad Samaritan, the passerby who would hurry past a person lying in the gutter, and who would do nothing to aid a person being attacked.

But when victims and potential victims did take collective action, it was often in ways as damaging to American life as crime itself. America had had a long and shameful history of lynch mobs, vigilantes, and frontier justice, in which the crowd reached its verdict and administered instant punishment without any hifalutin Eastern nonsense about due process, defense counsel, judge and jury, or constitutional rights. By and large, we had slowly grown away from all that—only to see it begin to reappear during the 1960s, not on the frontier and not in small southern towns, but in the heart of a number of our largest cities. In high-crime areas in New York, Dayton, Boston, Trenton, Detroit, St. Louis, and various other cities, citizen groups were formed—some of them Irish, some Polish, some Italian, some black, and some Jewish—to patrol and police their own areas. Most claimed they were performing only surveillance, but a number of them had police dogs and others carried arms; it is only a matter of time until some of these groups begin to administer back-alley justice to muggers they catch beating up an old man or a woman. Indeed, police suspect that such things have happened already, far more frequently than they can prove.

People fear the violent criminals who terrorize them; fearing them, hate them; and hating them, are interested in only one solution to the problem: the use of force by the police—this despite the conclusion of the most thoughtful and best-informed minds in the field that the use of force alone, even when deployed in massive amounts, is relatively ineffective and of limited value. It is true that when all restraining force is removed, as during a police strike, there is likely to be an upsurge in the number of robberies, burglaries, and assaults, as was the case in Montreal in 1969; it is true, too, that whenever a high-crime neighborhood is "saturated" with police, the crime rate in that neighborhood drops. But both phenomena are temporary, and both involve widespread publicity about the presence or absence of police; under more normal circumstances, the crime rate is relatively unresponsive to variations in police power. The Crime Commission, for instance, pointed out that in cities of over half a million the ratio of policemen per thousand population ranged anywhere from 1.07 to 4.04, but that the incidence of crime in those cities showed no correspondingly large variations. The obvious presence of policemen inhibits some criminals, in some degree; police power, however, does not of itself eliminate crime or even bring about major reductions in the crime rate. The Crime Commission did urge a number of steps designed to improve police effectiveness, speed up court procedures and improve correctional institutions, all toward the end of combating crime through the criminal justice system; but again and again the Commission stated in the most emphatic terms that while all these things might help, the only basic and lasting solution would be one that involved a full-scale assault upon the social conditions that breed crime:

> The Commission doubts that even a vastly improved criminal justice system can substantially reduce crime if society fails to make it possible for each of its citizens to feel a personal stake in it—in the good life that it can provide and in the law and order that are prerequisite to such a life. . . . Warring on poverty, inadequate housing and unemployment, is warring on crime. A civil rights law is a law against crime. Money for schools is money against crime. Medical, psychiatric, and family-counselling services are services against crime. . . . A community's most enduring protection against crime is to right the wrongs and cure the illnesses that tempt men to harm their neighbors.

Two years later the Violence Commission, having likewise drawn upon the knowledge and skills of a number of outstanding sociologists, criminologists, jurists, and historians, came to the same conclusion. After making numerous practical suggestions for immediate improvements in law enforcement and the administration of justice, the Commission continued:

> Necessary as measures of control are, they are only a part of the answer. They do not cure the basic causes of violence. Violence is like a fever in the body politic: it is but the symptom of some more basic pathology which must be cured before the fever will disappear. Indeed, if measures of control were this society's only response to violence, they would in the long run exacerbate the problem. The pyramiding of control measures could turn us into a repressive society, where the peace is kept primarily through official coercion rather than through willing obedience to law. . . . The way in which we can make the greatest progress toward reducing violence in America is by taking the actions necessary to improve the conditions of family and community life for all who live in our cities, and especially for the poor who are concentrated in the ghetto slums.

But almost no one was listening; or, more accurately, some were listening but only a few agreed, and fewer still really cared, truly *wanted* to see the nation make the herculean efforts and vast expenditures necessary to radically change the position of non-whites in American society. When imagining the mugger lurking in the darkness outside one's own house, one is far more likely to think only in terms of counterattack, involving force supplied by the police and punishment dealt out by the courts and prisons. These weapons are far more immediate, far easier to comprehend, and, above all, far more gratifying, for they fulfill powerful primitive wishes built into our very neurones. Beyond this, they have the huge appeal of costing only pennies in comparison to the staggering theoretical cost of creating equal opportunities for all citizens from the moment of their conception onward.

In 1964 Barry Goldwater ran for President on a law-and-order platform, but the fear of crime had not yet reached the critical point. By 1968 it had; Richard Nixon, running for President, appealed to frightened and angry people throughout the country in terms directly contradictory to those of the Crime Commission Report—"If the conviction rate were doubled in this country," he said in his first position paper on the subject, "it would do more to eliminate crime in the future than a quadrupling of the funds for any governmental war on poverty"—and, the time of that idea having come, he won.

Even in advance of his victory, however, Congress had written the vigilante spirit into law. President Johnson had sent up an Omnibus Crime Bill in 1967 which would have granted federal funds to the states to improve police training and equipment, speed up court procedures, improve correctional systems, and allocate a few dollars to preventive programs aimed at combating crime at its sources. By 1968, when a later version of the bill was finally enacted (the Omnibus Crime Control and Safe Streets Bill), the balance had shifted heavily toward police action: although some money was to go for the planning of court reforms and correction improvements, the bulk of the funds were "action money"—95 percent of which went to the police, with very little for the courts, probation departments, or prisons, and nothing at all for programs that attacked crime at its sources.

But most of the members of Congress, being successful politicians (whose "most distinctive characteristic," Richard Harris has tartly said, "is selective cowardice"), were merely heeding the wishes of the majority of their constituents. (Even 68 percent of the Negroes polled by Louis Harris on behalf of *Life* magazine were of the opinion that the best way to fight crime was to have more policemen.) Beyond giving money grants to police forces throughout the nation, the 1968 Omnibus Crime Bill also made significant efforts to override recent Supreme Court decisions liberally interpreting the protections the Constitution offered suspected or accused persons against police and prosecutors: specifically, the Bill granted the police new latitude to wiretap and to bug private citizens, and partially reversed the Supreme Court decisions that sought to protect accused persons, under the Fifth Amendment, against coercive police interrogation.

The quality of the preliminary hearings for the Bill, particularly in the Senate Subcommittee on Criminal Laws and Procedures headed by John McClellan of Arkansas, had shown how things were going. Senator McClellan had stacked the hearings with law-and-order advocates—Southern sheriffs, police chiefs, tough-minded D.A.s, and the like—studiously avoiding almost all liberals, criminologists, and civil-rights advocates. Hundreds and hundreds of pages of transcript of the Subcommittee hearings had been filled with testimony about the need to instill fear in potential criminals; with attacks on intellectuals, behavioral scientists, and Supreme Court justices who "coddled" criminals and "offered lame excuses and apologies" for their behavior rather than made them pay dearly; and with barely disguised attacks on the Bill of Rights, Senator McClellan himself making many a frontal assault on the American ideal of justice in terms such as these:

> I tell you we are going to have to forget about some of these trivialities—worrying with all this sentimentality that somebody who is innocent somewhere some time might suffer a little injustice.

He spoke not only for the rednecks of the Arkansas hills, but for Middle Americans nearly everywhere. In a poll taken not long afterward by CBS News, 58 percent of a random sample of Americans said they felt that if a man were tried and found innocent of a serious crime, and new evidence were later discovered, he should be tried again, and the same percent said that they thought the police ought to be allowed to hold in jail a person suspected of a serious crime until they could get enough evidence against him. The former of these opinions is, of course, in direct contradiction to the Fifth Amendment, which expressly prohibits double jeopardy, while the latter conflicts with the Fifth and the Fourteenth, both of which prohibit the deprivation of liberty without due process of law.

Months before Richard Nixon was elected, the 1968 Omnibus Crime Control and Safe Streets Bill was passed by a margin astonishing even to its proponents: only seventeen members of the House and four members of the Senate had the courage to vote against it, though many more deplored it and had argued against it. Since then Mr. Nixon has done a good deal to fulfill Mrs. Ambos' dream of a "leader," including the twin achievements in 1970 of getting Congress to pass a second and tougher crime bill (ostensibly aimed at organized crime, but chipping away at both the Fifth and Fourth Amendments) and a District of Columbia Crime Bill that he and Attorney General Mitchell viewed as forward-looking anti-crime legislation, suitable for the whole nation, two of the most striking provisions of which were the authorization of "no-knock" searches of private homes and the preventive detention of accused persons considered by the police and the court to be too dangerous to set free on bail pending trial. With these measures, the Administration had made a good start at reshaping American justice along the lines of criminal justice in nations in which the good of the state is put far above the rights of the individual, and in which it is considered right for the police to break in upon citizens they suspect may be up to something illegal, and for accused persons to be locked up without the right to bail or even the right to seek it in court.

The number of crimes being committed throughout the nation has, however, continued to increase by roughly the same amount each year. To be sure, the crime *rate*—the number of crimes per 100,000 population—rose less in 1970 than it had for some years, but this was more an arithmetical illusion than a real improvement, as we will see later; in any case, the slowing-down of the rise in the rate pertained to crime in general, not to violent crime in particular—the very kind Congress and the Administration had promised to control—which continued to rise, seemingly unhindered by the tough new legislation or the enlargement and modernizing of the nation's police forces. All of which must be cold comfort to the unheeded authors of the Crime Commission and Violence Commission reports, who had repeatedly stated that even the largest police force could only catch existing criminals, and could not prevent new generations of criminals from being created or stop them from seeking to commit crimes.

---

# IX   *Helmer Plays His Part in a Nefarious Symbiosis*

---

CERTAINLY, nothing the police were doing in 1964 and nothing they have done since then would have forestalled the criminal behavior of the youths who had decided to pull a score on Alexander Helmer. At the most, a patrolman on the corner of 160th Street and Melrose might have made them decide to choose another place in which to attack him, or deflected their aim to another target altogether; but even for such limited benefits one would need patrolmen on every block of the city at all times, or perhaps ten times as many as all those now in the New York Police Department, even assuming every one of them could be assigned to street duty—a level of policing not even the most repressive dictatorship in Europe or South America has come close to.

Nonetheless, the youths were a little ahead of their time in choosing to attack indoors, for it has been chiefly in the last several years that indoor mugging has become a fairly common adaptation to the increased efforts of police and vigilante efforts to patrol the streets. A common pattern of attack—much like that decided upon by the little band that was after Helmer—involves trailing an old and single person home, unobtrusively following him (or her) until he unlocks his front door, and then rushing him on inside, where the mugging can take place unobserved and uninterrupted.

It happens very fast—too fast, usually, for the victim to be aware of what is going on except in that vague, surprised, and disbelieving way in which one perceives himself to be in the middle of an automobile accident. Helmer had climbed two flights of stairs and was at the front door of his apartment, Number 2-B—the 2-series apartments were on the third floor, two levels up from the street—unlocking it with his right hand, the bag of groceries cradled in his left arm. As he got the door open, he put the bunch of keys back in his pocket and started on in; then from the stairway, to his left and behind him, there was the sound of racing feet, and in an instant he was violently propelled inside and shoved, stumbling, half a dozen steps along the narrow hall to the kitchen doorway on the right side.

Here he lurched into the doorway and turned, gasping in astonishment and fear. The shapes of two young men were hard upon him, and a third was at the front door, in the background. Inexplicably and wordlessly, as if preparing to do something to him, one of the two took the bag of groceries from his unresisting hands and set it on the floor just outside the kitchen. The other, meanwhile, slipped into the kitchen behind Helmer, who wheeled around in panic, beginning to shout in a cracked, aging voice and flailing out at the intruder with his feeble old arms. Behind him, whoever had taken the groceries from him now pinioned his arms to his sides, at which Helmer shouted all the louder. Then suddenly the man in front of him had a knife in his hand, with which he struck at Helmer backhandedly and powerfully, hitting him in the left side and pulling the knife out, and striking again and yet three more times, the blade disappearing into Helmer for an instant each time, then reappearing, bright red.

Helmer abruptly stopped shouting and grew limp; the arms holding him from behind let go and he pitched forward onto the kitchen floor, landing heavily on his face, his brown hat flying off and falling to the floor a couple feet away, and the flesh-colored hearing aid popping out of his ear and landing close to his face, still connected to him by its fine wire. He lay there without moving, the warm blood soaking his clothes beneath him and beginning to seep out onto the floor. He did not see them step around him to search the kitchen, or hear their hurried footsteps around his apartment or the opening and slamming shut of bureau drawers and lids of boxes. The grayness and the silence closed in; he was unaware of what they said to each other, and did not hear the front door slam shut as they left, running pell-mell down the two flights of steps, splitting up, and disappearing in opposite directions, unnoticed by anyone, their faces fading even from the memory network of Helmer's brain as it slowly cooled and its circuits shut down for the first time in seventy-two years.

# Chapter 2  The Investigation

## I  The Four-Two Precinct Gets a Seemingly Routine Call

NINE days later, on the morning of Sunday the 18th, a door-to-door representative of Jehovah's Witnesses was working his way through the building at 399 East 160th Street. On the second floor he rang the bell at a door marked 1-B, and when the tenant, a Mrs. Smith, answered, he switched on a saccharine smile and went into a rapid, well-rehearsed speech about God's Truth, at the end of which he offered her a copy of *The Watchtower,* the sect's official publication. While she was fishing some change out of her purse, he added in a confidential half-whisper, "You know, one flight up there must be a dead body somewhere, to judge by the smell." Mrs. Smith, hoping he had noticed nothing more serious than stale food odors in the muggy air of the hallway—the day was unusually warm for mid-October, and oppressively humid—fearfully tiptoed up the stairs a minute or two later, and suddenly collided with an invisible stench that assaulted her like a blow to the stomach.

She fled down the stairway to the ground floor, rang Mrs. Ambos' bell, and gasped out something to the effect that there was a dead man over her head. The elderly landlady, grumbling and muttering, spryly climbed the two flights of stairs with Mrs. Smith trailing her. At the third-floor hall she wavered, crying out and clapping a withered hand to one cheek; then, after hurrying around from one door to another and sniffing, her face screwed up in revulsion, she ran a few steps to the door of 2-A, whose occupant, a middle-aged Italian woman named Ena Varela, was a crony of hers, and rang urgently and repeatedly. When Mrs. Varela opened up, Mrs. Ambos wasted no time in greetings, but cried out, "Ena, kvick, call the police! It's an awful stink in the hall, like from a dead person!" And pointing to the door just to her right, she added, "I smelled on the door by Helmer—it's from there." Mrs. Varela, assaulted by a wave of foulness so powerful as to seem almost palpable, ran to her phone.

Number 399 is located in the very middle of the 42nd Precinct (or, in New York police lingo, the "Four-Two Precinct"), and about fifteen minutes later a Four-Two radio car, dispatched by a call from the Bronx Communications Bureau of the Police Department, pulled up in front. Two young policemen got out and were met at the front door by the agitated Mrs. Ambos, who rattled away almost unintelligibly while leading them up the stairs to the third floor. There, frozen-faced and tight-lipped, they strove to look calm and professional, despite the nausea that gripped them. Somewhat pointlessly, they tried Helmer's door, which Mrs. Ambos had already told them was locked; they then asked her for a key, but she said that a couple of years ago the tenant had demanded that she give him her key to his apartment. She added, however, that they might be able to get in through a bedroom window from an outside fire-escape they could reach through apartment 2-A.

Patrolman Edward Kacerosky rang Mrs. Varela's bell, and was soon standing on the iron fire-escape outside a partly open window of the Helmer apartment. But not for long: the vile odor that was seeping out, and a dense cloud of flies that filled the air of the room with wild humming, drove him back; he hurried downstairs to the car and radioed for Emergency Service, and in a little while two more police vehicles arrived, one a radio car bringing Sergeant Maizel of the Emergency Service, the other a small, specially equipped station wagon with two of his men. While Sergeant Maizel waited in the third-floor hallway, the two Emergency Service officers, Patrolmen Puvogel and Savage, went through Mrs. Varela's apartment to the fire-escape, put on gas masks, and entered Helmer's apartment. They found nothing much in the first room except a number of cans of paint, and hundreds of flies, ceaselessly and turbulently in motion, that bumped into every inch of their bodies and faces, and filled the air with continual and maddening buzzing. Puvogel and Savage moved through the cloud of flies to a doorway at the left, which led into a small, sparsely furnished living-room. There was no sign of life—or death—in it, but in the next instant they saw what they were looking for. To their right a long hallway ran from the living-room to the front door of the apartment; halfway down it, at the kitchen doorway in the left wall, they saw a paper bag standing on the floor and, just beyond it, a man's feet protruding from the doorway into the hall.

Puvogel and Savage, both experienced at this business, knew about what to expect and had long since grown hardened to such things; even so, when they walked down the hall through the ever thickening atmosphere of flies and looked into the kitchen, they were momentarily taken aback. Alexander Helmer was lying just where he had fallen, his hat and hearing aid still nearby, his head still turned to the right just as it had been nine days earlier, but he had changed greatly: throughout the trillions of cells of his body a pervasive ferment, systematically simplifying and recombining the proteins, carbohydrates, and fats of which he was made, had begun turning his skin and flesh into a liquefying mush; gases generated by these changes and by the eager multiplication of bacteria in his tissues and juices had distended his abdomen and made him larger than in life; and hastening the metamorphosis of his being were hundreds upon hundreds of white maggots, ceaselessly crawling in and out of his clothing, writhing in the large pool of thick reddish-brown liquid that had leaked out from beneath him onto the kitchen floor, and squirming to and fro all over his face (or what was left of it, since they had already eaten away his eyes, lips, tongue, and much of the flesh of his neck).

Puvogel edged around this mass of corruption, crunching some of the maggots underfoot despite his care; stepping over what he took to be a wrapped piece of candy in the middle of the floor, he flung the kitchen window wide open and tiptoed back to the hall. He and Savage then opened every window in the other rooms, after which they let Sergeant Maizel and Patrolman Kacerosky in at the front door. In the hallway, a handful of neighbors holding handkerchiefs over their noses tried to peer in, but Kacerosky quickly closed the door, leaving them to gossip in hushed tones and to drift back to their own apartments.

Which was just as well: the average city-dweller is emotionally unequipped to deal with the sight of death and bodily disintegration. Policemen, however, and especially those on the Emergency Service, learn, like combat soldiers, to suppress their emotional reactions to blood, viscera, and dismembered or rotting bodies, and to view such things as dispassionately as does the housewife the chicken she is cleaning. Even so, the four policemen found their duties that morning taxing their professionalism to the limit. Thousands of flies peppered them continually, crawled on their faces and hands, were part of the air they could scarcely breathe. As for the corpse, they could not bring themselves to turn it over (nor did any of them even suggest it) to see if it bore any signs of violence, and when Maizel ordered the rear pockets searched for clues to the dead man's identity and for valuables, Puvogel found a scissors in the living-room and cut the right rear pocket open, rather than reach into it. Kacerosky, assisting him, lifted out Helmer's wallet and found in it various business cards, receipts, a Board of Elections registration card, an identification card, and $189 in bills and 80 cents in coins. He also noticed a key chain fastened to a trouser belt-loop, and cautiously tugged on it; a bunch of four keys slithered out of the right-hand front pocket. The four men, choking and waving away the flies, looked briefly around the kitchen, noticing nothing out of the way, and hastily checked the other rooms for signs of unusual activity (there were none: a couple of dresser drawers were half open, but the place was generally neat and in order). They looked in all the drawers and in the closets for valuables that would need to be safeguarded, finding nothing but three bankbooks with a little under $650 recorded in them. Assuming from all appearances—including the cash in the wallet—that Helmer had died of a heart attack or stroke and, like many a big-city solitary, lain unnoticed and unmissed by anyone until his body was badly decayed, they took the wallet, keys, and bankbooks, and escaped into the comparatively breathable air of the third-floor hallway, shutting the door on the horror within.

A relief patrolman remained on duty in the hallway with the keys, to guard the body until it was removed for medical examination. Back at the 42nd Precinct Station, a foreboding old red brick building only two blocks away at 160th and Third Avenue, Kacerosky reported that he had found a D.O.A. (Dead On Arrival), and the desk officer phoned the detective squad, one floor up, since a routine check would have to be made before the body could be removed. It was then about 1:00 p.m., and accordingly Detective Stephen McCabe "caught" the case (that day he was responsible for—or, in cop lingo, would "catch"—any case that came in between 11:00 a.m. and 2:00 p.m.). McCabe, a short, strongly built man in his mid-thirties with pale blue eyes, wavy blond hair, and the clean, handsome, hard-edged features of a Scoutmaster or a Good Guy in an old-time Western, had been a policeman for fourteen years, the latter seven of them as a detective, and he knew about what to expect, though he hadn't had to deal with quite so badly decomposed a body as this before. But it would apparently be a routine dirty chore, followed by a little paper work—the very kind of unglamorous detail that occupies the larger part of the working hours of real detectives, though not of those the public knows best through fiction and television.

Hopefully inconspicuous but obviously a detective to any knowledgeable eye—the stigmata being the inexpensive double-breasted suit, the bulge at one side of his waist, the slightly too loud sport shirt, the slightly too close trim of the hair at the neck, and the cold, wary eyes and ready-for-anything look—McCabe arrived at the apartment building at about 3:00 p.m. and identified himself to Patrolman Joseph Landy, the young policeman guarding the door of 2-B and looking thoroughly unhappy with his assignment. McCabe, his ruddy face paling at the fetid stench, could understand why. Landy unlocked the door for him, and McCabe went in, clutching a handkerchief over his nose and mouth. Buffeted by the swirling cloud of flies that seemed (as he later put it) "as thick as smoke in a card game," he edged around the body, nearly slipping on the underfoot gruel of blood and squashed maggots. Steeling himself, he bent down to study the late Alexander Helmer more closely; although he had been talking tough to thieves, muggers, and knife-wielding junkies for years, and had once killed a man in line of duty and lost not an hour's sleep that same night, the sight and smell of death as he confronted it that day was more than he could stand, and he ran out of the apartment and slammed the door, his face white and pinched and his forehead beaded with sweat. Landy tactfully said nothing, and McCabe, after a minute or two of silence, lit a cigar, hoping the smoke would protect him from the odors and the flies, and went back in. This time he got somewhat further with his observations, but after a couple of minutes he suddenly gagged, the cigar flying out of his mouth and rolling out of sight under a table. Struggling to control his retching, and afraid the cigar might start a fire, he crouched down and frantically hunted for it, found it, and rushed outside again. And still he came back, and this time looked all through the four rooms, seeing nothing suspicious, and noticing, but paying no attention to, the bag of spoiled groceries in the hall, a wrapped piece of bubble gum on the kitchen floor, and the wrapper from another piece on the kitchen counter.

After what seemed a very long time—ten minutes, actually, for all three sorties—he had seen as much as he needed to see and left the apartment, said good-by to Landy (who remained on guard), and headed back to the station house, weak, weary, and thoroughly out of sorts. Back at his desk, he tapped out a brief report on the typewriter, stating that the death was apparently due to natural causes; as a formality, however, he left the case open until the corpse could be autopsied by the Medical Examiner. Late that afternoon he left and drove some thirty-odd miles to his neat little split-level home in Stony Point, New York, a clean, quiet suburb of Middle Americans who mowed their lawns, went to church on Sundays, and washed their own cars in their driveways. McCabe was greeted enthusiastically by his eleven-year-old son and two young daughters, his busty, bouncy Italo-American wife, his white-haired mother, and his dog, and, after washing up, went downstairs to the rumpus room and sank down in front of the TV, a cold beer in hand, and turned his attention to news from the world of sports.

The putrescent mass that had once been called Alexander Helmer had meanwhile taken a trip of several miles to a morgue operated by New York City in the Abraham Jacobi Hospital, a part of a large, dreary municipal medical center at Pelham Parkway and Eastchester Road. The morgue wagon, with a driver and a mortuary attendant, had arrived at 5:00 p.m., after McCabe's report had been turned in and the desk officer had phoned the Medical Examiner's office and asked to have the body removed for autopsy. The two mortuary employees, well versed in such matters, took one look at the thing they had to deal with and swiftly threw several of Helmer's scatter rugs on top of the pool of body liquids, stripped the shower curtain out of his bathroom and laid it down next to him, and, throwing a blanket from his bed over him to protect their hands, rolled him onto it, wrapped him up, and worked the untidy bundle into a mortuary bag. Aided by the policeman on duty, they carried the package downstairs to the wagon and drove with it to Jacobi, where in due course the corpse, still clothed and maggot-covered, was stowed away in a box and slid into the massive mortuary refrigerator.

At about 10:30 the next morning Detective Salvatore Russo of the Bronx Homicide Squad—a special unit not attached to any one precinct, but located in the 46th Precinct Station at 2120 Ryer Avenue—got a phone call from a long-time professional acquaintance, Dr. Charles Hochman, Deputy Chief Medical Examiner in the Bronx. Dr. Hochman, a loquacious elderly man who had been a medical examiner for thirty-five of his fifty-one years in medicine, told Russo in a breezy tone—he had performed some 10,000 post-mortems and nothing fazed him any longer—that he had something on a slab that Russo had better pop over and take a look at: namely, a homicide that had come in as a death from natural causes. Russo, a tall, heavy, stolid man of thirty-six and an old hand at homicide investigation, notified his superior, was assigned by him to the case, and arrived at the Jacobi Morgue a little later on. He looked on impassively as Hochman showed him the now naked corpse of Alexander Helmer, pointing out five small, clean-cut stab wounds on the left side of the body ranging from the area of the heart down to the upper abdomen, where a short loop of intestine protruded from one of them. Hochman himself had undressed the body earlier, meaning to perform a routine autopsy, and upon seeing this evidence of murder, had phoned Russo at once.

A few minutes later Detective Stephen McCabe, sitting in a courtroom at the Criminal Court building on 161st Street and waiting to testify in another case, felt a tap on his shoulder; turning, he saw a patrolman from his Precinct, who urgently whispered, "The old man you checked out yesterday was a homicide. They want you back at the squad." McCabe felt as if he had been punched in the stomach. His heart pounding, he mumbled an excuse to an assistant district attorney, hurried out, and all but ran around the block to the 42nd Precinct Station, cursing himself for having failed to spot the homicide during his investigation, and burning with shame that his reactions to the condition of the body had stopped him from examining it more thoroughly. Every homicide case, however challenging, means overtime, pressure, and the close supervision of the "bosses" (commanding officers); in this instance, McCabe not only dreaded the work ahead, but felt sick at having fumbled the case due to his weakness of stomach, and at having been caught doing so. For someone who, dealing with a street ruffian, could switch in a split second from affable good guy to fierce avenger and who took pride in his professional toughness, it was a wretchedly embarrassing beginning to a case that would prove anything but routine.

# II *A Policeman's Lot Is Not a Happy One*

IN most cases, of course, those who die alone and unnoticed do so from natural causes rather than from acts of violence; when their bodies begin to rot, neighbors call the police not because they think a crime has been committed, but because they automatically turn to the police for help with all sorts of disgusting or distressful problems of daily life. Yet while the public uses the police in this fashion far more often than in any other, it does not think of them as factotums and handymen, but as law-enforcers and keepers of the peace, praising or criticizing them for their performance in that role alone. Policemen themselves are drawn to their profession, and take pride in it, because of this latter image, and because the law-enforcing and peace-keeping role cloaks them with authority and gives them power; nevertheless, to their great discontent, the bulk of their actual work consists of mundane, boring, and often menial taks that have little or nothing to do with their major function and for which they get little thanks.

A staff study made for the Crime Commission a few years ago estimated that only a third of all police radio calls involve criminal matters, and a recent series of time-and-motion studies made by the New York Police Department bore this out in detail. On an average day the typical New York policeman spends six hours on patrol on foot or in a car, plus one hour actually responding to calls and performing specific police tasks. Of the time he spends responding to calls, two thirds involves non-criminal matters such as helping sick or injured people, getting passengers out of stuck elevators, freeing persons locked in their own apartments, disconnecting stuck auto horns, keeping traffic moving around accidents, and, of course, identifying dead bodies and seeing that they get moved to the morgue. And although the rest of his time on calls does involve criminal matters, the largest part of it—particularly on serious crimes—is spent making out reports (in quadruplicate or worse), traveling to and from court, and waiting endlessly to testify at arraignments, hearings, and trials. In 1969, in New York City, the average arrest took ten hours to complete; in the great majority of burglaries and robberies, however, the policeman never gets to arrest the wrongdoer or to see justice done, for there is no clue as to the identity of the criminal, and he can only ask questions of the victim and write out a report, knowing that nothing more can be done and that the victim will think him and his fellow officers indifferent and incompetent, if not corrupt.

Rather more in accord with the way the policeman likes to see himself are those many borderline calls which involve "keeping the peace" or maintaining order—that is, putting a stop (without making arrests) to such annoying or potentially dangerous behavior as quarrels in bars, unruly teen-age gatherings, noisy parties, and family fights. But while such interventions usually yield immediate results, give the policeman a gratifying sense of power and rightness, and involve little clerical work, they do have their own disagreeable side: policemen feel in such situations there may be danger, but that it is unpredictable and hence particularly to be feared. When a policeman has cornered an armed robber, he knows what to expect and is mentally and emotionally ready for it; when he accosts a drunk, asks a reckless driver to produce his license, or tries to stop a family fight, he never knows whether or not to expect violence, or in what form to look for it. The average citizen, when being questioned by or making a complaint to a policeman, feels uncomfortable, and senses (without understanding it) his hostility, coldness, and suspicion; what the citizen does not realize is that in the policeman's eyes anybody he has official reason to talk to may have something to hide—and hence may attack him without warning.

Most civilians—including most blacks—are therefore deeply ambivalent about the police. Only thoroughgoing conservatives see the police as the "finest," and only radicals and black militants see them wholly as "fascist pigs." To nearly everybody else they are a bewildering mixture of good and bad: ally and enemy, friend and foe; guardians of the law, but often corrupt; brave in combating criminals, but bullies toward those they dislike or suspect; defenders of justice and morality, but themselves deeply cynical about both.

These puzzling contradictions in the character of the police, and the resulting ambivalence felt about them by most of society, probably have deep historical roots. In our great period of national expansion, when the need for law-enforcers emerged, lawmen were often gunmen and desperadoes, hired because they were tougher and more expert with weapons than other men—but, unfortunately, easily bought off by anyone with money and illicit goals. As cities grew up in the West, the link between the police and crime grew with them, while in the East, as the cities developed powerful bosses and corrupt political machines, police forces fell under their domination and served their ends. Yet the police did protect the public in those exceedingly lawless and violent decades by combating and controlling street crime directly and at considerable cost to themselves, since their main job, according to criminologist David Dodd, consisted of hand-to-hand combat.

The middle-class public, while aware of their involvement in crime and corrupt politics, was nevertheless grateful for the protection the police provided and none too squeamish about the methods they used. In 1853, for instance, when a gang of thugs known as the "Honeymooners" was mugging and robbing well-dressed civilians in midtown Manhattan, a police captain named George Walling organized the first "Strong-Arm Squad," which was composed of husky officers who dressed in civilian clothes and carried clubs as inconspicuously as possible. Their *modus operandi* was simplicity itself: upon seeing any known member of the gang, they swiftly surrounded him and, without warning, beat him unconscious. The Honeymooners soon moved their operations elsewhere; the well-dressed midtowners breathed more easily, and if they disliked the illegal and brutal methods that had been used, they could blame them on the lower-class roughnecks who made up the police force.

That tradition has remained dominant in the police subculture to this day. Even now most policemen are recruited from lower-income groups to whom violence is a natural and legitimate way of righting wrongs; even now police training in most of the nation's smaller cities and some of its larger ones focuses upon the use of small arms and judo, with a bit of time for traffic control and the writing of tickets; even now most American policemen have less than a high-school education, and New York's police recruits in 1970 had an average I.Q. of only 98.2; even now the police tradition of "teaching them a lesson" is still alive in the form of the clubbing of peaceful (or at worst foul-mouthed) political demonstrators, the shoot-in raid on sleeping Black Panthers, and the gunning down of provocative but unarmed black college students.

The result is that, except for thorough-going conservatives, almost no one in America likes cops. Criminals see them as the enemy, non-white minorities see them as the occupying forces of the ruling white middle class, and much of that middle class regards them, with misgivings and distaste, as violent, sadistic, narrow-minded, vengeful—and unfortunately necessary—mercenaries. As a result, according to sociologists who have studied them, the police feel alienated, persecuted, and unappreciated; indeed, they themselves say so, the late Chief William Parker, for instance, explaining the bitterness of the police as due in part to the "shell of minorityism" within which they live, and a former New York Police Commissioner, Michael J. Murphy, saying in 1965, "The police officer, too, belongs to a minority group—a highly visible minority group—and is also subject to stereotyping and mass attack."

But not even the overt hostility of today's blacks and radicals is any more exasperating and embittering to the police than the hostility of the liberal intelligentsia, who for many years have attacked the traditions of the police subculture and fought a long battle (culminating in a series of important victories during the years of the Warren Court) to deprive the police of their historic practices of forcible entry, seizure of evidence, stopping and searching of "suspicious" persons, and incommunicado interrogation of suspects not yet under arrest.

Most police feel that they have been "shackled" and "handcuffed" by "bleeding hearts" who "give the criminal every benefit of the doubt" and themselves none at all; they find this outrageous and incomprehensible, since the very same bleeding hearts and their lawyers, judges, and political leaders want to be protected from criminals and are loud in their denunciation of the police for not doing a better job. But even more offensive to the police than this handcuffing is the denigration of their character and ethics implied by the landmark civil-rights decisions of the 1960s. A field study by a team of Yale law students of the effects of the *Miranda* decision—which guarantees all suspects, poor as well as rich, the chance to have a lawyer present at any custodial interrogation—found that to detectives, *"Miranda* is not merely a change in the rules to help the suspect . . . [but] a personal rebuke . . . a statement that police are nasty people, who cannot be trusted to treat a suspect in a civilized manner."

Thus the police feel that they try to make the streets safe for the decent members of the society that employs them, only to have the courts of that same society continually undo their work. In Manhattan, according to District Attorney Frank Hogan, there were 10,000 arrests for loitering in 1969, but the courts held only 4 percent of them to be valid. Even in cases of mugging, a vastly more serious crime, the fallout rate is astonishing: in a study of the first 136 persons arrested for mugging in 1967, *The New York Times* found that the courts dismissed nearly a third of the cases for lack of evidence or other legal reasons, and convicted not a single one of the rest on the serious charge of first-degree robbery placed against most of them by the police, and for which they could have been sentenced to as much as twenty-five years. Instead, the courts reduced their charges and sentenced them to comparatively trifling terms of six to eighteen months—which meant that, with time off for good behavior, most of them were back on the streets, unrehabilitated, in about four months, and the rest in about a year.

The alienation that all police suffer from has special power in the case of detectives. Theirs is the most prestigious form of police work and in many ways the most satisfying, since they deal only with criminal matters and thereby live up to the policeman's ideal self-image. Rank for rank, they get better pay than other officers, and feel themselves to be the élite of the Department; even their shields, at least in New York, are gold in color rather than silver. Unlike cops on patrol, detectives are not mere watchmen but something far more glamorous —avengers of wrongs already committed—and it is deeply gratifying to them that they get to make roughly four times as many arrests per year as uniformed policemen on patrol. Nevertheless, their work is filled with frustrations and their position in society with contradictions —perhaps even more so than other policemen because their favorite investigative methods have come under close scrutiny and been subjected to biting criticism by the Supreme Court in recent years. The "clearance rate"—the percentage of cases "solved" by arrest, though not necessarily by conviction—is the most important measure of their accomplishment, and it is no wonder that every court limitation on the techniques of investigation seems to them a senseless interference with the job they are expected to do, and makes them feel that they are laboring and risking their lives for an ungrateful and undeserving society.

From 1963 to 1969, the overall crime clearance rate declined steadily throughout the nation, and in 1970 remained at the 1969 low. Although many complex factors are responsible, the Warren Court decisions excluding evidence obtained by illegal searches and seizures, or by illegal interrogations, are blamed by detectives more often than any other factor. For in the past their success in solving tough cases often depended on their power to collar and frisk suspects without legal grounds, and to bring them in to the station house and interrogate them long and strenuously (often "working them over" to help soften stubborn resistance) until confessions were forthcoming. Detectives who did this were hard, tough men, but not necessarily sadistic; in many cases they had no alternative except to leave the case unsolved. For despite the existence of manuals and textbooks on investigative technique and all the talk about "scientific detection," the greater part of the science of investigation is a literary myth spawned by Conan Doyle and passed on down in a direct line to the authors of the latest whodunits. In actual fact, fingerprints are helpful only once in a while; blood samples and fingernail scrapings are even less frequently useful; Holmesian analysis of the habits and movements of suspects is seldom of great value; and, generally speaking, the gathering of collateral evidence from persons and things is feasible only when the crime is of a sort where witnesses or informers can point to a suspect, or where the criminal leaves objects or traces that can be linked with him. In most muggings—even those which involve murderous violence—there is practically nothing to go on, and no skills or techniques exist for collecting crucial evidence other than interrogation, assuming one is lucky enough to have a suspect and is unhindered by the enforcement of that suspect's constitutional rights. Not surprisingly, a recent study by the Rand Institute in New York City revealed that most of the robbers who get arrested have been unlucky enough to have a uniformed patrolman nearby when they committed their crimes; of those who escaped, however, and whose crimes were turned over to the detectives for investigation, fewer than 6 percent were ever arrested.

At the empyrean pinnacle of the criminal justice system, things look somewhat different. In the historic *Escobedo* decision of 1964, Justice Arthur Goldberg, speaking for the Supreme Court, declared:

> We have learned the lesson of history, ancient and modern, that a system of criminal law enforcement which comes to depend on the "confession" will, in the long run, be less reliable and more subject to abuses than a system which depends on extrinsic evidence independently secured through skillful investigation. . . .
> This Court also has recognized that "history amply shows that confessions have often been extorted to save law enforcement officials the trouble and effort of obtaining valid and independent evidence . . ." *Haynes* v. *Washington,* 373 U.S. 503, 519.

This seems to assume that there almost always *is* extrinsic evidence that detectives could discover if only they would work harder and were more skillful. But not even the most highly regarded detectives or detective squads have near-perfect records, and everywhere the clearance rates for robbery and burglary are particularly low because there is so seldom anything to link the victim to a specific suspect. We may wholeheartedly agree with the Court that interrogation is exceedingly subject to abuses of a despicable nature; we may even look forward to a time when no suspect will ever be interrogated without a lawyer by his side, even if he waives his right to have one there; but we ought not delude ourselves that skillful investigation can always independently secure extrinsic evidence good enough to convict. In any case, the empyrean view of detection requires all detectives to be brilliant, logical, systematic, and immensely skillful, whereas in fact most of them are rather ordinary men, without rigorous and scientific training, who go about their business in the same fumbling and slipshod way that other ordinary men do, and with commensurate results.

# III   *We Know a Lot Already*

IN many if not most crimes of violence, the collecting of valid extrinsic evidence is exceedingly difficult not only because there is almost nothing to collect, but because detective work, for all its odds and ends of technique, has no all-embracing logical procedure, no essential systematic method. And as if this were not bad enough, investigation is continually hampered by the distortions of human perception, the tricks of memory, and the "contamination" of evidence by outside influences.

Several examples of contamination greeted the upset and sweating McCabe—still smarting from an uncomfortable conference with his squad commander, Lieutenant Howard Norton, and the commanding officer of the Bronx Homicide Squad, Lieutenant Edward G. Clark—when he and two uniformed policemen from the 42nd Precinct entered apartment 2-B on the morning of October 19th. On the kitchen floor, all over the pool of brownish liquid and its maggots, there was a heavy sprinkling of white powder—disinfectant strewn there by Mrs. Ambos shortly after the body and the policeman on guard had left the previous evening. Not only had the powder partly obscured the traces of the body's position, but its presence meant that at least one person had been in the apartment unobserved by the police and hence that there was no guarantee that things were exactly as they had been.

Nor was this all. McCabe, although struggling to keep his stomach from heaving up his breakfast—the odor in the apartment was only a little less powerful than the day before—noticed with alarm that the fetid, leaking bag of rotten groceries no longer stood by the kitchen door but was in the living-room (he later learned that the mortuary attendant had moved it to make room when maneuvering the corpse out of the kitchen); he replaced it, but the result was a reconstruction rather than virgin evidence. Worse yet, as he wandered around the apartment looking for anything that might be revealing, he realized that Kacerosky and the other policemen who had preceded him yesterday had searched the place for valuables, undoubtedly obscuring any fingerprints that might have been on drawer handles and altering the condition of the drawers themselves.

While he was mulling all this over, Detective Sal Russo arrived and immediately lit up an acrid black Italian cigar to combat the foul odor throughout the apartment. He told McCabe he'd been assigned to work with him on the case, and McCabe felt better at once; though he knew Russo only slightly, he had heard of his reputation as a dogged, tireless homicide detective with an impressive record of arrests. Russo, a great bear of a man, but smooth and swift of movement, had been on the homicide squad three years, and had had a lot of homicide experience prior to that in his ten years of service, most of them as a squad detective, in a gang-ridden area of Brooklyn. Technically, he would be McCabe's assistant, but in actual fact he would be running things (under his own lieutenant's supervision) and McCabe would be *his* assistant. This, however, was standard practice; McCabe felt no pique, but only a sense of relief that a first-rate homicide investigator was with him on the case, and that the burden would be more on Russo's shoulders than his own.

Russo, his sallow, low-browed face intent but impassive, went through the apartment trailed by McCabe, drawing a floor plan with paper and pencil and tossing off to McCabe a dazzling series of deductions, hypotheses, and questions relating to the things he saw. There was a pair of binoculars on the kitchen table; why didn't the killer take them? Or was Helmer a "bushwhacker"—a long-distance Peeping Tom on whom someone had taken revenge? A piece of Bazooka bubble gum, still wrapped, lay on the kitchen floor, and a wrapper from another piece was on the kitchen counter; an old man with dentures would never have chewed such gum, so whose was it? Did he have a teen-age friend? Was there something queer about the relationship? Or was the killer a stranger—a junkie, with an addict's periodic craving for sugar? A tiny splatter of blood was on the refrigerator door—probably Helmer's, but perhaps not; perhaps he had fought and the killer had bled; the blood was worth checking. Then there was the bag of spoiled groceries: the old man hadn't had time to put his things in the refrigerator, so it was very likely that the killer had waited for him to open the front door and then rushed him. But what about the fact that his wallet, full of money, had been left on his person? A very tough question; but perhaps the killer was looking for something more, had expected to find money in the apartment and had ignored the body. Possible corroboration: there was an empty metal box in the kitchen that might have been his cashbox, but there was not one cent elsewhere in the apartment.

Russo told McCabe they'd need the fingerprint men and photographers, and McCabe got on the phone. While waiting for them to arrive, he unpacked the grocery bag at Russo's suggestion, gingerly taking out the rotten eggs, the mushy tomatoes, the carton of milk that had soured and burst open, the ice cream that had melted and gone bad—a stinking, useless mess. But on top of it all, unharmed, was a prize: a cash-register slip from the A&P, dated October 9th. Since no one would let a bag of such purchases stand around outside the refrigerator, this slip almost certainly fixed the date of the crime and was the most important piece of evidence to come to light that day. McCabe tucked the precious slip in his shirt pocket, and put everything else back in the bag, so that the photographers would be able to record the scene in as nearly pristine a state as possible.

In a little while the apartment was a beehive of investigative activity: policemen everywhere, flashbulbs popping, a detective delicately brushing fingerprint dust onto doorknobs, drawer handles, and cabinet doors, and scrutinizing them under a bright light, McCabe and Russo pawing through drawers and sorting out photos, correspondence, bills, and other papers that might give them clues. Though all this looked thoroughly professional and methodical, it was both unrewarding and shot through with little everyday errors. The Police Laboratory men neglected to collect scrapings of the dried blood on the refrigerator door, the fingerprint man found only useless smudges throughout the apartment except for a single print above the refrigerator door handle, and the photographers forgot to take any shots of the grocery bag in its place by the kitchen doorway (McCabe, not knowing this, had Mrs. Ambos throw out the rotten mess for him, thereby leaving himself with no proof of its existence or position except the recollections of police officers). And not only did McCabe keep the A&P sales slip in his own pocket, but he did the same thing with the gum wrapper and with the piece of bubble gum—which, from his perspiration, began to come unwrapped. Worse still, he later put these three items in his own locker at the Precinct and kept them there for months, although materials to be used as evidence are supposed to be entrusted to the Police Property Clerk in order to preserve their provenance. As for the search of Helmer's effects, while it yielded a picture of the old man's sad, barren way of life, it gave the detectives no clue as to identity of his assailant; all they came up with were the names of a few correspondents, his lawyer, a hearing-aid repair shop, a hospital where he had been a patient, and so on, and while one or more of these might conceivably lead them to something useful, it didn't seem very likely.

Not until mid-afternoon was Russo ready to leave the apartment; even then he showed no signs of fatigue, but seemed filled with energy and ready to launch a dozen lines of investigation at once, as soon as he could get back to the Precinct and confer with his superior and McCabe's. First, however, he and McCabe talked to a few people in the building, learning nothing whatever until they got to Mrs. Ambos. The aged landlady was well aware by now that Helmer had been murdered; indeed, on the pretext of putting down more disinfectant, she had even barged into the apartment in the middle of all the activity and been rudely ordered out by a red-faced and excitable McCabe. Interviewing her now in her bare, shabby living-room, the two detectives found that she had a very interesting—but hopelessly confusing —story to tell, which was made no clearer by her German accent and her aged-person's way of assuming that her listeners knew the people and events she was referring to.

Oh, yes, she could recall the last time she saw Helmer: it was a week and a half ago, a little after 7:00 p.m., because she was standing in the vestibule about to lock the front door for the evening, when he came in, carrying a little paper bag in one hand. (A *little* bag? How little?) Not big, not tiny, a little bag! (In his *hand,* not in his arm?) In his hand, in his hand! (Did he say anything?) No, just passed by without a word. (Why?) Because he never spoke to her, that's how he was. So he went upstairs, but the Spanish boys had left a few minutes earlier—(Spanish boys! *What* Spanish boys?)—two light-skinned young fellows who told Mrs. Ambos they were looking for their cousin, and went upstairs, and came down in a few minutes and left. (Left before Helmer came home, and didn't come back in?) Correct, and she herself had locked the door right after Helmer went up, and then she had gone upstairs to visit with Mrs. Varela, next door to

Helmer, and found the blood in the hall—(*Blood* in the hall! *What blood?*)—droplets of fresh blood sprinkled around the third-floor hallway; she had rung Mrs. Varela's bell and borrowed her mop, cleaned the floor—thinking someone had had a minor accident—and then gone into Mrs. Varela's for the evening, and she had never seen Helmer again. (But no one followed him up, and no one came down before you got to his floor?) No, absolutely not. (And what day was this?) Thursday. (*Thursday?* But Thursday was the 8th. Are you sure?) Positive. (Couldn't it have been Friday the 9th?) No, no; Thursday. Ask Ena Varela.

(That night, when Mrs. Varela came home from work, she was brought to the Precinct and interviewed; she recalled the episode of the blood, and spending that same evening chatting with Mrs. Ambos in the kitchen; yes, it had been Thursday, October 8th, and no, she had never seen or heard Helmer again. Which only made things worse, for as significant as some of Mrs. Ambos' details sounded—Puerto Rican youths reconnoitering the territory; Helmer coming home, bag in hand; blood on the hallway floor—her story didn't fit any reasonable hypothesis of the crime. For one thing, the date she gave was plainly wrong. For another, she spoke of a "little" bag, while the grocery bag in the apartment had been medium-sized. For a third, nobody could have gone up the steps after Helmer without her seeing him. And why would there be blood in the public hall if Helmer was attacked in his kitchen?—or, at least, why would there be no trail of blood from one place to the other? And if he had been attacked in the hall in those few minutes before Mrs. Ambos got upstairs, why had she heard nothing and seen no one running down the steps and out? It could be, of course, that she had seen the Puerto Rican youths, and Helmer, and the blood in the hall, on Thursday the 8th, and that they were all coincidental; it could be that Helmer had been killed on Friday by someone else. But her story was too close to being a meaningful one to be dismissed lightly, and they sent for Mrs. Ambos that same night and had her questioned again at the Precinct by several detectives; she held firm, and even grew waspish and sharp when one of them, getting tough, threatened to lock her up, so they apologized and drove her home.)

When Russo and McCabe had first returned to the Precinct, they found a full complement of "bosses" waiting for them in Lieutenant Norton's room—Norton himself, Lieutenant Clark (Russo's superior), Inspector August Harms, commanding officer of the 7th Detective District, and Assistant Chief Inspector Frederick Lussen, commander of all detectives in the Bronx. Lussen, stiff-backed, stern and formal, asked McCabe sharply why he had failed to report the death as a homicide after his first investigation; McCabe, inwardly shaking at being quizzed by so high-ranking a boss, stammeringly described the condition of the body and the apartment, and after a while Lussen appeared satisfied, if hardly pleased. The four bosses had been discussing the case while waiting for the detectives, and now, hearing what Russo and McCabe had to report, outlined the overall approach to be followed. There would be a general canvass—a door-to-door survey of people in Helmer's building and throughout the neighborhood, to see if anyone knew anything; there would be individual interviews with every person whose name appeared in Helmer's effects; there would be laboratory studies of the evidence collected in the apartment; there would be inquiries at mental hospitals to see if anyone from the Melrose area had recently been released; and so on. Russo, of course, was already familiar with these and other lines of investigation; the bosses, however, gave him and McCabe the go-ahead to use all these large-scale procedures, and assigned a number of detectives from several Bronx squads to assist them.

Finally the conference was ended, and Russo and McCabe were given permission to withdraw. Sighing with relief, they left and immediately started mapping out the details of the investigation. Unmindful of having had no dinner, they worked on feverishly and singlemindedly until midnight at McCabe's desk in the squad room, a noisy, barren, comfortless place of desks and file cabinets, naked light bulbs and peeling paint, bare windows and worn wooden floors. Russo, oblivious of his surroundings, sometimes chewed on a dead cigar or sipped bitter cold coffee, totally involved in his planning and doing what meant more to him than anything else in the world. The son of a city sanitation worker, he had grown up in a cold-water flat in Ocean Hill, a crime-ridden Brooklyn slum, but his father, an Italian immigrant who spoke almost no English, had Old World ideas and an Old World patriarchal command of his own home, and all four Russo children grew up good Catholics, unquestioning patriots, and right-minded citizens. Young Salvatore Russo, indeed, had always deeply admired the policemen who tried to combat the criminals in his area, and who, in his social circle, were looked up to as brave and important men. As a boy, he had even gone to the library and read about policemen as other boys read about explorers or war heroes. To be a policeman had remained his dream as he grew up, and after military service he had applied to the New York Police Department, been accepted, and had been a cop for fourteen years. It was not just a job, for him, but a calling: a hardworking, selfless bloodhound of a man, he lived with his wife and her invalid mother in half of a small, tidily furnished two-family house in a lower-middle-class residential part of the Bronx, but often saw little of it for days on end, working fourteen hours at a time day after day whenever he was on an important case. His wife accepted this without complaint, knowing that he put his job and his duty above all else. Curiously enough, however, he had also developed something of a taste for going to Broadway shows with his wife when he could, and for visiting art museums, but he never mentioned these things to his fellow detectives, most of whom would have found them rather suspect.

Such divertissements were far from his mind that night, however. With McCabe by his side, he was organizing the campaign—shapeless and non-logical, but covering practically every imaginable possibility. Before he was through, he had made plans which, over a four-day period, used the part-time services of some thirty detectives from four or five Bronx squads and resulted in the filing of fifty-five reports. An ordinary mugging, of course, might produce a routine inquiry or two by a couple of detectives, and a one-page report—and not even that, in many a city, if the victim were black, Puerto Rican, or Mexican-American; a felony murder, however, particularly of a middle-class white man, automatically is assigned fairly high priority by the police.

One detective was sent out to supervise a crew from the Department of Public Works, who dredged a number of sewers near Helmer's building in hopes of finding the murder weapon; they did find several knives, but none that fitted Helmer's wounds.

Another called on Helmer's lawyer, learned that the old man had left nearly $22,000 worth of stocks, and that he had willed some of his money to the Red Cross, and the rest to the aging switchboard lady from Sheffield's and to another elderly widow, neither of whom was a likely suspect, and neither of whom had really believed herself to be in his will.

A detective went to the nursing home, and found Helmer's brother suffering from senile dementia; he talked to the manager, but learned nothing except that Helmer had refused to be responsible for his brother's bills.

Another checked with the New York State Department of Mental Hygiene to see if any psychotics from Melrose had recently been released from mental hospitals; none had. Four detectives fanned out and visited Bronx hospitals, checking for patients with recent cuts or bites, since Helmer might have fought back; all cut or bitten patients, however, had adequate explanations. Another detective checked with the Police Lab to see what they had learned from Helmer's clothing (nothing useful) and from the blood on the refrigerator (the Lab man had forgotten to collect it, and Mrs. Ambos had since cleaned up). Still another checked to see what the fingerprint technicians had to say (nothing: the one print obtained didn't match any of Helmer's, or those of the policemen who had been in the apartment, or, later on, those of the suspects).

One detective went down to the A&P and spoke to both the assistant manager and to Annette Odierno, the checkout clerk. The former, looking at a picture of Helmer, said he had known the man by sight, but had no recollection of seeing him on the fatal Friday; neither did Miss Odierno. She identified the sales slip as coming from her machine, which meant that Helmer had been alive on the 9th, but she said that nothing on the slip would indicate what time of day he had been there. Mrs. Ambos' story thus was proven wrong—but she herself had already changed it, for when McCabe dropped in on her on Tuesday to go over it again, she said that she and Ena Varela had talked things over and decided they had been in error: it had been Friday night, the 9th, when the Spanish boys had been there, when she had seen Helmer come home, and when she had mopped up the blood in the hallway. She was as positive about this now as she had been, the previous day, that it had all happened on Thursday, October 8th. Her change of story was not wholly convincing, for she knew by now that the murder had taken place on the 9th, but even if this played no part in her altered recollection, her story still made it impossible for anyone to have entered and followed Helmer up the stairs. Yet the attack could not have occurred earlier, if Mrs. Ambos saw Helmer alive at about 7:15, and it could not have occurred later, for he would have had time to put his groceries away.

Clearly, Russo and McCabe could only hope to turn up someone else who knew something, since neither Mrs. Ambos' story, nor the

physical evidence in the apartment, nor the rundown of outside possibilities was yielding anything. On Tuesday, even before this had become clear, they began the canvass: more than half a dozen detectives
went out to ring doorbells in 399 and in neighboring apartment buildings, drop in on shopkeepers, and generally try to learn anything
they could from people in the neighborhood. No one in Helmer's
building had seen or heard anything that confirmed Mrs. Ambos'
story, or anything that offered clues as to the identity of the murderer,
though the few people who had known Helmer added to McCabe's
and Russo's general knowledge of the kind of man he had been and
thus fortified Russo's feeling about the kind of criminal who had
sought him out. A street crony of Helmer's, who knew him only
slightly, said that Helmer used to talk big about being in the stock
market, and a filling-station manager said that Helmer occasionally
passed the time of day with him and invariably mentioned that he had
stock in the oil company that owned the station. People in the local
candy stores and dry-cleaning shops did not recognize his picture or
know his name; the kind of women who lean out of windows and
watch the passing scene were unable to say anything useful about him;
and an auto-parts shopkeeper nearby did recognize his picture, but
said that Helmer and another oldster both used to wave at him and
say hello, and he wasn't sure which was which.

McCabe, an overwrought and hyperactive novice at this kind of
investigation, grew discouraged, pounded his fist on the desk, and
paced up and down, but Russo was imperturbable and rock-steady.
"Take it easy, Steve," he said. "We know a lot already. We know
this wasn't some ordinary mugger who needed a few bucks for a load
of junk, or he'd have hit the old man in the vestibule and grabbed his
wallet and run. *This* guy waited to take him in his apartment because
he knew Helmer lived there alone and he thought there was a lot of
money around. But he probably *was* a junkie, and strung out or
scared—and when the old man fought back, he panicked and stabbed
him, not once, but again and again. See what I mean? There's something there. We got something to go on."

And yet, with reports flowing in from all fronts, Russo and McCabe
had to admit, when asked by their superiors, that they still had not
one scrap of physical evidence pointing to any identifiable individual,
not one suspicious relationship to look into, and not one witness who
had seen a describable intruder.

But they were not without other resources; indeed, even though scientific detection and the effort to gather extrinsic evidence had produced not one suspect, they still had two other methods which might do so. And here McCabe was as well informed as Russo, for every detective in every investigative agency in the country knows that two of the most useful techniques for ferreting out suspects in such crimes have nothing whatever to do with analytical investigation or scientific detection; indeed, they are of ancient vintage and alien political tradition, having been practiced for many centuries by inquisitors, agents of the Crown, secret police, constables, and sheriffs.

The first is the round-up or dragnet, which formerly involved mass arrests—and still does in many countries—but which today in the United States takes the form of seeking out, questioning, or "inviting" to the station house for a talk any and all local probationers, parolees, and persons who have ever been arrested, and even those who merely strike the police as unsavory. The second is the use of petty criminals as "stoolies" or informers, who are sometimes paid off in cash, occasionally in drugs, but most frequently in the reduction or dismissal of charges pending against them. It is baffling and exasperating to most detectives that the nation's liberals, and many of its jurists, regard the first as unconstitutional and both as contemptible; but undeterred by this, the investigators continue to do what they feel they must, and to conceal their actions as best they can.

# IV *Suspectology*

DETECTIVES investigating a crime of violence, particularly a robbery-murder in or near a black or Puerto Rican slum, have a number of clear preconceptions as to the kind of person to hunt for. Although, like most police, they are contemptuous of "bleeding-heart" theories of crime causation, their own notions are, at least in part, pragmatic equivalents of the sociological and psychological explanations of crime. The sociologist speaks of the "transmission through culture of criminal roles, values, and patterns of behavior"; the cop means somewhat the same thing when he says that "any kid who has grown up in the jungle" is likely to have learned to be "rotten," a "scumbag," and a "punk." The criminologist speaks of "associational delinquency," or the influence of "criminal peer groups" and the pressure within them toward "cultural conformity"; the cop says that "anybody who hangs around with a bunch of bums" is almost surely a bum himself. The criminologist speculates about the role of "relative deprivation" and about "deviant reactions to the blocking of legitimate goals"; the cop is talking about somewhat the same thing when he says, "These no-good bastards want everything decent people have, but they don't want to work for it." The sociologist speaks of the "social disorganization" and "lack of group identity" among people in present-day slums; the cop says that today's slum-dwellers are "animals" who aren't "decent" even to their own, let alone to outsiders. The psychologist talks of "poor superego development" and of the "failure to internalize social values" due to faulty family relationships and the absence of a male model in many a slum home; the cop says that "the little bastards" spawned by "winos" who "took off" long ago, and whose mothers are "welfare bums," have never had "their asses whipped" when they should have been and consequently "have no goddamned idea of right and wrong."

Along with these sensible, if inelegantly worded, notions, most police also have a number of lower-middle-class and socially conservative prejudices as to what constitutes suspicious behavior or a criminogenic background. They regard anyone who is shiftless or lazy, unkempt or poor, outlandish in dress or boisterous, as "no good." More serious is any form of defiance or talking back to a policeman; anyone who does so is a "wise guy," and very likely "into something"; even without evidence of other wrongdoing, most police regard "disrespect" as a crime in itself, and a third to a half of police, in two separate studies, said they felt that defiance or verbal abuse warranted their "roughing up" the wise guy.

Policemen also are more prone to suspect black males, especially young ones, of criminality than white males, and they feel that young Negroes "need to be taught a lesson" more often than whites, the latter being more likely to benefit from a "break." (A recent study made in a large Eastern city showed that police let whites off with warnings half again as often as they did Negroes, even where equivalent crimes of violence were involved.) In part this is an expression of common lower-middle-class anti-Negro feeling, but in part it is the result of the policeman's observing the high rate of violent crime among Negro males, and daily experiencing the hostility of slum Negroes. A Crime Commission study in Boston, Washington, and Chicago found anti-Negro feeling widespread among all police, but severest among those who work in predominantly black precincts: over three quarters of the latter officers expressed "prejudiced" or "highly prejudiced" sentiments toward Negroes—as did almost 30 percent of the Negro policemen working in those precincts.

Policemen, and detectives in particular, also seem to feel that virtually everyone in the slums who uses any drug stronger than marijuana is involved in some other form of criminal activity, and that nearly all heroin addicts are muggers. But the evidence is far from conclusive; such statistics as the Crime Commission could collect indicated that drug addicts were considerably more likely to commit crimes against property than against persons, and that violent crime had risen considerably even in cities where there was no great drug traffic. A fair-minded way of putting it might be that although many muggers are addicts, many addicts are not muggers; the police, however, are not inclined to make such distinctions.

These several preconceptions are subsumed under the historic and most important police assumption about where to look for suspects: namely, among those who have already been in trouble. Police act as if anyone who has ever committed a crime or been accused of one —whether or not found guilty—is forever untrustworthy and most likely up to no good. Now, it is undoubtedly true that our courts and penal system rehabilitate relatively few criminals, and it is also true that many of those whom the police arrest go on to commit further offenses as soon as they are released on bail, probation, or parole. But police thinking goes far beyond considering the odds of recidivism, and even beyond the general lay feeling that a man once found guilty can never again be presumed innocent (a view forbidden in the courtroom, but held, consciously or unconsciously, nearly everywhere else). The police view is quite simple: anyone who has ever been convicted or even arrested, or about whom the police have ever heard any derogatory gossip, is very likely to be guilty of some present criminal activity.

Accordingly, when there are no specific leads in a serious crime such as rape or murder, detectives often make a list of all persons in the area who have ever been convicted or arrested, or who associate with anyone who has, and then canvass these persons, either conducting "field interrogations" or asking them to come to the station house "to clear up a couple of matters." From many years of exposure to detective movies and murder mysteries, many Americans think these are proper and harmless procedures. But they certainly are not harmless to the ego and the social status of the interrogated persons, particularly considering the hostile and belittling manner many detectives take toward them. Moreover, except for persons out of jail on probation, it is questionable whether either procedure is proper. Certainly, to be confronted in public or in one's home by a detective and treated like a suspect, when the detective has no "probable cause" to connect one to the crime other than one's color, background, and general lifestyle, is a violation of the constitutional right—guaranteed by the Fourth Amendment—to be "secure . . . against unreasonable searches and seizures." The same would seem to be even more true of the so-called "invitation" to come to the police station to clear up some matter: although the Supreme Court has not yet ruled as to whether such an invitation constitutes a seizure, civil-rights lawyers argue that it is, pointing out that for most people—and especially for persons with any sort of arrest record—the invitation has the psychological force of command (and is delivered that way). In the absence of sufficient cause to make an arrest the police have no legal right to compel the individual to come in for questioning, but they do so anyway, though not so openly or often as formerly or as the police do in totalitarian countries; in the District of Columbia, for instance, over one quarter of all felony arrests in a recent year were found to be lacking in probable cause, and thus illegal. On occasion, the police violate the Fourth Amendment so flagrantly and outrageously as to make legal history: in Meridian, Mississippi, a few years ago, a young black raped an elderly white woman, who was able to describe him only in the most general terms; police thereupon rounded up virtually every young black male in the community, fingerprinted all twenty-five of them, and identified the rapist, who was convicted. But the Supreme Court, seeking to deter such police actions in the future, set aside the conviction in 1969, saying, "Nothing is more clear than that the Fourth Amendment was meant to prevent wholesale intrusions upon the personal security of our citizenry, whether these intrusions be termed 'arrests' or 'investigatory detentions.' " The law-abiding middle-class citizen may find it difficult to see the justice of this decision unless he imagines how it would feel if he and a couple dozen of his neighbors were rousted out of bed by armed detectives and taken to a station house under arrest—and thereafter forever marked as having once been arrested—because some unidentified white man of approximately his age had committed a crime.

Such police-state methods are no longer widely used in the United States. But the police have other ways—more time-consuming, but nearly as effective—of achieving the same end. Most lower-class persons, even those who have never been in any trouble, are afraid to refuse to come to the station house, or are unaware that they need not go unless the detective has grounds to arrest them; realistically, too, they know that some detectives will, if provoked, use force—and then charge them with assault, beating them to provide some "evidence" for the charge. Often, to make it easier, detectives prefer to "con" a suspect into coming to the station house on some pretext (to straighten out a parking ticket; to clear up a question of the ownership of a stolen car), and once he is there, will surround him with detectives and subject him to strenuous questioning.

Field interrogation and dragnet procedures work best of all with those who are on parole, for such persons, being still technically prisoners, have only limited civil rights, and in any case are afraid to resist interrogation and detention even when there is no probable cause. Even people charged with some offense and out on bail, though still technically innocent, are treated much the same way and usually prove tractable, if sullen. As for those who have never been in trouble and are more resistant, the police have yet another useful tool: legal arrest on such vague catch-all grounds as "vagrancy," "loitering," "loitering for purposes of using narcotics," "disorderly conduct," and so on. In their own eyes, the police never use such statutes unfairly; they only arrest persons they can tell are bums and punks, and whom, they feel, it is perfectly all right to treat that way. But in the police view, it should be considered right to treat even the "clean" and law-abiding citizen the same way in order to solve a crime. Their outlook has been acidly paraphrased by Professor Herbert L. Packer as follows:

> Of course the police should be entitled to arrest a person when they have probable cause . . . but it would be absurd to suggest that an arrest is permissible *only* in that situation. The slight

invasion of personal freedom and privacy involved in stopping a person on the street to ask him questions or even taking him to the station house for a period of questioning and other investigation is necessary in a wide variety of situations that only by the exercise of hypocrisy could be described as involving "probable cause." . . . [As for] previous offenders, [they] should be subject to arrest at any time for the limited purpose of determining whether they have been engaging in criminal activities, especially when it is known that a crime of the sort they have committed has taken place. . . .

In addition to field interrogations and round-ups of persons they consider generally (but not specifically) suspicious, detectives often rely on the use of "stoolies" (or, more euphemistically, "confidential informants" and "special employees"), particularly in vice, narcotics, and subversion, and in felony murders in which there are no good clues. Police departments are extremely secretive about the extent of their use of informers because a large part of the public not only regards the latter as loathsome, but finds something detestable in the spectacle of law-enforcement officials rewarding certain criminals in order to catch and prosecute others. Even the underworld considers the informer system dirty, immoral, and proof that law enforcement is not clean of hand. To policemen, however, not only is the informer system essential and morally justifiable, but the informer himself is often admirable. As America's top cop, J. Edgar Hoover, has put it:

> Experience demonstrates that the cooperation of individuals who can readily furnish accurate information is essential if law enforcement is to discharge its obligations. . . . There can be no doubt that the use of informants in law enforcement is justified. The public interest and the personal safety of these helpful citizens demand the zealous protection of their confidence. Unlike the totalitarian practice, the informant in America serves of his own free will, fulfilling one of the citizenship obligations of our democratic form of government.

Mr. Hoover is ill-informed (to make the most charitable interpretation): everyone in police work knows that, except in espionage and countersubversion, informers are almost always criminals working for police who have caught them "dirty" (carrying drugs) or in some other criminal act, and who threaten to "bury them" if they don't cooperate, but promise to "get them off light" if they do. A leading manual of technique on the use of stoolies—*The Informer in Law Enforcement,* by Malachi L. Harney and John C. Cross—forthrightly admits that police, prosecutors, and courts almost universally reward informers, and that the reward usually consists of a lightened sentence, a more generous consideration of the request for parole or probation, and the like. Other sources suggest that informers are rewarded by being permitted to continue their criminal activities unmolested or with actual police protection. Customs Bureau agents and federal narcotics investigators rely heavily on informers, and federal law actually empowers judges to award up to half the fine imposed on a convicted smuggler to the stoolie whose information led to his arrest.

The public has little idea how frequently the police rely upon informers, for detectives make every effort to conceal the truth, both to keep their informers from being exposed and to protect themselves from public criticism. When informers' tips lead them to evidence, they write up their arrest reports and tell their stories in court so as to make it appear that they got the evidence by other means, or at least knew of it before making the arrest or search that yielded it. Very often the informer cannot tell them that any actual evidence exists; all that he has to offer is hearsay, gossip, or a suspicion, based on circumstances, that points to the suspect. But if, in the investigation of a serious crime of violence, the person named by the informer is black or Puerto Rican, associates with known offenders or loafers, uses drugs, comes from a broken home, is unemployed, and has a police record, the detective is not likely to suspend judgment or to approach him with a judge's regard for due process or the presumption of innocence. All the detective's training—and his prejudices—tell him he has a good suspect in view, and the makings of a "good collar" or felony arrest of a kind likely to bring him esteem.

To the detective, the good suspect is more than suspicious; he is probably guilty. The detective deals with such people all the time, and considers himself a specialist in recognizing criminals; in advance of collecting evidence of the kind that can be used by a prosecutor, he makes judgments of guilt or innocence based on clues, hearsay, and the suspect's past history, none of which, under our system of justice, is admissible in court. And having pretty much made up his mind, he is very apt to deal with the suspect as if he already had sound, legal, probable cause to connect him with the crime; viewing the good suspect as guilty until proven innocent, the detective behaves toward him as if he had already lost his civil rights and as if his punishment were overdue.

---

## V   Get Your Coat

---

ASSUMING that the killer was a junkie and a mugger, and therefore not likely to have ventured far in search of his victim, Russo marked off on a map an area some half-dozen blocks in radius all around the apartment building on 160th Street, and told McCabe they'd be looking for a suspect among the known criminals and punks within that zone. McCabe then spoke to local squad detectives, patrolmen with regular posts in the area, and others who patrolled the section in cars; he said things like, "I got a bad one, I need your help," or, "You have any punks who've been real hard up for a while, and all of a sudden been flashing a roll?" He made a list of the names they offered, adding to them a number of others gleaned from the Precinct's file of arrest cards, which he and Russo painstakingly thumbed through in search of anyone arrested within the last year or so who fitted Russo's criteria ("He's got to live in the area," Russo said, "and be on junk, and have been up to things like flat burglaries or muggings").

Having compiled some dozens of names, McCabe and Russo had had their commanding officers assign teams of detectives to the job of canvassing or bringing in the potential suspects even before all the other lines of investigation had come to dead ends. Occasionally the detectives who went out on this task were satisfied with a field interrogation, if the potential suspect resisted going to the precinct and had no charge hanging over him. One such field interrogation went about like this:

—Okay, Juanito, get your coat and come with us.

—What for? What I'm suppose' to have did?

—Never mind that.

—Lissen, man, I'm clean, and I ain' been in no trouble for almos' two years. I'm a family man now.

—They just want to ask you a few questions.

—You got nothin' on me. You got a warrant?

—Take it easy. Nobody's talking about arrest. . . . What do you do these days, Juanito?

—I been workin' regular, the las' six months.

—Where?

—The big laundromat on Courtlandt, you know?

—Did you work Friday a week ago—the 9th?

—Sure. I ain' missed a day for two months. From eleven a.m. to about eight at night. Ask the boss—he'll tell you.

—Okay. We'll ask him—and it better be right.

But it is an axiom of detective work that questioning works better and produces more information in the bleak, forbidding surroundings of the station house, so when the canvassing detectives anticipated resistance, they often "conned" the suspect into the station house. A typical episode:

—Look here, Leroy, we got a complaint against you—an abandoned car over on Grand Concourse registered in your name.

—You got the wrong man. I ain't never had no car.

—So how come it's registered in your name?

—Beats the shit out of me, boss.

—Well, we've got this complaint, and it says the car's yours. Let's go down and get it straightened out.

—Hey, man, I can't just leave my job in the middle of the day—

—Won't take but ten minutes, and we'll bring you right back. Let's go.

Many of the other names on McCabe's list belonged to youths or men who were out on bail awaiting trial for some offense or awaiting sentencing after trial; they came along, unprotesting, silent, bitter, and frightened. Others were brought in under arrest because they had been hanging around corners known to be pusher hangouts, or because they had been shouting and rough-housing in the street when the detectives found them, or because they had had a "bag" (an envelope of heroin) or "works" (hypodermic and needle) on them. Any of these persons might turn out to be the killer, if the detectives were lucky; but it was more realistic to hope merely that one or more of them might have some helpful information. This is part of classic investigative strategy: the rounding-up of punks who are already in trouble, or who can be arrested on new grounds, is essential to the informer system. As Mc-Cabe once explained it to a friend: "We try to locate all these fellows who have been in trouble, and hope that when we find them they'll be dirty, or that we'll catch them in the act of doing something, so we'll have this weight on them and can make them work for us. And even if we have nothing, but they were loitering or loud, we'll bring them in for that, so we have something we can work out a deal on."

Most of the men brought in, whether merely "asked" to come in and answer questions or arrested on some ground, were hurried up-stairs, through the detective squad room, and into a small interroga-tion room. Half a dozen detectives would crowd in, and usually one of them would start things off by asking to see the inside of the inter-viewee's arms; if he had recent needle marks, he was in real trouble, but even if he hadn't, the detectives would start firing questions at him that sounded as if he were. It might begin like this:

—What do you know about that job on 160th Street?
—Just what I hear around. Some old guy got done in.
—Come on. Let's have it, fellow.
—Let's have what?
—*You* know. We heard about you.
—Heard what? They ain't nothin' to hear. What you tryin' to to?
—You some kind of wise guy? We know what to do with a wise
    guy—
—Nos*sir!* Not me! I didn't mean nothin' bad—
—That's better. Now, do yourself some good, because otherwise
    you're in plenty of trouble. . . .

And the session would go on for an hour or two, questions ripping at him from in front and in back, now soft and now shouted, confusing him, trying to trip him up in his account of what he'd been doing on the 9th, what he ordinarily did on Fridays, who his friends were, who the junkies in his neighborhood were, what gossip he'd heard about anybody who'd suddenly had a few bucks to throw around, or who'd been bragging about his exploits, or who'd unaccountably dropped out of sight.

But although a stream of Puerto Ricans and blacks and Italians were interrogated, sweating and gulping, none of them seemed a real suspect in the Helmer case; each was told after a while that he could go, and slunk out like a whipped dog. And though a number of them agreed to help, none of their initial suggestions or tips led to anything until the arrival for questioning of a youth who, for legal reasons, will here be called Toro Ramirez, although that is not his real name.

Toro was a small, hardbitten youth of twenty who lived at 156th and Courtlandt, some five blocks away from the scene of the crime, in one of the high-rises of Melrose Houses. Tough as he tried to seem, he was clearly nervous, and he had reason to be: not only did he have four arrests on his record, but at the moment he was out on bail on a serious burglary charge and very much afraid of any further complications. McCabe does not now recall whether he himself made the offer that induced Toro to turn stoolie, but he says that if he did, he would have put it about like this: "Look, Mister, you're in trouble and you can get lots of time for it. You could use some help—and so can I. I could get you off light or out of it altogether, if you'd work for me. You interested? Good! But I don't want any games. If you're going to feed me a lot of horseshit, I'll come down on you like lightning out of the sky. I'll slam you into the can so fast you won't know what's happening to you."

What Toro replied is nowhere written down. He may have told of hearing someone boast about "taking off" an old man, or he may have told the detectives that he merely had put two and two together from things he had seen; one way or another, he tipped the detectives off to a name not on Russo's list of suspects, though it had appeared a couple of times among the lists of friends of junkies who had already been interrogated. The name was that of Doel Valencia, whom Toro knew well—whose pal and neighbor, in fact, he had been for four years.

Russo and McCabe hadn't had Doel Valencia on their list because his last arrest went back two years. Now, however, they reexamined the information in the Precinct's file of known criminals, and found that Valencia had been convicted of burglary four years ago, arrested in a shooting fracas (in which no one was wounded) two years later, was a known junkie, and, perhaps most significant, numbered among his regular friends two brothers, Alfredo and Carlos Ortiz, who lived at 406 East 160th, a building just three doors the other side of Melrose Avenue from Helmer's and in full view of the Helmer living-room window. As it happened, that very day one of the Four-Two patrolmen on the beat had told McCabe that "there were a couple of little bastards named Ortiz in 406 who might be worth looking at—and one of them has just been busted for junk." Neither Ortiz brother had yet been pulled in for questioning, but when McCabe and Russo took a second look at the Precinct records, they found that Carlos had been in and out of court starting at age twelve, for various sex and drug offenses, truancy, and stealing, while Alfredo had recently been convicted of robbery and, as a youthful offender, given a three-year suspended sentence; at that moment, however, he was in jail again, having been arrested the previous week for possessing works and heroin, and selling some of the latter. Russo and McCabe looked at each other meaningfully; the case was at last "getting hot."

It was already well into the evening, and Alfredo would be easy to find; indeed, as a quick phone call to the jail revealed, he was due in court in the morning, around the corner from the 42nd Precinct, and in all probability his family would be there, including brother Carlos. The person to start with tonight, therefore, before going after the Ortiz brothers, was Doel Valencia, and McCabe asked Detective Anthony La Rocco and another man to go bring him in at once. He had no legal ground for ordering Valencia arrested, but, to his way of thinking, he was not asking for an actual arrest; and while it was true that if Valencia were to refuse to accompany the detectives they would have no legal way to make him do so, he was not likely to know anything about his constitutional rights, or, if he did, stand upon them against the authority and assertiveness of the police.

For although he might almost have passed for a mainland white—at five feet eight, he was taller than most Puerto Rican men, and while his skin was olive and his hair almost kinky, his open, boyish features bore no trace of Indian or Negroid ancestry—Valencia was scarcely part of the American culture and understood very little of the world beyond the streets of Melrose. Born in Ponce, Puerto Rico, the youngest of eight children, he had come to New York at the age of three and grown up in Melrose. The oversized, impoverished family, jammed into one slum apartment or another, spilled out into the streets at every opportunity, and Doel Valencia's acculturation was largely to the limited society of ghetto streets. School did little to augment his education; he was, in fact, so unmotivated—and perhaps so dull—that at sixteen, when he finally dropped out of a slow-learner eighth-grade class, he could barely read or write.

His ailing (and by now husbandless) mother exercised no control over him, and neither, apparently, did his brothers or sisters, most of whom were scattering out to live on their own. At sixteen he and two friends stole some $300 worth of copper roofing material from a schoolyard and got caught, Valencia receiving a suspended sentence. At seventeen he began using heroin regularly, and at eighteen he had a "wife"—a teen-age Puerto Rican girl to whom he was not faithful, but whom he visited frequently at her mother's apartment, and who in due course bore him a child.

Valencia's skills being limited to what he had learned in the streets, he had almost nothing to offer an employer, and was hardly likely to enjoy such work as he got. In August 1964 he was hired as a packer by Consolidated Millinery on East 38th Street in Manhattan, where, before deductions, he earned $60 a week when he worked full-time—which was rarely, probably because of his addiction. For he was then using heroin continuously at the rate of two or three bags a day, costing anywhere from $40 to $100 a week. In addition, he sometimes gave his common-law wife money for the child, but later on, when asked how he could spend so much money if he had so little income, he could offer no good explanation. At least his rent and food cost him little or nothing, for he lived with his older sister, Idalia (their mother having long been hospitalized), in an apartment in one of the high-rise buildings of Melrose Houses, and he only occasionally gave her a few dollars toward expenses; Idalia, an attractive, bleached-blonde, Americanized girl of twenty-four who worked as a nurse's aide at Columbus Hospital, paid the bills, fretted about him, and was unable to make him change his ways.

That evening there was a knock on her door; she answered it and was confronted by two detectives who flashed their badges and asked for Doel Valencia. Idalia let them into the living-room, where they found him. As he and Idalia tell it, one of them said, without preliminaries, "Get your coat. You're coming to the Precinct with us." "What for?" Valencia asked. "You know what for," said the detective. Valencia insisted that he didn't. "We want to ask you some questions," said the detective, and Valencia meekly got a black pea-jacket from the closet and put it on. Idalia, playing the part of mother-surrogate, persisted in asking what was going to happen; they said again that they only wanted to ask Doel a few questions, and that he would be right back. Living in Melrose and being Puerto Rican, she didn't believe them, and if her account is true, she was right not to, for although she waited for him all night, he never returned.

On the way to the station house the detectives told Valencia that he was wanted in connection with an armed robbery, but revealed nothing else. When they got to the 42nd Precinct Station, they hurried him through the gloomy, high-ceilinged Muster Room, past the high old oaken desk and switchboard where shirt-sleeved cops were dealing with sullen youths, tearful women, and various local crises. They went up the stairway to the second floor, and there through the squad room, where half a dozen detectives were working at desks, into the Lieutenant's room, a small, dingy office with peeling paint, battered lockers, an assortment of "Wanted" posters on a bulletin board—and McCabe, seated behind a table, his lips a thin line, his eyes piercing blue below his tufted golden eyebrows.

Valencia and McCabe both later said, under oath, that they had a conversation that night in the Lieutenant's room, but this was almost the only thing they agreed upon. McCabe testified that he questioned Valencia by himself, starting around 10:30 p.m. and finishing by about 11:00, at which point Russo took his place and questioned Valencia alone until about 11:40 p.m. Valencia, however, testified that although McCabe was present, it was two other detectives (whose names he did not know) who did most of the questioning from near midnight until about 1:00 a.m. He had no recollection of being interrogated by, or even seeing, Russo that night—a detail that casts serious doubt on Valencia's accuracy or truthfulness, since it is unimaginable that Russo, an interrogator deeply devoted to his work, would have gone home, whatever the hour, without taking a crack at the suspect.

On the other hand, McCabe's account, in court, of that night's interrogation has an artificial, stilted flavor, typical of much police testimony, in which interrogator and suspect discourse in dead, neutral, polite phrases that one cannot imagine actually being spoken. First, McCabe "advised him of his rights," telling him that anything he might say could be used against him; then, as the detective told the tale, it went as follows:

"I asked him his name. He told me his name was Doel Valencia. I asked him where he lived. He gave me where he lived. . . . I asked him if he was working. He stated that he was working. I asked him how long he was working and where he was working. He stated that for two and a half months he worked for Consolidated Millinery on 38th Street. I asked him if he was married. He stated that he was married and he had a child. . . . I asked him where his wife lived. He said his wife lived with her mother. I asked him if he had worked in the week between October 4th and October 11th and he stated he did work and he worked between the hours of nine a.m. to six p.m."

And so on. McCabe, writing on a long yellow pad, asked Valencia when he had gotten home that day, and Valencia said he had arrived home at 7:00 p.m., had eaten something, had gone to visit his wife for a little while, taken a walk, gone to Brook Avenue at 9:30 p.m. (he admitted to McCabe that he went there to get some heroin, but McCabe was not permitted to mention this in court), and had come home again by 11:30. Valencia denied ever having been at 399 East 160th Street, said he didn't know of anything that had happened there, didn't know the area, and didn't know anyone who lived around there. This concluded the talk; McCabe then left, and shortly Russo came in and took over.

Russo's narrative sounds much the same, although, being an older hand at homicide interrogation, he asked more biographical and background questions than McCabe. He asked Valencia, for instance, to name his close friends, and Valencia complied, naming seven—but not mentioning either of the Ortiz brothers, although he was known to spend much of his time with them. He did say, however, that he usually hung out at 156th Street and Melrose Avenue, which fitted perfectly into Russo's general theory of the crime. Russo's account of the interrogation concluded as follows:

"When asked if he knew of anything happening on 160th Street and Melrose Avenue the past couple of weeks, indicating prior to October 9th, the defendant stated that he knows of nothing happening. The defendant then stated that he would be glad to help us if he can. That completes the statement of October 22nd. This statement was completed about 11:40 p.m. on October 22nd. The defendant was then told that he can go home, at which time I observed the defendant leaving the 42nd Squad Office."

That is not at all the way it went, according to Valencia. Granted that he later would have had good reason to lie, and that there are serious inconsistencies in his story, many of its minor details do have the authentic sound and color of what generally happens in an interrogation room. He had never seen McCabe before being led into the room, but, being a street youth, he undoubtedly knew at once that he was facing a hard-nosed type. McCabe, a handsome and genial man with his friends, can look and sound very mean, his fair Irish complexion flushing easily with anger. He was, in fact, an old hand at dealing with Melrose youths—he himself, the son of a bricklayer, had grown up in a cold-water flat at 153rd and Courtlandt, one block from where Valencia had just been picked up, and in his childhood he had had to contend with young Italian toughs; he had learned to deal with them—and perfected the technique as a policeman confronting black and Puerto Rican hoodlums—by "giving these guys the impression: 'Mister, if you tangle with me, it's going to be the worst thing that ever happened to you!' "

McCabe brusquely told Valencia to empty his pockets, and looked carefully through the things the youth put on the table. He and two other detectives then began to question Valencia, McCabe asking him first where he had been on October 9th. Valencia said he didn't know, but, "They told me, 'The 9th, think back, it was a World Series or some kind of game was on.' " Valencia said he guessed he had been working that day. But what had he done at night? McCabe asked. Valencia didn't remember, tried, couldn't remember, and suddenly and terrifyingly McCabe barked, "Come on! A woman saw you running out of the building where the man was stabbed to death."

Valencia leaped to his feet. "A woman seen me runnin' out of the building where a man was stabbed?" he cried. Yes, and Valencia was the one she saw. "I tol' him, 'Tell this woman to come here. It's a mistake.' " One of the detectives picked up the phone, dialed, and spoke to someone. "Madam, can you come down here?" he asked. "We've got a boy here we want you to identify." He hung up and announced that she would shortly be on her way. While waiting, one of them, perhaps McCabe, said to Valencia in a kindlier tone, "How come you don't get it off your chest?" but Valencia denied that he had anything on his chest. The detectives went back over his story again and again for about an hour, at which point Valencia asked where the woman was. One of the officers asked him if he was getting smart; he replied that he wasn't, he just wanted to go home. A detective then telephoned again, sometime after 1:00 a.m., and said, "Madam, are you coming? . . . Come down ten o'clock tomorrow morning."

"I'm suppose' to stay here until ten o'clock tomorrow morning?" asked Valencia, dismayed. Yes, McCabe said, ending the session, and took Valencia out, through the squad room, to a smaller room just off the hallway in which there was fingerprinting equipment, a row of lockers, and, in the far corner, a detention cage—a small cubicle of steel bars. He shoved Valencia into the cage and locked him in, telling him he was going to be booked for homicide. "Why?" cried Valencia. "I didn't kill no one!" But McCabe turned off the lights, went out, and left him alone.

Detectives never give details of this sort in the courtroom, but the textbooks of investigative technique used in police academies do; among other things, they advise interrogators to sound as if they already know a lot and have other sources of information, to employ at times a kindly father-confessor approach, and to utilize various bluffs and tricks (including fake telephone calls) that can elicit the truth from some suspects. McCabe himself, not in court but in his own home, commented later on some of his own favorite techniques:

"You try to show up the lies he's telling. So you make it up, you look around or out the window, like you know it's a lie. Or you might even make a telephone call while the questioning is going on, and then say to him, 'I don't give a damn if you tell me or if you don't. I *know* you were there, I got somebody who knows you were there.' And you ask him questions for a long while, and whatever he says, you throw it at him later and say, 'That isn't what you said before.' And you play it this way and that, because if he's lying, he's got to figure he's going to stumble somewheres along the line, and when you tell him you've just caught him in a lie, he's never sure you haven't, no matter how good a story he made up."

One might reasonably suppose that what actually happened that evening was a combination of both versions of the story: one can imagine that McCabe blustered, cajoled, threatened, and attempted to trick Valencia, but in the end was forced to take down a formal statement in which Valencia admitted nothing and professed total ignorance of the crime. One might also reasonably suppose that Russo did interrogate Valencia, who, being not overly bright and probably somewhat beclouded by heroin, got it mixed up with later events; or perhaps that Valencia simply forgot to tell about Russo's interrogation in his overpowering desire to tell the jury how he was illegally locked up for the night without being formally arrested.

For that is the most important of all discrepancies between the two versions. Police regulations forbid keeping a man overnight in the cage, or even in one of the regular cells on the first floor, unless he has been booked at the front desk—that is, formally arrested and charged with an offense. Ordinarily, the desk officer would see detectives bringing someone in for questioning, and would get his name, but on a busy night, with a number of policemen, complainants, and prisoners in the Muster Room, it would have been possible for someone to be hustled through without any record being made. Had Valencia confessed, he would certainly have been booked at once and locked up overnight in the regular cell area; but since he had not, what could one do with him? For if he were guilty and the detectives released him, he would probably disappear. One long-time Bronx detective (who has no direct knowledge of the events of that night) says, "Once you have your man, you're not going to turn him loose. It's strictly illegal to hold him if you can't book him, but if you let him go, you might never find him again. So you keep him, but you never admit that you did—and even if some of your fellow officers know about it, they can be relied on not to admit it. No good cop would do that. It wouldn't be *right.*" *

But this, of course, is pure conjecture. McCabe and Russo, both of them good men doing their job to the best of their abilities, swore under oath that Valencia was released sometime around 11:40 p.m.; Russo said he last saw him leaving the squad room, and McCabe said he saw Valencia going down the stairs by himself, a free man. And unless Doel Valencia, Stephen McCabe, or Salvatore Russo ever decides to change what he said in court, the actual truth—which is not necessarily the same thing as the probable truth—will never be known. But this is neither strange nor rare; indeed, it is the case more often than not, in the workings of criminal justice.

---

* This is not an idiosyncrasy of Bronx cops, but an almost universal police characteristic. Albert Deutsch, for instance, writes in *The Trouble with Cops:* "A perverse sense of loyalty tends to brand as a traitor to his group any police officer who exposes dishonest colleagues," and sociologist William A. Westley, in his classic study, *Violence and the Police,* reported that "secrecy among the police stands as a shield against the attacks of the outside world," including the newspapers, the public, the courts, and the underworld.

## VI   *No Good Cop Would Do That*

IF no good cop would unmask a brother officer's illegal conduct or admit to his own, that does not necessarily mean that he is a criminal. There are, of course, crooked cops: the existence of police corruption, in every form from the petty "gifts" required of local shopkeepers to the massive bribes taken from big-time heroin dealers, is well known; so, too, is the fact that some policemen maltreat or needlessly beat up drunks, panhandlers, addicts, hippies, blacks, and political dissenters, later denying any accusations made against them or offsetting them in advance by booking the abused person for resisting arrest or assaulting an officer.

But these are kinds of misconduct of which the majority of policemen disapprove, even though they will not betray their brother officers, and which police departments and civilian complaint review boards deal with, more or less.* What is subtler, far more profound, and infinitely harder to control is a species of illegality inherent in the police role and for which justifications are offered by even the most honest cops—namely, a broad range of practical and effective ways of dealing with suspects which the policeman knows to be technically improper but considers morally justified.

If a cop frisks a seedy-looking fellow in an alley without legally adequate grounds for suspicion, and finds a few decks of heroin in his

---

* Less, when the investigating body is run by the police department itself. A 1970 Rand Institute study of the New York Police Department found that more than one quarter of policemen studied stole from homes or businesses already robbed, shook down traffic violators, and the like, but that only 8 percent of formal allegations of criminal conduct resulted in convictions by departmental trial. As for the Civilian Complaint Review Board—which is run by the Police Department, although some of its members are civilians—83 percent of the complaints it received in the year studied were dismissed, and only one resulted in a major fine.

pockets, he may testify in court that the suspect threw the envelopes to the ground when he saw the policeman approaching.* If a detective opens a door with a pass key or rings a bell and forces his way in, finding the occupant using drugs or committing some other illegal act, the detective may well testify, blandly and clear of eye, that the door was slightly ajar and that he could see a crime being committed. If he wants to interrogate someone he feels sure is guilty but against whom he has no legal grounds for arrest, he may lure or browbeat the suspect into coming to the station house, and later testify that he "invited" him to come down and that the suspect did so willingly.

To the patrolman or detective who has tracked down a criminal, the important thing is to arrest him and submit him to the courts along with sufficient evidence to convict him. The most effective ways of doing so are themselves often violations of law, but the latter seem to the policeman inconsequential compared to the crimes he is seeking to control; similarly, the lies he tells to conceal his methods seem to him not real perjury but trifling prevarications, indulged in for the sake of highly desirable goals.

Left-wing cop-haters miss this obvious point: they see the police as having only evil ends, whereas in fact most of those ends are good; it is the means the police use to achieve them that are often evil. Right-wing cop-lovers, on the other hand, see the police as having only good ends, and using means which are justified by them; but in fact the means the police use often do more damage to the moral fiber of society than their goals could ever warrant.

These contradictions stem from a basic dilemma that the police, and the society that employs them, have faced since the beginnings of our system of government, and which may never be fully resolved. Professor Herbert Packer, in *The Limits of the Criminal Sanction,* suggests that we have two separate and disparate sets of values within our criminal justice system: he labels these the Crime Control Model, which views the efficient repression of criminal conduct as the most important function of that system, and the Due Process Model, which assigns top priority to the protection of the innocent and the safeguarding of liberty through strict judicial procedures.

American society has never chosen between the two value systems.

---

* This practice has become so common since 1961, when the Supreme Court, in *Mapp* v. *Ohio,* banned illegally seized evidence, that arrests on such evidence are known around the courts as "dropsy" cases.

We want both, but of course we cannot have both simultaneously. We can achieve optimum police effectiveness against crime only by giving the police unlimited power and discarding those protections that make us a free people; but we can fulfill the due-process promise of the Constitution only by so controlling the police as to prevent their behaving illegally toward the innocent—or the guilty.

But it is the policeman himself who is most acutely pained by the tug-of-war between society's conflicting value systems. Like any other American worker, he wants to *produce* and be rewarded for high yield —yet the society that rewards him for it also forbids him to use techniques by which he can best achieve it. As Professor Jerome Skolnick puts it, in *Justice Without Trial,* the conflict between the Crime Control Model and the Due Process Model of criminal justice is, for the policeman, a conflict between the American *work ethic* and the American *legal ethic.* The policeman sees himself as a craftsman, trained to turn out a given product and, like other craftsmen, rewarded for productivity; unlike the others, however, he is forbidden by the system to improvise, to invent, or to show initiative. In this situation he can best obey the work ethic by violating the legal ethic and concealing the violations, even as factory workers often increase their productivity by taking short-cuts, their pride in their high output blinding them to the fact that the product they make is unsafe.

For many reasons—a major one being the struggle of American Negroes to win their civil rights—the Supreme Court sought during the 1960s to make the legal ethic dominate the work ethic in police behavior. The Court cannot, of course, supervise or control the nation's 40,000 police departments, but it can and did seek to make those police actions which violate due process unrewarding by designating the evidence such actions yield unacceptable in court.

This involved using the due-process clause of the Fourteenth Amendment* to make various parts of the Bill of Rights—especially the Fourth, Fifth, and Sixth Amendments—binding upon the states, although until then they had been binding only upon the federal government. (Since the great bulk of criminal trials are held in state courts, this was legitimately seen by many observers as a "criminal-law revolution.") In 1961, as mentioned above, the *Mapp* decision made it useless for police to seize evidence illegally, no matter how

---

\* Which forbids any state to "abridge the privileges" of citizens or to "deprive any person of life, liberty, or property without due process of law."

good that evidence turned out to be; in 1963 *Gideon* assured poor defendants of counsel at their trials, which meant closer scrutiny of police evidence; in 1964 *Malloy* threw out confessions obtained by police through long imprisonment, and *Escobedo* gave the suspect the right to have his lawyer present during questioning in custody; and in 1966 *Miranda* went beyond *Escobedo* to require that the police tell the suspect that he can have a lawyer present during such questioning, and that a lawyer will be furnished him free if he has no money.

In addition, no less than forty-nine Supreme Court decisions during that decade dealt with Fourth Amendment questions of "search and seizure," many of them spelling out the conditions under which arrests were illegal and thus under which any evidence obtained as a result would be of no use. The police, however, adapted to the growing body of restrictions by making illegal arrests less often, and by resorting more often to "detention," which, unlike arrest, involves no formal charge and no entry or record on the police blotter. By not calling it arrest, the police could question a suspect and even hold him in custody without probable cause; if a confession was forthcoming, however, they could then formally arrest him, and not be plagued by the complaint of illegal arrest.

Or so the theory goes, and the practice with it. Yet the Constitution says nothing about "arrest" and "detention"; it uses only the term "seizure." But isn't detention a form of seizure? Granted that it is socially necessary, and legal, for a policeman to briefly stop and question someone on the street if he has reasonable grounds to think that person may have some connection with a crime, does this also mean that he can question such a person for a prolonged period? Or require him to come to the station house and question him there? And for how long? And if he has no probable cause, but only "suspicion," how reasonable must his grounds for suspicion be?

There are no final answers, as yet, to these questions. Prosecutors and police generally hold that if the subject comes to the station house "voluntarily"—or even unwillingly, as long as he is not booked—he has not been subjected to arrest. (Most police actually know that anyone taken unwillingly to the station house has, in effect, been arrested; very often, however, they stoutly maintain in court that there was no unwillingness and hence no arrest, in order to safeguard their evidence from attack.) Due-process partisans disagree strenuously with the assertion that detention is not the same as arrest; Professor Caleb

Foote of the University of California at Berkeley, for instance, has vehemently argued that "no matter what you call it, an imprisonment has taken place. The constitutional use of the word 'seizure' certainly contemplates a right against unreasonable imprisonment." Detention, he feels, should be governed by the requirement of probable cause as strictly as formal arrest. The Supreme Court, too, without actually ruling on the matter, had defined an arrest many years earlier as "the seizing of a person and detaining him in the custody of the law," adding, "The term arrest may be applied to any case where a person is taken into custody or restrained of his full liberty, or where there is the detention of a person in custody for even a short period of time."

But suppose a detective has a pretty good idea who might have committed a serious crime, basing his belief on biographical background that could not be used in court, plus an informer's hearsay tip—

And suppose he has no physical or eyewitness evidence, and is not likely ever to have any—

Suppose, that is, that he cannot show anything like probable cause, in its legal sense, and has no chance of doing so—

But suppose he has a deep sense of duty to his society, plus a powerful desire to solve his case by making a "good collar," thereby advancing his own career—

And suppose he can achieve these goals only by somehow managing to get the unwilling suspect into the station house and interrogating him under conditions factually resembling arrest but legally definable as detention—

Suppose all the above: what, then, is that detective likely to do?

## VII   *I Believe It Was Voluntarily*

RATHER than drive thirty-odd miles to his home at midnight, McCabe had stayed at the Precinct, sleeping restlessly on a lumpy, bare mattress in the dorm room with only a scratchy blanket as bedding. But with the case getting hot, he was too keyed up to care, or to feel weary. Having dressed and eaten early, he was, as he tells it, on his way before 8:30 a.m. to pay a call to a well-known junkie who lived in Helmer's block, and who might know something about the Ortiz brothers. Driving west on 159th Street, McCabe stopped for a light at Melrose, and was surprised to see none other than Doel Valencia walking down the avenue from 160th Street, even though Valencia had said the previous night that he knew no one in that area. McCabe called out, "Valencia, come over here!" He did, and McCabe said he'd like to ask him some more questions; then, according to his sworn testimony, he uttered the following unlikely sentence: "Do you want to come with me to the station house?" Valencia did, and came along voluntarily; McCabe, abandoning his other errand, took him up to the squad room, told him to sit down in a chair against a wall, and left him there, becoming involved in other matters. Valencia, he says, remained sitting in the squad room unguarded and unconfined all morning and well into the afternoon, when at last the detectives got around to talking to him.

Valencia, naturally, tells a very different story. He says that he slept on the floor of the cage that night, using his coat as a pillow, and that in the morning a detective took him out briefly to go to the toilet, and then locked him in again. He remained there without food or water until some time late that morning or early that afternoon, when another officer brought him a sandwich; he never got to eat it, however, because a detective, ready to interrogate him at that point, said there was no use in his eating it, since the interrogation process would only make him throw up.

Russo arrived at about 9:30, and he and McCabe immediately had a conference about the morning's plans. Shortly after ten o'clock, they went around the corner to the Criminal Court building at 161st and Washington. As usual, the smoky halls were thronged largely with ill-dressed blacks and Puerto Ricans—worried-looking mothers, sullen teen-age boys and young men in sweaters and sneakers—and natty, officious lawyers clutching armloads of papers and pushing their way through the throng or urgently palavering with clients before going inside. In the plain, high-ceilinged courtroom, nearly all of the seats were filled with an anxious, whispering audience; lawyers bustled to and fro continually, stopping for whispered conferences, while courtroom attendants tried to keep them quiet; inside the railing, a dozen or more people—lawyers, assistant district attorneys, a prisoner, and two detectives—were gathered in front of Judge Edward Breslin, their backs obscuring the proceedings from the spectators, their voices an unintelligible mumbling. To the right, guards stood over half a dozen prisoners awaiting their turn, and from time to time, through a door to the right of the magistrate's bench, others would arrive or someone whose hearing had been completed would go out.

The smallest, palest, and thinnest prisoner brought out that morning was Alfredo Ortiz. Accompanying his mother, when she came forward to the railing before the bench, was his equally small, almost as pale and thin brother, Carlos. The two hardly resembled desperate or violent criminals. Although Alfredo was eighteen and Carlos seventeen, neither looked more than thirteen or possibly fourteen. Both were mere boys in size—scarcely more than five feet tall, skinny, weighing not much more than a hundred pounds, and with the gaunt, small-chinned faces of underfed children. Alfredo, in fact, though a year the elder of the two, had delicate and childlike features, faintly olive in hue, topped by a mass of wavy dark hair; Carlos, fairer in complexion, had a somewhat stronger mouth and a slightly sturdier body. But neither of them, except to the eyes of specialists like McCabe and Russo, would have appeared to be anything worse than truants and mischievous kids.

And that was how they seemed to their nervous and tearful mother, though she had reason to know better. Luisa Ortiz Pomales—in Latin fashion, using the matronymic, she called herself Mrs. Pomales rather than Mrs. Ortiz—was a tiny, frail, light-skinned woman, attractive but worn, defeated, and seeming much older than her thirty-five years. Despite her best efforts nothing had gone right in her life since her teens. She had been a pretty fifteen-year-old in a village in Puerto Rico when she unwisely yielded to the wooing of Alfredo Ortiz, a dapper, mustachioed, but almost illiterate young fellow; she became his wife (legally, she says, although many years later a probation investigator for the New York Supreme Court reported that it had been a common-law alliance), and thereupon ended her education, producing two sons and a daughter within four years. Ortiz was an unskilled knockabout, and in 1949, when all these new mouths to feed proved too much of a burden, he decamped for New York to seek his fortune there. Luisa Pomales, the children, and her mother followed him some months later, but everything seemed to turn out badly: they lived in a squalid, rat-infested tenement on East 116th Street, in Spanish Harlem, with scarcely any furniture, little hot water, and often no heat; Ortiz earned a bare subsistence wage, often squandered much of it on drink, was flagrantly unfaithful, and flew into violent rages when Luisa reproached him; and one day he walked out, never came back, and never bothered himself again about his children.

Mrs. Pomales was on her own in the teeming slum of the great city, without any command of the language, any skills, or any idea of how to escape the trap of her circumstances. For a while she worked as a general helper and saleswoman in local stores of one kind or another, while her mother, a simple, old-fashioned peasant woman, took care of the children, but after a few years the older woman went back to Puerto Rico and Mrs. Pomales, in order to be at home with her children, went on relief and became part of the immobilized, habituated welfare class. She drifted into a pattern of aimless domesticity and idle visiting among neighbors and relatives, tried to make a home for her children but could never accumulate more than a few bare essentials of furniture, cooked such food as she could afford but was less and less able to make her vagabond sons come home and eat regularly.

For by the time Alfredo was eight or nine, and Carlos a year younger, they had acquired the manners and skills of the street boys of Spanish Harlem and were beyond her comprehension or control. She scolded and lectured them about their ways, and, typically like Latin-American males, they revered her—and deceived and disobeyed her. They were always ragged and dirty; they stayed out till all hours, eating sandwiches instead of her dinners; they got into numerous fights, but stuck together, tiny and nimble, and survived, though they often came home bruised, bleeding, and defiant. Very early they fell into the habit of cutting school whenever they felt like it, either to work for a few hours in some produce market or merely to rattle around the streets with a gang of friends, playing ball, swimming in the foul Hudson until the police chased them, and getting in and out of a dozen kinds of trouble by way of apprenticeship training for the things they saw the older street-corner youths doing.

Mrs. Pomales knew only part of all this; the boys lied to her fluently and successfully about much of what they did. But she learned more of the truth when Carlos—who had always been the scrappier, more daring, and wilder one—was arrested at the age of twelve and brought into Children's Court on a neighbor's complaint that he had induced her five-year-old daughter to perform fellatio upon him several times. He told the judge that it was a frame-up, and that the child's mother had put her up to telling a lie; the judge was unconvinced and sentenced him, but put him on probation. He was hardly chastened by the experience; if anything, he became bolder, wilder, more of a problem for school authorities, and generally readier for anything. He needed to be: the family moved to 156th Street, in Melrose, when he was fourteen and Alfredo fifteen, and for a while, as new "spicks" in a neighborhood filled with Italian and Negro toughs, the Ortiz brothers had plenty of savage fights, and more than once dragged themselves home bleeding and missing a tooth or two.

But they went through their initiation rites, were accepted, and fell into a pattern of street living which they found thoroughly agreeable. To an educated middle-class person the life of a slum youth might seem filthy, violent, boring, and hopeless, but many slum youths do not perceive it that way; they live a continual round of diversions and pleasurable activities, enjoying the noisy, convivial life in the streets, "goofing off" and "rapping," playing ball and shooting pool, drinking beer, smoking pot or "snorting" heroin, getting into fights, avoiding the police, panhandling a little, stealing a little, dancing and fooling around with girls, and proving their sexual prowess whenever and wherever they can.

Mrs. Pomales knew some of this and deeply disapproved, but was unable to make them change; she felt, however, that her boys were basically good and would eventually turn out all right. But it took considerable rationalizing to think so. When Carlos was only fifteen, for instance, he was back in court, charged with being a persistent sexual aggressor toward an older girl; the judge also heard evidence that he was ungovernable in school, a chronic truant, a user of barbiturates and marijuana, and out of his mother's control. The judge sent Carlos to Newhampton, a state reformatory for youths near Middletown, New York; there, during a five-month stay, he fought his fights, learned how to get along, worked on the farm and in the shops, and picked up a fair amount of prison know-how. He came home worldly-wise, toughened, but not in the least reformed; indeed, three months later he was in court again, charged with stealing a purse, but was treated generously and put on probation. He never went back to school—he had reached only the seventh grade, at which time he had a verbal I.Q. score of 80, or dull normal—and for the next few months occasionally worked a little as a car polisher, delivery boy, and janitor's helper; he kept none of the jobs more than a few days, however, perhaps because he was a confirmed marijuana-user and was continually high from morning until night. For about two months prior to the death of Alexander Helmer he had been out of work, but not in the least unhappy about it or worried about his future. "When you a ghetto kid," he later said, looking back, "you don' be thinkin' about the future. All you thinkin' about is what you goin' to do for the day, hangin' out with your little group, an' foolin' aroun' an' goofin' off."

Alfredo, more delicate of feature and less of a battler than Carlos, seemed the brighter of the two and did better in his first years in school. As he picked up the values of the street culture, however, he became a chronic truant—sometimes in order to make money, but more often in order to run with the pack; guilt-ridden liberals always assume that slum schools fail the children, but it is also true that the slum children fail the schools. At fourteen, Alfredo had a verbal I.Q. of only 73, or just four points above the upper boundary of mental retardation; throughout junior high school he was a borderline student, often uncooperative and hostile, always uninterested, and finally, at sixteen, failing all subjects in ninth grade, he dropped out.

By then, however, he needed all his time not only for the same kind of activities Carlos was engaged in, but for another: the pursuit and use of hard drugs. He had been contented with marijuana for a while, but among the friends he made in Melrose, the three he spent most of his time with were already heroin addicts, and he felt isolated and ridiculous for not joining them. As he later recalled, "They was shootin' up an' I was smokin' a reefer, an' they'd be noddin' an' sleepin', an' I'm groovin' by myself an' lookin' stupid. So after a while, bein' with them, I started sniffin'. Later on, one time, I took my first shot, an' after that I always used the needle."

One thing led to another. Half a year after dropping out of school, he and two friends were arrested and charged with breaking into an apartment in mid-afternoon, holding up a Puerto Rican woman (one of Alfredo's friends put a screwdriver to her throat), and robbing her of $80 in cash and $1,000 worth of jewelry. Alfredo, awaiting trial in the Brooklyn House of Detention, suffered the miseries and terrors of jailhouse life, but survived, growing as wily and adept as a trapped rodent. He pleaded guilty (telling his mother, however, that he had had nothing to do with it, and had taken the rap for a pal who already had a conviction on his record); the judge sentenced him to three years, but put him on probation, and he came home in March 1964 and at once resumed his old friendships and old habits.

But with a difference: he now used heroin every day, needed it desperately, would drink whole bottles of cough syrup when he couldn't get it, and suffered from such fits and horrors when he lacked a "fix" that even Luisa Pomales scraped up money for him and sent him out to buy it, while pleading with him to take the cure at a city hospital. It was, he says, a continual round of activity: "All you doin' is goin' from here to there gettin' money to buy you some dope, an' after you get off, you might spend half an hour or so on a stoop noddin'—an' then you start in tryin' to look for some more money to get high again."

Alfredo sometimes thought about getting a job, and he actually worked for a short while alongside his friend Doel Valencia at Consolidated Millinery, packing hats for $55 a week; all too soon, however, he was laid off for absenteeism. For some weeks he remained unemployed; then on Thursday, October 15th, six days after Alexander Helmer was murdered (but three days before his body was discovered), Alfredo was arrested by a detective on his old block, East 156th Street, from which the family had moved to 160th Street half a year earlier. The officer charged Alfredo with possessing heroin and works, and making a sale to him; Alfredo was arraigned in Criminal

Court, shipped back to the Brooklyn House of Detention to await a hearing, and there for three or four days went through the agony of "cold-turkey withdrawal," shaking and moaning on his bed, rolled up in a blanket but hopelessly cold, unable to eat for days or even to tolerate the voices and noises of men in the recreation room. Finally he got over it, and on the morning of Friday the 23rd, skeletally thin, haggard, and feeble, he was taken back to the Bronx by prison van to appear before a magistrate in Part 3 of the Criminal Court, and to enter his plea.

His mother had hired a lawyer named Wallace Pruzansky to represent him, and Pruzansky was present that morning and conferred briefly with Alfredo before his case was called up. McCabe and Russo, seated nearby, expected from everything they had seen in court on innumerable similar occasions that Alfredo's attorney would seek a postponement, hoping to have the case grow stale and to have some months of good behavior, on bail, to show the court before it finally came up. But when Alfredo's name was called out and he and Pruzansky stepped up to the bench, with Luisa Pomales and Carlos coming up to the railing behind them, McCabe and Russo were astonished to hear Alfredo plead guilty. Alfredo says he was merely copping a plea (pleading guilty) in return for an informal assurance, by the D.A., of a light sentence. McCabe thinks otherwise: "He was supposed to plead not guilty—the D.A. told us so—and then he saw Sal and I in court, and we seemed to be interested in him, and he got nervous. So what better place to go than into the can? I can't talk to him when he's in the can, right? So all of a sudden he changes his plea to guilty." Judge Breslin accepted the plea, adjourned the case for a week to await a probation report before sentencing him, and a guard led Alfredo back through the door and returned him to the cage beyond it. At once Russo and McCabe, according to plan, split up, McCabe remaining in court to try to get Alfredo out, and Russo hurrying off to intercept Carlos.

Russo's account of what happened is simplicity itself. Before Carlos and his mother left the court building, Russo approached them and, according to his later sworn testimony, "asked [Carlos Ortiz] if he would accompany me to the 42nd Squad, in that I had an investigation which I was conducting, at which time he stated that he would." They then went around the corner together and arrived at the squad room of the Precinct at about noon.

Carlos' version is, as so often is the case, somewhat different. In his sworn testimony, he said that Russo asked him if he was Carlos Ortiz and then asked if he owned a blue Oldsmobile. Carlos replied that he didn't own a car and didn't even know how to drive. Russo persisted, seeming to disbelieve him, and finally said, "Well, come to the Precinct with me." Mrs. Pomales anxiously asked where the detective was taking him; Carlos replied, "He wants me to go to the Precinct," and Russo added, "Don't worry, he'll be right back." And off they went, around the corner and up to the second-floor squad room.

McCabe, meanwhile, was having a far more complicated problem. He whispered urgently to the assistant district attorney who had just handled Alfredo's case; then, with the D.A.'s okay, McCabe went back to the cage, motioned to Alfredo, showed him his shield, and said, "Come along with me." They went to another courtroom, presided over by Judge Walter Gladwin, where another assistant D.A. asked on McCabe's behalf to have Alfredo temporarily paroled in McCabe's custody. McCabe could have done this in the courtroom where Alfredo's case had just been heard, but, according to a lawyer who defended Alfredo later on, he was seeking to get away from Wallace Pruzansky, who might still be within earshot and would certainly intervene to see what was being done to his client and to protect his interests.

Equally intriguing—and equally moot—is the matter of what grounds were offered Judge Gladwin for the parole request. Had he been asked to parole Alfredo in McCabe's custody for questioning at the police station, the judge might well have refused, protecting Alfredo's rights by telling McCabe to interrogate him in jail. But had he been asked to parole Alfredo so that McCabe could take him to the Probation Part of the Supreme Court to clear up the probation violation created by his present drug offense, the judge could have seen no harm in it. There is no record of what grounds were offered him, but what happened thereafter is at least suggestive. Alfredo was paroled as requested, McCabe signed him out (considering Alfredo his prisoner as of that moment) and drove with him across 161st Street to the imposing white Bronx County Courthouse on the Grand Concourse, where he went to the Probation Part; there, in due course, he stood before Justice William Lyman of the Supreme Court,* with the

---

* The nomenclature is somewhat confusing. In New York the Supreme Court is not the highest court of appeal, as in many states and the federal system, but a trial court of high powers and extensive jurisdiction; in criminal cases it handles felonies. The court of last resort in New York is called the Court of Appeals.

pale, wordless Alfredo at his side, and had an assistant district attorney ask on his behalf that Alfredo, though a probation violator and hence subject to arrest, be released on his own recognizance in connection with other pending matters. Justice Lyman so ruled, and McCabe and Alfredo turned and left the courtroom, Alfredo being free until such time as he was due to reappear both in this court and in Criminal Court.

But his freedom was a metaphysical reality, not a material one, for outside the door—as Alfredo tells it—McCabe slammed handcuffs onto him and without a word led him to the elevator, took him downstairs, and drove with him to the 42nd Precinct. McCabe has always denied most of these details, maintaining that Alfredo, no longer a prisoner, came along with him of his own volition. Much later, when a lawyer for Alfredo asked in court, in heavily sarcastic tones, "Did Alfredo Ortiz go to the 42nd Precinct with you *voluntarily?,*" McCabe evenly replied, his handsome face a study in ingenuousness, "I told him to come along with me. I *believe* it was voluntarily." And clarifying the point, he added, "If I ask a person to come along with me and they come along with me, then it's voluntarily. If I ask a person to come along with me and they say, 'No, I'm not going to come with you,' and I *bring* him along, then that's involuntary."

The distinction was lost upon Alfredo Ortiz; handcuffed or not, he could not have known that he was technically not under McCabe's control, or that he had a right to disobey this man who had hustled him through two courts and various arcane procedures.

And there was one other thing that he did not know, but that McCabe did. While waiting for Justice Lyman to return from lunch, McCabe had phoned the Precinct to let Russo know how things were going. It was then a quarter to two, and Russo had been at the station house with Carlos over an hour and a half; when he came to the phone and heard McCabe's voice, he made an effort to keep his own cool and professional. "Steve," he said crisply, "we've got Bazooka."

"We *what?*" gasped McCabe.

"The kid's opening up," said Russo. "Get that guy out and bring him over here!"

"Right, Sal!" said McCabe—and he did.

# Chapter 3   The Interrogation

## I   Opening Up

AT the time of McCabe's phone call, Carlos had made nothing like a confession to Russo; instead, he had offered an alibi. Nonetheless, it constituted a real break in the case, for after failing to satisfy Russo that he knew nothing about the murder, Carlos had finally remembered meeting three people opposite Helmer's building at noon—Alfredo, Valencia and a friend known as Negrito—and seeing them enter the building, shortly after which he again encountered them on the street and observed that they had a good deal of money they had not had earlier.

As incomplete as this might be, it was the all-important first opening, the crucial breach in the defense of total denial. Russo had gotten the story from Carlos in an hour and a half of questioning, using only legally permissible techniques—or so he says; Carlos, not surprisingly, has always told his brother, his lawyers, and his friends a very different version of the first interrogation. It would be naïve to suppose that either Russo or Carlos must be telling the truth and the other one lying; though this is often the case in fiction, in real life nearly everybody involved in a criminal case lies—some a little and others a lot, some only about trifles and others about major matters, some for such trivial ends as to look braver than they really are and others for such weighty ends as to conceal their own guilt.

Still, the natural tendency in most lying is toward parsimony: one tells a story as close to the truth as he can in order to minimize the effort of invention and the risk of self-contradiction. Accordingly, two discrepant accounts of a crime, an interrogation, or an arrest may both be partly false and both partly true—a psychological reality judges acknowledge when advising jurors that they may believe any part of a witness' testimony without believing all of it, reject any part without rejecting all of it, and assemble for themselves a probable truth made up of whatever they find credible in each story they have heard.

Even if one has good reason to doubt most of what Carlos says about his first session of questioning, some aspects of his account ring true; even if one has equally good reason to believe most of what Russo says about it, some of what he says rings false. In the account of the questioning that Carlos gave in court some five months later, his feelings, as he reported them, seem entirely credible; many of the details he gave of the detectives' methods, however, sound like jail-house clichés assembled into a run-of-the-mill repudiation of what he had told Russo. Both the plausible and the implausible are apparent in the opening sentences of his courtroom narration:*

> When [Russo] took me into the [Lieutenant's] room, he tol' me, "Have a seat," so I sat down, an' then he went out of the room. An' he came back in with Detective McCabe an' then he tol' me, "We want you to tell us why did you kill that man?" So I jump up from the seat I was sittin' in. I say, "What you talkin' about? I don' know what you talkin' about." So he say, "Come on, knock it off, start tellin' us about the murder." I say, "Look, I don' know what you talkin' about, I don' know who even got kill." He say, "You better start talkin' or we will bounce you all over this room." . . . [Russo] say to me, "You better say that

---

* Court reporters do not customarily transcribe dialect or accented speech phonetically, but use conventionally correct spellings. In Carlos' speech above, and elsewhere in this book, I have slightly modified the trial record to make spoken sounds conform to those I heard and tape-recorded in my interviews. I have not, however, altered the wording.—M.H.

you did this, because if you walk out of this building, I'm goin' to pick you up when I get off duty, put you in my car, take you out in the country, an' shoot you dead." . . . [McCabe] say, "All right, you ready to talk?" I say, "I can't tell you anything about this, because I don' *know* anything about it." He grab me by the jacket an' kick me between my legs. . . . He say, "Valencia, he tol' me that you, your brother, an' somebody else had something to do with this crime."

Years later, relating the same events informally to a visitor,* he retold it with even more color and with sharpened emphasis on his mistreatment; once again, both the credible and the incredible were freely intermingled:

Now, when I get to the police station, they take me into one of the rooms an' tell me to sit down. McCabe was sittin' at the desk. McCabe say, "Now, tell us why you kill that man." So I laugh, you know; I thought it was a joke. So he grab me by my leather coat an' throw me against the wall, an' say, "Look, fuck, I ain' bullshittin', I want to know why you kill that man." Then I get *scared!* Then he show me a whole stack of pictures of people I been hangin' out with in the neighborhood an' axe me if I recognize them, an' I recognize every one except this old dude. I say, "Well, I don' know *him.*" He say, "Whacha mean, you don' know him? That's the guy you kill!" I say, "I ain' kill nobody," an' he kick me in the nuts, an' they threaten to pick me up outside an' shoot me, an' start tellin' me about how they think this crime was committed an' givin' me the answers they wanted from me.

But both his versions of the story are gravely flawed by the presence in them of McCabe, who did not return to the Precinct until 2:15 p.m.; even Carlos' own brother testified to that. Both accounts are further contradicted by Carlos' own admission, during his cross-examination, that the interrogation began not in a slam-bang fashion, but with a series of quiet, neutral questions by Russo, about his name, age, residence, arrest record, and the like—which is exactly what Russo says is his normal way of starting off an interrogation. But

---

* Unless otherwise noted, these and other recent remarks by Carlos and Alfredo Ortiz were made in the course of two days of tape-recorded conversations with the author in December 1970.

if Carlos was lying about McCabe's kicking him in the groin, he may well have been telling the truth about being bellowed at and threatened, for a colleague who worked on many cases with Russo says that while he never saw the detective beat a prisoner ("He might slap him, but that's nothing, *that's* not brutality"), he had heard him yell and swear ferociously at prisoners a number of times. And considering that Russo, blue-chinned and dark of countenance, was six feet two inches in height and weighed 225 pounds, while Carlos was five feet one and weighed about 115, one can well believe what Carlos says about how the interrogation *felt* to him, even if one cannot credit many of the details he gives.

As the interrogation continued, Russo asked him to account for his time on October 9th, got him to name all of his close friends, and ferreted out many other items of background information. Then, Carlos says, Russo got to the matter of the crime itself, and told him that he already knew that Carlos, Alfredo, Valencia, and Negrito had planned it, that they had waited on the corner opposite 399 East 160th for Helmer, that after he had gone in, Alfredo had run across and rung a bell to gain entry, and that Valencia, Negrito, and Carlos had gone upstairs, pushed the aged man into his apartment, and there murdered him. Carlos steadfastly insisted that he knew nothing about any of this, that he hadn't been there, hadn't heard any details about the crime, and hadn't even known that one had been committed. Eventually Russo wearied of this unprofitable process and took Carlos into the dorm room, where he handcuffed him to a bed and darkly threatened, "We'll take care of you in a little while." This first interrogation, as Carlos tells about it, lasted an hour and a half, but yielded not one syllable of self-implication or implication of others.

Russo's account agrees with Carlos' as to the duration of the interrogation and the opening sequence of questions about name, age, and what he'd been doing on the 9th; for the rest, the two differ greatly. For one thing, Russo says that although he hinted that he knew a lot, it was Carlos, not he, who named the time of day and actually gave an account of the entry of the building. Recalling the interrogation recently, Russo said that he made it clear to Carlos, after the opening phase, that he was investigating the murder at 399 East 160th Street and already knew plenty, and that names had already been named. He didn't have to mention Valencia's, since Carlos had already seen him outside, but Russo did say that another detective was even now bringing Alfredo in for questioning. With these and similar "knowledge bluffs," he unsettled Carlos, who, for all his usual air of bravado, was actually a "weak sister," according to Russo; it was not necessary to "lean on" him, nor would Russo have beaten him, threatened to murder him, or used other coercive tactics. "That's not my cup of tea," he says. "If you treat a junkie or a mugger that way, you're no better than he is. You're degrading yourself, you're making yourself just what you're supposed to be against." Russo described the rest of the interrogation as follows:

> I got him to tell me his story before I talked about the crime at all. Then, after I got around to that, I started to look for little discrepancies in everything he said. I'd ask, "By the way, where did you say you were at that time?" or "Where did you say your brother was?" I'd catch him in little contradictions, and he'd fumble around and say things like, "Wait a minute, I wasn't there yet, I think I was still on my way," or, "I think my brother was downtown, not home," and I'd say, "Wait a minute, now, that doesn't fit with what you told me a little while ago"; and he was getting more and more nervous, feeling that I could see through him and was catching him in lies. When I felt he was getting panicky, I laid it on him—I said, "All right, now, you know the case I'm investigating. If you're going to be implicated, it might behoove you to tell it your way first, because we'll be speaking to the other people and we'll find out. If you did the stabbing, we'll know about it, but if you didn't, you might as well say so." This gives him the feeling that maybe I'll make it easy for him if he talks, or maybe if he just tells me enough to pin it on someone else, I'll be satisfied with that and leave him out. So after a while he finally says, "Oh, yeah!—I guess I know what you're talking about—but I wasn't in on it," and he tells me a story about the other three, excluding himself completely, maybe hoping I'd buy it and make him a witness against them, or maybe hoping that even if we figured him for a participant, he'd have cut himself a piece of cake by giving us information first.

Russo's account is largely, but not completely, convincing: If Carlos had really been part of the crime, could he have imagined that the accomplices he named would not name him in return? Or if he felt the detectives would eventually know about his role in the crime, could he have supposed they would let him stick to his alibi? But he was young, small, poor, ill-educated, not overly bright, and already a loser in the eyes of the law; he was probably incapable of handling the situation with good judgment. Probably, too, Russo did terrify him by his mere presence and manner (and perhaps by some suitably fierce talk), and out of fear Carlos responded by offering one or two details, found Russo acting far friendlier and more reassuring, and so went ahead with it.

Whatever the explanation, Russo finally got Carlos to tell him a valuable, if manifestly incomplete and partially untruthful story, which Russo took down in longhand. Carlos said he remembered Friday, October 9th, because he had gone downtown looking for a job that day; he didn't get it, returned by noon, and in front of his own house met Alfredo, Doel Valencia, and "Negretto" (as Russo misheard the nickname Negrito), a one-armed, dark-skinned Puerto Rican whose real name he said he didn't know. Alfredo asked him to go upstairs and bring down some water; he needed it to take a shot of dope, but had his own reasons for not wanting to go upstairs at that time.

Carlos got him the water, but when he returned, he found the three had crossed the street and were standing in front of 399, the "nice" building on the corner. He saw Alfredo go into the vestibule and ring a bell; then all three went inside the building. He did not wait for them, but visited a nearby girl-friend for a few minutes; when he came out of her house, he saw the three of them again, approached them, and heard them talking about going downtown to buy some heroin. Alfredo, at that point, flashed a roll of bills that Carlos thought amounted to about $100. Russo's handwritten notes conclude:

> [Carlos] states that his brother Alfredo and the two others must have robbed someone in the building they went into because they didn't have any money before they went in there. He knows his brother didn't have any money so they must have robbed someone or broke into somebody's apartment. States his brother did not tell him where he got the money from. States that Negretto hangs around the Melrose projects on Co[u]rtlandt Avenue and that people give him food.
>
> States he didn't know anyone was killed in 399 East 160th Street. States he saw the police cars there on Sunday but didn't think anything of it.

And this, Carlos told him, was everything he knew about it. But it was enough; it was all Russo needed to crack the case, for now he could confront the other three with the testimony of a real witness rather than the vague hearsay of an informer.

Russo acted as if he were satisfied with Carlos' story, and parked the youth outside in the squad room, near Valencia, where both of them sat, silent and withdrawn, under the watchful eye of one or another of the crowd of detectives working in the room. It was just about then that McCabe phoned in and heard that Carlos was opening up; Russo referred to him as "Bazooka" because he had heard somewhere that this was one of Carlos' nicknames, and because he expected that eventually he would find that it had been Carlos who left the bubble gum and the wrapper in Helmer's kitchen. But that would come later in the day, after he had had a chance to use Carlos' story against the other suspects—and could then use their stories to pry the rest of the truth out of Carlos.

Whatever psychological tactics Russo may have used up to this point or later on, Carlos himself has always maintained that it was sheer physical brutality that finally forced him to talk, and to assent to a completely false confession prefabricated by Russo and McCabe. Carlos says that the morning's interrogation, lacking brutality (except for the kick in the groin), got nothing from him but the truth—in the form of total denials—but that he did name names and make a confession late in the afternoon, after several hours of savage beatings and physical torture.

Describing this process in court, Carlos said that a few minutes after Russo had handcuffed him to the bed in the dorm room, several detectives came in and told him they wanted him to say that Alfredo was known as Bazooka. (They may have, at that; this would have been one way to trick Carlos into identifying himself as Bazooka.) He refused, saying his brother was known only as Freddy, and at once they began punching him in the stomach and smacking him in the face until he was doubled up in pain and unable to breathe; he then agreed that Alfredo was sometimes called Bazooka.

But this bought him only a moment's respite, for he was brutalized off and on for the next four hours. His account, confused and disjointed, tells of being dragged from the dorm room to a small interrogation room, then into the squad room, then back to the dorm room, for various sessions of questioning and beating. Groups of detectives —several at a time, and sometimes half a dozen—kept visiting him, barking questions at him, demanding that he admit to details they said they already knew, and, when he refused, kicking him, hitting him in the head, smacking him on the ears, and punching him in the stomach, until he had agreed to the beginning of their story of the murder. A sample of the process, reconstructed from his testimony:

> First Detective: When you went in the building, where did you go?
>
> Carlos: I di'n' go in that building.
>
> First Detective: You *went* in that building! Now, where did you go? You went up the stairs, didn't you?
>
> Carlos: Look, I never went up no—
>
> Second Detective (*smacking Carlos in the face*): What's the matter with you? We *know* you went up. What do you want to put yourself through all this for? (*Smacks him again.*)
>
> Carlos: All right, I went up the stairs.
>
> First Detective: How many flights?
>
> Carlos: I don't know how many flights, I ain' been there.
>
> First Detective: You *know* how many flights! You *know* it was two flights!
>
> Carlos: I don't know that, man—
>
> Second Detective (*punches him in the stomach*): *Why* are you making it hard on yourself?
>
> Carlos (*doubled over, unable to breathe*): Yeah . . . two flights.

But he kept resisting at every step, until a fat detective came into the dorm room, ordered him to kneel on the floor, buttoned Carlos' jacket backward over his arms, and then pulled his head back and clapped a rag soaked in ammonia over his face. In mortal terror, his mouth and lungs on fire, Carlos strangled and struggled until the fat detective took the rag away and asked if he was ready to tell about the killing. Carlos answered, "How can I tell you I kill somebody if I don' know anything about this?" The detective grunted, "Oh, you're a wise guy," threw him on his back, and put the rag on his face again, keeping it there until Carlos blacked out. The detective removed it, and when Carlos came to, he surrendered and told them he'd say anything they wanted him to.

At 5:30 p.m. he was led into the Lieutenant's room, from which he had just seen Alfredo emerge. Russo and McCabe were inside, and as

Russo asked him questions, both detectives wrote down his answers on long sheets of lined yellow paper. This time Carlos gave a detailed story of the crime, naming himself as one of the criminals. When he met the other three at noon on the 9th, he said, they were planning the score, and he joined them. They waited across from 399 East 160th until Helmer appeared and went inside; then Alfredo ran across, pushed a button, and held the inner door open. Doel and Negrito went in and up the stairs, and Carlos followed them after a moment's hesitation (Alfredo remaining downstairs); he found Doel at the door of Helmer's apartment, and Helmer and Negrito inside in the kitchen. Carlos went in, grabbed the bag of groceries from the old man, and set it on the floor. Helmer began to yell and fight, Carlos seized the old man's arms, and Negrito stabbed him—only once, as far as Carlos saw. He admitted that he had chewed some gum while in the apartment and left a wrapper on the kitchen table, but despite this seeming casualness, he said he was panic-stricken after the stabbing and had nothing to do with the search for money. Negrito, however, shortly appeared with a fistful of bills, and all of them thereupon rushed down the stairs, out of the building, and over to the Ortiz brothers' apartment. A little while later the other three left him and went downtown, presumably for drugs; Carlos, not a heroin user, did not go with them.

This ended the "Q&A"—technically, a confession, even though taken by detectives rather than a district attorney and not written or signed by Carlos. The Q&A had taken only half an hour; on this point there is no conflict between Carlos, Russo, and McCabe; all agree, moreover, that every question written down by the two detectives was actually asked, and that every answer they recorded was actually given. The only two points of disagreement are as to the truthfulness and the voluntariness of this confession: Carlos maintains that the story was completely made up by the two detectives, and that he was forced to say it by over four hours of beatings and threats, and by the ammonia treatment. Russo and McCabe, of course, hold that, aside from one or two minor details, the story represents the truth, and they have said both privately and under oath that neither they nor, as far as they know, anyone else used physical violence upon Carlos, who voluntarily told the truth as a result of being closely questioned and learning that Alfredo had just told everything.

## II    *Forcibly Obtained Truth: A Contradiction in Terms*

ALMOST every suspect who confesses to a serious crime while being interrogated later tries to repudiate his confession, generally by claiming that it was wrung from him by physical or psychological force. Such a charge is a dual attack on the confession: it challenges both its legality (since the Fifth Amendment forbids any compulsion to bear witness against oneself) and its credibility (for common sense tells us that anyone being physically or mentally tormented may confess falsely in order to end his suffering).

Of the two reasons, the latter would seem easier for the average person to understand and agree with: the Fifth Amendment, after all, is only a man-made rule, and not long or widely in use; but should it not be obvious to any man, in any time or place, that a tortured prisoner might say whatever his tormentor wants him to in order to end his agony? Is it not self-evident that, without physical evidence or other witnesses, such confessions are inherently unworthy of belief?

It should be, but it has not been to a great many of the people who have lived on earth. Torture has been a standard part of the judicial process in many societies, and endorsed by some of the finest minds in Western culture. Aristotle and Demosthenes regarded it as the surest means of obtaining evidence—primarily, however, from slaves. In Rome, during the Republic, the same view was generally held, but during the Empire freemen as well as slaves were often tortured in criminal cases, the Romans believing that the rack, the barbed hook, the heated metal plate, and similar instruments were efficient means of ascertaining the truth. From the thirteenth century on, the Inquisition was authorized by the Pope to inquire after truth in much the same way, the inquisitors breaking their suspects upon the rack, flogging them, hanging them by their thumbs, searing their feet over coals, and pulling their arms and legs out of their sockets by means of windlasses. All through the late Middle Ages and up to the eighteenth century, the French, English, Scots, and others sometimes resorted to similar techniques, including the use of the boot, the iron gauntlets, the thumbscrew, and occasionally the *peine forte et dure* in which ever heavier weights were piled on the suspect's body until he confessed or was crushed to death.

But how could any prosecutor, inquisitor, or magistrate suppose that what some poor wretch shrieked out, as his bones were splintering or his flesh was smoking under the red-hot iron, was the truth? Easily enough: torturing authorities have always been convinced, by the very nature of their profession, that they do, in fact, have in hand wrongdoers whose refusal to confess signifies not innocence but stubbornness, and who must therefore be dealt with by more and severer torture until a confession is forthcoming. And so they doubted only the denials of what they wanted to hear, and believed only the confirmations of their suspicions. Fifteenth- and sixteenth-century inquisitors, for instance, were certain that witches not only could and did stir up storms, cast spells, turn themselves into animals, and fly through the air, but that they all copulated with various devils and sometimes even with Satan himself; accordingly, they believed all such stories told to them by tortured suspects, and burned some 30,000 confessed witches during a century and a half. Hardly any of the condemned managed to leave us any denial of their confessions, but one Johannes Julius, a burgomaster of Bamberg, somehow got a note off to his daughter before being burned at the stake in which he urged her to believe none of it, saying, "It is all falsehood and invention. . . . They never cease the torture until one says something." *

Century after century, in a thousand dungeons, towers, prisons, and public squares, shattered wrecks of humanity have recited the confessions desired by the agents of every kind of tyranny from monarchy to fascism, from the Inquisition to the French Revolution, from the Puritan theocracy of Salem to the "cultural revolution" of Maoist China. And yet, though we know all this, and despise and condemn the torturers, most of us still secretly feel that it is not always wrong to force

---

* It is only fair to add that some of the confessed witches accused themselves without being tortured, apparently because of compulsions or delusions. See Notes on Sources.

a confession from a suspect: the worse the crime, and the more certain we are that we know the villain, the more we feel it is justified to make him talk, if it is only through his confession that he can be convicted and punished. But of course this reasoning is totally specious: it assumes (as did the inquisitors) that the truth is already known and needs only to be verified.

Such feelings, all too human and common, are bound to lead to the abuse of suspects by those with power and the task of law enforcement unless such abuse is expressly forbidden and controlled. In this country, however, there had been no state or local police at the time the Constitution was drawn up, and its framers therefore did not think to ban forcible police interrogation. It was probably inevitable that when police forces grew up in the latter half of the nineteenth century and began to be charged with the job of crime investigation, they freely used every means available, and therefore resorted to various forms of brutality to get their suspects to talk. Often they got confessions which led to confirming outside evidence; sometimes they got confessions which did not. In either case, the crime was considered solved, the public was grateful, and even gentle, moral people viewed the "third degree" as an ugly necessity, made less opprobrious by the thought that vicious criminals deserve the punishment they get.

American police never adopted the rack, boot, thumbscrew, or other alien instruments of torture, but used their own homespun and informal methods, many of which were exceedingly savage, and which were widely used well into the present century. In 1931 the Wickersham Commission (President Hoover's National Commission on Law Observance and Enforcement) reported that the third degree, as employed by various American police departments during the 1920s, had included cases of starving the suspects, keeping them awake for many days, beating them with fists, blackjacks, rubber hoses, or telephone books, whipping them with straps and bullwhips, kicking them in the shins, torso, and crotch, twisting their arms, twisting or squeezing their testicles, administering tear gas, scopolamine injections, and chloroform, and, in one instance, hoisting a man aloft repeatedly by his sex organs.

Public revulsion at these disclosures began to moderate the inquisitorial methods of detectives but did not eradicate them. Not until the Supreme Court, in 1936, began to intervene in confession cases in state courts did the third degree decline in popularity. The 1936 landmark case *Brown* v. *Mississippi* involved three illiterate black murder suspects who had been spread-eagled over chairs by local sheriffs and beaten with straps that had metal buckles until their flesh was torn to shreds. The beatings continued until the suspects confessed, adjusting or changing their confessions as the whippings continued until every detail met the wishes of the sheriffs. The suspects were, naturally, convicted, but the Supreme Court reversed the judgment on the narrow ground that the use of torture had deprived the prisoners of their rights without due process of law. But in other cases both before and after this one the Court also said that the aim of the rule making involuntary confessions inadmissible was to exclude false evidence.*

Over the ensuing decades the Court ruled out a number of other forms of physical coercion, including all types of infliction of pain, withholding of food or sleep, and prolonged imprisonment. But although brutality in interrogations decreased, it did not disappear; rather, it went underground and there was used more selectively and cautiously. It was, nonetheless, common knowledge among lawyers, police reporters, and criminals that when other methods failed, a certain amount of physical violence was still likely to be used in nearly every detective squad throughout the country. Even when the third degree had become uncommon, there still were scattered revelations of interrogation brutality as late as the 1960s. In 1962 in New York City, for instance, where the third degree had virtually disappeared, police in Brooklyn not only beat and kicked a potential witness in order to get a statement, but placed lighted cigarette butts on his back; and in 1964, at the 41st Precinct in the Bronx, another suspect required six weeks of hospitalization after his interrogation.

Still, in New York City brutality of this order had become rare by the 1960s and even ordinary beatings had become infrequent; according to several former detectives, such physical coercion as still existed in interrogations consisted chiefly of "bouncing a guy off the wall a couple of times" or administering a few roundhouse wallops on the side of the head. Since then it has become even rarer; the educational process of having tainted confessions thrown out of court has led most detectives to feel that suspects have to be questioned very circumspectly, and that confessions are often more trouble than they are worth.

But even while the use of physical force was decreasing, the use of

---

* In later confession cases the Court further broadened and deepened the grounds for its reversals, as will appear in Section IV of this chapter.

psychological force was not; indeed, it was being expanded and refined
—and few of the new psychological methods were reviewed or ruled
upon by the state courts or the Supreme Court until the mid-1960s.
The clearest picture of the psychologically coercive methods in common use at that time is given by the more widely used manuals of investigative technique cited by Chief Justice Earl Warren in 1966 in
the *Miranda* decision—*Criminal Interrogation and Confessions,* by
Fred E. Inbau and John E. Reid, *Fundamentals of Criminal Investigation,* by Charles E. O'Hara, and a number of others. Inbau and
Reid, for example, stress the importance of questioning the suspect in
the police station, away from home and in "an atmosphere [that]
suggests the invincibility of the forces of the law." They recommend,
among other things, that the interrogators make false statements
about having other evidence, so as to bluff the prisoner into talking;
accuse him repeatedly of lying; accuse him of other crimes of which
he is actually innocent to frighten him into an admission; deprive him
of cigarettes or other tension-relieving devices, and keep him seated in
a straight, hard chair; put him in a "fixed line-up," in which he is
"identified" by a supposed witness, or even in a "reverse line-up," in
which he is pointed out as the supposed perpetrator of other and
worse crimes than the one under investigation; and whipsaw him with
the "Mutt and Jeff" (or, in New York City, "Good Guy and Bad
Guy") routine, in which one detective is savage and vindictive but the
other is sympathetic and helpful—as long as the suspect cooperates.
Professor Inbau recognizes the immorality of these devices, but considers them justified by need: "Of necessity," he has written elsewhere, "criminal interrogators must deal with criminal offenders on a
somewhat lower moral plane than that upon which ethical, law-
abiding citizens are expected to conduct their everyday affairs." Professor Inbau was formerly a police official; it is not surprising that he
views the suspect as an offender even in advance of interrogation or
prosecution, and so justifies the use of techniques which would not be
used on the innocent person.

O'Hara, who suggests many of the same devices dealt with in Inbau
and Reid, also recommends the "bluff on a split pair" (in which the
suspect is falsely informed that an accomplice has squealed and accused him), the use of faked laboratory evidence or faked lie-detector
reports, and, in general, the maintaining of a terrifying and relentless
attitude:

[The investigator] must rely on an oppressive atmosphere of dogged persistence. He must interrogate steadily and without relent, leaving the subject no prospect of surcease. He must dominate his subject and overwhelm him with his inexorable will to obtain the truth. . . . In a serious case, the interrogation may continue for days, with the required intervals for food and sleep, but with no respite from the atmosphere of domination.

Psychologist Philip Zimbardo, perhaps overstating the case a little, concluded in an article in the June 1967 issue of *Psychology Today* that "the secret inquisitorial techniques of our police force[s] are sometimes more highly developed, more psychologically sophisticated, and more effective than . . . those of the Chinese Communists."

No one knows, however, how many confessions obtained in recent years by means of psychological coercion have been false and have resulted in wrongful punishment, for almost none of those who claim they falsely confessed under duress have any way to prove their innocence. Nor, in the absence of other evidence, have we any way to be sure they are guilty. But we can judge from the example of the confessions used in Stalinist show trials—later proven to be false by the "rehabilitation" of the convicted persons—how great the potential is for injustice in the use of psychological coercion. We have long told ourselves that nothing of the sort is possible under our system of law, but the Supreme Court concluded that it is: this was one of the reasons the Court sought, in *Miranda,* to protect suspects against even subtle forms of psychological coercion to confess. For any toleration of coercive methods, any temporizing with the principle of voluntarity, opens the door to injustice.

A footnote in the *Miranda* decision refers to the most recent and celebrated case in point, the interrogation and confession of George Whitmore. A dull-witted Negro youth of nineteen, he was arrested in Brooklyn on an attempted rape charge in April 1964; during his interrogation a photograph in his wallet led to the suspicion that he might also have been the murderer of two young career girls, Janice Wylie and Nancy Hoffert, who had been stabbed to death in their Manhattan apartment the previous August. He was interrogated first about the rape, then about an unsolved homicide, and finally about the Wylie-Hoffert case, for a total of some twenty hours (but was not, apparently, beaten); after having confessed to the first two crimes, he went on to make a full confession to the double murder, although he did not know at the time that the two girls had died of their stab wounds. The questions he was asked and the answers he gave about the Wylie-Hoffert murders filled sixty-one typewritten pages and included specific details as to how he came to enter the apartment, surprised Janice Wylie coming out of the shower, knocked her and her roommate unconscious with a soda bottle, bound the two of them with torn sheets, stabbed them repeatedly with carving knives, washed his hands of their blood, and left the apartment. The only trouble with this was that he had not done any of these things: the details had been deduced by the detectives, but Whitmore was not the one who had done them. Tremendous psychological pressure, fatigue, fear, and the limitations of his own intelligence had led him to accept the suggestions of his interrogators step by step, or to suggest various answers of his own to each of their questions until he hit on one that was close enough to the facts to be acceptable. Time and again, ignorant of the right answer, he would flounder around until he perceived what was wanted of him, and would give it; in the end, he had made a complete and coherent confession and was booked for the double murder by jubilant detectives who believed that they had solved the case.

Half a year later an informer told the police that they had the wrong man: a junkie friend of the informer's, one Richard Robles, had murdered the girls and told him about it. Four months later the police had collected enough evidence to arrest Robles and convict him; not only was their case against him thoroughly convincing, but by that time detectives had established beyond question that Whitmore had been in Wildwood, New Jersey, on the day the murders had been committed. Had Robles never been named and investigated, Whitmore would probably have died in the electric chair or spent his life in prison, and no one but he would ever have known that his confession was a complete fiction wrung from him by a psychological *peine forte et dure.**

Nor can his case be comfortingly regarded as a pure fluke: the year after Whitmore made his confession—when its falsehood was first revealed—charges against six other murder suspects in New York, all of

---

* But Whitmore was convicted of the earlier charges of assault and attempted rape, where there was corroborative evidence and identification by the victim as well as his confession.

whom had confessed, were dropped, the prosecution conceding the defendants to be innocent in each case. Most likely, however, the majority of confessions obtained by psychologically stressful interrogations in recent years have been true; the justice system, at least in that respect, is largely just. But is largely just good enough? How legal should a law-enforcement system be? How much risk dare we run of convicting a few innocent men in order not to let many guilty ones go free? There are many who, today, think we are more virtuous than we need be, who think some risk of doing someone a wrong is justified, who would agree with Senator McClellan when he deplores our "worrying" and "sentimentality" that some innocent person, somewhere, some time, might suffer "a little injustice." But there are others who regard even a little injustice as too much, and view any permission to coerce a suspect as an infection that can sicken the entire system and bring about the unintended death of civil liberty.

---

## III *Anything You Say May Be Used Against You*

ALL things considered, it would seem very unlikely that Carlos Ortiz was intermittently beaten for more than four hours and asphyxiated by ammonia fumes. Not only had severe physical coercion become rather rare by 1964, but police photographs of Carlos in the nude, taken the day after the interrogation, show no marks or discolorations whatever, not even around the mouth, where, he later said, the ammonia had left him badly reddened and chapped; moreover, the physician who examined him at the Brooklyn House of Detention found no evidence of trauma, and reported that Carlos made no physical complaints.

On the other hand, he was undoubtedly subjected to various psychological stresses, some of which would be ruled out a year and a half later (but not retroactively) by *Miranda*. But even if these stresses were coercive, it also seems unlikely that they could have made Carlos agree to a wholly fictitious confession of murder; it is far more likely, in view of the facts, that they made him tell the truth. For although his tale of how he came to confess does have echoes of the Whitmore story about it, he was interrogated only one quarter as long as Whitmore, his confession was corroborated by two other persons, and he never was able to supply a provable alibi. Coincidentally—but perhaps most importantly—two months before he described his interrogation in court the news broke that Whitmore's confession had been wholly false and a product of something akin to brainwashing—news that could not have failed to reach Carlos in jail, awaiting trial for murder, and make a profound impression on him.

But even if it seems unlikely that what was wrung out of him was a false confession, he probably did feel about the afternoon's interrogation much as he says he did—badgered, harangued, frightened, and overpowered—and quite possibly he was shaken, shoved, or smacked several times by one or another of the ever changing crews of detectives working on him, all of which made him finally yield and give the account of the crime that Russo and McCabe took down at 5:30 that day.

Much the same sort of explanation may account for the confessions which they got out of Alfredo Ortiz and Doel Valencia the same afternoon, and which both later similarly repudiated. Alfredo, in fact, was the first of the three to give a complete account of the crime, and even his own later disavowal of it makes it clear that he gave in fairly soon and without being subjected to pressures in any way comparable to those applied to Whitmore, although, to be sure, Alfredo was greatly weakened by his recent drug-withdrawal experience and at a severe psychological disadvantage from having both a drug charge and a parole violation outstanding against him.

Even before entering the squad area, he says, McCabe made him untie his shoelaces so that he couldn't run. "I said, 'Run for what? I don' know what you want me for.' " He found out soon enough: McCabe and Russo took him back into the dorm room—where Carlos says *he* was at the time, though Alfredo says nothing about that—and there demanded he tell them why he killed the old man, adding that they knew he and his friends had done it. "What old man?" asked Alfredo. "I don' know what you're talkin' about." When this first confrontation yielded nothing, they took him into the Lieutenant's room and Russo got down to business, telling Alfredo his friends had already said he'd been with them on the score; Alfredo, however, stuck to his astonished denials and whining assertions of complete mystification.

Russo then challenged him to account for his time that day, and Alfredo spoke of having been downtown with a friend, but the detective said that his own brother had seen Alfredo and the two others going into Helmer's building a little after noon. "I don' know what you're talkin' about, man," Alfredo repeated. "I haven' seen my brother on the 9th. I di'n' see him all the day until the night." According to Alfredo, McCabe, infuriated, threatened to hit him with a baseball bat, but Russo restrained him; McCabe began to kick Alfredo in the shins, but Russo said it would leave marks; McCabe punched Alfredo in the stomach, and Russo said nothing.

When Alfredo could speak, he said he wanted to hear Carlos make his accusations against him face to face, and got his wish:

> They brought my brother into the room an' he say something, an' I say, "Carlos, why don' you tell him the truth?" So they took him out of the room, an' from there McCabe an' Russo took me by the arms an' started pickin' me up an' throwin' me back down, an' I say, "Yes, it was *me*, it was *me!*" That was aroun' four-thirty, aroun' there. I tol' him, "Yes, it was me." So he tol' me, "All right, tell me what happen."

But although they began to write down his answers to their questions, he continued to profess ignorance on various points, and, item by item, they had to make him agree to their conception of what had happened. When he resisted, Russo would say, "Listen, man, you want to go through what your friends went through?" and Alfredo would say no, he didn't, and answer his questions. Later, when he refused to say that he heard the old man scream, McCabe punched him in the face, and Alfredo said, "Yes, I heard the old man screamin'." So it went, to the end, his confession being completed some three hours after he and McCabe had entered the Precinct.

As stories of forced confessions go, it is rather pale; Valencia's is far more lurid. But no doubt he was much harder for the detective to deal with: two years older than Alfredo, half a head taller, and solidly built, he was made of tougher stuff, as was evident from his having admitted nothing the night before. As he tells it, he was interrogated and brutalized by teams of detectives for nearly seven hours that day before he finally began to answer Russo's questions to Russo's satisfaction. Hour after hour he was bullied, browbeaten, pummeled, smacked, and knocked down, behind closed doors, in various private rooms, and even quite openly in the squad room. At one point he was confronted by Carlos, at another by Alfredo, with their damaging admissions. Somewhere in the midst of all this there came an ammonia episode much like Carlos':

> He had like a rag in his hand. Something started to smell in the room. I don' know what it was. He came an' put it closer to me an' they put my coat down over my back. He held me against the wall an' he put it in my face. Then I started goin' down, an' I reached the floor an' my back was towards the floor, an' he had his knees in my chest. He kept puttin' it. I was tryin' to hold my breath, shakin' my head to avoid the rag. Then I couldn' breathe any more. That's when I started like to pass out.

When he revived, another detective gave him a rough outline of how they thought he, the Ortiz brothers, and Negrito had murdered Helmer; the detective began coaching him on the story from the beginning, beating him whenever he refused to give the right answer. A sample of the procedure:

> Then he was tellin' me we went upstairs. I tol' him, "Sir, I don' know what happen upstairs." He tol' me, "You *know* what happen upstairs." I say, "I don' know." He keep hittin' me, hittin' me. All right, I went upstairs. "What did you do up there?" I say, "We jumped a man." "No, no, stop right there—you waited an' you opened the door and you pushed him in."

At various times McCabe was in on the proceedings, punching Valencia repeatedly in the stomach and smacking him on the ears; others did the same things to him, and also hit him in the neck, kicked him in the chest, and slammed him backward into metal lockers again and again. According to his narrative, Valencia must have been hit in the body at least a hundred times, and kicked, smacked, and knocked against the wall at least as many more times during his seven-hour ordeal, in addition to getting the ammonia treatment.

And finally he capitulated and began to agree to everything they wanted him to say—with one important exception: he claimed he had been working at Consolidated Millinery the day of the crime, and after a detective had gone out to make a phone call, presumably to check on this, he returned and told Valencia to say that the murder had been committed at 9:00 p.m., a time when Valencia could have been part of it. Valencia agreed to this, and eventually, after both Ortizes had made their confessions, he was brought into the Lieutenant's room at about half past six to repeat the whole thing for McCabe and Russo while they wrote it all down.

After his statement was completed, McCabe took him out and locked him in the cage, pending the arrival of an assistant district attorney. Valencia protested his innocence once again, and this time, he says, McCabe cynically and smugly admitted that the whole thing was a frame:

> I say to McCabe, "I have nothin' to do with this. What that man wrote there in that statement, that's lies." He tol' me, "Yes, I know. But tell that to a jury or to the judge." I tol' him, "I'll tell him." He say, "You think they're goin' to believe you, a spick?" He tol' me just like that. "I've been on the force I don' know how many years—you think they're goin' to take your word [rather] than mine—and [when] there are more officers to back me up?" So then he went out of the room.

Detectives Russo and McCabe, as one would expect, give a very different account of the afternoon's activities. In court, of course, they said nothing about the various opening maneuvers and tactics used in both interrogations, or about the cat-and-mouse questioning, the knowledge bluffs, the doubling back to catch each suspect in inconsistencies, the confrontations with fellow suspects. They merely told of having "conversations" with each one, after first warning him that he did not have to say anything and that anything he said might be used against him as evidence; the conversations apparently proceeded in a straight line from name and address to an orderly account of the day's activities and the committing of the crime. Neither detective said anything about bullying, bluffing, shouting, or threatening the suspects, much less shoving them around or hitting them, although one is entitled to suppose that some of all this—short of real beatings— might have been part of the mix. (Incidentally, as with Carlos, the police photographs show no marks whatever on Alfredo or Valencia, nor did the medical examiner record any signs of trauma or any complaints except that Valencia had a case of athlete's foot.)

Out of court, however, the detectives give a more detailed and credible story of the interrogations. They say they did talk to all three of their suspects before taking down Q&As (and by evening had talked to the fourth, Negrito, whom they had identified as one Angel Walker, and had had picked up and brought in). But between 2:30 and 5:30 p.m. they spent most of their time in the Lieutenant's room, concentrating on Alfredo, the most vulnerable of the group, and letting teams of other detectives hammer away at Carlos and Valencia elsewhere. Sitting behind the desk in the Lieutenant's room, Russo started off shortly with his typical opening questions (McCabe, who had a toothache and was inexperienced at homicide interrogations, said little, but sat in back of Alfredo in order to make him nervous) and then moved on to more sensitive matters, asking Alfredo what he had done on the 9th, querying him about his use of drugs and his previous conviction for burglary and assault, and finally telling him what the present investigation was about. For a while Alfredo denied knowing anything about it, but was badly shaken by the news that his brother had already named him, and shaken even worse when Carlos was brought in and repeated his assertion in a hangdog mumble. With this, Alfredo's resistance collapsed; after Carlos was taken out, he admitted his role in the crime and began to talk.

Oddly enough, however, he first told the story so as to confirm Carlos' alibi, leaving him out of it altogether. Russo let Alfredo go on, since the main thing at this point was to get him to pin himself down; perhaps Alfredo was playing the older brother, or perhaps, since he was already in trouble on two other counts, he saw no reason for both of them to be in trouble on this one. But after having led Alfredo through the whole narrative, Russo tackled him about the omission of Carlos, reminding him that two other suspects would be telling their stories and that there was no point shielding Carlos—who had given Alfredo away, anyhow—and that it was up to him to do the best for himself by cooperating. Alfredo struggled briefly and then gave in; they started at the beginning again and went through the whole story, McCabe and Russo writing everything down a second time.

Now Alfredo's story was that he and Carlos had met Valencia and Negrito that morning and been invited by Valencia to come along on a score. They agreed to do so, and all four stationed themselves across from Helmer's building at about noon. Carlos went off to get Alfredo water for a fix, and while he was away, Helmer appeared and went in. Alfredo crossed over, pushed a button, and opened the inner door, waving to the other two; they ran across and went upstairs, and when Carlos appeared a moment later, he followed them, Alfredo remaining downstairs as a lookout. He heard yelling and a crash from above; though badly frightened, he stayed by the inner door, and some minutes later, when the others came running down the stairs, Negrito (or perhaps it was Valencia) told him there was $80 for each of them. The Ortiz brothers ran off toward Courtlandt Avenue and the other two down Melrose; they met a few minutes later in the park of the Melrose project, where they divided up the money, Negrito and Valencia getting $80 each and Alfredo the same amount to split with Carlos, the brothers' proceeds being less than the others because it hadn't been their score. Alfredo concluded his statement by saying that Carlos had told him "the old man was cut bad."

Alfredo's two confessions took until half past five. Russo and McCabe were now hot for total victory, but there was a great deal to be done: Alfredo's second confession implicated all three of the others and would aid interrogation, but was of no use against them in court: under Section 399 of the Code of Criminal Procedure then in effect in New York (and under Section 60.22 of the Criminal Procedure Law which replaced it in 1971), a person cannot be convicted of a crime solely on the testimony of an accomplice; there must be corroborative evidence tending to connect the defendant with the crime. (The New York rule on accomplice testimony is more stringent than that in effect in many other states and even in the federal courts.) In this case there was virtually no such evidence except the Bazooka gum and the wrapper. But, paradoxically, though Alfredo's confession could not convict his accomplices, it might send *him* to the electric chair or to life imprisonment even though he had been only a lookout, for under the Penal Code of New York (as under the codes of many other states) anyone who plays any part, however minor, in a felony murder is as guilty as the one who does the actual deed.

As soon as they were through with Alfredo, therefore, they took him out and brought Carlos in. He, knowing nothing of the Code of Criminal Procedure, had no idea that Alfredo's confession was inadmissible as evidence against him, and after learning that his brother had just told all, he did too. There were some minor discrepancies between his version and Alfredo's—he said, for instance, that he was not upstairs getting water at the moment Helmer returned, but across the street with the others—but Russo and McCabe made no effort to clear up the discrepancies; there always are some, and in any case Carlos had admitted to the central facts of the crime.

With two confessions in hand, one of which was an eyewitness account of the stabbing by Negrito, Russo and McCabe felt a good deal more confident—so much so, indeed, that they phoned downstairs and asked the desk officer to book all four suspects officially. (Normally, they would have taken the suspects downstairs and booked them in person, but they wanted to waste not one minute.) Russo now had Valencia brought into the stale, smoky room, rancid with the odor of sweat, and told him about the two existing statements. He asked if Valencia was ready to make one of his own; Valencia was, but despite the earlier pressure to make his story conform to those of the Ortiz brothers, he stubbornly maintained that he had worked that afternoon, and that the crime had taken place at night. His narrative was substantially the same as Carlos', with the usual curious but trifling discrepancies, but the discrepancy in time was no trifle; it was far too great to be explained by errors in recollection, even where the memories were those of narcotics users. Russo told him his story didn't match those of the Ortiz brothers, but Valencia stuck to it, and Russo, feeling that any self-incrimination in the murder was probably worth something, decided to let the jury worry about it, and accepted it as Valencia told it.

By about seven o'clock in the evening, they were through with Valencia, had confessions in hand from three of the four suspects, and needed only one more to have a complete wrap-up of the case. Too exhilarated to feel weary or even hungry, they phoned the District Attorney's office and asked to have an assistant D.A. and a stenotypist come over to take formal confessions. Then they brought in the last suspect, the man said to have done the actual stabbing: Angel Walker, also called Angel Oquendo, but known to all his friends as Negrito (a nickname often given to Puerto Rican babies who are dark-skinned and Negroid in appearance). Negrito, a stocky, powerful man in his early twenties, scowling and hostile, was clearly a far tougher fellow than even Valencia. But Russo and McCabe had three confessions naming him, two of which included eyewitness accounts of his use of the knife, and they expected that with these tools they would be able to open him up in short order.

For they supposed that Negrito, like the other three, would be ignorant of the crucial provision of the Code of Criminal Procedure that made those confessions, by themselves, insufficient to convict him of Helmer's murder. They hoped that he, like the others, would convict himself out of his own mouth, for no other admissible evidence existed against any of them. Assuming that the three who had already confessed had been subjected only to pressures considered acceptable at the time, one can suppose that their confessions were essentially truthful; yet had any one of the confessing youths had a little more stamina, or a little knowledge of the Code of Criminal Procedure—or had the law given him a little greater protection from psychologically stressful methods of interrogation—he might never have talked or been tried for murder.

# IV   *Truthful Confessions and the Doctrine of Fairness*

BUT why should any society so thoroughly protect all who are suspected of crime that the guilty are enabled to escape justice? Granted that the use of force is abhorrent because it so often produces false confessions, why cannot the police use temperate methods—logic, confrontations, facts, appeals to conscience, trickery—which will produce, if anything, only the truth?

Yet even gentle methods can be coercive. Criminals do not, by and large, *want* to incriminate themselves; whatever makes them do so, even if not brutal, is a type of coercion, the proof being that gentle methods succeed not with the strong-willed and knowing, but only with the weak-willed and inexperienced. However civilized and painless a technique may be, if it succeeds in making a weak man incriminate himself despite his original intention, it violates his Fifth Amendment privilege not to be compelled to do so.

The Fifth Amendment seems unreasonable to many good and law-abiding people: since no innocent man needs to take refuge in silence, what good is a law that protects only the guilty? But they are wrong on two counts. First, the history of forced confessions teaches us that only where there is no compulsion whatever can we believe what a suspect says against himself; only where he did not have to talk can we believe him if he does talk. But, second and far more important, the Fifth Amendment sets a limit on the power the state may exert over the lives and thoughts of its people; the Amendment may sometimes allow the guilty to escape justice, but it gives the innocent a decent chance of escaping injustice.

For the privilege against self-incrimination has its roots in the revolt against judicial tyranny. In England, inquisitorial methods of trial like those commonly used on the Continent were employed until the seventeenth century, when Puritans and dissenters were compelled to testify in the Star Chamber (a special court) to matters of conscience and belief for which they could be severely punished. But in 1641 a rebellious Parliament abolished the Star Chamber, and in 1689, following the expulsion of the Stuarts, further barriers against coercion were erected. English criminal justice became adversarial rather than inquisitorial, and instead of an all-powerful court that accused the defendant of guilt and then used every means it could to prove its case out of his own mouth, the court became an impartial referee before which the prosecutor and defendant were adversaries in a contest to determine the truth—a contest governed by rules of fair play which gave the individual a reasonable chance against the might of the government. The key rule of fair play was that the defendant could not be forced to convict himself; the privilege against self-incrimination was thus a crucial limitation upon the power the state could exert over the individual.

In England the privilege became a part of common law, but in America the colonists so prized it that when they became a nation they made it part of their Constitution. In that form it protected an accused person during his trial, but the later development of police investigation created a situation the Founding Fathers had not anticipated: station-house interrogation became in effect a kind of trial held according to old-style inquisitorial principles, yielding evidence which determined the outcome of the supposedly fair adversarial trial later held in court.

The Supreme Court eventually took note of this, and in the confession cases it reviewed from 1936 on, it extended the adversarial concept to those pre-trial activities in which the police were involved—not only to keep them from extorting false confessions, but to protect the adversarial system from erosion, and to preserve and even extend the central idea of the fairness of our legal system. In the 1936 torture case referred to earlier (*Brown* v. *Mississippi*) the Court reversed the conviction because of a violation of due process—but made it clear that this was no merely technical matter; such a violation, the Court said, "offends [a] principle of justice rooted in the traditions and conscience of our people"—namely, fairness. From then on, the Court laid down ever stricter rules concerning interrogation, holding that anything that overcame the suspect's will to be silent violated either due process or the privilege against self-incrimination, or both—and that, in any case, the unfairness involved was a larger issue than the question of truth or falsehood. Said the Court in 1941:

> The aim of the requirement of due process is not to exclude presumptively false evidence, but to prevent fundamental unfairness in the use of evidence, whether true or false.

And twenty years later the Court went much further, saying that even truthful confessions were not worth the price, if they meant violating the principles of the system:

> In many of the cases in which the command of the Due Process Clause has compelled us to reverse state convictions . . . independent corroborating evidence left little doubt of the truth of what the defendant had confessed. Despite such verification, confessions were found to be the product of constitutionally impermissible methods in their inducement.

All of which inevitably led to *Escobedo* and *Miranda*—hardly radical departures from the past, but only steps along the same road. *Miranda,* the last such step, has been seen by its opponents as an extreme departure from legal tradition and without constitutional foundation; yet all it did was insist that the adversarial system operate in the police station for the poor and ignorant as it had already long done for the well-to-do and knowing. For in its fourfold warning, and the offer of free counsel to the poor before questioning began, it only sought to make sure that all defendants really knew and understood their rights and chose either to exercise them or "knowingly and intelligently" to waive them. But to let them waive their rights or fail to exercise them out of ignorance was to be unfair to them, and hence unjust. As Mr. Justice Goldberg had forcefully said, in *Escobedo:*

> No system of criminal justice can, or should, survive if it comes to depend for its continued effectiveness on the citizens' abdication through unawareness of their constitutional rights. . . . If the exercise of constitutional rights will thwart the effectiveness of a system of law enforcement, then there is something very wrong with that system.

Unhappily, violent crime was increasing rapidly in the very years during which the Supreme Court was seeking to assure all Americans the use of their rights; Middle Americans, wanting tougher handling of criminals rather than greater protection for the poor, became antagonistic to the Court, regarding it, says Professor Joseph W. Bishop, Jr., of the Yale Law School, "as a little clique of merciful asses, brimful of what Learned Hand once called the 'watery sentiment that obstructs, delays and defeats the prosecution of crime.' " Even some of the justices themselves spoke in similar terms: Justice Harlan, dissenting from *Miranda,* scathingly called the goal of the majority opinion "voluntariness in a utopian sense . . . voluntariness with a vengeance," and Justice White, complaining that the majority opinion was unworldly, wrote, "The values reflected by the [Fifth Amendment] privilege are not the sole desideratum; society's interest in the general security is of equal weight."

But if our society cannot make good on its promises without incurring chaos, then there must be a basic flaw in its ideal of justice: if there were such a fatal flaw, *Miranda* should have revealed it. And at first most police chiefs, district attorneys, and political conservatives held that *Miranda* would indeed produce chaos and anarchy, some of them offering early evidence that law-enforcement efforts were rapidly failing: a year after the decision District Attorney Arlen Specter of Philadelphia told the McClellan Subcommittee that just before *Miranda* 32 percent of arrested persons were refusing to make statements, as compared to 59 percent after it; District Attorney Aaron Koota of Brooklyn said that in his felony cases the percentage had jumped from 10 to 41; and District Attorney Frank Hogan of Manhattan said that, apart from homicides, in his bailiwick the figure had risen from 51 to 85 percent.

But there was plenty of other evidence showing that while interrogation had become more difficult, it had not become impossible, and that even if *Miranda* was allowing some criminal suspects to slip away, it was not creating anarchy. The authoritative *University of Chicago Law Review* pointed out that *Miranda* ruled out the use of threats, trickery, or cajolery only in regard to getting the suspect to waive his rights; if he once waived them, these techniques could still be used. (Indeed, Inbau and Reid cheerfully asserted, in a post-*Miranda* edition of their book, that after a proper waiver all but a few of the methods they had presented in earlier editions would still be valid.) Other studies have reported that *Miranda* has had limited impact because the warning is often delivered in a perfunctory manner; because it is often given after questioning is well under way; and because it is often robbed of force by such follow-ups as, "Now, of course you don't *have* to say anything, but how can you explain . . ." etc. The New Haven field study of the effects of *Miranda* made by a team of Yale law students showed that it had adversely affected interrogation in only about 10 percent of the felony cases, and that by and large "the police continue to question suspects, and succeed despite the new constraints." A study in Pittsburgh found that the percentage of cases with confessions had dropped from 54.4 to 37.5, but that the clearance rate had fallen only a little and the conviction rate not at all. Even some police chiefs said *Miranda* had done no real harm: Richard Anderson, Chief of Police of Omaha, for instance, told the House Select Committee on Crime in 1969 that the new rules had added to the burdens of his men, but not decreased the number of arrests they were making. And while critics of *Miranda* point to the declining clearance rate throughout the nation as one of its dire results, the FBI data show that the rate declined no more steeply in the two years after *Miranda* than it had in the two years before it.

From all the foregoing, it seems fair to suppose that *Escobedo* and *Miranda* have made crime-solving harder, but have not seriously affected arrest or conviction rates. Only in crimes where there is no other evidence—crimes of stealth, most typically—has it noticeably interfered with police functions and enabled more criminals to escape trial than formerly. But this latter result has been partly offset by the methods police have found to sidestep the *Miranda* requirements, and by the willingness of prosecutors and judges to accept police testimony at face value, in keeping with the public's present fear of crime and desire for revenge.

The price of the "judicialization" of the law-enforcement system is twofold: it places an added burden on the system, and it allows more criminals to go unpunished than formerly. The price of evading the judicial restraints and enforcing the law more easily and more effectively is the adulteration of American justice. The dilemma is one no court can resolve except the court of public opinion; in the coming years the people themselves, through their political leaders, will choose either to preserve or to destroy their heritage of freedom.

# V  *I Don' Remember Nothin'*

LACKING the protections soon to be provided by *Miranda,* Alfredo Ortiz, Carlos Ortiz, and Doel Valencia had all succumbed to the interrogation process, but the fourth suspect in the squad room—Angel Walker, also known as Angel Oquendo, "Santana," and most often "Negrito"—was made of different stuff. Older, harder, and wiser in the ways of the police and the courts, he exuded defiance, his black-skinned Negroid features knitted in a scowl, his eyes glittering with hatred, even the limp, empty right sleeve of his leather jacket conveying an air of danger rather than of weakness. McCabe and Russo had briefly emerged from the Lieutenant's room at 5:00 p.m. to have a look at him, and when McCabe told him they'd be talking to him later about what had happened on the 9th, Walker stared at him and said, "I don' remember nothin'." McCabe snapped that he'd better try to remember something before they got back to him, and the two detectives returned to their interrogation of Alfredo. But neither this, nor the sight of his friends coming out of the Lieutenant's room and being taken out to the detention pen—nor even the fact that he himself was ordered into the pen along with them as soon as the request to book him had been phoned in—seemed to unnerve him; when McCabe came out at a quarter past seven, unlocked the door of the pen, and ordered him to come along, Walker looked at him in a bold and truculent manner that McCabe recognized as boding ill for the interrogation.

For Walker had had plenty of experience with the police, not to mention problems of his own that had armor-clad his psyche. Always a fighter, he had wanted to be a boxer until, at nineteen, he lost his right arm, and despite this handicap he had since then been arrested three times for assaults and for robbery. In addition, he had been a heroin addict for three years, and had once spent half a year in jail for having made a sale to a narcotics detective.

Like his three friends, he was the product of a broken home and had, in fact, been living mostly on his own since his later teens. He had come to New York when he was twelve with his father, Herbert Oquendo, a sober, hardworking carpenter (his mother, Daniela Walker, remained in Puerto Rico), and in Spanish Harlem learned the ways of the streets years before the Ortiz brothers. He dropped out of a trade school after eighth grade, at sixteen, and worked off and on at odd jobs and as an assistant to a silk-screen printer. Either because he was headstrong or because he fought with his father, he moved out and roomed in a squalid tenement on West 77th Street, but he had made friends with Puerto Ricans from the Melrose area and on the fateful night of Friday, November 3rd, 1961, went up there on the subway and attended a dance in a Puerto Rican social hall on Willis Avenue. He had a good time there, during which he drank two whiskeys and six or seven bottles of beer, and got into a brief fight; then, a little before 3:00 a.m., he left for home.

At 3:30 a.m., still waiting on the southbound platform of the subway station at 149th Street and Third Avenue, he impatiently went to the edge of the platform to look for the train, and fell off onto the tracks. Stunned, he rolled under the platform overhang, his right arm still lying across the track. A moment or so later, when a work train slowly pulled in, the foreman of the crew saw something moving ahead and yanked the emergency tripper, slamming the brakes on, but the train was only thirty-five feet from Walker and the wheels of the first car passed over his arm before it stopped. Even as the horrified crew scrambled out, Walker struggled to his feet, his arm hanging useless by his side and blood beginning to drizzle down out of his sleeve. The crew boosted him up to the platform and called for an ambulance, while Walker, stupefied, said again and again, "My arm, what's the matter with my arm?"

At Morrisania Hospital a doctor cut away Walker's clothing and found the arm attached by only a few shreds of mangled flesh. He amputated it just below the shoulder, made the necessary repairs, and assigned Walker to post-operative care in the hospital, but even as the wound was beginning to heal, Walker grew unmanageable: he cursed, raged, screamed, talked of suicide, and threatened to kill various persons in the hospital, and after a couple of weeks was shipped off to Bellevue Hospital for psychiatric treatment. Several weeks later he had recovered sufficiently to be discharged, but although he was given an artificial arm and trained in its use at the Institute for the Crippled and Disabled, he never adjusted to his new condition and soon abandoned the prosthesis altogether. Instead, he dreamed of becoming rich: he and his father engaged a lawyer, who filed suit for them against the New York City Transit Authority, asking for half a million dollars for Walker on the grounds that he had slipped on a newspaper lying on the edge of the platform, and that the Transit Authority had been negligent to let it lie there. But what with innumerable court delays and legal maneuvers, the case had not yet been heard nor had Walker realized any of his dreams when he was brought to the detective squad room of the 42nd Precinct, three years later, to be interrogated about the murder of Alexander Helmer.

During those three years he had become a drifter and a heroin addict. He had moved up to Melrose and lived for a time with an uncle; then he shifted about, stopping briefly with one friend or another. He lived on welfare and handouts of food from residents in the Melrose project, shot up every day, and spent his time on the streets with youths like Valencia and the Ortiz brothers. Deformed, brooding, and laconic—he sometimes spoke barely a word to his friends—he was a mysterious figure on the street; the gossip about him was that he had been a subway mugger and lost his arm in the course of plying his trade, that he would be rich any day now, that, tough as he was, he sometimes forgot about the missing arm and tried to use it—in a handball game, for instance—and when others laughed, would burst into tears of impotent rage. This was the man Carlos and Valencia said they had seen stick a knife into frail, terrified old Helmer, and then calmly search his apartment for cash; this was the man from whom Russo and McCabe now sought to extract a full and self-convicting confession.

Later, as one might have expected, Walker and his fellow suspects said that Russo and McCabe used brutality in their efforts to make him talk; Carlos, for instance, says that Walker's face was so badly burned by ammonia that the skin peeled off, leaving white marks, and that he was so savagely beaten that his stump broke open and bled. But the photographs taken the following morning show no trace of such injuries; moreover, since Russo and McCabe expected an assistant district attorney to appear in a few minutes, they would hardly have used methods the effects of which he could not have failed to see, and which he would, in conscience, have been obliged to report to his superiors.

As soon as Walker was seated, with Russo across the desk from him and McCabe behind him, Russo gave him the standard warning and began with the usual opening questions, both detectives taking notes on their long yellow pads. Walker freely gave his name, age, current address, and admitted that he knew both Ortiz brothers and Doel Valencia. Then Russo said rather formally, "I now direct your attention to the day and night of October 9th. That was the Friday before Columbus Day, which fell on a Monday. Do you remember the Friday I'm talking about?" When Walker said he did, Russo asked what made him remember it.

Walker replied without hesitation, "That was the day I ate with my cousin, Rubio." Since this was apparently going to be the crux of the alibi, Russo sought to get Walker to spell it out in detail so that he could look for inconsistencies and lead Walker into efforts to extricate himself; unfortunately, almost at once it became clear that Walker knew better than to let himself fall into that trap:

Russo: What time did you get up that Friday?
Walker: Ten-thirty.
Russo: Where did you go when you left the house?
Walker: Over to a hunner-fifty-sixth an' Melrose.
Russo: What time did you get there?
Walker (*after a pause*): I don' remember.
Russo: Whaddya mean, you don't remember?
Walker: I don' *remember*!
Russo: Was there anyone there?

Walker: I don' remember.
Russo: Was Carlos Ortiz there?
Walker: I don' remember.
Russo: Was Alfredo Ortiz there?
Walker: I don' remember.

Russo kept his temper; he could sense that Walker was not one to crack when yelled at. Going back to the scrap of alibi Walker had offered, Russo asked how long he had stayed at 156th and Melrose, and Walker, surprisingly, gave a concrete answer, saying he'd been there until noontime and that from there he'd gone to meet Rubio at a restaurant at 115th and Madison. But although Russo hoped he might now get something to start working on, Walker again put up an impregnable defense:

Russo: Was there anyone else there?
Walker: Don' remember.
Russo: What time was it when you and he were eating?
Walker: About three o'clock.
Russo: What time did you finish?
Walker: Don' remember.
Russo: What time did you get back to 156th Street?
Walker: Don' remember.

Although Russo now began to feel fairly certain that nothing he could do would get Walker to talk, he pressed on, hoping to catch him in a contradiction—and actually did so, but without any useful result:

Russo: Did you see the Ortiz brothers and Doel Valencia that night?
Walker: No, I di'n' see them that day or that night.
Russo (*sharply*): Why is it, when I asked you before if you saw them, you said you didn't remember, but now you're sure you didn't see them?
Walker (*firm, unruffled*): I di'n' see them. *An'* I don' remember.

The blatant inconsistency and boldness of this answer made Russo sure, at this point, that he would get nothing useful from Walker; he says he felt deep anger and frustration, having gotten the story from three others and knowing that he was talking to the alleged killer—and could get nothing out of him. Trying one last breakthrough tactic,

Russo put down his pen, looked intently at Walker, and said, "Listen, the others have told me the whole story, and you don't stand a chance of convincing anybody with yours. The other three guys make it look like they were only spectators there and you're the only bad guy. Get smart—tell your story, tell it the way it was. *They* didn't hesitate to put you on the jackpot, so *you* better tell it the way you want me to hear it." But Walker's expression of stubborn defiance did not change; he stared back at Russo without saying a word. Russo went on in this vein for a while and then gave up, picked up his pen, and continued the interrogation largely as a formality:

> Russo: Do you remember going to an apartment on East 160th
>    Street and stabbing an old man to death?
> Walker: No, it wasn' me. I don' know what you're talkin' about.
>    I don' remember nothin'.
> Russo: Was it Carlos who stabbed the man?
> Walker: I don' know nothin' about that.
> Russo: Was it Alfredo or Doel?
> Walker: I don' know nothin' about that.
> Russo: Are you friendly with Carlos, Alfredo, and Doel?
> Walker: I see them aroun'.
> Russo: Why should they tell us that *you* stabbed the old man?
> Walker: I don' know why. I don' know nothin' about it.

Russo doubled back to the earlier questions that Walker had answered, but by now Walker had dug into his line of defense and was not to be budged:

> Russo: What time did you leave 156th Street that night and where
>    did you go?
> Walker: I don' remember—I don' remember nothin' now.
> Russo (*suddenly*): Do you own a knife?
> Walker (*forgetting his stance for a moment*): No!
> Russo: Did you have a knife on you that night, Friday the ninth?
> Walker (*regaining his poise*): No, I di'n' have a knife, don' have
>    any knife, don' know what you're talkin' about. I don' re-
>    member nothin' now.

Russo looked at his watch: it was 7:55 p.m., and he had been interrogating Walker for forty minutes with no results whatever, had been interrogating one suspect or another for seven and a half hours, hardly stopping to go to the bathroom or take a few bites of a sandwich, and now, at any moment, the assistant district attorney and the stenographer would be arriving to take formal confessions. Russo looked at McCabe and said, "Okay, that's it, let's get him out of here," thinking to himself bitterly, but with an effort at resignation, *That's not the first or the last killer who'll get away from me.*

McCabe stood up. "Come on, you," he said to Walker, and it was all he could do to keep from smashing a fist into that dark, malevolent, stony face.

---

# VI  *The Dispensability of Confessions*

WHAT would become of American society if detectives could put no pressure whatever on suspects they were interrogating, or if every criminal clung to the Fifth and Fourteenth Amendments and refused to say anything? There are two hopelessly disparate views of what would happen: one, that the crime-control efforts of the police and the courts would be critically damaged and that our society would crumble into an anarchic ruin; the other, that a slightly larger percentage of criminals would escape punishment than do so already, but that this cost would be more than offset by the subtle, widespread benefits of having our criminal justice system treat all citizens with equal fairness.

Those who hold the apocalyptic view say that our efforts at crime control would collapse without confessions. Nine tenths of all convictions are the result of guilty pleas made by suspects who realize that if they go to trial they run a considerable risk of being convicted and sentenced for their real crimes, while if they strike a bargain with the prosecutor and the judge and plead guilty to lesser ones, they will get off far more lightly. In a real sense, therefore, the guilty plea, though it offers no details, is an implicit confession that the suspect did commit a crime at least as serious as—and probably more serious than—the one he is pleading guilty to. But what criminal, the apocalyptic prophets ask, would ever plead guilty if he had a good chance of beating the charge at a trial? And if confessions become rare or non-existent, is that not exactly what would happen?

Former District Attorney Koota of Brooklyn—now a justice of the New York Supreme Court—said in 1967 that, no matter what other kinds of evidence the police gave him, nothing was as important in his jury trials as confessions: "Since a conviction depends on the prosecution['s] convincing a jury of the defendant's guilt beyond a reasonable doubt," he said, "a confession is almost indispensable to a conviction."

Still more alarming, if there were no confessions many a criminal might not even be tried. District Attorney Frank Hogan of Manhattan, gravely concerned about the effects of *Escobedo,* said in 1965 that in more than one quarter of his current homicide cases the suspects would not even have been indicted by the Grand Jury, had there been no confessions. And going still further, Michael J. Murphy, the New York Police Commissioner at that time, stated that in half of all homicide cases confessions or damaging admissions had been essential in making the arrests possible. Even at the opposite end of the criminal justice spectrum there were a number of judges who agreed, including some on the United States Supreme Court: Justice White, for one, wrote in his *Miranda* dissent,

> The rule announced today will measurably weaken the ability of the criminal law to perform [its] tasks. It is a deliberate calculus to prevent interrogations, to reduce the incidence of confessions and pleas of guilty, and to increase the number of trials. . . . There is, in my opinion, every reason to believe that a good many criminal defendants, who otherwise would have been convicted . . . will now, under this new version of the Fifth Amendment, either not be tried at all or acquitted. . . .

But the prophecies that the criminal justice system would virtually collapse as confessions became scarcer and harder to get have not proven true. The overall crime clearance rate did decline, but no faster than in the years just preceding *Escobedo* and *Miranda,* and in 1969 and 1970 the decline leveled off. Even in crimes for which it had always seemed most important to be able to obtain confessions, detectives were learning to find and use other kinds of evidence as grounds for arrest: the clearance rate for murder has declined only slightly since *Escobedo* and *Miranda,* and the clearance rate for robbery, though it showed a serious decline for several years, leveled off in 1969 and even rose slightly in 1970.

Nor are confessions as important to conviction as Mr. Koota had claimed. Justice Stanley Mosk of the Supreme Court of California reported in 1968, on the basis of a survey of the records, that the landmark civil-rights decisions of the Supreme Court had caused no decline in convictions in California—and, what was even more interesting, where convictions had been reversed and the cases sent back for retrial on grounds such as the use of improperly obtained confessions, 95 percent of the retrials, though lacking the disallowed evidence, resulted in new convictions. In Illinois, incidentally, Ernesto Miranda himself was retried after the Supreme Court's reversal of his conviction on kidnapping and rape charges; the illegally obtained confession was, of course, omitted, but Miranda was reconvicted.

Similarly reassuring experience has been reported from other quarters. In the New Haven study referred to earlier, the researchers concluded that in only twelve of the ninety cases they observed were confessions or admissions needed to provide evidence enough to convict, and in only half of the twelve—that is, in 7 percent of all cases—were detectives unable to get such confessions after giving *Miranda* warnings. In the Pittsburgh study also mentioned above, the authors reported that while confessions had dropped off 20 percent after *Miranda,* there was no decrease in convictions; perhaps the Pittsburgh police had begun seeking evidence in ways they had not fully used until then. As former Attorney General Ramsey Clark writes in his book *Crime in America,* "The long-range effect of *Miranda,* when old and ineffective habits are broken and emotions subside, will be to compel law enforcement to use efficient, scientific, reliable methods of investigation."

It would be naïve to think that scientific methods could solve every case that interrogation formerly cleared, but it is plain that confessions are not nearly so important to the justice system as interrogators and prosecutors have long believed. Often police seek confessions as a matter of habit, even when they are unnecessary: a post-*Miranda* survey by staff members of the District Attorney's office of Los Angeles County reported that police had obtained confessions in half their felony arrests, but that confessions had been essential to conviction in only 12 percent of cases tried. And Mr. Hogan's fear that without confessions the indictment rate would drop seems unfounded: even before *Miranda,* Justice Nathan Sobel reviewed 1,000 felony indictments in Brooklyn and found that confessions constituted part of the evidence in less than 10 percent of them, all the rest relying upon physical evidence such as drugs found on the suspect, or on personal knowledge of the offender by the victim or by other persons.

Yet, unfortunately, the crime that is most frightening to Americans today—the mugging—rarely involves either physical evidence or witnesses who can identify the offender. Confessions would seem to be the principal possible source of evidence here, and coercive interrogations would thus seem indispensable. But would this make a major difference? Years before the Court ever began limiting interrogation techniques, when the third degree was still widely used, the police were unable to solve the majority of robberies for the simple reason that in most cases they had no idea whom to interrogate. Even if the Supreme Court, tipped in the conservative direction by President Nixon's appointments, were to reverse *Miranda* and perhaps even *Escobedo,* or if a conservative Congress were to make a major assault upon the Fifth Amendment, police would not be able to clear any large percentage of muggings by using old-style interrogation techniques unless they also located suspects to interrogate by means of large-scale canvasses, round-ups, informer networks, and quasi-legal arrest procedures.

None of this, of course, would be possible without a huge and costly expansion of our police forces. But the financial cost would be as nothing compared to the social and spiritual cost—the abandonment of our rare and priceless traditions of civil liberty, fairness, and the dignity of the individual. Until we make those far deeper and more daring changes in our society which will eliminate the major psychological and social causes of violent crime, we will either have to pay for our freedom by dealing ineffectively with the violent men among us, or pay for effectiveness in dealing with them by giving up our freedom.

# VII   *Do You Want to Tell Me What Happened?*

McCABE had just locked Angel Walker in the cage, within which the
other three defendants were now sitting on the floor, when Assistant
District Attorney Vincent Vitale and a court stenographer named
Irwin Wasserman came up the steps and entered the squad room.
Vitale, a heavy-set, meaty-faced man nearing forty, went into the Lieutenant's room with McCabe and Russo, leaving Wasserman outside,
and asked them to brief him before he took the confessions of the
three who had talked. (Technically, the statements the two Ortiz
brothers and Valencia had already made to McCabe and Russo were
confessions, but while the detectives would be allowed to relate in
court what the defendants had said, they would not, under the existing rules of evidence, be permitted to read aloud from their handwritten Q&As; it is usual, therefore, to have such confessions repeated
to an assistant district attorney and recorded by a trained stenographer, whose transcript can be put in evidence.)

Russo and McCabe reviewed the essential elements of the crime
and the several defendants' versions of it for about fifteen minutes,
Vitale jotting down names and salient facts on a pad. They candidly
admitted to him that while the general outline of the crime was the
same in all three confessions, they were concerned about the serious
time discrepancy between the statements of the Ortiz brothers and
that of Valencia, and pointed out that there were also a number of
minor conflicts among the confessions, a couple of extremely awkward details (the cash-filled wallet and the time problem created by
Mrs. Ambos' testimony), an almost total lack of other evidence connecting the defendants with the crime, and the total refusal to talk by
the defendant who was said to have done the actual knifing.

Vitale chose to take the two most compatible confessions first, and to pursue the time discrepancy in Valencia's story last. Alfredo was brought in, pale and wilted, and ordered to sit in a chair across from Vitale, who was behind the desk, with McCabe and Russo off to one side. Carefully speaking in a neutral, businesslike way, he started out by saying, "My name is Vincent Vitale, and I'm an assistant district attorney in Bronx County. I understand you told the police what happened. Do you want to tell me what happened?" Alfredo, whispery and defeated, said he did. Vitale warned him that he need say nothing, and that whatever he did say might be used against him; then he questioned Alfredo step by step about the crime, and Alfredo, though barely audible, answered every question as he had in the Q&A. Having heard it through to the end, Vitale called in Wasserman, who stationed himself at his stenotype machine, and started in at the beginning again. The confession went swiftly: Vitale now knew the questions, Alfredo neither delayed nor argued, and the reporter softly tapped away at his little machine, the ribbon of white paper tape issuing forth from its innards and folding itself neatly into the little drawer on the far side of it with Alfredo's fate hidden in its arcane ciphers.

The recording of the confession took less than ten minutes; then Vitale declared the statement completed and asked the detectives to take Alfredo out and bring in Carlos next. The procedure was the same, and Carlos, though he sat up a little straighter and spoke in a slightly less cowed and terrified manner, offered no more resistance than Alfredo. He told Vitale substantially the same story he had told the detectives two hours earlier, though he added one odd new detail —he said he had never received any of the money—and, at the very end, gratuitously offered a comment neither the assistant D.A. nor the detectives had expected: Vitale, concluding, had routinely asked if there were anything else Carlos wanted to say, and he replied, "The only thing I can say, I am guilty for what I did."

Vitale was now ready to tackle the problem of Valencia and the time discrepancy, but McCabe, after taking Carlos out to the cage, returned alone, flushed and furious. Valencia, he said, seemed to be changing his mind and now refused to repeat his confession to the assistant D.A. Vitale turned to Russo, who for the first time that day seemed completely taken aback and at a loss. "I would never have believed it," muttered Russo, "I would never have believed it." He hurried out to the cage and came back in a moment, scowling blackly. Vitale asked if he thought it was worth a try, and Russo said he doubted it; Valencia had been positive about it. But Vitale, after considering this for a moment, said, "That's all right; bring him in anyhow. He did make a statement to you, and I have to try."

Valencia was led in, his face tight with resolve. Whether he had, on his own, had second thoughts about his confession, or whether he had been talking to Angel Walker in the cage, he was now firmly defiant, despite the presence of the two detectives to whom he had made a detailed confession little more than an hour ago. Vitale started off by identifying himself, and then said, "I understand you want to make a full statement concerning these charges," but Valencia immediately shook his head and said, very distinctly, "No."

Vitale looked at him hard. "What do you mean, no?" he asked.

"I di'n' do it," said Valencia.

Vitale, in a cold, knowing tone, said, "Well, I understand that you admitted to the police that you *did* do it. I understand you told the police what happened."

Valencia, avoiding the detectives' eyes, said in a tense, sullen voice, "I di'n' do it—an' I never told the police I did it." Vitale stared at him in silence for a long moment, but Valencia stared back, saying nothing more, and finally the assistant D.A. turned to the detectives and said, "Take him away." After Valencia was out of the room, Vitale told them that he would not question Valencia further, and that there was nothing more for him to do. He called Wasserman in to pack up the stenotype machine, and the two of them then left.

Russo and McCabe looked at each other and said nothing for a moment, not knowing whether to feel elated or depressed at this point; they had solved the case, but the man they considered the real murderer had successfully defied them and might well go free, while of the three they had gotten to talk, the one hardest to break down had found the strength to defy them to their own faces only an hour and a half after giving in. It was now a little after 9:00 p.m., the air in the room was spent and sour, and the two men were rumpled, rank, and weary. McCabe finally said he guessed that that wrapped it up; that was all they could do. Russo agreed, but said they weren't through for the day—they had to take the prisoners downstairs to the cell block, make out their reports, put their papers in order, and arrange to have someone else take the prisoners to court in the morning to be arraigned. "Sal," said McCabe, filled with admiration, "you know what you are?—you're nothing but an old guinea laborer. You could work in the fields from sunup to sundown and never stop except to have a bite to eat. I'm dragging my bottom, and you're still ready for action." Russo chuckled, lighting a fresh cigar; then he said, "All right, let's get to it."

After a while the long day came to its end. Alfredo Ortiz, Carlos Ortiz, Doel Valencia, and Angel Walker were herded down the stairway and into the cell block in the back of the building, where an elderly uniformed policeman ordered them into separate cells, clanged the iron doors to, and turned a key in the clashing locks. They found themselves in tiny iron-walled cages, each containing nothing but a seatless toilet bowl and a bare wooden slab to sleep on. Their stomachs grinding from emptiness, they could do nothing but lie down on the scarred boards of their beds, their bones bruising their chilled flesh, and try to sleep. Throughout the endless night they would doze off now and again, only to start up, their hearts racing in sudden alarm at the nightmare not of their sleep but of their waking lives.

Mrs. Luisa Pomales was but little better off, though she lay in a softer bed in her dreary tenement apartment on 160th Street. Late that afternoon, when Carlos failed to return, she had gone looking for him; it had not occurred to her that he was in serious trouble, and she searched for him in his usual haunts, asking friends of his if they had seen him. No one had, and she grew more and more alarmed; finally, in the evening a youth known as Bimbo told her to try the police station because, he said, the detectives were investigating the murder case and talking to all the boys who lived nearby. Mrs. Pomales, not permitting herself to think that Carlos might be wanted for more than questioning and having no idea that Alfredo was also at the station house, hurried over to the Precinct and told a policeman just inside the front door that she was looking for her son Carlos Ortiz, who had not come home. The policeman took her over to the desk, where the duty officer told her that they had both of her sons in custody, and that both were accused of murder. Mrs. Pomales uttered a small, stifled cry of agony; when she could speak, she asked if she could see them, but a detective came down from the second floor and, she says, told her she would have to see them at the Criminal Court building in the morning. She walked slowly home, a small, broken, weeping woman, and went to bed, praying to her God even though He had let her sons get into dreadful trouble in this strange and evil part of the world, and wondering how to endure her night thoughts until the morning came.

Salvatore Russo and Stephen McCabe each went to bed in quite another frame of mind: each felt the voluptuous exhaustion that comes after work well done, and the inner contentment of having achieved something admirable. Russo arrived at his tidy apartment by midnight, McCabe at his split-level suburban house even later. Each had a sympathetic, distraught wife waiting for him; each spoke at length of the day's trials and achievements while eating and drinking with long-delayed gusto; each undressed, bathed, and sank into clean sheets with groans of relief, thinking back on the triumphs and disappointments of this endless day (had it really been only this morning that they went to the courthouse to pick up the Ortiz brothers?) and of the things they had seen and done since the investigation began so very long ago (had it really been only five days since Dr. Hochman phoned with his surprising news?); and at last each one fell asleep into a rest as pure and deep as any a man can have.

Except, in a sense, that of someone like Alexander Helmer, who lay that night in a brand-new resting-place from which he would never arise. That very afternoon, while the interrogations were going on and his name was being mentioned a hundred times, Helmer—his ruins mercifully unseen inside a sealed wooden casket—was the subject of a modest funeral ceremony at the Walter B. Cooke funeral parlor at 1 West 190th Street in the Bronx. His lawyer had arranged it, but did not come, nor could he locate any relatives who would; in fact, listening to the Lutheran minister who presided were only four mourners (the word is scarcely appropriate)—the two elderly ladies Helmer had left money to, though he had not seen them for many years; the aged sister of one of them, who had known him slightly; and Mrs. Ambos, who came out of a sense of propriety rather than of personal loss. Afterward Helmer's body was transported in a hearse to the Veterans Administration cemetery in Pine Lawn, Long Island, where, under a gray sky and in a chill wind, his casket was swiftly lowered into the ground and sealed in by six feet of damp earth topped with sod. Yet even from that blackest and most silent of resting-places, removed from all that breathes and moves on the surface of earth, this wretched remainder of what had been an unimportant and unloved old man would continue for years to concern and affect scores of living people above in various offices, jails, and courts up to and including the Supreme Court itself, and would control the lives of some of those people to this very day, and until they die.

# Chapter 4  Detention

## I  Keep Your Mouth Shut

AT 6:30 a.m., before the thin autumnal sun had leaked down into the city streets, a policeman was pounding on the steel doors of the occupied cells in the 42nd Precinct. He told the prisoners to get ready for a trip downtown, and let them out, one at a time, to wash up at a grimy sink at the far end of the cell block. A little after 7:00 a.m., Detective Bartholomew Jiacobello—McCabe's regular partner, a tall, massive man in rumpled street clothes—came into the cell block, handcuffed the suspects in the Helmer murder in pairs, and herded them into a dirty-green police van along with a handful of other prisoners.

It is a long ride—nine miles, through city streets—from the 42nd Precinct in Melrose to Police Headquarters at 240 Centre Street in lower Manhattan; along the way they could catch glimpses, through the dirt-encrusted barred windows of the back doors of the van, of a thousand different sights that only the previous day would have meant nothing, but now seemed strangely important, and even touching, merely because they were on the other side of the bars: a refrigerator truck backing up to a supermarket unloading ramp; a brown mongrel trotting thoughtlessly across a busy avenue; a white-aproned grocer setting out boxes of vegetables and fruit on a stand in front of his store; a sweating black janitor struggling up the steps from the bowels of a brownstone with a heavy can of garbage; huge office buildings, lifeless and sterile on this Saturday morning; an ample-bellied doorman, resplendent in braid and brass buttons, bowing as he opened the glass front door of a luxurious high-rise apartment building for a well-dressed tenant; young women in mink and willowy homosexuals in khaki pants taking their poodles out for a quick curbside evacuation; chic East Side movie houses and rundown Irish bars, bright antiseptic drugstores and dim cluttered antique shops, public schools and department stores; and everywhere, even before 8:00 a.m., people walking the sidewalks—free people, going where they wanted to go, unaware of their liberty, and heedless of the green van passing by and of the young men in it, cut off from the rest of the world.

At Police Headquarters they shuffled into a former gymnasium for the morning "show-up"—the displaying of new prisoners before an audience of detectives from all over the city, there to see if they could spot anyone they wanted for another crime. When no one picked out Alfredo, Carlos, Valencia, or Walker, Jiacobello took them to the police photo studio in the basement, where they stood side by side facing glaring lights and were photographed first in their dirty, wrinkled street clothing, and then totally nude, from the front, rear, and both sides. Alfredo, naked, was a bony, hollow-chested boy with open space between his scrawny thighs; Carlos was also boyish, but a trifle sturdier; Valencia, though far taller and more manly, was round-shouldered and glazed of eye, perhaps because he was beginning to have withdrawal symptoms; and Walker, scowling, husky, and with a great hawser of a penis, was distorted of body, his powerful black frame askew to the right to balance the arm so oddly missing below the ragged stump.

Jiacobello ordered them to dress again and herded them into the van for the long ride back to the Bronx, where by mid-morning they were sitting on benches inside a crowded detention pen in a Criminal Court building across the street from the one Alfredo had been in yesterday for his drug hearing. This courthouse, a dreary brick building with innumerable sprayed-on graffiti on its white stone base, was older, dirtier, and more crowded than the other: crowds of people, mostly dark-skinned, pushed and shoved their way through the smoky, sweaty hallways and into the jammed courtrooms, dozens of policemen and lawyers came and went, and in front of the judge's bench there was a continual procession of persons arriving and departing. For this was arraignment court—the intake hopper of the Bronx criminal justice system, into which police and district attorneys were desperately cramming new cases at the rate of one every minute or two; the court, in the person of the judge, was struggling to choke down the influx, jamming the mass of raw material under pressure into the city jails, to be contained there, fermenting and explosive, until bit by bit it could be processed at hearings and trials, and passed further on into the system's machinery.

For, unlike lower-echelon magistrates' courts that quickly dispose of minor cases, slapping small fines and brief jail sentences with machine-like speed upon a dismal procession of drunks, derelicts, peddlers, and other minor offenders, the arraignment court is concerned with the intake—for later handling—of persons accused of having committed misdemeanors (crimes carrying penalties of up to a year in jail) and felonies (serious crimes carrying penalties of more than a year, up to and including, in 1964, the death penalty). Every minute or so, the clerk of the court would call out a name, and from a seat out front or from the door opening to the detention pen someone would step up before the bench—usually a black or Puerto Rican youth in denims or a leather jacket, sometimes a white tough, sometimes a brassy, overdressed girl still in last night's working make-up. The courtroom guards would stand behind the prisoner, the arresting policemen or detectives would move in to join the huddle, an assistant D.A. with a sheaf of papers would read the charge aloud to the judge in a rapid monotone, a young Legal Aid or other defense attorney would quickly enter a plea of not guilty and, in a sentence or two, ask for low bail or sometimes for dismissal of the charges, and the judge, brusque and quick, impassive and hardened to the endless stream of unrepentant thieves, whores, addicts, pushers, muggers, armed robbers, knife-wielders, and rapists, would listen, occasionally interrupt with a question or two, then snap out his orders, and ask the clerk for the next one. But he could do nothing else: nearly a hundred prisoners were still waiting, and all had to be arraigned and either released or turned over to Department of Correction officers by mid-afternoon. There could be no let-up for an instant, and so the accused came up one after another to stand before him, hearing a smattering of phrases fly back and forth, and being led away almost before they knew what he had said, most of them disappearing through the door back to the pens; a few others, released because the judge had dismissed the charges against them or paroled them without bail, hesitated for a moment before quitting the courtroom, unable to believe that they too had not been swallowed by the system.

Eventually Alfredo, Carlos, Doel Valencia, and Angel Walker were summoned from the pen and led through the door into the front part of the courtroom. Another prisoner was still before the judge, and they had a moment to look around: they saw McCabe and Russo standing inside the rail, and Luisa Pomales seated all the way in the back, where she could scarcely see them. Then their names were called out and the guards led them before the bench. The judge asked if they were represented by counsel; one by one they said no, and he said he would appoint counsel for them, for this arraignment, in order to protect their rights. In 1964 the accused in murder cases were being represented not by Legal Aid, but by private defense attorneys hired by themselves or, if they had no money, appointed by the court; the judge therefore looked past them to the first row of spectator seats, where a few lawyers—a couple of young hopefuls and a couple of old hangers-on—were watching and waiting to volunteer their services at just such moments on the chance that among those to whom they gave a minute or two of free time there would be one or two who might retain them. The judge beckoned to a short, rotund, graying man with a bristly mustache. "Mr. Carney," he said, "would you represent these defendants for purposes of arraignment?"

The lawyer said he'd be glad to, and waddled forward. Early in his career James Carney had practiced more dignified law than this; he had even, long ago, been an assistant D.A. in the Bronx for a while, but eventually left the job because of the low pay. For the last eighteen years he had been doing better for himself by hanging around courthouses and picking up criminal cases by virtue of his mere presence. Most of his clients were burglars, robbers, prostitutes, drug-users, purse-snatchers, or people who, when drunk, had hit or knifed someone; like many attorneys who represent such clients, he often did little more than plead for lower bail, ask for delays, and try either to get the charges dismissed or to strike a bargain with the assistant D.A. and get a reduced charge in return for a plea of guilty. Only ten or fifteen times a year did he get a client whose case involved a sizable fee or went to full-dress jury trial; and like other lawyers with the same sort of practice, he often felt it necessary to collect in cash, out in the hall, before even going into court to represent his client.

This morning his function was nominal, although with luck it might net him one or more of the accused youths. First he went over to the assistant D.A. and learned that the charge was "Murder One" (murder in the first degree); then he joined the four defendants and whispered to them, "Don't say anything here. Let me do the talking." He then nodded to the judge, and the assistant D.A. and McCabe and Russo stepped in close, the D.A. swiftly reading the complaint aloud. The prisoners could catch their own names, the word "murder," and the name of Alexander Helmer, but little else. The judge said something to Carney, who replied that his clients pleaded not guilty. The assistant D.A. asked for an adjournment to prepare the case against them; the judge granted it, said there would be no bail—judges of the Criminal Court are not empowered to grant bail in homicide cases; justices of the Supreme Court are, but rarely do so—and thereupon ordered the case adjourned until November 6th and the defendants remanded to the Department of Correction. "Next case," he said, and the guards led them off, the entire proceeding having taken a little over two minutes—a long time, as arraignments go in the crowded courts of America's larger cities.

Carney asked the guard to let him have a moment with the defendants; away from the bench, he had a whispered conference with them, explaining that they would be coming back later for trial, and passed out his card to all four. He told Alfredo and Carlos to let their parents know if they wanted him as their lawyer, and then said to all of them, emphasizing his advice with a stubby, wagging forefinger, "Don't talk to anybody without me being present, or some other lawyer. Keep your mouth *shut*. Don't talk to anybody, any more, about this case." Neither of the Ortiz brothers said anything, but Valencia and Walker whispered to him briefly, and Walker said he would use him as his attorney. Then all four were taken out through the door leading to the pen. Carney went back to his front-row seat, looking mildly pleased, McCabe and Russo headed out through the courtroom, and Luisa Pomales, who had neither heard nor understood anything, wavered uncertainly another minute or so before leaving, by which time another defendant had been brought before the bench, arraigned, and led off, and still another brought on.

After interminable, dreary hours in the pen, Walker and the other adults were taken out and shipped off to the Bronx House of Detention; a little later Alfredo, Carlos, and Doel Valencia, along with other prisoners under twenty-one, were loaded into a couple of vans bound for the Brooklyn House of Detention, which at that time was a jail for males from sixteen through twenty who were awaiting trial. Alfredo knew the place well: he had been there for the past week— except for last night—and earlier in the year had spent several months there while awaiting trial on the robbery charge for which he had received a three-year suspended sentence in March. Valencia, too, had been there a couple of years ago; Carlos had not, but the others had told him enough for him to know that, as jails go, this was a passable one—modern, fairly clean, and not particularly severe as to discipline. Not that it was anything like a treatment institution: it was only a place of confinement, with almost no therapy, relatively little recreation, no industry or training, and no schooling—nothing, really, but 800-odd tiny cages for the captives, plus barren, tile-walled day-rooms in which, a few hours a day, they could play cards or watch television, and two gymnasiums in which, once or twice a week, they could get some exercise. Most of the time they spent here, however, was heavy, smothering, useless time, waiting hour after hour, through endless days and interminable weeks and months, for their cases to come up in court.

The Brooklyn House of Detention is a trim, modern, ten-story building with a façade of glass brick and solid gray sides located on Atlantic Avenue, a shabby business street in downtown Brooklyn not far from the courts and municipal buildings of that borough. In late 1964 the unaware passerby might mistake it for an office building, never realizing that within it there were over 800 imprisoned teen-age youths and young men, some of them vicious, some of them merely lawless, some of them guilty of nothing but having been in the wrong place when the police came along—and none of them convicted of the crimes for which they were locked up. In the eyes of our justice system, none of them had yet been found guilty; at least two thirds of them could have been free on bail while awaiting trial, had they had the money or the property to put up for collateral. But they did not, and they remained in jail, only vaguely aware of the monstrous unfairness of it all.

The van pulled up behind the jail, and its passengers were led in by a rear door and shunted into several large holding pens—tile-walled chambers with benches—along the sides of the long, noisy receiving room; at desks in the center, clerical workers made out papers for each of the new arrivals. A batch at a time, the prisoners were taken out of the pens to a disrobing and showering room on the other side, and then, naked and clean, were led into an adjoining medical office for a physical examination. Afterward they dressed again, went into pens at the other end of the receiving area, and eventually were herded by guards to the elevators and distributed to the various floors above. Alfredo went back to his own floor, and Carlos and Valencia were sent to different floors, it being standard procedure to keep accomplices separated so they could not perfect their stories.

Each of the three, by late afternoon, was locked in a cell of his own. The cells were an improvement over those they had slept in the previous night, in that each had its own washbasin and seatless toilet, a thin mattress on a narrow bunk, and a tiny metal table and seat fixed to the wall. But each was a psychologically suffocating steel box about five feet wide and eight feet long, with painted walls and ceiling, and nothing to look at through the vertical bars at the open end except a catwalk where guards patrolled, silhouetted against the bright wall of glass brick.

One could not even pace back and forth in such a cell, or look out through a barred window at the sky or the ground; one could only lie on his bunk or sit at his little table reading or staring at the blank walls, sometimes shouting back and forth to unseen inmates in adjoining cells, and dully waiting for breaks in the day—the mealtime visits to the day-room, the three periods of card-playing or television in those same rooms, the once-a-week or twice-a-week bouts of volleyball in the gymnasium, the occasional half-hour chat with a relative seen through a tiny window of reinforced glass and heard on a telephone in the visiting cubicles.

Many prisoners, and especially all those who were fairly sure they would be convicted of the crime they were charged with, felt they were already "doing time," since their incarceration here would be credited against their sentences. But all those who were innocent, or felt they had been unfairly charged, or thought they would stand a chance of a suspended sentence, felt their detention to be worthless; worse than that, it was punishment without conviction. Yet in 1964 they did not rage against the system, rioting, destroying their own day-rooms, taking guards as hostages and threatening to kill them; all that would come later, when the growing court congestion and the backlog of untried cases forced the Department of Correction to jam two men into each of those closet-like cells and keep them there for months and sometimes even a year or more without trial.

In 1964 the delays, though not that long, were bad enough. Youths arrested on misdemeanors were locked up for an average of a week—some of them for many weeks—before the court could get around to finding them not guilty and freeing them, or finding them guilty and sentencing them; those accused of felonies had to wait an average of a month to two months, and some of them far longer. If, at the end of the time spent waiting for the courts to get around to them, they were found not guilty, all the time in jail, all the degradation, all the boredom had been for nothing—punishment that had been undeserved, and that would not have been inflicted on anyone able to post bail.

At the moment, this was an academic matter as far as the Ortiz brothers, Doel Valencia, and Angel Walker were concerned. But even if Helmer had survived the stabbing and the Criminal Court judge had set bail for them, they would probably have been unable to raise it. Presumed innocent by the laws of the land, they would have been treated as guilty persons until tried. And they knew this; at least, they knew that two weeks of imprisonment would pass before their next hearing, and thought that several weeks more would pass before they would have a chance to assert their innocence before a judge and jury. But they were unaware that even then the backlog of cases as serious as theirs was so severe that they would spend the rest of that fall and almost the entire winter waiting, that they would have slept and awakened, dressed and undressed, stood up and lain down, read and dozed off, sighed and cursed, urinated and defecated, in those same tiny cages for nineteen weeks—134 days—before getting the "speedy and public trial" guaranteed to them by the Sixth Amendment of the Constitution of the United States.

## II   *The Law's Delay*

WHAT should the state do with a man it charges with a crime, while preparing its case against him? The common-sense answer is, of course: Lock him up so he won't disappear or commit other crimes. But this is an inquisitorial answer—it has, indeed, long been the answer given by inquisitorial systems—for it assumes that the accused man is actually guilty and that the trial is only a way of validating the charge; this being the premise, one hardly does the accused man any wrong to imprison him before conviction.

In an adversarial system of justice, however, no matter what the police and the prosecutor say, we are supposed to assume the accused man to be innocent until proven guilty; any time he spends in jail before his trial, therefore, seems inherently unjust—all the more so if the charges are later dismissed or if he is proven innocent. Yet if he is in fact guilty, to let him go free while awaiting trial would give him the opportunity to escape, and would be unjust to society and to his past and future victims.

It is a dilemma without any perfect solution. An imperfect one is to jail him but make the period of detention as brief as possible, thus minimizing the injustice done if he should prove innocent. This is why the right to a speedy trial is considered basic to the Anglo-American system of justice; indeed, it was one of the rights wrested from the tyrannical Crown by the Magna Carta of 1215, repeatedly reasserted in English law later, and guaranteed to Americans by the Sixth Amendment and by statute in nearly all of the states.

Another useful but imperfect answer is to release the accused until trial, provided he can guarantee his return; even if his trial is delayed, this minimizes the harm done him. Accordingly, the right to bail is of ancient provenance in Anglo-American law, dating back to the

Middle Ages and having been assured to Americans by the Eighth Amendment, which forbids the fixing of bail at excessive amounts, and by federal and state codes of criminal procedure.

These devices have made the system reasonably fair to the state as well as the individual until recent years; now, however, neither is doing so. In the past decade the right to a speedy trial has become a broken promise; scores of thousands of persons have been jailed for many months without having had the chance to defend themselves in court. As for bail, more and more accused persons have been using it to escape justice altogether, either by disappearing before trial or by having their lawyers delay so long, while they remain out on bail, that their cases grow too stale to be successfully prosecuted. The system is still dispensing justice now and then, but injustice—both to accused persons and to society—has become endemic.

The most obvious form this takes is the prolonged imprisonment, in city and county jails, of unconvicted persons who cannot make bail or are not eligible for it. In Washington, D.C., the average delay between a felony arrest and trial in 1969 was ten months; in New York the average time spent in jail by persons defended by the Legal Aid Society in 1969 ranged from half a year in Manhattan to nine months in the Bronx, and over 40 percent of persons who were detained until they had been tried were held in jail more than a year; and in many other large cities the situation was and is almost as bad. A decade ago trials were delayed weeks; today the delays are generally measured in months and sometimes years. Yet from 40 to 60 percent of all jailed persons awaiting trial are eventually found innocent or have the charges against them dismissed, and although they are not all innocent in fact, our system is supposed to punish no one it has not proven guilty. All things considered, the guilty—and the innocent—who are held in jail for weeks, months, or years, and then released unconvicted have fared little better than the political enemies of the kings of old and the dictatorships of the present.

The present erosion of our constitutional right to a speedy trial is not, however, political in nature, but the result of what sociologists call "culture lag." Crime has increased hugely and rapidly in recent years, but our society has scarcely begun to expand and to adapt the criminal justice system except for its front line of defense, the police. But without a corresponding expansion and modernization of the rest of the system, the emphasis on police activity only results in a considerably larger number of cases which have to pass through the narrow, inflexible bottleneck of the criminal courts. The result is an ever growing backlog of untried cases, ever lengthening delays, and ever longer imprisonments of innocent and guilty alike.

In New York City, according to a study made in 1970 for the Mayor's Criminal Justice Coordinating Council, 52 percent more serious crimes were entered on the court dockets in 1968 than in 1959—but the courts managed to dispose of only 16 percent more. What is even more alarming is that, if one includes the less serious crimes (except for traffic violations), the annual backlog of undisposed cases in New York was fifteen times greater in 1968 than in 1959—yet the courts disposed of 19 percent *fewer* cases in 1968 than it did in 1959. The pressure of the backlog, it seems, pushes not more but fewer cases through the bottleneck, for the backlog itself decreases court efficiency, which then adds more to the backlog, which then decreases efficiency still further. If each new case were assigned a trial date only once, and were heard or tried on that date, this feedback effect would be minor, but in most criminal courts today every case—especially every serious case—is called up and postponed a number of times. In New York's Criminal Court the average case was adjourned four times in 1970, and many an armed robbery, attempted murder, or other major felony was adjourned ten to twenty times, the resultant waste of time paralyzing the courts, severely overloading the jails, discouraging the police, embittering the uncomprehending public, and bringing the entire criminal justice system to the verge of total breakdown.

But whose fault is it? Everyone's. The judges' fault: many of them start the day late and end it early—and being, in consequence, short of time for the conducting of trials, grant adjournments hastily and without adequately inquiring into their legitimacy. The jail clerks' and correction officers' fault: sometimes they fail to get prisoners to the right courts on the right day. The court stenographers' fault: they often fail to have the minutes of previous proceedings ready in time. The court clerks' fault: files are sometimes not located and sent to the courtroom in time (in one New York court 10 percent of arraignments had to be adjourned for this reason alone). The prosecutors' fault: overworked, and without enough process-servers, they often fail to notify or to subpoena witnesses they need. The police officers' and witnesses' fault: they often fail to appear because of other business, or lack of motivation. The defendants' fault: often a defendant who has clamored for trial will quixotically dismiss his lawyer at the last moment and obtain an adjournment until he can get another and the case can be prepared again.

More to blame than any of these, however, are the defense lawyers themselves. "Judge shopping" is one of their favorite techniques: in many court systems each trial date comes up before a different judge, unfamiliar with the case, and lawyers can unabashedly ask for postponements again and again, claiming they need more time to prepare their case, until they come before a judge known to be lenient toward their client's particular kind of crime. Even more important, delay itself generally helps the defense, because with each trip to court, each tedious wait that ends only in adjournment, witnesses become less cooperative, victims lose their fervor to see justice done, judges and prosecutors grow wearier of the case and more willing to settle for a reduced charge and nominal sentence in return for a plea of guilty just to be rid of it. With persistence, the defender may do still better than this: one lawyer interviewed by *Life* magazine said that a client of his had shot and nearly killed another man, but that he, the lawyer, pleaded for adjournments and got them eight or nine times, and "finally the victim just got fed up, I guess, because he stopped coming to court, and then it was the district attorney who had to ask for adjournments. After the victim failed to show up three times, the charge was finally dismissed." But prosecutors, too, sometimes seek delays for strategic reasons: if they are not confident about winning a case before a jury, they may seek repeated adjournments in order to keep the defendant in jail until he pleads guilty in return for a bargain sentence—an outcome which saves prosecutorial time and eliminates the risk of failing to get a conviction.

If the worst injustices of long imprisonment are visited by society upon the innocent, the worst injustices of the bail system are visited by the guilty upon society. For bail often permits the guilty to escape justice altogether: with the jails as crowded and explosive as they now are, judges are inclined to adjourn bail cases on almost any pretext, in order to give priority to those being held in jail. As Justice James Leff of the New York Supreme Court puts it, "The horror is that as it looks now [1970], the bail cases are never going to get tried, because the pressure is on to try all the jail cases first. So the bail cases get put off, and grow staler and staler. For all practical purposes, you can forget about the guy who is admitted to bail unless he commits another crime, and then bail is fixed high enough to make him a jail case."

But the setting of high bail to keep a man in jail is unconstitutional. As Justice Jackson once pointed out in a United States Supreme Court case,

> The practice of admission to bail, as it has evolved in Anglo-American law, is not a device for keeping persons in jail upon mere accusation until it is found convenient to give them a trial. On the contrary, the spirit of the procedure is to enable them to stay out of jail until a trial has found them guilty.

Many prosecutors and judges see things differently: they regard the prisoner—especially if he has a record of any sort—as a menace to be kept off the streets, and accordingly they try to set bail high enough to keep him in jail until his trial, thereby making bail an instrument of punishment for guilt not yet proven. One typical New York Criminal Court judge puts it this way: "Legal Aid is always fighting to get lower bail for their junkies and muggers, but I'm not about to help put these fellows back out on the streets any sooner than necessary. The least I can do for society is to keep them out of the way for a while." With the kind of young man most often accused of mugging, it does not take much to achieve this end: a judge can be fairly sure of keeping nearly any mugger in jail by setting bail at a mere $1,500, and practically certain of it by setting bail at $2,500.

In a way, it may seem only reasonable that a person who has a bad record, who is accused of a violent crime, and who seems likely to be a continuing danger to society ought to be confined until tried; this is the basic argument for preventive detention, which is the practice in most foreign countries. But, despite its seeming reasonableness, it is so antithetical to the American concept of justice (and, in particular, to the presumption of innocence), and so grave a threat to civil liberty, that it is bitterly opposed by a wide range of knowledgeable persons and groups—civil-rights advocates, of course, but also the American Bar Association and the National Bar Association; James V. Bennett, former director of the federal prison system; the conservative constitutionalist Senator Sam Ervin; and many others. On the other hand, it is now favored not only by many police chiefs, prosecutors, and political conservatives, but by enough middle-of-the-roaders and liberals to enable the 1970 District of Columbia Crime Bill—which made preventive detention the law in the nation's capital—to pass by solid margins in both the House and the Senate.

But at least preventive detention is supposed to be based on a careful evaluation of the prisoner's dangerousness made by competent personnel. This is hopelessly unrealistic, since reliable tests of dangerousness do not yet exist, and since the probation departments of most courts are already overworked, but it is hardly worse than the way in which bail is widely used for the same end right now. For judges in most courts have no time to evaluate the prisoner's character and lifestyle, and to set bail just high enough to ensure his reappearance in court; instead, they set bail according to fixed schedules, the amount being determined by the seriousness of the alleged crime. This preventively detains a great many people while freeing others charged with the same crimes but financially better off. A study made a few years ago by the Vera Institute of Justice, a private foundation in New York, reported that 25 percent of all defendants in that city cannot make bail even when it is as low as $500. A Census Bureau survey of all U.S. city and county jails in 1970 revealed that over half of all inmates in such institutions, or roughly 83,000 persons, had not been convicted but were awaiting arraignment or trial, and that the great majority of these detention cases, though bailable, were unable to finance their freedom. The use of bail to keep defendants imprisoned makes headlines in the case of Black Panthers and other defendants for whom public protests are made, but the same practice, in the case of run-of-the-mill defendants accused of common misdemeanors and felonies, is the far greater inequity and one the average citizen rarely hears about.

But if it is grossly unfair that so many should linger in jail because they cannot afford bail, it is equally unfair that so many others should use bail as a way of escaping justice altogether. In New York City, according to unpublished research data gathered by the Mayor's Criminal Justice Coordinating Council, some 60,000 to 70,000 of the persons arraigned on misdemeanors and felonies in 1968 were released on cash bail or bail bonds, or on their own recognizance (in effect, zero bail)—and over 10 percent of them never came back to court: that is, roughly 8,000 persons accused of crimes ranging from the fairly serious to the very serious used bail-jumping as a bargain way to escape trial.*

* Even more alarming figures were released in early 1971, with suitable fanfare, by State Senator Roy M. Goodman, who asserted that 347,000 crim-

But with the jails as badly overcrowded and trial delays as long as they now are, judges are being forced to grant low bail a good deal more often than they would like to. The wave of jail riots in New York and elsewhere in 1970 made judges sharply aware of the suffering they were inflicting upon anyone they jailed pending trial. Such detention had been bad enough in most of the nation's jails a decade ago; by 1970 it had become almost insufferable. When men rebel against overwhelming odds, knowing that they face certain defeat and punishment, they are plainly desperate.

For even though many of the charges made by rebelling inmates during the riots were exaggerated for political value, the conditions they were protesting were dreadful enough. The Census Bureau's 1970 survey of 4,000 city and county jails revealed that many inmates—the unconvicted as well as those serving sentences—were living in abominable conditions. (Convicted prisoners serving short sentences remain in city and county jails; those serving long sentences generally go to state prisons, where the conditions are usually somewhat less horrendous. Many jails are dark, gloomy, dank, and filthy (one out of ten now in service was built in the nineteenth century), and cells are often chilly in winter and stifling in summer. In many jails, roaches abound and mice and rats run over the prisoners in their sleep, especially in those big-city jails where overcrowding forces some inmates to sleep on the floor. Mattresses are often dirty and infested with bedbugs; body lice are common and uncontrolled; hot water and soap are rare, prisoners being lucky to get one shower a week; toilets are seatless and often out of order; the food is frequently gray, greasy, tasteless, and unvaried. Of the more than 3,000 jails in our larger communities, nine tenths have no educational facilities, over four fifths make no provision for recreation or exercise, half have no medical facilities, and a quarter do not even make provision for visitors.

In every jail, but particularly in those where prisoners are kept in dormitories or are allowed into day-rooms, the younger and frailer are

---

inal defendants had jumped bail in New York in 1968, 1969, and 1970. The Senator made headlines but badly misinformed the public: his data included a large number of persons who had merely failed to show up when issued a summons, and many others whose cases involved domestic matters such as non-support rather than dangerous criminal activities. Senator Goodman's claims, unfortunately, quickly became part of the litany of New York's sins, and have been frequently repeated.

in constant danger of assault—particularly homosexual rape—by the older and stronger, not so much for sexual pleasure as to express anger and aggression. The rapist, having a score to settle with society, settles it with the hapless victim, taking away his manhood and "making him a girl"; once this happens, the victim remains an object of sexual degradation as long as he is in jail. Although homosexual rape is uncommon in some jails, it does occur sometimes in all of them, and is endemic in many. A suggestion of what such rape must mean to the defenseless victim is conveyed by a typical statement taken by a team of researchers investigating sexual assaults in the Philadelphia jails:

> Right after the light went out I saw this colored male, Cheyenne—I think his last name is Boone. He went over and was talking to this kid and slapped him in the face with a belt. He was saying come on back with us and the kid kept saying I don't want to. After being slapped with the belt he walked back with Cheyenne and another colored fellow named Horse [into E Dorm]. . . . I looked up a couple of times. They had the kid on the floor. About twelve fellows took turns with him. This went on for about two hours.
>
> After this he came back to his bed and he was crying and he stated that "They all took turns on me." He laid there for about twenty minutes and Cheyenne came over to the kid's bed and pulled his pants down and got on top of him and raped him again. . . . Then about four or five others got on him. While one of the guys was on him, Horse came over and said, "Open your mouth and suck on this and don't bite it." . . . The kid hollered that he was gagging and Horse stated, "You better not bite it or I will kick your teeth out."

And of course there are the guards: a few of them sadistic brutes who delight in beating up and punishing prisoners they consider defiant or troublesome, many more of them martinets who bully prisoners and on little provocation accuse them of infractions and take their privileges away, or lock them, for days, in a "strip cell" or "hole" without light, reading matter, or even a bed or chair to sit on—they have to sit on the cement floor—sometimes even taking away all their clothing except underwear to maximize their discomfort and humiliation. Even those guards who are humane toward prisoners have to issue orders to them continually ("Line up!" "Knock it off!" "Clean up that mess!" "Get a move on!" "Don't talk back to me!"), command them to strip and submit to frequent searches, lock them in and let them out and lock them in again, and throughout the long day and the night continually pass by their cells and stare in at them as if they were the animals they feel like.

Even in 1964, when conditions were not as bad as they are today, one group of legislators concluded, after surveying the local jails in their own state:

> The indignities of repeated physical search, regimented living, crowded cells, utter isolation from the outside world, unsympathetic surveillance, outrageous visitors' facilities, Fort Knox-like security measures, are surely so searing that one unwarranted day in jail in itself can be a major social injustice.

Today all those same factors exist, but much exacerbated by overcrowding and delays, and by the inflammatory activities of the black militants. And so the prisoners, many of whom were violent men outside, become even more so in jail; indeed, there could hardly be a better way to breed violence than to hold unconvicted men in jails like most of those now operating in our cities and counties.

It is hard to say what useful purpose is served by our present method of dealing with those who are awaiting trial for muggings and other crimes of violence. Certainly it is not that of correction or rehabilitation; hardly that of punishment, since there should be none before conviction; scarcely that of the segregation of dangerous persons —or at least not in significant numbers; and surely not anything like impartial and certain justice. Perhaps the only end it serves is that of partly gratifying the public's need for vengeance through sporadic and symbolic acts of retribution.

The situation looks hopeless; yet there have been numerous commission reports, sociological and juridical studies, legal and penological analyses which have offered scores of detailed suggestions for making the system work. But most of the suggestions have been ignored because they involve spending money and effort to lessen the misery of those who most of us are secretly pleased to see suffering. The most promising and creative proposals for change would entail a sweeping reconstruction and vast expansion of our courts, our probation services, our jails, and our prisons, but we as a people prefer to

wage the kind of war on crime advocated and in part already legis-
lated by the Nixon Administration: a war waged largely by means of
expanded police forces and increased police powers, tougher laws and
rules concerning investigation, detention, trial procedures, and sentencing, and the reversal of the long-term trend, in Supreme Court
decisions, toward the extension and increased protection of civil liberties.

But if we wage the war against crime only with such weapons,
where are we going to put all the prisoners accused of crimes? How
are we going to try them all before they grow old in jail? What will
keep the growing influx of cases from breaking down all orderly court
processes and producing epidemics of uncontrollable rioting in our
jails? And what will save us from the wrath of the jailed when they are
free again to walk the same streets as those who called this justice?

## III  *What's Happening? Anything Happening?*

ALFREDO ORTIZ, Carlos Ortiz, and Doel Valencia experienced none of
those subhuman living conditions so common in the nation's jails;
indeed, the Brooklyn House of Detention was then—and still is—in the
top tenth of American jails in terms of cleanliness, facilities, and general attentiveness to the needs of the prisoners. The cells were light and
fairly well ventilated; the food was plentiful, nourishing, and no worse
than that in a typical short-order diner; the mattresses and blankets were
reasonably clean; the guards or, in inmate slang, "hacks" or "C.O.s"
(Correction Officers) were quick to write up infractions—penalized
by a loss of privileges, or even by solitary confinement (euphemistically called "administrative segregation")—but they carried no guns,
brass knuckles, or even billy-clubs, and only occasionally "used
muscle" on an obstreperous prisoner or "handed out a rap in the
head"; the prisoners received no rehabilitative training or therapy to
speak of, but did get several periods each day of free time in the day-

rooms, where they could socialize, play cards, or watch television; and once a week they saw a movie, visited the gymnasium, and could have a relative visit them.

Yet even without the squalor, the physical discomforts, and the brutality so often reported elsewhere, it was hardly an agreeable place in which to wait for one's trial. A jail or prison is, in sociologist Erving Goffman's phrase, a "total institution"—a sub-society within society, separated from the enveloping one by a sharp discontinuity, social as well as physical. The prisoner is keenly aware of this: he lives in a rigid two-class society (staff and prisoners), according to rules and relationships unlike those of the world he used to live in, and the discontinuity between the two worlds is so complete that, despite an occasional letter or visitor, he feels forgotten, lost, and as good as dead in the eyes of those on the outside. He cannot help feeling that no one out there is really capable of, or interested in, helping him get out; the question that haunts him day and night, whenever he is alone with his own thoughts, is, "What's happening with my case?" —a question to which he fears the answer is, "Nothing." And this may be as dreadful a torment as any, for what makes waiting in today's jails—including the Brooklyn House of Detention—almost unbearable is not having any known goal, any fixed date toward which each day is at least a tiny step. (In the 1970 riot at the Brooklyn jail, it was the "trial prisoners"—unconvicted men awaiting trial—who were most daring, ferocious, and demanding; the "time prisoners"—convicted men with definite sentences, assigned to this jail to work in the laundry and the kitchen—put up only a token demonstration of discontent.)

But even if every trial prisoner had a definite end to his waiting in view, the waiting itself would still be excruciating, particularly when long drawn out, for life in a jail, even one as relatively civilized as the Brooklyn House of Detention, is constricting, humiliating, and, above all, boring, with the same tedious schedule every day, the same empty activities, the same interminable mornings, afternoons, and evenings. Each day began for Alfredo, Carlos, and Doel at 5:30 a.m. (when it was still pitch black outside the glass-brick façade) with the switching-on of the lights in their cells and a bellowed command shouted down each tier, "On the wake-up! Everybody out of the sack!," sometimes accompanied by a clangorous shaking of the gate at the end of the tier. Then a groaning and grunting all down the line, the sounds of urinating, farting, flushing of toilets, a few voices shouting back and forth, the sounds of nearly a hundred youths on each floor getting ready for a day of nothingness. Then another shout: "On the chow! Everybody out!" A rumbling sound as fifteen steel gates at a time, operated by a master control, trundled open, the prisoners shuffling out and getting into line, their clothes drab and shapeless from the cramped life in the cells, their faces neutral and watchful, their eyes wary and darting. In the hall at the end of the tier they picked up filled food trays from the stainless-steel portable food wagons manned by convicts, and took them into the day-room, a bare, noisy, tiled chamber with yellow plastic tables and long wooden benches, where they ate, talked, complained, joked, and boasted until, when they got too noisy, a guard would shout in at the door, "Knock it off!" or sometimes, "On the noise!"

Another shout at 6:30 a.m.: "On the lock-in—everybody out!" Back at their cells, they next heard, "Get your heads back inside your gates!" A rumbling, and a thud, as all the gates slid closed and locked at the same time. "On the G.I.—clean up your houses!" Mindlessly obedient, they made their beds, mopped their floors, and then waited, bored and fidgety, while the guards made the body count, peering in at them, dispassionate and impersonal. After a tiresome wait, another yell: "On the lock-out! Into the day-rooms!" A couple of hours then, listlessly playing cards or watching soap operas or morning talk-shows on television in the cold, comfortless day-room, or sitting and staring at nothing—the walls, the floor, but never outside, there being no windows but only translucent glass brick, except for screened openings too high to see out of. Back to the cells at 11:00 a.m. for another body count; then dinner at 11:15, always different but always the same, the various bean soups much alike, the canned ham and franks and hamburgers all curiously akin, so that by evening one could hardly remember what he had eaten at midday.

So it went, throughout the days and the weeks, forever being locked in, counted, let out, eating, being ordered back and locked in again, let out to sit around and do nothing, listening to the same tiresome complaining and joking, dealing the same greasy cards, lying on one's bunk and staring at the ceiling, thinking the same chewed-out, tasteless thoughts, and waiting for something, anything, to happen.

Now and then something did. Every once in a while they were notified by the guards that there was a visitor downstairs for them. The

first time, when the brothers met on the first floor, they hastily ex-
changed news. "They got me on the floor with all them bugs," said
Carlos, referring to prisoners under mental observation, "but I been
rappin' with them dudes an' some of them's all right. How about
you?" Alfredo said that he was on a "heavy" floor—one reserved for
youths accused of very serious crimes—but that he had met friends
there and was getting along all right. An officer ordered them to their
position, and they went into a narrow, low-ceilinged corridor lined on
both sides with fixed stools, on which other prisoners were taking their
places. At the assigned stool, Alfredo sat down, Carlos standing behind him; directly in front of Alfredo, in the wall, there was a tiny
square of wire-reinforced glass through which he could make out the
tense, anguished face of his mother. He picked up a telephone handset
hanging in a cradle on the wall, and she did the same on her side,
beginning to weep when she heard his voice. As they now recall, the
conversation went about like this:

"Moms, don'!" said Alfredo.

"Freddy," she sobbed, struggling to compose herself, "they say you
confess that you help kill the old man."

"Moms," said Alfredo quickly, "I di'n' do it. I di'n' do *nothin'!*"

"Then why you confess, if you don' do it?" she asked.

"They beat me," said Alfredo. "They beat Carlos an' Doel, too."
He couldn't help it, he said; he had had to say everything they wanted
him to say, but in court he would be able to tell the truth. She looked
somewhat relieved. "You foun' out anything about the case?" he
asked. "You look for a lawyer yet? What's happening? Anything happening?" No, she hadn't found out anything yet; no, she hadn't begun
looking for a lawyer. Money was the big problem. Since they had
none, the court would appoint a lawyer to defend him and Carlos, if
they requested it, but who could trust a court-appointed lawyer? She
would try to get one of their own and finance the fee by asking her
relatives for contributions.

She asked to talk to Carlos, and Alfredo changed places with him.
The phone wasn't much good, and it was hard for each to hear the
other, what with the babble of voices of other prisoners on his side
and other visitors on hers, but he managed to tell her what things to
bring him (he had arrived with nothing but the clothes he had been
wearing). All too soon the half-hour visit was over and a bell
sounded; they said good-by, went back to their floors, and began

waiting, once again, for something to happen.

The days dragged on, each one so slowly that sometimes they would forget whether it was morning or afternoon, or what day of the week it was. They could keep track of time by remembering how many days since they'd been up to the barber shop to get shaved (the prisoners weren't permitted their own razors or blades), or to the roof to play volleyball, or to the chapel to see the weekly movie.

Valencia, on his floor, was having comparable experiences. At first he had had to go through a severe cold-turkey withdrawal for several days, "kicking pretty bad," as a guard put it, with chills, shakes, vomiting spells, and an epileptic seizure that had to be treated by the doctor; then he got over it, and began adjusting to the routine and living the life of endless waiting. His common-law wife, Josie, came to visit him, brought him clothes and other necessaries, and told him that his sister, Idalia, was going to find him a lawyer and pay for his defense; but despite this reassuring news, as soon as she left he felt alone again, and abandoned and helpless.

Even fierce, tough Angel Walker, up at the Bronx House of Detention, felt much the same: after only two days in jail, he wrote to the lawyer representing him in his damage suit against the Transit Authority, telling him what had happened and concluding, "HELP me. It is *very hard* being here for something I did not do." (The lawyer replied, regretting that he was unable to handle the criminal case, and Walker went ahead with his original intention to use Carney, the courthouse lawyer who had stood up for him at the arraignment.)

Hard as it was to be in jail, Walker and the three others were all seasoned ghetto street-youths, and all had been in penal institutions before; they knew what to do, how to spot the tough guys, what things to say and not to say, and how to survive in the subculture of the jail. The most important thing for each of the diminutive Ortiz brothers was to make friends with other Puerto Ricans, in order to be protected from any blacks, Irish, or Italians who might be spoiling for a fight, or for the rape-conquest of a despised spick. Alfredo, recalling his own first days at the Brooklyn jail, says, "It wasn' no problem for me. I had friends there already. If you growed up in New York an' ran all over different neighborhoods the way I did, you got to meet a lot of different people. An' those people in the ghetto, you goin' to meet some of them in jail. So when you get there, right away you fin' somebody you know an' get you a little group to hang with, an' to help you if anything happens. To avoid messin' with all them, the other inmates leave you alone, but the people that don' know nobody that's goin' to help them, they're the ones that get in trouble, an' get raped an' all that. But also, it depends on the way you conduct yourself, 'cause if you goin' aroun' sellin' tickets [offering insults or verbal challenges] to somebody else, somebody's got to *try* you, but if you min' your own business, most of the time nobody goin' to bother you."

Carlos, with his cockier and generally rowdier manner, was involved more often in selling tickets or having them sold to him than Alfredo, but feels that it wasn't his fault. As he puts it, "If some dude sells me a ticket an' I don' tell him I'm goin' to see him outside, well, when he get the opportunity to see me alone, this is his shot. If you don' buy the ticket, you goin' to be his punk.* If you do buy it, you gotta be ready to fight—but then he's not goin' to sell you no more tickets." Carlos caught tickets fairly often, and even had to go to the infirmary a few weeks after arriving at the jail to have two stitches in his cheek, but most of his fights were one-punch affairs due to minor disagreements at cards, and he considered them part of the game.

Alfredo, who preferred to avoid such entanglements, fought the problem of boredom and despair by asking the guards on his floor to put him on the work detail; they did, and in consequence he was out of his cell nearly all day long manning the food wagon, mopping the floor, polishing brass, and thereby not only passing the time but staying on the good side of the guards.

The days and the weeks dragged on, with no word of what was happening, but then one morning, right after breakfast, each of the three was told by a guard on his floor that he would be going to court that day, and to make himself as presentable as he could. The trip to court was an exciting break in the routine; nevertheless, it involved a number of discomforts and humiliations—the quick frisk (hands against the wall while being "patted down" by a guard) before leaving the floor; stripping to the skin in the receiving room to be searched (how many times can a man bend over and spread his buttocks without losing the last shreds of pride?); dressing again, and having a handcuff clamped on one wrist, connecting him to another prisoner; outside for a moment—seeing the sky for the first time in weeks—and into the van, with its merciless wooden seats, for the long, jolting ride to Criminal Court in the Bronx; another frisk, then upstairs, uncuffed,

* If you don't stand up to him, you will have to be his sexual servant.

and pushed into the holding pen, muggy and stale with the sour smell of too many men in sweaty clothes. And there, none other than Negrito was shoving his way through to greet them (surly as ever) and to ask if they had lawyers in the courtroom today (he did—Carney would be there on his behalf), though he knew no more than they about what was going to happen.

Almost nothing did. They waited in the pen for what seemed endless hours until at last they were called out, led into the courtroom, and paraded before the bench. Rotund little Mr. Carney came forward and stood beside Walker, and a heavy, middle-aged man with thin brownish hair and a double chin that crushed his shirt collar asked the others which of them were the Ortiz brothers, and told them he was James Hanrahan and had just been retained by their mother to represent them. Then he motioned them to be silent. The assistant D.A. was saying something to the judge about needing a further adjournment because his office was waiting for the Grand Jury to return an indictment in the case; Carney and Hanrahan agreed to the adjournment; and in a moment all four defendants were being hustled back to the pen. The Ortizes, bewildered, saw no more of Hanrahan that day, and after long hours of waiting, they were handcuffed again and taken downstairs to the van for the ride back to Brooklyn, where they underwent another strip and search, then went up by elevator to their own floors, had a final frisk, and were back in their cells seven hours after they had left them, all for a minute or two in the courtroom.

A week later they went through the same routine; and again a week later. On that third trip to court, however, something important did happen: when they stood before the judge, the assistant D.A. read aloud the indictment that had now been returned against them by the Grand Jury, whereupon the judge said something about the case being "dismissed" (did their ignorant hearts leap foolishly, for one instant, at that word?) and about the defendants' being remanded in the custody of Detective McCabe (who was standing by with warrants all prepared). Except, however, that Angel Walker, also known as Angel Oquendo, had not been indicted by the Grand Jury, and lawyer Carney, sounding as if he personally had brought this about, asked for the dismissal of charges against his client; the judge said the charges were indeed dismissed. Various papers were handed back and forth, and shortly the Ortiz brothers and Doel Valencia were handcuffed again, this time by McCabe and another detective, taken downstairs to a squad car and driven across 161st Street to the Bronx County Courthouse, and locked in a detention pen on a floor where the Supreme Court convened.

They had no idea what was happening—McCabe had volunteered nothing on the short ride across town, and none of them had felt like asking him any questions—but soon enough they found out. For in a moment, James Hanrahan appeared in the aisle outside the pen, and beckoned the Ortiz brothers to come over to the bars. By his side was another lawyer—a brisk, natty little fellow in his thirties, with crinkly blond hair and a boyish pug-nosed face; he called out Valencia's name and, when Valencia came over, introduced himself as Kenneth Kase, his lawyer, hired for him by Idalia.

All three defendants had heard, by this time, that they would soon be having their first real meeting with their lawyers, but hardly expected it to take place in these circumstances—with two dozen other prisoners a few feet from them in the same pen, listening to every word. It turned out, however, that neither lawyer could talk to them for more than a few minutes at this point, but each explained that it didn't matter, since today's proceedings would be only a formality: their cases had been technically dismissed in Criminal Court because it lacked jurisdiction over murders, but now they would be rearraigned in this court and a new calendar date set for their next appearance. Their questions, and the lawyers' answers, went something like this: *But what about Walker? How come he ain' here?* Because he wasn't indicted by the Grand Jury. He's out of it now. *Out of it! You mean they're lettin' Walker go an' they're keepin' us? . . . Oh, man!* Just don't concern yourself about that—and don't say anything down there today. Just keep quiet. I'll plead you not guilty and come over to talk to you in Brooklyn. *Yeah, but what's goin' to happen? How long we goin' to be stuck over there?* Hard to say. A few months, most likely. Don't be in a hurry—this is a tough rap. *Yeah, but, man, it's hard, waitin'.* We have to take our time and see what we can work out. This is a capital case. It's Murder One, and that could mean life—or even the chair. *The chair! Man—you bullshittin'? The chair?* Now, take it easy. I'm not going to let that happen to you. I'm going to do everything I can. I can probably get you a deal if you plead to Man One or even Man Two,* which would mean only five to fifteen. *But listen, man, we di'n' do it. We wasn' there, we never seen that old*

* Manslaughter in the first degree, or in the second degree.

*man, we don' know nothin' about it, nothin'!* All right, all right, don't worry about a thing. I'll be over to see you in a day or two, and we'll talk the whole thing over. I'm going to do everything I can for you. Don't worry.

And somehow, because the lawyers held briefcases in their hands, and rustled papers while they were talking, and seemed to know exactly what was what, the three defendants did feel better, as a critically ill patient does the moment the doctor walks in. The lawyers left and after a while the prisoners were called out by a guard and led down a flight of steps and into the courtroom. McCabe was waiting inside the railing, as were Hanrahan and Kase; outside, in the spectators' section, were Luisa Pomales, Idalia Valencia, and Josie. But there was no time to do more than exchange a glance with their people, for they were led straight before the bench—a higher, more imposing one, in a grander, more awe-inspiring room than the other—and at once some crisp, formal statements were being made by an assistant district attorney, and then by their own lawyers; aging, gentle Justice William Lyman then said there would be no bail, and that the defendants were remanded in the custody of the Department of Correction pending their next hearing. And that was that: the guard beckoned them, and they stumbled out and were led back to the pen, and eventually taken back to their cells in the Brooklyn House of Detention, where they still felt isolated and powerless, but a little less afraid of the unknown future because someone was now in charge, someone who knew what was happening.

# IV   *Defenders of the Faith*

IN 1957 Justice William O. Douglas visited the principality of Swat—a part of Pakistan—and discussed the law with its ruler, the Wali. Upon learning that there were no lawyers in Swat, Justice Douglas asked who represented the accused in a criminal case, to which the

Wali replied, "The defendant himself—but the judge, of course, sees that he gets a fair trial." But, asked Justice Douglas, what if the defendant felt that he did need a lawyer? "None would be appointed," said the Wali. "You see, Mr. Justice, up here in Swat we have concluded that a lawyer only makes a lawsuit complicated and confusing."

With this last point, no sensible American could disagree; he might, however, find himself totally at odds with the Wali's belief in a system of justice that supposes a paternalistic judge can be fair while acting as prosecutor and defender at the same time. Americans put their faith in a very different system which seeks to assure fairness by making the criminal case a contest between the prosecutor and the defendant, and giving each approximately equal rights and powers. But the subtleties and complexities of the law are so great that, except in minor infractions, the accused cannot adequately defend himself without professional help; as lawyers never tire of saying, "He who is his own lawyer has a fool for his client." Criminal lawyers—or, as they prefer to be called nowadays, defense lawyers—are therefore the defenders not only of their clients but of the adversarial ideal, and of the faith we place in it. Ideally, they are protectors of their clients' rights, searchers after the truth, and exposers of falsehood and wrongdoing; more often they are nags, poseurs, windbags, ham actors, connivers, tricksters, defamers, and sowers of confusion—yet unless they are free to be any and all of these things, without allegiance or obligation to the prosecution, they cannot do their best to defend their clients—who thus cannot do their best to defend themselves.

The defense lawyer is therefore a figure of paradox; he is indispensable to the maintenance of fairness in court, though he seeks not fairness but the freedom of his client, regardless of the latter's innocence or guilt; he is essential to the noblest goals of the justice system, though he strives less for justice than for personal victory; he is crucial to the carrying-out of our highest ideals, but is held in low esteem both by his fellow lawyers and by the public.

In consequence, he is regarded by his fellows and the public with great ambivalence. The general impression of the defense lawyer is a pastiche of opposites, made up, on the one hand, of the stereotype of the courageous, selfless defender of poor people, social outcasts, radicals, and framed innocents, and, on the other, the stereotype of the crooked "mouthpiece" of mobsters and swindlers. We think of criminal lawyers either as dedicated idealists, struggling against lying witnesses and unscrupulous district attorneys, or as flamboyant pragmatists brilliantly rescuing vicious criminals from the punishment they deserve; indeed, we think of them as a mixture of both, and feel admiration and loathing, respect and contempt for them in equal parts.

But very few of the nation's defense lawyers resemble either of these models. Criminal law practice is, by and large, underpaid, insecure, tedious, unglamorous, and lacking in prestige. The typical criminal lawyer is a solo practitioner who makes only a fifth as much money as the average corporation lawyer belonging to a firm. Most of the working hours of the criminal lawyer are spent not in carpeted offices or in paneled, dignified courtrooms, but in courthouse hallways, jails, and crowded, stuffy criminal courtrooms; most of his clients are ignorant, malodorous, suspicious persons with whom he can scarcely communicate, and many of whom he would find frightening if they were not behind bars; and much of his work in defending them involves neither challenging intellectual activity nor courtroom drama, but the making of routine appearances, the concocting of excuses for delays, and continual maneuvering, blustering, persuading, dickering, and bargaining.

It is, indeed, so unappealing a specialty that in a recent survey of the students at Harvard Law School, only 3 percent said they hoped to go into criminal law after graduating, and only 2 percent of the privately practicing lawyers in America accept criminal cases more than occasionally. The need for defense lawyers far exceeds the supply: the Crime Commission found that as of 1967, somewhere between 8,300 and 12,500 full-time criminal lawyers were needed in this country, but that only a third to a half that number were available, many of whom were doing criminal work only part-time. (The estimate included 2,500 to 5,000 private practitioners, and some 900 lawyers on the staffs of public-defender agencies in a number of states.)

In romantic tradition, the defense lawyer is a man of unquestioned probity and standing who temporarily takes leave of his regular practice to fight for the rights of some wretch so despised that no ordinary trial lawyer will take his case: the classic example is that of John Adams and Josiah Quincy, Jr., who undertook the defense of Captain Preston and his soldiers, accused of murder in the Boston Massacre, after several Crown lawyers had refused to touch it. But most criminal lawyers have been, and are today, small-time hustlers who defend accused persons in order to earn a living, depending on volume and quick turnover to make up for the smallness of their fees, and rarely if ever being motivated by any deep sympathy for their clients.

Indeed, almost the only contemporary defense lawyers who identify strongly with their clients are those who specialize in representing political radicals: William Kunstler, for instance, has said, "I only defend those whose goals I share. I only defend those I love." But this seemingly idealistic attitude is, by another paradox, a hidden and virulent form of illiberality, for if all defenders were to serve only those whose goals they share, who then would defend those whose goals no one shares—or those with no goals, but who stand accused (perhaps wrongly) of peddling drugs, mugging, rape, or murder? Mr. Kunstler's view is a chilling repudiation of the tradition of fairness in Anglo-American law; to see what would happen if his view prevailed, one need only look at the Communist show trials in which the defendants can obtain only court-appointed lawyers—whose anxiety to show their dislike of their clients is so great that they all but help to convict them, limiting their "defense" largely to pleas for clemency.

It is not, therefore, idealists but mercenaries who make the law operate justly for all of us; it is the uncommitted hirelings of the profession who make a reality of the system's ideals. Ironically, this noble achievement rarely brings them any substantial reward: though a top-flight criminal lawyer may charge a big-time extortionist or gangster $10,000 or $20,000 to try his case, the great majority of misdemeanors and felonies are handled for minor sums, $500 to $1,000 being about par for seeing a mugging through to trial, $250 taking care of plea-bargaining in a marijuana bust, and $50 or so buying an appearance to arrange bail or win an adjournment. One must take what he can get: 60 percent of the people accused of crime cannot afford a lawyer at all, and most of the others have difficulty scratching up anything more than modest sums.

Since the *Gideon* decision, of course, every jurisdiction must provide a person accused of a felony with a lawyer if he cannot pay, and even before *Gideon* many jurisdictions did so in the most serious felonies. Much of criminal defense is now subsidized, the lawyers being volunteers or persons listed on panels, who are assigned by the court in rotation, and paid for—at fixed economy-class rates—out of public funds. In some cities and counties, and throughout some states, most of the defense of the indigent is done by legal-aid societies or public-defender agencies funded by federal or local governments; here the cases are handled by harried, overworked staffs of salaried lawyers who earn even less than the seediest courthouse hangers-on, and who, burdened with masses of cases not of their own choosing, are often unable to meet their clients, much less establish rapport with them, until a few minutes before their appearance in court.

But one would suppose that at least there would be considerable emotional reward in fighting for the innocent man, particularly when he is poor, uneducated, black, and incapable of defending himself against the subtle machinations of the prosecution. A few criminal lawyers—particularly those eager young men who go straight from law school into public-defender agencies—do see themselves at first as champions of the oppressed and helpless, but it does not take long before they discover that most of the people they represent have already been convicted of other crimes, are evasive, suspicious, surly, and hostile, and are chronic liars. In almost every case where the client has made a confession, he tells his lawyer he was beaten or threatened into making it; if he was caught by a policeman carrying a TV set, he claims he found it in a back alley; if he had a knife or gun on his person, he swears that some passing stranger stuck it in his hand a couple of seconds before the policeman came along; if he is accused of a mugging or shooting, he protests that he was nowhere near the scene of the crime, never saw the victim, and has been mistaken for someone else or is being framed. The stories are so standardized that after a while the novice defender becomes disillusioned and cynical, and doubts even the most outraged or anguished protestation of innocence. But what else could one expect? The lawyer is a college man, a law-school graduate, washed and shaved and articulate; whether his skin is white or black, he is part of the Establishment in the eyes of the criminal. He may provide a defense, but why trust him, why tell him the truth? Better to deny, lie, swear to one's story, and hope to beat the system with its own weapons.

For all that, the accused man *may* be innocent: the slum-dweller's suspiciousness, his manner of talking, his clothing and odor, his habits and way of life make him unfathomable to the lawyer. Innocent or guilty, he sounds unpleasant, alien, incomprehensible. Slowly the defense lawyer realizes that in most cases he will never be really sure of the truth, even though he does have reason to suppose that most of the people he defends probably did commit the crimes they are charged with, or something close to them.

How, then, is he to feel about the value of what he does in the courtroom and in society? It would be only natural for him to feel pleased and proud any time he got an innocent man acquitted; but since in most cases he is exceedingly doubtful of his client's innocence, how can he find heart to fight for him or take pleasure in whatever success he achieves? How can he avoid seeing himself as anything but a legal whore and an enemy of his own society?

Most criminal lawyers resolve this conflict, when it begins to trouble them, by telling themselves that they are defending not just individual men—some of whom are innocent, many of whom are guilty—but the justice system itself: unless they defend every man as if he were truly innocent, there would be nothing to prevent the system from becoming inquisitorial and tyrannical. And did not the Fifth Canon of Ethics of the American Bar Association, in force for six decades, state that the defense lawyer should do everything he can to get his client acquitted "regardless of his personal opinion as to the guilt of the accused . . . to the end that no person may be deprived of life or liberty but by due process of law"? * So he shuts his eyes to his client's apparent guilt, telling himself, in the well-known words of the noted English barrister Sir Patrick Hastings, "Counsel has no right to believe or disbelieve either his client or his case; he has a duty to perform; he must perform it." Criminal lawyers conclude after a certain amount of exposure to the reality of criminal law that they are not so much protecting the downtrodden from being unjustly punished as they are protecting the system from an inherent tendency to subvert its own principles. Mary Tarcher, Assistant Attorney-in-Chief of the Legal Aid Society of New York, says, "Much of the time you would be very discouraged if you thought only of the client you represented and what it means to society if you get him off and turn him loose. But if you think of the part you play in keeping intact and viable a system designed to exculpate the innocent, it's somewhat dif-

---

* The clarity of the Fifth Canon was muddied in the 1969 Code of Professional Responsibility (a revision of the long-standing canons), but much the same principle prevails in its relevant sections. E.g., "The duty of a lawyer, both to his client and to the legal system, is to represent his client zealously within the bounds of the law. . . . The obligation of loyalty to his client applies only to a lawyer in the discharge of his professional duties and implies no obligation to adopt a personal viewpoint favorable to the interests or desires of his client" (Canon 7: EC 7-1 and EC 7-17).

ferent." Daniel Sullivan, formerly a public defender in Nassau County, New York, and now head of the Appeals Bureau of the Bronx District Attorney's Office, says, "Many a time I've defended some rotten bum who ought to have been locked away for the good of society, but I did my best to get him off, and I had no problem of conscience about doing so. The only way to preserve our system of justice is to put the prosecution to their proof in every case. Better the worst bum should walk the streets free than that the police should be able to arrest citizens without probable cause or the prosecution should be able to use illegally seized evidence."

Yet one can hardly utilize such grand justifications every day without their wearing thin. The average defense lawyer, dealing all day long with men and women he would hate to encounter at night on a dark, deserted street, and who, he knows, will probably commit further crimes if he defends them successfully, cannot continually comfort himself with the thought that he is defending the justice system. What he does instead is stop looking at the consequences of his work and go about his business blindly, doing it for his own benefit even as the combat soldier ceases thinking of the ultimate goals of the war and commits his butcheries solely to survive and to win. As Jay Goldberg, a former prosecutor and now a private criminal lawyer, told a *New York Times* reporter, "I am a mercenary. A person who is accused of something comes into my office and he wants me to be his sword, he wants me to protect his rights. I must, if I accept his case, close my eyes to the needs of society." With public defenders—who do not even have the choice of accepting or rejecting a case—the situation is still more clear-cut: one of the top defense lawyers in New York's Legal Aid Society, Martin Erdmann, put it with ultimate bluntness in an interview in *Life* magazine: "If you say I have no moral reaction to what I do, you are right. I'm not concerned with the crime committed or the consequences of [my client's] going free. The only reason I'm any good is because I have an ego. I like to win. . . . I have nothing to do with justice." *

Not many defense lawyers are so outspokenly cynical or so unsparingly honest with themselves. But most of them come to function, day

---

* But Mr. Edward Carr, his superior, said in a subsequent letter to the Editor, "The pervasive cynicism that has engulfed Mr. Erdmann's underlying idealism does not represent the views of the Legal Aid Society or of any significant number of our staff attorneys." Mr. Erdmann was subsequently shifted from trial work to administrative duties.

to day, on much the same emotional and intellectual basis. Only once in a while—but less and less often as the years go by—do they bother to remind themselves that, but for the part they and other defense lawyers play, there would be no adversarial system, no reality to the presumption of innocence, no insistence that guilt be proven beyond reasonable doubt, and no fulfilling of the constitutional promise of fair trial.

# V   *Leave It to Me*

LUISA POMALES had sought and found a lawyer for her sons on her own, and agreed to pay him a fee which represented nearly half her year's income. In 1964, only one year after *Gideon,* impoverished persons accused of crime were not yet accustomed, as many of them have since become, to asking the court to appoint and pay lawyers to defend them. But even had it occurred to Mrs. Pomales to do so, she would probably have dismissed the idea: the poor, especially those of ethnic minorities, prefer to find and pay lawyers of their own if they possibly can, especially in very serious cases, for they cannot see how a court-appointed lawyer or public defender paid by the same government that is prosecuting them can really be on their side.

Such people seek their lawyers haphazardly: they haunt courthouse hallways and ask sympathetic-looking persons for a name, or consult neighbors who have been in trouble, or walk the streets in a court-house area looking at the signs in windows, trying to decide which name sounds good. Mrs. Pomales had yet another method: she remembered having read an account in a Spanish-language newspaper four years earlier about the trial and acquittal of the "Umbrella Man" —a Puerto Rican youth accused of murder, and identified by the umbrella he generally carried—and decided to visit his lawyer, James J. Hanrahan.

Too timid to go alone, she begged a neighbor to accompany her to Hanrahan's office. As soon as they got off the subway, Mrs. Pomales felt a little easier, since the address turned out to be in Spanish Harlem, in an area much like the one she had lived in before moving up to Melrose. Hanrahan's office was on the ground floor of a tenement building on East 110th Street, among the cracked front stoops, battered garbage cans, stray dogs, and noisy children she knew so well. Outside there was a sign saying, reassuringly, "Abogado"; inside, in a cramped, glaringly lit waiting-room, sitting on plastic-covered chairs and a sofa, were several other Puerto Rican people; and on the walls there were yellowing framed newspaper clippings telling about cases Hanrahan had won on behalf of Spanish-named people accused of muggings, drug-pushing, and murder. Mrs. Pomales felt a good deal better.

On the wall at the inner end of the waiting-room was a mirror—actually, a one-way glass through which Hanrahan and his secretary could keep an eye on his clients from the inner office. After a long wait, Mrs. Pomales' turn came, and the secretary showed her into the inner office, a small, shabby, windowless room, carpeted but dingy, cluttered with shabby furniture, and heaped high everywhere with legal papers, folders, and correspondence. Behind a desk sat Hanrahan, a bulky, flaccid man of forty-eight whose broad, flabby face was like a balloon that had slightly deflated. The balloon was decorated with sparse, fading brown hair, a small, thin-lipped mouth, and pale blue eyes behind heavy-framed glasses—a face as reassuringly unpretentious as the waiting-room itself.

Hanrahan greeted her soberly in flat, American-accented Spanish, and asked what he could do for her. She poured out her story and he listened closely, jotting down a note or two and asking questions from time to time. He seemed to know a great deal—how people are interrogated, why there was no bail for her sons, where they now were being held in Brooklyn, what the next steps were—and soon she was convinced that he was the very man to defend them. She asked him to do so, and he replied that if he accepted the case, he would do the best he could for them but that it would be expensive: he would have to defend not one but two clients, both accused of Murder One, and both of whom had confessed. Mrs. Pomales, alarmed that he might not take the case, asked how much, and he said it depended on many things. If they had to go to trial and he was tied up in court for two or three solid weeks, his fee might run to $1,500. She looked stunned; Hanrahan quickly added that if they settled the case without trial, it would come to less, and in any event she could pay him in installments. After hastily reckoning on what she might raise from various relatives, she agreed. "Leave it to me," he said, "I'll do everything humanly possible." She thanked him tearfully and left his office, relieved and proud that she had found Alfredo and Carlos a defender.

Hanrahan, for his part, was pleased; it was a serious case, and the clients were the very kind of people he knew best, although he had grown up among the Irish and Italians. His parents had come to New York from Ireland in 1906 and settled in East Harlem, which was then largely white and thoroughly working-class. He grew up without ever leaving the neighborhood, going to parochial school and then to a small Catholic college; even after the war, when the area was becoming Puerto Rican, he and his family remained, while he struggled through Fordham Law School, and after graduating, he went into practice in his own neighborhood. The more ambitious graduates of law schools seek positions with big downtown firms, or with city or state governments, but Hanrahan preferred to go into "storefront" private practice, handling matrimonial matters, leases, and the everyday problems of the poor. He soon decided, however, to make criminal law his specialty, partly because he found this more in demand in East Harlem than other kinds of legal service and partly, he says, because it fitted in with his own ideals: "I've been with poor people all my life," he says, "and I found criminal law a great challenge. I'm not in the business of making a great living, but I had an ideal, I kept faith with myself. I believe in the future of this country, I believe in its judicial system, I'm interested in the small people, and I live by my conscience and sleep well at night." He delivers such comments in an unabashedly orotund manner and, indeed, has even run for Congress twice, addressing the electorate of East Harlem (where he and his wife live) in his best Irish-American Spanish, but without winning either election.

Though Hanrahan had accepted the Ortiz brothers' case, he made no moves on their behalf, pending the Grand Jury hearing, except to show up briefly at their hearings in Criminal Court. The Grand Jury is an ancient device, still used in about half the states, to protect citizens from unjust or malevolent prosecution: it does not try cases, but hears the prosecutor present some of the crucial evidence he has gathered; if the Grand Jury feels, from what it has heard, that the accused should be prosecuted, it returns an indictment and the prosecutor proceeds, but if it finds his grounds insufficient, it does not and he must drop the charges. Since Hanrahan could play no part in the Grand Jury hearing —defense lawyers are not permitted to attend—and chose not to exercise his right to send his clients in, unprotected, to be witnesses for themselves, he simply waited, doing no work on the case; any work he did would be wasted if no indictment was returned. But the Grand Jury listened to what the assistant district attorney and McCabe had to say, and did indict the Ortiz brothers and Doel Valencia, whereupon Hanrahan got to work.

First of all, he went by subway to Brooklyn, signed in at the reception desk of the House of Detention, and was ushered into the counsel room, where he was assigned one of a score of tiny cubicles separated by shoulder-high partitions. Shortly, a guard brought in Alfredo and Carlos, and left them alone with him. Hanrahan took out a legal-sized notepad and a pencil, and started asking questions and scribbling down notes of their replies. The conference lasted over an hour, but none of what was said was unusual: in the past seventeen years Hanrahan had asked similar questions and heard similar answers countless times. It went something like this:

What can you tell me about all this? How did you get involved in the case? *We don' know nothin' about it! We ain' been there, we di'n' even know that old man!* But what about those confessions you made to the police? *Listen, man, they beat the shit out of us till we can't take no more an' we say what they tell us to say.* But why did they pick you? *They would of picked anybody they could pin it on, an' we happen to look good. The way we figure, somebody in the neighborhood must have name' us to get himself off the hook.* Where were you that day? Anybody see you? *I was downtown lookin' for a job an' then I was with this girl, Marie. No, I don' exactly know her address. Alfredo, you was with Manny, wasn' you?* What were you doing, Alfredo? *Jus, goofin' off, hangin' around.* I understand both of you have had some previous difficulties. That isn't going to make it any easier. *Yeah, but, man, we di'n' do none of that stuff. I di'n' have no part in that robbery—I was jus' takin' the rap for a buddy of mine. And Carlos, he was framed, he di'n' bother that woman's daughter. She was his girl-friend, he had a right!* An' drugs?—*they hit me with a sell, but I di'n' make no sell. I was usin', but I wasn' sellin'.* You know what could happen if we go to trial and lose—and we might, because the D.A. does have your confessions. But I could try to work something out with him. You know—offer a guilty plea to something less, and get a much better deal. *We ain' goin' to take no plea. They got nothin' on us but those confessions, an' those is all lies. They beat us up an' kick us in the nuts an' put ammonia on our faces until we confess. When we tell about that in court, they goin' to convict us?*

By the time he left, Hanrahan says, he was convinced that the Ortiz brothers were innocent; or perhaps, realizing that they were going to insist on a trial, he made himself think so, for today he talks about it more like an actor who persuaded himself to feel the emotions he needed to play a part. "They didn't look vicious to me," he says. "Of course, they didn't have a good record, but I didn't think they could have done it—I had a psychic feeling about it. And the way the police beat the daylights out of them!" Does he really believe the police did so? Does he actually consider McCabe brutal, vicious, and dishonest, as the Ortiz brothers claim he is? "Let's say, at that *moment* I thought so, I certainly did, at that *time*. But I have no fault to find with McCabe; he's all right." Had he no doubts about the truthfulness of the Ortiz brothers' story? "Usually, when I go to trial I actually believe my clients are innocent. Truthfully! If I think they're guilty, I try to work out a deal for them, but the Ortiz boys insisted they were innocent and I told them if they wanted me to go all the way, I'd go all the way. So I *had* to go to trial—and I felt the boys were telling the truth."

Not that he had much to go to trial with. He could see no obvious legal flaws that would merit a dismissal of charges or a suppression of the confessions, though he made futile motions to those effects at various hearings. He could see little value in delaying the trial, since the detectives and the assistant D.A., unlike other witnesses, were unlikely to lose interest in a murder case, and their written records guaranteed that their memories would not fade. Hanrahan did try to establish the Ortiz brothers' alibis, personally going in search of the people they named, but the woman Carlos said he had seen at an employment agency was no longer working there and the agency had no record of his visit, the girl Marie could not be found, and Alfredo's pal Manny denied even knowing him. Mrs. Pomales, though she might be an affecting character witness, had not seen her sons all that day.

Hoping to ferret out something helpful about the prosecution's case, Hanrahan applied in writing to the court for a Bill of Particulars, asking that the assistant district attorney in charge of the case be ordered to give him some twenty pieces of information for the use of the defense, including the details of the understanding among Carlos, Alfredo, and Doel to commit the crime, a description of the actual knifing, the coroner's report, and the complete text of all admissions and confessions made by the two brothers. The District Attorney, of course, rebutted, as Hanrahan knew he would, saying that, except for the coroner's report, everything Hanrahan had asked for was evidentiary and could not, under law, be made available to the defense before trial, and Justice Lyman ordered only the coroner's report and the time and place of the alleged crime to be sent to him. Hanrahan then offered another motion in writing to the effect that he be permitted to inspect the secret Grand Jury minutes, on the grounds that there had not been enough evidence offered to warrant an indictment; Justice Lyman denied the request (as Hanrahan must have known he would) on the reasonable grounds that the adequacy of the evidence would be reviewed at the trial itself.

As the weeks passed and the trial date, set for early March, approached, all Hanrahan could plan to do, if the case did go to trial, was to cross-examine the detectives closely in the hope of finding illegalities in their detention and interrogation of the Ortiz brothers, harp on the brutality claimed by the defendants, stress the discrepancy between the time given in their confessions and that given by Doel Valencia in his, and point out repeatedly that there was no other evidence. He might persuade the jury that a reasonable doubt existed as to his clients' guilt; he had sometimes been lucky before, and perhaps would be this time too.

At about the same time, Idalia Valencia had gone looking for someone to defend her brother, Doel. Idalia, though a little flashy-looking, was a serious and responsible girl, and decided to hire someone on her own; since, however, she would have to pay him out of her modest salary as a nurse's aide, he could not be the kind of high-priced criminal lawyer from downtown who defended *Mafiosi,* big-time heroin dealers, crooked politicians, and union bosses. Through a friend, she heard about a young lawyer in the Bronx who, though reasonable in price, was said to be clever, energetic, and very good at getting off persons accused of robberies, knifings, liquor-law violations, and other run-of-the-mill felonies; he sounded good, and she phoned and made an appointment to see him.

His name was Kenneth Kase, and his office was part of a well-appointed suite, shared by several other lawyers, on the fifth floor of an office building on East 149th Street, a broad commercial avenue. Kase, though younger than Hanrahan (he was only thirty-eight at the time), was already doing nicely for a criminal lawyer, considering that he was not in the big time. A hustler and a charmer, he was cocky and worldly, yet genial and open, with as ready a flow of Bronx-accented talk as a typical New York cabbie; indeed, he had actually driven a cab during part of his college and law-school years. The son of a dress salesman, he had grown up in a middle-class, largely Jewish section of the east Bronx, and after high school had spent the World War II years in the Air Force as a navigator. Afterward he came home and idled around for a year, trying to find himself; then, suddenly galvanized by some sense of lateness, he entered Adelphi College, went to classes twelve months a year, and zipped through in two and a half years, after which he went to the law school of St. John's University in Brooklyn. Short, peppy, and boyish-looking, with a pug nose and frizzy blond hair, he was clearly cut out for the more active kind of law work—court appearances and trials—rather than real-estate closings, the drawing up of wills, the merging of corporations, or the writing of appeals based on precedent and interpretation.

At first he worked for another lawyer on routine commercial matters, but after handling a few liquor-license applications and spending some time in bars talking to their owners, he found himself being sought out by minor criminals, released convicts, and other patrons and friends of the bar owners. Breezy, knowing, and cheerful, he got along with such people easily, and soon found himself doing more criminal work than anything else, dealing for the most part with misdemeanors and routine lesser felonies. "I did real good," he says, grinning at his own immodesty. "I got them off easily, no trouble, no sweat—not because I was brilliant, but probably because most of the charges were throw-outs. But I started to get a bit of a reputation, and things built up. Also, I found out that the more you bounce around in bars and grills, the more of that kind of work you get." He became the partner of a lawyer specializing in commercial work, and prospered; his marriage broke up, and he took to wearing spiffy clothes and became something of a man-about-town.

By the time Idalia Valencia sought him out, he had been in criminal law for nine or ten years; she was sufficiently impressed by his manner and credentials to engage him for $1,500 to $2,000, depending on the time involved. Actually, although he had handled hundreds of felonies, he had never had a murder, and considered Doel Valencia's case an exciting challenge. A few days after first meeting Valencia at the Supreme Court arraignment, he went to Brooklyn and spoke to him at length. Kase was pleased to learn that Valencia, despite having confessed to the detectives, had refused to repeat his confession to Assistant D.A. Vitale; this would lend credence to the argument that the confession had been extorted. Kase's own feelings about his client's guilt or innocence were mixed; though Valencia fervently denied any part in the murder and told him a rambling, semi-coherent tale about mistreatment, Kase had heard such things before (except for the use of ammonia), and took it at something less than face value. "I did believe," he says, "that there was some kind of force or pressure used. Psychological, but maybe physical, too—what sort and how much I don't know. Steve McCabe was a good friend of mine and I couldn't believe he himself would have done the things Valencia said he did, or Russo either, but I did believe unfair pressure was brought to bear."

After hearing Valencia's story, Kase said, "Look, suppose I could get you a Man One or Man Two—would you take it?" Valencia said absolutely not; he was innocent, so why should he take anything? Kase, wanting to believe him but knowing that even if Valencia were guilty he would undoubtedly stick to that position until he could see how things were going, agreed. "All right," he said, "that's it. We'll go to trial, probably in two or three months. I'll do everything I can. Leave it to me." In the next few weeks, between appointments and court appearances, he tried to establish Valencia's alibi, but without much success. The crime had occurred at 9:00 p.m., according to Valencia's confession, and he did find Idalia ready to swear that Doel had been with her at that very hour, packing their belongings in preparation for their move to another apartment. But the Ortiz confessions (which named Valencia) said that it had happened shortly after noontime, and a jury might believe them instead; besides, a jury might well suppose that a sister would lie to save her brother's life. Kase visited Consolidated Millinery and found that Valencia was credited with having put in a full day's work on October 9th—but although his time-card showed a morning punch-in, it had not been punched out in the afternoon (on Fridays, at Consolidated, all time-cards were collected early in the afternoon by the bookkeeper), and no one could remember having seen him there all day.

Feeling that there were no motions worth making, and that asking for particulars or an examination of the Grand Jury minutes was useless, Kase saw little else to do until the trial. His main strategy would be to hammer away at the detectives as to whether they had detained Valencia illegally overnight and used force to obtain his confession, point up the time conflict between that confession and those of the Ortiz brothers, and stress the fact that there was no evidence—at least, he hoped there would be none—other than the confessions.

If this approach succeeded, it would hardly matter what Kase himself thought. "No matter what, an accused man has a right to his day in court," he says. "I've represented many clients I *feel* are probably guilty, although they haven't admitted their guilt to me—but I can't plead them guilty just because I might think they are. If a man says, 'Don't cop me out, I want to try it,' I owe it to him to do just that. He has constitutional rights, and I have to protect them at all costs, because when I defend one man, I'm defending the rights of all Americans." He pauses, chuckles at his own lofty words, then adds, "Well, maybe that's partly baloney. I don't really think I'm protecting the whole American people every time I defend a client. I do it for a fee—that's important—but also for my ego; when I win a tough case, I feel great and I'll take a lot less money. I love pitting my talent against that of the other guy, the D.A., who usually has the odds in his favor, and when I win, it's a wonderful feeling."

So he went about his other business, and Doel Valencia was a file folder in his active drawer, a mere name that became a real individual once every couple of weeks when he saw him in court for a minute or two at a calendar call. In all, he met Valencia, Hanrahan, and the two Ortiz brothers at five such hearings. To him they were time-wasting and useless, but to the three accused youths they were major events which, though incomprehensible, interrupted the dreary, interminable round of days and weeks in jail and gave them brief glimpses of the outside world. They hungered for those interruptions, for by late February they had been in jail four months and were still not scheduled to appear again in court until early March. They could not understand the reasons for the long delay, or the brief, arcane rituals performed at their appearances and adjournments; still less could they understand why the three of them had been in jail so long and were going to be tried for the murder of Alexander Helmer, while Angel Walker had been a free man for the last three months and would never be tried at all.

They had no idea what Walker was doing with his precious freedom, but might have been surprised to learn that he was trying to look straight, at least for a while—he even briefly held a job in a photoprocessing laboratory on West 54th Street in Manhattan—perhaps because his $500,000 damage suit against the Transit Authority was now scheduled to be tried in April. If Walker ever thought about his old friends and their desperate situation, he never wrote them or offered to appear as a witness on their behalf, although, had they been telling the truth, his testimony might have been helpful to them. And neither James Hanrahan nor Kenneth Kase ever contacted Walker or asked him to appear as a witness, although if their clients and Walker were innocent, his account of how he had spent his time on the 9th might have helped offset their confessions. But both lawyers were specialists in their trade, and knew what they were doing.

# VI    *A Matter of Convictions*

THE defense lawyer is far from a free agent in his choice of strategy; what he does is determined in large part by what the prosecutor does, much as the possible strategies of Black, in chess, are limited by the opening chosen by White.

The prosecutor, however, has many more advantages than that of making the opening. If he thinks himself likely to lose, he can choose not to play the game at all; prosecutors have great discretionary power to pick and choose which arrested persons to prosecute, and which to let go. This discretionary power, euphemistically called "selective enforcement," is justified on the grounds that the prosecutor's and the court's limited time must be used to society's greatest advantage against the worst and socially most destructive criminals; in practice it often means that prosecutors go after the sure wins and drop the chancy cases, in order to look as good as possible.

The prosecutor also has a powerful tactical advantage in being free to choose from a range of applicable charges for any given crime. Generally he pursues a middle course, but he can charge very lightly if the accused is willing to sign himself into a rehabilitative program of one sort or another, or he can charge far higher than the crime ordinarily brings if he feels certain that the accused has been doing more than he was caught doing and wants to "burn" him. Most importantly, he can change his mind at the next-to-last moment, reducing the charge significantly if the prisoner cooperates by pleading guilty and waiving his right to a trial.

Although the prosecutor is strictly required to tell the defense lawyer anything he learns that is favorable to the accused, he need divulge little else; in most states, the greater part of what he has learned from the police or his own investigators remains his secret until he springs it on the defense at the trial. The defense lawyer has some idea, of course, based on his conferences with his client, what sort of information may be forthcoming, but most of the time he does not know exactly what witnesses will appear, what physical evidence will be introduced, or what statements will be offered for the record. He does his best to prepare his case in advance without knowing what evidence he will have to try to discredit on the spot, and, like every defender in war, has no idea until the enemy attacks whether or not he has disposed his forces wisely.

Finally, the prosecutor's motions and objections are more apt to be favored by the judge than those of the defense, for, although judges are supposed to be impartial, and although some are actually defendant-oriented, most feel themselves to be defenders of the social order and therefore basically on the same side as the prosecutor. The prosecutor, indeed, is cloaked in dignity and rectitude, for, as he always points out to juries, he is counsel for the People and is presenting the People's case. Nonetheless, his job is a full-time one only in large cities; the majority of American prosecutors work on a part-time basis and, in order to live, practice law privately on the side—a situation that is fraught with possibilities for conflict of interest. Most prosecutors' offices include no more than one or two appointed assistants on salary (the prosecutor himself being an elected official), and only in the largest cities is the prosecutor a full-time functionary with a staff of dozens or scores of assistant prosecutors, detectives, stenotypists, and others. But even when this is the case, the pay is poor compared to that of most other forms of private legal practice: in Bronx County, for instance, the starting salary of an assistant D.A. was only about $6,000 in 1964, at a time when such assistants were appointed "right out of the political clubhouse," and moonlighting with a private practice was not only permitted but was particularly useful because of one's official status. More recently, under District Attorney Burton Roberts, private practice has been forbidden and assistants are hired on merit, beginning at $11,000 (or $12,000 if they have already been admitted to the bar), which is at least a living wage; unfortunately, there is little financial future in remaining long in the D.A.'s office, for even after ten or fifteen years an assistant, unless he finds favor with the District Attorney, may still be earning only $16,000 or so, a small fraction of what he might have been earning had he spent those years in a downtown law firm.

In the smaller communities, where the D.A.'s job is part-time, his pay is sometimes absurdly small: a 1965 survey found that some of the prosecutors in twenty-one different states were getting under $4,000 a year—hardly more, hour for hour, than the cleaning ladies who came after hours to do their offices. Those offices, incidentally, were no better than the pay: assistant D.A.s and the D.A.s themselves generally rate cheerless, economical chambers, often equipped with wooden chairs, linoleum on the floor, and pale-green institutional paint on the walls, rather than the leather sofas and chairs, deep-pile carpeting, and wood-paneled walls that are the classic perquisites of the successful lawyer.

What sort of men (or, occasionally, women) choose to undertake such heavy responsibilities at such inadequate pay? Two kinds: the idealistic and the ambitious. The idealists are bright young men right out of law school who sign on as assistant D.A.s, hoping to do important and constructive work for their society. The ambitious, a much larger group, are somewhat older men—usually practicing attorneys with an eye toward politics or a judgeship—who see the office of prosecutor as a steppingstone to better things and who run for office as part of the local slate put up by their political party.*

* In only half a dozen states and the federal system are prosecutors appointed, and even there, according to the Crime Commission, partisan politics plays a large part in their selection.

Only a few of the gifted and a few hacks remain in office (or remain as appointed assistant D.A.s) for a long while; most others move on in a few years. The idealists leave because of the lure of more money—a move made easier by the fact that their idealism soon turns sour. They intend at first to help protect society against the ravages of crime (and at the same time to protect individuals against the invasion of their civil rights); they mean to question the police closely and to reject cases which are not legally meritorious; they mean to spend their time prosecuting not just the sure things but the cases in which conviction will benefit society the most. But all too soon, their high ideals are eroded by everyday reality. There is, for one thing, the unbelievable pressure of the caseload: as of 1971, there were somewhere on the order of 20,000 to 25,000 prosecutors and assistant prosecutors in the fifty states, handling close to a million felony indictments, plus part of some five to six million misdemeanor indictments, per year. (The rest of the misdemeanors were handled by police courts and magistrates' courts without prosecutors.) With workloads that often run to over a hundred cases per man, per year, in large cities, prosecutors hardly have time to interrogate the police painstakingly, evaluate their truthfulness, and exercise the kind of supervision over them that they had had in mind. The vast influx of new cases, the huge backlog of old untried ones, the horrors of jail conditions, the intolerable delays in bringing jailed persons to trial, the inequities brought about by the bail system, the frustrating dilatory tactics of defense lawyers—all these and other hard facts of everyday prosecutorial life gradually induce feelings of despair and cynicism or, at the very least, of doubt about the value of what they are doing. One very bright young lawyer, upon leaving the Manhattan D.A.'s office after four years as an assistant, spoke for many young men like himself:

> Often I felt I did significant public service—I sometimes got cases dropped that didn't warrant prosecution at all, I got others dismissed where there had been incorrect police conduct (and maybe educated the police a little by so doing), and, most important of all, I protected the public by getting some of those who were likely to harm them out of the way for a while. But sometimes when I'd look at the volume of cases we couldn't handle or had to drop, or had to bargain down to almost nothing,

I would wonder what good my long, hard hours of work were doing. It was like putting a Band-Aid on a mortal wound. And even when I did get a really vicious criminal sent away, I'd wonder what I'd accomplished, because what with parole, he'd be back in a few years, worse than ever after his prison experience. Sometimes it would seem to me we'd be better off not sentencing him at all, unless we could send him away for the rest of his life. But as long as I was in the D.A.'s office, I had to fight against such feelings; they made my day-to-day life impossible.

Many prosecutors quit; those who stay on, hoping to make something of a career within the system, must make an accommodation with themselves—one surprisingly like the adjustment reached by the typical defense lawyer, for even though they tell themselves they are fighting crime and seeing to it that the law is fairly and properly used, in actual fact they become all-absorbed by the need to obtain convictions in the specific cases they are handling, feeling successful and fulfilled when they get them either at trial or through plea-bargaining. They come from law school armed with the courage of their convictions; after a while, it is through convictions of another sort that they find the courage to go on. "My ultimate objective is to get some bad egg off the street for a while," says one typical assistant D.A. in Washington, "and each time I succeed, I feel I've done some good. I feel I've beaten an enemy. It's a wonderful feeling."

But except in the largest cities, idealists—whether new-minted or worn—do not make up the bulk of the prosecutorial forces. The great majority of elected heads of the local offices—the District Attorneys, County Attorneys, County Prosecutors, or any of several other names by which they are variously known—are, basically, politically motivated, and though most of them have some real interest in combating crime and in seeing the law decently and fairly administered, their more compelling aim is to look good in office, to make a good name for themselves, to gratify the public, and to become politically valuable to their parties as future candidates for better and more rewarding offices, especially judgeships.

Few of those who remain for any length of time are highly talented; on the other hand, few of those who stay for many years, being periodically reelected, or who remain as paid assistants in big-city D.A.s' offices, are incompetents. Like most civil servants, most of those who make a long-term career as local prosecutors are mediocrities. Probably it does not matter: most prosecutions call for doggedness, thoroughness, and the use of proven legal weapons rather than brilliant improvisation, subtle interpretations, and legal innovation. Whatever achievements the present prosecutorial system can be credited with, they are largely the by-product of political ambition on the one hand, and of *petit fonctionnaire* mediocrity on the other.

There might well be a better way for a justice system to prosecute criminals, but this one, considering its defects, works somewhat better than one might suppose it would, actually managing to achieve convictions in a little over half of the serious crimes for which police have made arrests.* Actually, rolling up a large number of convictions is not the most important goal of most prosecutors, according to sociologist Jerome Skolnick. After intensive field observation, he reached the conclusion that the prosecutor's goal is not so much to win as it is not to lose. It is not his total score of victories that matters, but the ratio of wins to losses, for, says Professor Skolnick, "he seeks to maintain, insofar as possible, a reputation for utter credibility, inevitable truth, almost of invincibility."

This is his goal not so much because it will get him reelected, but because it is the by-product of his upward striving within the justice system. For his social status in that system lies somewhere above that of the policeman and below that of the judge: when he first listens to the policeman presenting evidence, the prosecutor acts in a somewhat judge-like fashion, questioning him closely, obeying the rule of law, ferreting out untruthfulness, rejecting improperly gathered evidence; but when he decides to press charges, he himself becomes accusatorial and appears in the courtroom as the ally of the policeman, and is subject to rulings, orders, and rebukes coming from the judge. His chief desire is to enhance his role and elevate his status, dissociating himself from whatever is police-like in his role; he seeks esteem, says Professor Skolnick, in the form of recognition that he is a judge-like official, and often yearns to be chosen by his party to run for a judgeship. Nothing would damage his posture more than a series of courtroom defeats, nothing would enhance it more than a series

---

* But this reflects the effectiveness of prosecution, not of the whole criminal justice system. Police learn of only about half of all serious crimes, and make arrests in only one fifth of these cases; prosecutors carry through on four fifths of the arrests and achieve convictions in about 70 percent of these cases. The net result is that the system manages to produce convictions in only 5.6 percent of all serious crimes. This overall figure is even lower than that for robberies in particular (see page 27 above).

of courtroom victories. So he pursues victories—and, even more so, non-losses—not so much for their own sake as for the light they shed upon his character and his acumen as a true judge of guilt and innocence.

Thus it comes about that the bulk of prosecutions handled within our system are the work not of the idealistic but of the ambitious; that ambition and vanity, rather than ethics, make them drop most of the cases in which the evidence is of doubtful legality; and that in the end a considerable degree of fairness characterizes the prosecution of crime in this cpuntry because such conduct on the prosecutors' part helps them to rise higher in the scheme of things.

The recognition of these realities need not make one cynical. Human beings are not so much weak as they are malleable; an evil system can make them evil, but a good system can make them good. A justice system which encourages prosecutors to harass or punish, with impunity, people they dislike or disagree with, or to try accused persons by unfair means, will make merciless inquisitors out of ordinary men; but a system which subtly encourages prosecutors to be fair out of self-interest, and to a considerable extent succeeds in making them so, is a good system. The worst thing about our criminal justice system is its dreadful inefficiency; the best thing about it is its ethical impact upon the people within it.

# VII  *I'm Proud of My Record*

ON the southwest corner of the sixth floor of the Bronx County Courthouse, Mr. Isidore Dollinger, District Attorney of the Bronx, had a spacious, carpeted, well-furnished corner office befitting his rank; down the hall on that floor and the one just above it, in a series of drab, spartan rooms, were his 39 assistant D.A.s and 62 assorted investigators, clerks, stenotypists, and other ancillary personnel, their distance from Dollinger's office being roughly indicative of their status. One of those rooms, fairly far from the District Attorney's center of power, was occupied by Alexander E. Scheer, an assistant D.A. assigned primarily to the trying of Bronx murder cases. Scheer was an old hand at it: in fifteen years on the D.A.'s staff he had handled thousands of criminal cases, including hundreds of murders, and had actually tried fifty or more of the latter before juries. In his office, preparing those cases, he had heard almost everything there was to hear about modern urban murder: detectives, special investigators, relatives, neighbors, coroners, assistant D.A.s, accidental eyewitnesses, stenographers, and defense lawyers had told him innumerable tragic, sordid, revolting, and sometimes merely absurd stories, and while the accused persons themselves were almost never brought to that room to tell their tales, even they were often present in a fashion, in the form of their statements or confessions.

Although the tales recounted in that room could have made an *Arabian Nights* of modern urban homicide, the room itself had no special aura, being only a bare, institutional office such as might be occupied by the chief clerk of a small-town highway department. It had a drab, brownish asphalt-tile floor, pale-green walls much scarred by chair backs, and one large window half covered by an aged, cracked, rain-stained tan windowshade. Against the walls were several straight-backed wooden chairs, a long library table loaded with fat folders of legal papers, and a row of battered dark-green filing cabinets. In front of the window, commanding the room, was a large metal business desk covered with correspondence, briefs, and miscellaneous papers, its one decorative touch being a tiny American flag stuck in a penholder.

The décor of Alexander Scheer's office was only in part a matter of departmental budgetary limitations, for his own personal touches, on the walls, were of the same genre: framed photographs of his gray-haired boss, District Attorney Dollinger, and of the late Justice Brandeis; two landscape paintings executed by filling in numbered areas with colors from numbered tubes; his law-school diploma, various certificates, plaques, and citations; and a faded banquet photograph, taken many years earlier.

Behind the desk (whenever he was not in court) Alexander Scheer sat like a spider in the center of a web, patiently waiting his time and then seizing, paralyzing, and wrapping up in testimony whatever prey came within reach. At the time of the Helmer murder, Scheer was in his mid-fifties, though he had looked much the same for twenty years, being one of those short, pudgy, inflexible men who seem middle-aged from their early years on. His large, round head, with neat graying hair, seemed attached directly to his body without any neck and unable to turn freely. Nothing about him, in fact, moved freely, least of all his features: with his hooked nose, tight, down-curving mouth, and emotionless eyes behind steel-rimmed glasses, he resembled a turtle perhaps more than a spider, rigid-faced, inscrutable, and expressionless. His whole body style, indeed, was inflexible: he stood very erect, leaning a little backward to counterbalance his belly, and when seated at his desk, he tilted back a little in his chair but never slumped, leaned on one elbow, folded his arms, or crossed his legs. When questioning a detective or witness, he stared fixedly at his visitor, his face impassive and his stubby fingers sometimes drumming idly on the desktop; those he questioned would often feel uneasy in his presence and try hard to please him with their answers. He was, above all, painstaking and careful; indeed, every sentence he uttered, even among friends and associates, sounded as if made for the record. All of which had its advantages: though many judges have long considered him exasperatingly cautious and slow-moving, they have also acknowledged that he is a thoroughly competent trial prosecutor, and his principal satisfaction in life is the fact that he has won nearly all his cases by his careful preparation and relentless courtroom manner. "I try a hard case," he says, permitting himself a tiny self-congratulatory smile. "My percentage of convictions is very, very high—about ninety percent. I'm proud of my record."

It has been a bitter disappointment to him that, despite this record, he has risen no further than his present position. Considering how far he had come by his thirties, he used to think there would be still greater things ahead. Alexander Scheer was the youngest of eight children of a Russian-Jewish immigrant who peddled shoes from a pushcart on the lower East Side, and whose huge family, jammed into a four-room apartment, lived in conditions no better than those which seem today to breed the kind of persons Scheer prosecutes for murder. Young Scheer, however, like so many sons of immigrant Jews, Italians, and Irish, fought to belong to the society around him. He earned a few dollars whenever he could, made his way through City College, and worked his way through the law school of St. Lawrence University, in Brooklyn. He went into private practice, handling damage suits, contracts, wills, and various other matters for some years, and did middling well at it, but he had to leave for several years of military service and afterward decided not to start all over again in private practice but to go into government work. He served as a staff lawyer on first one city agency and then another, and, being still a bachelor (he did not marry until he was thirty-nine) and having his widowed mother to keep house for him, he had plenty of time to dabble in clubhouse politics and do grass-roots work for a Bronx Democratic club. Eventually he got his reward, being appointed an assistant D.A. in 1950 by the then District Attorney of Bronx County, a loyal Democrat.

But this, which seemed the important step toward greater things, proved a dead end. He remained an assistant D.A. year after year, advancing only to the extent of being assigned as a trial specialist in murder cases and not even becoming the head of that bureau. Yet he continued to work hard, and at night often left his wife and son to take part in organizational activities (he belongs to the Lions Club of the Bronx, the National Conference of Christians and Jews, the American Legion, a variety of lawyers' organizations, and, of course, the local Democratic club). But all in vain. "For all his clubhouse politicking," says a former colleague, "he hasn't gotten anywhere. He just hasn't got whatever it is that makes a man succeed in that game." A criminal lawyer who has known him for years says, "It used to be that if you stuck it out long enough as an assistant D.A., the party would get you appointed a Criminal Court judge, but somehow they never gave Al Scheer the break. He's a very frustrated man."

Which is pure speculation; no one can see behind the façade of his face. He still works as hard as ever, tackling every case as if there were all the time in the world, and as if every grubby felony murder were the *crime passionel* of the decade. He has the grudging respect of many of the defense lawyers who have opposed him in court, though some of the latter have been known to say that Scheer cares nothing for justice but only for convictions. Even young assistants in his office have been heard to apply to him (in jest, of course) an old prosecutorial wheeze: "Anybody can convict the guilty, but only Al Scheer can convict the innocent."

The Helmer murder case came to his attention only after the Ortiz brothers and Doel Valencia had been indicted by the Grand Jury. As soon as the defendants were arrested and charged with the crime, the case became the responsibility of the District Attorney's office, and various assistant D.A.s handled it up to the point of the Grand Jury hearing. There, one of them named Theodore Eppinger explained to twenty-six men and women assembled in a large, wood-paneled Grand Jury room in the Bronx County Courthouse why the District Attorney's office thought the Ortiz brothers and Doel Valencia ought to be prosecuted, and why Angel Walker, though indicated in the others' confessions as the guiltiest of the four, was beyond the reach of the law and should not be indicted. He then called in a few witnesses one at a time, and, questioning them, led them through quick, informal versions of the testimony they would give if there was a trial. McCabe was the principal witness, but even he testified briefly and from memory, without notes or documents in hand, since Grand Jury hearings require only a *prima facie* showing. The Grand Jury, having heard this much of the evidence, did what Eppinger had asked them to do (Grand Juries, indeed, are generally responsive to the D.A.'s suggestions and advice), voting no true bill against Walker but an indictment against the other three which read as follows:

The Grand Jury of the County of Bronx, by this indictment accuse defendants

Alfredo Ortiz, Doel Valencia, and Carlos Ortiz

of the crime of MURDER IN THE FIRST DEGREE committed as follows:

The said defendants, acting in concert with each other and with another person in the County of Bronx, on the ninth day of October 1964 wilfully, feloniously and of their malice aforethought, did strike, stab and wound one Alexander Helmer, with a certain knife, and did thereby inflict divers wounds upon the said Alexander Helmer, of which said wounds, the said Alexander Helmer, thereafter, to wit on or about and between the said ninth day of October, 1964 and the eighteenth day of October, 1964, in the County of Bronx aforesaid, did die.

The case was thereupon assigned to Scheer, who gathered all the available materials—the court records to date, the minutes of the

Grand Jury testimony, the texts of the confessions, the medical examiner's report—and began to study them. When he could find time, he invited the key witnesses in to discuss the evidence with him, and explored in detail the strengths and weaknesses of his case, seeking to anticipate the defense's counterattacks and making sure he would be able to deal with them.

Either he never felt any doubts about the justice and fairness of the People's case, or he has since erased these doubts from his mind; or perhaps his long years as an assistant D.A. have made it impossible for him to think about his work except in the form of pietistic certitudes. For instance: Was he never troubled by the thought that the police had cut corners in order to detain the suspects and make them talk? *It is incumbent upon me to determine that the rights of the defendant have been protected. I did inquire as to the surrounding circumstances of the statements taken from the suspects, and I was impressed with the fact that their rights had been protected.* But did he feel quite sure that the detectives had told him the truth, without cleaning things up a little? *From my close association with the arresting officers in this case over many years, I believe they are excellent and dedicated investigators, truthful officers, doing a magnificent job.* But don't investigators—even excellent and dedicated ones—misuse their powers sometimes in order to get a confession where they feel certain the recalcitrant suspect is guilty? *I have no recollection of any case—any case—where the powers of police officers have been misused or have exceeded proper bounds. Of course, if I had confessions I felt were not obtained voluntarily, I certainly would not offer them into evidence.* Wasn't his belief in the confessions—at least those of the Ortiz brothers—weakened by Mrs. Ambos' statement that she saw Helmer alive a little after 7:00 p.m. that day? *She was an elderly woman, and in view of the confessions, her recollections of the time had to be faulty. She did not seem worth calling as a witness.* But mightn't her testimony seem important to the jury? Shouldn't they have a chance to judge things for themselves? *It could very well be that her thought processes were not too accurate, and I wouldn't want to put someone on the stand under these circumstances.* Didn't it trouble Scheer that there were no corroborating fingerprints, no eyewitnesses, nothing to verify the confessions? *Not at all. Besides, we did have confessions not from one but from three defendants.* But how could all three be guilty? How could all three confessions be true, considering their discrepancies? *We can't attempt to account for the discrepancies in confessions, and it really doesn't make much difference; they all admitted that they acted in concert. Actually, when I have several stories that fit perfectly, I'm not happy; I relish the idea of slight differences in testimony—it shows truthfulness.* Then he never felt, even momentarily, that the defendants might have been the innocent victims of police error, or of excessive diligence in the quest for confessions? *The D.A. is not the judge and jury. It isn't for him to decide that the defendant is innocent or guilty. He presents the evidence in open court, and it is up to the jury to decide where the truth lies. Of course, if he feels the evidence he has is insufficient to convict, he's not going to prosecute.* Didn't it ever trouble him that he was prosecuting for Murder One and possibly sending to the electric chair three youths who had not intended to murder anyone nor actually done so, and one of whom had only been a lookout downstairs? *They all understood what they were going in for before the crime was committed. They knew what they were doing.* Didn't it bother him—didn't it make the whole prosecution seem wrong, somehow—that the person named in the confessions as the real killer had gotten off scot-free because the New York law is stricter, concerning accomplice testimony, even than federal law? *The New York rule about accomplice testimony is a hardship on the prosecution; no question about it.*

Weeks passed. Although Scheer was busy with scores of other cases, he found time, here and there, to gather and stuff into a bulging manila folder everything he needed to present his case against the Ortiz brothers and Doel Valencia—pictures, diagrams, police data as to the past records of the defendants, medical reports on their condition when received in jail, notes about his conferences with witnesses, correspondence with the jail warden, Hanrahan's applications for information and his own rejoinders. Scheer even got to know the defendants by sight, having appeared in court several times at calendar calls concerning their case, though he and they never spoke to each other.

The closer the trial date came, the readier both sides were to strike a bargain and save themselves the uncertainties and the protracted exertions of an actual jury trial. Scheer saw both Hanrahan and Kase in the courthouse hallways from time to time and at several of the calendar calls on the case, and casually sounded them out as to the chance of settling the matter without trial. But he made it clear that while he would bargain, he would insist that the defendants plead to something serious enough to result in a sentence of some consequence. *I try to be as fair as one can be in recommending lesser pleas, but the plea has to be one that gives the court adequate scope to impose a fair sentence. Obviously we cannot try all the cases on the calendar, but the plea has to be a sufficient one. If they had been serious about pleading guilty to manslaughter in the first degree, for instance, I might very well have recommended it to the court, keeping in mind their youth and the fact that someone else did the stabbing. But they wouldn't take it, and I certainly wouldn't recommend anything less.*

Hanrahan was blocked by the obduracy of the Ortiz brothers. "The D.A. approached me to see if we wanted to take a plea," he says, "but we never got down to real bargaining because the boys wouldn't go for it." Kase's recollections are similar: "Scheer came up to me one day —I think it was right after one of our hearings on the case—and said something like, 'Look, would you be willing to take a Man One on this?' I said I'd see what I could do, because I thought it was a pretty good offer. I went to Valencia and told him, 'They're ready to offer you something. They don't want to try this case. You could get a good deal.' But I couldn't get him to take a thing."

Which meant that the defense lawyers had a lot of hard work and courtroom time ahead of them; that the defendants would be exposing themselves to the risk of life sentences or even of the death penalty; that a judge, a battery of stenographers, a court clerk, a courtroom, a handful of guards, and fourteen citizens would be committed to the case for two or three weeks; and that Alexander Scheer, who would have been happy to settle the matter cheaply in five minutes, content to see the defendants get five years or so, now had to try with all his skill to convict them of Murder in the First Degree.

# VIII   *Justice Without Trial*

EVERY American knows how accused persons are dealt with by our courts: they are tried before juries of their peers and found either guilty or not guilty. Every American knows this because he has learned about it in school and seen it innumerable times in the newspapers, in drama, and in fiction. What he knows, however, happens to be untrue. Although the Sixth Amendment guarantees each accused person the *right* to a jury trial, in reality criminal trials are only flags bravely fluttering on top of the structure—the edifice of criminal convictions obtained by private, unseen bargaining in which confessions are offered and given in trade for the reduction of charges and the minimizing of punishment. Our courts handle nine tenths of criminal cases not through trials but through guilty pleas, most of which result from unofficial deals; the system is geared to "dispose" of cases rather than put them to the test of truth, and punishes the accused not according to what they did but according to the going rates for copping a plea. In Professor Jerome Skolnick's acerbic phrase, criminal justice in the United States is mostly "a system of justice without trial."

Not that this system forcibly deprives the accused of their rights: by and large, they participate in it willingly because they know a good thing when they see one. Those who plead guilty almost always get much lighter sentences than those who put the prosecution to the test; in one recent study of U.S. District Courts, defendants who pleaded guilty averaged sentences only half as weighty as those who were convicted of the same crimes through jury trials. The worse court congestion is, and the more eager court officials are to avoid trials, the harder a bargain the accused person can drive: the *New York Times* survey of muggings mentioned earlier showed that 62 percent of accused muggers were permitted to plead guilty to lesser offenses, and that, as a result, their sentences averaged 12.4 months, although in early 1967, according to law, the crimes they committed should have cost them up to seven years for unarmed robbery and up to twenty-five for armed robbery.

Prosecutors and judges hand out such bargains today because they have no alternative: the jails and the courts are so jammed with accused persons, and the continual influx of new cases is so huge, that it has become absolutely impossible to try more than a tenth of the cases that merit prosecution. The criminal justice system would collapse if the courts had to try all, or even a substantial minority, of the indicted. Chief Justice Warren E. Burger recently pointed out to the American Bar Association that if only 80 percent of defendants rather than the present 90 percent pleaded guilty—that is, if 20 percent rather than 10 percent insisted on trial—we would need twice the number of judges, reporters, bailiffs, clerks, jurors, and courtrooms we now have. If a movement to insist upon trial were to become widespread among defendants, the system would completely break down.

Meanwhile every prisoner knows the advantages of cooperating in plea-bargaining and the penalties for refusing to do so. The stubborn prisoner may remain in jail many months before being tried—and if he is convicted, the prosecutor and judge are likely to consider that he "deserves" severe sentencing for his refusal to cooperate. The stubborn prosecutor, on the other hand, knows that unless he cooperates with defense lawyers, they may retaliate by demanding trial for every case they have on hand, thereby strangling his office. Everyone knows, in short, that cooperation is necessary; but it is also necessary to talk tough, demand more than one expects, haggle like a fishwife, and then —not a moment too soon, not a moment too late—strike a bargain.

Thus the system of justice that guarantees fair trial to every defendant cannot presently make good on that guarantee today, but has to depend on a kind of sharp trading which was never intended by the lawmakers who framed the Constitution, and which, according to a Task Force Report to the Crime Commission, is a source of unease and ethical discomfort to nearly everyone in criminal law.

This may be why plea-bargaining has been discussed so little in public, and has almost no official status nor any regulatory mechanisms. It exists as an open secret, an everyday transaction conducted off the record, often in whispers or behind closed doors. Everyone knows what is happening and what kinds of things are being said, but everyone lies for the official record, talking as if no deals, inducements, and understandings existed. Sometimes a participant will renege—a defendant may, at the last moment, refuse to go through with the guilty plea, or a judge may, depending on the state of his digestion, slap a tougher sentence on the defendant than he said he would—but such things are rare: the viability of plea-bargaining depends on the personal confidence prosecutors, judges, and defense lawyers have that all parties will stick to the unofficial deal—the existence of which is explicitly denied by all hands in court.

The bargaining process was excellently depicted in the March 11th, 1971, issue of *Newsweek,* in a major study of the criminal justice system. In a Chicago case involving armed robbery, the key persons spoke to each other as follows:

"Plead guilty, jackass, you could get ten to twenty for this," [Public Defender] Xinos whispered when they finally got to trial. *Ain't no need for that,* said [defendant] Payne. "You really want a jury?" the assistant state's attorney, Walter Parrish, teased him. . . .

Xinos took Parrish aside. "Let's get rid of this case," he said.

"It's Christmas," Parrish said amiably. "I'm a reasonable man."

"What do you want?" Xinos asked.

"I was thinking about three to eight."

"One to five," said Xinos.

"You got it."

*It's an absolute gift,* Xinos thought, and he took it to Payne in the lock-up. "I can get you one to five," he said. Payne said no. . . . "You may get ten to twenty going on with the trial."

"Well, even if I take the one to five, I'm not guilty."

But would [Judge] Fitzgerald buy it? . . . [In his chambers] Fitzgerald scanned Parrish's prep sheet, outlining the state case. Xinos told him glumly, "We look beat."

"Walter," asked the judge, "what do you want?"

"I don't want to hurt the kid," Parrish said. "I talked to Connie [Xinos], and we thought one to five. . . ."

"Will he take it?" the judge asked Xinos.

"I'll go back and see," Xinos replied. He ducked out to the lock-up and put the offer to Payne.

"Let's do it," said Payne. "Right now."

But after such negotiating, the judge usually asks the prisoner in open court, for the record, whether anyone has made him any promises or inducements that have led him to plead guilty, and whether the prisoner understands that the judge is making him no promises as to the sentence he will impose. The judge asks all this quite earnestly, the prisoner dutifully utters the right lies, the stenographer takes everything down accurately, and the prosecutor and defender look on seriously without so much as a shadow of a smile, the entire charade being necessary to prevent the prisoner from later asking for a new trial on the grounds that his guilty plea was induced or coerced.

Plea-bargaining, the basic *modus operandi* of our courts today, is thus a wholly different method of dispensing justice from the truth-seeking, adversarial trial by jury guaranteed by our laws and idealized in our cultural mythology. Yet we have come so far that without some vast enlargement of the present system—vaster by far than we now have personnel available for—we cannot do without it. The Crime Commission recommended that we not even attempt to do away with it but bring it out in the open, legitimizing it and making the bargaining process part of the record; the American Bar Association and various state and federal courts have recognized the propriety of plea-bargaining in recent years, provided there were proper safeguards upon it; and in May 1970 the United States Supreme Court, under Chief Justice Burger, ruled six to three that it is constitutional for a state to extend a benefit (in the form of a reduced sentence) to a defendant who in turn is extending a benefit to the state by willingly admitting to his crime and sparing the state the need to try him. A few months later the Court went still further; it held that even if a defendant maintains he is innocent, he can be allowed to enter a guilty plea in order to get a bargain conviction.

One might suppose that criminal defendants would regard plea-bargaining as a boon, and would feel grateful to their defense lawyers for getting them good deals. By and large, they do not. The mythology of prisoners and convicts—the posture they adopt and come to believe in—is that they were innocent, or at least could have been acquitted, but were pressured into pleading guilty by their own lawyers, who were playing the prosecutor's game. They suspect their lawyers of wanting to get the case over with quickly and easily, of wanting to curry favor with the D.A., of getting payoffs of one kind or another for inducing them to plead guilty. A defense lawyer may quite truthfully point out to his client that the evidence against him is very strong, that defendants are convicted in the great majority of jury trials, that judges are often harder on those convicted in a jury trial than those who plead guilty, that bargaining can (and often does) reduce a felony charge to a misdemeanor charge, which means not only a far shorter sentence but little or no loss of civil rights, and that, all things considered, the defense lawyer has managed to get him a very good offer. All this may be true, and may cause the defendant to take the deal; but after his first feeling of relief, he rapidly becomes resentful, cynical, and embittered, and feels that he was sold out.

Not, however, because he is innocent and was unjustly convicted, but because he senses and interprets as corrupt the interaction between defense lawyer and prosecutor, and between each and the judge. Convicted prisoners and members of the militant left even see public defenders as agents of the Establishment: in the New York *Village Voice,* an article on the Legal Aid Society was entitled, "Defending the Poor: Lawyer as Hangman." But this view is not wholly paranoid, for, according to Abraham S. Blumberg, professor of sociology and law at the John Jay College of Criminal Justice, it is not so much by combat that the defense lawyer and the prosecutor each achieves his own goals as by a species of cooperation. The defender does not sell out his client, but he does work for both sides, acting as a necessary intermediary between the client and the prosecution. "In his role as double agent," Professor Blumberg says, "the criminal lawyer performs a vital and delicate mission for the court organization and the accused. Both principals are anxious to terminate the litigation with a minimum of expense and damage to each other"—the defense attorney being ideally situated to bring this about through the plea-bargaining process. Both sides ought to be grateful to him, for he has served both. He gets no gratitude from his client, however, who belongs to a subculture which sees the dominant society and all its representatives as enemies, but the prosecutor, who may have been arguing with him hotly only a little while ago, now smiles, shakes his hand, and treats him as a friend.

Most prisoners are firmly convinced that public defenders are particularly loath to go to trial and quick to pressure them to plead guilty. Even if true, however, it may well be that public defenders, not having to impress their clients, do not bother to strike a posture of vigorous defense, doing instead what they think most realistic and effective. In a study of felony cases made in Cook County (Chicago), lawyers of the public-defender agency pleaded their clients guilty 82 percent of the time as compared to 68 percent for private defense lawyers, reserving for trial those cases where they felt that the time and effort—and the additional risk to the client—were justified. Apparently they were right: when they did go to trial, they got their clients acquitted half the time, while private defense lawyers won acquittals at trial less than a quarter of the time.

The best one can say of plea-bargaining is that it works—which is also the worst one can say of it. It preserves the criminal justice system from total collapse, but perverts the central ideal of fair trial and abandons the search for truth. It benefits society by achieving convictions in a majority of criminal cases, but only by giving up any effort to administer just punishment and by handing out sentences so short as to negate any value imprisonment may have. It punishes (even if inadequately) many of the guilty, but it also punishes a certain number of the innocent who, because of a bad record or some other factor, dare not risk going to trial, or who plead guilty to end the indefinite wait for trial.

We can be thankful that plea-bargaining exists (but grieved that we need it), for without it we would have no criminal justice system at all; we can also be deeply chagrined that in letting it become essential, we have badly damaged the most precious aspect of our system of law: its ethical idealism. The Supreme Court, in sanctioning plea-bargaining, avoided plunging the nation's courts into chaos, but did nothing to show us how to regain our lost ideals. The Court's endorsement of plea-bargaining as an exchange of benefits between state and criminal is wholly pragmatic—and wholly lacking in the kind of vision that created a society whose members once were proud of it.

# IX *Are You Ready?*

THEY came together at last, nearly five months to the day after Alexander Helmer, having considered the weather, had dressed himself warmly for his walk to the A&P. Since then fall had deepened into winter, Christmas had passed, the New Year had begun, and after passing slowly through the outer barrens of winter the northern hemisphere was slowly beginning to tilt back toward the sun. But Monday morning, March 8th, was one of those end-of-winter days when the pale, chilled city-dweller feels as if the spring, with its warmth, light, and new life, is still unbearably far off. It was raw and chilly, the sky gray and heavy, the trees black and bony in the park next to the Bronx County Courthouse, the grass dead and matted, like the hair of some drowned creature. People coming to the courthouse hunched their shoulders against the wind, hurrying up the steps and into the shelter of the stately white building. They crowded into the elevators, preoccupied with their own thoughts—lawyers with briefcases, policemen unbuttoning their heavy blanket-like coats, worried-looking men and women with sullen youths in tow, secretaries and officious-looking clerks, burly, cold-eyed detectives, and a miscellany of people carrying newspapers and books to while away the hours of sitting in the jury room.

One case on which some of them would be called got under way a little later that morning in a large, impressive courtroom on the sixth floor—one of the courtrooms in which the New York Supreme Court in Bronx County holds hearings and trials. It was a chamber to enter with awe, one's voice dropping to a whisper—wood-paneled, two stories high, with many-branched brass chandeliers hanging from the ceiling, an imposing, elevated bench for the judge, a spacious jury box with chairs upholstered in green leather, and a large, stage-like area before the bench, with long counsel tables and a number of chairs, set off from the spectator section by a handsome, heavy wooden banister.

In that room, a number of people had assembled by 11:00 a.m. The half-dozen uniformed courtroom attendants, the clerk of the court, and a stenographer had come from their modest apartments and row houses in different parts of the Bronx. Justice Irwin D. Davidson, seated behind the bench, magisterial in his black robe, a short but commanding presence, square-jawed and firm-fleshed, a former United States Congressman and long-time judge, had come here this morning on loan from Manhattan, where he lived in a Fifth Avenue apartment house that was impeccable, orderly, and utterly unlike the building at 399 East 160th Street. Below him at the counsel table to the left (as seen from the spectators' section) was Alexander Scheer, small but stiffly erect, stony-faced and on guard, here ostensibly to seek retribution on behalf of society for the murder of an old man no one cared about, but really, like some latter-day Leonidas making his hopeless stand at Thermopylae, to fight against the wave of criminality sweeping upward from the south Bronx and westward from Melrose until it had all but reached his own nearby middle-class apartment area. At the defendants' tables were Kenneth Kase, in from New Rochelle, jaunty and smiling after a busy bachelor weekend; near him James Hanrahan, ponderous and serious, the self-styled idealist who had come here this morning from the shabby streets and dingy tenements of East Harlem where he preferred to live and to serve the people he knew best; and, finally, Alfredo Ortiz, Carlos Ortiz, and Doel Valencia, all three of them pale, silent, and expressionless, freshly shaved early that morning in the jail barber shop and dressed shabbily but cleanly in slacks and zipper jackets, sitting here almost like anyone else although they had just come from jail, with handcuffs clamped on their wrists during the ride, to defend themselves against the accusation that five months ago they had helped to murder an old man in his kitchen, half a dozen blocks from this quiet, formal chamber in which all was so orderly, lawful, and under control.

Back in the spectator seats were other people who had business here this morning: on one side of the center aisle, sad, pale little Luisa Pomales, hoping against hope that her sons would be found innocent, her life totally disarranged by now—her welfare cut off, her daughter sent back to Puerto Rico to live with the grandmother, her neighbors become so hostile (always pointing her out as "the mother of the murderers") that she had sold her few poor things and moved in with a cousin; a handful of courtroom buffs—retired white-collar workers and middle-aged housewives—who came to Supreme Court every day to shop around for an interesting case to watch; and, on the other side of the aisle, some fifty or sixty potential jurors—a mixed lot of people, mostly men, some youthful and some not, some black and some white, some poorly dressed and some better-dressed, their coats on their laps, hopeful that after days of tedious waiting in the jury room they were at last going to be in on something, and curious as to what the three pale, meek boys at the defense table could possibly have done to make the ponderous machinery of the law bring all these people together here this morning.

Others who would eventually be here had not yet been summoned. McCabe, Russo, various other policemen, and the medical examiner had been notified that they would be called in on short notice when needed to testify, as had Rose Pavese and Ena Varela, Helmer's neighbors. Mrs. Ambos, however, had heard nothing and was going about her chores at the apartment house this morning unmindful of Helmer, of whom every trace had long since disappeared, some of his furniture and possessions having been sold off by the lawyer and the rest carted away by the Sanitation Department, his apartment re-painted and inhabited now by a young Southern housewife with child, whose husband was away in the service.

Justice Davidson looked over at the clerk of the court, Joseph Jay, and nodded. Jay rose to his feet, a paper in his hand, and proclaimed, "People of the State of New York against Alfredo and Carlos Ortiz and Doel Valencia. The Assistant District Attorney is present, each defendant's counsel and each defendant is present." Then, looking at Scheer, he asked, "Are you ready?"

Rising partway from his seat and directing his reply to Justice Davidson, Scheer said, "The People are ready."

Jay turned to the defense tables.

"Ready," said Hanrahan.

"Ready for Valencia, your Honor," said Kase.

Jay looked up at Justice Davidson, who nodded for him to proceed. The trial was about to begin.

# Chapter 5    *A Matter of Credibility*

## I    *Voir Dire*

EVERY adult and normally intelligent American thinks he knows the essential elements of trial by jury: the parading of physical evidence before the jurors, the testifying of witnesses—some for the prosecution and others for the defense—and the cross-examining of each by the other side to pry out the truth, the summations in which the lawyers make their best arguments, and the deliberations by which the jury decides where the truth lies.

But if the adult and normally intelligent American actually becomes involved in a trial, either as juror or as spectator, he discovers how simple-minded his concept was, and how many of the essential elements are hidden from the public's and the jury's view. He perceives that many important transactions between judge and lawyers are conducted in arcane language that he is not meant to understand, that crucial discussions are often conducted in whispers at the bench or out of sight altogether in the judge's chambers, that much existing information is ruled out and forbidden, that various notes, documents, and transcripts of conversations that bear directly on the case can be alluded to but not read aloud, even though they lie in full view on one lawyer's table or another, and that the attorneys often ask questions of witnesses in indirect, euphemistic ways that suggest they know important things they may not reveal. All in all, the novice juror or spectator may well feel that a trial by jury is something like a magic act which he watches from out front, never being permitted to go behind the scenes to see what is really going on.

In the trial of Carlos and Alfredo Ortiz and Doel Valencia for the murder of Alexander Helmer, this was apparent even in the *voir dire* —the questioning of prospective jurors by lawyers for both sides to see if they could, as the ancient French phrase has it, "speak the truth." Some of the questions Assistant District Attorney Scheer asked the first group of people in the jury box seemed pertinent enough (*What do you do for a living, sir? Do you have any particular dislike for the police? Would you hesitate to reach a verdict of guilty just because there is a possibility of capital punishment in this case?*); others, however, seemed pointless, or perhaps designed to ferret out something more than appeared on the surface (*Are you married? Do you have children? Have you sat on a jury before?*); and still others seemed excuses for interminable repetitions of very obvious points (*Do you agree that "reasonable doubt" is not the same as "no doubt"? Would you accept the law as the judge gives it to you, no matter how you feel about it?*). Hanrahan and Kase, in their turn, asked some of the same brief questions about the jurors' work, friendships with police officers, and attitudes toward Puerto Ricans, and spent much of their time asking long rhetorical questions—actually, little lectures—as to whether the juror knew that the "burden of proof" always rests on the prosecution and that the "presumption of innocence cloaks the defendants" despite arrest, imprisonment, and indictment, unless the jury itself, as the "sole trier of the facts," decides that the defendants are guilty. Oddly, too, the two defense lawyers repeatedly asked a number of questions to which only a fool could have given wrong answers (*Do you feel that if you are selected as a juror you will be able to avoid being swayed by sympathy, bias, fear, prejudice, or favor? Would you feel that a policeman's testimony is necessarily more credible than that of a defendant, just because a policeman is an official and the defendant happens to be Puerto Rican and unemployed?*).

Some prospective jurors seemed reluctant to sit on a capital case, some said they could not afford to be tied up on a long one, and some could not seem to grasp the rhetorical questions about the law: all these were rapidly excused by Justice Davidson. But some who answered intelligently and fair-mindedly, and were very willing to serve, were peremptorily challenged (excused without cause) by one side or the other after questioning, often for no apparent reason. Still more peculiar, and certainly more annoying, was the fact that Scheer, Hanrahan, and Kase went through their rhetorical questions and quasi-lectures on the law all over again whenever more prospective jurors were called up from the spectator section to fill the empty seats left by those who had been excused. Whenever prospects, after questioning, were excused, one could feel, though not hear, the groans of the jurors who had been accepted and sworn in, for once again they would have to sit and listen to the same questions about the presumption of innocence, the nature of reasonable doubt, and all the rest. Why did the lawyers do it? Could they not cut it shorter? Or had they some purpose in mind other than getting answers to their questions?

The day wore on with excruciating slowness: prospective jurors were excused and left, new candidates were called up and sidled into the jury box, the lawyers went through their *voir dire* again and again, and the jurors accepted by both sides were sworn in and slowly filled up the jury box. Toward 4:00 p.m., when seven of the seats had been filled, Justice Davidson called a halt to the tedious proceedings and ordered everyone to appear again at 11:00 a.m. the next day. Inexplicably, it went faster then, and shortly past noon the full complement of twelve, plus two alternates, had been sworn in.

The jurors—serious, aware of their own importance, and eager to have things begin—were a mixed lot: six white men and one white woman, four Negro men and one Negro woman. (Scheer may or may not have been admirably free of bias in putting so many blacks on the jury; one former colleague of his says, "Al hinted to me at the time that he had put five Negroes on because there was a lot of ill-will between them and the Puerto Ricans and he hoped they'd be tough—even though he'd look good for having accepted them.") The jurors were a mixture such as a casting director might have selected: one elderly Retired Bank Clerk, Jewish; one muscular, middle-aged Factory Worker, black; one florid, white-haired Old Irishman; one attractive young Lady Bookkeeper, black (but not very); one middle-aged Bored Housewife, Jewish, whose wonderful, wonderful children had grown up and left her with nothing to do; one nondescript Young Man, Irish-American and temporarily unemployed; one Assistant Personnel Director, black but very bourgeois; one Toll Collector, black and very proletarian; and so on.

When Clerk of the Court Jay had sworn in the last of them, he read aloud their names—a list that was to become oppressively familiar, since he would call it aloud every time the jury returned to the box after an overnight adjournment, a luncheon break, or even a five-minute recess:

"Trial jurors will please answer to their names. Irving Arrow [*Here!*], William Steele [*Here!*], George Sackel [*Here!*], Danetta Black [*Here!*], Thomas Ryan [*Here!*], Conrad Bellamy [*Here!*], Carl Brown [*Here!*], Eve Israel [*Here!*], John McNeil [*Here!*], Stanley Edelman [*Here!*], Thaddeus Patterson [*Here!*], Sylvia Perella [*Here!*]. Alternates—Mildred Gurven [*Here!*], Frederick Evert [*Here!*]. The jury is all present, your Honor."

(Why, the jurors came to wonder, did their names have to be called every time? Wasn't it obvious they were all there? Couldn't anyone recognize them by sight, after a while? But still the roll-calls went on, three, four, five times a day: "Trial jurors will please answer to their names. Irving Arrow [*Here!*], William Steele [*Here!*] . . .")

And now, chosen, sworn in, and all present, they were ready, attentive, and earnest—and in for an immediate disappointment, for first of all the judge said, addressing the lawyers, "Gentlemen, will you come up here?" and whispered to them at the bench, then announcing to the jury, as the lawyers returned to their seats, "When I excuse you folks today, I will excuse you until Monday the 15th." (*A six-day delay after all this? Why? What was going on?*) "This court will be engaged in certain very important matters, with which you will not be concerned, for the balance of this week." (*But why aren't we concerned? Are we not triers of the facts, and you only the trier of the law? Why do you make a secret of what's happening?*) "We will have a session this afternoon; this jury will not be concerned with that session." (*No fair, no fair! You're only tantalizing us.*)

"All right, members of the jury," said Justice Davidson, "you're excused until Monday the 15th at a few minutes before 10:30. In the meantime, do not discuss this case with anyone. Do not even stand in the presence of anyone who may be discussing some phase of this case. Neither form nor express any opinion as to the guilt or innocence of the defendants until the matter is submitted to you for that purpose." That, at least, was a little better; it gave them a feeling of importance, and of possessing a secret of their own.

The afternoon session with which the jury was not concerned was crucial to the case: it consisted of a technical inquiry, requested by Hanrahan and Kase and known as a Huntley hearing, in which the judge determines whether the confessions made by the defendants were genuinely voluntary. If they had been obtained by beatings, threats, or coercion of any kind, the judge would find them involuntary, and hence inadmissible—and if so, the jury would not be allowed to know they existed, even if they were completely truthful. (In this instance, of course, if the confessions were ruled out there would be no trial, for there was almost no other evidence.)

The hearing lasted all afternoon, and was resumed and completed the next morning. Only three witnesses were called—Russo, McCabe, and Vitale—all of whom steadfastly denied that there had been any illegal detentions or arrests, beatings, threats, or coercion. Although Hanrahan and Kase could have put the defendants on to swear that there had been, they chose not to, in order not to give away their defense to Scheer. That left them with no way to contest the confessions except to cross-examine the detectives and Vitale, asking questions which implied that there had been coercion but which impressed Justice Davidson not at all, since questions put by a lawyer are not evidence. Hanrahan, who surely knew this, nevertheless cross-examined Russo at length and with mounting indignation and volume.*

> Hanrahan: Officer, during the time that you were questioning [Carlos] from 12:15 to 1:45, did you ever place any ammonia on his face?
> Russo (*flatly and without expression*): I did not.
> Hanrahan: Did you use a handkerchief to cover his mouth?
> Russo: I did not.
> Hanrahan: Did you ever actually handcuff him to a chair—*did you do that?*

* In what follows and in other courtroom scenes throughout this book, I have relied upon interviews with persons who took part in, or were present at, the trials, plus my own observations of the principals, to reconstruct actions and inflections. Official trial records preserve exactly what was said, but do not report gestures, grimaces, or tones of voice.—M.H.

Russo: I did not.

Hanrahan: Did you handcuff him and place him on the floor in a
bent position—*did you do that, Officer?*

Russo: No, sir.

Hanrahan: Did you grab him and with a gun in your hand tell
him to make a statement to you—DID YOU DO THAT?

Russo: No, sir.

Kase, for his part, repeatedly asked both detectives when and how
Valencia had been released at night after his first questioning, implying that perhaps the defendant had never been released, or that if he
had, McCabe had not just "invited" him to the station house the next
morning but illegally arrested and detained him. Russo and McCabe,
of course, stuck to their stories. Justice Davidson, who knew what the
lawyers were up to, finally got very short with Hanrahan when the
lawyer asked McCabe several times whether an attorney had tried to
visit the Ortiz brothers in the police station and been refused permission. "Listen, now," the judge broke in. "You are trying this hearing
without a jury, and you are in front of *me* now. Are you going to give
any evidence that an attorney came to see these people?"

"Your Honor," Hanrahan said, stalling, "I may do that."

"You better tell me now," snapped Justice Davidson. "I am asking
you. If I ask a question, you *answer* me."

Hanrahan stammered something about "certain information" he
was seeking, and asked for a recess, but Justice Davidson denied the
request and gave him a sharp dressing-down on the difference between
a closed hearing and a trial by jury: "If you have got a question to
ask, if it is based on some facts, I will be happy to have it, but don't
try to create atmosphere with me. I am not a jury. I am sitting as a
judge. I know the Escobedo case as well as you, and if there is anything factual behind your question I want it right away. If there is
nothing factual about it, I don't think you should ask such a question.
I don't think it is ethical for you to do so." (Nonetheless, just such
questions are asked by lawyers all the time in front of juries, and
while judges advise the juries that the questions are not, of themselves, evidence, they do not, in the juries' hearing, label the "creation
of atmosphere" unethical. The jury has to figure out for itself what is
going on.)

In the end, Justice Davidson ruled that there had been no evidence
that the confessions were not voluntary; the prosecution would there-

fore be entitled to introduce them at the trial. The jury, which would return on Monday—the balance of the week being taken up with another trial, already begun—would have no idea that the two star witnesses had already told their stories in part and been cross-examined, that many of the questions and answers they would hear had in effect been rehearsed and were known to everyone but themselves, and that the defense lawyers, who would stress the coercion issue and have their clients testify to it, could have done so before the judge at the Huntley hearing but made no attempt to do so. The jurors would eventually have to render a verdict—another word whose roots mean "truth-speaking"—provided they could perceive the truth while wearing the blinders put on them. For in our system of justice it is held that although jurors are the triers of the facts, they will be unable to be fair and impartial if they hear facts illegally obtained and that, in order to speak the truth, they must often know less than the whole truth.

Which may not be as absurd as it sounds, if there is more than one kind of truth—if, that is, the jurors need to know less than the *factual* truth in order to speak the *legal* truth.

---

## II   *The Purposes of Trial by Jury*

FACTUAL and legal truth are not necessarily different, but neither are they necessarily identical. A man may be innocent of a crime in actual fact, but if a jury is convinced otherwise by misleading circumstantial evidence or perjured testimony, it will find him legally guilty. Far more commonly, a man may be actually guilty of a crime, but because the crucial evidence against him was illegally obtained and hence inadmissible, the jury finds him legally innocent. Not that the jury perceives the distinction: nearly always it supposes that it is seeking the factual truth, when actually it is able and empowered to ascertain only the legal truth.

These days, when prosecutors and courts are more constrained by constitutional guarantees than ever, and when, as a result, a certain number of obviously guilty persons escape conviction, many people put part of the blame on the institution of trial by jury. From many quarters—from laymen, lawyers, and even judges—we hear that trial by jury is a poor way to go about ascertaining the facts, that it has little to do with the truth, that it is only a game between opposing attorneys, that it is outmoded, inefficient, and unnecessary. If the real purpose of trial by jury were to find the factual truth, there would be some merit to these harsh accusations; but if its real purpose is to find the legal truth—and in so doing to uphold due process, the very heart of our judicial ethos—then trial by jury is up-to-date, efficient, and, indeed, indispensable.

The confusion about its purposes has deep historical roots. In the early Middle Ages, accused persons underwent "trials" by ordeal or by combat, it being thought that the Lord would intervene on behalf of the innocent, but by the thirteenth century trial by jury had replaced both of these. The early *juratores* (swearers) were, however, more like witnesses to the facts than judges of the evidence presented to them; they were neighbors who, by virtue of their own knowledge of the case or of the persons involved, could swear that the accused was either innocent or guilty. But as cities grew larger and social life became more complex, the role of the jurors changed: by the fifteenth century their personal knowledge was being supplemented by evidence given by other witnesses, and by the eighteenth century the jurors had altogether ceased acting as witnesses and become impartial triers of the facts offered by others.

But the transformation of jurors into impartial triers of the facts was curiously affected by other and more profound developments in the English system of justice. During the seventeenth and eighteenth centuries, accused persons won the privilege against self-incrimination and the right to confront their accusers in court, trials became adversarial, and due process emerged as the paramount principle of criminal law. These changes subtly but significantly altered the purpose of trial by jury: the search for factual guilt or innocence, though still ostensibly its business, was becoming subordinate to a larger aim—the enforcing of the due-process principle. Jurors were required to presume the defendant innocent unless they heard convincing evidence to the contrary, but they had to ignore—indeed, they were supposed never to hear—any evidence, no matter how pertinent, that had been unfairly obtained. Similarly, any unfair revelations made by the prosecutor in their hearing would be considered irremediably prejudicial, and would bring about a mistrial. If these and other changes in the nature of trial by jury meant that vital information was sometimes excluded and that guilty men sometimes went free, they also protected the liberties of the innocent and preserved the ethical character of the justice system. The jury, unbeknownst to itself, had come to try not only the accused, but the police, the prosecutor, and even the judge; it had acquired the function of seeing to it that the system was, above all, fair.

Despite this lofty purpose, jury trials today account for a numerically insignificant proportion of criminal prosecutions. The vast majority of criminal cases involve minor matters which, by statute, are not entitled to jury trial, and are tried before a magistrate or lower-court judge. Even of that minority of crimes serious enough to warrant trial by jury, nine tenths are, as we have seen, settled without trial, by guilty pleas. Finally, of the small number that actually do come to trial, two fifths are heard and decided by judges without juries, such "bench trials" being an option chosen by defendants in cases where legal technicalities, rather than jurors' sympathy, offer the best chance of acquittal, or where the defendants feel judges will be less swayed against them by appearances or by local sentiment than will jurors.

The net result is that out of a grand total of perhaps six to seven million prosecutions per year, nearly a million of which are for serious crimes, only something like 125,000 result in jury trials. Nonetheless, they are of immense importance: they are the test cases, the examples, the models which guide the rest of criminal justice behavior. The cop about to make an arrest, the D.A. interviewing witnesses, the defense lawyer conferring with his client in jail, each bases much of his behavior and many of his decisions on his estimate of what would happen if the case went to trial and a jury undertook to decide the guilt or innocence of the accused.

If deciding guilt or innocence were identical with ascertaining the factual truth, the jury would be an outlandishly inefficient mechanism. First of all, in many parts of the country, jury commissioners, though directed by statutes to compile lists of persons of normal intelligence and good character, interpret those statutes as they see fit, in the South excluding most Negroes, and elsewhere many of the poor and

members of ethnic minorities—the very persons who might best understand and appraise the testimony offered by persons of their own
background. Lawyers for both sides then comb over the persons
called up from these lists, excluding by means of peremptory challenges jurors they feel would not be fair and open-minded—that is to
say, jurors who would not be biased in their favor. Prosecutors favor
salaried and managerial persons who accept and give orders and who
therefore expect others to do the same, but they mistrust actors,
writers, and artists, who might be somewhat lenient toward deviancy,
and they avoid women if the defendant is a handsome male but favor
them if the defendant committed a sexual or violent crime. Defense
lawyers try to eliminate managerial types, educated or sophisticated
persons who might guide the jury along logical lines, and virtually
everyone who knows something about the law or police; they prefer liberals, creative people, poor people, and members of minority
groups. (Each side, meanwhile, restates its views *ad nauseam* in its
rhetorical questions in order, as Manhattan D.A. Frank S. Hogan
says, to "brainwash the jury," or as lawyers often put it, to "try the
case in the *voir dire.*") Since each side can peremptorily challenge a
certain number of the very kinds of jurors the other side wants, the
end result is something of a Least Common Denominator: a collec-
tion of persons of no special training or knowledge, no notable intel-
lectuality, no particular awareness of the problems at issue, no strong
ideology, no previous trial experience, and no clear ideas about the
causes or control of crime. The principal qualification of the ideal
juror is that he be an ignoramus about all the subjects to be discussed
in the case at hand, and thoroughly underqualified to make expert
judgments about the evidence he will be hearing.

Compounding the problem still further, this ideal juror is prevented
from knowing much that would help him ascertain the factual truth.
Any evidence obtained by illegal search or seizure may not be heard
by him, even though it is both true and essential to the determination
of factual guilt. Notes or memos jotted down by a policeman during
the investigation may not be read aloud or shown to him, even
though the policeman may look at them while testifying, in order to
refresh his memory. A witness may not say what another person told
him about the crime, however significant it might be, for such second-
hand statements are "hearsay"—a species of evidence generally ruled
inadmissible because the witness knows only that it was said, and not

that it was true. Most important of all, in order not to create prejudice in the mind of the juror, the prosecutor may not mention or seek to elicit anything about the previous criminal record of the accused person unless the latter takes the stand; the juror may, for instance, have to decide whether or not the defendant committed rape on the basis of scanty and confusing evidence, without ever learning that he has previously been convicted of half a dozen sexual offenses and been diagnosed as a psychopathic personality.

If the defendant does take the stand, however, the prosecutor is then, paradoxically, permitted to ask him questions about his criminal record—ostensibly for the purpose of showing the jury that he is not a truthful witness, but in actual fact sneaking across to the jurors the very kind of information that will make them view the defendant as a bad person who probably committed the crime he is being tried for. An accused rapist may not actually have committed the rape at issue, but if the jurors hear that he has a history of six previous sexual offenses, how impartially are they likely to weigh the evidence in the case? But this is only one of the ways in which the prosecutor, rather than merely parading evidence before the jurors, seeks to influence and prejudice them. He may, for instance, hint at the existence of some piece of inadmissible evidence; the defense will violently object, and the judge will order the remark stricken from the record and instruct the jurors to disregard it—but they heard it and cannot really erase it from their minds. He talks to his witnesses beforehand, not actually telling them what to say but subtly coaching them by suggesting the ways in which the defense may attack their testimony unless they testify carefully. His most pervasive tactic is, however, his role-playing: he is righteous, decent, accusing but fair, self-controlled in the face of provocation by the defense lawyers and their defense witnesses, calmly self-confident without being cocky, smart without being too smart—the kind of man, in short, whom the jurors cannot help trusting, and whose witnesses, they feel, must be telling the truth.

But the defense attorney also makes it hard for the jurors to see the facts clearly. He acts as if he were trying to help reveal the truth to them (and occasionally does so), but most of the time he seeks to confuse them, to engage their sympathies, to portray himself and his client as underdogs, and, above all, to create in them some feeling of doubt about the prosecution's case. He leaps to his feet with innumerable objections, many of which are groundless but which enable him to appear harshly dealt with by the judge; he offers motions for mistrial which he knows will be denied but which may make the jury think the judge is being unfair to the defense; he acts outraged toward the prosecutor, indignant toward the judge, contemptuous toward the other side's witnesses. If he suspects his client is guilty, he tries to keep him off the witness stand, lest the truth come out, or at least makes it plain to him what may happen if the defendant admits certain things under cross-examination. He does not tell his client to commit perjury, but neither does he stop him in the middle of doing so and let the jury know the facts.

Both he and his opponent, the prosecutor, cross-examine each other's witnesses to help present the facts to the jury and to unmask falsehoods; at least, such is the theory behind cross-examination, termed by John Henry Wigmore, the noted authority on evidence, "the greatest legal engine ever invented for the discovery of truth." Sometimes it is just that, but often it is an engine for laying down a smoke screen in front of truth. If he can, a lawyer will use cross-examination to reveal lies; if he cannot, he will use it to make the witness seem inconsistent, stupid, confused, dishonest, and generally unworthy of belief. He nags, badgers, bullies, and pesters the witness, twisting his words, repeating his answers sarcastically, trying to make him seem an ass, a liar, and a nitwit. Quite simply, in the words of one leading New York trial lawyer, "You have to try to destroy the other side's witnesses. Whether they were telling the truth or not doesn't matter; you have to destroy them."

The judge, meanwhile, is supposed to be the referee, allowing full scope for each side to do whatever is legal and proper, but offering the jurors caveats to aid them in excluding from their deliberations anything they have heard that is not evidence. The judge plays a role characterized by fairness, learning, wisdom, strength, and patience; he is a somewhat godlike or at least Old Testament patriarchal figure, fierce, brooding, and concerned that he do what is right. But this demanding part is generally played by very ordinary men. According to Professor Blumberg, the majority of the 7,500 state, county, and city judges in the lower criminal courts of the United States are lawyers of marginal ability who played clubhouse politics until they were rewarded with an appointment or with a sure-fire nomination to the slate. In higher courts the judges may have been more competent lawyers or district attorneys, but they too have usually had to give generously of their time and money to their party, or even pay secretly, for their judgeships. As recently as 1960, according to a massive study of New York City government, the going rate for a judgeship was the equivalent of two years' salary contributed to the party. Merit selection of judges by impartial panels exists in about one fifth of the states and has helped somewhat, but it, too, is subject to political influence and to favoritism. Even at the very pinnacle of the judiciary, party politics may count for more than judicial temperament and intellectual power, as was made clear by President Nixon's two unsuccessful nominations to the Supreme Court.

The judicial temperament, in most criminal courts, is distressingly rare: every trial lawyer knows that most judges have their prejudices and partialities, many being frankly People-oriented and a few openly defendant-oriented, many brusque and dictatorial and some languid and almost passive, some harsh toward drug-sellers and lenient toward sexual offenders and others just the reverse, some socially liberal in their rulings and others conservative. But whatever the judge's particular bent, he maintains the stance of infallibility: he listens to both sides, perhaps even looks up the references, and then makes what is supposed to be a strictly legal decision, based upon unquestionable authority. But judges themselves know how human and biased are many of their decisions: as one noted jurist said more than a century ago, "I might once in a while be embarrassed by a technical rule, but I almost always found principles suited to my view of the case."

With so much built-in role-playing, deception, and confusion, and such frequent exclusion of information, the jury trial is obviously not a very good way of getting at the factual truth. Professor Packer, after closely studying a number of major criminal trials, concluded that the adversary process "simply is not well adapted to the intelligible sequential ordering of complex factual information," and, as a technique for ascertaining factual guilt or innocence, is unequal to the demands placed upon it. But even if it serves its ancient purpose poorly, it serves its more recently acquired one better: the very factors that make it so hard for juries to perceive the factual truth lead them to verdicts that represent legal truth—verdicts based on only what it is fair for them to know.

There are undoubtedly far more efficient ways of seeking truth and convicting the guilty, but none manages to do what trial by jury does— namely, to seek only the kind of truth that is consonant with the principle of due process, and thereby to make a reality of our promises of liberty for all. It is on this basis that one should judge whether trial by jury today is a success or a failure, an anachronism or a vital component of the criminal justice system.

---

# III   *The People's Case*

---

NOTHING about jury duty is as irksome as the way it wastes time. On Monday, March 15th, the jurors in the Ortiz-Valencia trial read and reread their newspapers all morning in a barren, comfortless jury room, sighed and squirmed on the hard chairs, and stared unseeingly out of the windows; at last, when a uniformed court attendant opened the door a little before 1:00 p.m., it was to tell them that they would not be needed that afternoon, and were to come back the next morning. But when they did, they spent that whole morning the same way and, after scattering out to have lunch in local cafeterias and short-order joints, returned only to wait some more. They were offered no explanation; Justice Davidson's other trial had dragged on longer than he expected, and he had ordered them kept on hand in case it ended suddenly, but no court attendant would tell them that and risk making them resentful of the judge.

At last, in mid-afternoon the attendant opened the door and invited them to follow him into the courtroom. They filed in and self-consciously took their seats, aware that the key characters in the drama were assembled and watching them. The only one missing was Justice Davidson, who, during his undergraduate days, had wanted to become an actor; he did not, but the role of judge has long given him the pleasure of making a star's entrance. When the jury was in its place, a guard pounded twice on a door and called out, "The Honorable Justice of the Court! All rise!" and as everyone stood up, Davidson swept in, short but majestic in his flowing black robe, mounted the dais, and seated himself behind the massive bench, the flag on his right, and above his head on the wall in neat gold letters, the motto "In God We Trust."

He nodded to Clerk Jay to begin, but no sooner had Jay called the roster of jurors than Hanrahan stood up and asked for a two-day adjournment on the grounds that he had just received important new information and needed to verify it. (*Oh, no! Not now—not after all the time we've sat in that damned room!*) But Justice Davidson, a dark-haired, square-jawed man who spoke in a growl and had cold, piercing eyes behind his heavy dark-rimmed glasses—a judge who likes to say that he "runs a tight ship"—would have none of it; there had been delays enough already, and he insisted that they at least make their openings without further delay.

Davidson, who had been a judge for fourteen years after long service as lawyer and Democratic legislator, began by making a little speech to the jurors of a kind he had made many hundreds of times before, dealing with certain fundamentals of jury-trial procedure. He told them that nothing any lawyer might say could be considered as evidence, and no question any lawyer might ask meant that what he asked about had actually taken place. The Court would be ruling out some questions, but the jurors were not to let themselves speculate as to what answer a witness might have given to any barred question. He concluded, with a wintry little smile, "My rulings of law are my business. All questions of fact—namely, what happened here—are your business. So you stay out of my business and I'll stay out of yours." The jurors chuckled dutifully, and felt important, as he had meant them to.

Davidson then asked Scheer to make his opening statement. Scheer arose, pudgy and stiffly erect, and in a detached, businesslike manner read the indictment aloud; he then said that the People expected to prove that the three defendants here on trial, plus one Angel Walker, had planned the hold-up that resulted in Helmer's murder, and he gave the jury a condensed account of how and where, according to the People, the crime had taken place and what part each of the four accomplices had played in it. (*So where is Angel Walker? Why isn't he on trial? Why doesn't the D.A. say anything about that?*)

When Scheer had concluded, Hanrahan arose to make his own opening. His manner was grave, shocked, and offended: having little else to offer, he was seeking to create atmosphere. "The District At-

torney has told you that the actual killer of Mr. Helmer was Angel
Walker," he said, "yet if you examine this indictment, you will not
find the name of Angel Walker—"

Scheer popped up, shouting an objection, and Davidson at once
sustained him and told the jurors that they were to infer nothing from
Hanrahan's remark. Undaunted, Hanrahan continued, saying that he
expected to prove that the Ortiz brothers had not even been in the
apartment when the crime was committed, that the date of Helmer's
death was uncertain, that any confessions made by the Ortiz brothers
had been involuntary, and, finally, that the jurors ought to give their
utmost energies to the case, since it was one in which two young men
might lose their lives—

"Just a *moment,* please!" barked Scheer, leaping to his feet, his
hand upheld like a traffic policeman's. "Sustained!" said Justice Davidson immediately; juries are not supposed to consider the potential
penalties, but only what happened or did not happen. All the same,
Hanrahan had scored a point, and now, like a bull beset by picadors
and gaining ferocity from their thrusts, he plunged on, somber and
indignant. "We intend to prove," he intoned, "that the actual killer is
Angel Walker—but that he has been free to roam the streets of the
Bronx *without being indicted!*" It was an extraordinary thing for him
to say: the only evidence that Walker had stabbed Helmer was the
confessions of the defendants—confessions Hanrahan had said he
would prove to be involuntary and false. But at this point the jurors
did not know that there was no other proof; they knew only that Hanrahan had spoken of this trial as if it were a travesty of justice, and as
if the police, the Grand Jury, and the prosecutor had bungled things
and were making the defendants their scapegoats.

Hanrahan sat down, and Kase arose to make his opening. He began
by stressing the point that the District Attorney would have to prove
the guilt of the defendants beyond a reasonable doubt, but Justice
Davidson broke in, glowering at him. "Look," he said, "don't give this
jury your version of the law."

"Yes, your Honor," said Kase meekly, although what he had said
was perfectly standard theory and not anything of his own.

Davidson, not mollified, rapped out, "Tell us what, if anything, you
intend to prove!"

Kase looked intimidated, and hesitated; then he said he would
waive his opening. This was pure play-acting. He had realized, during

the Huntley hearing, that Hanrahan and Davidson disliked each other, and that during the trial the former would be obstreperous and combative, the latter severe; he had decided, therefore, to make himself a contrast to Hanrahan, appearing humble, polite, diffident, and perhaps somewhat abused by the judge—a clean-cut young fellow with whom the jury could sympathize. Davidson, a little surprised, asked Kase to repeat his waiver, and then ended the session with the usual warning to the jury not to discuss the case with anyone, or read about it, or form any judgments about it as yet.

The following morning Scheer brought on a series of minor witnesses, partly to establish the identity of the dead man (since his body had been unrecognizable), and partly to give the jury a sense of the thoroughness of the People's case. Mrs. Rose Pavese and Mrs. Ena Varela, both long-time neighbors of Helmer's, described the recluse and identified as his a hearing aid Scheer showed them. Mrs. Varela also told about the Sunday morning when the police had come, at her call, and had passed through her apartment to gain access to Helmer's place by a window.

All this was dull and innocuous stuff, but Hanrahan frequently objected (Kase sometimes joining in), and was nearly always overruled. (*What is he objecting to? Why is the judge always against him? What's going on?*) Things got a little livelier when Patrolman Puvogel, of the Emergency Service, was about to describe the corpse as he had first seen it in the apartment; before he could do so, Hanrahan arose and made a deeply impassioned speech of a kind he would repeat scores of times in the next two weeks. "Your Honor," he said, "I am going to object to this entire examination and move to strike it from the record. And I am asking further for the withdrawal of a juror and a declaration of a mistrial.* It is merely to prejudice these defendants; it has nothing—it is not relevant, not germane, to the issues here." (*Declaration of a mistrial? What happened? What was so terrible?*) "Motion denied," Justice Davidson said as soon as Hanrahan stopped, "objection overruled." ("I was trying to put the judge off," Hanrahan recalls, "and to give the jury the idea that we were getting an unfair trial. I did it deliberately.")

Puvogel, resuming, described the condition of the apartment, the

---

* "Withdrawal of a juror" is a somewhat archaic phrase referring to a way of ending proceedings by removing one juror and so having an incomplete jury; essentially, it means the same thing as "declaration of a mistrial."

activities of the policemen who first arrived there, and the retrieval of the wallet from Helmer's body. After a good deal of this, and a perfunctory cross-examination by Hanrahan, who tried to make Puvogel seem incompetent ("Did anybody place any identification mark on this wallet?"—"I don't know."—"I *see*"), the trial grew stormy and contentious when the elderly medical examiner Dr. Charles Hochman took the stand. Dr. Hochman described the condition of the body— maggot-covered, bloated, and rotting—as he had first seen it in the Jacobi Morgue. There was not a sound from the jurors, whose faces had all become studiously expressionless. Scheer opened a folder and took out of it a color photograph, which he held out to Hochman, asking if it was a fair representation of the face of the corpse he had seen in the morgue. Hanrahan was on his feet instantly; this, he shouted, was "a deliberate attempt by the District Attorney to not only inflame this jury but prejudice the rights of these defendants." Kase added a similar, though milder, objection.

The judge called all the lawyers to the bench, where the jury could see much earnest whispering, gesturing, and head-shaking. Finally Justice Davidson told the jurors to go to lunch early; he and the lawyers had some work to do. In the jury's absence, Davidson said he agreed with the defense lawyers that the picture was gruesome and disgusting, but unless they would stipulate (that is, formally agree) that Helmer's body had indeed looked as Dr. Hochman said it did, the picture would be admitted into evidence and shown to the jury. But neither Hanrahan nor Kase would so stipulate, and in the afternoon the picture was introduced into evidence, and handed to the foreman, who studied it and passed it along. The women jurors, as stiffly impassive as the men, looked at the purulent wreckage of Helmer's face in complete silence; then the foreman handed the picture back to an attendant. Dr. Hochman, an old hand at trials, next described in clinical detail his autopsy findings, including the location, size, direction, and appearance of each of the five wounds. The precise cause of death, he said, had been cardiac tamponade—the filling of the pericardial sac with blood from one of the wounds until the resulting compression of the heart had stopped its beating.

Hanrahan sought in cross-examination to shake Dr. Hochman's estimate that the death had occurred a week to ten days prior to the autopsy. Hochman had based this on the extent of decomposition of the tissues and on the size and number of maggots on the body, the latter point being the one Hanrahan returned to again and again.

*(Why doesn't he stop that? Who cares about the maggots?)* Hanrahan's purpose soon became clear, however: if Hochman's dating was uncertain, and if Helmer had actually died considerably earlier or later than October 9th, the confessions—all of which named the 9th as the date of the crime—would seem less than credible. Hochman was not to be budged, however, and Hanrahan finally resorted to the very kind of question the judge had warned the jury originally not to take as evidence:

> Hanrahan: Is it possible, Doctor, that the death could have occurred *two* weeks before [the autopsy]? Is it *possible?*
> Scheer: Objection!
> Davidson: Sustained.
> Hanrahan: Is it possible that the death could have occurred *three* weeks before?
> Scheer: Objection!
> Davidson: Sustained.

Hanrahan sighed a little, shook his head dolefully, and sat down, hoping he had created some doubt among the jurors.

Kase began asking questions along the same line, but Davidson called him to the bench and scolded him for dwelling on the subject, in a growl the tone of which, if not the words, was audible to the jury. "You're merely parading before this jury the fact that this body was covered with maggots that were eating away the flesh," he said, "and by the same token you object that these things are inflammatory. You told me that your defense in this case was going to be alibi. I don't know where your brains are."

"Well, Judge," Kase began feebly, but Davidson cut him short, saying, "I don't want to say any more to you." Kase returned to his place before the witness stand, halfheartedly asked Dr. Hochman two more routine questions, and then sat down. Justice Davidson said that everyone had had enough for one day, and the jurors filed out, avoiding each other's eyes while putting on their coats in the jury room as if they feared to reveal to each other, prematurely and against orders, the thoughts and questions in their minds.

On Thursday afternoon, after another entire morning wasted in waiting, the jurors were called in, and listened to the morgue-wagon driver and a series of policemen—Patrolman Kacerosky, the first policeman on the scene; Patrolman Landy, who stood guard outside the apartment; and Patrolman Perrone, who had relieved Landy and helped the morgue attendants. Along the way, the jurors heard about each and every card in Helmer's wallet, saw his false teeth, and looked at various photographs of the street, the front of the building, and the interior of his apartment. It was a dull afternoon—even Hanrahan and Kase scarcely bothered with objections or cross-examinations—but Scheer dragged in all this material to establish the provenance of the body, and meanwhile to make his case sound massive and well prepared.

At the end of this third day of the trial, the jurors had still heard no direct testimony about the actual crime, nor any evidence against the defendants. Nor were they about to: the judge excused them until Monday (he had to be in another court all of Friday), and when they returned, they were subjected to more of the same kind of tedious background material: a store manager told them what make and model of hearing aid Helmer had used and read aloud the record of his repairs and his purchases of batteries; Kacerosky's partner, Patrolman John Flynn, repeated the story of the first police visit to the apartment; a detective told how he dusted various surfaces for prints and found only one that was legible; and another detective said he had compared that one print to those of various suspects but found none that matched.

Finally, in the middle of that afternoon—two weeks after jury selection had begun, and six days after the trial had gotten under way—Detective Salvatore Russo was called to the stand. The jurors first thought him just another detective—a burly, dark-jowled man, ice-cold in his manner—but soon enough it became evident that he was a key witness and the principal investigator of the crime. Scheer, staring owlishly around, now at the jury, now at the spectators, as he asked his questions, got Russo to tell how he had been assigned to the case, had visited the morgue and viewed the corpse, and had begun his investigation at the reeking, fly-blown apartment. Hanrahan periodically objected to such details as the abundance of maggots or the pool of body fluids on the kitchen floor, and Davidson crisply and quickly overruled him nearly every time. But just as the jury finally got a clear idea of the evidence Russo had found on the scene and was ready to hear how these things had led him to the suspects, the dialogue made a curious leap:

Scheer: Continue, please, with what further investigation and action you took, Detective Russo.

Russo: I left 399 East 160th Street and proceeded to the 42nd
    Squad.
Scheer: Continue, please.
Russo: On October 22nd, some time between 9:30 and 10
    o'clock, the defendant Doel Valencia was present at the 42nd
    Squad.
Scheer: Did you have a conversation with him?
Russo: I did.

Of all that happened in between, and of the processes by which the detective had come to suspect Valencia and to get him to the station
house, he said not a word. (None of that would have been valid evidence—but it would have made the "conversation" with Valencia a
good deal more comprehensible and real to the jurors.)

Looking at a photostated copy of his own notes, Russo described
that first interrogation, during which Valencia had denied all knowledge of the crime and had even omitted the names of Carlos and Alfredo Ortiz when listing his close friends. At one point, while Russo
was looking at his notes, Scheer asked for a bench conference; after a
huddle with both sides, Justice Davidson told the jurors that they might
have observed some heavy black markings on the notes. "Pay no attention to those black lines," he said. "Those are deletions which were
ordered by the Court, deletions of matter which we're not concerned
with at all in this case." (*Why not? Isn't it all part of the interrogation?
What are they hiding?*) The deletions, technically known as "redac-
tions," had been ordered by Davidson earlier for good reason: they
were admissions by Valencia about his use of heroin and, under the
rules of evidence, were considered prejudicial, since the jury might
well suppose that such a man was very likely to commit other crimes,
even if the evidence was insufficient.

Russo went on to recount the entire next day's activities, with its
crop of confessional statements. He said nothing of the struggle to
ferret the confessions out of the suspects, but merely related, in a
level, expressionless manner, the substance of the statements made by
the three defendants at the end of that day, again using his own notes
to remind himself of his questions and their answers. It sounded like
this:

At about 4:20 p.m. Detective McCabe and myself spoke to Alfredo Ortiz. We told Alfredo that his brother Carlos had stated to
us that he observed the defendant Alfredo Ortiz, Doel Valencia,

and Negrito entering the building at 399 East 160th Street. . . .
Detective McCabe and myself [then] proceeded to take a statement from Alfredo Ortiz. . . . The defendant was asked if he remembered what he did, if anything, on October 9th, 1964. The
defendant stated, "Yes, that's when all that happened." The defendant was asked what he meant by "That's when all that happened," and he stated, "That's when we were pulling a score."

(*Was it really like that? Did they just "speak" to Alfredo? Did they all
sit around having a conversation, the detectives asking him things and
Alfredo "stating" answers?*) In this almost trance-like fashion, Russo
recounted the story of the crime as told to him and McCabe by each
of the three defendants; it was left to the jurors to imagine, if they
could, the human realities behind his desiccated narrative.

Early in this process, while Russo was telling about the first interrogation of Carlos Ortiz, Justice Davidson stopped the questioning
briefly and gave the jurors another short lecture, advising them that
whatever Carlos said was evidence only against himself, and not
against any of the others whom he named or whose actions he described. "You cannot consider what he may say, if believed by you,
against anybody other than himself," he said. "It must be evaluated
only in connection with your consideration of *his* guilt or innocence.
Is that clear? Have I made that clear?" The jurors nodded, but it
could hardly have been clear to them, for the point is almost meta-
physically subtle: under our rules of evidence, a statement made by
an accused person outside the court cannot be used as evidence against
his accomplices (even if they, too, confessed) because, unlike a live
witness in the court, the statement cannot be cross-examined; hence,
while it is evidence against the speaker, it is only hearsay as far as
anyone else in it is concerned. Whether such statements should even
be heard by a jury that has to disregard them in the case of some defendants had been argued up to the Supreme Court in 1957, the
Court holding that if a jury was given sufficiently clear instructions, it
could manage to ignore the things said in a statement by one defendant
about his co-defendants. (*Why can't we consider what he said against
the others? He saw them, didn't he? He was a witness to what they
did, wasn't he? What kind of law is that?*)

(If the jurors found it puzzling, the defendants found it—and
nearly everything else about the trial—totally incomprehensible. Al-

fredo, for instance, reminiscing about the trial, has remarked, "It meant *nothin'* to me. I di'n' understan' anything. In fac', I spent most of the trial sleepin' on the seat, gettin' nothin' out of it.")

It took two hours for Russo to complete his direct testimony; Scheer then turned to Hanrahan and said, "You may inquire." Justice Davidson, however, said that since it was already 5:30 p.m., all hands should go home and return at 11:00 a.m. the next day.

The following morning Hanrahan began his cross-examination. Working hard to make it seem that he was being blocked by the judge and Scheer in his efforts to reveal the truth, he asked innumerable questions which he knew would be ruled out, but which might, by the mere fact of their being asked, make some impression on the jury— questions, for instance, implying that the evidence was inadequate ("Isn't it a fact that you were unable to secure anyone who *saw* this alleged stabbing?"), and that there had been no legitimate reason to interrogate the Ortiz brothers ("Isn't it a fact, Officer, that you had *no information* concerning either boy on October 23rd, prior to 4:30 p.m. —isn't that correct, sir?"). And of course he repeatedly asked about details of physical coercion, naming them as if he and Russo knew the truth:

> Hanrahan (*slowly and positively*): Isn't it a fact, Officer, that you
>     spoke to Carlos Ortiz and that you placed ammonia over his
>     face—is that correct?—in a handkerchief?
> Russo (*coldly*): I did not.
> Hanrahan: Did you at any time *kick* this defendant?
> Russo: I did not.
> Hanrahan: Did you ever pick him up and *throw him against the
>     wall?*
> Russo: I did not.

Hanrahan also managed to overstep all normal bounds in arguing with the judge, succeeding in getting himself so sharply called down that he could look martyred:

> Scheer (*objecting to a remark Hanrahan had made*): Objection.
>     Immaterial.
> Davidson: Sustained.
> Hanrahan: *I* believe it is *very* material!
> Davidson (*sarcastically*): You know, it really doesn't make any
>     difference as to what *you* believe, either to the jury or myself.

Hanrahan: I take *affront* at that remark. . . . I object *strenuously* to that remark, Judge.

Davidson (*very angry*): Let the record show that you are affronted and that you take exception. . . . I am going to tell the jury to disregard what you think, because what you think *is* immaterial, and as a lawyer you should know that! It's what *they* think about what the evidence in this case shows, not what *you* think.

Hanrahan: Your Honor, I object to that remark as to what I think.

Davidson (*furious*): That will be the *end* of that! Ask your next question! I am not here to argue with attorneys, nor am I here to have attorneys argue with me.

Hanrahan: Your Honor, I take exception to your remarks.

(Hanrahan was rather pleased by this and similar clashes. "He was pretty rough, and I felt very upset by it," he says. "But I also was glad about it, because there are many cases where a judge's remarks before the jury are grounds for reversal, or where they actually swing the jury over to feeling sympathy for the lawyer. I guess he didn't know what to make of me because I stood up there and kept going.")

Kase, when his turn came to cross-examine Russo, sought chiefly to cast doubt on Russo's statements that Valencia had been allowed to leave the police station on the night of the 22nd, and had freely and voluntarily returned the next morning and waited in the squad room all day. Russo, though his manner grew somewhat grim, held fast to his statements. Finally, Kase resorted to the technique Hanrahan— and nearly every other defense lawyer—often uses: the question that suggests a fact contrary to the witness' sworn testimony:

Kase: Detective Russo, isn't it a fact that the defendant Doel Valencia *never* left the 42nd Precinct from Thursday, October 22nd, until he was brought to court on Saturday, October 24th?

Russo: It is not.

Kase: Isn't it a fact, Detective Russo, that he was detained against his will on October 22nd, 1964?

Russo: He was not.

Kase sat down. Scheer, on redirect examination, asked Russo a few questions to patch up the weak spots made by the defense lawyers;

then Hanrahan and Kase asked a few questions on recross-examination to weaken the patches; and at 3:40 p.m. Russo, who had been on the witness stand since the previous afternoon, was excused. Justice Davidson, saying he assumed everyone was as tired as he himself, called it quits for the day.

In the morning Stephen McCabe was called as a witness. The jurors, who knew who he was from Russo's testimony, found him an intriguing contrast to Russo. Bouncy, handsome, and smiling, he looked almost too clean, wholesome, and self-assured to be real. (In the jury room, after lunch, Bored Housewife, Jewish, said she thought he was too cocky, but Retired Bank Clerk—the foreman—mildly reminded her that they were under orders not to discuss the case yet; she looked offended, but said no more.) McCabe began with an account of his first sickening examination of the apartment, when the corpse was still there, but he ran into trouble when he identified the red, white, and blue Bazooka gum wrapper ("Young America's favorite") that he had found in the kitchen: it lacked any identifying markings, but McCabe said he'd kept it in his locker ever since finding it. This immediately produced a minor row, since he should have turned it over to the Police Property Clerk; Hanrahan moved for a mistrial, but Davidson denied his motion and allowed the gum wrapper to be entered as evidence. ("He's a very fair judge," Scheer has said; certain defense lawyers, however, have sometimes referred to him as "the other D.A. in the courtroom.") Hanrahan put on an extraordinary performance from then on, leaping to his feet with objections and motions literally scores of times during the morning; at one point, in a four-minute period, he made five objections, four motions for mistrial, and took exception five times. (An exception is a formal refusal to acquiesce in a judge's ruling, and is potential grounds for a later appeal; lawyers need not actually request exceptions in court, but often do so for the jury's benefit.) Justice Davidson, his mouth curving downward ever more grimly, told Hanrahan he would do better to listen than to jump up every minute, ordered the jury to disregard some of Hanrahan's remarks, and finally lost his temper in an embarrassing exchange:

Hanrahan: Your Honor, may it be noted for the record that the detective is turning over papers and reading from those papers.
Davidson (*reasonably*): Well, he can't refresh his recollection from the paper if he doesn't turn it at the proper page.

Hanrahan (*ignoring the reply*): May it also be noted that he's
  reading from questions and answers made on those papers?
Davidson (*curtly*): It will *not* be so noted.
Hanrahan: Your Honor, if it is not so noted, I move for the with-
  drawal of a juror and the declaration of a mistrial.
Davidson: Denied.
Hanrahan: I think that's a prejudicial remark by the Court to
  the jury, and I renew my objection.

At this point, Davidson glared down at Hanrahan and barked, "I've
had *enough* of this! Sit *down!*" but Hanrahan, mule-stubborn, and
courageous in his own way, remained on his feet, fighting:

Hanrahan: All right. May I make objections for the record that
  the Court has ordered Counsel to sit down in a harsh tone?
Davidson: Yes, I do so in a harsh tone!
Hanrahan (*bloody but unbowed*): And may I move for withdrawal of a juror and declaration of a mistrial as a result of
  what the Court said?
Davidson: Denied. (*To McCabe:*) Go ahead.

(*They shouldn't carry on like that in the courtroom! It isn't right!*)
  So it went all morning, as McCabe told of his first investigation of the
apartment, his return the next day with Russo, the gathering of physical evidence (including the vital A&P slip), and the various interrogations of the three defendants. Although he made some effort not to
read directly from his notes of those interrogations but only to use
them to "refresh his recollection," Hanrahan kept making a great to-do
about it and was repeatedly rebuffed by the judge in a dozen scenes of
this sort:

McCabe: He [Carlos] was asked, "When you came back, did you
  go home?" He answered "Yes."
Hanrahan: Your Honor, may the record show that this detective
  has been reading from questions and answers?
Davidson: It will *not* so show. That is *not* the fact.
Hanrahan: He *has* been looking at the papers—
Davidson: I'm not here to argue with you. The jury will see. This
  man has been looking at his notes, as he has a right to do. He
  then lifts his head. He looks straight forward, and he answers
  with his memory refreshed.

Hanrahan: For each and every question, he's been looking down
at his notes, your Honor, as I see him from here.

Davidson (*exasperated*): BE SEATED!

Hanrahan: Your Honor, may I then sit on the side and observe
whether he's doing that or not? May I make objection—

Davidson (*caustically*): If you're unable to observe, what are
you arguing for?

Kase, in contrast, politely and earnestly asked that all references to
Valencia's name be stricken out of McCabe's account of the interrogations of Carlos and of Alfredo, and although Davidson denied the requests, he looked approving, replied that Kase's concern was entirely
proper, and instructed the jurors once again that any statement by a
defendant could be taken as evidence against himself but not against
the other people he named in it.

Scheer took the whole morning to elicit McCabe's story; by the time
he was done, the jurors had heard the crime described six times in
the words of the defendants, each detective having recounted three
such statements. But no one had said a word about the various discrepancies in their confessions—particularly the one great discrepancy having to do with time. (*Two of them say it happened at noon,
and one at night. How could there be such a difference? Is someone
lying—and which one? And why? Why don't the D.A. or the detectives say something about it?*) Neither Scheer nor the detectives had
said anything about the time discrepancy for one simple reason: they
couldn't explain it. They merely hoped the jury would believe all
three confessions as far as the murder was concerned, and disbelieve
either one or two of them in regard to the time of day when it happened.

In the afternoon Hanrahan cross-examined McCabe, using every
weapon in his arsenal. First he sought to make McCabe's testimony
seem rigged: "Well, now, how many times have you talked this matter over with the District Attorney?"; then tried to make him seem
an incompetent investigator: "Are you testifying that on October
18th you didn't speak to *any* tenants—is that correct?"; then slipshod
and lazy: "Did you ever go to the home of Carlos Ortiz in your investigation?" (McCabe had not, and had had no reason to); then
sought to imply that the statements written down by the detectives
were fraudulent: "Officer, did you have any one of these defendants

initial *any part* of the *alleged* statement that you have taken from either one of these defendants?" (the answer was no, but Hanrahan, Davidson, and Scheer knew—though the jurors did not—that a detective's notes of an interrogation need not be initialed by the suspect to be credible as evidence); and, of course, he asked about beatings, the use of ammonia, and other forms of abuse, getting firm, almost cheerful denials from McCabe, who had been forewarned by Scheer to expect such questions.

When Hanrahan was all done, Kase took over and managed to do more damage to McCabe's credibility in fifteen minutes than Hanrahan had in two hours. Kase began by harping on the implausibility of McCabe's story that he had accidentally come across Valencia the morning after his first interrogation and invited him back to the Precinct:

> Kase: Were you out looking for him the next morning?
> McCabe: No, I was not.
> Kase (*with heavy sarcasm*): You just *happened* to see him?
> McCabe (*smiling a little*): That is right.
> Kase: When you saw him, will you tell us the exact words you
>      used—
> McCabe: I said, "Valencia, come over here. Do you want to come
>      with me to the station house?"

Kase turned to look at the jury, wide-eyed, and asked him to repeat it; McCabe, reddening, did so in a gritty, determined voice. Kase pestered him as to whether Valencia, sitting in the squad room all the next day, had really been free to come and go, or had, in truth, been under detention prior to being booked. McCabe, growing flustered, said first that Valencia had been free to come and go all afternoon, but then admitted that by 2:30 p.m. he, McCabe, had "formed an opinion that he was *not* free to come and go." (*Formed an opinion? What does that mean?—that he gave an order to hold Valencia? Why doesn't he talk plain English?*)

Kase's finest moment, however, came when he read aloud from the Grand Jury minutes (which he was free to see and to quote from, now that the detective had testified directly in the trial) and got McCabe to admit having told the Grand Jury that Valencia had said the crime took place a little after 7:00 p.m., while now McCabe maintained that Valencia had said 9:00 p.m. McCabe, flushing, was not allowed to explain the difference in his testimony (he had rushed off to the Grand Jury hearing without his notes and relied on memory); it was left to the jury to figure out whether he had been mistaken or had lied, which version to believe, or whether to disbelieve him altogether.

After McCabe, the rest was anti-climactic. Dark-haired little Annette Odierno, the A&P checkout clerk, verified the sales slip as having come from her machine on October 9th, though she couldn't tell from any symbols on it what time of day Helmer had made his purchases, nor did she remember having seen him. The next morning Irwin Wasserman, the stenographer who had recorded the formal confessions taken by Assistant D.A. Vincent Vitale from Alfredo and Carlos Ortiz, read his transcript of those confessions in an expressionless drone. Hanrahan and Kase interrupted his reading with numerous objections and motions; they accomplished nothing concrete but had to make the effort, because Wasserman's official transcripts were bound to be even more convincing to the jurors, though they had no greater legal validity, than the statements the defendants had made to the detectives. In the afternoon Hanrahan briefly cross-examined Wasserman, trying to show that he kept imperfect records of when and where he reported interviews, but it was only a halfhearted effort. Kase asked what had happened when Valencia was brought before the assistant D.A., and Wasserman said that Valencia had refused to make a statement, and that there had been nothing for him to record.

With that, the first phase of the trial came to a sudden ending:

Kase: I have no further questions.
Davidson (*to Scheer*): Anything further with this witness?
Scheer: Nothing else, your Honor.
Davidson (*to Wasserman*): Thank you. (*Wasserman steps down and leaves.*)
Scheer: That's the People's case, your Honor.

Justice Davidson at once summoned the lawyers to the bench and invited Hanrahan and Kase to make their motions. This was a charade of known outcome, the purpose of which was only to put on record things that might later be needed in an appeal. Hanrahan and Kase each moved for dismissal of the case on the grounds that the People had not only failed to prove the guilt of the defendants, but had also failed to prove the elements of premeditation and conspiracy that were necessary components of the charge against them. Davidson listened patiently, denied their motions, and asked if they had anything else. They said they did not, and were ready to proceed with the Defense.

"All right," said Davidson, and as soon as they had returned to their seats he nodded to Clerk Jay to proceed. Jay got up and called out the first name given him by Kase. It came as a total surprise—and an unpleasant one—to Assistant District Attorney Scheer to hear Jay call out, "Mrs. Anna Ambos, for the Defense."

---

# IV  *Credibility*

---

JURORS, though responsible for ascertaining the facts, have almost no chance to do so directly. They are passive listeners who know only what other people tell them, and their decision as to the guilt or innocence of the defendant is based, in large part, on which of the witnesses they believe and which they do not. Physical evidence is often put before them—packets of drugs, guns, knives, photographs, specimens of handwriting, fingerprints—but nearly always it has to be linked to the crime and to the defendant by the sworn testimony of witnesses. Even where there is a laboratory analysis linking the blood of a murder victim to the blood on the clothing of the defendant, the vital element is the jury's belief in the persons who say they found the stained clothing and turned it over to the technicians, and in the technicians who tested it and came to some conclusions. A gun may have been found upon the defendant and a bullet in the victim's body, but in themselves these things are of no significance unless the jurors believe the policeman who says he found the gun in the defendant's possession, the coroner who says that the bullet in evidence is the same one he found in the body, and the ballistics expert who says that his tests show that the fatal bullet was fired from the gun in question.

Which is, of course, why both the prosecutor and the defense lawyer spend so much time and effort attacking the credibility of each other's witnesses. One way to do so is to make the witness seem befuddled, forgetful, confused, or generally unreliable, by stressing any inconsistencies or gaps in his testimony, however minor. Another way, particularly useful with an expert of any sort (a doctor, coroner, or technician, for instance), is to make him seem incompetent by asking questions implying there were steps he failed to take to preserve the evidence, or double-check it, or keep closer track of it, or label it better, and the like. Still another is to harass the witness by picking at words and challenging his knowledge until he becomes unnerved or angered, and seems untrustworthy. And perhaps the most important is to probe for evasions, contradictions, improbable claims, and other indications that the witness is a liar, and to suggest in one's questions that he not only has reason to lie, but is the very kind of person who would do so.

Indeed, even though lawyers try to make every honest mistake by an opposition witness seem a deliberate deceit, there is no doubt that many of the distortions and errors contained in sworn testimony are the result of deliberate lying under oath. For perjury has always been quite common, according to historians of the law, and if this was so centuries ago, when men believed they might be punished from on high for swearing falsely, it must be more so today, when most people fear nothing except being caught by their fellow men—a risk which, in the case of perjury, is very small. H. Richard Uviller, an assistant district attorney in Manhattan for fourteen years and now a professor at Columbia Law School, speaks from a wealth of first-hand experience: *"Everybody* lies under oath. Fortunately, few of the lies are big ones, but even the most honest witness will try to make his story a little better, under oath, than it really is."

Cumulatively, however, even the little lies have a profound effect upon the character of trial by jury, making the jurors' search for truth something like feeling one's way through a strange room in the dark, or perhaps even like a long, fevered dream in which the solid things before one's eyes shift and change shape, or the people one is with become, somehow, other people even as one looks at them. Most jurors (particularly white ones) assume, at first, that the police will be telling the truth—they are, after all, figures of authority and protectors of social order—and find it deeply disturbing when the cross-examination and the testimony of defense witnesses cast doubt on their truthfulness. But that which the average juror finds so disconcerting is taken for granted by all who work in the courts for any time: the police do frequently lie on the witness stand, not to frame innocent persons and not even to cover themselves with glory but the better to play their part in the convicting of the guilty. "As a cop, you're *supposed* to lie on the stand," says one New York detective assigned to undercover investigation of his fellows, "but it doesn't seem like perjury. It's just a thing you've seen other cops doing in order to make sure they put the criminal away, so you do it too." Paul Chevigny, an angry civil-liberties lawyer who described police abuses in New York in his recent book, *Police Power,* writes:

> Police lying is the most pervasive of all abuses. . . . The Criminal Court is not viewed as a tribunal for the determination of fact, but as a sort of administrative adjunct to the police station for the purpose of obtaining desirable results. . . . The police feel that they have made a mistake if they fail to obtain the conviction, not if they lied to obtain it.

A policeman who has interrogated a suspect and gotten incriminating statements from him, and who only belatedly gave him the required warnings, can be counted upon to swear in court that he gave the suspect the warnings beforehand. A policeman who searches a person or a person's car without probable cause will, if he finds anything incriminating, invent a probable cause. In California, for instance, highway patrolmen have recently been swearing, in case after case, that they searched the suspect or his car because, when pulled over to the side of the road by the patrolman, the suspect made a "furtive gesture," as if to hide contraband. As Justice Stanley Mosk of the California Supreme Court recently wrote, "The furtive gesture has on occasion been little short of a subterfuge in order to conduct a search on the basis of mere suspicion or intuition." Comparable deceptions have been used elsewhere—particularly in New York—in connection with drug arrests: in the "dropsy cases" mentioned earlier, narcotics police swear straight-facedly, in case after case, that just as they approached the defendant, whom they had no valid reason to stop and search, he happened to drop a packet of heroin or marijuana, which the policeman then picked up and because of which he made the arrest. In September 1970, Judge Irving Younger of the New York Criminal Court caustically observed in a decision, "The very language of the testimony is identical from one case to another. . . . Surely, though, not in *every* case was the defendant unlucky enough to drop his narcotics at the feet of a policeman."

But only professional civil-libertarians, radicals, and cop-haters believe that perjury is entirely or primarily a police practice. It may be, in special kinds of cases—those growing out of civil-rights demonstrations, for instance—but in the majority of criminal cases it is the defendants who, if they testify at all, lie fervently, sweepingly, and—unfortunately for themselves—unimaginatively. Prosecutors, defense lawyers, and judges all grow hardened and cynical after hearing the same threadbare clichés used by hundreds of defendants: the same insistence that they never even heard of the victim, the same tales about having been given the wallet by a stranger or having found the jewelry in the gutter, the same ingenuous suggestions that someone must have planted the drugs on them for a joke or to frame them, the same claims that they were with strangers (whose names they cannot furnish) at the time of the crime, the same assertions that the police gave them no warnings, smacked them around, threatened to pin tougher raps on them if they didn't cooperate, and refused to let them see their lawyers. These statements, made under oath, are heard so often and so predictably that every judge, prosecutor, and trial lawyer knows them by heart; no wonder defense lawyers are eager to avoid jurors who have sat on criminal cases before. "The police do lie," says Professor Leo Loughery of the John Jay College of Criminal Justice, "but defendants lie far more often. It stands to reason: they have a lot more to lose than the police by telling the truth and a lot more to gain by lying."

A lot more to gain, and with little risk. For as the Crime Commission pointed out, perjury itself is very common but successful prosecution of that crime is very rare because of the special common-law rules governing perjury trials. For one thing, the falsity of the testimony has to be established by more than one witness; for another, circumstantial evidence alone, no matter how pervasive, is insufficient to convict. "The integrity of the trial," the Commission said, "depends upon the power to compel truthful testimony and to punish falsehood"—and concluded gloomily that as things now stand, most courts and prosecutors have little power to do either thing.

Guilty defendants generally perjure themselves on their own initiative, but their lawyers often help them decide to do so—not by urging them to lie, but by giving them advice that makes it apparent how necessary lying will be. Monroe Freedman, professor of law at George Washington University, caused consternation among members of the bar a few years ago by candidly exposing—and justifying—certain practices of many defense lawyers, in an article published in the *Michigan Law Review:* he argued that to be truly ethical, a defense lawyer must give his client legal advice even when he has reason to think it will tempt the client to lie under oath, and that he must let his client take the stand even when he knows the client is going to commit perjury. (The defense lawyer's paramount obligations, Professor Freedman argued, are to preserve the confidentiality of his relationship to the client and to give him the maximum chance to defend himself; these override the conflicting ethical obligations not to suborn perjury and to disclose a crime planned by his client.)

But at their lawyers' advice, guilty defendants—and even innocent ones—often prefer not to take the stand, forgoing their chance to explain things to the jury. It is not so much that they risk breaking down under cross-examination and blurting out the whole truth; that regularly happens only on the screen or on stage. "In real life," Louis Nizer says in *My Life in Court,* "the witness's fortitude in the face of exposure [by cross-examination] is as remarkable as a human body's resistance to incredible torment," and even when the witness is trapped in obvious contradictions, "he continues to fight back and clutch for the remote chance that the tide will turn and he will not go under."

It is not the fear of being caught that keeps defendants off the stand, but the fear of something less direct and at least as damaging; the revelation of the defendant's previous criminal acts, and the jurors' resulting feeling that he is the kind of man who would be likely to commit other crimes, and therefore probably did commit the one for which he is on trial. This represents only common sense on the part of jurors: in everyday life we judge people and interact with them on the basis of our cumulative experience of their behavior. But in court we dare not use common sense; no one who has ever done wrong could be tried fairly if his past were automatically taken as proof of fresh guilt, no suspect—in particular, no political dissenter—could avoid lifelong harassment and repeated imprisonments if hostile police and prosecutors had only to reveal his past in order to get him convicted anew. And therefore evidence of prior crimes is admissible only when it tends to prove guilt—when it directly connects the previous crimes with the present one—but inadmissible when all it shows is bad character—that is, a *disposition* to commit crime.

Accordingly, in most prosecutions the district attorney cannot introduce such evidence as long as the defendant does not take the stand. The moment he does, however, a peculiar change takes place in the rules of evidence: the district attorney is suddenly entitled to ask him questions about his previous criminal behavior, not for the still impermissible purpose of showing his general disposition toward crime, but presumably only to prove that he is a person not worthy of belief. It is a pure fraud; as Erwin N. Griswold, formerly Dean of Harvard Law School and now Solicitor General of the United States, has acidly asked, "We say that the evidence of the prior convictions is admissible only to impeach the defendant's testimony . . . [and] juries are solemnly instructed to this effect . . . [but] is there any-one who doubts what the effect of this evidence in fact is on the jury?"

And not just on the jury, naïve though jurors may be. For Professors Harry Kalven, Jr., and Hans Zeisel of the University of Chicago Law School report in their massive study *The American Jury* that judges gen-erally agree with verdicts rendered by juries in serious cases where the criminal records of the defendants have been revealed. This suggests that judges, when they know the defendant has a record, are no more fair-minded than jurors and no better able than they to abide by that special form of reasoning which flouts common sense in order to be utterly fair, and which we call Justice.

---

# V   *The Defense*

---

UNTIL the defense lawyers told Justice Davidson they were ready to proceed, Assistant District Attorney Scheer had not known whether they would call any witnesses or put the defendants themselves on the stand. In many a criminal trial the best defense, or at least the only sensible one, consists of offering no evidence whatever, but simply attacking the credibility of the prosecution's witnesses in an effort to create doubt in the minds of the jurors. Scheer had hoped things would not go that way with this trial. "I love to cross-examine," he has told friends. "I love to have the defendant on the stand, twisting and turning, and trying to change his story around. Besides, only if he takes the stand can I bring out his record—and if he has one, that's worth a great deal to the prosecution. Of course, the law says a defendant shouldn't be tried on the basis of his past conflicts—and I think it's a *good* law—but the average juror, as a practical man, will certainly consider it if I can bring it out."

Kase and Hanrahan had decided, long before the trial began, not to rely on attacking the People's witnesses, but to mount a full-scale defense, with their key witnesses being the defendants themselves. "I felt strongly that these boys had to explain their confessions to the jury," Hanrahan recalls. "Jurors want an explanation from the defendant, they're just waiting for it—and if you don't give it to them, your chances aren't good. And if the defendant is a youngster, and small, and decent-looking, the jury is all set to be sympathetic."

Kase was of much the same mind. "I could have summed up for Valencia without putting him on, and brought out all the important points," he says, "—the sloppy detective work, the lack of any evidence except Valencia's admissions to the detectives, the issue of his overnight detention, the fact that the whole thing looked like a frame. But I felt the jury would prefer to hear him tell it himself, and especially to have him explain why he admitted the crime to the detectives and then a little while later refused to repeat it to Vitale. I knew Scheer would drag out his record, but it was a calculated risk and I felt we had to take it."

Kase also planned to put on Valencia's sister and his former employer, each of whom would offer an alibi for part of the day, but he kept wishing he could find someone or something to contradict the confessions more directly. A day or so before he was to start his defense, he dropped by 399 East 160th Street in the morning before going to court. He meant only to have a look around inside—for what, he could not even say—but the front door was locked. As he was trying it, however, Mrs. Ambos appeared inside, opened it, and asked if she could help him. He asked her who she was, and whether she had known the murdered man or seen anything having to do with the crime, and was astounded to find that she did—so much so, in fact, that she had been interrogated by detectives and assistant D.A.s a total of five times. "I thought, 'Omigod, why didn't they bring her in to testify?' " he recalls. "It could only be that her testimony would have made trouble for them and hurt their case." After talking to her at length, his suspicion was fully confirmed; he felt excited—and shocked—by his discovery. As one of Kase's good friends put it, "Ken is too nice a guy to say this, but what Scheer did was revolting— he had vital evidence that could have helped the defendants, and he concealed it."

So Kase subpoenaed Mrs. Ambos as a defense witness and put her on first for dramatic effect. Up to the witness stand she came, a quick, fidgety skinful of brittle bones, her hair wispy and disordered, her gnarled hands shaking a little. Kase gently and deferentially got her to identify herself and tell of her ownership of the building and long-time acquaintanceship with her tenant Alexander Helmer. Then he asked if she recalled October 9th, 1964. "Correct!" she said. Did she recall what happened on that day? With the tart forthrightness that the elderly take as their privilege, she ignored the niceties of procedure and bluntly asked Kase, "You vont me to tell the story the vay it happened?" The judge and jurors smiled, and Kase asked her to go ahead. She told of the two "Spanish" youths she had seen in her vestibule a little after 7:00 p.m. that evening (she did not, however, identify them as the Ortizes or Valencia), and how, just after they left, Helmer had come in, she had locked the front door after him, and had gone upstairs a moment later to visit Mrs. Varela, discovering fresh blood in the third-floor hallway when she got there. Kase asked if anyone could have followed Helmer up the steps. Absolutely not, she said; she herself had been there all the time. Furthermore, she had stayed with Mrs. Varela all evening, and had heard no noises from Helmer's adjoining apartment. Kase kept his questioning brief; he was content to have introduced testimony that contradicted vital elements of all three confessions (especially Valencia's), and was all done with Mrs. Ambos in five minutes.

Scheer stood up, displeased at what he had to do to this nice old lady, but unflinching. First, he managed to make Mrs. Ambos look obstinate and a trifle unreasonable:

Mrs. Ambos: So I rang her bell. So I says, "Do you know that it is blood, out here in the hall?"

Scheer (*reasonably*): You don't *know* whether it was really blood, madam, do you?

Mrs. Ambos (*testily*): It *vos* blood! Blood spots!
Scheer (*still reasonably*): It *looked* like it, didn't—
Mrs. Ambos (*quite crossly*): Like *blood* spots, very fresh!

He asked if she was relying solely on her memory, on certain crucial points; she snapped back, "That's *exactly* vot happened," and again, "That's *chust* the vay it vos!" Whenever possible, he managed to convey the impression that she was difficult, stubborn, and possibly a trifle senile:

Scheer: You don't *know* whether Mr. Helmer left his apartment after that [7:15], do you, madam?
Mrs. Ambos: No, I don't know, I can't tell you if he vent in the apartment.
Scheer (*patiently, a little more loudly*): I say, you don't know whether he *left* the apartment?
Mrs. Ambos: Oh, *left* the apartment—no, ve heard notting.
Scheer (*a hand to his forehead, in apparent exasperation*): I didn't ask you that!
Mrs. Ambos: Oh, no, I didn't see him, unt heard no apartment opening. Notting.
Scheer (*wearily*): Mrs. Ambos, *please* bear with me, yes? At least, between 7:15 or thereabouts and 10 o'clock, you don't know whether Mr. Helmer left the apartment to go shopping and come back. You don't *know*, do you?
Mrs. Ambos (*shrugging*): No.

The more he seemed to seek clarification, the more he was able to obtain confusion. (*He shouldn't be so hard on her. She's an old lady; she can't help it if she gets things a bit mixed up.*) Finally, Scheer played his trump card—a point he had remembered about her story from his conversations with the detectives:

Scheer: And do you remember telling Detective McCabe that you saw the two [Spanish] boys on a Thursday?
Mrs. Ambos (*uncomfortably*): That time I vos confused, yes, mit the Thursday, the Friday—
Scheer (*suddenly harsh and demanding*): Now, madam, did you mention *anything* about a Thursday to Detective Mc-

Cabe when you spoke to him—*yes* or *no,* please!
Mrs. Ambos (*defiantly*): Vell, yes—I said it vos Thursday.

(*It's a shame, it's too bad. But maybe he has to do it.*) Kase was
seething; when Scheer had concluded and was passing by on his way
back to his own table, Kase whispered to him, "They murdered the
wrong Alexander." Scheer stared at him and smiled faintly.

Mrs. Varela, the next defense witness, seemed to verify Mrs. Ambos'
story; she said she remembered the evening when there had been
blood in the hall, and that it had been a Friday. But Scheer asked her
if she, too, had not first told McCabe that it had been a Thursday, and
while she did not recall telling him that, she said she'd take his word
for it that she had. Kase was disappointed at her backing down, but
hoped that the jurors would at least feel some doubts creeping in.

The following day he called as his next witness Assistant District
Attorney Vincent Vitale. (*A district attorney for the defense? What
kind of business is that?*) Kase had only a few questions for him, one
of which was exceedingly important: he wanted to know exactly
what Valencia had said when he was brought in to make his formal
confession. Vitale was very precise: "He said, 'I didn't do it, and I never
admitted to the police that I did it.' That's the extent of the conversation." Kase, feeling he had at last scored solidly, next called Irving
Goldstein, the traffic manager for Consolidated Millinery, who testified
that, according to the payroll record, Valencia had worked eight
hours on the day of the murder. This seemed to eliminate him from
any reconstruction of events that placed the crime at midday; Scheer,
however, thumbed through the pile of papers and investigation reports
on his table, found what he was looking for, and asked Goldstein if
the time-card showed when Valencia had left (it did not), and if he
could recall seeing Valencia there all day (he could not).

Valencia's chief alibi witness, however, was his sister, Idalia, who
came next. (*A little jazzy-looking, but she speaks well, she seems very
respectable.*) Idalia, answering Kase's questions in a firm, low-pitched
voice with almost no Spanish accent, said that on the night of October
9th she had met Doel coming out of the elevator on the ground floor
of their building at about 8:30 or 9:00 p.m. He had gone back upstairs with her and remained there all evening, both of them packing
for their move from the apartment. Kase did not belabor the point or
make her repeat it; it was obvious that if Valencia had been with her

the whole evening, his confession had to be partly or even wholly false. Kase therefore went on to the matter of Doel's detention: Idalia said that the detectives had picked Doel up for questioning on the evening of the 22nd, and that he had never come home that night. Thoroughly alarmed, she had gone to the Precinct the next day and had inquired about him upstairs in the squad room, but had been told by several detectives that they had no one named Doel Valencia there and did not know where he was.

Illegal detention and the refusal to let a close relative see a suspect would both be defects in the legality of the People's case; accordingly, when Scheer got his chance to cross-examine Idalia Valencia, he assaulted her credibility head-on, using a highly effective device that he knew in advance would be objected to and ruled out, yet would surely get across to the jury:

Scheer (*reasonably*): Now, you are here to help your brother, aren't you?
Idalia Valencia: Yes.
Scheer: You know what he is charged with, do you?
Idalia Valencia: Yes, I do.
Scheer (*like a schoolteacher*): What is he charged with?
Idalia Valencia: First-degree murder.
Scheer (*louder, a trifle nasty now*): Madam, you say you want to help him, don't you?
Idalia Valencia (*puzzled*): Yes, I do.
Scheer (*very loudly, looking at the jury while speaking*): And would you *lie* to help him out of this charge, madam?

Kase leaped up, shouting his objection, and Justice Davidson sustained him (the question was thoroughly improper for a number of reasons), but Scheer was satisfied; he had made his point. (*He really sneaked that one over! The judge ruled it out, but Scheer might have something there.*)

Scheer next asked her to recall exactly what Doel had done on the several days before and after the day of the murder; she could not, and he suggested that she claimed to remember the 9th in detail only because that was the day for which an alibi was needed. He contrived to make her seem recalcitrant and evasive ("I didn't ask you that, did I?" and "Madam, *please!*") and often repeated his questions in a hectoring and exasperating way ("Is that correct, madam—is that correct?" and "You don't know where he was, do you? *Do you?*"). She grew nervous, faltered, stalled for time by asking him to repeat his questions, and, when he nagged her for twenty minutes for a precise description of the squad room (implying that she had never been there), became vague and confused. Finally he flung out the impermissible question once more: "Madam, you'll tell us *anything* to help your brother, won't you?" and although Kase angrily objected and Davidson sustained him again, Scheer sat down with a faint, frozen smile of satisfaction.

"You're next," Kase whispered to Valencia at the counsel table. "Are you ready?" Valencia nodded. Kase stood up and said, "I call Doel Valencia to the witness stand." There was a faint murmur, and a palpable feeling of excitement in the courtroom; nothing that had gone before could compare with hearing an accused man tell his own story. (*Good, good! We're going to get to hear them and find out what they're like.*) Valencia got up and shambled to the stand, where he spelled out his name for the stenographer in a virtual whisper and took the oath inaudibly. Kase led him through the usual background questions—his age, birthplace, and so on—and then got to more awkward matters: his common-law marriage, and his burglary conviction. (Since Scheer would have brought them both up anyway, Kase did so first, hoping to make Valencia look like an open and honest witness.)

Then came Valencia's account of the day of the murder. Speaking very rapidly and slurringly, in a barely audible voice, he said he had worked all day on October 9th, come back to Melrose by subway, stood on a front stoop talking to some friends for a few minutes, and gone home by 8:00 p.m. At 9:00 he had gone out to look for his sister; he had met her as he was coming out of the elevator, and gone back upstairs with her and spent the evening packing.

He was hard enough to follow when giving this alibi, but when he began telling about his interrogations, he became almost wholly unintelligible. He jabbered away faster and faster, in a mumbled, hiccupy, half-hysterical fashion, and the court reporter, his own lawyer, and the judge all repeatedly asked him to slow down, to speak louder, and to enunciate more clearly, but although he agreed to, he could not seem to control himself. He spoke of the first night's interrogation, when (he said) McCabe accused him of being part of the murder team and told him a woman had seen him running out of the building. A little before 1:00 a.m. McCabe locked him in the cage, and he remained in it until midday, when, shortly after he saw Carlos being brought in, he himself was taken out of the cage and his day of agony began. A team of detectives began to interrogate him, and each time he professed ignorance of any detail of the crime they would smack him in the face or on the ears, punch him in the stomach, kick him, and knock him against the wall, all the while telling him exactly how they thought the crime had occurred and what his part in it had been.

When he came to the ammonia episode and the subsequent confrontation with Alfredo, his speech became so incoherent that Justice Davidson stopped the proceedings several times and lectured him on the need to make himself understood. But it did not help; he kept running on like a hysterical child, his words jumbled together and scarcely articulated, the language barren, the thoughts disjointed:

> So [Alfredo], he put down his head, he say, "Yes, Doel an' Negrito came down, an' they say the man was hurt," an' I tol' him, *"What* are you sayin'?" an' the officer with the blond hair, McCabe, he hit me against the stomach, knocked me against the wall, he say, "I tol' you, don' say nothin'." They pull me out of the room, they started hittin' me again, an' say, "I tol' you, I tol' you," I say, "No, sir, that's a lie," an' then they take me to this other room an' the other officer say, "You *know* you tol' the other officer you did it," I tol' him, "Yes, when they were hittin' me." . . . I tol' him, "I don' want to get hit any more," that's what I tol' him, he say, "Handcuff him again an' take him back to the room," an' McCabe came an' started backing me against the ears, an' I tol' him, "I ain' got nothin' to do with this," "Yes, you do"—hittin' me again, he say, "Why don' you answer?" an' punched me.

On and on went his bewildering account of innumerable beatings, questionings, and unidentified tormentors who forced the story of the crime upon him a bit at a time until he knew everything they wanted him to say. Finally, unable to stand any more punishment, he gave in, was brought in to McCabe and Russo, and answered all the questions they asked him while they took notes. But immediately afterward, when McCabe was locking him up, Valencia said to him that everything he had just admitted was a lie; McCabe said he knew that, but who would believe a spick if police officers said otherwise?

A little later, when he was led into the Lieutenant's room to repeat his confession for Assistant D.A. Vitale, he told him he had nothing to do with the crime, and that the detectives had been trying to make him say he did; he did not explain to the jury, nor did Kase ask him to, what had made him decide to take this step, or how he had dared to do it in view of the fact that afterward he would be in the hands of the same police who had been torturing him all afternoon. (*Not a word? Isn't he going to say a thing about it?*)

Kase spent only an hour on the direct examination of Valencia, but by the time he was through everyone in the courtroom was exhausted from the effort to hear and to understand the manic, disjointed narration. As an ordeal, however, it was nothing compared to what followed, for Scheer cross-examined him for two hours that afternoon, and on Monday (the next trial day) spent the entire morning and afternoon at it. Infinitely persevering and energetic, untroubled by his own repetitiousness, he stalked Valencia like Javert pursuing Jean Valjean. He began by extracting from the dossier of documents, notes, and exhibits on his table certain papers on which he had full details of Valencia's burglary conviction and of his later arrest in a shooting incident, and questioned him about each episode at considerable length. From this, he went on to review Valencia's testimony, laboriously seeking to show at every step of the way that the defendant was a liar, and not a very good one at that. Sometimes he did so by nagging Valencia about the things he claimed not to remember: Valencia had been vague, for instance, about the identity of the detectives who questioned him the first night, and Scheer pounded away at him on this point:

Scheer: Was Detective Russo there?

Valencia: I don' remember.

Scheer (*exasperated*): Did you hear Detective Russo testify that he asked you questions on the evening of October 22nd, 1964?

Valencia: Yes.

Scheer (*with heavy irony*): Does that refresh your recollection, now, that he spoke with you that evening?

Valencia (*cornered, nervous*): I still don' remember, I don' remember seein' him.

Scheer (*jabbing at Valencia with forefinger*): Do you *deny* that you spoke with Detective Russo the evening of October 22nd?

Valencia (*almost whining*): I don' *remember* talkin' to him.

Scheer (*shouting each word*): I . . . AM . . . ASKING . . . YOU . . .

Kase (*aggrieved*): Your Honor, I object—

Scheer (*turning angrily on Kase*): *May* I?

Davidson: It is cross-examination. He can ask him that.

Inch by inch, Scheer went over Valencia's testimony, seeking to make him look evasive, obstinate, or perjurious (*"Look* at me, please!" . . . "I didn't ask you that, did I?" . . . "Did somebody suggest to you, in any form, to say that to this jury?" . . . "Aren't you saying that because you are charged with a crime here?"). He asked Valencia to repeat the story of the beatings and physical punishment at such length that it began to sound exaggerated, improbable, and unreal; he then asked whether Valencia had made any complaints of physical illness when he was interviewed at court the next day by a Department of Correction officer, and produced the interview record to prove he hadn't; he then asked whether Valencia had made any such complaints to the examining doctor at the jail in Brooklyn, and produced medical records which showed Valencia had no signs of trauma. Had Valencia told Assistant D.A. Vitale he'd been beaten into making a false confession? No. Or Mr. Carney, his lawyer at the arraignment? No. Or any judge at any of his hearings? No.

When Scheer got to the matter of Valencia's heroin addiction, he seemed intent on extracting enough material for a dissertation, asking so many questions about the price per glassine, the number of shots Valencia used per week, his method of using it, and his withdrawal symptoms in jail that Kase asked for a bench conference and protested to Davidson that Scheer was attempting to prejudice the jury against his client. With a perfectly straight face, Justice Davidson cited precedent and said, "I believe the District Attorney is doing that for the purpose of impeaching his credibility—is that right?," to which Scheer gratefully said, "Yes, your Honor." ("A strict judge," Scheer later said of Davidson, "but fair.") With his sanction, Scheer went back to the topic of drug addiction and pursued it for another half-hour.

The greater part of the Monday session, however, was devoted to a

word-by-word review of every question and answer in Russo's notes of
the final interrogation. Scheer systematically forced Valencia to deny
every incriminating answer, and to maintain that the whole confession was a fabrication:

> Scheer: Now, was this question asked of you: " 'Who was
> there?' Answer: 'Freddy Ortiz.' " Do you remember that
> question?
> Valencia: Yes, sir.
> Scheer: "Question: 'Who else was there?' Answer: 'Carlo and
> Angel.' " Do you remember that question being asked of
> you, and you making that answer?
> Valencia: No, sir.
> Scheer. Do you *deny* making that answer?
> Valencia: Yes, sir.
> Scheer (*staring at him, speechless; then, finally, in a sarcastic
> tone*): Do you know where the detectives got the name
> "Angel"?
> Valencia: I don' know.

Beyond making Valencia deny everything repeatedly, this technique
enabled Scheer to state and restate each detail of the crime as given in
Valencia's own words; the repeated details would presumably be far
more vivid in the jurors' memories than Valencia's repeated denials:

> Scheer: Was this question asked of you, Mr. Valencia: " 'What
> did the old man say or do, if anything?' Answer: 'He was
> telling them to get out. Then Carlos grabbed the old man
> around the neck, and then Angel stabbed him.' "
> Valencia: He [Russo] *tol'* me Carlos grabbed him and then Angel
> stabbed him.
> Scheer (*with mock surprise*): You didn't tell *him* that?
> Valencia (*sincerely*): No, sir.
> Scheer (*sarcastic again*): Do you know how Detective Russo got
> those details in that answer, Mr. Valencia?
> Valencia: No, sir.
> Scheer (*bellowing*): It came off *your lips,* didn't it—
> Valencia: No, sir—
> Scheer: —because it's the *truth,* isn't it?
> Valencia: It's not, it's not the truth, sir, it's a lie!

After what was an endless torment to everyone in the courtroom,
Scheer came to the end of the confession and abruptly said to Justice

Davidson, "No other questions." Kase, who had been suffering agonies for his hapless client all day but been unable to do more than register an objection now and then, saw no point in going back over any of the material; despite Scheer's terrible persistence, Valencia had stuck to his story that the whole confession had been fabricated by the detectives and forced upon him by brutality. Kase stood up and announced, "The defendant Doel Valencia rests at this particular time," and the judge declared the trial recessed until late the next morning; the jurors staggered out, punch-drunk and exasperated by what they had been put through. (*He has to do it; it's his job. But what a bore he is, what a grind!*)

When the trial resumed late the next morning, it was Hanrahan's turn to put on his defense. He called Carlos to the stand—(*He's so little, so harmless-looking!*)—and began by asking him his age, height, and weight, and what kind of work he had been doing. Carlos said he'd been out of work, but had been helping a building superintendent remove trash. Hanrahan asked if he had ever been convicted of a crime, and Carlos said he had not, an answer Hanrahan had told him would be legally correct, since in his previous difficulties with the law he had been under sixteen and thus technically a delinquent "child," not a convicted criminal.

Carlos gave his own account of October 9th, including the fruitless trip downtown to look for a job, the afternoon spent in the apartment of the girl named Marie, a few hours hanging around with a man named Tom, and the evening at home, watching television. On the 23rd, he said, Russo duped him into going to the Precinct; there, in his first terrifying encounter with Russo and McCabe, the detectives accused him of being part of the crime, and then turned him over to others, who, beside giving him the ammonia torture, took turns questioning, slapping, punching, and beating him all afternoon until they broke his will to resist: he surrendered and agreed to every detail they had been seeking to force upon him. ("When they used to ask me something—I mean *tell* me something—an' I say, 'How could I say this if I di'n' do it?,' they used to hit me an' I have to say yes to stop them from hittin' me.") He told his story in a calmer, simpler fashion than Valencia—indeed, sometimes giving a bitter little laugh—but the details were very much like those given by Valencia, and he even attributed a racial slur to McCabe that sounded very much like the one in Valencia's story:

He say, "You know somethin'?—I hate spicks." No, he say, "I hate *niggers*," that's what he tol' me, an' then I look at him an' he say, "You know somethin' else?—I hate spicks." An' when he say that, he stuck his finger in my eye an' started twistin'.

(*Did McCabe really say anything like that? Could Carlos be putting in the part about "niggers" because five of us on this jury are Negroes?*)

Hanrahan, knowing Scheer was likely to produce medical records showing that Carlos had had no signs of trauma the day after the beatings, sought to counter such testimony in advance: he asked Carlos if he had told the examining doctor at the jail of any pains he felt, and Carlos said he had told the doctor he had pains in the chest from the ammonia, but the doctor had said it was nothing and ignored it.

Hanrahan's direct examination lasted only half an hour. (*Is that all? Where are those people Carlos says he saw during the day?*) Justice Davidson called for an early luncheon recess, and in the afternoon Scheer went to work on Carlos. The process was painfully familiar to everyone by now, but it went a little more quickly with Carlos than it had with Valencia; instead of becoming excited and voluble under attack, he grew sullen and laconic, sticking to simple answers and repeating them doggedly despite Scheer's shouting and table-pounding. (Mrs. Pomales, recalling that afternoon, says, "Every time the District Attorney would yell and hit hard on the table, I felt as if a knife was being stabbed into *me*.")

Scheer went through various opening maneuvers, asking Carlos if he had attributed a racial slur to McCabe because there were five Negroes on the jury, hammering away at the fact that he had made no physical complaints the day of arraignment, needling him about his having been out of work and without money at the time of Helmer's murder. With this opening barrage out of the way, Scheer dug in, as he had with Valencia, and proceeded to go through every question and answer in both of Carlos' interrogations and in his confession to Vitale. Carlos freely admitted making all the answers that were non-incriminating; he insisted, however, that all those that linked him with the crime had been "told" to him during his beatings, and repeated by him during the Q&A only to avoid further physical abuse. For instance:

Scheer (*reading from the Q&A*): " '—Then I saw Negrito with some money and then we left the apartment and ran downstairs. We all ran to my house. Then we stayed in the apartment a few minutes, then they said they were going downtown to buy some dope. They were going to buy dope.' " Do you remember making that answer?

Carlos (*sullen*): *He* say that to me, an' I repeated that.

Scheer (*sarcastic*): He gave you all those details?

Carlos: He say that to me earlier, an' I repeated that.

Scheer: Listen to the question: Did he give you all these details to say—yes or no?

Carlos: Yes.

The boring, repeated denials, the continual assertions that Russo and others had told him what to say, began to sound unreal, as Scheer knew from experience that they would. And once again the method permitted Scheer to dwell upon the details of the crime, going over them again and again, and imprinting them indelibly on the minds of the jurors:

Scheer (*shouting, pointing at Carlos*): Isn't it the truth that while you were holding the old man's arms, Angel plunged that knife into the chest of the old man—

Carlos (*interrupting, desperate*): No!

Scheer: —five times?

Carlos: No!

Scheer: And you didn't panic or run out, isn't that the truth?

Carlos: I wasn' *there!*

Scheer also often suggested that Carlos had been coached in his testimony ("Did anybody *tell* you to say you were handcuffed to a bed?"), used sarcasm to suggest the impossibility of Carlos' claims of physical abuse ("For about *six hours* or more, off and on, you were beaten by various detectives?"), and made much of his trifling inconsistencies ("You made a 'mistake' before, when you said nobody kicked you in your legs?"). (*Will it never end? How much of this do we need?*)

But it did end when Scheer came to the last and most damning answer in the transcript of Carlos' confession to Vitale—an answer Carlos acknowledged, either forgetting to make a disclaimer or being caught short by Scheer's sudden ending of the cross-examination:

Scheer: "Question: 'Is there anything else you wish to tell me about this, Carlos?' " Do you remember that last question that was asked by Mr. Vincent A. Vitale?

Carlos: Yes, sir.

Scheer: And do you remember making this final answer: " 'The only thing I can say, I am guilty for what I did.' " Did you say that to him?

Carlos: Yes, I did.

Scheer (*instantly*): Your Honor, I have no other questions.

Hanrahan, who had been trying to protect Carlos by objecting now and again to Scheer's questions, and had even earned himself a couple of tongue-lashings by Justice Davidson, now tried on redirect examination to salvage something by getting Carlos to say once more that he had been afraid for his very life, and that the doctor at the jail had simply ignored his complaints and his pain. But Scheer, on re-cross-examination, showed the medical records of the jail to be fairly detailed—he even had Carlos pull up his left sleeve to show the jurors the tattoo "Luisa," which was recorded on the medical form—and finally both sides were done, the day was over, and everyone left, exhausted and relieved to get away from it for a few hours. Only Alexander Scheer, gathering up his bulging files and heading for his office, seemed unwearied by the day; to look at him, one might have thought he could have gone on for hours, until everyone around him had collapsed.

The next day was largely devoted to Alfredo, the palest, thinnest, and least audible of all. ("The people can't hear you," Justice Davidson told him repeatedly. "The people on the jury are indicating to you by raising their hands that they cannot hear you.") In a whispery and whining fashion, he told of being questioned by McCabe and Russo, of being punched, kicked, thrown to and fro, and generally terrorized into agreeing to say whatever they wanted him to say, a process he said had taken about two and a half hours from beginning to end. He had repeated his confession to Vitale in the evening because, quite simply, he was afraid of being beaten again if he refused to do so.

Scheer, cross-examining him, began by asking about his burglary conviction; Hanrahan objected that this had been a "youthful-offender matter" and hence should not be brought out in court, but Davidson said Scheer had a right to try to impeach the witness, and permitted it. Scheer next got to the matter of heroin; Alfredo admitted having used it regularly, and having been arrested for possession and works. Scheer wanted to know how often he used it, how much he paid, what technique of shooting-up he used; Hanrahan objected, but Davidson brushed him aside like a fly.

Once again, however, the largest part of the cross-examination consisted of the insufferable rehashing of all the questions and answers written down by Russo and McCabe in the Q&A. Alfredo, a feebler witness than either of the other two, squirmed, writhed, and, time after time, surrendered:

> Scheer (*reading from the Q&A*): "Question: 'Why did you want water?' 'Because I was sick, and after we do the job I would get off.' " Did you say that to Detective Russo?
>
> Alfredo (*in a whisper*): No.
>
> Scheer: What does that mean, "I was sick"—what is that expression? (*Hanrahan objects; Davidson overrules him.*)
>
> Alfredo (*after a long pause, giving in under Scheer's stare*): You would say that when you need drugs.
>
> Scheer: And, "after we do the job"—what would we mean by that expression? (*Hanrahan objects; Davidson overrules him.*)
>
> Alfredo: I don' know.
>
> Scheer: No idea? No idea what that means?
>
> Alfredo (*stalling*): No idea, what? (*Hanrahan objects; Davidson overrules him.*)
>
> Scheer (*coming close to Alfredo and speaking loudly and slowly*): What does that expression mean—"I would get off"?
>
> Alfredo (*hanging his head and whispering*): When you shoot up.

But at least Alfredo never wavered on the major issue: he maintained consistently that every incriminating answer had been forced upon him by the detectives, and that none of them was true:

> Scheer: "Question: 'What happened after your brother went upstairs for the water?' Answer: 'Negrito said, "Let's go," and I ran into the building to ring the bell for them.' " Did you make that answer to Detective Russo?
>
> Alfredo: I *repeated* that.
>
> Scheer (*contemptuously*): You *repeated* it. . . . Do you know

where Detective Russo got the information that you ran
across the street and rang the bell?

Alfredo: I don' know.

Scheer: Didn't *you* tell it to him?

Alfredo: *He* was tellin' *me* all that.

Scheer (*sarcastic*): Russo is putting everything in here?

Alfredo: Right.

Scheer: And charging you with murder in the first degree?

Alfredo: That's right!

(*Why is the D.A. keeping on at it? Why do we have to hear it over
and over again?*) Scheer was like a bulldozer smashing away at the
underbrush, roaring and bellowing, working over the same ground
again and again. The jurors squirmed, the judge leaned back and
stared at the ceiling, Alfredo cringed and feebly bleated out his answers, Hanrahan leaped up with objections, a spring shower rattled at the windows, and the afternoon dragged on interminably.
Somehow, at last, Scheer was done and Alfredo went back to his seat
at the table, looking smaller, frailer, and more pathetic than ever.

The rest was anti-climactic. Hanrahan called Mrs. Pomales to the
stand—a tiny, frightened woman who burst into tears from time to
time—and got her to tell of not being allowed to see her sons at
the police station on the night of their arrest. She also told of seeing
"something like brown"—ammonia burns—around the mouths of
both her sons when she went to visit them at the Brooklyn House of
Detention. (*But Alfredo never said anything about ammonia being
used on him. Could this poor little woman be lying? Or is she just
confused?*)

In the morning, when the court was called to order and everyone
was ready to resume, Hanrahan announced, "The Defense for Carlos
and Alfredo Ortiz rests"; Kase said that defendant Valencia rested
likewise. But Scheer was far from through: he had some rebuttal
witnesses waiting—rebuttal is an optional final stage of presenting
evidence—and brought in a whole series of persons to verify the
medical records of the defendants and the nude photographs taken
of them the day after the interrogations, and half a dozen detectives to
say that they had seen no one in the cage overnight on the 22nd
or on the morning of the 23rd and had neither seen nor heard any
beatings taking place that day.

At last, in mid-afternoon, Scheer said he had no further questions. "Do both sides rest?" asked Justice Davidson. Kase and Hanrahan both said they did, and, mercifully, Scheer said, "The People rest, your Honor." "All right," said Davidson, "suppose we take five minutes' recess, and then we will start on our summations. Ladies and gentlemen of the jury, notwithstanding the fact that both sides have rested, the case still is not yours for a decision." Warning them not to discuss it, he sent them out to the jury room while he entertained and denied the standard motions for dismissal.

In the jury room, the jurors stretched and groaned, avoided each other's eyes, made vapid remarks ("Feel like I've been here half my life"), wondered what the others were thinking, and felt eager to hear the summations by both sides and the charge by the judge, hoping these might somehow help them discover what they themselves thought.

# VI   *The Jury on Trial*

BY the time a juror has endured days or weeks of service on a case like that of Doel Valencia and the Ortiz brothers, he may well be somewhat disenchanted with the whole institution of trial by jury. In fiction and drama, and even in most news writing, the jury trial is rarely portrayed warts and all, but is dramatized and idealized to conform to our prevailing culture myths about it; the juror, however, having seen the warts close up, may find himself sympathizing with the increasingly numerous and outspoken critics of the jury system who hold that it is unsuited to modern social conditions, that it is ineffective at determining the truth and inequitable at dispensing justice, and that it ought to be discarded and replaced by a more scientific or professional system.

Attacks on the use of the jury are nothing new. Those who are

more concerned about punishing the guilty than protecting the innocent, those who doubt that ordinary people can be fair or use good
judgment, those who want criminal justice to be in the hands of professionals and who feel that amateurs should have no part in it, have
been damning the jury system for centuries. Twenty-five hundred
years ago, Anacharsis, a Scythian philosopher, acidly said of juries,
"Wise men plead causes, but fools decide them." More recently Alexander Pope jested that both judges and jurors were less interested in
justice than in their stomachs:

> The hungry judges soon the sentence sign,
> And wretches hang that jurymen may dine.

Even in America, where the right to trial by jury was so highly regarded that it was one of the few things easily agreed upon by the
Founding Fathers at the Constitutional Convention, juries have long
been the subject of caustic satire and harsh criticism. Mr. Dooley
echoed Pope's comment several generations ago in his own inimitable
style:

> Whin the case is all over, the jury'll pitch th' tistimony out iv the
> window, an' consider three questions: "Did Lootgert look as
> though he'd kill his wife? Did his wife look as though she ought
> to be kilt? Isn't it time we wint to supper?"

Professionals within the justice system have often been far harsher.
An eminent California lawyer, Bruce G. Sebille, railed against juries in
the *American Bar Association Journal* in 1924:

> Too long has the effete and sterile jury system been permitted to
> tug at the throat of the nation's judiciary. . . . Too long has
> ignorance been permitted to sit ensconced in the places of judi-
> cial administration where knowledge is so sorely needed.

And recently Erwin N. Griswold, when still Dean of the Harvard Law
School, termed the jury trial "the apotheosis of the amateur," and
asked why anyone should think that twelve people brought in from the
street and selected for their lack of general ability should have any
special capacity for deciding controversies.

One might dismiss such comments as nothing more than the inevitable complaints against an unpleasant necessity, as universal and ineffectual as griping about taxes. But today there is something ominous about the attacks on the jury system, for they are more frequent and more virulent than ever, and come not from one part of the political spectrum but from many.

Liberal critics see trial by jury as archaic and unprofessional: Dr. Karl Menninger, for instance, recently wrote in *The Crime of Punishment:*

> The jury and the adversarial combat are not so cruel as the rack and the thumbscrew, but they are only a little less clumsy, outworn, and inquisitional. . . . To most psychiatrists, or at least to this one, the rigmarole of installing and instructing a mixed assembly of strangers, then presenting them with intricate problems, is an appalling mechanism.

Members of the New Left and militant blacks see the jury trial as rigged, and as part of the apparatus of control used by the capitalist-militarist-racist power structure. People like Rennie Davis and Bobby Seale have insisted they cannot possibly get a fair trial within the existing system; when Davis was convicted in Chicago, it proved his contention, in his eyes, while when Seale won a mistrial and dismissal of charges in New Haven, he and his supporters felt not that the system operated fairly, but that he had beaten it.

Middle-of-the-roaders and conservatives view jury trials as too often "soft" on criminals, and hopelessly ineffective at dealing with the contemporary crime wave. No less a person than the Chief Justice of the Supreme Court, Warren E. Burger, has repeatedly criticized the role of trial by jury in the American justice system. Prior to his becoming Chief Justice, he was instrumental in persuading a study group at the Center for the Study of Democratic Institutions to omit the right to trial by jury from a suggested new Constitution for the United States, and since becoming Chief Justice he has spoken out openly on the matter a number of times in words like these:

> When we look at the administration of justice in such enlightened countries as Holland, Denmark, Norway and Sweden, we find some interesting contrasts to the U.S. They have not found it necessary to establish a system which makes a criminal trial so complex or drawn-out as it is in this country. They do not employ our sys-

tem of 12 jurors. Generally, their trials are before three professional judges. They do not consider it necessary to use a device
like our Fifth Amendment under which an accused person
may not be required to testify. They go swiftly and directly to
the question of whether the accused is guilty.

But even the views of the nation's top judge are not as influential in
shaping our national mores as the daily practice of thousands of judges
and prosecutors throughout the land who see trial by jury as an undesirable last resort, and who do everything they can to handle the
vast majority of criminal cases by far speedier and more "practical"
methods.

Although nearly all of the major arguments against jury trials are of
ancient vintage, some of them have particular significance today. For
instance:

—It has often been said that jury trials take too long (several times
as long, on the average, as bench trials). But this is particularly serious today, when jury trials have become more dragged-out than ever
due to pre-trial hearings and other time-consuming legal innovations of
recent date, stemming from Supreme Court decisions of the Warren
era. Jury trials take so long, indeed, that they are the major bottleneck
in the criminal justice system.

—Jurors are amateurs trying to function in an area where professionalism is essential. This has always been so, but it has added significance today, for a virtual revolution occurred in American criminal law during the 1960s; today many serious criminal cases involve
complex and subtle legal issues that are difficult even for the trained
to understand and are all but incomprehensible to the novice.

—Jury-selection techniques effectively eliminate almost all of the
better and better-informed minds. As true as this may have been in
the past, today *voir dire* questioning has become a monstrosity, often
taking longer than the presentation of the evidence, its legitimate
purposes subverted by the effort of both sides to pre-sell their case to
the jurors. Moreover, in our age of mass communication the task of
finding jurors who are uninformed and unprejudiced about any important or notorious defendant has become exceedingly difficult: in
1970–71, for instance, at the trial of Bobby Seale and Mrs. Ericka
Huggins in New Haven on charges of having murdered a suspected
police agent in the Black Panther ranks, 1,550 veniremen were called

and 1,035 of them were questioned over a four-month period before a full jury had been assembled. Major publicity may even make it all but impossible to try an accused person: when the jury could not agree about Seale and Mrs. Huggins, the judge dismissed the charges because the trial had had such massive news coverage as to make it virtually impossible to select another jury who knew nothing about the case and had no preconceptions about it.

—The histrionic displays of trial lawyers, and their techniques of cross-examining the opposing side's witnesses, mislead jurors; judges are far better able to see through these tactics. But recently, as part of the general rebelliousness and anomie endemic in our society, defense lawyers have become far more flamboyant and daring than formerly, and presumably are influencing jurors more than ever.

—The presence of jurors causes the "game" aspects of trials, inherent in adversary law, to become dominant; the trial becomes a spectacle rather than a search for truth, whereas bench trials minimize these elements of the adversary contest. Modern news coverage, in important trials, has made this emphasis on theatricalism and game-playing in jury trials far worse; where there is press or television coverage of a trial, every lawyer becomes a performer for a vast audience, and the ends of law and of justice become secondary to making a hit.

—Juries often ignore or depart from the law when they disagree with it. This is an old criticism, but it has new and ominous significance in an era when the fear of crime is widespread and when there is an intense desire in many people to set an example and to experience the satisfaction of punishing the enemy. Conversely, jurors from minority groups are more likely than ever, given the present climate of dissent, to depart from the law in order to set one of their own kind free.

—The Fifth Amendment and the rules of evidence keep jurors from receiving much information that bears upon the actual guilt or innocence of the accused; the restrictions on what they may hear have increased considerably in recent years. And the contemporary news media, once again, greatly accentuate the problem: in a trial of any notoriety, the case may end in a mistrial if jurors are exposed to inadmissible evidence in any news source. Sequestration is sometimes the only answer, but this works an undeserved and intolerable hardship upon the jurors: in the celebrated "Manson family" trial in California in 1970–71, the jurors were forced to live in a hotel under the eyes of bailiffs, apart from their families and friends and without access to magazines, papers, or television, for seven months; even the windows of the bus they rode to court in were painted over to prevent them from accidentally reading headlines.

The complaints that the jury system squanders time, money, and human energy are essentially trivial: the requirements are minuscule compared to our national outlays on space exploration, on military intervention, or even on police protection and private security systems. If we must choose between doubling or even quadrupling our expenditures on jury trials, on the one hand, and, on the other, giving up the right to such trials and the protection they provide against the abuse of power, there can be but one choice—unless it be proven that jury trials yield a brand of justice inferior to that of trials heard by judges alone.

But those arguments which have to do with the difficulty of finding jurors who are unbiased and keeping them that way during the course of the trial, in a milieu of instant national news dissemination, are weightier. Yet these problems, too, can be handled by changes in the law far less drastic and far less damaging to our democratic traditions than doing away with the right to trial by jury. The *voir dire,* for instance, could be put in the hands of judges, where it would be quicker, less wasteful, and purer in purpose than it is in the hands of trial lawyers; indeed, this has for years been the practice in federal courts, and was recently initiated in the courts of New Jersey. Again, without limiting the freedom of the press, it would be possible to pass laws restricting the kind of details published prior to trial about persons accused of crime, as is the practice in England; police and prosecutors eager for personal publicity, as well as newsmen eager for a good story, could be held to account for violations of such laws.

The most serious arguments against trial by jury are those which hold that jurors are gullible and impressionable, understand neither the evidence nor the law, and arrive at wrong verdicts a good proportion of the time. But most of the critics who make these charges are biased: criminals convicted by those jurors; defense lawyers, who, as we have seen, lose two thirds or more of their jury trials; and police and prosecutors, who consider jurors too lenient in general, not because they acquit a majority of defendants but because they acquit any of them.

A fairer and more accurate picture of how well or ill juries perform their function might be obtained by asking judges what they think of the decisions juries have reached in those trials over which they themselves have presided. To be sure, judges are fallible human beings, and most of them (as was said earlier) are lawyers of only modest talent who did political hackwork until they were rewarded with judgeships; accordingly, they are not likely to evaluate jury decisions with scientific objectivity or perfect judgment. But they are less likely to be biased than any of the other principals concerned with criminal trials, and in any case are the very professionals who, according to the critics of jury trials, are far better able than the common man to reach just verdicts as to legal guilt or innocence.

For such reasons, Professors Harry Kalven, Jr., and Hans Zeisel, co-authors of the pioneering study *The American Jury*—the only major sociological investigation of juries yet published—sent queries to judges throughout the country who sit on criminal trials, asking how their juries had decided recent cases, and what verdicts they themselves would have handed down, had they tried the same cases without juries. Professors Kalven and Zeisel received usable reports from 555 judges, covering 3,576 criminal jury trials. Astonishingly, the judges agreed with their juries in three quarters of the cases, viewing the jury verdicts as "quite correct" in 69 percent and "one a judge might also come to" in another 8 percent. Even of the remainder, more than half were rated "tenable for a jury," and only the small balance—9 percent of all verdicts—were "without merit."

In the great majority of all cases, judges felt their juries had understood the evidence and been able to comprehend the legal guidelines given them. Even when the judges disagreed with their juries' verdicts, they almost never attributed the disagreement to the jurors' gullibility; there was almost no difference, for instance, between judges' and juries' attitudes toward repudiated confessions or the testimony of accomplices who have turned state's evidence. The authors concluded that, in general, "judge and jury do not display different habits of mind or different criteria of judgment in evaluating credibility."

There was only one notable exception: where a person accused of a serious crime testified in his own behalf and had no previous record, the jury was distinctly more likely to believe him than was the judge. Indeed, when judges and juries differed, the difference was almost always in the direction of greater caution, on the part of the juries, about convicting; in only 3 percent of the cases did juries convict where judges would have acquitted, while in 19 percent the juries acquitted where judges would have convicted. In some kinds of crimes, the jury evidently felt the laws to be so unfair, archaic, or harsh that they could not enforce them (juries were more lenient than judges 44 percent of the time with persons accused of indecent exposure and less lenient only 3 percent); in murder cases, on the other hand, the jury was simply more willing than the judge to give the defendant the benefit of the doubt.

Oddly enough, in their differences from the judges, the juries appear to play two contrasting roles. In departing from the law when they consider the law wrong, they are a mediating factor, tempering legal tradition with contemporary social attitudes; but in being somewhat more insistent than judges that guilt be proved beyond a reasonable doubt, they are supporting a fundamental American tradition and saying, in effect, that ours is a society which believes it better to let ten guilty men go free than to convict one innocent man. "This is, to be sure," say Professors Kalven and Zeisel, "an almost heroic commitment to decency. . . . The jury, as an expression of the community's conscience, interprets this norm more generously and more intensely than does the judge."

For all its drawbacks, therefore, the jury represents a subtle and valuable way of distributing official power, of maintaining checks and balances within the justice system, and of building discretion and flexibility into criminal trials. Although juries do differ from judges a quarter of the time, they rarely do so because they are incompetent or biased, but, rather, because they are a mediating and humanizing force within the justice system. "Whether or not one comes to admire the jury system as much as we have," Professors Kalven and Zeisel conclude, "it must rank as a daring effort in human arrangement to work out a solution to the tensions between law and equity and anarchy."

## VII    *The Sole and Exclusive Judges of the Facts*

BEFORE the jurors in the Ortiz-Valencia case could play the last and most important part of their crucial role in the drama, they still had to hear summations by all three lawyers and the charge by the judge, all of which, one might suppose, would greatly clarify matters for them. But one would be wrong. Judges' charges are, for the most part, safe, standard, ritualized speeches on broad principles of law; when a charge also deals with the specific evidence in a case, it is usually only to summarize that evidence, not comment upon it. (Most states, in fact, do not permit judges to comment upon the evidence in their charges.) And in summations, prosecutors and defense lawyers seek not to clarify the factual truth (or even the legal truth), but to persuade, confuse, sway, worry, or move the jurors—in a word, to win by any allowable means; if summations do sometimes help jurors see things more clearly, this is only a by-product of their primary purpose.

In mid-afternoon, when the jurors had returned to their places, Hanrahan delivered the first such effort. Using only brief, scribbled notes, he rambled along almost extemporaneously in that oratorical but disjointed style to which the jurors had become accustomed during the past three weeks. He called Scheer a "crafty district attorney," and said he had "raved," "ranted," "bellowed," and "screamed," sought to "bamboozle" the jury, and tried to "play a game" upon them. Detectives McCabe and Russo hadn't been able to solve the case legitimately, so "they solved it by applying ammonia to a youngster seventeen years of age," and by mercilessly beating the defendants—and detectives, he added, know how to hit without putting marks on their victims. As he went on, he grew more impassioned—or, possibly, desperate—and his oratory became ever foggier: "When it comes down to the fundamental facts of whether or not there is a time element here in the opening, that wasn't done," he said, by which he apparently meant that Scheer, in his opening statement, had not explained how the time discrepancy in the confessions could be resolved.

He offered numerous suggestions designed to sow doubt in the minds of the jurors ("How is this [A&P] slip so clean if it was in a grocery bag that contained all groceries that were broken?" and "Do you mean to tell me they [the defendants] are laying the bubble gum on a table while allegedly this crime is being committed?"). The prosecution had talked a lot about the grocery bag, but failed to produce it; maybe it had never existed. There had been no eyewitnesses and no identifiable fingerprints; the weapon had not been found; and while money for drugs was said to have been the motive, Helmer's wallet had been stuffed with cash. His clients were really nice boys: "He [Alfredo] *told* you that he had a drug addiction. . . . He gave you an honest story," and Carlos "was clean of any crime—the District Attorney would have proven otherwise if he had committed any crime."

The defendants had been found in their own neighborhood after the crime, which showed that they were innocent; if they had not been, "one or two of them would have disappeared and taken off, as you always do," he said, not meaning that the jurors had committed crimes and fled, but merely improvising speech loosely like an untalented pianist noodling inaccurately at the keyboard. Near the close of his summation, Hanrahan's discourse became almost wholly impressionistic and non-syntactical: "I leave this—and I know that I leave it in good hands—I leave it with you, and I know that when you consider this case from all of its aspects, every part of the statements, and the beatings, and the lack of will, and lack of intellect—do *you* think that these boys, lacking practically any education (that's *another* item to be considered by you)—I say that the resistance here was overcome by force!" He concluded by referring obliquely to the penalty that conviction would bring: "I say, in your individual judgment, don't destroy their lives in this type of case. This is a Murder One charge, and you and I know what it means to these defendants, and you and I know what it means to your responsibility."

Kase was briefer and more lucid, but permitted himself flights of fancy and dramatic posturing such as the jurors had not known him capable of. "During this trial and for many moments," he said, "I would look up there and see, 'In God We Trust' "—he turned and gazed reverently at the motto over Justice Davidson's head—" 'In God We Trust'—and in the jury system! And thank God for the jury system, for it's with the jury system that we can determine where truth lies in this particular case." He reviewed the evidence, making many of the same points Hanrahan had, but spending most of his time attacking the detectives' account of how and when Valencia had been interrogated. He was ironic and incredulous about McCabe's claim that he had accidentally seen Valencia the morning after the first interrogation and had politely invited him to return to the station house for more questioning; Kase even went so far as to assert flatly that Valencia had never been released the night before. As for the official claim that Valencia's confession was voluntary, Kase grew heavily sarcastic: "He is questioned at 2:30 and he denies anything or any complicity in this particular charge. At 6:20 he is questioned again—and then, nice as you please, without any kind of duress, threat, or force, he says, 'Yes, fellows, I did it, I will tell you all now.' . . . You can believe *this?*"

Kase reminded the jurors of Valencia's refusal to repeat his story to Vitale, of the time discrepancy between his confession and those of the Ortizes, and of the conflict between his confession and Mrs. Ambos' testimony. And finally, after a few comments on beatings, he alluded as openly as he dared to the Whitmore confession—the product of psychological rather than brute force—which had recently been front-page news: "This won't be the first time that somebody has been convicted on a false confession. Need I say more about that, ladies and gentlemen of the jury?"—and raising a forefinger and wagging it significantly, he added, slowly and clearly, "No, not one *whit more* do I have to say about that kind of thing!" Scheer reddened, started to his feet, and then thought better of it. Kase, proud of himself, asked the jury to find Doel Valencia not guilty, and sat down.

It was late afternoon, but Justice Davidson wanted the summations completed this day and asked Scheer to proceed. Scheer offered various conjectures to counter those made by Hanrahan and Kase (perhaps the A&P slip was not soiled because it had lain on top of boxes in the grocery bag), but primarily he sought to repair the credibility of the two detectives. In dramatic and emotional terms, he asked the jurors not to be misled by the dramatic and emotional terms used by defense counsel. "We hear a lot of testimony about the beatings," he said. "Did you feel the impact during the course of Mr. Hanrahan's summation?" He doubled a fist, and looked at one juror after another. "Did you feel the punches? Did you feel the kickings? Did you feel the blows to the head? Did you feel the blows to the body?" he cried, hitting his paunch, and doubling over; then holding a hand to his mouth and nose, he shouted, "Did you feel the ammonia?" Abruptly, he was calm, quiet, and rational: "Do you believe that, Mr. Foreman and ladies and gentlemen? *You* have seen Detectives Russo and McCabe on the stand—do *you* believe that?"

There was no evidence, he said, that the defendants had been beaten, other than their own testimony—which the jurors had a right to regard as a "big, deliberate lie." If Russo and McCabe were "ruthless and heartless" brutes who framed innocent persons, they would hardly have left the awkward time discrepancy in the confessions. Concerning which, incidentally, it was up to the jurors to decide what really happened; they were entitled to believe, from the testimony, that Helmer had been alive at 7:15 p.m., that the blood on the floor had not been his, that he had gone out again, come back, and been attacked at about 9:00 p.m., as per Valencia's confession, and that the Ortiz brothers' confessions were correct in every respect except for the time they gave.

Then, growing grave, he said he had hesitated to bring up his next point, but felt obliged to do so: "I tell you, it is hitting below the belt when one of the defendants gets on the stand and tells you good ladies and gentlemen that Detective McCabe told him he didn't like Puerto Ricans . . . [and] didn't care for Negroes. Detective McCabe—you saw him, you heard him, you saw his partners of the Negro race. . . . [The defendants] are cunning, they are sly, they are using you to extricate themselves out of something they have done. How low, how *low* could anybody be in charging Detective McCabe with such a statement!"

And he concluded with a touch of Law Day rhetoric, telling the jurors that on the Supreme Court building in Manhattan there was inscribed the motto, "The true administration of justice is the firmest pillar of good government," and that if jurors did not administer justice fairly and impartially, without relation to creed, color, or background, the pillars of government would crumble. The only verdict that would be fair and impartial to the People of the State of New York in this case, he said, would be to find all three defendants guilty as charged. He sat down, and Justice Davidson asked the sagging jurors to be back at 9:30 a.m., and sent them home.

In the morning, when all hands were present, Davidson read his charge to the jury. It was a speech running some fifty typewritten pages, and to the jurors it seemed as if Davidson had gone to great pains to give them advice specifically pertaining to this case; actually, much of what he said was a basic, reusable lecture on legal principles that could be applied to almost any criminal case, consisting of classic statements such as, "You are the sole and exclusive judges of the facts," "You and you alone determine the credibility of the witnesses who testified at this trial," "Take into consideration the appearance and demeanor of each witness upon the witness stand," "Consider the interest of the witness, if any, in the result of the trial," and "If you find that any witness lied in a material aspect of his testimony, you have a right to disregard all of the testimony of such witness [but] you may believe any portion of it to which you give credence."

In the same fashion, he explained that the presumption of innocence put the burden of proof on the prosecution, that the phrase "beyond a reasonable doubt" does not mean "to a moral certainty," that the potential punishment is not to be considered by the jury, that circumstantial evidence is not necessarily inferior to eyewitness evidence, that anyone who assists in a felony murder is as guilty under the law as the person who commits the violent deed, and that any statement made to a policeman by a suspect can be used as evidence against him unless it was extorted by fear produced by threats or beatings.

After this little talk on law, he reviewed the evidence—not selectively, as Scheer and the defense lawyers had done, but painstakingly, completely, and in the sequence in which it had been given, without saying how he himself felt about any of it. His purpose, he said, was to refresh the jurors' recollections, but if their recollections on any point were different from his, theirs were controlling, and not his. (He was not actually relying on recollection, however; he and his law assistant had worked from typed transcripts of the stenographic record in preparing this part of the charge.)

Justice Davidson concluded by telling the jurors that there were only two possible verdicts for each defendant—guilty of Murder in the First Degree, or not guilty, that the verdict did not have to be the same for all three defendants, and that in each case there could be no verdict unless all twelve jurors were agreed on it. Finally, a little after noontime, he uttered the words the jurors had sometimes felt they would never hear: "The twelve jurors will retire to the jury room and commence your deliberation." They arose and filed out past the defendants, solemn and self-conscious, and acutely aware of their gaze.

In the jury room, they sat down around the long green composition-topped table; another spring shower was drumming at the windows, and it seemed very long ago that they had first sat in this room waiting to be called in to hear the case. Actually, it had been less than three weeks, but in that time they had heard some two dozen witnesses, listened to a third of a million words of testimony and argument, and vicariously experienced a whole series of human acts and feelings that were alien to their own lives. And now they were going to find out whether they could make sense of it all.

The foreman (the retired bank clerk), a mild-mannered little man, asked who would like to speak first. Hesitantly, at first, they spoke up one by one; then they gradually became bolder, and after a while were interrupting each other, some speaking loudly, some pounding on the table for order, in a free-for-all of agreements, disagreements, rejoinders, irrelevancies, and shifts of subject:

—I think McCabe is a hot-head. Did you see him get red in the face? He's just the kind who might wallop the hell out of a suspect in the back room.

—So he gets red in the face—what's that prove? Who *says* he beat them? You believe what punks like that say? Junkies and juveniles like that?

—The time thing bothers me. How could all three be telling the truth? I think the detectives rammed nine o'clock down Valencia's throat after they found out he was working that day.

—I don't buy that. The time thing is just what makes me think they didn't force anything on anybody. Like the D.A. said, why would they leave it that way if they were framing these guys?

—If Scheer couldn't break those three down, drilling away at them all the time like he did, they must have been telling the truth.

—Mister, where I live I see lousy kids like them all the time, and they lie like it was second nature. They're tough and rotten, and they're not about to break down just because some D.A. is asking them questions.

—I've lived in the ghetto all my life, and I've never seen cops being brutal. Don't laugh, I'm *telling* you! They only get rough when people are rough with them.
—Man, you got to be kiddin'! That Russo, that's a *mean* cop. And McCabe?—he get you up a back alley and you goin' to be a sorry mess, if he got somethin' against you.

—I'd like to ask just one question—where is Angel Walker? Why didn't they bring him in? I think they're hiding something.
—The judge told us that's not for us to speculate about. We're not supposed to be taking that into account.

—Whose blood was on the floor?
—Who says it was blood? Only the old lady.
—And it might have been there the day before the crime!
—It *couldn't* have been Helmer's blood.
—It *had* to be his—it's too much of a coincidence.
—Yes, but she said nobody went up the stairs after him. Or came down. The whole thing doesn't make any sense.

—I'd feel wrong to convict them just on their confessions, and that's really all we have.
—That's *all?* How much do you need? All three tell the same story except for the time, and all three name each other—
—Wait a minute. The judge told us twenty times not to take one defendant's statement against another—
—But they *did* name each other, and they all said they did it together. How are you going to ignore that?

—I think McCabe is a racist. What those boys say he said sounds real to me. It don't mean nothin' that he's got black partners—they're cops, and they're probably just as racist as him.
—The defendants have every reason to lie. And they see five people on this jury who they think might respond to that kind of thing, and it's only natural for them to try it.

—We're not supposed to consider the fact that the death penalty could be involved. Well, I don't know how all of you feel, but it's on *my* mind!

—All right, but it doesn't have anything to do with whether they're guilty or innocent.

—Why should a person who was only a lookout face the same penalty as the one who did the stabbing? It isn't right.

—But that's the law, and we all agreed to follow the law.

It was close to lunchtime, and the foreman suggested they take a vote to see how things stood before having lunch sent in. He went around the table, asking each one: nine jurors thought the defendants were guilty, but the toll collector, the assistant personnel director, and the lady bookkeeper—all black, as it happened—voted not guilty, and the first two of them were very positive about it. The foreman said they'd better have lunch and continue afterward; he rang, and a court attendant brought in sandwiches and coffee. They made desultory conversation while eating and then resumed deliberations, the argument going around and around, and leaping from topic to topic. They spoke about reasonable doubt ("I don't want to have them on *my* conscience if I don't feel certain—and I don't"), and whether Hanrahan had been unfairly treated by the judge ("Hanrahan's a fake—he's a ham actor"); they argued about the discrepancies among the confessions ("There's a lot of little things wrong—I don't believe *any* of it"), and the reliability of Mrs. Ambos' memory ("All right, so she's a nice old lady—but she's mixed up"); they went over and over Valencia's refusal to talk to Vitale ("He wised up—or somebody in the cell wised him up—just in time"), and the credibility of Mrs. Pomales' testimony ("She said they were both burned around the mouth—and even *they* didn't claim both of them were"); they wrangled about whether Justice Davidson had been unfair to the defense or not ("He never gave poor Kase a chance—he put him down every time"), and why none of the people that Alfredo and Carlos had been with that day had come in to testify for them ("I'll tell you why not—because those punks are lying"). Some of them were polite and reasonable, some were loud and vehement, a couple of them were silent and inarticulate. It was difficult to know whether any of them were being convinced by the arguments of the others until another vote was taken well along in the afternoon;

it turned out then that there were five for acquittal and seven for conviction. Someone groaned; clearly, no verdict would be forthcoming for a long time.

In the courtroom, the three lawyers, the two detectives, Mrs. Pomales, and Josie, Valencia's common-law wife, were all suffering acutely, although for different reasons. At any moment something might happen, yet each moment passed without anything happening. Scheer read the newspaper, did a crossword puzzle, and leafed through some files brought him by an assistant, but, for all his years in service, he could scarcely concentrate. Hanrahan chatted affably with Russo and McCabe, worked over the rough draft of a brief, and occasionally went off to make a phone call. Kase fidgeted around, talking to one person or another, sometimes trying to read a newspaper but without any interest. In spacious chambers a floor above, Justice Davidson relaxed on a sofa and read material pertaining to other cases coming before him, then had lunch served him, with proper linen, dishes, and silverware, at the long conference table in the middle of the room. Outside the courtroom and up a flight of steps, in a holding pen, the three defendants sat on hard wooden benches with nothing to do but wait, minute by minute, for the answer. As Alfredo recalls it, "We was smokin', an' lookin' at each other, an' rappin' a little—di'n' feel like sayin' much—an' feelin' those people got our lives in their han's. It was *bad,* man!"

The day wore on, the sun peeped through the clouds from time to time, the guards stood around the courtroom making small talk with one another, and whenever a door opened, every head snapped around to see whether there was any word yet, but there never was. At 6:00 p.m. Justice Davidson sent down word that the jury should be taken out to dinner by bailiffs, and that the lawyers could leave and be back by about 8:00 p.m. After dinner, the deliberation continued; it had narrowed down by then chiefly to a discussion of indications within the confessions themselves that there might have been coercion. The length of time each defendant was in the police station before the Q&A began to seem important ("They grilled him for five or six hours—and he was just a teen-ager"); so did the brevity of the Q&A sessions ("They had those boys pretty well rehearsed"); and so did the wording of some of the answers ("A slum kid like that wouldn't say, 'I panicked'—the detectives were putting words in their mouths").

The vote had reached six to six, but there it seemed stuck fast. Someone suggested that it might help if they would look at the Q&As to see which of their recollections about them were correct. The foreman rang for an attendant and handed him a note for the judge, and shortly before 9:00 p.m. everyone was back in the courtroom, although no one but Davidson and the jurors knew what the reason was. Kase's heart was pounding, Hanrahan was mopping his face, Scheer was drumming the tabletop with his stubby fingers, and the defendants were pale and trembling. ("When they call us out to tell us the jury comin' in," says Alfredo, "we jump, we start shakin', butterflies an' goosepimples all over us, waitin' to see what these people gonna do. Man, we was scared to death!")

"I have a note from Mr. Irving Arrow," said Justice Davidson, "which reads as follows: 'May we have the original statements of the three defendants to Detectives McCabe and Russo and the statements of the District Attorney Vitale.'" Everyone slumped; the moment was not the one they had expected it to be. Justice Davidson explained that the Q&As were not in evidence and could not be lent to the jurors, but that whatever the detectives had said about them under oath could be read back. "It might take a couple of hours to read this to you," he warned, "but we'll do it if that's what you would like us to do." Most of the jurors nodded, and at his order, the court reporter began reading back testimony; with various interruptions and questions by jurors, the process took an hour, and a little after 10:00 p.m. the jurors went back to their room, and the waiting began again for everyone else.

After another round of discussion, they voted; this time there were nine for acquittal, but the three who voted to convict—two white men and one Negro—seemed unimpressed and adamant. The discussion went on, repetitious, tedious, and fruitless. A guard summoned the jurors back to the courtroom near midnight, and the judge asked if they were close to agreement; the foreman said they needed more time, and Davidson suggested they go to bed and resume deliberations in the morning. Bailiffs took the jurors to the Concourse Plaza Hotel and locked them in (only a few of them had had the foresight to bring toothbrushes and overnight things), while the other people in the courtroom scattered out into the night and made their way home, the defendants getting to their bunks in the jail in Brooklyn well after 1:00 a.m., and tossing feverishly until they were awakened, before 6:00 a.m., and readied themselves to go back to court.

From the general tenor of the jurors' queries and the length of their deliberations, Scheer must have sensed that the prospects of conviction were fading; in the morning, therefore, he made a last-minute effort to secure a conviction by offering the defendants an attractive bargain. As Kase tells it, "That Saturday morning Scheer and Peter Stowe, the judge's law secretary, came over to me in the courtroom and asked me how would I like to talk to the defendants and see if they'd plead to some lesser felony. If they'd go along with it, the judge would sentence them to Elmira and to a maximum of five years. I ran up to the pen and told Valencia, while Hanrahan talked to the Ortiz boys—we had to work fast, because who knew what that jury would do at any minute?—but the answer was still no, they wouldn't buy it. So we had to go back and tell Scheer nothing doing; we had to sweat out the jury."

The jurors, meanwhile, were arguing hour after hour about the same issues they had already gone over so many times. The balloting settled down, during the morning, to eight for acquittal and four for conviction, and there it remained, the majority growing ever more exasperated at the holdouts, the holdouts feeling harassed and defensive, and nearly everyone growing unhappy and frustrated at the prospect of having to report themselves a hung jury. For the lawyers and others waiting in the courtroom, and for the three defendants in the pen, the day was an endless torment; they sighed, squirmed, paced back and forth, watched the clock, and suffered a hundred false alarms and momentary hopes whenever they heard a footfall in the hall or the sound of a door opening.

At last the jurors reluctantly agreed that they were getting nowhere and could not reach a verdict. At about 4:00 p.m. the foreman sent another note to Justice Davidson, and shortly everyone was reconvened in the courtroom. Davidson carefully masked any feelings he had about the matter, but it is almost universal among judges to feel frustration and resentment when a jury hangs. None of the others knew what the jurors had decided; with damp hands and the blood pounding in their ears, they looked at the jurors as they came in and took their places, but could read nothing in their faces.

In a moment, however, the secret was out: Davidson asked the foreman if it was correct that the jury had been unable to reach a verdict, and the foreman said that it was. For a moment, all was quiet in the courtroom; most people looked befuddled or dazed. Kase, wilting, knew he should be pleased that the trial had not resulted in the conviction of the defendants, but he felt a severe letdown; he had begun to think an acquittal was in the making. Hanrahan felt a great weariness at the prospect of trying the case all over again, and consoled himself with the thought that he might get a more kindly judge next time. Russo and McCabe were not present that afternoon, but both, when they heard the news, felt sharply disappointed ("You feel like you've done the right thing," says Russo, "and you want the success, you'd like to see yourself get the conviction. When you don't, it feels like all of your work was for nothing"). As for the defendants, they scarcely knew how to feel: they had had a reprieve from the worst that might have happened, yet they had to face trial all over again. They had gained nothing; still, the terrible moment of doom had come and been postponed, and they felt a strange mixture of relief and despair.

The three of them were taken back to the holding pen, to wait for the van to the Brooklyn House of Detention. Justice Davidson hurried up to his chambers, slipped out of his robe, and headed downtown by cab; he would be able, after all, to go to a Saturday-night dinner party he had been invited to. Hanrahan, Kase, and Scheer all remained for a while, talking to those few jurors who were willing to stay and answer their questions; each wanted to know how the jurors felt about the trial, why they had voted as they had, and how the voting had gone. Scheer was troubled by what he learned; he could not understand how so many—or, indeed, any—of the jurors could have been for acquittal. The assistant personnel director tried to explain: "Mr. Scheer," he said, "I'm a courtroom buff and I go to a lot of trials—and I haven't seen anyone batter a defendant harder than you did. And if you couldn't break them down, we had to figure they were telling the truth and those confessions had been beaten out of them." Scheer looked unconvinced, and properly so: in actual fact, only a few of the eight who had voted for acquittal had felt the same as the assistant personnel director. Most of the others, after thinking things over, had simply not felt sure whom to believe, and hence not certain where the truth lay—and therefore unwilling to convict the defendants. They knew they had failed to punish three persons who were, probably, guilty—but they also knew that they had not unjustly punished three persons who were, possibly, innocent. After twenty court days, they had achieved neither conviction nor acquittal, and the case would have to be tried all over again, but they had performed their duties with all due seriousness, protected the feeble individual against the mighty state, and affirmed once again our national credo that the jury is a vital and central part of the American system of justice.

# Chapter 6 *The Presumption of Innocence*

## I    Cast Changes

"ALL right," said the judge, "let's proceed. Get the defendants out." Several courtroom attendants went out and returned in a moment with Alfredo, Carlos, and Doel, all three still wearing wrinkled cotton slacks, white shirts, and zipper jackets, all three still pale, boyish, and harmless-looking. They saw Mrs. Pomales and Josie sitting, as usual, in the spectator section, took their places at the same tables, and heard the clerk of the court intone the familiar words: "The People of the State of New York against Alfredo Ortiz, Doel Valencia, and Carlos Ortiz." Even the weather seemed much the same: a raw March wind moaned at the tall windows, but the deep-hued blue of the sky foretold spring.

It was, in fact, March 21st—but of 1966. A whole year had passed since the first trial. Spring had blossomed and decayed into the stagnant New York summer, which had finally yielded to a crisp, lovely fall, and that, in turn, had slowly withered away into winter; holidays had come and gone, rains and snows had fallen, plays had opened and closed, buildings had been torn down and others had sprung up in their places; wars and revolutions had blazed around the world as usual, and countless millions of persons had continued to make love, marry, work, eat, laugh, and play. All the while, Alfredo, Carlos, and Doel had been imprisoned within the brick-and-tile walls of the Brooklyn House of Detention, waking up every morning to the same shouted orders of the guards, hearing the same excretal noises from nearby cells, eating the same dull meals, making the same tedious small-talk with fellow prisoners, waiting for each interminable day, each endless hour, to be over.

Valencia got a note from his sister now and then, though she did not visit him; Josie came all year, but seemed to be losing interest. Mrs. Pomales still visited Alfredo and Carlos every week, but neither of them heard anything from their relatives or friends during the year. Most notably silent was their old friend Negrito—Angel Walker—although during their early hearings when they met him in the detention pen at the Criminal Court building, he would tell them and Valencia that as soon as he won his upcoming lawsuit against the Transit Authority and became rich, he would help them out.

Whether he would actually have done so is anyone's guess, but he had had no opportunity. Less than three weeks after the end of the first Helmer murder trial, in which his name had so often been mentioned, Angel Walker had boldly walked into the same Supreme Court building on Grand Concourse with his lawyer and been plaintiff and principal witness in the $500,000 damage suit for the loss of his arm. After four days the jury—perhaps not quite convinced that the Transit Authority had been negligent, but sorry for Walker anyway—gave him a handout of $30,000 plus hospital expenses. It was a cruel awakening from his daydreams; all the same, it was more money than anyone he knew had ever had. Justice Harold Baer, however, was exasperated: he considered the evidence so grossly insufficient that he set aside the verdict—in most states, judges are empowered to take the case from the jury or to set aside a verdict of guilty where the evidence is clearly inadequate—and dismissed the charges; he then added insult to injury by giving the Transit Authority the right to recover $150 in court costs from Angel if it chose to. (It did not.) Angel's lawyer filed an appeal, but Justice Baer's decision was upheld by the Appellate Division; the lawyer then took it up to the Court of Appeals, New York's highest court, but the matter had not yet been decided at the time the second Helmer murder trial began. By that time, however, Angel Walker was being fed and sheltered by the City of New York—in its jail on Rikers Island, where he was serving an eight-month-to-three-year sentence for a new drug offense.

Like Walker, Hanrahan had dropped out of sight. When the first trial ended in a hung jury, Luisa Pomales had stopped making payments to him, and Hanrahan, having received only half his fee, asked the court to relieve him of the case. Kenneth Kase, who had likewise been given short shrift by Idalia Valencia, also asked to be relieved. In June a judge of the Supreme Court asked the three defendants if they had any money, and when they said they did not, assigned other lawyers to defend them at no cost to themselves, the fees of $1,000 per lawyer to be paid by the City of New York. Each defendant was assigned two lawyers, one as the primary defender and trier of the case, the other as his courtroom assistant. Because almost no work was involved in being assistant, the judge offered to put Kase and Hanrahan on in that status, to make up in part for the money they had lost. Kase accepted, and was assigned as a defense lawyer for Alfredo Ortiz this time, assisting Mrs. Mary Johnson Lowe. Hanrahan dropped out; in his stead, defending Carlos, the judge named Samuel Bernstein, assisted by Thomas Casey; and for Valencia the judge appointed Herbert Siegal, assisted by Philip Peltz.

So things did look somewhat different, after all: six defense lawyers sat at the tables this time, instead of the two of last year, only one of the six being a familiar face. (At the prosecutor's table, however, was the all-too-familiar face of Alexander Scheer, still coldly implacable, eying the defendants, as they took their places, as impersonally as if they were laboratory animals ready to be sacrificed.)

The three chief defense lawyers were remarkably dissimilar. Samuel Bernstein, representing Carlos, was a mild-mannered, nondescript little man nearing sixty, balding and with a thin, prissy bit of mustache; he had practiced ordinary household civil law in the Bronx during most of his career, had none of the pugnacious style and personality of a good criminal lawyer, and was thought of by his colleagues as a "nice guy" and easy to deal with.

Mrs. Mary Johnson Lowe, defending Alfredo, was a rarity even in New York—a Negro woman criminal lawyer. Trim, well dressed, and in her early forties, she was a pleasant-looking woman with a wide, friendly mouth, her skin medium dark but her features semi-Caucasian, her eyes light brown, her hair nearly straight. Her voice was low-pitched and her manner invariably ladylike, even though she was a zealous and dedicated champion of criminal defendants from the ghetto against a system she regarded as cruel and oppressive—a system with noble ideals, in theory, which are ignored in practice by the police, the prosecutors, and the judges who serve the power élite. The third child of seven in a Harlem slum family, she grew up in poverty (both of her parents had gone to college in the South, but could get only relatively menial jobs in New York City); she managed, nonetheless, to graduate with high honors from Hunter College, studied law at Brooklyn Law School, and took a Master of Laws degree at Columbia University. Then, instead of going into a downtown firm to make good money, as she could easily have done, she chose to stay in the Bronx and defend the poor.

As a result, she has long worked out of cramped, cheaply furnished offices in a rickety wooden house in Melrose, where her secretary has to keep the door locked all the time, and in recent years her clients have nearly all been technical "paupers," to whose cases she has been assigned by the court at rates that are little short of insulting. "They pay $10 an hour for out-of-court time and $15 an hour for in-court time," she has said, "but I handle all I can, even at those rates, and willingly, because I see around me so much oppression and so many people with nobody to turn to for help. Ordinarily, in my profession, money is the name of the game, but I consider I do well if I break even at the end of the year. As long as I don't have to ask my husband for anything for my car, my office, my secretary, or my lunch money, I'm satisfied." Her husband, a successful Negro lawyer in civil practice, has encouraged her in her work and not been in the least dissatisfied with her income.

Herbert Siegal, Valencia's defender, was a very different sort. Then sixty years old, a gray-haired man with a vast belly, a monumental face whose pendulous folds overlapped his shirt collar, and a gravelly voice that could go from a confidential growl to an ear-splitting bellow in an instant, Siegal was a highly successful criminal lawyer who dressed his great bulk excellently, wore a diamond ring and diamond cufflinks, and had a suite of offices in the Wall Street area complete with sculptured wall-to-wall carpeting, oil paintings, plants, and air conditioning.

Though Siegal had long accepted occasional court assignments by way of rendering service to the system, in his private practice he charged anywhere from $10,000 to $15,000 for defending such big-time criminals as syndicate members and leading heroin packagers. His name had never become a national byword, but he was well known to fellow lawyers and regarded with respect in New York and in the District of Columbia, in both of which jurisdictions he was a member of the bar. Entitled to argue cases before the United States Supreme Court, he prided himself not only on having often made the pages of the tabloids, but on having helped bring about three important appellate court decisions limiting the prosecution's use of certain kinds of evidence.

Siegal, unlike Mrs. Lowe, rarely feels that his clients are oppressed and downtrodden innocents; he does what he does for them because he enjoys the adversarial combat of criminal law, likes making prosecutors toe the line, and because, when he gets a murderer or mobster off on the grounds that the evidence was insufficient or the testimony false, he feels that he has done a good deed. He is primarily interested not in the people he defends but in their cases; as Mrs. Lowe has said, with grudging admiration, "Herb doesn't get involved with his clients—he doesn't care about their guilt or innocence, or even what they're like as human beings—and in that way he's far superior to me as a lawyer, because unless I'm emotionally committed to a client, I can't do my job properly. But he can, any time and every time."

Besides these new faces in the courtroom, there was another, seated at the bench—an old face, actually; the tired, pale face of an aging, ailing man with a gleaming bald head, a fringe of white hair, and weak, watery eyes. Justice William Lyman—the same judge who had released Alfredo into McCabe's ready hands a year and a half earlier —was seventy-three, or three years beyond retirement age, but still sitting on the bench, thanks to an extension granted by the Appellate Division. William Lyman, like so many other judges, had come up the long route: an ambitious Jewish youth from the Bronx, he had become a lawyer, involved himself in party politics and worked hard as a district leader, run successfully for the state assembly, and after many years of service been rewarded by being put on the slate for a judgeship. As a judge, he had made no great reputation, but most lawyers considered him reasonably competent. In his aging years, however, and particularly after the death of a son and another close relative, he had faded and weakened; he seemed distracted and forgetful, spoke as little as possible in court (perhaps in order not to make judicial errors by mistake), and kept his law assistant near at hand to whisper to him whenever he needed guidance or a reminder. The work had become difficult for him, but not as difficult as giving up the $37,000 pay and the dignity and status of being a judge, and as long as he wanted to hold on, there was almost nothing the administrative offices of the state judiciary could do to make him step down.*

The cast of characters had thus changed somewhat, but the stage setting and the script had the eerie familiarity of a *déjà vu* experience. First of all, *voir dire*. Justice Lyman ordered up a panel of jurors; seventy-five people trooped into the courtroom, and the familiar process of jury selection began with the same kinds of questions as last time, the same rhetorical devices, the same speeches on reasonable doubt, the presumption of innocence, and other cardinal principles. But this time the *voir dire* was far lengthier and more numbing than it had been the previous year: Siegal, who did the bulk of the questioning for the defendants, went to great pains to have jurors he mistrusted excused for cause, and only when he could not, took no chances and used one of the twenty peremptory challenges allotted to the defense. "I didn't want any little old ladies on that jury," he recalls, "or any fellows who had worked in a bank for fifty years, or anyone who had never had any problems."

Scheer, who had won so many cases in his career but nearly lost this one, was particularly finicky and long-winded; he no longer needed to ask jurors how they felt about the death penalty—it had been abolished by the State Legislature during the past year—but he went into other matters at great length and used peremptories to excuse several Negroes and one Puerto Rican who had answered all his questions faultlessly. (Mrs. Lowe fumed silently, and later, in the hallway, told Scheer in uncharacteristically strong terms that he was a "prejudiced bastard"; he angrily replied that she should mind her own damned business, and that *she* was prejudiced in favor of anyone whose skin was colored.)

Group after group of prospective jurors sat in the box that first afternoon and, except for one man, were weeded out by one means or another. All the next day the same wearisome process went on, only three more jurors being accepted by all hands. The entire panel had

---

* The problem is not New York's alone: in most states, as the Crime Commission observed in its final report, there exist no adequate mechanisms for retiring aging or infirm judges without publicly humiliating them.

now been used up; on Wednesday morning a new batch of seventy-five was ordered up, but in the course of the whole morning not one additional juror was sworn in. The defense, however, was running out of peremptory challenges, and Siegal asked Justice Lyman to exercise his discretion and allow them more peremptories on the grounds that there were three defendants. "If your Honor rules against us," he said politely but firmly, "we think, most respectfully, that we are entitled to a declaration of a mistrial."

Justice Lyman thought a moment, then rallied himself. "That's the law," he said, "that's what's in the statute." Siegal argued the point, but Lyman waved him away and asked him to proceed. Even without more peremptories, however, it took until the middle of Thursday afternoon—over three days in all—to complete the selection of twelve jurors and the alternates out of the total of 150 persons called up.

Somewhere in the midst of all this, Burton Roberts, the second-in-command of the Bronx District Attorney's office and soon to become top man, quietly entered the courtroom and sought to arrange a conviction rather than risk losing the trial. As Mrs. Lowe remembers it, he leaned over her table and whispered, "If they'll take a plea to Man One or Man Two, we'll recommend Elmira, with five maximum—and with time already served and good behavior, they can be out in a year or so." Mrs. Lowe and the other defense lawyers all hopefully urged the deal upon the defendants, but they shook their heads stubbornly; they knew how close they had come to acquittal last time, and by now they were desperate to get out of jail and could envision themselves walking out the front door in two or three weeks and heading for the dear, dirty streets of Melrose.

By the time jury selection was completed, they may have had some misgivings: twelve white middle-class men sat in the box, some youthful, more of them middle-aged, but all solid, respectable citizens somewhere in the middle of the political spectrum, as nearly as one could tell. One was an engineer and one a chemist; several were civil servants, working for the Post Office and other government agencies; others were white-collar technical and administrative employees of the New York Telephone Company, Con Edison, and other giant companies. Although they included no representatives of the Bronx's black or Puerto Rican population, they did include the other major components—Jewish, Italian, Anglo-Saxon, Irish, and Polish, as the roll-call indicated. "Trial jurors will please answer to their names," sang out Clerk Jay. "Gilbert Waltzer [*Here!*], Isidore Horowitz [*Here!*],

Hamlet Mucelli [*Here!*], Eli Mazer [*Here!*], James Ferry [*Here!*], John Purcell [*Here!*], Arnold Giuliani [*Here!*], William Pawlowski [*Here!*], Rudolph Pietrangeli [*Here!*], Thomas V. Gilbert [*Here!*], George D'Rall [*Here!*], Irving Zimmerman [*Here!*]."

The judge excused the jury until the next morning. As soon as they had left, Siegal, who by common consent was the principal spokesman for the defense, asked for copies of the Q&As and the Grand Jury minutes; Scheer, of course, vigorously opposed the request; and Justice Lyman, seemingly unsure what to do, avoided taking any action by saying, "I will rule on it as we go along." Siegal, trying to build a record and, perhaps, to set the tone for the coming days, next asked for all the detectives' reports; Scheer replied that they were not under his control and that Siegal could subpoena them from the Police Department. Siegal's massive face contorted, grew alarmingly wrathful. "It is *abominable*," he burst out, "for an assistant district attorney in charge of a Murder One trial to tell us we can subpoena these records. *He* should furnish us with the records." He carried on, waving his arms, until Scheer made some slighting remark about his theatricality; at this, Siegal wheeled his great belly around at Scheer and bellowed, "Don't tell me that! Don't ever do that to me because I will walk over there and *flatten* you, right in the courtroom!" Considering Siegal's size, age, and general physical condition, this might have struck an outsider as funny, but the other defense lawyers, the guards, the clerk, the defendants, and the judge were all dumb-struck. Scheer, at first taken aback, rallied and told Siegal not to raise his voice to him, but Siegal only got louder; finally Scheer's adrenaline began to flow and he barked, "I will knock *you* flat, too!" The two short, fat, graying men stood a few feet apart, bellies thrust out, and shouted at each other while the court stenographer dutifully took down their billingsgate, which went about like this:

> Siegal: You will knock nothing flat!
> Scheer: Don't you talk to me, you big, round, fat—just because you are a big blubbermouth, you are not going to talk to *me* like that!
> Siegal: I'll blubber *you* in a minute!
> Scheer: You are not going to dictate to me what you are going to do, whether your name is Herbert Siegal or anything else.
> Lyman: Stop it! I am going to hear no further argument. Remand the defendants!

The guards hurried the bewildered defendants out, but the shouting and the threats continued; finally Justice Lyman, banging on his desk, bleated, "Wait a *minute!* We won't have any fist fights around here. Adjourned!"—and got up and rushed out. No one made a sound; Scheer gathered up his papers and left, as did Siegal, neither of them saying another word about the matter then or later. (Each insists, of course, that they are "good friends"; Scheer adds that his friend Herb Siegal tries to do a good job, and that this often includes play-acting, while Siegal says that his friend Al Scheer "likes to take advantage when he can get away with it," and that his own outbursts are one way of keeping Scheer in line.)

Clearly, it was going to be a thoroughly adversarial trial, a contemporary version of the trial by combat of old. Scheer had had time to correct the weaknesses that had shown up in his case the first time, but he now had a tougher, quicker, wilier, and more aggressive opponent than formerly. The question was whether any of this would make any difference, and whether the jury system would function adequately despite the divertissements and distractions that lay ahead.

# II  *The Sequelae of* Gideon

THE second trial of the Ortiz brothers and Doel Valencia was going to be somewhat different from the first one not just because different lawyers were in charge, but because the criminal justice system in 1966 was undergoing major changes due to that series of Supreme Court decisions, handed down during the 1960s, which made nearly all the rights guaranteed by the Fourth, Fifth, and Sixth Amendments binding upon the states.

Of these decisions, the most wide-reaching in its influence was the Court's 1963 ruling, in the case of *Gideon* v. *Wainwright,* that the states were obligated to furnish lawyers to persons it prosecuted who could not afford their own. The decision was epochal: as Professor

Herbert L. Packer puts it in *The Limits of the Criminal Sanction,* *"Gideon* v. *Wainwright* will remain for a long time the watershed decision in the evolution of the criminal process. . . . The norms of the process have been ineradicably changed [by it], and in far more than the mere insistence that counsel must be provided." For *Gideon* is the practical embodiment of our basic belief that the right of citizens to be treated fairly is more important than the right of the government to enforce the law by the most efficient means possible. In dealing with criminal suspects, the federal government had always been bound by the Constitution, but the states, under their own constitutions, had not been as restricted by guarantees of civil rights, and had had their police, prosecutors, and judges deal with many criminal defendants simply, economically, and unfairly. Many states would try an accused person without a lawyer if he was too poor to hire one; this was very generally the case with misdemeanor defendants, and in some states was true even of felony defendants facing severe penalties.* The accused person could, of course, speak up for himself, but this was virtually worthless; a layman, especially if poor and ignorant, is as helpless when pitted against any trained prosecutor or any tough-minded judge as a flabby, short-of-wind desk worker facing a karate instructor. A criminal trial in which the defendant has no lawyer is in no real sense adversarial, and is certainly not fair.

Yet such trials were common enough all throughout United States history because the right to counsel, guaranteed in the Sixth Amendment, was part of the Bill of Rights, and hence binding upon the federal government, though not upon the states. Yet there was a curious inconsistency in the Constitution: the Fourteenth Amendment said that no state could deprive any person of life, liberty, or property without due process of law, and for decades lawyers and judges argued as to whether prosecuting a defendant who had no lawyer was a violation of due process. For if it was, then the Fourteenth, which *was* binding upon the states, made the Sixth binding too. But the Supreme Court, which alone could settle the matter, ignored the issue for many years, or dealt with it equivocally and only in very special situations.

The states therefore remained free to deal with things as they chose, which generally was to the serious disadvantage of the indigent defendant. At the beginning of the 1960s, according to a survey made

---

* Even in federal courts it was not until after a Supreme Court decision of 1938 (*Johnson* v. *Zerbst*) that indigent defendants had to be furnished counsel.

by sociologist Stuart S. Nagel, 12 percent of all felony defendants throughout the country were being tried without any lawyer at all, and a great many others—anywhere from 25 to 80 percent of felony defendants in the various states, according to the Crime Commission— were being defended largely by unpaid or underpaid lawyers appointed by the court, or by volunteers furnished by bar groups, the defense thus provided often being perfunctory and nominal. In a few states and some cities, legal-aid societies and public defenders existed, but they were seriously limited by inadequate funds and insufficient staff.

Thus a great many felony defendants in state courts—perhaps even a majority of them—were getting nothing like a fair chance to defend themselves. One indigent defendant, however, a harmless, middle-aged drifter, gambler, and occasional thief named Clarence E. Gideon, made legal history by getting the Supreme Court to face the issue squarely. Gideon had been convicted and sentenced to five years in a Florida prison for breaking and entering a poolroom in order to steal money; at his trial, in 1961, he had said, "I request this court to appoint counsel to represent me in this trial," but the judge had replied, "Mr. Gideon, I am sorry, but I cannot appoint counsel to represent you in this case. Under the laws of the State of Florida, the only time the court can appoint counsel to represent a defendant is when that person is charged with a capital offense." Gideon, who had no particular knowledge of constitutional subtleties, petitioned the Supreme Court for redress, claiming that to try a poor man for a felony without giving him a lawyer was to deprive him of due process of law—maintaining, in other words, that his rights under the Fourteenth Amendment made the Sixth binding upon the state of Florida.

And this was the very conclusion the Supreme Court came to in reversing his conviction in 1963. (Significantly, when he was later retried with the help of a paid lawyer, he won acquittal.) As Justice Black said, in delivering the Court's opinion:

> The right of one charged with crime to counsel may not be deemed fundamental and essential to fair trials in some countries, but it is in ours. From the very beginning, our state and national constitutions and laws have laid great emphasis on procedural and substantive safeguards designed to assure fair trials before impartial tribunals in which every defendant stands equal before the law. This noble ideal cannot be realized if the poor man

charged with crime has to face his accusers without a lawyer to assist him.

But the decision affected not only trials, for the Sixth Amendment guaranteed the right to defense counsel in criminal *prosecutions*—and prosecution starts before, and ends after, the courtroom phase. But how far before and after? Within a few years the *Escobedo* and *Miranda* decisions spelled out one answer: the right to counsel began as soon as the defendant was taken into custody; and other decisions extended the right all the way until appeals were exhausted. After *Gideon,* the poor were able to do for themselves for the first time what the middle class and the wealthy had always been able to do, and what the philosophy underlying the Constitution had always meant them to.

As a result of *Gideon,* the states had to set up mechanisms to provide lawyers for the poor that were more reliable than the volunteer and unpaid-appointee systems. Within a few years two such mechanisms were in existence. In the *assigned-counsel system,* lawyers in private practice are assigned on a case-by-case basis to defend indigent persons. They are paid, from public funds, according to a fixed (and rather low) schedule of fees. By contrast, the *defender system* relies on agencies which operate either as a department of the government, or as a private service supported by government funds, and which employ a staff of salaried lawyers to defend the indigent. Although the assigned-counsel system exists in a great majority of the counties of the nation, there are now ten states that have statewide defender systems, and among the other forty, a number of individual counties or cities have such systems of their own; some, too, have both defender and assigned-counsel systems working side by side. The need for such defense has proven greatest in the largest cities, where crime and poverty are at their worst: in 1971, for instance, over four fifths of criminal defendants in New York City signed affidavits of indigence, and were defended by counsel provided them by the city, which paid the Legal Aid Society $4,000,000 to handle the bulk of the work, and paid over another million to private defense lawyers appointed in capital cases or cases where there was a conflict of interest with Legal Aid.*

---

* For all that, New York City's legal aid to the accused is relatively meager. The 1965 County Law requires the city's five counties to provide representation for all indigent defendants accused of any crime (other than a traffic in-

With paid lawyers defending them, the poor suddenly had available to them the many legal devices long used by wealthier persons plus all the new obstacles to conviction growing out of Supreme Court decisions. In nearly every serious case, there now were motions to suppress evidence, lengthy pre-trial hearings, motions for pre-trial disclosure of the prosecution's evidence, hearings to reduce bail, longer and greatly intensified questioning of prospective jurors, innumerable objections and motions during the trial to build a record for the appeal, and the like. All of this put serious new burdens on the existing facilities: trials ran two to three times longer than formerly, court congestion was intensified, the conviction rate dwindled, sentences grew lighter—and a large part of the alarmed middle class and blue-collar class promptly and simple-mindedly blamed the Supreme Court for having brought about the crime wave of the 1960s, regarding its liberal criminal-law decisions not as a fulfillment of the promises of the Constitution but as the expression of a sentimental and absurd sympathy for wrongdoers. Many who shared the Court's social aims wondered if it had not gone too far too fast, or strayed beyond its proper bounds: Fred Graham, *The New York Times*'s Supreme Court correspondent, echoing Chief Justice Hughes, called the hostility the Court had aroused by its liberalism and activism a "self-inflicted wound." Even some of the defenders of the poor had misgivings: as one high-ranking officer of the New York Legal Aid Society puts it, "We've fought to extend constitutional rights to all criminal defendants in the states, but as good as these acts have been, they also have had some attending evil consequences. We have made criminal sanctions very hard to impose; we have actually interfered with justice while making the system more just—but those of us who are on this side of things are afraid to face up to the truth."

As for law enforcers, the majority of them regarded the Warren Court as the enemy, and as the chief reason the entire justice system had to come to the brink of disaster. As Evelle J. Younger, District Attorney of Los Angeles County, told the House Select Committee on Crime in 1969:

> The impact of these cases extends well beyond the bounds of legal precedent. It is the spirit of these decisions which perme-

---

fraction) for which any imprisonment can be imposed, but generous as this sounds, the total amount spent on such defense in 1971 came to only one half of one percent of the city's outlay for criminal justice.

ate[s] our courts. . . . Defense attorneys, understandably so, urge every conceivable argument, and some inconceivable ones too, to assure an adequate trial record as their prolog [sic] for appeal. Appellate courts thirst for theories of reversal, converting their task on appeal, as Justice Frankfurter said, into a quest for error. This spirit—this syndrome—permeates the entire judicial system; and no case can ever be final, apparently, until the defendant dies.

The effect of this spirit spreads beyond the courts where its trail may be seen in the logjam of trials and appeals. It injects the people with a virus no society can tolerate—a loss of confidence in the courts and ultimately in the entire system itself.

More recently, in an address to the National District Attorneys' Association in June 1971, the nation's chief lawyer, Attorney General John N. Mitchell, spoke warningly about "the preoccupation with fairness for the accused" which, he said, "has done violence to fairness for the accuser." He added that the Nixon Administration would shortly propose legislation designed to "make the courtroom a place where fact is determined and innocence or guilt decided, rather than a place where fact is obscured and justice frustrated through the triumph of sophistry over common sense."

The "preoccupation with fairness" of which Attorney General Mitchell complained is a phenomenon less than a generation old; the preoccupation with efficient crime control is ancient, and has been the dominant motif of justice systems in most other lands, and even in our own, throughout most of history. For two centuries our state courts have largely ignored the intention of the framers of the Constitution that all men should be treated alike by the law, and that no man should be convicted without a fair chance to combat the power of the state. But for many decades each modest strengthening of the hand of the defendant against the state has produced loud outcries from those who fear that the justice system, and society itself, are about to succumb to lawlessness. Thus far, the justice system and society have survived by a series of adaptations and modifications—but they might very well perish in a holocaust of revolution if the historic rights which have only recently become a reality in state courts were to be taken away by repressive and reactionary legislation.

The criminal justice system, in moving toward the due-process ideal, has become unwieldy and cumbersome, but there are better solutions than trying to turn back history or to restore the unfair advantages the state formerly possessed over the individual and the rich over the poor. Conceivably, the notion of fairness embodied in the Constitution is unworkable, but it is so decent, so noble, a concept that it deserves to be tried. And perhaps it will work, after all; perhaps, despite its awkward, clumsy, and inefficient way of achieving justice, it will prove able to command the loyalty of the great majority of citizens, including those downtrodden groups who have always felt that there was no such thing as justice for them, and who had recently begun to think they could achieve it only by revolutionary violence.

# III   *The Best Defense*

EVEN in jurisdictions whose courts long furnished lawyers to poor defendants accused of serious crimes, many of the poor preferred until recent years to scrape together money, by whatever desperate means they could, to hire their own lawyers. But by 1965 *Gideon* was changing the outlook of such persons, and the Ortiz brothers and Doel Valencia, like many others in their economic category, had suddenly become aware of, and willing to use, court-assigned counsel after their first trial, particularly since all the money spent on their behalf thus far had been wasted.

One of the penalties in using court-assigned counsel, however, is delay: such lawyers are greatly tempted to give their private, better-paying clients priority, and to seek delays in their assigned cases until they have free time. Whether or not this played a part in the long delay suffered by the Ortiz brothers and Doel Valencia, at least one other reason was the existence of the first trial itself: the typed transcript of the proceedings ran to nearly 1,500 pages, every word of which the defense lawyers had to study closely before going ahead with other preparations or setting a trial date. And so the interminable months crept by, with adjournments and hearings and more adjournments, until Alfredo, Carlos, and Doel sometimes felt their rage and despair rising in their throats like bile, choking and bitter.

Mrs. Lowe, who could not afford law assistants and was chronically overburdened with work, made her own analysis of the transcript in spare hours of her evenings and weekends, diligently cross-indexing every topic in order to unscramble the chronology of the events and to ferret out inconsistencies in the testimony. Not until she had been through the foot-deep pile of typescript four times, over a three-month period, was she ready to proceed. She then began seeing the persons important to the defense, beginning with Mrs. Pomales and Mrs. Ambos, visited the former Helmer apartment and studied the building, the halls, and the layout of 2-B itself, and went to Brooklyn a number of times to talk to Alfredo and Carlos. She was deeply disturbed by what the brothers told her, and believed their story, with only minor reservations: "They weren't model youngsters by any means," she has since said. "They were typical children of the ghetto —little bastards who would steal, smoke pot, snort heroin or shoot up, and were into all sorts of things. Alienated kids, yes, to whom society held out no promise—but not vicious kids, not savages. I believed them when they said they had had nothing to do with this crime and had been given a rotten deal, and I suffered for them and wanted to do my damnedest for them." She even tracked down Angel Walker, spent three hours talking to him in the jail on Rikers Island, and believed him, too. "He impressed me as being a guy who knows where it's at," she says. "He told me, 'They tried to make me confess, but they would have had to kill me, because I knew it would mean I'd be tried for murder. I could take it, but the kids couldn't, and when the cops beat the hell out of them, they told the story.' "

It rang true to her. "I grew up two doors from a precinct station in Harlem," she says, "and I used to wake up at night hearing men and women screaming as they were being beaten, and would see them being taken out in ambulances. I *know* what happens in police stations, and when I hear in court that 'the rights of the defendant were protected' or that 'the suspect was given the warnings before interrogation,' it eats me up inside. It sounds so fine, but it means *nothing*. The truth is that deprived people are almost utterly defenseless against the system." She knows better than to think that all her clients are wronged innocents, but she does believe their stories rather more often than do most defense attorneys, and becomes passionately concerned about them, chain-smoking, working late at night, and tossing sleepless in her bed, her victories sweeter and her defeats more bitter than those of her harder-headed colleagues.

But while she believed what Alfredo and Carlos told her about their interrogations and confessions, she doubted that most jurors would, and this, she says, posed a serious dilemma: "I desperately wanted to have the jurors hear from the boys themselves how the confessions were tailored to fit the case and beaten out of them, but the fear of drugs and drug-users was rising rapidly in the Bronx and juries were getting their backs up. Scheer had hammered away at the narcotics thing in the first trial until you'd think these kids were the criminals of the age, and I felt no jury could give them a fair shake if they heard all that—but the only way to keep it from them was to keep the boys off the stand. I agonized over it for months; it's the hardest decision a lawyer ever has to make."

Herbert Siegal helped her decide; he was never in doubt as to what to do. Siegal had skimmed the transcript and quickly concluded that, as witnesses, the defendants were no asset to themselves. He had little personal contact with his client, Doel Valencia, speaking to him briefly in court and sending an assistant to talk to him in jail, but he did think Valencia had been beaten and might even be innocent. Siegal weighed his strategy, however, in terms of whether or not it would work, not whether it would give a wrongly accused person a forum to be heard in. "You put the defendant on the stand," he has told younger lawyers, "and if the jury doesn't like his looks or the manner of his testifying or whatever, it'll turn against him and ignore his story. You never know what will happen. I never put a defendant on unless there's no other way out." He felt that the evidence against all three youths was so limited, and included so many inconsistencies and so many questionable acts by the police, that the best defense for all three would be no defense at all, but an attack on Scheer's witnesses and evidence. "I told counsel for the other defendants," he recently recalled, "that I felt I could create and prove the defense by cross-examining the People's witnesses; I could develop a defense out of their own mouths." With such talk and the weight of his reputation, he persuaded Mrs. Lowe, Samuel Bernstein, and the others to go along with him, and to let him do the lion's share of the attacking. ("When I'm in," he says with a toothy smile, his chin all but vanishing into the bag of fat under it, "they let me handle it.")

On Friday morning, March 25th, the day after he and Scheer had threatened to trade blows in the courtroom, the trial finally got under way. Scheer made an opening statement which, much like his previous one, was a brief account of the crime as seen by the prosecution and a summary of what the People expected to prove. When he sat down, Justice Lyman called upon Mrs. Lowe for her opening, but in accordance with the overall strategy the defense attorneys had agreed upon, she replied, "Alfredo Ortiz waives the opening." Siegal said the same thing for Doel Valencia, and Bernstein for Carlos Ortiz. Most of the jurors, not having sat on a criminal case before, were unable to imagine why the defense had nothing to say for itself, but Scheer suspected rightly that the defense lawyers meant to rely on the presumption of innocence and the creation of reasonable doubt, rather than offer a case of their own.

Scheer began with Helmer's neighbors, Mrs. Pavese and Mrs. Varela, who told their stories again just as they had a year earlier. Siegal, in turn, cross-examined each, but mildly and briefly, since there was no real value, from the defense viewpoint, in attacking either one's credibility. But the third witness, Patrolman Puvogel, was a different matter: any policeman was a prime target.

Under Scheer's methodical questioning, Puvogel told again about entering the apartment, discovering the body, looking around, and cutting open the pocket of Helmer's pants with scissors he found in the living-room so that Patrolman Kacerosky could remove the wallet. It was a straightforward account by a policeman who had done his job, but Siegal heaved his great bulk up from his chair and attacked, seeking to make Puvogel look like a dunderhead. He asked if it was correct that Puvogel had instructions not to touch anything that might have fingerprints on it (yes, he had), and whether Puvogel had thought to bring a pair of scissors with him from the emergency truck (no, he hadn't); then, like a cat that has been toying with a mouse, he sank his teeth into his prey:

Siegal (*accusingly*): Now, you went to a sideboard, I understand, and got a scissors?
Puvogel: Yes, sir.

Siegal (*pulling off his glasses and pointing them at Puvogel*):
You didn't *know* at the time that you got that scissors, or
took that scissors, whether or not that was the murder
weapon, did you?

Puvogel (*looking uncomfortable*): No, sir.

Siegal: And where did you find the scissors?

Puvogel: In a drawer in the sideboard that was located in the
living-room.

Siegal (*shocked, disgusted*): Did you put your *hand* on it?

Puvogel: Yes, sir.

Siegal: And you *used* it?

Puvogel: Yes, sir.

After ten or fifteen dreadful minutes, Siegal let Puvogel go. Scheer
next called Kacerosky to the stand and got him to give an account of
what sounded like a perfectly sensible and workmanlike investigation
of the apartment and the corpse. But Siegal, in the cross-examination,
managed to make poor Kacerosky sound thoroughly incompetent:
growling at him one moment and shouting the next, yanking his glasses
off and jamming them back on, turning to stare at the jury while
Kacerosky was explaining and then wheeling back at him with the next
question, his vast, fleshy face undulating with successive waves of disbelief, sarcasm, perplexity, and scorn, he got the policeman to admit,
first, that it had not occurred to him that a crime might have been
committed; next, that in searching the apartment he had touched
dresser drawers without considering that he might be ruining fingerprints; and finally, that although he had looked closely at the body,
he had neglected to turn it over and so failed to notice the cuts in the
clothing. As a last touch, Siegal made him look ridiculously squeamish:

Siegal: The first thing that you see as you look into the apartment is the window. That's nearest you, isn't it?

Kacerosky: The first thing I seen was the flies on the window
and in the apartment—and the odor—and I backed off the
fire escape and went back into apartment 2-A.

Siegal (*solicitously*): Were you . . . *afraid* of the flies?

Kacerosky (*stalling*): Was I *afraid* of the flies?

Siegal: Yes—did you run away from them? (*Then, quickly:*)

I'll withdraw that question. (*Siegal sits down, leaving Kace-rosky looking furious and foolish.*)

So it went, all day long. The other defense lawyers occasionally made a few objections or asked a few questions during cross-examination, but it was clear that the trial was a contest between Scheer and Siegal, the former assembling his case piece by piece, the latter systematically spoiling each piece by making fools of the prosecution witnesses and hence, in a way, of the prosecutor. The opponents even clashed personally as the day wore on, interrupting each other, arguing, and shouting until Justice Lyman would bang on the desk and call out, in his weak old voice, "Stop it, please!" or "*Will* you stop!"

On Monday, Patrolman Landy was called first, followed by Patrolman Perrone, then by the morgue-wagon driver, Helmer's lawyer, and the hearing-aid man. Siegal bided his time; the other defense lawyers did some minor cross-examining, but the credibility of these witnesses was not important. When the fingerprint man, Detective McGuire, took the stand, however, Siegal cross-examined him minutely, asking him about every surface he had not bothered to dust until it seemed as if McGuire had done a hasty and slipshod job. After the luncheon recess, McGuire's superior, Detective Goldstein, testified that only one partial fingerprint had been found that was clear enough to be usable, and Siegal at once asked him what finger it had been part of; Goldstein said he couldn't tell (as it happens, distinguishing which finger a partial print comes from is almost impossible); Siegal, vastly scornful, repeated, "You couldn't *tell?*," turning to stare at the jury knowingly, as if Goldstein were yet another incompetent cop.

Siegal did not unleash his full powers, however, until Dr. Charles Hochman, the elderly medical examiner, took the stand the following morning. In response to Scheer's orderly and detailed questioning, Hochman professionally and dispassionately described the condition of the body at autopsy, the size and direction of the wounds, and the cause of death. Scheer did not, however, ask him to reckon the probable date of Helmer's death, because at the previous trial when Hochman had used the development of the maggots and flies as an indicator of elapsed time, he had nearly been tripped up by Kenneth Kase. But Mrs. Lowe had spotted this in her careful analysis of the first trial, and alerted Siegal to it (every morning she brought in index cards on which she had outlined the testimony of the witnesses at the first trial, and briefed Siegal so that he could make the most of his opportunities). Siegal therefore asked Hochman whether he had an opinion as to the date of death; Hochman said he did, and discoursed learnedly on the number of hours it takes the new adult fly to lay her eggs, the number of hours before they hatch into larvae (maggots), the number of days the maggots actively feed and grow, and the number of days they are inert in the pupal stage before hatching out as young adult flies. Based on all this, he said, Helmer must have been dead from ten to twelve days at the time of the autopsy.

What authority, Siegal asked, did he have for all those figures? Hochman said he based them on his own observations of flies; he had watched them. Watched them where? When he was at school. Siegal, affably: "That's a long time ago, isn't it, Doctor?" Hochman, chuckling: "I think *so!*" Siegal, still affably: "Since then, have you read any authorities on the subject of flies and maggots and pupae?" Hochman, beginning to see the trap closing, said no. Did Dr. Hochman know a Dr. Halpern? Of course; he was Hochman's superior—the Chief Medical Examiner of New York. Had Dr. Hochman read Halpern's book on legal medicine, pathology, and toxicology? No (squirming), he had not. Would Hochman agree with the statement in that book that from one generation of common blowflies to the next, twenty-four days, rather than ten or twelve, were involved? No; ten or twelve days. But could he cite no authority for this opinion? No, only himself.

And now the *coup de grâce:* Could Dr. Hochman tell whether the flies in the room had been the original ones, or a second generation that had been grown upon Helmer's corpse? Well, the policeman had said the flies were small, so they must have been recently hatched. Which officer had told him they were small? He couldn't remember. Could he tell, by looking at a maggot, whether it had come from an egg laid by one of the original flies, or by a second-generation fly? No, he couldn't. Yet, based on what the officers said about the flies, he still held to his opinion about the date of death? Yes, he did.

Siegal thanked him; Dr. Hochman, mopping his face, left the stand, and everyone sighed with relief. It had been deeply embarrassing: the elderly doctor had been made to appear opinionated, uninformed, foolish, and perhaps a little senile. Whether it had been worth the effort was another matter: Mrs. Lowe felt she had just seen "one of the technically most tremendous cross-examinations ever done—from a law student's point of view. But it really had very little to do with the guilt or innocence of the defendants." Two of the three defendants felt the same; Valencia was pleased that his lawyer had been so busy, but the Ortiz brothers were mystified and suspicious. "Halfway through," Alfredo later told a friend, "I felt I was gettin' railroaded. On the first trial, our lawyers worked for us; on the second trial, they ain' did nothin', but Siegal doin' everything. Seem like they was sayin', 'Let's give up these two an' get *one* out.' Mostly all them questions about maggots di'n' matter, anyway; the jury wants the facts about the *crime*." He was both wrong and right: at the time, most of the jurors felt that Siegal had damaged the People's case, and only later on, after they had heard other and more pertinent evidence, did the maggot-and-fly issue seem unimportant.

The one person thoroughly pleased with the cross-examination of Dr. Hochman was Siegal himself. "Wasn't that beautiful?" he said, chuckling, to a friend some time later. "Hochman tells that story to everyone; he thinks it's fantastic what I did to him. I did it even though he's a friend of mine; I had to show that the People aren't always right. He was a good sport about it—he even sent me a hell of a case a couple of months later."

Mrs. Ambos was called next—this time as a witness for the prosecution ("If you didn't want her at the first trial," Kase asked Scheer in the hall, "why'd you put her on in this one?" Scheer, making an effort to smile, admitted, "So *you* wouldn't make us look bad by bringing her in.") She herself never knew the difference, and, indeed, had always thought the defendants innocent: "I told the cops right up unt down," she said to a friend, "that these boys couldn't have killed him the vay they confessed it, because the time vos so short, unt I vos there, unt heard not a sound unt saw notting." Scheer, who had been so harsh with her last year, now very gently and politely got her to tell her story as if it somehow proved his case. In actual fact, it still conflicted not only with the Ortiz confessions but with the Valencia confession, and could have been useful to all three defendants if left unchallenged, but Siegal, who had been preoccupied with Dr. Hochman, rose to do battle without taking time to confer with Mrs. Lowe or go over her index cards. She tried to stop him, but he brushed her off, whispering, "Later, later." She was frantic: "He had no idea where Mrs. Ambos fit into the picture—she was the one witness who could make the difference for the Ortiz boys, because she had seen the man alive seven hours after they said that he had been killed. But there was no stopping Herb once he got going."

Siegal began gently, but soon was hounding Mrs. Ambos about when she had seen the blood in the hall and had last seen Helmer alive:

> Siegal: Did you tell them in the police station that the last time you saw Helmer alive was on the 8th?
>
> Mrs. Ambos (*ignoring the question*): On Friday.
>
> Siegal (*slowly, loudly*): Did you tell them at first it was on Thursday?
>
> Mrs. Ambos (*bristling*): Correct! Ve corrected it afterwards.
>
> Siegal: Who corrected it, McCabe?
>
> Mrs. Ambos: No, no, mine friend unt I. Ve talked it over. (*Siegal turns toward jury, raises hands helplessly, lets them drop to his sides again.*)

The more he questioned her about the blood, the less reasonable her behavior seemed:

> Siegal: After you saw the blood, you knocked on your friend's apartment.
>
> Mrs. Ambos: Right!
>
> Siegal: And you directed the attention of your friend to this fresh blood?
>
> Mrs. Ambos: Right!
>
> Siegal (*pulling off glasses, peering at her closely*): Did you *tell* her then that you had just seen Mr. Helmer come upstairs?
>
> Mrs. Ambos (*shrugging*): No—there vos no need for it.
>
> Siegal (*perplexed*): Did you knock on Mr. Helmer's door to see if, perhaps, something was wrong with him?
>
> Mrs. Ambos (*annoyed*): No. I just *saw* him!—a few minutes, maybe.
>
> Siegal (*slowly, as if talking to someone of limited intelligence*): But then, *after* you saw him, you saw *fresh blood,* isn't that right?
>
> Mrs. Ambos: Right. I did! (*Siegal shakes head in wonderment.*)

Mrs. Lowe was writhing in her seat. "He was destroying her," she says, "he was making her look like a foolish old lady. I was furious with him—he didn't care, because it had nothing much to do with Valencia's confession—he was just having a good time showing off his expertise. I felt like getting drunk and staying that way for the next two weeks; I felt he had taken the guts right out of my case."

After the destruction of Mrs. Ambos, the judge called a luncheon recess. As soon as the jury left, Scheer turned over to the defense lawyers the Q&As he was about to use in upcoming testimony, and immediately got into a furious wrangle with them. Siegal and his assistant, Philip Peltz, argued that a recent decision of the New York Court of Appeals justified drastic redacting (editing) of the Q&As to eliminate from each confession the names of the other defendants and substitute letters of the alphabet for them. Scheer protested that this was not the intent of the Court of Appeals, and would make the confessions unintelligible. Justice Lyman, his head propped up on one hand, listened to the debate both before and after lunch without saying anything; finally, when Siegal pressed him, saying, "We ask the Court to decide," Lyman ignored him and said only, "All right, proceed. Bring the jury down." Siegal insisted that unless the issue were resolved in advance, questions would be asked which would do damage even if ruled out; Scheer argued the other side; and Justice Lyman made no reply, allowing the discussion to go on and on. Finally he lifted his hand for silence and said, "Let's not argue about it. Go ahead. Bring the jury down."

In this most unsatisfactory fashion the trial resumed with Detective Russo being called to the stand. He told his story almost precisely as he had a year earlier, but as soon as he arrived at the first interrogation of Valencia, Siegal arose and formally declaimed, "I object to any questions at this time unless the District Attorney is prepared to abide by the decision of the Court of Appeals to see that only proper questions and answers are permitted at this time." Justice Lyman called everyone to the bench, where the jury could see an argument going on; after a while he sent them out for half an hour; and finally he had them called back in and told to go home for the day, there being some legal research to be done before the case could proceed. That afternoon Lyman and his law assistant studied the recent decision cited by Siegal and the other defense lawyers, and Wednesday morning he announced that it was impossible to eliminate the names of co-defendants from each confession without making them meaningless, and that in such cases, according to the higher court, there was no alternative but to allow the confession into evidence, and to instruct

the jury to consider it as evidence only against the one who confessed.

With Russo free at last to talk about the interrogations, Scheer
called him back and continued. Siegal and the other defense lawyers
now put on a virtual circus: one after another they popped up with
objections, motions to strike out testimony, motions for mistrial, requests for *voir dire* privileges in the middle of Scheer's direct examination, and requests that the judge instruct the jury again about cross-
implicating evidence. Sometimes they interrupted merely to break up
the flow of testimony (Siegal, naïvely: "At this time, if your Honor
please, may we know from this witness who is 'Alfredo'?" and again,
"And who is 'Negrito' who you mentioned?"). Sometimes they sought
to suggest that Russo was doing something unfair in the way he testified: Mrs. Lowe objected at great length to his reading from his
notes rather than "refreshing his recollection" from them. Justice
Lyman, who had heard all this and much more a thousand times before, denied the many motions for mistrial, ruled on some objections
and ignored others, weakly ordered the lawyers, again and again, to
"stop it" and to "stop the nonsense," and sometimes pleaded, in a
weary tone, "Let's go ahead."

In such fashion, Scheer's direct examination of Detective Russo continued until mid-afternoon. Siegal then arose to do what damage he
could, though he recognized that Russo was a seasoned witness and
not easily ruffled or tripped up. For a while, indeed, Siegal achieved
little more than to make Russo seem somewhat uncooperative, but
eventually he found some of the weak spots he was seeking:

Siegal: How did you know there was gum in there [in the
     wrapper]?
Russo: I felt it.
Siegal (*astounded, indignant*): You *felt* it? You put your *fingers*
     on it?
Russo (*coldly*): I felt it; yes.
Siegal: Were you ever told not to touch anything at the scene of
     a homicide so that the fingerprint men would have an op-
     portunity to dust objects for fingerprints?
Russo: Of course I was told.
Siegal: Nevertheless, *you touched this object!* Is that right?
Russo: I did.

He next got Russo to repeat that he first heard from the Ortiz brothers that the crime occurred at noontime, learned later that Valencia was supposed to have worked all day, and then got a confession from Valencia placing the crime at 9:00 p.m. Siegal suggested that there was something fishy about all this; no honest investigator would have accepted two such discrepant accounts of the same crime:

Siegal: And he now told you that he was implicated in a crime that was committed at 9 p.m., is that right?

Russo: He did.

Siegal (*openly unbelieving*): Well, did you tell him, "Look, son," "boy," or whatever, "do you know that your two associates in this crime say that it happened at noontime?"

Russo: We did.

Siegal (*pointing at the papers in Russo's hands and shouting*): Is it ANYWHERES in ANY of these notes?

Russo: It is not.

Siegal (*cupping a hand to his ear*): WHAT WAS THAT?

Russo: It is not in the statement.

Siegal (*triumphantly*): It is *not* there—*that's* what you're telling me, isn't it?

Russo (*surly*): That's right. (*Siegal nods, as if his point has been proven.*)

Several times, moreover, Siegal brought up the matter of brutality, even though he knew his questions about it would be ruled out or at least discounted as evidence:

Siegal: What kind of persuader did you use? (*Scheer objects; Lyman sustains him and tells the jury the question is not evidence; Siegal rewords the question.*) Did you use a persuader?

Russo (*tight-lipped and scowling*): Did not!

Siegal: Did you use your hands?

Russo: Did not!

Siegal: Your feet?

Russo: Did not!

Siegal: Did you kick him?

Russo: Did not!

Siegal: McCabe do anything in your presence?

Russo: He did not!

Siegal: Any other police officers do anything in your presence?
Russo: Did not!
Siegal (*nodding sarcastically*): Not a *thing*. . . .

And having made Russo blackly angry, Siegal contentedly sat down. Mrs. Lowe asked her partner, Kenneth Kase, to take a crack at Russo next, feeling his style to be more suitable for rough going than her own. Kase, far less nervous and diffident than he had been a year ago, made some good points: for one thing, he got Russo to admit that he had never asked any of the defendants where they had found the money in the apartment. For another, Kase made much of the fact that Russo claimed he had written down the fifteen pages of Alfredo's Q&A in a mere forty-five minutes; Kase's implication was that they must have been written out later. And he managed to catch Russo in a piece of pure fakery about Valencia's status during the afternoon of the 23rd:

Kase: Was he under arrest at two-thirty in the afternoon?
Russo: No, he was not under arrest. No, he wasn't.
Kase: Did you have anybody guarding him at that time?
Russo: Yes, there was someone there.
Kase: He was under guard?
Russo (*hastily backtracking*): *I* said there was someone there. *You* said he was guarded. That doesn't mean he is being guarded because somebody is there, counselor. . . .
Kase: You mean he could have gotten up and left?
Russo: Yes.

But Russo, sensing that this answer was patently unbelievable, tried to fix it up and only succeeded in making things worse:

Russo: He may not have gone too far, but he could have gotten up and left.
Kase: In other words, you would have detained him?
Russo (*tight-lipped*): We would have gone out and gotten him back.
Kase (*enjoying himself*): He was *not* under arrest?
Russo: He was not under arrest. He was entitled to leave the squad office.
Kase (*with great gusto*): But you just *told* me you would have detained him!

Russo (*cornered, but still fighting*): He wouldn't have been detained. He could have gone home, and we would have gone out and brought him back.

Kenneth Kase, clearly, had learned something in the past year. Pleased with himself, he sat down and let Samuel Bernstein tackle Russo for a while. Bernstein questioned him chiefly about the presence of ammonia, rubber hoses, and baseball bats in the station house (Russo said he didn't know of any such things being there); Mrs. Lowe then asked Russo why some of the detective reports seemed to be missing from the file (he didn't know why); and when, after nearly two days on the stand Russo thought he was about to be released from his misery, Siegal arose once more and dealt him the worst blow yet, on a seemingly minor point. Russo, while being questioned by Scheer on redirect that morning, had corrected some minor point in his previous day's testimony, and Siegal, an old hand, knew exactly what had happened and made the most of it:

Siegal: Prior to taking the stand here today, did you tell Mr. Scheer that you had made a mistake in that answer to that question?

Russo (*carefully*): I told him that—

Siegal (*shouting*): Did you, YES OR NO?

Russo: I did.

Siegal: And weren't you instructed by the Court that while on cross-examination, you were *not* to discuss your testimony with *anyone?*

Russo (*sagging*): I was.

Siegal (*triumphantly*): And *nevertheless*—disregarding the Court's instruction—you *talked* to Mr. Scheer! IS THAT RIGHT?

Russo (*grimly*): I did talk to Mr. Scheer.

Siegal at once turned to the judge and moved to strike out all of Russo's testimony because he had violated the Court's instructions; Lyman denied the motion, but the episode made Russo look bad. With that, he was excused, and lurched out of the courtroom, shamed and bested, but annoyed at himself more than at Siegal and Kase. "I have no animosity towards defense lawyers," he says. "If getting me up on the stand and accusing me of atrocities and lies does good for them and their client, I figure that's part of the job. That's what they have to do. Afterward they come up to me and say, 'Hey, Sal, you know there's nothing to all of that, it's all in the game,' and I go right along with them."

Mrs. Lowe next spent some fifteen minutes, with the jury out of the room, earnestly and carefully offering to prove that Alfredo had been spirited out of Criminal Court and arrested without probable cause, and that any statement taken from him was therefore inadmissible— "the fruit of the poisoned tree," as she put it, slightly misquoting a famous phrase of Justice Felix Frankfurter (who had said "poisonous" tree). But having listened to her with a slightly blank look on his face, Justice Lyman conferred in a whisper with his assistant and ruled that the Huntley hearing held by Justice Davidson had covered the issue adequately. Ever ladylike, she replied, "Thank you, your Honor," and accepted her defeat. Actually, she had expected nothing more, but her application for a new hearing and Lyman's denial of it were now on the record for purposes of appeal; she had done far more than the sullen and discontented Alfredo realized. ("The second trial," he has said, "I don' think they were tryin' their best, I think they were tryin' to save time." Carlos, too, was growing restless and dissatisfied: "What kind of lawyer they give me? That old fellow Bernstein, he make jokes like 'I ain' won a case in twenny-five years' —now, what kind of lawyer is that to give me?")

When the jury returned, Detective Stephen McCabe was called to the stand. Scheer had scarcely begun getting his story from him, and was about to offer the bubble gum and the wrapper in evidence, with McCabe identifying it, when the defense launched a full-scale attack, Siegal making a great to-do about the fact that McCabe had kept the gum and wrapper in his own locker and never turned them in to the Police Property Clerk. This, Siegal said, failed to establish continuity of possession: there was no proof that the gum and wrapper were the same ones McCabe had found in the apartment—if he had found any at all—and McCabe had violated police regulations by keeping items of evidence in his locker. With other defense lawyers joining in, the fight got even louder and more disorderly and lasted nearly half an hour; although Justice Lyman finally admitted the exhibits into evidence, the jury had been thoroughly exposed to the idea that McCabe could short-cut the rules in his zeal.

The next hour or so of McCabe's testimony went more quietly.

Using his notes, McCabe repeated for Scheer the Q&A statements of all three defendants, relating every question asked by Russo and himself, and every answer made by each defendant. His account had, of course, the unreal and formal quality of all police testimony: "Detective Russo and myself took Alfredo Ortiz into the boss's office and we spoke to him in there. Detective Russo told him that he was going to ask him some questions, and . . . [asked him] if he wanted to answer these questions. And Alfredo answered, Yes, he would." By midafternoon McCabe had repeated all three confessions very much as he and Russo had taken them down, and completed his testimony on direct examination; he never imagined that he was going to spend the rest of the afternoon, the whole next day, and part of the following Monday being raked over the coals.

It began with his cross-examination by Siegal. At first McCabe was feeling lively and scrappy, and gave Siegal a few jabs by way of opposition:

McCabe: The slip from the A&P indicating the date of October
>9th was found in the shopping bag that contained ice cream,
>milk, apples, eggs, and various produce.

Siegal (*sarcastically*): Did the ice cream and cake and the various
>products help you solve this crime?

McCabe (*pretending great seriousness*): I did not state "cake,"
>counselor. (*Discreet chuckles from the jury box.*)

Siegal (*irked*): Well, whatever you saw in that bag, did it help
>you solve this crime, in your opinion?

McCabe: In my opinion, if I had purchased—

Siegal (*harshly*): Yes or no! Did it help you solve this crime?

McCabe (*turning to Lyman*): Your Honor, I don't believe I
>can answer that with a yes or no.

Siegal (*hastily*): I'll withdraw it.

But there were few such minor victories for McCabe; once Siegal hit his stride, he bullied and bloodied the detective for hours. In the remainder of that afternoon, reviewing McCabe's investigation of the apartment, he found a dozen ways to make him look amateurish: for one thing, he got McCabe to admit that on the first visit he had thought it a natural death, and missed any evidence of murder; for another, that he had always known the rules about depositing evidence with the Property Clerk, and simply had not done so with the

A&P slip, the gum, and the wrapper; for still another, that he had picked up the bubble gum without marking its position on the floor and replaced it, from memory, for the subsequent photographs; and for yet another, that he had touched the gum and the wrapper without considering whether this might ruin any fingerprints on them, and then removed the bubble gum and the wrapper without having the specialists try to dust those objects.

On Friday, Siegal quoted McCabe's testimony before the Grand Jury to the effect that Valencia placed the time of the murder at 7:00 p.m., though now McCabe claimed Valencia had said 9:00 p.m. McCabe, after wriggling around, admitted the discrepancy, and Siegal made him repeat it like a bad boy being forced to confess his naughtiness:

Siegal: Did you make that answer to that question?

McCabe: If it is stated in the Grand Jury minutes, then it must have been stated at that time, and I must have made the statements that are mentioned in there.

Siegal (*with heavy irony*): *Thank* you, sir. And sir, when you made that answer, was it the *truth?*

McCabe (*all but choking*): I must have made a *mistake*. If it is stated that I said seven o'clock or seven-thirty, then I was mistaken at that time.

Was it McCabe's talk with Mrs. Ambos that led him to change the time? McCabe angrily denied it. Was it McCabe's discovery that Valencia had been working all day that led him to change the time? McCabe angrily denied it. Siegal sensed that McCabe was losing control, and managed to elicit another denial that struck even novice jurors as plainly unbelievable:

Siegal: Now, once having made a charge of homicide against Doel Valencia, at 5:55, without any eyewitnesses and without any admission from the defendants, it now became your duty to see that you got some admission from Doel Valencia, isn't that so?

McCabe: It *never* became my duty to get an admission from the defendant! If the defendant *volunteered* this information, then it was up to me to record this information, which I did.

Siegal turned and looked silently at the jurors; the answer was so absurd that no comment was necessary.

On and on went McCabe's torment without surcease. Was Doel beaten up, or threatened, or given the ammonia torture? No. Had McCabe ever gone back to the Ortiz brothers to ask them to clear up the time discrepancy? No, he was not going to put words in their mouths. How long had Russo and McCabe interrogated Angel Walker? Forty minutes. Only forty minutes for the man alleged to be the actual killer? That is right.

Siegal did not finish with the perspiring, red-faced McCabe until late in the morning; then the detective was tackled for a while by Bernstein, and then by Mrs. Lowe, who needled him about how and when he had taken Alfredo out of Criminal Court, and whether or not Alfredo had been his prisoner when he took him from Supreme Court to the Precinct. McCabe ingenuously maintained that when he took Alfredo to the Precinct he did not consider him his prisoner, and that although he had told Alfredo to come along with him, Alfredo had done so voluntarily. Mrs. Lowe was incredulous, but McCabe explained, not very convincingly, that if a suspect obediently came along when "asked" to do so, it was a voluntary act; only if he had to be brought in by force was it involuntary.

On Monday morning Mrs. Lowe nagged McCabe for another hour or two about various mistakes and imperfections in his investigation; when she was done Kase took a crack at him; and when he was done Casey, Bernstein's co-counsel, took a turn, despite the judge's obvious annoyance with the length of cross-examination.

Everyone, in fact, was beginning to act ill-tempered, and for good reason: it was lunchtime, stomachs were rumbling, and blood sugar was running low, but Justice Lyman felt that in view of the approaching Passover and Good Friday holidays, the trial should continue without recess until 2:00 p.m. and then adjourn until the following Monday. The squabbles among the lawyers grew louder and nastier until Lyman croaked, "Stop the nonsense!" and called for a five-minute cooling-off period; things were quieter thereafter, and eventually, by 1:30 p.m., no one had any more questions to ask McCabe. The detective, exhausted and in a foul mood, and embittered by what he had been made to look like in these past three court days, was excused without so much as a word of official thanks from anyone: "All right," said Justice Lyman with unaccustomed crispness, "step down!" And he turned to Scheer and said, "Call your next witness."

In the remaining half-hour, and in the morning session on the following Monday, lesser witnesses came and went without much drama. Annette Odierno, the A&P clerk, told her brief story and left. Irwin Wasserman, the stenographer, again read his transcripts of Alfredo's and Carlos' confessions. Assistant District Attorney Vitale narrated the taking of the confessions. Justice Lyman asked who was the next witness. "People's case, your Honor," said Scheer.

There was a buzz of surprise at the defense tables; they had heard, in the hallway during a recess, that Scheer had four more witnesses lined up. Justice Lyman sent the jury off to lunch, gave the defense lawyers a few minutes to confer, and then listened to their motions: Siegal, Mrs. Lowe, and Casey (speaking for Bernstein) each moved for dismissal of the indictment on the grounds that the People had failed to make a *prima facie* case because of the time discrepancy and because of the lack of evidence other than the confessions. They learnedly quoted various cases, sections of the Penal Law, and parts of the Code of Criminal Procedure, but, as they knew in advance, they were only building the record: the case had in fact been strong enough that no judge would have taken it away from the jury at this point. And indeed, Justice Lyman said only, "Motion denied, all motions are denied. We will resume at two o'clock." With that, he hurried out, eager for his lunch and a few minutes of catnap in his chambers, for, as far as he knew, they might be about to present a full-scale defense.

And for a while even they did not know what they were going to do. Despite the earlier strategy decisions, the defense lawyers were now unsure whether their attacks on the People's case had really been sufficient. At the end of the luncheon recess they would have to commit themselves one way or the other, taking their chances on the basis of what they had done thus far, without having the defendants tell their story, or letting them tell it and running the risk of undoing the doubts the lawyers hoped they had created in the minds of the twelve men who even now were making their way, in twos and threes, to various nearby restaurants, carefully talking about the April weather, air pollution, the Knicks, and other safe and neutral topics, though all they really hungered to talk about was the People's case and what the defendants might have to say for themselves when they took the stand, if they ever did.

---

## IV   *The Presumption of Innocence*

---

AT every criminal trial by jury, the jurors are repeatedly informed by the judge and lawyers for both sides that the defendant is presumed innocent until the jury reaches its finding, and that this presumption holds good even if he offers no defense witnesses and says nothing in his own behalf. From the sonorous and reverent fashion in which judges and lawyers speak about the presumption of innocence, often calling it one of the basic principles of Anglo-American law, one might expect it to be among the rights guaranteed by the Constitution; oddly enough, the phrase does not even appear there.* It is, rather, an *attitude* toward the individual human being and toward the proper balance between freedom and authority—a cultural assumption, deeply entrenched in common law but rarely made statutory, that the individual is more important than the central government and personal liberty more valuable than social order and efficiency.

The presumption of innocence is thus central to our concept of justice, at least in theory; in practice, it often seems a manifest absurdity, a credo to which we pay lip service but in which we believe no more than we do in miracles. Suppose, for instance, that an unemployed young black, arrested by police who catch him running away from the scene of a shooting with a recently fired gun in his pocket, is arraigned before a judge and held without bail, indicted by a Grand Jury which hears some of the evidence collected by the police, and brought to the courtroom to be prosecuted by an assistant district attorney who values his own professional reputation: which of us, at that point, would not be inclined to suppose the defendant had indeed committed a crime? When we read in the paper that the police have

* It does, however, appear in some state codes of criminal procedure, written long after the Constitution and its Bill of Rights.

made an arrest in some notorious murder or bombing case, or that a city official has been indicted by a Grand Jury for graft, do we not assume that the individual has done something wrong, rather than that he is the guiltless victim of error or malice?

And yet most of us know that, whatever our common-sense reaction, we expect another and nobler response in all who play a part in our courts. We expect them to achieve the nearly impossible: to presume even the most seemingly guilty person innocent until he has been legally proven guilty beyond a reasonable doubt. This is why so many thoughtful people were deeply shocked when, on August 3rd, 1970, in the midst of the trial of Charles Manson and several members of his hippie "family," President Nixon said during a press conference, "Here is a man who was guilty, directly or indirectly, of eight murders without reason." If the lawyer running the nation, responsible for the policies of the Justice Department, and empowered to nominate Supreme Court justices, could openly forget this basic principle of Anglo-American law, which of us was sure to remember it? Which of us could feel that, if charged with a crime, he could still be sure of getting a fair trial?

Mr. Nixon, of course, recognized almost at once that he had made a real blunder and issued a "clarification," saying that he did not know whether the defendants were guilty in fact or not, and that at this stage of their trial they should be presumed innocent. But it was not a unique or insignificant slip: President Nixon has long sought to promote preventive detention—a concrete expression of the presumption of guilt—and various members of his Administration have belittled the principle of the presumption of innocence, Assistant Attorney General Will Wilson, for one, labeling it a "mere rule of procedural evidence."

But it surely is not a mere rule. Even the moderately educated person who knows very little of law has heard that the major difference between Anglo-American criminal law and criminal law in continental European countries is that in our system the accused person is innocent until proven guilty, and in the other, guilty until proven innocent. This is a misstatement, or at least an overstatement; the presumption of guilt is not written down as an explicit principle in continental codes of criminal law. But it does exist as an attitude expressed by specific procedures. To arrest a man on suspicion, to hold him incommunicado while investigating the crime, to have the police's and prosecutor's evidence, unfiltered by rules of evidence, studied by the very judges who will decide the case, to require the defendant to testify or have his silence taken to imply guilt, is to treat him as if he were guilty until proven innocent. In contrast, to arrest a man only on probable cause, to guarantee him the right to see his lawyer at once, to exclude from the jury's or judge's knowledge any hearsay or unfairly gathered evidence, and to grant the accused the right to remain silent without allowing inferences to be made from that silence, is to treat him as if he were innocent until proven guilty.

The attitudes expressed in these differing procedures have ancient origins. The continental or inquisitorial system is the descendant of the criminal law of imperial Rome, a centralized despotic power in which the primary goal of criminal law procedures was to maintain an iron-fisted control over disruptive or troublesome elements in society. The judge, typically, has great power: he inquires into everything, hears whatever the police and the prosecutor have learned (the prosecutor himself is a quasi-judicial figure), questions the accused and the witnesses himself (though he also listens to what defense lawyers have to say), decides the question of guilt or innocence, and determines the punishment of the guilty. With wide variations, this is what one finds today in Paris, Moscow, and most points between.

The Anglo-American or adversarial-accusatorial system, on the other hand, had its remote origins in the homespun, quasi-democratic forms of procedure which were used in small Anglo-Saxon communities and which, as the power of the king became greater, developed into a series of protective devices shielding the individual against him and his agencies. In this system, overall control of the trial is more or less distributed among the several participants: the judge is essentially an umpire, overseeing a contest between prosecutor and defender; these two contestants have roughly equivalent standing and powers, the former trying to convey as much incriminating information as he can and the latter trying to keep out as much as he can, each having the right to call his own witnesses and to attack the other side's; and the jury, after passively hearing the evidence and arguments, determines guilt or innocence and, in some cases, fixes the penalty.

The Anglo-American system is the product of many centuries of accretion. The protection of the accused against the power of the state was assembled piecemeal as democracy evolved: it included the right not to be arrested except for legal cause, the right of *habeas corpus* (a legal mechanism by which arbitrarily imprisoned persons could obtain either their release or an open hearing), the right of the accused not to testify against himself, and the right to be released, pending trial, on reasonable bail. The unstated implication of this growing body of rights was that the accused might very well be innocent, and therefore should not be treated in advance of conviction as if he were guilty and deserving of punishment. In creating an adversarial balance between individual and government, English common law thus expressed the emerging democratic conception of the moral worth of the average man, and in the United States that attitude was embodied in the very structure of government and formalized in the Constitution, in the guarantees of the Bill of Rights.

Over the years, moreover, some of those rights have been strengthened by laws and court rulings making the presumption of innocence more nearly a working reality. Some states, for instance, long permitted prosecutors or judges to comment unfavorably to the jury on the refusal of the accused to testify; in 1965, however, the Supreme Court ruled that "comment on the refusal to testify is a remnant of the inquisitorial system of justice which the Fifth Amendment outlaws. It is a penalty imposed by courts for exercising a constitutional privilege."

Again, statutes and court rulings have increasingly excluded jurors who, by reason of bias or information, might be unable to presume innocence in the defendant. A suspect may, for instance, confess to the police and later plead not guilty—and, conceivably, may have confessed falsely—but if jurors have heard about his confession, they may be unable to presume him innocent. The Supreme Court, in 1963, reversed a Louisiana conviction because a local TV station had repeatedly shown a film of the defendant confessing to a sheriff and two state troopers, and not only had three of the jurors in the case seen the film but the community at large knew about it. (The simple remedy, the Court pointed out, would have been change of venue.)

Yet even where unbiased jurors can be found, they see before them in court a defendant who has been seized, charged, investigated, and brought to trial by responsible public officials and representatives of the state; how can the jurors believe that the accusation is without foundation in fact, or that the defendant is guiltless? The late Charles P. Curtis, a respected lawyer and author, sourly commented that "no one who has been indicted and formally charged with a crime is really presumed innocent by anyone but his friends or well-wishers, or somebody who happens to know that the government was wrong." Not even the professionals manage to presume the innocence of the accused in their hearts: prosecutors certainly do not, defense lawyers generally assume that their clients are guilty, and many judges would agree with the federal jurist, quoted by Martin Mayer in *The Lawyers,* who admitted, "The truth of the matter is that I never see a defendant in a criminal case without assuming he's guilty."

But the obligation to presume innocence in the defendant rests more upon the untrained amateurs in the jury box than upon the lawyers or the judge, and even if they fulfill it imperfectly, they do so better than the professionals. Professors Kalven and Zeisel, for instance, found in their study of the American jury that in serious crimes, if the defendant takes the stand and has no previous record, the jurors are distinctly more likely to acquit him than the judges would have been; in such cases, the presumption of innocence has special force.

It has less force, however, if he has a previous record or fails to take the stand. To presume someone innocent when his previous history and especially his silence are against him is to willfully defy common sense in the name of fair play, and this is not easy to do. Defense lawyers and their clients, indeed, believe silence to be so damaging to the presumption of innocence that three quarters of defendants with criminal records do take the stand, judging it less hurtful to have their past revealed than to remain silent.

Yet there is no proof that juries automatically convict anyone who refuses to testify. The Kalven-Zeisel data indicate that while juries are swayed by the silence of the defendant, this is only one of the factors influencing the outcome: whether the defendant testifies and reveals a record, or refuses to and so creates a suspicion in the jury's mind that he has one, there is still anywhere from a 12 percent to 38 percent chance of acquittal, depending on the strength of the prosecution's case. If juries are not as good at presuming innocence as one could wish, they are far from being as poor at it as cynics and pessimists say.

And even if they are imperfect at it, the mere existence of the presumption of innocence as an ideal results in a very different criminal process from that in any inquisitorial system. George Feifer, having listened to many a criminal trial in Soviet courts, reports in *Justice in*

*Moscow* that trials and verdicts are, in large part, preordained by the preliminary investigation, and that defending the accused is considered bourgeois and not quite respectable:

> Even the law students on my floor in the dormitory thought of the trial as something of a formality and, consequently, of the lawyer's role as superfluous. "In *this* case, he is clearly guilty," I used to hear from students when we went to court. "Why must the lawyer confuse the issue and waste our time?" The idea that guilt is determined only by the court, only after the arguments are heard, is not firmly entrenched. And so the feeling lingers on that the accused is guilty and represents a bother, if not a danger, to the state and that to defend him is somehow disreputable, obstructionist, opportunistic, and a waste of time.

The Soviet and other inquisitorial systems are probably more practical and sensible than our own, and considerably more efficient at maintaining social order, but while we pay a price for our impracticality, we get something in return: the privilege of living in a society in which every man has a fair chance to defend himself against overwhelming official power—a society which fails to convict all who should be convicted, but which sustains the dignity of the individual and preserves his right to defend himself against the government itself.

---

# V  The Defendants in This Case, Gentlemen, Failed to Take the Stand

AT lunchtime, just before leaving the courtroom, Justice Lyman had said to the defense lawyers, "I would like to get through with it. Try to have some witnesses to get started at two o'clock." As far as he knew, the defense was planning to present a case; indeed, Bernstein and Kase had asked him for a one-day delay—which he had refused them

—claiming that they hadn't known the prosecution was about to rest, and therefore hadn't advised their witnesses to be on hand. Actually, they had made no plans to call in any witnesses, the defense strategy still being what it had been from the beginning; but when defense lawyers intend to present no case, the approach of the critical moment when they must announce "The defense rests," forgoing any chance of presenting evidence for their side, fills them with misgivings. All but Siegal were, at this juncture, apprehensive and vacillating in their feelings, and none felt the case was anything like clear-cut for acquittal. Despite Siegal's ferocious attacks on key prosecution witnesses, there had been no dramatic revelations or breakdowns on the witness stand, and the dozen assorted middle-class men on the jury were so thoroughly reserved, not to say stolid, that it had been impossible to sense or even guess where their sympathies now lay.

The six defense lawyers went to lunch together to discuss their next move. Siegal, speaking in an *ex cathedra* rumble, said that they should rest their cases; they had badly damaged the People's case already, could do further damage in summation, and had nothing to gain by offering weak and imperfect alibis. Mary Lowe, looking anguished and smoking furiously, said she was having second thoughts; she wondered if they shouldn't put the boys on the stand after all, to let the jurors know how they had been beaten into making false confessions. Did she really believe they had been? someone asked. Absolutely, she said; it made sense, it felt like the truth; besides, Alfredo had been eager, all during the trial, to testify, and had even urged her to bring in Angel Walker to tell about the beating he, too, had received. And she had been impressed by the genuine agitation Alfredo and Carlos had shown at many of the things Russo and McCabe had said on the stand, Carlos even muttering something several times about "lies," and once shouting out loud and being promptly squelched by the guards and the judge.

Siegal brushed all this aside. He'd seen and heard the same sort of thing hundreds of times—and often from guilty defendants; they wanted so much to be believed innocent, and told their stories so often, that after a while they half-believed everything they were saying. No, it would be a mistake to put them on the stand; if the jurors were to learn about their previous records, it could only weaken the doubts they must feel about the prosecution's case. But what about bringing in Walker? Wouldn't his testimony about the beatings make the confessions much less credible? Siegal pooh-poohed the idea: who would believe a man with Walker's record—a man brought from jail to testify—particularly when he himself was named in the confessions as the actual murderer? Back and forth went the arguments, until the food, idly picked at, turned cold on their plates and the ashtrays grew full. Finally they arrived at the same decision they had come to weeks ago: they would rely on the presumption of innocence and on the reasonable doubts they had tried to create.

Troubled and unsure (except for Siegal), they returned to the courthouse, where Mrs. Lowe went up to the detention pen to tell the defendants of their decision and to urge them to accept it. Alfredo and Carlos protested at first, but soon agreed; in the courtroom a little later on, however, when Siegal, Mrs. Lowe, and Bernstein asked them to sign statements saying they had voluntarily chosen not to testify, Alfredo suddenly refused. For a few moments the trial was delayed while there was much fierce whispering at the defense table. Then Valencia, who felt Siegal had been doing well by him, signed; Carlos meekly followed suit; and Alfredo, sulking and muttering to himself, gave in and did likewise.

The jurors entered and took their places, and Justice Lyman asked the defense to proceed. Mrs. Lowe stood up and said, rather formally, "May it please the Court—Mr. Foreman—members of the jury—the defendant Alfredo Ortiz rests." Scheer, though he had suspected this all along, felt a pang of disappointment and a wave of apprehension; without a chance to expose the defendants, it was possible he might lose. The jurors, most of whom had never sat on a criminal case before, were not only disappointed but astonished, finding it hard to believe that the defense was not going to offer them anything by way of explanation or alibi. Mrs. Pomales, following the case as best she could, felt betrayed ("Mrs. Lowe, she seem very nice," she said later to a friend, "but she let us down").

As soon as Mrs. Lowe sat down, Siegal half rose and said that Valencia rested, and Bernstein followed with the same announcement for Carlos Ortiz. Justice Lyman called all the defense lawyers and Scheer to the bench; the jurors, as usual, wondered what they were up to, and for once found out, Lyman turning to them and explaining that the lawyers were merely discussing how long they would need for their summations. In a few moments the conference was over, and Lyman excused the jurors until the following morning; the jurors, still surprised and disappointed at the sudden, anti-climactic end of the presentation of evidence, went their separate ways to their homes, wondering about the many unresolved questions that now would never be answered for them and about which they would have to make up their minds in some fashion or other.

The next morning, when everyone was assembled, Kenneth Kase took over for Mrs. Lowe and made the summation on behalf of Alfredo. Surer of himself than the previous year, and no longer playing the role of the meek young man, he opened with a flourish of arm-waving rhetoric: "Ye shall seek the truth, and the truth shall make us free," he quoted ringingly if a little inaccurately; and again, "Alfredo Ortiz sits there cloaked with the presumption of innocence, and thank God for it!"; and yet again, looking at each juror in turn, "You people have an awesome burden, you people have a great responsibility!"

Having got this fanfare out of the way, he said that the prosecution bore the burden of proving Alfredo guilty beyond a reasonable doubt, but that there were many reasons why the jury might have such doubts. There was the strange business about McCabe's keeping both the gum wrapper and the A&P slip in his locker all this while; there was the matter of the grocery bag, which for no good reason was never photographed; the Ortiz confessions put the crime at a little past noon, but Mrs. Ambos had seen Helmer alive after 7:00 p.m.; there was not one eyewitness, not even anyone who could testify to seeing the defendants near the building on the day of the murder; neither Russo nor McCabe had ever asked where the money had been found or where the murder weapon was; and though robbery was alleged to be the motive, a full wallet had remained on the victim's person.

Speaking well and emoting freely, Kase felt pleased with his performance and let himself get carried away: "The fingerprint compared negatively to the defendants," he said, and triumphantly cried out, "It *eliminates* them, gentlemen!" (Even as he said it, he knew it was absurd; so did the jurors, none of whom, later on, proved to have been taken in by it.) Hastily he dropped the subject and went on to deride the formal confession taken down by Wasserman: seventy questions and answers had been recorded in a mere six minutes ("Take *that* into the jury room and deliberate over that," he said, "as to whether that is good credible evidence"). And he ended with another burst of rhetoric: "I said before that these defendants are cloaked with the presumption of innocence. It is worn like armor. We *all* wear it, as citizens of this country, the presumption of innocence—and thank God for it!" Dropping his voice and speaking slowly and emphatically, he intoned, "They have not pierced this armor, this presumption of innocence. They have not *dented* it on these defendants." Then, rather spoiling his simile, he added, "They haven't even *bruised* it!" He asked them to bring in the only verdict he felt was possible for Alfredo Ortiz—a verdict of not guilty—and sat down.

Bernstein was next, summing up on behalf of Carlos. Uncomfortable in the role of criminal lawyer, he strove to sound dramatic and to use a wide range of expression, but only succeeded in blundering into a number of blind alleys of thought. Helmer had gone upstairs, he said at one point, and nobody followed him, yet there was blood on the floor a few minutes later, from which it was clear that "either Mr. Helmer was standing outside somewhere, came upstairs by his doorway—" He paused, apparently unable to remember what point he had meant to make, and finished lamely, "*I* don't know, but the fact of the matter is that the blood was there after Mrs. Varela had gone into her apartment and before Mrs. Ambos came upstairs." Which, of course, proved nothing.

Struggling out of this dead end, he went on to make an assortment of unrelated points. Most detectives gave straight yes or no answers, but McCabe was always making some kind of explanation. As for the confession, who could believe that a suspect would ever stop to unwrap chewing gum in the midst of a murder? McCabe and Russo were "rotten cops," McCabe in particular, because he "had never been on a homicide case before, and was looking for glory." Bernstein waved an admonishing finger at the jury. "Ladies and gentlemen," he said, and then stopped, suddenly realizing there were no women in the jury box after all. "I'm sorry, *gentlemen* of the jury. When I bring these things to your attention, I tell you they absolutely create a reasonable doubt." The jury, he said, could only resolve that doubt in the favor of the defendants. He sat down, much to the relief of all concerned, including Carlos, who felt that Bernstein was "jammin' me up."

After Bernstein's potpourri of non sequiturs and clichés, Siegal arose, moved in huge-bellied majesty to the center of the floor, and took over, authoritative, forceful, and fluent. "Of necessity, because I am last," he said to the jurors in a gracious tone, "I hope you will forgive me if I seem to be repetitive in some of the statements that have already been made by associate counsel." But having begun with formal and graceful language, he shook the jurors awake with plain and harsh words: the police had offered only a "lame-brained" excuse for not trying Angel Walker; McCabe and Russo had "had the nerve" to try to put over "tripe" and "nonsense" on the jury; McCabe had "lied" to the Grand Jury, and faked evidence for this trial, putting the gum wrapper on the floor to be photographed but removing it before the fingerprint men arrived because none but his own prints could be found on it. "And we are going to hear the District Attorney," Siegal bellowed, flinging an arm in Scheer's direction, "ask for a conviction of murder in the first degree!—upon the testimony of a man like McCabe!" That was why the law, over the centuries, had created the presumption of innocence—"because of the many McCabes and Russos before."

He fell silent for a moment, looking at his notes; then, starting from a *pianissimo,* he went into the matter of the time discrepancy, his voice rising in volume and intensity as he talked, until it slowly reached a new *fortissimo.* Why was noon given by the Ortiz brothers, when Mrs. Ambos had seen Helmer alive after 7:00 p.m.? Because the Ortiz brothers never said it: it had come from McCabe, who, for some reason or other, figured that the crime had been committed at high noon and forced that time upon them. Then why did McCabe have Valencia say it happened at 9:00 p.m.? Because he had found out that Valencia had been working all day. Why didn't he and Russo change the Ortiz confessions to fit? Because it was too late: Vitale and Wasserman had already recorded them and they couldn't be changed.

This last point was wrong, of course; McCabe and Russo did have nearly an hour in which they could have changed the Q&As or reinterrogated Alfredo and Carlos. But Siegal had carefully advised the jurors when he began that if anything he said about the evidence did not accord with their own recollection of it, it was their recollection that counted, and not his. With this safeguard, he could afford to be inaccurate, whether accidentally or deliberately. He misstated the evidence even more flagrantly a little later: "Don't forget," he said, "that the landlady, sitting on the stand, said, 'I saw, a little while before Mr. Helmer went up there, two Puerto Rican boys go into the building and didn't come out.' Don't forget that! And when I asked her to please look at these defendants and see whether those boys that she saw were any of these defendants, what was her answer? No!" (Mrs. Ambos had explicitly said that she did see the two Puerto Rican boys leave before Helmer came in.)

The major part of Siegal's summation, however, was given over to a series of reasons why reasonable doubt existed: he did what Kase had already done, but with a pounding, roaring, driving energy, his ungainly body seeming almost agile as he strode up and down, his monumental face billowing and quivering with sarcasm, outrage, and indignation. Where was there any proof that Helmer had been robbed, as alleged? Where—except in the so-called confessions—was there any proof that Angel Walker had stabbed Helmer? How could a man possessing only a left arm have inflicted wounds of the size and direction of those on Helmer's body? When Valencia denied everything before Vitale, why didn't McCabe speak up and confront him with the Q&A in which he had admitted his part in the crime? What proof was there that Valencia had ever really made any such statement to the detectives? Why were there no fingerprints on the grocery bag? Why were there no fingerprints of the detectives on the cupboards and furniture they had touched? And so on, and on, for nearly forty-five minutes, until he reached his resounding peroration:

"The defendants sit there presumed innocent. They have no burden of proving anything in this case. The District Attorney must prove the defendants' guilt beyond a reasonable doubt on each and every allegation of the indictment." But the case presented by the District Attorney "is so full of reasonable doubt that there cannot be any problem in your minds as to how to arrive at a proper verdict." And shifting to a deep, earnest, heartfelt manner, he ended: "I ask you, gentlemen of the jury, Mr. Foreman, can you in good conscience convict these defendants of the crime of murder in the first degree upon the tools—the evidence—and the likes of McCabe, that was in the courtroom? I ask you, Mr. Foreman and gentlemen of the jury, to bring in a verdict of not guilty."

(Later on, discussing the case with an acquaintance, Siegal said, "Oh, McCabe's all right. I wouldn't pinpoint him. Police officers who make up their minds that a particular person is guilty don't have too much compunction about, let's say, *exaggerating* in their testimony." McCabe, for his part, looks back on what Siegal did to him as being "a normal thing—after all, he's a good attorney. If I was in trouble, I'd like to have him on my side.")

It was 12:30 when Siegal finished. Justice Lyman sent everyone to lunch before calling on Scheer to sum up—an inconspicuous way, perhaps, of aiding the prosecution, since it gave Scheer two hours to prepare rebuttals of what had just been said in the defense summations. When everyone was back in place after lunch, Scheer arose to do battle. Standing very straight, as if to make his short, rotund body a trifle taller, and leaning backward a little against the weight of his belly, he started out with the usual pieties: the defendants were entitled to every right under the law, and the jury should respect their rights. But, he added, the People of New York had rights under the law, too, and the jurors had taken an oath to respect the rights of all concerned. He then reread the indictment charging the defendants with murder; he reminded the jurors that he had told them at the outset that there were no eyewitnesses; nor had the criminals left some mark, like Zorro, to identify themselves; but though the People had no such direct external evidence, they did have confessions. (Alfredo had never heard of Zorro; later on, when he found out who he was, he concluded that Scheer had been appealing to racial prejudice.) Like the Zorro allusion, Scheer's other literary devices left much to be desired: in the opening minutes of his summation he said, "The ball is being thrown to the People's witnesses to divert your attention from these defendants, and it is very cute," a moment later adding, "I don't think you will watch a red herring go by in front of you and miss the critical evidence," and still later saying, "It is human to err—that's why we have erasers on pencils."

But finally he got down to the real issues and systematically reviewed the testimony of his witnesses, seeking to plug the holes made by the defense in its summations. At times schoolteacherish, at times angry, at times righteous, he supplied what he hoped were plausible answers to some of the more troubling questions they had raised. Had the gum been planted in the kitchen by McCabe? No, Officer Puvogel had seen it there before McCabe ever arrived on the scene. Had the grocery bag been only a fiction? No, the first policemen on the scene had seen it, and the morgue-wagon driver had moved it. Could Walker have inflicted the wounds with his left arm? Yes, Dr. Hochman had said it depended on the relative positions of the assailant and the victim. Why did Helmer still have his wallet in his pocket? Because the attackers had probably intended to get into his apartment to look for a hoard secreted there. Was it credible that an assistant district attorney could ask seventy questions and get seventy answers in six minutes?

Scheer dramatically pulled out a watch, put it on the table and rapped once to signal the beginning of a minute, and stood in dead silence for what seemed a very long while before saying, "You saw how long that minute was." But what about the time discrepancy among the confessions? The jurors were entitled to believe everything in the Ortiz brothers' statements without believing that the crime happened at noon.

Finally, and most important of all, there was the matter of the credibility of the detectives. Speaking with such fervor that he grew red in the face, he expostulated, "Did Detective Russo dream this up? Did Detective McCabe dream this up? For what purpose? This is a Murder One charge against these three defendants—would he sleep nights if he dreamed that up? I say this is *cruel*, it's *inhuman*, it's *unmerciful* to charge Russo and McCabe with such conduct!" Indeed, he added, pounding on his table, there was only one real issue in the case: credibility. The jurors had to decide whether they believed Russo, McCabe, and the other members of the Police Department who had been involved in the case; if they did, they could only find the defendants guilty. And he ended as he had the previous year by saying that the rights of the People of New York should be respected, quoting the motto "The true administration of justice is the firmest pillar of good government," and warning them that unless they reached a verdict fairly and courageously, the walls of justice would come down. "I am sure," he said, "that in fairness to all, you will come out with the only fair verdict that could be rendered in this case, and that verdict is guilty as charged."

When Scheer sat down, Justice Lyman announced that he would charge the jurors in the morning, and released them for the rest of the day. Off they went, their minds congested and throbbing with the pros and cons of what they had heard in the four summations. Their bewilderment, however, was very different from that of the jurors at the previous trial. Those jurors had had the problem of deciding which of two wholly contradictory stories they believed, and which of the human beings who had appeared before them they judged to be truthtellers, which liars. The present jurors, however, were striving to keep the unnatural presumption of innocence in their minds, and to decide whether the story told by the accusers was so convincing that they could condemn three young men about whom they knew nothing, and who had mystifyingly said not a word in their own behalf.

Nearly all of the jurors, like those at the first trial, hoped that the judge's charge would clarify things for them. But although what Lyman said the next morning sounded authoritative, it was no more interpretive or clarifying than Davidson's charge had been the year before—which was hardly remarkable since it was Davidson's charge warmed over. Mary Lowe, who had a transcript open in front of her, saw with astonishment and indignation that Justice Lyman was reading to the jurors Davidson's charge of last year, merely edited so as to omit the references to defense testimony. The first part of it—the lecture on legal principles—was unchanged, and some of the jurors were rather surprised to hear the enfeebled and absent-minded Lyman giving a clear and cogent, if somewhat droning, talk on the law. Following this, his review of the evidence was likewise only a verbatim repeat of Davidson's charge up to the point where Justice Davidson had reviewed defense testimony; there, of course, Justice Lyman stopped short and said, instead, "The defendants in this case, gentlemen, failed to take the stand and testify in their own behalf. Under the law, a defendant—every defendant—has a right to do so, but his failure to take the stand and testify in his own behalf creates no presumption against him." He then quoted the relevant statute (Section 393 of the New York Code of Criminal Procedure), which said the same thing, using not the pejorative term "failed" but the equally pejorative expression "neglect or refusal to testify." (Could not a defendant simply "choose" not to take the stand, or "prefer not to testify"?— would this not be closer to the spirit of the presumption of innocence?)

When Justice Lyman had finished, Siegal asked for various exceptions and, for the record, requested the Judge to give the jury certain additional instructions; Lyman refused most of these requests, as he had twenty-five others made before his charge. Mrs. Lowe, who had had relatively little to say during the trial, now got up and made a long, highly articulate, and rather fervent speech, sometimes clasping her hands and sometimes gesticulating freely, as she asked Lyman to "marshal the evidence"—that is, to indicate to the jurors exactly what items in each confession could be held against each defendant, so that what one said about any other would not be held against that other. Lyman listened to her patiently for many minutes, leaning his head against one hand; when she had concluded, he said—as she had fully expected him to—"Decline to charge as requested." (He could hardly have done what she asked him to without hours of preparation, and in any case he had precedent for merely cautioning the jurors about cross-implicating testimony; Mrs. Lowe, again, was only building the record for an appeal in case the jury brought in a conviction.) Bernstein then asked Lyman to charge that if the jury believed Angel Walker had not committed the crime, the defendants must be acquitted; Lyman said, "I so charge," apparently forgetting that the same request had been made earlier and that he had denied it.

No one had any other requests, and Lyman told the jurors, "If you want any exhibits, of course you are entitled to any." He nodded to an attendant and said to the jurors, "All right, you may step up." They arose, sidled from the box, and followed the attendant across the courtroom, the lawyers and the three defendants looking at them as they passed—twelve average-looking, businesslike men of varying height, age, and build, their faces all uniformly expressionless—and wondering what they were secretly thinking, and what certainty or doubt they were feeling about the things they had heard.

---

# VI   *The Benefit of the Doubt*

---

IF the defendant is presumed innocent until proven otherwise, it follows that the prosecution bears the entire burden of proving him guilty; neither his previous record nor his silence is supposed to weaken the presumption, and it remains the task of the prosecution to offer evidence so convincing that of itself it convinces impartial jurors of his guilt "beyond a reasonable doubt."

This, it is often said, is one of the three great principles of Anglo-American justice (the others being the presumption of innocence and the exclusion of unfair, or unfairly gathered, evidence). Yet, important as it is, it is not named in the Constitution, for, like the presumption of innocence, it too is an attitude deeply rooted in the traditions of English common law but not specifically made statutory. Even where, in this country, it has been formally set down in various state codes of criminal procedure, it is neither defined nor explained but merely named, as if its meaning were self-evident. This is hardly the case. A flaw or contradiction in the evidence that is sufficient to make one juror doubt the guilt of the defendant may bother another not at all; moreover, even if both jurors harbor exactly the same degree of misgiving or uncertainty, they may differ as to whether it feels like a strong enough doubt to preclude a finding of guilty. For no objective test, no quantitative scale, exists with which to measure the intensity of doubt; it remains a subjective perception, like each person's inner experience of a flavor, a sunset, cold water, or a touch.

Subjective though reasonable doubt is, however, the justice system cannot allow each juror to define it as he pleases, for it is not a purely personal experience but one with profound effects upon the life of the defendant and the well-being of the society that is seeking to convict him. Judges therefore always attempt, in their charges to the jury, to clarify the meaning of reasonable doubt. Unfortunately, the standardized "pattern" or "boiler-plate" jury instructions used by many judges generally give only circular definitions which do little to make it more concrete. An example:

> A reasonable doubt is a doubt based on reason. It is a doubt for which a juror can give a reason if he is called upon to do so in the jury room. . . . A reasonable doubt is defined as an actual doubt, a doubt that you are conscious of having, after going over in your mind the entire case and giving consideration to all of the testimony and every part of it. If you then feel uncertain and not fully convinced that the defendant is guilty, and if you believe that a reasonable person would hesitate to act because of such doubt that you are conscious of having, then that is a reasonable doubt. . . .*

Judges also often say that a reasonable doubt is not just a whim, hunch, or fantasy, but the product of logical reasoning from the evidence; this helps, but not much, for even logical reasons for doubt may be trivial, and not "reasonable" in the broader sense of "worthy of serious consideration." Sometimes another explanation is offered

* This was the explanation offered the jurors by Justice Davidson at the first trial of the Ortiz brothers and Doel Valencia, and repeated by Justice Lyman at their second trial. Similar explanations are to be found in the standard instructions used by many judges in a large proportion of the states.

which says that proof beyond a reasonable doubt requires a higher order of proof than that normally required in civil proceedings; that is, proof by a preponderance of the evidence. But how much higher? The answer is not self-evident, and the boundaries remain unmarked.

Various judges and appellate courts have sought to answer the question in one fashion or another, but with limited success. One classic and widely cited explanation, offered by the Court of Appeals of the District of Columbia in 1923, says that proof beyond a reasonable doubt requires more than a strong probability; it requires "a reasonable and moral certainty"—but immediately adds that this is not the same as absolute certainty. (One remembers Byron's words in *Don Juan*: "I wish he would explain his explanation.")

Another celebrated effort, made in 1925 by the Supreme Court of Appeals of West Virginia, also used the criterion of "moral certainty," but explained that this did not exclude every "possible or imaginary doubt"; then, seeming to have one foot on solid ground, it promptly slid back into the quicksand of tautology, adding that proof beyond a reasonable doubt is proof such as satisfies "reasonable men . . . applying their reason to the evidence before them . . . [and finding that] no other reasonable conclusion [is] possible" except that the defendant is guilty. A judge of the Supreme Court of Illinois, despairing of all this, curtly wrote in a majority opinion in 1927, often quoted since then, "The term needs no definition," and although this is patently untrue, it has undeniable appeal.

Thus there exists no quantification of reasonable doubt, no rule such as, say, "If there is more than a five [or ten, or fifteen] percent chance that 'guilty' would be a wrong verdict, then reasonable doubt exists and a 'not guilty' verdict must be returned." Lacking any such rule, jurors have to make do with the blurred and indistinct parameters they are presently offered, which can be summed up by saying that in order to convict, they need a sense of conviction but not of utter certainty. And this is precisely what makes jury duty in criminal cases so difficult: the jurors have to make a moral choice, which is far harder than carrying out instructions that leave no room for individual decisions.

Professors Kalven and Zeisel, in their study of the American jury, sought to determine how often the choice is a difficult one. According to the evaluations offered by the judges they surveyed, in two out of every five criminal trials the evidence presented is close to the reasonable-doubt threshold, while in half the cases it is clear-cut for conviction and in one out of twenty clear-cut for acquittal. It is in the close two out of every five cases that jurors face the mental and moral struggle to decide whether their doubts are of such reasonable magnitude as to require acquittal, or are smaller than that and leave them no alternative but conviction.

Whatever judges may tell them, jurors base their reasonable doubts less often on logical deductions from the evidence than on a feeling that the law is too harsh in the case at hand—a feeling which they translate not into open revolt against the law, but which, according to Kalven and Zeisel, they express by unconsciously seeking grounds for doubt or magnifying such doubts as they feel. As British jurist Lord Devlin has pithily said, "I do not mean that [jurors] often deliberately disregard the law. But if they think it is too stringent, they sometimes take a very merciful view of the facts."

Yet even when jurors give the same weight to the evidence as the judge, even when they feel the same about the credibility of the witnesses, and even when they have the same sentiments about the laws applicable to the case, they still are a little less likely than the judge to feel certain of the defendant's guilt, and somewhat more likely to give him the benefit of the doubt. Perhaps this is only due to inexperience: it is harder for the raw recruit to kill than it is for the combat veteran, harder for the intern to cut than for the surgeon; perhaps the juror would find it easier to lay aside his doubts and convict if, like the judge, he had already done so a number of times. Or perhaps the explanation lies in the different perspectives from which they view the human race: judges, seeing a daily parade of repulsive and vicious persons being brought before them, become somewhat misanthropic and pessimistic; jurors, whose daily sampling of mankind is likely to be more normal, may retain a slightly more benign view of their fellow man, and feel slightly readier to doubt his guilt. If jurors sometimes err in this direction, it is the better of the two possible errors they could make, for the principle of reasonable doubt is something like that principle taught to beginning medical students: *Primum, non nocere*—first of all, do no harm. Even as it is better not to treat an ill patient than to make him worse with harsh or wrong medicines, so it is better to let reasonable doubt stay our hand than to convict and punish so freely that ailing democracy perishes of its cure.

# VII  *How Say You, Gentlemen of the Jury?*

As soon as the jurors were seated around the long conference table, the foreman, a diffident and soft-spoken young man, suggested that there be an expression of opinion all around. By a remarkable coincidence, three jurors were for a verdict of not guilty—exactly the same number as on the first ballot at the previous trial—while the other nine were for convicting all the defendants. The mood of the three, however, was very different from that of their predecessors. At the first trial, the minority in favor of acquittal had heard the defendants tell their own stories, and actually believed them to be the innocent victims of police error and brutality. This time the minority for acquittal had no idea what the defendants were like and had heard neither alibis nor tales of brutal interrogations; they felt that the defendants might well have committed the crime, but that the evidence was not strong enough to leave no reasonable doubt in their minds.

The foreman, being a good deal younger than most of the others, hesitated to play the role of a strong chairman, and the discussion, undisciplined, leaped from topic to topic, with side discussions and cross-talk slicing through the main deliberation somewhat as follows:

—There are three confessions. How much does it take to make you certain?

—The trouble is, they can't all be true. Two say noon, one says nine p.m. How do you know which to believe?

—The judge said you can believe part of a confession and reject part of it. So you could figure all three guilty, if you disbelieve them only about the time.

—*Personally, I wouldn't put any stock in what the detectives say. They pulled a lot of funny stuff.*

—*That's the way the defense lawyers made it sound—false arrest, frame-up, lies, all that. Baloney! So the police made some mistakes; who doesn't? One thing they didn't do—they didn't fake this case.*

—But everything in the Ortiz confessions makes noon the only possible time—and the landlady says she saw Helmer alive in the evening. So how can I accept their confessions at all?

—Maybe they got this job mixed up with another one. They might be junkies who didn't know the time—

—That's just guesswork—

—All right, all right; the fact is that they *confessed*—all three of them—and gave just about the same story, except for that.

—*If you ask me, the old lady was mixed up. I wouldn't throw out any confessions on the basis of what she said.*

—*She wasn't mixed up at first. Siegal got her mixed up, same as he did the old doctor, with that stupid business about the maggots and the flies.*

—*What was the point of all that, anyway? To make the date of death uncertain? But we know the date from the grocery slip and the confessions—*

—*If you believe them!*

—I beg your pardon; their stories differed on lots of important things. Like whether Carlos held the old man around the neck or by the arms. Where they ran to afterward. Who handed out the money.

—I don't remember that. You sure of that?

—Pretty sure. . . .

—Maybe we ought to have another look at the Q&As—

—*The Ortiz boys don't look like they could murder anybody. I could put them in my pocket! Now, Valencia—*

—*If they assisted in a murder, they're murderers. That's the law.*

—*Are you willing to convict Alfredo of murder when he was only a lookout? And when the real murderer isn't even being tried for it?*

—*It isn't up to me to decide what the law should be.*

—*Well, just the same, it doesn't seem right.*

—While we're at it, maybe we ought to have another look at what the landlady said about what day it was that she saw the blood and the old man.

—What about another look at Valencia's first statement? The one
 he made before he admitted anything? He had an alibi until
 they got to work on him.

—We don't *know* that they got to work on him! Just because
 some lawyer asks about beatings and ammonia, that doesn't
 mean anything.

—Maybe not, but nobody denied it, did they? I find that suspicious. It makes me wonder.

 —*There were hints about these guys having been in trouble
 before. It would help if we knew the truth—*

 —*We're not supposed to guess what's behind hints. We don't
 know that they ever did anything wrong.*

 —*The important thing about Valencia is that he wouldn't repeat his confession to the D.A. That makes me feel he
 only talked to the detectives because they were beating up
 on him.*

 —*If they were, why didn't they get him to say noon, like the
 other two? They could have, easily.*

—Would you like me to send a note to the judge, asking to hear
 the Q&As read again?

—Yes. And Valencia's first statement when he didn't confess.

—And the landlady's testimony about what day it was when she
 last saw Helmer, and when she saw the blood.

—And what McCabe told the Grand Jury said about the time of
 the crime.

—Aren't we asking for a lot?

—We have a right to. It's a matter of life imprisonment. We'd
 better be sure.

The foreman scribbled a note to Justice Lyman, and by 12:30
everyone was in the courtroom again. Scheer and the defense lawyers
were all fairly calm, feeling it unlikely that the jury had reached a
verdict in only a little over an hour. Alfredo, Carlos, and Doel, however, were pale and sick with fear. "When they call us out to go
down," Alfredo recalled later, "it really scared me, it gave me the
shakes. I *expected* to get convicted this time, I felt it comin', because
the jurors, they sat there like they was half asleep durin' the cross-
examinations. I felt like the only chance for us was to take the stan'—
an' we di'n' get that chance, an' now they were goin' to put us away
for life."

The suspense was over in a moment: Justice Lyman announced that it was time to go to lunch, and that during the lunch recess the court reporter would locate the various parts of the transcript that the jury wanted reread. He read aloud the foreman's note naming the sections and discussed it with him; the lawyers could tell that they were in for a long, tedious afternoon and an even longer wait for the verdict. After lunch everyone sat and listened to court reporter droning on until late afternoon; then the jury returned to its room, the defendants were sent back to the pen, and the lawyers resumed their efforts to pass the time.

In the jury room, it was disappointing to discover that the rereading had resolved only minor issues. But although the details of the discrepancy as to time were now very clear in everyone's mind, clarity was no guide to deciding what was true and what was false. Also clear were the many trifling differences among the confessions, but it was not at all certain that these differences were reason enough to doubt the confessions or to suppose they had been extorted. Several of the older and more conservative jurors finally expressed impatience with the discussion, one of them summing up his viewpoint succinctly: either you believed in the Police Department or you didn't. If you did —admitting, of course, that cops can make errors—then the Q&As were all the evidence needed to convict the defendants. The time discrepancy was not the cops' fault: it was the result of faulty memory, or deliberate lying on Valencia's part, or something like that. In any case, all three had admitted their guilt, and there was no reason to disbelieve them on that score. "If we vote all three of them guilty," he concluded, "I'll go home to sleep tonight with a perfectly clear conscience."

One of the younger men—a juror who had been for acquittal at the beginning—said he had thought it over and changed his mind about the Ortiz brothers; he now thought them guilty. But he felt more strongly than ever that he could not vote to convict Valencia. A pro-conviction juror debated the point with him:

—Would you tell me how you figure Valencia innocent?
—I don't, I only say I can't find him guilty.
—Oh, for Christ's sake!
—What I'm saying is, we're supposed to find him not guilty unless the case against him is beyond reasonable doubt. And I feel the case against him isn't that good.

—He confessed the whole thing—

—But wouldn't repeat it to the D.A. And that makes me less sure about him than about the other two.

—Well, both of the Ortiz brothers said Valencia was with them on the job.

—Look, we were told time and again *not* to take what any one defendant says as evidence against any other. What the Ortizes said about Valencia has no weight. If we stick to the law, there's doubt about Valencia, and that means not guilty—even if he did it.

He won over one juror to his view: on the next vote, the count was ten to two to convict the Ortiz brothers, but only eight to four to convict Valencia.

Shortly after 6:00 p.m. the deliberations were interrupted by a guard who asked the jurors to follow him back to the courtroom, bringing their coats with them. There, Justice Lyman told them they would now be taken out to dinner, and were not to discuss the case until they got back. They went to a rather pleasant Italian restaurant, but dinner was a chore: no cocktail or wine was permitted, and since the one topic in which they had a common interest was banned, they could only talk self-consciously and dispiritedly about neutral subjects. It was a relief to return to the jury room at 8:00 p.m.

All evening long, Scheer, the defense lawyers, Mrs. Pomales, Josie, the clerk of the court, and the courtroom attendants kept their dreary vigil, some of them reading papers and magazines, some trying to work, some making sporadic conversation. The lawyers always hoped this part of the trial would be over mercifully soon, but knew better: it is common knowledge, verified by survey, that the longer a case has lasted, the longer it generally takes the jury to arrive at its verdict. The courtroom was a cheerless place, at night, drab and bleakly lighted, tomb-like and resounding to every movement. Kase, though restless, was not especially nervous, but Mrs. Lowe was jumpy and tense, and sometimes seemed close to tears. Siegal, exuding confidence, was annoyed at the waste of his evening, and kept making trips to the phone booth in the corridor. Scheer worked fitfully on a couple of other cases, and sometimes chatted with Russo and McCabe, who dropped in for a while during the evening. Upstairs in the pen, the defendants were enduring the same torment they had known last year; this time it was even worse, for the jury, it seemed to them, had been hostile, and their lawyers (except for Siegal) had been far less rambunctious and hard-working than Hanrahan had been at the first trial. They could not understand why the lawyers had summoned no witnesses and offered no evidence on their behalf; the presumption of innocence, a phrase they had heard a hundred times, had no real meaning for them, and they did not for an instant expect the jurors to presume them innocent.

The evening wore on with infinite slowness as the jurors struggled back and forth over the muddy, trampled ground of their deliberation. The two who had held out for acquitting the Ortiz brothers were weakening a little, but put up a last-ditch fight to maintain their reasonable doubt:

—Can you really send those two kids to prison for *life* on no better evidence than what the police claim they told them?

—Not just the police! They told it to the D.A., too.

—Well, maybe we ought to have that reread, so we see if it's really the same as the Q&As.

—What do you think you're going to hear that you haven't heard already? There's no reason to think those boys are innocent. Listen, all through the trial I was just waiting for *something* to make me think they were innocent, but the defense gave me *nothing*.

—Right—if those kids had wanted to say something, they would have. I know *I* would, if I was innocent. But still, before I send anybody away for life, I want to be absolutely sure—

—You don't need to be *absolutely* sure. The judge told us that.

—Well, surer than I am now. I would like to hear those confessions once more.

As for Valencia, the mood of a couple more jurors had swung the other way as the case against him had come to seem less clear-cut than they had first thought. Still, the discussion went on and on, unresolved, the air grew heavy and eye-smarting with smoke, and men looked at their watches and shook their heads dolefully, realizing that they would not get home until very late, or might even have to stay in a hotel overnight and continue in the morning.

The latter proved to be the case. At 11:30 p.m. Justice Lyman, pale and drawn, summoned everyone back to the courtroom and announced a recess for the night. A Carey bus took the jurors to a motel a couple of miles away, stopping en route at an all-night drugstore to let them buy toothbrushes; in the morning, unshaven and seedy in their stale clothing, they breakfasted in a diner and arrived back at the courthouse by 9:30 a.m. It was a crisp, sunny spring morning, the sky purest blue and the air tangy but soft; reluctantly they went inside and took the elevator up to their small, bleak room and their labors.

As soon as they started talking, they agreed that the first order of business was to ask for the rereading of the confessions the Ortiz brothers had made to Assistant District Attorney Vitale; this might resolve the lingering doubts of the two holdouts. And since Mrs. Ambos' testimony had conflicted with these confessions as far as the time was concerned, they also wanted to hear everything she had said —not just the part they had heard yesterday, but all of it, including the cross-examination.

Shortly they were ushered into the courtroom, where the judge and the lawyers, in fresh clothing but tired-looking, were waiting; the three defendants, haggard and shabby, stared at them with the hunted, unblinking eyes of cornered animals. Justice Lyman announced the order of business, and there was a faint sigh from some of those who had desperately wanted an answer and yet been afraid to hear it. Everyone settled back, and the court reporter thumbed through his pile of transcript and began reading aloud. On and on he read, sometimes stopping to hunt for the next part, or being interrupted by brief discussions between the lawyers and the judge. The jurors listened, staring out of the windows or looking unseeingly at the flag, the bench, the attendants, the familiar faces, while trying to hear something new and meaningful.

It went on all morning; not until a little before noon did the court reporter stop and announce, "That's the end of it." There was a moment of silence; then the foreman asked Justice Lyman, "May we go up?" Yes, said Lyman, they could; the jurors returned to their room, ordered their luncheon sandwiches and coffee, and fell to work discussing what they had heard. One of the jurors who was for conviction pointed out that Mrs. Ambos' testimony was clearly self-contradictory and unbelievable: it eliminated any possibility of attackers being upstairs between the time Helmer entered and the time she went up after him, yet it was just in that brief time that she said the blood was spattered in the hallway. It made no sense; besides, she had definitely changed her mind about which day all this had happened. But if her testimony was not particularly credible, there was little reason to feel any doubt about the Ortiz confessions.

One of the two holdouts admitted that he had now changed his mind. "If they had put somebody on the stand, made some attempt to explain, I'd feel better," he said. "At least I could choose between two sides. This way, I have only one side and silence, so I've felt very doubtful, but now I think I have no real reason to doubt." Everyone waited to hear from the last remaining holdout, one of the jury's younger men. He nodded slowly. "All right," he said, "I said yesterday I don't put much stock in what the detectives said they got from the boys, but I guess the confessions to the D.A. are something else." There was a mumble of approval all around the table. The foreman called for a vote on each Ortiz brother: all twelve jurors said they were guilty. Then he called for a vote on Valencia, and, to no one's particular surprise, the balance had shifted a little further the other way and stood now at six for conviction and six for acquittal.

Doggedly, but with a sense of impending defeat, they tackled the problem of Valencia once again. No new arguments were advanced, no new suggestions were offered; the six for conviction were unshakable, but the six for acquittal, no longer a defensive minority, were self-confident and adamant. The young man who had been the last to switch to guilty on the Ortizes became the most outspoken of them. "I wouldn't *like* acquitting him," he said, "because I don't see how he can be really innocent. But I feel the evidence doesn't justify convicting him. It would be wrong to do so, even if we would like to."

They fell silent, started in again, and fell silent once more. Another vote—six to six. More talk, more silences, a sense of hopelessness. Another vote, still six to six. Finally one of the not-guilty faction said that if they reported themselves deadlocked, they could all feel more or less satisfied: they wouldn't be turning in a verdict of either guilty or not guilty, and probably the prosecution would try him again. This seemed to relieve their minds, and after another few minutes of talk and one last six-to-six vote, they decided to report a disagreement on Valencia and sent word to Justice Lyman that they had reached a verdict.

A little before 3:00 p.m. they filed into the courtroom, their faces carefully blank, avoiding the eyes of the defendants and their lawyers.

Scheer's pulse raced; he could almost taste his victory ("If they keep their gaze away from the defendant when they come back in," he says, "that generally indicates there's a conviction." Mrs. Lowe, hoping against hope, refused to let herself believe the signs; with her stomach gathered into a hard knot, she sat and waited, the familiar words and procedures unreal and infinitely remote. Alfredo, Carlos, and Doel, their legs trembling, were led forward, flanked by guards, to stand before the bench and listen to the verdict.

"The foreman will please rise and answer," called out the clerk. The foreman got up and stood at attention. "Gentlemen of the jury," said the clerk, "have you agreed upon a verdict?"

"We have," said the foreman in a strained, rather shaky voice.

"How say you, gentlemen of the jury? What is your verdict? Do you find the defendant Alfredo Ortiz guilty or not guilty of murder in the first degree?"

"Guilty," said the foreman. Alfredo gasped and seemed about to faint. "Hey, Freddy," whispered Carlos, "hey, man, be cool!" But Alfredo, dazed, heard nothing except the voice of Valencia, seemingly a great distance away, rapidly mumbling a Hail Mary in Spanish. Mrs. Lowe, totally numb, like one who has just been injured but has not yet begun to feel the pain, could not help looking at Scheer; she saw with revulsion that his normally cold, homely face was transformed by a beatific smile.

"Do you find the defendant Doel Valencia guilty or not guilty of murder in the first degree?" asked the clerk.

"We are deadlocked on that," said the foreman. Valencia was stupefied; once more he did not know whether to feel despair or joy. Siegal, however, grinned toothily and triumphantly; he regarded this second disagreement on Valencia as a victory, and doubted that there would be a third trial. He glanced at his opponent, Alexander Scheer, and was delighted to catch him in a moment of astonishment and anger, the joy momentarily gone.

"Do you find the defendant Carlos Ortiz guilty or not guilty of murder in the first degree?"

"Guilty." Bernstein sighed and shook his head, Mrs. Lowe began to feel the pain seeping through her numbness, Scheer beamed again, and Carlos glared at the jurors with wild and hate-filled eyes, though inwardly he felt completely impotent ("They look right back at me," he recalls, "an' what could I do?").

Some formalities followed: the judge set a date to hear Siegal argue that charges against Valencia should be dropped, the defense lawyers made their usual unsuccessful motions to set aside the verdict, the jurors were asked one by one to affirm that they found both Alfredo and Carlos guilty of murder in the first degree, and Justice Lyman set June 10th as the date for sentencing. Finally, he thanked the jurors for their attention during the trial, and for rendering a verdict according to their consciences. With that, the trial was over, and the jurors—uncertain for a moment—got up, stumbled out of the jury box, and drifted away.

Outside in the hallway, a woman was screaming. Mrs. Lowe knew who it had to be, and hurried out. She had urged Luisa Pomales to remain outside when the verdicts were announced, but by now someone had told her the news; when Mrs. Lowe got outside, Mrs. Pomales was lying on the floor in a dead faint. Two court attendants struggled to pick up her limp body, and carried her to an anteroom. Mrs. Lowe, sick with pity, hurried back inside to visit Alfredo. On her way to the pen she saw Scheer smilingly accepting the congratulations of several young assistant D.A.s, and of McCabe and Russo, who had been among the spectators. McCabe grinned at her as she passed by. "You bastard," she said, "you'll live to regret what you did here."

"What do you mean, Mrs. Lowe?" he asked, astonished and hurt.

"You've got two innocent boys doing a life sentence," she said. "I hope you sleep well tonight." She saw him growing red, and left, satisfied, hurrying through the door and up the flight of stairs to the detention pen. There she found Alfredo and Valencia both crying, while Carlos leaned against the wall, stony-faced and silent. Mrs. Lowe sat down on a bench next to Alfredo and put an arm around his thin shoulders; he laid his head in her lap and burst into racking sobs. Kase and Bernstein, arriving a moment later, tried to help her comfort both him and Carlos, and Philip Peltz arrived to assure the weeping Valencia—on behalf of Siegal, who had rushed off on other business —that he had been very lucky. Mrs. Lowe stayed on after the others had left, and sought to calm and encourage Alfredo and Carlos. "I di'n' even want to rap with her," Alfredo remembers, "I couldn' believe what happen. It was hard . . . ah . . . *man!* . . . But she say she never goin' to let us down, she goin' to fight the thing the whole way for us, it was a rotten deal, she goin' to get us out—an' after a while I felt a little better. Moms came to visit us in the jail that night, cryin' an' carryin' on, but I tol' her about Mrs. Lowe an' tol' her not to worry because we goin' to be back in court on an appeal, an' we wasn' goin' to do life for this thing that we ain' done."

By 4:00 p.m. the courtroom was empty and locked for the night. In his chambers, Justice Lyman was signing the last of a batch of papers and preparing to go home to his comfortable apartment and his solicitous wife; Scheer, in his office on another floor of the courthouse, was laughing and joking with colleagues and feeling very pleased with himself; the twelve jurors had all taken subways or buses, or their own cars, and headed off to their various homes, bursting to tell their wives, children, friends, and cronies of the high drama of the trial and of the verdict they had reached; Mary Lowe, getting somewhat drunk in a bar near the courthouse, was bitterly complaining to another woman criminal lawyer about the corruption and injustice of the whole system and about her loss of faith in it; Mrs. Pomales, revived by smelling salts, was lying on her bed in her rented room, sobbing and praying; Detectives McCabe and Russo were back on the job, the cases piled on their desks already making them forget the glow of pleasure and sense of vindication they had felt in the courtroom; and in the detention pen, waiting for the bus to take them back to jail, Doel, Alfredo, and Carlos were sitting in silence, Doel beginning to feel that there was a real chance for him now, and the two Ortiz brothers trying to comprehend the disaster that had befallen both of them and to tell themselves that there must be some hope, that their lives could not be over so soon.

# Chapter 7　Correction

## I　*Is There Any Legal Cause to Show Why Judgment Should Not Be Pronounced Against You?*

FOR nearly eight weeks Alfredo and Carlos Ortiz wasted away the weary and useless days in the Bronx House of Detention (to which they had been moved, from Brooklyn, at the beginning of the second trial) while awaiting their scheduled reappearance before Justice Lyman for sentencing. The long delay, typical in felony convictions, had a worthy purpose: it gave the Probation Department of the Supreme Court time to prepare presentence reports on both youths. Such reports bring together biographical details and psychological evaluations of a sort that would not be admissible as evidence during a trial but that help judges measure out the amount and type of punishment appropriate to the given case. A case worker in the Probation Department therefore visited Scheer and made note of some of the information in the D.A.'s files, talked to McCabe, got the Ortiz brothers' arrest records from the Police Department, looked up their school records in the files of the Board of Education, interviewed

**336**

Luisa Pomales, and visited both brothers in jail.

The reports he wrote on the two brothers, which reached Justice Lyman a week before the date set for sentencing, were several pages long, neatly typed, and couched in the disembodied terms of professional diagnosis. The one on Alfredo, for instance, described his behavior between his robbery conviction and the arrest for Helmer's murder as constituting a "poor adjustment to probation," specifically citing his "irregular reporting" to the probation officer, his "apathy in the employment area," and his rearrest on the drug charge. It also included a brief family history, frigidly clinical and detached in tone, that named all the right entities without conveying any of the actual feeling of Alfredo's upbringing:

At the time of this report, defendant's mother was 37 years old, one of six children. She had a 9th grade education. She entered into a non-legal union with defendant's father at the age of fifteen. (It is to be noted that defendant believed his parents were legally married and subsequently divorced.) This union, which lasted about five years, was marked by considerable friction and discord and intermittent separations, certainly due to father's tendency to drink excessively, consort with other women, and provide inadequately for his family. In New York City, defendant's mother worked for a relatively brief time as a packer in a garment factory, but for the most part she has been living on Public Assistance.

Alfredo, accordingly, had become a chronic problem; in school, even before his troubles with the law, he had been "aggressive, at times," "absent excessively," had "compiled a poor efficiency record," and "had lacked motivation." Even now, after a year and a half in jail and a conviction of murder, he struck the investigator as being "assertive and argumentative, vehemently denying his guilt in spite of his conviction by jury trial." Taking everything into account, the report concluded, "The instant offense impresses us as a carefully planned, brazenly executed crime, perpetrated by four aggressive youths, each of whom has a prior record."

The report on Carlos was similar in style and content, but the capsule history and diagnosis were somewhat more sympathetic, portraying him as the victim of forces larger than himself:

Ineffectively reared in an emotionally unstable, broken-home environment, the defendant experienced neglect and deprivation during his formative years; hence he was an early behavior problem in school and eventually came into contact with juvenile authorities, culminating in his admittance to the New York State Training School. . . . He has a poor employment record and is completely unable to furnish any verifiable employments since his discharge from school. . . . He impresses us as a basically anxious, insecure, impulsive youth with low frustration tolerance; he lacks vocational aspirations and tends to associate with delinquent, criminally involved persons, including his codefendants herein.

Unfortunately, all this research and analysis was in vain. Even if Justice Lyman had considered the Ortiz brothers the hapless but salvageable victims of their upbringing, he had no choice: the Penal Law of New York State made life imprisonment mandatory for Murder One. A year later, under a revision of the Penal Law, judges would be able to impose an indeterminate sentence, with some leeway to make the minimum term longer or shorter, according to what they learned from presentence reports, but in 1966 nothing Justice Lyman read in them could change the sentences which he had to impose, and which, all things considered, were surely very harsh. For the Ortizes, according to their own admissions, had meant to aid only in a mugging, and every day New York City judges were sentencing the average mugger to about one year in jail. But another person's unexpected use of violence had made them technically murderers, and even with perfect behavior and the earliest possible release on parole, they would each spend a total of twenty-six and a half years in prison. If they had been apathetic, lacking in motivation, and basically anxious before, what would they be after spending their youth and more than half their adulthood in such a fashion?

Alfredo and Carlos were unaware of this: they assumed that the judge would take things into account and would mete out punishment according to the circumstances. On the morning of June 10th, fearful but hoping for the best, they sat, silent and pale, in the detention pen in the courthouse. The day was drizzly, humid, and unseasonably hot, and nervous sweat soaked through the armpits of their shirts and trickled down their thin, bony backs; they spoke to each other rarely and only in curt monosyllables. Finally a guard unlocked the gate and called out, "Carlos Ortiz!" Carlos, terrified but trying hard to look tough, got up and went out, preceding the guard down the stairway and into the courtroom. There he found a familiar scene: Mrs. Lowe, Kase, Bernstein, and Casey were at their tables and Scheer was at his; the white-haired clerk of the court was at his desk, his features starkly illumined by the green-shaded lamp shining on his papers; Justice Lyman was ensconced above all at the bench; and in the spectator section sat Luisa Pomales clutching a handkerchief to her mouth, her face a mask of grief.

Cultural tradition in the West portrays the handing down of the sentence as a portentous and impressive occasion: there is a grim pageantry in the spectacle of the sinner approaching the throne, the stern, white-bearded figure above looking down upon him, pronouncing judgment in echoing, sepulchral tones, thunder and lightning marking the dread words, the earth opening and swallowing the condemned man.

But it was not much like that in the Supreme Court, Bronx County, on the morning of June 10th, 1966. Carlos, tiny and rumpled, was led before the bench by the guard, where the aging Justice Lyman whispered to his assistant and shuffled helplessly through the papers before him. Pudgy little Mr. Bernstein came over and stood next to Carlos, and the clerk of the court called out in his bored, train-announcer's singsong, "Carlos Ortiz, is there any legal cause to show why judgment of the court should not be pronounced against you?"

"There is, your Honor," said Bernstein without any hint of conviction. "At this time I ask your Honor to rest judgment on the ground that the People have failed to prove the indictment." He explained that he was referring to the discrepancy between the time of the murder given in the confession and the time suggested by the prosecution in its opening. When he ended, after a brief speech, Lyman looked up for a moment and said only, "Motion denied."

The clerk, on cue, then called out, "What have you now to say before judgment is so pronounced?" Bernstein again spoke briefly and pointlessly to the effect that it was still *his* belief that Carlos was innocent, and lamely concluding, "Since the court hasn't any leeway in this particular case, and it's a mandatory sentence, I could only state to you our position herein."

"All right," said Justice Lyman, nodding. Then, as quietly and impersonally as if he were a magistrate fining someone for speeding, he said, "The defendant Carlos Ortiz was tried before a jury, the jury returned a verdict of guilty, the sentence is mandatory. I have no discretion about it. You, Carlos Ortiz," he said, reading from the papers before him, "are sentenced to state prison for a term of natural life, through Elmira Reception Center. Judgment accordingly."

It was done; it had been irrevocably uttered in an ordinary voice in less than half a minute. Carlos scarcely realized that it was all over until the clerk asked if he had been advised by his counsel of his right to appeal and Bernstein whispered something to him; then he heard himself croaking out loud, "Yes, sir." Did he intend to appeal? Yes, sir. Did he know how to institute his appeal and to obtain a transcript of the testimony? Yes, sir. He signed a form the clerk offered him, and his brief moment was over; a guard told him to sit down, and the judge ordered Alfredo brought in.

Alfredo, smaller, thinner, and paler than ever, appeared at the door and was led before the bench. Mrs. Lowe stood by his side and whispered to him briefly. "Alfredo Ortiz," intoned the clerk, "is there any legal cause to show why judgment of the court should not be pronounced against you?"

"Yes," said Mrs. Lowe firmly, "there is legal cause."

"Proceed," said Lyman, nodding to her.

Knitting her hands tightly before her breast, Mrs. Lowe launched into a lengthy review of Alfredo's arrest by McCabe. "The defendant," she said, "under the doctrine of *Wong Sun* versus *the United States,* was taken into custody and taken to a police precinct, when the testimony in this case shows there was no probable cause to believe this defendant was guilty of this crime." Both the arrest and the statement taken from him, she said, therefore violated his constitutional rights. McCabe had indulged in a complicated subterfuge to spirit Alfredo away from his attorney and out of the Criminal Court; moreover, Justice Lyman himself had refused to hear evidence to this effect offered by Mrs. Lowe during the trial. Furthermore, the judge had failed to marshal the evidence so as to make sure that nothing the other defendants said would be used as evidence against Alfredo. Finally, Alfredo's statement, of itself, did not contain proof that a robbery, stabbing, or homicide had actually been committed. "Based upon these facts, your Honor," she concluded, "counsel moves to set aside the verdict as against this defendant."

Alfredo had felt hope wildly fluttering within his chest as she spoke:

what she said seemed so reasonable, so learned, so full of legal references, that for a moment he thought his future hung in the balance. But Justice Lyman, after asking Mrs. Lowe if her motion was complete, said merely, "Motion denied." Then, looking at the papers on his desk, he said, "Alfredo Ortiz, you were convicted by a jury after trial for the crime of murder in the first degree. The sentence is mandatory. You are sentenced to state prison for a term of natural life, through the Elmira Reception Center. Judgment accordingly." Alfredo was stupefied. He scarcely realized that the clerk was asking him if he had been advised of his right to appeal until Mrs. Lowe prompted him; then he whispered, "Yes," and after a few more formalities sat down next to Carlos. Justice Lyman scribbled his signature twice on the back of the indictment, where the sentence had been entered, and the business of the day was finished.

With Lyman's permission, Alfredo and Carlos were allowed to remain in the courtroom another minute of two in order to talk to their mother at the railing separating the trial area from the spectator section. Luisa Pomales came forward, sobbing uncontrollably; Alfredo whispered soothingly that they would appeal and everything would be all right, but she hardly heard him. Carlos recalls that he grew angry, and the conversation went somewhat as follows: "Don' do that to me!" he snarled at her. "I'm gettin' life—and I got to stan' here an' watch you cry?" She grew quiet and stared at him. "I got convicted, so I got to go upstate," he said in his bluffest, most Spartan tone. "What you goin' to do, worry yourself to death?" She looked apologetic and said she wouldn't cry any more, promised to write and to visit them, and said she would pray and hope for the best. A guard said it was time for them to go, and in a moment they had disappeared through the door. Mrs. Lowe, Bernstein, Kase, and Casey left, the clerk called out another name, another prisoner was brought out and another lawyer came forward, and Justice Lyman, leafing through his papers, proceeded with the morning's calendar, the Ortiz brothers and their twenty-six or more years of imprisonment already gone from his thoughts.

Doel Valencia, meanwhile, was still a prisoner. Scheer, wanting more time to consider his case, had delayed the hearing at which Siegal planned to ask for a dismissal of the indictment. Scheer was not eager to try Valencia again ("Who likes cooked-over food?" he says) but hated to see him escape. Three days after the sentencing of the

Ortiz brothers, however, the Supreme Court handed down its decision in the case of *Miranda* v. *Arizona,* which held that from then on, no admission or confession would be admissible as evidence unless the suspect had first been given the four-part warning outlined in the decision. It was a moot point whether Valencia's confession could be used in the future, for a retrial might be viewed not as a continuation of the old one, but as a new one, and hence subject to the *Miranda* rule. After mulling it over, Scheer and most other lawyers in the Bronx District Attorney's office concluded that although *Miranda* was not retroactive and would not affect the Ortiz convictions, Valencia's mistrials had been, in effect, no trial at all, and thus his confession could not be used against him in the future.

When Siegal appeared in court with Valencia a few weeks later, Scheer offered to agree to a "discharge on own recognizance," setting Valencia free but not dismissing the charge, in case it later turned out that a retrial was possible after all. Siegal, growling in righteous indignation, pointed to the two hung juries and the many months in jail, and asked for dismissal of the charge, but the judge chose to free Valencia on Scheer's terms. Later that day, after more than twenty months of imprisonment, Valencia walked out of the front door of the Bronx jail; he looked and felt like a free man, though legally he was in limbo and could be picked up again by the police any time the District Attorney decided to reinstitute proceedings.

If Valencia understood this, it made little difference to him. He wanted nothing but to walk the streets, to talk and laugh with people in a normal way, to get himself a girl (he was no longer on good terms with Josie), and to enjoy life once again. But in the following days, as he prowled his old haunts and told his story again and again to any number of friends, he came to think of himself as having been found innocent; that being the case, he felt that he had been wrongfully imprisoned all those months. After a while he telephoned Siegal, who was delighted to hear that Valencia was on the line. "I thought he was calling me to thank me," Siegal recalls. "He hadn't said a word of thanks to me at the end of the trial, and not even when I got him discharged. But what did he want? He asked me to sue the city for two million dollars for false arrest! I laughed. I told him, 'Forget it! You should be grateful for the result—the Grand Jury indicted you, so there must have been probable cause. You have no suit.' He got mad at me and slammed the phone on the hook, and I never heard from him again. That's the way it is with these guys. If you lose their case, you're a bum, but if you win, they think they had it coming to them."

But how could it be otherwise? Valencia's arrest and trial had cost him a slice of his life, and yet he had not been proven guilty; accordingly, he felt wronged by the police, the prosecutors, and the judge— and as for the motives and feelings of the intelligent, tricky, verbose, fat Jewish lawyer who had defended him, Valencia understood them no more than he would have those of a Brahman priest or a Costa del Sol playboy. Although Siegal had saved him from life imprisonment, Valencia regarded him as another alien, incomprehensible enemy, which was only fair, since Siegal, in his turn, saw him and others like him in much the same way.

---

# II  *The Dilemma of the Criminal Sanctions*

THE sentencing of Alfredo and Carlos Ortiz, for all its ironies and absurdities, was hardly unusual; the weakest part of our criminal justice system is that which follows upon conviction, from the sentencing procedures through the carrying-out of the sanctions imposed upon the convicted offender to the penalties and disabilities inflicted on him after his punishment is supposedly completed.

To begin with, there is no consistency in the kinds or amounts of punishment imposed by law upon convicted defendants for any given offense: a crime for which one state may send a man to prison for a minimum of twenty-five years may bring five or less in another. (Even within a single state, one county may be very much harsher than another in sentencing practices.) Again, beyond the minimum penalties set by law, judges have a good deal of latitude to set maximums; this, too, results in gross inequities, since some judges are harsh and others lenient by nature, and since some treat certain crimes with undue severity while others treat the same crimes with undue gentleness. One recent study of sentencing within a single federal circuit, for instance, showed that federal prison terms handed out in Delaware averaged 13.7 months, but those in nearby central Pennsylvania averaged 53 months, although the range of crimes and the federal laws were the same in both areas.

An even more widespread inconsistency concerns the use of background information, relating to the offender's character and past history, to temper or increase the severity of the sentence. In most jurisdictions, judges are generally provided with presentence reports on persons convicted of felonies, but almost never on persons convicted of misdemeanors. The felon is thus judged according to the interplay of two standards—his crime and his character—while the misdemeanant is judged only by the first. (Judges do try to incorporate the second in sentencing misdemeanants, on the poor basis of appearance and guesswork.) Even felons are sometimes sentenced without the use of background information; in about a quarter of the states, in jury trials it is the trial jurors themselves who are the sentencing authority, and who almost never get a presentencing report, there being no time to prepare one before they are dismissed.

Such inconsistencies and inequities are peripheral effects of the central dilemma of the criminal sanctions. Deeply embedded in our cultural traditions—and hence in our feelings—are two contradictory ideas as to their purpose: one, that it is retribution, the other that it is the prevention of anti-social behavior.

The former involves the inflicting of hurts on the criminal to "make him pay" for his wrong acts; it seeks revenge, rather than deterrence or reform. This ancient, barbaric ethic is still operative today: the death sentences imposed on Sirhan Sirhan and on Manson and his followers, for instance, are hardly likely to inhibit other fanatics and cultists from committing murders; they serve no real purpose other than to satisfy the public's desire for vengeance.

The prevention of anti-social behavior is quite another thing: when this is the purpose of punishment, pain and deprivation are inflicted upon the criminal in order to make him and others like him fear the consequences of criminal acts and so avoid committing them. (Prevention of anti-social behavior through rehabilitation of the criminal is another, and very recent, alternative, as we shall see in a moment.) This being a rational aim rather than an emotional one, the punisher tends to choose humane methods rather than brutal ones, and to prescribe their severity according to the nature of the criminal rather than the gravity of his crime.

The two purposes are clearly at odds, what serves one often negating the other. The death sentence, for instance, or life imprisonment, may gratify the desire to retaliate, but only at the cost of frustrating the desire to use humane punishments to inhibit the criminal from repeating his behavior, and to restore him to society. Harsh sentences and brutal prison treatment achieve retaliation but fail to achieve general deterrence; very severe punishments may inhibit some criminals, but only make others more vicious—the armed robber, for example, shooting to kill rather than risk being identified and imprisoned for life. On the other hand, there are crimes which either need no deterrent to prevent repetitions (a person who commits a homicide during a family quarrel almost never commits another), or are the relatively harmless result of compulsions that do not respond to deterrence, though they do to treatment (exhibitionism, kleptomania, alcoholism); but when such crimes go unpunished on the ground that punishment is unnecessary or unavailing, a large part of the law-abiding public is outraged and loses faith in its government's ability to enforce the law and the moral norms.

This confusion as to the proper purpose of the criminal sanctions is the product of tradition and social evolution. Early hunter-warrior peoples generally avenged wrongs by personal retaliation (a life for a life); later on, more settled cultures transformed personal physical revenge into a demand by the victim or his family for compensation paid by the wrongdoer. Still later, as society became more centrally governed, the state came to regard crimes as offenses against social order and appropriated to itself the right to administer justice; even then, however, criminal sanctions sought to make the criminal suffer physically, financially, or socially for what he had done. In the civilized Renaissance and even later, convicted criminals were still put in stocks and pelted with garbage, banished to remote colonies and condemned to hard labor, branded with hot irons or flogged with rawhide whips, mutilated or blinded, hanged or burned at the stake, torn apart by horses, and drawn and quartered.

But with the advent of the Enlightenment, such practices came to be regarded by social philosophers as primitive and contrary to a sensible philosophy of social control. Man was a rational animal: if he chose to do evil rather than good, punishment should be administered in order to correct his calculations of the pleasure and pain inherent in the acts he was capable of performing. Social theorists like Bentham and Montesquieu rejected brutality and favored the use of prolonged solitary imprisonment (a sanction which had been quite rare throughout history), the English philosopher and divine William Paley eloquently arguing that it was "calculated to raise up in [the prisoner] reflections on the folly of his choice and to expose his mind to such bitter and continued penitence as may produce a lasting change in the principles of his conduct."

By the end of the eighteenth century, penal institutions in Pennsylvania and New York were trying out the new idea, but it soon became clear that total solitary confinement was expensive and unwieldy. Early in the nineteenth century, however, an economical and manageable modification of it was invented at Auburn Prison in upstate New York and soon widely copied: in this system, prisoners worked together by day, making products that paid for their keep, but were forced to maintain total silence not only at work but at meals, in their cells,.and even when marching from place to place in lock-step.

But such measures, however rational the theory behind them, made men desperate and vicious rather than penitent and contemplative; moreover, the appeal of slave labor to legislators and prison administrators led to innumerable abuses. Eventually, after the Civil War, these defects produced a new wave of prison reform, based upon a new concept of the use of the criminal sanctions in which their purpose, though still said to be the prevention of anti-social behavior, was to be achieved not through the fear of punishment but through controlled educational and reconstructive experiences. The new penology was essentially a product of the emerging science of psychology, which deterministically explained the individual's behavior as the result of his sum total of experience; the criminal, so viewed, was not to blame for what he had done and hence there was neither any moral justification for retribution nor any point in using punishment to influence his future behavior. Criminal acts were the result not of rational decisions but of immaturity, defective development, or unconscious conflicts; instead of being punished, the criminal should be *treated*— with warmth, understanding, curative human contacts, education, and individual and group therapy of various sorts—until he was whole, normal, and could be reintegrated into society.

With the emergence of this view and its adoption by the intellectual and liberal *avant-garde,* the dilemma of the criminal sanctions became far more acute. In place of the conflict between retribution and deterrence—both involving punishment—there now was a more basic conflict between punishment and treatment. The alternatives of the former dilemma were only partly antithetical: both assumed that the choice of a criminal act was the product of a free will, and therefore punishment or deprivation was both deserved and essential. The alternatives of the latter dilemma are almost wholly antithetical: they agree only that the end result of the criminal sanctions should be to prevent anti-social acts, but they are diametrically opposed as to the explanation of criminality, the moral evaluation of the criminal, the right of society to punish him, and the nature of the methods which will best modify his behavior.

The two alternatives ought, indeed, to call for wholly different systems of dealing with the convicted offender; in actual fact the two coexist and contest each other within one single system of laws, penal codes, sentencing procedures, and penological practices. From the courtroom to the cell block, from the legislative chamber to the parole officer's cubicle, the handling of criminals in America today is hopelessly conflict-ridden, inconsistent, and paradoxical.

Most jurisdictions do not, for instance, punish convicted persons under sixteen, but seek to treat them by means of probationary programs, training schools and camps, and reformatories; yet all but probationary programs involve isolation from society, regimentation, and strict discipline, and thus are both punitive and prison-like. Similarly, even in the most progressive prisons, where group therapy, counseling, and other rehabilitative programs exist, the inmates still wear uniforms and march to mess halls, are locked in their cells from late afternoon to early morning, and are subject, for disobedience or disrespect, to the loss of recreational and other privileges, and even to solitary confinement on a bread-and-water diet. Again, drug addicts are often sentenced to prison and simultaneously enrolled in treatment programs, thus being dealt with at one and the same time as guilty persons deserving of punishment and as guiltless victims of psychosocial forces beyond their control.

The public, like the criminal justice system, is of two minds as to the purpose and value of the criminal sanctions. The large majority are traditionalists who regard probation, parole, and the provision of recreational facilities, educational services, and psychotherapy in prisons as "coddling" the criminals; on behalf of these people, most legislators strenuously resist spending more than token amounts for treatment programs or for anything that makes prison life less dreadful. A highly vocal minority of liberals and intellectuals, on the other hand, regards all prisons and all forms of punishment as barbaric, harmful, and immoral. They would substitute treatment and training programs, without imprisonment, for all offenders except the most dangerous and the uncontrollably violent; even the latter, however, they would want to see not in ordinary prisons but in institutions more akin to mental hospitals, from which they would be released as soon as the staff considered them sufficiently improved.

The two viewpoints seem irreconcilable on nearly every issue concerning the criminal sanctions. The traditionalists believe that the imposition of harsher punishments would reduce the crime rate through general deterrence (the inhibiting effect of fear of punishment on would-be criminals); liberals, ex-convicts, and reformers vehemently deny that punishment has any general deterrent value. Both sides are right in part, and wrong in part. There is no factual evidence, according to criminologists Norval Morris and Gordon Hawkins, that the severity of punishment has any correlation to the crime rate. But if the liberals are right that severity does not help, they are wrong that punishment never deters: a number of recent research projects have shown that for offenses ranging from parking violations to homicide, the swifter and more certain (but not the more severe) the punishment, the lower the offense rate. Which is not to suggest that general deterrence, achieved by punishment, can ever eliminate crime, for it has always existed throughout history, no matter what the forms of punishment in vogue. The important—and still unanswered—questions are not categorical but quantitative: How fast, how certain, how severe must punishment be to achieve a significant degree of general deterrence? What part of the crime potential can be thus deterred? At what point does increasing severity fail to yield further benefits?

So much for general deterrence; on the matter of special deterrence—the inhibiting effect of punishment on the convict himself—the debate between the punishers and the treaters seems just as deadlocked. Treaters say that prisons fail to deter convicts from returning to crime after their release, and maintain that about two thirds of released prisoners commit new crimes and return to prison. Punishers, for their part, are equally certain that old-fashioned imprisonment does work and that the liberal and therapeutic measures recently introduced into some prisons have no effect on recidivism rates.

Again, both sides are right in part and wrong in part. The assertion that two thirds of prisoners commit new crimes is based on methodological error: surveys of prison inmates generally do show that two thirds are recidivists—but recidivists come and go repeatedly, and tend to accumulate in the prison, while the minority of inmates who have never been there before represent a steady stream that flows through and does not return. Inmates, in short, are the wrong sample; ex-inmates are the right one. The proper way to measure recidivism is to do follow-up studies of released prisoners, seeing how many remain free and how many return to jail. Such studies, made in many parts of the world, indicate that about one third to one half, rather than two thirds, of those who leave prison eventually return. The rest—anywhere from half to two thirds—do not, and one can reasonably suppose that to some degree they were influenced by their prison experiences to avoid doing things they feared would subject them to more of the same.

But if treaters are wrong to think that imprisonment never works, punishers are wrong to think treatment valueless. Treating inmates within the punitive setting of the prison gives them conflicting signals —opposing views of themselves, contradictory sets of stimuli, incompatible systems of reward and punishment—but when treatment techniques are applied in non-punitive settings, they show much better results. Experiments in Scandinavia and elsewhere with "open prisons," with "work release" programs in which prisoners work on the outside, with unrestricted visitation rights, conjugal visitation, regular home leave, and halfway houses and hotels, have all yielded encouraging results.

So has the use of probation under normal living conditions, particularly where supervision is adequate and is combined with some form of treatment. The California Youth Authority, for instance, tried giving one group of juvenile delinquents individually tailored, intensive programs of therapy and tutoring in their own communities, while giving a matching control group the regular treatment available within youth institutions; after half a dozen years only 28 percent of the experimental group had had their provisional freedom revoked, as compared to 52 percent of those who were institutionalized and later released on parole.

If the promise of treatment has not yet been kept in this country, it may well be because treatment nearly everywhere remains entangled with punishment. The sensible answer would be to attempt to separate the two: to treat, outside of prisons, all those who seem to classification boards to be treatable; to punish, within prisons, only those who are diagnosed as deterrable but untreatable; and to isolate from society under maximum-security conditions those who cannot, in the best judgment of the professionals, be influenced constructively by either method.

If we clearly distinguished the two purposes in our thinking, and carried out the distinction in our laws, our sentencing procedures, correctional institutions, and treatment programs, we might go far toward solving the dilemma of the criminal sanctions and achieving the goals of each alternative.

## I I I   *Prognosis Is Guarded*

ON a fine hot day in mid-June 1966, eighteen-year-old Carlos Ortiz took a trip that under other circumstances would have been both pleasant and interesting: he boarded the "Phoebe Snow," an Erie Lackawanna passenger train westbound out of Hoboken, New Jersey, and traveled for six hours, through northern New Jersey and Pennsylvania, far into the clean air, the undulating hills, and the luxuriant farmland of western New York. Except for a flight to Puerto Rico three years earlier, he had not been outside New York City since his early childhood; now he sped through countryside such as he had never seen before, the train snaking through valleys flanked by wooded hills, racing along straight stretches past green fields and lonely clapboard farmhouses baking in the sun, speeding past crossings where insistent bells and semaphore arms kept a car or two at bay, and sometimes slowing down in a town or small city to stop, with screeching brakes and a vast hiss of released air, to discharge and take on passengers at places whose homespun American names were all unknown to Carlos—Summit, Blairstown, East Stroudsburg, Mount Pocono, Gouldsboro, Scranton, Clark's Summit, Hallstead.

On the long stretches between stops, it rushed past billboards and signs on the neighboring highways, telling of motels and guesthouses, summer camps, restaurants, and ski lodges, all of them things quite outside Carlos' experience; sped alongside clear streams and blue lakes totally unlike the greasy, malodorous city river he had often swum in years ago; and roared through drowsy villages such as he had never visited or even seen except on television shows. It eased slowly into the shabby, busy city of Binghamton, stood for a while in the station, and then proceeded on westward, winding alongside a narrow river through quiet upstate New York villages and towns with stately old houses, broad lawns, and unfamiliar names, some exotic, like Apalachin and Owego, some foursquare American, like Endicott and Smithboro; and finally in mid-afternoon it rattled through a region of apple orchards, dairy farms, and tree-cloaked hills into the decaying little city of Elmira, a formerly busy marketplace and light manufacturing center geographically 226 miles northwest of the Bronx but culturally light-years away from it.

Carlos did not much enjoy the trip. The entire time, except for one visit to the toilet, he remained in his seat handcuffed to another prisoner and stared almost unseeingly out of the window. He was one of some two dozen prisoners, watched over by half a dozen armed guards, occupying one coach of the train; people on the platforms at the stations saw their faces at the windows, and had no idea who the shabbily dressed young men were. (Alfredo, who had remained behind due to a clerical error, followed a week later on the same train and under the same conditions.) It was a long, dull, hot ride, with nothing to do but look out of the window, make small-talk, and wait to see what lay ahead in Elmira. Shortly before they got there, the guards had shackled their handcuffs to their waists, and at the station the prisoners clumsily lurched off in pairs, were shepherded into a small fleet of waiting taxicabs, and were driven through city streets to a residential area, where, at the top of a rise, they stopped in front of a large brick building set back behind a broad lawn and somewhat resembling a college hall or dormitory—except for the high brick walls extending to either side of it and running far back, enclosing other brick and stone buildings and a large yard, and topped by gun posts manned by armed guards.

In front of the main building, they got out and were herded through iron doors which clanged shut behind them, cutting them off from the strange, unknown world they had been looking at all day. As unfamiliar and incomprehensible as that outside world was to Carlos, so familiar and understandable was this one and all that happened to him in it during the next hour or two: the unshackling, the shouted commands, the rude frisk, the strip and shower, the quick, rough physical examination, the coarse gray dungarees and shirt slapped on a counter for him to pick up and put on, the questions snapped out by a clerk at a receiving desk and the assignment of a number in place of his name, the long silent walk in front of guards to a cell block where he was ordered into the tiny cubicle that would be his, the sound of the steel door crashing shut, and the silence and the overwhelming loneliness that washed over him as the guards' footsteps died away.

Yet familiar as all this was, he could already see differences from the milieu he had known for the past twenty months. Unlike the high-rise Brooklyn House of Detention, this place was a sprawling compound enclosed by the high wall; the gun posts on top of it were something new, and the machine-gun muzzles protruding from those posts were a statement to him and the others that their relationship to the world outside had now been defined by the courts. The uniform Carlos had been issued was another statement: at Brooklyn, the few convicted inmates on hand wore just such uniforms but most of the prisoners, including Carlos himself, were still awaiting trial and, being presumed innocent, wore their own clothes; now he was a convict, and was dressed as one. Even the architecture of the cell block reinforced his sense of isolation and total immurement: above the tiers of cells there was a high cathedral ceiling, and sounds reverberated so confusingly in the whole area that it was impossible for him to hold an intelligible conversation with inmates in other cells. Now and then prisoners did shout to each other briefly, but there was nothing like the convivial racket of sustained talk that he had been used to on the tier in the Brooklyn House of Detention.

Despite appearances, Elmira was not classified as a prison for incorrigible or exceedingly violent convicts: on the contrary, it was listed by the New York State Department of Correction as a reformatory, and its inmates, some thousand-odd teen-agers and young adults, had all been committed to it for lesser felonies, for which they had been sentenced to no more than five years. As part of the Department's effort to reform and rehabilitate these people, Elmira had shops, gymnasiums, schoolrooms, teachers, counseling rooms, and guidance personnel; at the same time, however, the prisoners were marched to and from mess halls and assignments, were forbidden to get up for any reason in the mess hall until ordered to do so, were drilled in the yard with dummy wooden guns, and were rigidly disciplined by the guards, who would report any minor infraction of the rules or trifling bit of back-talk to the deputy warden, who in turn would order a temporary loss of privileges or even send the offender to solitary confinement for several days.

Within the main building, but operating its own programs with a separate staff, was the Reception Center, which occupied two cell blocks in which some 300 young prisoners were in residence, each for six to eight weeks of evaluation culminating in assignment. All adults and youths committed to the New York Department of Correction (now known as the Department of Correctional Services) go through a reception and classification procedure. Adults are received at any one of three prisons with reception facilities, where they are given a medical examination, intelligence and academic tests, and an interview, and are then assigned to one prison or another, according to their personal traits and their sentences. Mentally ill prisoners, for instance, go to a prison hospital, drug addicts to prisons far from New York City, extremely dangerous prisoners to maximum-security prisons in rural areas, and young low-security risks to correctional camps. Prisoners between sixteen and twenty-one, however, all go to the Elmira Reception Center for a far more thorough program of orientation, testing, interviews, and observation, the extra effort being based on the assumption that the younger prisoners have a greater potential for rehabilitation, if carefully treated, than the older ones. The bulk of them are then assigned to reformatories of one sort or another, some of which have strict security facilities, one of which specializes in dealing with low-intelligence inmates, another with normal-intelligence inmates who can profit by additional schooling, and so on. A few of the most serious offenders are transferred to one or another of the prisons in the system, rather than to a reformatory.

The first part of the reception procedure—after an initial interview, barbering, and some clerical matters—was given over to orientation. Officially, this consisted of a series of lectures by guidance counselors,

parole-board members, chaplains, and the warden, about the classification program and the mores of prison life. Unofficially, another
kind of orientation went on at the same time, consisting of a number
of everyday experiences which gave new prisoners an emotional
understanding of who and what they are in the eyes of their keepers
and of society. During their stay in the Reception Center, for instance,
they were allowed no reading material in their cells, could receive no
packages from their families or friends, could have only one visitor,
and were brought up short any time they showed any sign of defiance
or independence. Alfredo, relatively passive and compliant, ran into
no difficulty, but Carlos learned at some cost the need for total submis-
sion. In the mess hall one morning, he accidentally dropped a crust of
bread on the floor, and picked it up and put it on his tray. A guard
standing nearby watched to see what he would do with it—the rules
state that prisoners must eat everything they take—and when Carlos
left it on the tray, the guard came over and asked him, in a gritty tone
of voice, "You going to eat that?"

"I ain' eatin' that, man," said Carlos. "It fell on the floor."

"Okay," said the guard, "that's it!" He wrote something down in a
little notebook, and later that morning Carlos was called into the
office of the deputy warden, questioned about the incident, and ordered to the guardhouse for three days. He recalled the experience
years later as follows:

> You get a mattress an' a blanket, but dudes have pissed on the
> mattress an' they don' wash it or nothin'. They take away the
> mattress an' the blanket aroun' five in the morning, an' you got
> only your shorts on, an' the rest of the day you got to lay on the
> floor. You don' get nothin' to read, nothin' to smoke, an' when
> they feed you they put everything in one bowl, all slopped to-
> gether. You don' get no shower, an' you *stink*. You get madder
> an' madder, but if you mess aroun', you goin' to stay in there, or
> get right back in soon's you out. An' all for "disrepectin' an
> officer"! You got some hacks that's all right, but some others
> don' care for the inmate an' want to make his time as hard as
> they can, so they joog at you, an' you say somethin' in return—
> an' you locked up for three days. It's rough, man.

Aside from this, however, Carlos went through the evaluation period smoothly enough. After a couple of weeks of preliminaries, in-

cluding several long private interviews with guidance counselors and a chaplain, Carlos (and a score of other prisoners) spent three long mornings taking a battery of tests of intelligence, academic achievement, personality traits, vocational aptitude, and the like, puzzling over the questions, scratching his head, and marking off questions with a pencil clutched in sweating fingers. From then on for the next four weeks, he was assigned to various periods of shop work, school, recreation, and clean-up duty on the cell block, with the persons in charge of each activity observing him and the others and making notes of their behavior. Alfredo, who was assigned to the same tier of cells as Carlos when he arrived a week later, went through the same procedures in his turn.

In the interviews, Carlos and Alfredo were asked to relate their life stories and give the details of their previous difficulties with the law. (The interviewers, of course, already had all the records on hand, including their presentence reports, but wanted to see what their present attitudes were.) In some ways, Carlos and Alfredo were run-of-the-mill cases, typical of the kind of incoming young prisoners the interviewers at Elmira saw all year long, and even of the incoming adult prisoners at the prison reception centers. Of the 5,000 new commitments sent by the courts to the Department of Correction in 1966, for instance, more than half came from New York City, over 40 percent were between sixteen and twenty-one years old (Carlos was eighteen at the time, and Alfredo nineteen), one out of six was Puerto Rican and nearly one out of two was Negro, four fifths had dropped out of school at the high-school level or even earlier, and nearly two thirds had no occupation or were listed as laborers.

But the interviewers and the Ortiz brothers' fellow prisoners found them far from typical in the crime they had been convicted of and in the sentences they had drawn. Among the 2,000-odd young convicts processed at Elmira that year, only fifteen—including Carlos and Alfredo—had been convicted of murder. (Had the brothers copped a plea, they would have been among the 52 convicted of manslaughter, and had it not been for the unexpected stabbing, they would have been among the 161 convicted of robbery—if they had ever been caught and convicted at all.) Still more unusual, and earning them commiseration from their fellow prisoners and even from some of the staff, was their sentence: of the young criminals processed at Elmira that year, nine tenths had no minimum sentences set, but could be released as soon as the parole boards thought them fit to be; four fifths would serve no more than three years, no matter what the parole boards thought; and only ten persons, including the Ortiz brothers, had been sentenced to life, which had as its absolute minimum, with time off for good behavior, twenty-six and a half years.

In such company the Ortiz brothers stood out, and although they told their fellow prisoners and the interviewers that they were innocent and had murdered no one, they got only respectful disbelief for their pains. The respect was all the more remarkable because they were frailer and feebler than ever. They had grown no taller in jail, and the two months of waiting to be sentenced had melted the flesh from their bones; Carlos, at the time of his arrival at Elmira, was a stringy, child-like creature of 106 pounds, and Alfredo, at a mere 99, was sunken of cheek, large-eyed, and looked like the victim of a famine.

Carlos, small and frail though he was, acted his usual tough-guy part, even in his interviews. At the first one, he answered the guidance counselor's questions sourly but somewhat flippantly, offering jocularly paranoid explanations of everything on the record against him. After Carlos left the room, the counselor jotted down, "Appears to be a cocky, argumentative, disdainful youth who originally made full admissions but now denies it and says he only agreed with the statements read to him to avoid further beatings and maltreatment." He added that Carlos told him he thought the real murderer might be the son of a woman who lived on the same floor as Helmer; that Helmer had been wearing a money belt containing thousands of dollars which the police stole; that Helmer had been Jewish, and that a largely Jewish jury had convicted him and Alfredo out of prejudice; and that Mary Lowe had some secret information which she was going to use in an appeal on his behalf.

In a later interview another case worker tried to dig deeper, but got only a similar series of excuses and rationalizations. The case worker's notes included these comments: "Could not be tricked into admitting that he had any part in the murder. . . . Was only twelve when he performed fellatio with a five-year-old child, but this again he denies. He does admit to having been unruly in school, claims he did have difficulty in learning." Carlos was still trying to be "cool," but showed some anxiety, perhaps because of the Elmira orientation procedures: "There is a slight tremulousness in his voice. When the interviewer pointed out to him that he did not appear to be too indignant about receiving a natural life sentence, in view of his statement of innocence, he made the remark that there was no sense in letting himself become emotionally involved or he would go crazy." The interviewer apparently found Carlos' tough-guy stance less than convincing, for he concluded: "Study here reveals a rather immature, subculture-type individual . . . [who] has shown a passive form of aggression in the form of defiance, refusal to conform"—this referred to the bread-crust episode—"but has never shown any overt acting out of his hostility." He diagnosed Carlos as an "inadequate personality with dissocial trends," whose respect for authority was probably not too good, but whose "general conformance" was satisfactory.

A psychologist, meanwhile, evaluated Carlos' intelligence tests, finding him no great shakes, but potentially brighter than he seemed: "Verbal IQ 80," he reported, "non-verbal 107. Present testing produced borderline and dull-normal verbal scores, with distinctly higher non-verbal scores in the normal and bright-normal range." The shop supervisor sent in word that Carlos was fair at using tools, but quick and impulsive, and inclined to make careless mistakes. The recreation leader noted that he seemed to have average coordination, but was a rank beginner at most sports and sometimes seemed to be a loner. The company officer who commanded the inmates of Carlos' cell block said that when Carlos did associate with other inmates, he generally chose the louder and more immature ones, but also noted that Carlos' performance on routine work details was satisfactory, and concluded optimistically that he was "capable of making a conforming adjustment within the institution."

The problem for the Classification Board—the warden, the guidance counselors, the psychologist, the academic analyst, the chaplain, the company officer, and a couple of others—was how to choose a program for Carlos that would make sense. How could one get him to make a "conforming adjustment" that would last the better part of his adult life? How could one keep him from collapsing into total apathy or exploding from suppressed rage? How could one offer him schooling designed to make the most of his latent abilities, when he would be in prison most of his life? How could one hope to rehabilitate him, when his sentence would leave him so little time to use his new lifestyle? Even if one could remold and improve him, what was the point of doing so?

But the members of the Board could not permit themselves to be immobilized by such sensible considerations; if they began to doubt the value of treatment in a punitive setting, they might lose all heart and all hope. After talking it over, therefore, they decided to send Carlos to Auburn Prison because, for one thing, it was a maximum-security prison, suitable for very serious offenders (convicted murderers, no matter what their age or psychological make-up, could not be sent to reformatories), and because, for another, it had the only adequate grade and high school in the state prison system, a series of shops offering training in barbering, auto repairing, and the like, and a prison factory where license plates were made. Even so, the final opinion of the Board was less than optimistic; they summed up the outlook for Carlos in the pallid words, "Prognosis is guarded."

Alfredo went through the same evaluation procedure and with rather similar results. Carlos had said he would like to be sent to the same institution as Alfredo; Alfredo said he wanted to be where Carlos was. Alfredo's account of the arrest, interrogation, trial, and conviction, and his theories about them, were nearly identical to his brother's; the guidance counselor even sourly noted that they clearly had had time to practice their stories in the many months they had been in incarceration. Alfredo explained nearly every previous conflict he had had with the law as the result either of prejudice, error, or outright lies on the part of the police. As for the murder case, he told the counselor that McCabe knew that he and Carlos were innocent, but had not had a day off in two weeks and had pinned the murder on them because he was tired. Like Carlos, Alfredo said he had made the confession the police demanded of him only because he was being tortured and pressured; he knowingly likened himself to Whitmore, and, indeed, claimed that all the inmates on his floor at the Brooklyn House of Detention had been, like himself, innocent youths tortured by the police into making false confessions. Despite the paranoia and the controlled anger implicit in these statements, Alfredo offered them in a soft-spoken and diffident manner, and the counselor, finding him a lot less abrasive than most incoming prisoners, commented in his report, "He impresses me as a very pleasant, docile, and cooperative youth, who does not fit the role of a killer. He does not verbalize as his brother, and seems to be the quieter and less aggressive of the two."

The psychologist who tested Alfredo found his verbal I.Q. to be 85, a trifle higher than Carlos', but added that on non-verbal tests Alfredo had scored 112—within the bright-normal range; according to the verbal I.Q., he was educationally retarded by only two years, but according to the non-verbal score, he had the potential for five or six years' more educational achievement than he demonstrated. The other observers, watching Alfredo in his regular duties and activities, had little to say about him except that he was quiet, inoffensive, unimpressive, and lacked enthusiasm or spark. The shop supervisor wrote that Alfredo had been friendly and respectful toward authority, showed satisfactory work habits and average mechanical ability, and "with stimulation and guidance, could do well in his area of interest." (This, at the moment, was tailoring—a subject Alfredo had asked about, although it had never intrigued him until his imprisonment, when he discovered that a prison tailor could earn favors and protection by modifying uniforms to give them some slight touch of individuality.) The recreation leader found Alfredo disappointing: Alfredo, he said, had no skills, little interest in sports, and would go through the motions if prodded, but would quit as soon as he was let alone. The company officer found him orderly and cooperative in routine gallery assignments, and in need of only average supervision; Alfredo, he commented, "seems to be accepting his incarceration in a favorable manner." (Alfredo himself, years later, wrote to a friend that at the time he felt overwhelming shock at being among "the living dead," and "actually witnessing my own life after death.")

The company officer also found Alfredo to be distinctly more intelligent than his brother, but merely less talkative and more guarded, "offering nothing in the way of conversation." This withdrawal may well have been the outward symptom of Alfredo's private despair, but none of the members of the evaluating team recognized it as such. One guidance counselor, in fact, took Alfredo's lack of perceptible anger or energy to signify a childish incomprehension of his plight. "Inmate reveals himself as a rather immature, happy-go-lucky sort," he wrote, "who is lacking in motivation toward social goals and is following a narcissistic pattern." Rather more accurately, however, he added, "There is nothing vicious in him and he is not hostile. He has no sense of remorse because he has no sense of guilt and wrongdoing. Appears to be passive, dependent, and easily led and manipulated."

After reviewing each other's reports, the Classification Board faced the problem of what to do with Alfredo. He could benefit from further education, would not be a disciplinary problem, and was malleable enough to be a good prospect for genuine rehabilitation; yet every form of treatment the Board could prescribe would have to be administered in the setting of life imprisonment. How could a man be improved, or improve himself, when ahead of him stretched an infinite desert of weeks, years, decades of gray tedium in the same cell and mess hall, the companionship of the same stupid and vicious men, the domination of the same arrogant and hostile guards? One might as well make no effort to salvage him at all, but reckon him—in Alfredo's own words—one of the living dead, and forget him. But the Board did not. Its members, hoping against hope, did what they had been trained to do and assigned him, like Carlos, to Auburn Prison, recommending that he be enrolled in the school and concluding, honestly enough, with the same glum words they had applied to Carlos: "Prognosis is guarded."

Yet the Ortiz brothers could count themselves lucky, in a manner of speaking: compared to the other prisons they might have been sent to, which had poor or no school facilities and where most of the inmates were severe disciplinary problems who were dealt with by harsh methods, the assignment to Auburn was a prize. And men being the absurd but sometimes wonderful creatures that they are, each of the brothers felt some stirring of hope when he climbed into a Department of Correction station wagon, two months after arriving at Elmira, and started off toward what would be, for all he could tell, his only home for the larger part of his life.

# I V   Functions and Dysfunctions of the American Prison

WHATEVER side one takes in the punishment-treatment controversy, and whatever fault one finds with the theory of correction through imprisonment, it is clear to anyone but the radical or the visionary that we cannot do without prisons. For there are always some persons who, though sane, cannot be prevented by reason, education, therapy, or fines from committing anti-social acts; in the end, society must forcibly restrain them. Aside from the death penalty, imprisonment is therefore the inevitable and necessary last resort of the justice system. Despite the polemic attacks of many reformers and radicals upon the entire concept of imprisonment, no modern regime, whatever its political color, has ever been able to do without prisons, and it is unreasonable to suppose there will ever be any complex urban society which will have no need to restrain anyone.

Yet although prisons are necessary, we seem to use ours in ways that are not only inefficient but often self-defeating. For one thing, we restrain in them only a tiny fraction of all dangerous criminals (about 1.5 percent of serious crimes result in actual imprisonment), and the average period of such restraint is only a few years. It may be, of course, that the number of those who are restrained and the duration of their incarceration are less important to the protection of society than the deterring effect their punishment has upon them, and upon all others who witness it and consider it a possible consequence of acts they themselves might commit. Here, too, however, we use our prisons in ways that undermine our own goals. If we subjected convicts only to legal, humane, and authorized punishment, and if all punishment were administered by impartial, objective correction personnel, it might prove a reasonably efficient deterrent, even as the fines imposed on income-tax violators are grudgingly accepted by most offenders and generally lead to stricter compliance. Instead, we allow sadistic guards and savage inmates to inflict upon many prisoners suffering far worse than anything specified by law or ordered by the court, and bearing no just relation to the crime committed. This is well known in the subculture from which most criminals come; it, as much as anything else, creates a deep mistrust and hatred of the law, the criminal justice system, and the society of which they are a part, and so endows the criminal act with special allure and emotional justification. As for those who are actually caught, convicted, and sent to prison, the unauthorized degradations, brutalities, and atrocities committed upon them in prison may prove a deterrent to future crime for some, but only turn others into hate-filled, vengeance-seeking monsters, for the latter regard these torments as society's intention. As one convict writes, the vile things done to him "cannot be a deep, dark secret known only to a few, any more than Hitler's

crematoria and concentration camps were unknown to the people of
Nazi Germany. The people know. They just don't give a damn. Or
they want it that way."

It is true, of course, that state prisons are generally a cut above the
city and county jails. Most prisons have some recreational facilities,
provide medical care of a sort, and make some provision for visitors;
a few even have ambitious rehabilitative programs. But for the most
part, the more destructive aspects of incarceration in jail are all present in most prisons—the overcrowding, the boredom, the helpless-
ness, the dictatorial and often sadistic treatment by guards, the use of
brutal punishment, the exploitation of weak inmates by strong ones,
and so on. For instance:

—Physical conditions in many prisons are abominable. Reports
cited in Violence Commission studies and many other sources tell of
filthy living quarters, spoiled food, uncontrolled infestations by ver-
min, shortages of soap and of laundering services, and the like. Overcrowding alone breeds innumerable problems, including constant assaults and rape, but protests are often met with official brutality. In
1971, for example, inmates at the state prison in Raiford, Florida, were
jammed in, ten to a cell, in cells built for four; in sheer desperation, they staged a sit-down strike to protest, but the director of the
Board of Correction, Louie Wainwright, promptly ordered them peppered with birdshot (sixty-three were wounded), explaining, "I did
it to protect the inmates themselves."

—In a number of prison systems, unauthorized physical tortures
are frequently and routinely inflicted upon inmates for disciplinary
purposes. One recent study of prisons of the Mississippi delta region
cited, as common, beatings with chains and belts, floggings, electrical
tortures, and lengthy confinement to underground dungeons. At the
Tucker Farm in Arkansas, according to a report released in 1967 by
Governor Winthrop Rockefeller, a favorite torture device used on
fractious inmates was the "Tucker telephone"—a generator from a
ring-type phone, hooked up to the big toe and penis of the inmate,
which when cranked, shot an excruciating charge into his private parts.

—Even where such direct brutality is uncommon, "strip cells"—
common in many supposedly enlightened states, including California,
New York, and Ohio, until very recently, and still in fairly wide use—
provide a major assault on both body and mind. Prisoners being disciplined are confined in such cells nearly naked and without furniture

(they sit on the cement floor and sleep on a thin mattress or piece of canvas), or wash basins, toilets, soap, and water; they live, sleep, and eat amid the stench of their own sweat and excreta. Grand Juries and judges who regularly tour prisons to check on conditions are never shown these cells, and rarely believe that they exist.

—Guards, with little prestige and poor pay—nationally, they earn an average of about $5,000 yearly—come chiefly from the lower middle class, are generally conservative in outlook, and tend to regard themselves as appointed punishers of the wicked. Many of them seek out and multiply the opportunities to dress down, insult, bully, and demean prisoners, and to "write them up" for infractions as trifling as having their hands in their pockets or having a button unbuttoned. In many prisons, unofficial "jack-up squads" of guards deal with defiant or disobedient prisoners by making unauthorized nighttime visits to their cells and swiftly and quietly beating them senseless with clubs, paying particular attention to the abdomen and genitals, where the blows will leave no marks. Ken Jackson, an ex-convict and a member of the Fortune Society, says that after he served time for burglary, he became an armed robber—and hoped his victims would resist: "The thing I wanted *second* was their money—the thing I wanted *first* was to beat their brains out, because I felt they had been paying to have done to me what had been done in prison."

—Even in the best state prisons, inmates considered troublesome by the staff because of their political views or their organizational activities are often severely penalized. At California's Soledad Prison —physically one of the finest, and penologically one of the more liberal, in the country—the more active political agitators are put in isolation cells, allowed no reading matter except in the fields of law and religion, and permitted no mail; they are not even allowed out for meals, their food being shoved in to them on a tray through a slot in the door.

—Some of the worst punishments are those which prisoners suffer at the hands of fellow inmates. In many prisons, according to the Crime Commission,

> certain inmates—often the most aggressive—assume control over the others with tacit staff consent; in some adult institutions this situation is formalized through the use of "trusties"—sometimes armed—to carry the burden of close supervision. Rackets,

violence, corruption, coerced homosexuality, and other abuses may exist without staff intervention.

In the most overcrowded and understaffed prisons, the guards cannot safeguard any prisoner from the others, assuming they want to, except by keeping him in solitary confinement; even so, he may have boiling coffee flung through the bars at him, or may be silently "crowded" and stabbed during any of the brief periods when he is taken out for exercise, a shower, or a visit to the infirmary. At Moundsville Penitentiary in West Virginia, after a series of stabbings and poisonings that were largely occasioned by robberies, gambling debts, and homosexual rapes among the inmates, the deputy warden admitted in court, "We can't guarantee the protection of anybody in there, not even in their cells." (Not all homosexuality in prisons involves rape, however; indeed, most of it is seemingly consensual—but much of it actually involves the consent of a small, frail prisoner to serve as the regular punk or "catcher" of a large, tough one, in return for protection from rape or abuse by others.)

Thus, many of the most punitive experiences of prisoners are not explicitly authorized by legislators or intended by judges and juries; they are simply permitted to happen by an indifferent or unconsciously vengeful public. It is little wonder that many ex-convicts are not deterred from further crime by their experiences, but are filled with a rage that overpowers their fear and impels them to wage a continuing feud against society, and to commit crimes worse than those they were imprisoned for.

Yet even where prisoners are subjected to nothing but legal and proper punishment, imprisonment in its present-day form is often counterproductive because it forces the prisoner to be infantile and dependent, and thus makes him unfit to take up a productive, responsible life afterward. Many psychologists and criminologists feel that the most damaging aspect of present-day prison life is the deprivation of all need or opportunity to make reasonable choices. In the traditionally run, wholly authoritarian prison, inmates are told when to get up, to wash, to eat, to exercise, to work, and to sleep; they may write to and receive mail from no one but their relatives and lawyers, they may not appeal to or be interviewed by representatives of the mass media, and they may not sign contracts or buy or sell property except by special permission; they may receive only certain kinds of food, clothing, or reading material from outside sources, and they may wear only authorized uniforms, any modification of which—even the addition of an extra pocket—is a punishable violation. Sociologist Gresham Sykes concludes, in *The Society of Captives,* that

> the prisoner's inability to make choices, and the frequent refusals of the staff to provide any explanation for its regulations and commands, involve a profound threat to the prisoner's self-image because they reduce the prisoner to the weak, helpless, dependent status of childhood. . . . [He] finds his picture of himself as a self-determining individual being destroyed by the regime of the custodians.

As with the goals of restraint and deterrence, the goal of rehabilitation is ill-served by our prisons—not only because the punitive milieu conflicts with the whole concept of rehabilitation, but because rehabilitation is the stepchild of the correctional system. Treatment personnel exist only in token numbers (when they exist at all), and are chronically overworked and underpaid. Less than 10 percent of the employees in American prisons and reformatories do teaching, counseling, and other rehabilitative work, and they are paid less for their work than comparable specialists elsewhere in our society. And all too often, they unwittingly absorb and adopt some of the attitudes of the security staff and begin to think about the inmates punitively rather than therapeutically.

Despite these handicaps, they manage to provide moderately good group and individual therapy in some institutions—but participation is often required of certain kinds of prisoners (drug addicts, for instance), and it is a truism that significant improvement rarely comes about through psychotherapy that is forced upon the patient. They operate reasonably good schools within some prisons, but most of their pupils are motivated by the desire to escape other duties or their cells rather than by any real interest in education. And though some inmates do acquire academic or vocational skills in prison, they all too often cannot find anyone willing to employ them afterward, or are legally forbidden to practice many trades and professions involving their new skills. (In nearly every state, convicted felons are barred from practicing a number of occupations, cannot obtain various kinds of licenses—including drivers' licenses—and are not permitted to own or operate various kinds of businesses ranging from restaurants to investment services.) As a result, according to one study of prisoners released from federal institutions, three months after release only 40 percent had found anything like steady full-time work, and nearly 20 percent had found none at all. Unemployment, the author of the study concluded, "may be among the principal causal factors in recidivism of adult male offenders."

Another obstacle to rehabilitation is built into the mechanism of release from prison. More than 60 percent of adult felons throughout the nation are now freed on parole (conditional early release, under supervision), which is an essentially rehabilitative scheme, since it offers early freedom in response to the prisoner's apparent readiness to "go straight." Unfortunately, its virtues are to a large extent canceled out by the presence within the parole system of punitive thinking: parole boards generally operate in the same autocratic and absolutist fashion as prison administrations, and ex-prisoners see the board members as hostile, gimlet-eyed, merciless inquisitors who study secret information given them by the guards and warden, neither reveal it to the inmate being questioned nor allow him to challenge it, fire questions at him for a few minutes and then dismiss him, and never explain their reasons for denying his parole application. Long fixed sentences without any chance of parole offer the prisoner no incentive to demonstrate rehabilitation, but the parole system, when it turns him down without reason or recourse, fills him with rage and despair and undoes the good the treatment staff may have accomplished. Even the "indeterminate sentence" laws enacted in California, Hawaii, Washington, and New York, which permit parole boards to release prisoners much earlier—or retain them much longer—than formerly, depending on their progress or lack of it, seem to many convicts not a boon but another form of power wielded over them by enemies they have no redress against, and who penalize them for any show of independence or any lack of humility.

Like the parole-board members, the parole officers who supervise released convicts also exercise power in ways that sometimes disserve the end of rehabilitation. Their uncontested word is enough to send the parolee back to prison if he commits a violation as trivial as having drunk a beer in a bar in the presence of other ex-convicts or having gone beyond a territorial limit in the course of a weekend outing. (In half the states, the parolee has no right to a hearing on the revocation of his parole; in the others, even when he gets one he usually cannot cross-examine witnesses, examine reports about him, or have a lawyer present to act on his behalf.) Parole officers are rarely the sadistic monsters they seem to convicts, but since they almost invariably have caseloads two to three times as large as they can adequately supervise, and since the pressure of their duties gives them time only to be law-enforcers rather than therapeutic case workers, it is not surprising that they often seem curt, cold, and authoritarian to the parolee, and that they sometimes revoke parole hastily and for minor causes.

Probation—the supervision of the convict in the community with-out his having spent any time in prison—seems to offer more hope of preventing anti-social behavior than does imprisonment and parole. Recidivism rates have been no higher—and in some studies have been considerably lower—among probationers than among parolees. The use of probation has, in fact, increased rapidly in the past few years, with the result that prison populations have somewhat declined. But the promise probation offers is not being fulfilled. Rapidly growing caseloads have been piled on probation departments without corre-sponding increases in personnel, to the great detriment of the goal of crime prevention. An extreme case is that of New York City, where by late 1971 the burden of preparing presentence reports and super-vising probationers was so great that the average person on probation was getting only about fifteen minutes of direct attention from his probation officer per month; not surprisingly, the violation and re-cidivism rates were taking a sharp upturn.

Ironically, too, the increasing use of probation has made prisons considerably worse: they have become the repository of the more vio-lent and incorrigible cases, their populations being more selectively chosen than formerly, and increasingly consisting of those who are not amenable to treatment and hardly even deterrable by punishment. Coinciding with and reinforcing this trend is the increase in the pro-portion of blacks in the prison population; their contemporary dis-affiliation from white values, and their growing acceptance of the radi-cal view that they are not criminals but prisoners of war, make it almost impossible to use liberal, permissive, treatment-oriented pro-cedures with them. Even as enlightened administrators try to make prisons more rehabilitative and to provide steppingstones to the out-side community, prison populations are becoming radicalized, riot-ous, and unreceptive to treatment; even as new legal rights are being won by inmates, the ideal of the humane and collaborative institution has become less feasible than it was only a few years ago.

After two centuries of reform and two generations of liberal psychological influence, prisons may be swinging back toward serving purely custodial and punitive functions. This might be a sensible and legitimate way to use them, if at the same time we vastly enlarged and greatly improved the facilities for rehabilitation outside of prisons; failing to do that, however, we will be but one more example of a people who turned backward in their effort to solve a crisis, and so brought about their own doom.

# V  *A Classic Example of the Institutionalized*

"YOU'LL find year 'round enjoyment at FINGER LAKES," a multicolored travel folder assures the reader, promising innumerable pleasures: swimming, boating, and water-skiing in any of the eleven narrow glacial lakes of central western New York; horse racing, hunting, and fishing throughout the area; camping, skiing, and soaring; visits to historic mansions, classic rose gardens, and wineries; and the scenic beauty of the region's densely forested mountains and its flat, fertile valleys, deep in corn, wheat, and grapevines.

A Department of Correction station wagon taking Carlos Ortiz, handcuffed and shackled, from Elmira Reception Center to Auburn Prison passed through just such countryside on August 10th, 1966 (Alfredo, once again, made the trip a week later). The seventy-mile drive took Carlos northeast from Elmira and then northward, between Lakes Seneca and Owasco, the station wagon speeding along narrow black-top roads past weathered old farmhouses with tree-shaded porches, past meadows where black-and-white Guernseys grazed, past apple orchards, ponds, and faded red barns, past dogs sleeping in driveways and children playing on lawns, and finally down the quiet streets of Auburn.

Situated just north of Owasco Lake, Auburn, a city of 34,000 people, is typical of the small shopping and manufacturing centers that were vital to the rural outlands a century ago but now are somewhat obsolescent. Along broad streets well outside the center of the city are large, rambling old homes set far back on deep lawns; closer to the heart of town are dingy brick factory buildings and rows of the small, shabby houses of working-class people; in the very center of town, along a dozen blocks of the intersecting main streets, are an assortment of stores, short-order restaurants, lawyers' offices, banks, the hotel, and the offices of the local newspaper. Auburn was once an active trading center for farmers of the area, and had a fair amount of manufacturing, but with the conquest of the land by the automobile and the truck, much of the trading was drained off by larger cities nearby; as for its manufacturing, one major local product—glass milk-bottles—went out of style, and, by unhappy coincidence, International Harvester, Auburn's largest employer, shut down its local plant in 1955. Today a number of Auburn's factories are silent and lifeless, its stores empty and for rent, and its railroad passenger station, unused for some years, is weedy and decaying.

For all that, the city still looks appealing to the casual passerby: the wide streets, the spacious old homes with their bay windows and cupolas, the easy familiarity with which people greet each other on the sidewalks, the archetypal main-street business center all suggest the innocence, peacefulness, and completeness of American small-town life, that legendary paradise from which we were expelled for the sin of economic growth.

Not far from the center of town is one important place of employment that shows no signs of shutting down—Auburn Prison, or, as it has recently been renamed, Auburn Correctional Facility. It is the second oldest prison in New York State (the oldest is in New York City), inmates having been first admitted in 1817; ever since, it has been an integral part of the life of Auburn, and yet totally apart from it—a silent, alien enclave in the heart of the city, within which nearly 2,000 men live unseen and unknown by their neighbors except for the gossip of those townsmen who work inside as guards and employees, and the occasional news stories grudgingly given out by the prison administration.

Auburn Prison has, in fact, made important news from time to time: in 1823 the "Auburn System" of prison management was inaugurated here, and soon copied by many other prison administrators; not until the end of the century was its severity ameliorated, and it was not wholly abandoned at Auburn until 1910. The prison also won renown as the site of the world's first electrocution; this ostensible advance in penology took place on August 6th, 1890, and made headlines across the nation. The first man electrocuted was a nonentity, but in subsequent years Auburn had the distinction of doing away with such celebrities as Leon Czolgosz, the assassin of President McKinley, and Chester Gillette, the man whose life and crime inspired Dreiser's novel *An American Tragedy.*

Auburn Prison, a "maximum-security" institution, today occupies twenty-one acres enclosed by high stone-and-concrete walls; within them, tan brick buildings with heavily barred windows rise up somewhat higher, but from the streets of the city one sees none of the inhabitants except for the guards at the massive iron front gate and in the gun posts around the top of the walls. At the time the Ortiz brothers arrived, the prison population consisted of some 1,700 convicted felons, more than half of them blacks and Puerto Ricans from New York City, guarded by 300 uniformed officers and fed, clothed, supervised, taught, and occasionally counseled by about 100 other employees. The total payroll was close to $3 million, making Auburn Prison an important part of the city's economy; news about the institution is always prominently featured in the Auburn *Citizen-Advertiser.*

Upon arrival, Carlos and Alfredo went through the usual admission procedures: frisk, medical exam, cell assignment, redesignation by a number, brief interviews with a guidance counselor and a chaplain, and an orientation lecture by the deputy warden. From their cell neighbors and from prisoners they spoke to in the yard, they learned that in the eyes of inmates, Auburn was the best and most humane prison in the state. Though it was under heavy security, and had a wing of isolation cells—and even (according to some of the inmates) a handful of strip cells—the atmosphere was generally relaxed, reflecting the warden's progressive ideas. Prisoners had a number of unusual privileges: they were allowed to wear white shirts, if they liked, and zipper jackets of non-uniform design; in the mess hall they could get up without asking permission—the first time Carlos saw this happen, he feared a riot was about to start—and could go out to the yard for recreation, conversation, or televiewing without waiting for orders to do so. Some of the guards were tough and antagonistic, but a number of others were easy-going and even friendly. "The younger hacks are okay," one inmate told Carlos. "Most of the older guys—especially the locals—would like to take it out on the inmates, but the warden don't allow it. If some hack tells you something you don't like, and you get all wound up and tell him to go fuck himself, you get locked up and get your movie taken away, but that's about all. Now, at Clinton or some other places in this state, you'd get the shit beat out of you and lose ninety days good time, and maybe the hack would even claim you had threatened him and you'd get thrown in the segregation box for a week."

Yet even though Auburn was far better than Brooklyn or Elmira, it was still prison. There was always the familiar pervasive tension hanging heavy in the air; there were insults, threats, fights, and sexual exploitation (but little rape) among the prisoners; there were guards who "agitated" the prisoners in order to demonstrate their power and to provoke back-talk for which they could penalize them; there were punishments and deprivations for infractions as trifling as being ten seconds late at line-up time; there was continual gambling, for cigarettes and food, with all its consequences—"shylocking," bad debts, beatings, knifings; there were trafficking in smuggled drugs, the making of "home brew" from pilfered foodstuffs fermented in a slop bucket, the constant sexual soliciting, the triangles, quarrels, and assaults; there were strict limits on outgoing and incoming mail, and censorship that delayed letters—particularly if written in Spanish, as were those from Luisa Pomales—for days or weeks; there were the hateful jangle of the morning bell, the breakfast march to the mess hall, the din of hundreds of plates, forks, and knives, the shouted orders over the loudspeaker to line up and march to the shops and schools; all day long there were bells, announcements, marching, formations, the locking and unlocking of gates. In the afternoon there was free time to talk in the yard, play ball, go to the library, and wander in to have dinner in the mess hall, but all too soon the order would come for all prisoners to return to their cells at 5:00 p.m., at which time the gates would rumble shut, locking them in for the next fourteen hours. At 7:00 p.m. the "silence bell" would signal the prisoners to cease all noise and talk, and at 10:00 p.m., with the turning-off of the lights and headphone radios, the long, lonely, shut-in night would begin. It was, in a word, prison.

Alfredo and Carlos, being well versed in jail and prison mores, fell in with the local routines and quickly made the necessary friendships, mostly among fellow Puerto Ricans, that gave them a relatively safe place in the prison society. After their assignment to adjoining cells and their initial processing, they were painlessly absorbed into the life at Auburn and virtually disappeared from the sight of the front office. The guards and the civilian employees who dealt with them directly came to know them, as did some of their fellow inmates, but to the warden and his deputy they were only names in the card file. "I get to know the troublemakers," the warden once told a visitor. "The model prisoners I never have any reason to see."

The Ortiz brothers were, indeed, model prisoners and not only obeyed all orders without making any trouble, but outwardly showed no signs of tension or emotional distress. (Carlos, to be sure, had a couple of minor fights and Alfredo got caught gambling once, but these were isolated and trifling infractions.) At first the Assignment Board made Alfredo a porter (general clean-up man) on his own tier and Carlos an assistant in the kitchen; both were also assigned to school half of each working day. Alfredo's achievement tests had put him at the fifth-grade level, but after only two months his English teacher reported to the Service Unit—the guidance and therapy department—"Inmate is a superior student; has learned to read, write, and do spelling remarkably well in a very short time; is now taking advanced work in higher grades, primary and intermediate. Above-average student, doing A grade work." When he got to still more advanced work, Alfredo was unable to maintain his A average, but his teacher continued to rate him "very cooperative and pleasant" and said he seemed genuinely interested in learning. At the end of only a year Alfredo had made an enormous leap in literacy and general knowledge, passed High School Equivalency examinations in three subjects, and, with great pride, received a High School Equivalency Diploma. Reinterviewed by a case worker shortly before completing his schooling, he was said to be "attentive and courteous during course of interview," "apparently well adjusted," and "lacking emotional or personal problems."

Carlos was a less apt pupil. He began school when Alfredo did, but proved uninterested and inattentive, fared poorly, and asked to be transferred to the auto-license shop, where he could make a little money. There, however, he got bored, grew jealous of Alfredo's swift progress in reading and writing, and soon asked to be transferred back to school, this time proving more cooperative and earning C's. He, too, made considerable progress toward literacy, though without equaling Alfredo's new-found verbal fluency, and received his High School Equivalency Diploma a year and half after entering Auburn Prison. His behavior was, in general, exemplary: when he was working at the license-plate shop, the supervisor noted that Carlos had "very good attitudes in relationship to other people as well as a very good disposition," and a case worker who interviewed him after he had been at Auburn a year reported, "Inmate claims to be experiencing no problems and appears to be adjusting favorably to institutional situation."

After completing their schooling, Alfredo and Carlos tentatively tried several work assignments and eventually wound up side by side in the prison laundry, where, along with a score or so of other inmates supervised by a guard and a civilian foreman, they ran huge churning machines and steamy pressers, and not only made half a dollar or so a day—a good rate of pay, by prison standards—but earned favors from various inmates by doing extra laundering and pressing for them. Both of the brothers did their work responsibly and competently, Carlos being particularly handy at maintenance and minor repairs; the foreman, when asked about them by a Service Unit case worker, praised them enthusiastically and said he wished he had twenty more like them in the laundry.

Even their cells evidenced adjustment to imprisonment. Alfredo made his as comfortable as the rules would allow: he built shelves and a couple of lamps, covered the steel cabinet he used as a desk with blue plastic on top of which he put a sheet of glass, bought a dictionary, books on law, and notebooks, hung several pictures of Spanish dancers on the walls, and beneath the glass of his desktop put pictures of his mother and sister. Carlos was less ambitious, but he too added shelves and a homemade lamp, hung a couple of Chinese prints on the wall, and kept a few law books on top of his cabinet. A case worker not long ago characterized both cells as "denoting a feeling of human inhabitation," Alfredo's in particular being practically "homey," and added that, all things considered, the Ortiz brothers were "a classic example of what sociologists call the institutionalized"—persons who have become so well adapted to the special social conditions within an institution that they scarcely seem anxious to leave it.

The brothers themselves sometimes say things that seem to confirm this diagnosis. Carlos, for instance, after being at Auburn for several years, said recently, "You hear a lot of rumors in the street about how you goin' to do a bad bit [i.e., sentence], fightin' all the time, or locked in your cell, but it's not like they say it is. The people in here are okay. The only difference from the ghetto is the walls an' the police." Alfredo, listening, agreed. "I've read articles written by inmates after they get out," he said, "an' there ain' no penitentiary like they say—not that I know of. Maybe twenty years ago there were prisons like that, but not now. The hacks are hard on guys mostly in youth joints—I guess they figure the youths have to have more discipline—but not here."

Beneath this façade, however, both brothers live with a misery so deep and pervasive that they survive only by ignoring it (as one does the thought of his own inevitable death), except when, from time to time, something makes them lose hope or forces them to face the terrible reality of their situation. "I might go months bein' happy," Carlos says, "an' then one day I get up an' I'm depressed an' can hardly do my work. Because you don' want to spend your life in a place like this, you think about bein' with people on the outside, an' marryin', an' havin' children an' a nice job, an' you get into a bag where you don' want to talk to nobody or nothin'. But you got to get out of that bag, because you suffer too much an' you goin' to flip out. So you jus' keep a hold, an' make yourself pull out of it."

These spells, which last anywhere from a day to a week or more, are most commonly brought on by the failure of lawyers or court clerks to answer their letters about the status of their appeals, or, alternatively, by answers that dash their hopes of winning a reversal. When Alfredo had been at Auburn for over half a year, for instance, he suffered an alarming, week-long spell of depression, worse than any he had ever known, because, despite many months of waiting, he had heard nothing to indicate that his appeal was going forward. A court clerk had sent him a routine acknowledgment that his notice of intent to appeal was on file, but Mrs. Pomales, in her letters, never seemed to have any information about its progress, and Mrs. Lowe had not written him a single word. He finally wrote to Mrs. Lowe telling her of his despair, assuring her of his gratitude for her past efforts, and begging for news. But even though he heard nothing from her, he and Carlos both filed applications with the court, affirming that they were indigent and asking to have Mrs. Lowe appointed to pursue their appeals.

After a long delay the Appellate Division replied that it was obliged to appoint Legal Aid on his behalf unless Mrs. Lowe was willing to serve without fee; eventually Mrs. Lowe did apply and was appointed to handle Alfredo's appeal on that basis, but for tactical reasons she had to separate the cases of the two brothers, and advised Carlos to let his case remain in the hands of Legal Aid. But these preliminaries took place with excruciating slowness, and nearly a year and a half after the Ortiz brothers had come to Auburn, there still had been no concrete actions taken on either of their appeals. Carlos in particular was depressed and angry; he had heard nothing for many months from Legal Aid, the court, or Mrs. Lowe. The latter's silence was particularly hard for him to comprehend: could the person he had so respected during the trial really find it too much trouble to answer his letters or keep him informed? Like many other prisoners, he was growing deeply suspicious of everyone outside, including the person who was doing the most for him. He finally wrote to Mrs. Lowe—he had become moderately literate in the prison school—telling her exactly how he felt, and expressing his growing bitterness and loss of faith.

Mrs. Lowe, whose poor performance as a correspondent was the result of a heavy workload and an income insufficient to maintain more than one secretary, had in fact been poring over the trial record in her spare hours for the previous two months (it had not been transcribed and printed by the court until a year after the trial, due to the backlog of work) and painstakingly assembling a brief for Alfredo's appeal, which she had just sent to the printer. Instead of being angered by Carlos' tone, she answered him with great compassion:

> I have been in constant touch with your mother, and have been under the impression that she tells you about the things we talk about. Perhaps it is just that she does not completely understand. What I want you both to know is that I have never forgotten my promise to you. I requested to be assigned to Freddy. I could not be assigned to both. After my assignment, I had to wait for the transcript of the trial to be printed, to begin work on the brief. I did not receive the transcript until September 23rd [1967]. Since it was over 1200 pages, it took a great deal of time to not only read but set up all the errors upon which we are appealing. . . . I know how you both feel, and please be assured that I am doing everything in my power to keep my promise to you. Don't give up—I haven't.

A month later, when the printer delivered the briefs, she sent a copy to Alfredo for him and Carlos to read, promising to deliver another one to the lawyer Legal Aid eventually named to represent Carlos. The Ortiz brothers read her brief and considered it brilliant (it was hardly that, though it was competent and workmanlike). Both brothers were practically giddy with relief and hope: they felt as if a great weight had fallen from them, as if the future, instead of being black and hopeless, was bright and promising. Mrs. Lowe, far from being another betrayer, now seemed almost saintly, and both of the brothers —Alfredo in particular—felt deeply ashamed that they had doubted her and, at times, had almost hated her. Alfredo begged her forgiveness for having doubted her, and told her what joy the brief had brought to him and Carlos.

Their joy was only in part the result of seeing spelled out in print the legal grounds on which their conviction might be reversed; equally, it was the result of knowing that after all, someone outside had not forgotten them and was actively working on their behalf. For despite Mrs. Lowe's letter of a month earlier, a year and a half had passed since they had arrived at Auburn, and they had heard almost nothing from anyone but their mother, and been visited by no one but her— and just once in the year and a half—and suffered from the chronic nightmarish feeling that they had been utterly lost and forgotten by the world.

But even when they felt most forgotten, they still appeared adjusted to prison life; indeed, once they had completed their schooling and settled into the routine of work, recreation, reading, and writing, the staff gradually came to regard them as trustworthy, genuinely rehabilitated, and quite capable of living peaceful, productive lives outside the prison. As Warden John Deegan put it in 1970, "If we could turn those fellows loose today, we'd never see them again. We're proud of them—not everybody who comes here makes it like this." But, unfortunately, "making it" did not entitle them to use their new skills or personalities in the world outside; Warden Deegan's file card for Carlos bore the notation, "Eligible for parole 1/8/92," and for Alfredo, "Eligible for parole 1/10/92," and neither the warden nor the Parole Board could change that. The system had punished them, educated them, transformed them—and given them no chance to be model citizens, but only model prisoners.

Yet despite their adjustment, imprisonment has not become easier for them to bear, but harder, for the longer they remain at Auburn and the more avenues of appeal their lawyers exhaust, the more they are forced to face the reality that they may remain there until January 8th and January 10th of the year 1992. In a recent letter* Alfredo sought to describe the feelings that burn inside him, unseen:

I look over my shoulder to see if hopelessness has caught up with me. The terrifying experience of going to sleep at night with the subconscious fear that you will wake up in the morning with that feeling of hopelessness. The law has been my salvation— strangely enough. But visitors have another effect on a man, they make him aware of the unimaginable loneliness; To see a loved one on an occasion, for a few uninterrupted hours, brings a feeling of pure joy. But, when the visit is over and they walk out that door,—then you feel part of the *real* punishment of prison life. . . .

Prison is just what its creators meant it to be: mental torture and a hell of punishment. So, you start out in prison by being locked in a cell—sleep; [are] let out—eat; you walk, work and talk, then you are locked up again, because the day has come to an end. You just keep getting up in the morning; try to get a good night's sleep; and make the time in between go by as fast as possible. . . .

The things that may seem common to you [i.e., persons outside], and are taken for granted, [cause] the acute feelings that plague me when I am in my cell; It is quiet, I am thinking of the aggravating sounds of children running on hardwood floors, yelling and screaming, playing, laughing, crying; well, I would just love to hear those sounds right now. Or, to just be standing on a subway platform waiting for a train; Riding a bus, sitting next to a woman, breathing the aromatic scent of her most expensive perfume. What about that small crowded restaurant at lunchtime, with the sound of dishes, voices and music. Perhaps, I could be just sitting in some quiet place, concentrating on a conversation with some young lady. All of these things that you people out there take for granted; mean so much to me. Foolish family arguments; hollering, nagging, complaining; Is heaven compared to this. The cold unsharing, uncaring, regimentable at-

* To the author of this book.

mosphere of prison, is what takes the place of everyday living in life; Its a task to retain self-respect, when you are required to be a participant in mans game of inhumanity.

The criminal justice system has both punished and rehabilitated the Ortiz brothers, but in continuing to keep them imprisoned after having remade them, it is inflicting a punishment so cruel and senseless as to be wholly antithetical to our stated moral values. For it has opened their eyes and minds, given them the capacity and desire to lead a normal life, and then denied them the chance to do so; it might have been less cruel to send them to some hellish Devil's Island or work them to death in chains under the broiling sun, rather than breathe new life into them and then condemn them to living death.

## VI    *The Purpose of Judicial Review*

NEITHER the dreaded announcement that the jury finds the defendant guilty nor the sound of the prison gate slamming shut behind him means that he need abandon all hope; as every layman knows, he can appeal to higher judicial authorities to review his case and to reverse the verdict. That, however, is virtually all the layman knows about appellate review; for the rest, he has a number of impressions and beliefs about it which are either naïve, fragmentary, or dead wrong.

For one thing, most people seem to think that convicted defendants have an inalienable—and perhaps constitutional—right to be heard and reheard at ever higher appellate levels up to and including the United States Supreme Court. Actually, the right to appeal is guaranteed neither by the federal Constitution nor those of the states. In some of the latter it has been established by law, and in others by custom, but in either case there are distinct limits upon it: in some states, lower appellate courts are generally permitted by law to refuse to hear certain kinds of cases; in most states, higher appellate courts can refuse to hear a good many of them; and the Supreme Court of the United States has complete discretion to select the cases it wishes to hear and to turn down all others.

Again, it is commonly supposed that in an appeal the case is presented again before the judges of the appellate court; in actual fact the judges do not retry the case, but simply read the printed record of the trial that has already been held and listen as lawyers for both sides argue about it, their arguments dealing primarily with the legality of that trial rather than with the truth or falsehood of the testimony. (On rare occasions, however, an appellate court will reverse a conviction on the ground that the facts obviously and incontrovertibly do not warrant the conviction.)

Finally, most people seem to assume that the major purpose of appellate review is to rescue innocent persons from undeserved punishment. It may indeed occasionally do so, but its major purpose is the righting of another and more serious kind of wrong, namely, the convicting of guilty persons by unfair methods. In more than four fifths of the cases, appellate courts affirm the judgment of the lower court, but even when they reverse it, they usually do so for a reason unrelated to factual guilt or innocence—the discovery of "prejudicial error" in the proceedings—and far from finding the defendant innocent, they generally send him back to be tried again.

Prejudicial error consists of any act by a policeman, prosecutor, judge, or juror which deprives a defendant of any of his substantial rights: a policeman may, for instance, arrest a suspect without probable cause, a prosecutor may comment adversely to the jury on the defendant's refusal to testify, a judge may allow some piece of inadmissible evidence to be heard by the jury, a juror may vote guilty against his belief just to get it over with, and so on. But the discovery of such errors and the resulting reversal of the conviction do not mean that the defendant has been "cleared," although this is how reversals are often interpreted by the mass media and the public. The importance of most reversals consists of what they do not for the appellant but for the entire citizenry: as Professor Delmar Karlen of New York University succinctly puts it, "Many appellate decisions grant new trials not because of any fear that an improper result has been reached, but because of the desire of the appellate judges to discipline trial judges, lawyers, and police officials, reminding them sharply of what they are expected to do and refrain from doing."

That this is the larger and more valuable purpose of appellate review appears most plainly in the case of the United States Supreme Court. In a typical recent year, the Court accepted only 3 percent of the cases offered it; in choosing which of them to hear—particularly in the area of criminal law—its concern was not to rescue a relative handful of individuals from undeserved punishment, but to choose those cases through which, by spelling out what kinds of behavior on the part of police, prosecutors, and trial judges are impermissible, it could exercise a clarifying and corrective influence upon the criminal justice system of the nation.

This is why appeals are so numerous and yet so rarely result in the freedom of the appellant: our higher courts, and in particular our Supreme Court, have granted prisoners easy access to the appellate machinery, but for larger ends than those of the defendants themselves. The odds in favor of any defendant's winning his freedom through the appellate process are minuscule: many appeals are not heard at all, less than a fifth of those that are heard result in reversals, and the great majority of these result in reconviction after retrial. Even appeals that reach the Supreme Court face no better odds at that august level; in a recent year, only a little over 5 percent of the criminal appeals that were submitted to the Court resulted in reversals, and most of these, again, sent the appellants back for retrial. Yet despite these discouraging odds, the volume of appeals has been growing rapidly in recent years: in New York State, for instance, the number of appeals reaching the Court of Appeals (the state's highest tribunal) has doubled in the past decade, and much the same is true in other states, while in the same period the number of appeals presented to federal courts has quadrupled.

There is more than one reason for this huge increase. The rise in crime has produced more arrests, more trials, more convictions, and hence, obviously, more convicted defendant appellants. More important, a number of Supreme Court decisions of recent years have made appellate review far more available to defendants than ever before. (Surprisingly enough, it was not available at all to convicted criminals until less than a century ago.) Among the key decisions were those in *Griffin* v. *Illinois,* in 1956, which required state courts to furnish free copies of the trial transcript to indigent defendants; *Douglas* v. *California,* in 1963, which required states to furnish free counsel to indigent appellants; and various others which expanded the "post-conviction remedies" of defendants, granting them the right, for instance, to petition state appellate courts or even federal courts to order their cases retried, even after all normal review procedures had affirmed their convictions.*

One unfortunate result of all this has been a huge increase in appeals and petitions presented to state appellate courts, many having little merit and even less chance of being heard or of succeeding. But the appellant has nothing to lose: if he is indigent, the appeal costs him nothing, and if he is in prison, it hardly takes time away from more pleasurable pursuits. Similarly, the federal courts have been inundated by *habeas corpus* petitions nearly all of which are, in the curious terminology of the law, "frivolous," or clearly lacking in legal sufficiency. The result has been the overloading of review calendars in both state and federal courts, and a serious lengthening of delays for appellants. Even the seemingly simple matter of transcribing trial notes has become a critical bottleneck: court reporters are now so burdened with work that in most places they hold up the appeals process by months, and sometimes years, because until they transcribe their notes of the trial, defense lawyers cannot write and file their appeal briefs.

Unlike appeals, *habeas corpus* and *coram nobis* petitions can be reinstituted again and again on new pretexts; this results in a troublesome loss of "finality." Formerly, when a defendant had exhausted the appeals process, his conviction became final and the question of his guilt was settled once and for all. Today, after using up all his appeals within the state courts, he can petition state or federal courts to reopen the case all over again. Most of these petitions are denied without a hearing for having offered no facts, and even those that do win a hearing rarely result in the order for a new trial or review. The increased use of these devices has not, therefore, noticeably opened the prison gates, but it has taken up a good deal of additional time and effort by judges, courtroom personnel, and district attorneys.

The ease with which convicted defendants can now appeal, and the lack of finality created by their expanded rights to post-conviction

---

* Such post-conviction remedies differ from appeals in going beyond the facts as adduced at the trial. A petition of *habeas corpus* to the federal court, for instance, alleges that the state acted unconstitutionally in some fashion not brought out at the trial; a petition of *coram nobis* to a state appellate court alleges that some pertinent defect, not in the record, should be considered.

remedies, are viewed very differently by partisans of the Crime Control Model of justice and partisans of the Due Process Model.* The former deplore the new freedom of defendants to file worthless appeals just because funds are available to them, and to file any number of post-conviction petitions simply because they may. This freedom, they point out, makes the appellate machinery terribly inefficient; costs go up, valuable time and energy are wasted, delays grow longer, more guilty persons win their freedom. Moreover, the granting of these legal rights to prisoners leads many of them to spend their time and energy fighting legal battles rather than straightening themselves out; as Attorney General Mitchell told the Alabama State Bar Association in June 1971, "The process of rehabilitating offenders is seriously impeded when they never reach the point of recognizing their own guilt." Among the solutions Mr. Mitchell suggested was limiting prisoners' use of *habeas corpus* to claims bearing on real guilt or innocence, and excluding attacks on procedural defects.

And this is the crux of the matter. Partisans of the Crime Control Model would solve the problems of court congestion and delay, and the loss of finality, by limiting the use of due-process mechanisms and by withdrawing some of the legal rights granted prisoners in recent years by higher courts of review. In July 1971, at the meeting of the American Bar Association in London, a number of spokesmen for the law-and-order position charged that *habeas corpus* proceedings and other extensions of legal rights to prisoners had damaged the justice system, and Mr. Mitchell won enthusiastic applause from conservatives when, as the nation's leading prosecutor, he warned that the United States was "in danger of drowning in a sea of legalisms," and called for a reappraisal of the "hydra of excess proceduralisms," naming among them the abuse of appellate review and of collateral attack.

In rebuttal, adherents of the Due Process Model say that efficiency is not the goal of our justice system, and that a certain degree of inefficiency is the necessary and tolerable price of extending constitutional guarantees to all. Furthermore, the increased rights permit very few guilty persons to win their freedom—and this loss is more than offset by the fact that those rights also permit some innocent persons to win their freedom. The loss of finality is not critical, but merely annoying and costly; in any case, our society would be better served

* Once again I am using the valuable dichotomy suggested by Professor Herbert L. Packer in *The Limits of the Criminal Sanction;* see above, page 80.

if we dealt with the heavy burden of appeals—and of delays and court congestion in general—not by retrenching on legal rights but by spending whatever is necessary to expand our courts to meet the challenge. As for the negative effect of legal rights on rehabilitation, the truth is that very few prisoners have ever seen imprisonment as a golden opportunity to improve themselves; in any case, even if the government is trying to rehabilitate the prisoner, this is no justification for denying him the opportunity to prove that he should not be in prison at all. As Justice Brandeis wrote in one of his sharp dissents, "Experience should teach us to be most on our guard to protect liberty when the Government's purposes are beneficent."

If one considers due process the legal embodiment of the concept of fairness, and the extension of its protections to all persons as the realization of the democratic ideal, he can hardly sympathize with attorneys general, state prosecutors, or judges (overworked though they may be) who see the recent growth of appellate review and collateral attack as a sea of legalisms and a hydra of excess proceduralisms. There is no fundamental conflict between the fight against crime and the extension of due process; it takes only money and manpower to have both at the same time. If we choose not to allocate the money and manpower, we have only ourselves to blame for the lessened effectiveness of crime-control efforts, or the withering away of democracy, or both.

# VII *The Defendant Appeals from the Judgment of the Supreme Court, Bronx County (Lyman, J.)*

WHATEVER the larger social function of appellate review, the imprisoned man sees only that it may be an avenue of escape from his conviction and sentence. Particularly for long-term prisoners like Alfredo and Carlos Ortiz, the hope that lies in appellate review is often the rock upon which their personalities stand; without it, they are apt to sink into total apathy, or else to become chronic troublemakers and violence-prone disciplinary cases. The initial shock of being committed for "natural life" was moderated for the brothers, when they first arrived at Auburn, by their vague and naïve expectation that they would soon be rescued by their appeals; it was only after many months had passed without any word of progress that they began to fall prey to spells of depression and to the prisoner's typical anger toward, and mistrust of, the very people who are trying to help him.

The anger and mistrust were abruptly dispelled when Mrs. Lowe's brief finally reached them, nearly a year and a half after they had come to Auburn. It began with the exhilarating announcement, "The Defendant appeals from the Judgment of the Supreme Court, Bronx County (Lyman, J.) and each and every part thereof entered on the minutes of June 10, 1966." The first fifteen pages were a summary of the evidence given at the second trial; in it Mrs. Lowe carefully highlighted the contradictions and discrepancies brought out by defense cross-examination, noted those key defense objections and motions which Justice Lyman had denied, and gave a good deal of space to Lyman's charge and to her unsuccessful request that he marshal the evidence.

In her next ten pages she got to the heart of the matter, naming and explicating in dense legal jargon, further congested by batches of references, the errors that she claimed had been committed. Her first point was that because Justice Lyman had not marshaled the evidence, his charge had been prejudicial:

> It is fundamental that the statements made by co-conspirators or accomplices after the crime had been consummated are incompetent and inadmissible as against the non-confessing defendant. *People* v. *Ryan,* 263 N.Y. 298; *People* v. *McQuade,* 110 N.Y. 284; *People* v. *Kief,* 126 N.Y. 661; *People* v. *Vaccaro,* 228 N.Y. 170. It was therefore highly prejudicial to this defendant for the Court to charge the theory of the prosecution that this defendant was involved in a felony murder when the only evidence adduced of felony murder was that extracted from the statements of his co-defendants (1153–1156, 1186).

This, of course, did not mean that Alfredo had not been guilty, but only that the court's procedure had been unfair: Alfredo himself had not seen the robbery-murder, but the judge had connected him with it by means of the evidence given by his co-defendants. If the judges of the appellate court agreed with her, they would reverse Alfredo's conviction not because they thought him innocent, but because they wanted trial judges to adhere strictly to the principles of due process.

Mrs. Lowe's second point was that Alfredo's confession should not have been admitted as evidence. McCabe had had no probable cause to arrest him, and therefore any statement Alfredo made as a result of the unlawful arrest was the fruit of the poisonous tree and a violation of the Fourth Amendment.

Her third claim of error was that the judge should have ordered all co-defendant names redacted from each confession, or else should have ordered each defendant tried separately. Justice Lyman had, of course, warned the jury not to accept as evidence anything any defendant said about his co-defendants, but according to Mrs. Lowe it was error even to allow the jury to hear such evidence. (Her view had no firm basis in higher-court rulings at that point, but she was anticipating the possible outcome of *Bruton* v. *United States,* even then under consideration by the U.S. Supreme Court, in which this issue was at stake.)

Finally, she maintained that Alfredo's guilt had not been proven beyond a reasonable doubt. If the jury had not used impermissible evidence from co-defendant statements, she said, they could not have found Alfredo guilty as charged; the evidence he gave against himself would, at worst, have warranted a conviction of a conspiracy to rob, but not of actual robbery, much less murder.

Technical and clerical delays, both on her part and that of the clerk of the court, kept her from formally filing this brief for nearly two months after she had sent a copy of it to the Ortiz brothers— every day of which Alfredo, unknowing, waited for his mail all atremble, hoping to receive good news—but at last in March 1968 her twenty-seven-page brief and the weighty three-volume trial record arrived together on the desk of Daniel J. Sullivan, Chief of the Appeals Bureau in the office of the District Attorney of Bronx County. In appellate proceedings, the prosecutor, or his aides in charge of appeals, examine the appellant's brief and prepare a "respondent's brief" rebutting the points made by the former; both briefs and the trial record go to the appellate judges, and lawyers for both sides then appear in person to argue their points orally. The bulk of brief-writing and oral argument in Sullivan's busy bureau is handled by assistants, but he himself handled all murder cases, and he lugged the weighty trial record and Alfredo's appeal brief home, and went to work on the case in his evenings and on weekends.

Sullivan first studied Mrs. Lowe's brief to see what issues he had to respond to; then he pored over the trial record and dipped into various law books and journals, mostly at home, away from the jangling phone and the incessant conferences of his daytime hours. Brief-writing is essentially a scholarly task, far removed from the ugly realities of criminals and victims, police stations and jail cells, and although Sullivan's plain, bare office is only a couple of doors down the hall from Alexander Scheer's, he had never seen the Ortiz brothers and had neither any need nor desire to see them now, or to talk to the detectives or any of the witnesses. His task was a purely intellectual exercise in rebuttal, using the trial record, the body of existing law, and the interpretations of it made by higher courts.

Oddly enough, Daniel Sullivan is not at all the kind of man one would expect to find in such a cerebral and detached line of work. Short and wiry, lank-haired and jug-eared, he has, at forty-odd, the lined, caved-in, humorous Irish face of a young Barry Fitzgerald and a crackling, peppery manner of speech in which legal erudition is freely intermingled with jailhouse slang and delivered in a tough-guy street-corner New York accent. Sullivan had, in fact, grown up father-less on the streets in a West Side slum area, been orphaned by nine-teen, and had knocked about aimlessly for a while, drifting into bad company and teetering on the brink of a life of petty criminality. Luckily, he was taken in by the family of a friend, straightened him-self out, proceeded to put himself through college and law school, and unhesitatingly chose the field of criminal law, spending part of his professional life as a public defender and the rest of it as a district attorney.

Sullivan therefore knows the look, feel, and smell of crime and pun-ishment more intimately than nine tenths of the assistant district at-torneys who write appeals briefs or judges who sit on the appellate benches. When he says that he has no doubt whatever that the Ortiz brothers are guilty, he is not being automatically and rigidly pro-Establishment; rather, he is judging their guilt from the printed record —and from his experience as both friend and foe of accused persons. When he dismisses their lawyers' talk of coerced confessions, it is not because he is a naïve cop-lover; rather, it is because he is a hard-headed realist who knows that police are sometimes brutal, but that guilty persons nearly always lie. "It's absolutely standard to charge brutality in these cases," he says, "because when you're faced with a confession you admittedly gave, what can you do but swear they beat the bejesus out of you? It's always the same damn story with these guys—no marks, no outcry, no complaint to their lawyers or the judge, just the claim that the cops tortured them unmercifully—because what the hell else are they gonna say?"

In rebutting Mrs. Lowe's brief, of course, Sullivan sounded nothing like this; though his prose was occasionally a trifle florid, most of the time it was formal, rigorously logical, and so stuffed with learning and dependent clauses as to be almost impenetrable. In answering Mrs. Lowe's argument, for instance, that Alfredo's confession included no direct evidence of murder and did not warrant a conviction on that charge, he wrcte:

Where there is independent evidence establishing the fact of death by criminal agency, a conviction for felony murder may be had on the strength of a confession either to robbery alone or to a killing during the commission of a robbery, albeit there is no corroborative evidence as to underlying felony [*People* v. *Louis,* 1 N.Y. 2d 197 (1956); *People* v. *Lytton,* 257 N.Y. 310, 312–315 (1931)]. Accordingly, the plaint of the defendant-appellant Alfred[o] Ortiz about the absence of corroborative evidence identifying the underlying felony as robbery, is baseless (Brief, pp. 17–18, 23–24).

He dismissed Mrs. Lowe's argument that Justice Lyman should have marshaled the evidence by pointing out that the judge had repeatedly warned the jury to consider against each defendant only the evidence of his own statements; this was all that the existing law required. As for McCabe's arrest of Alfredo, Sullivan said that even had it been unlawful, the resulting confession had been purely voluntary (as far as the record showed), and cited precedents in New York law to show that the voluntariness of the confession "attenuated" any "primary taint" of technical illegality in the arrest, thus making the confession admissible after all.

Finally, he denied that the combined use of all three confessions by the prosecution had been prejudicial. The confessions were generally consistent and similar; their simultaneous use therefore did not prejudice the appellant because it did not provide crucial and otherwise unavailable details against him. The one serious discrepancy among the confessions was the matter of time, but the resolution of that discrepancy was the jury's business; no proof had been offered to show that the jury had dealt with it improperly. For all these reasons, he concluded, the arguments of Alfredo Ortiz were devoid of merit and the judgment of conviction against him should be affirmed.

Mrs. Lowe's brief reached the chambers of the judges of the Appellate Division, First Department, at 25th Street and Madison Avenue, New York, in March 1968; Sullivan's brief arrived in April; and by late May the judges, familiar with both, called upon Mrs. Lowe and Sullivan to appear before them. The ornate, hushed courtroom, with its stately domed ceiling, elegant brass chandeliers, and general air of dignity and opulence, was in striking contrast to the dingy, malodorous courtroom of Criminal Court where all this had started, and even to the dignified but cold and barren courtroom of Supreme Court in which it had been tried. The procedure was as elegant and formal as the surroundings: Mrs. Lowe and Sullivan greeted each other politely, took their places at tables before the imposing, high bench, and then took turns addressing the five serious, intent judges sitting behind it. Standing at a lectern before the bench, Mrs. Lowe argued her four points in her typically earnest, hand-wringing, heartfelt manner, the effect of which was somewhat spoiled by the sharply worded questions with which one or another of the judges frequently interrupted her. Sullivan, in his turn, was all rapid-fire rhetoric laced with references, and he seemed rather less disconcerted than Mrs. Lowe by the needling questions of the judges. (In view of the fact that detailed briefs are prepared for them, one might wonder why appellate judges bother to hear oral argument in so many cases—in New York they do so about half the time—the answer being, most likely, that they like debating with different prosecutors and defenders, and demonstrating their own brilliance.) The whole procedure was the practice of law on the level of intellectual inquiry; if no one in the courtroom during that hour was thinking of Alfredo Ortiz as a real person, or envisioning him in the slum streets, the police station, or the living death of prison, it was not because the participants were inhuman theoreticians, but because their business, that day, was of a larger order than concern about one young man and his doom.

In less than an hour of fast-paced, driving, but courteous give-and-take, the oral arguments were completed, and Mrs. Lowe and Sullivan thanked the judges and withdrew. Later that day the five judges discussed Alfredo Ortiz's appeal in private, and found themselves in unanimous agreement that no substantial prejudicial errors had been made in the trial. Since, moreover, they felt that the legal issues were governed by existing law, they saw no need to produce a written opinion to serve as a clarification for similar cases in the future; as they do in about half of all cases coming before them, they issued a simple affirmance without opinion, which read in its entirety:

> Said appeal having been argued by Mary Johnson Lowe, of counsel for the appellant, and by Mr. Daniel J. Sullivan, of counsel for the respondent; and due deliberation having been had thereon,
>
> It is unanimously ordered and adjudged that the judgment so appealed from be and the same is hereby, in all things, affirmed.

Carlos' appeal, meanwhile, was traveling the same route, though it lagged behind by some months. After long delays the Legal Aid Society had finally gotten Emanuel P. Popolizio, one of a number of volunteer lawyers listed by the New York Bar Association, to work on Carlos' brief. (Appeals by indigent defendants had so overtaxed the staff resources of the Legal Aid Society that they had had to ask for unpaid volunteer help to take up the slack.) In his brief, Popolizio, who had a copy of Mrs. Lowe's brief at hand, made substantially the same points as she, but laid even heavier stress on the claim that it had been judicial error to try the defendants together, for, he said, despite Justice Lyman's warnings the jury was very apt to have combined elements from all three confessions in judging the guilt of each defendant. Popolizio made much of this issue because in late May 1968 the U.S. Supreme Court had finally held, in the *Bruton* case, that confessions by co-defendants were hard for juries to ignore, and if made only outside the courtroom and not subject to cross-examination, were very likely to prejudice the rights of the defendants and should generally be held inadmissible.

Sullivan read Popolizio's brief as soon as it arrived, and rose to do battle. He whipped together another respondent's brief, reusing much of what he had written against Alfredo's appeal but drafting a new section in which he argued that the *Bruton* jury could have found

Bruton guilty only by using details from the statements of his accomplices, while Carlos Ortiz could have been found guilty on the basis of his statement alone; Carlos' rights had therefore not been prejudiced by the use of statements of his co-conspirators. Moreover, Carlos had not even asked, through his counsel, to be tried separately—probably, Sullivan said, because defense counsel wanted the contradictions between Carlos' story and that of Valencia to confuse the jury and sow doubt in their minds.

Carlos, waiting to learn his fate, expected the worst, for Alfredo's appeal had been heard and denied by the end of May; still, when he heard that his case had finally been assigned, he kept hoping against hope that some miracle would happen. The summer waxed and waned, fall slowly displaced it, the days grew shorter and the air in the yard chillier, and finally in late October, two years and four months after Carlos had been convicted, the alleged errors in his trial were the subject of discussion in the courtroom of the Appellate Division, First Department. Not that Carlos knew what was happening that day; to him it was only another monotonous gray day, like all the days at Auburn; but in the courtroom at 25th Street and Madison Avenue, Popolizio and Sullivan were arguing the matter before the same five judges with particular fervor and excitement because the *Bruton* decision had given it new relevance.

Afterward, in their deliberations the judges found themselves divided. Justice Benjamin Rabin felt that *Bruton* applied, and that the use of the unredacted confessions had violated Carlos Ortiz's Sixth Amendment rights. The other four still felt as they had when Alfredo's appeal had come before them half a year earlier. Justice George Tilzer, writing the majority opinion, held that "unquestionably, a joint trial was desired by all defendants to take advantage of discrepancies in their confessions introduced at the prior joint trial"; if the joint trial was a faulty one, the fault had not been the court's. But the crucial point, he wrote, was that except for the question of time, the confessions were substantially similar, and therefore, even by the standards set forth in the *Bruton* decision, prejudicial error had not existed:

"Not every admission of inadmissible hearsay or other evidence can be considered to be reversible error" (*Bruton* v. *United States, supra,* p. 135). Applying the standard formulated by the

Supreme Court to test the gravity of constitutional error, we are convinced beyond a reasonable doubt that if there was error it did not contribute to the verdict obtained against appellant. (*Chapman* v. *California,* 386 U.S. 18, 24.)

The judgment should be affirmed.

News of the result of Alfredo's appeal in May and of Carlos' in November plunged each of the brothers, in turn, into new depths of despair. Each, however, felt new hope when Mrs. Lowe and Popolizio wrote to let them know that their appeals would be carried on up to the Court of Appeals, the highest bench in New York State. But again the mills of justice ground exceeding slow: the formalities of merely obtaining permission to carry the appeal on up took half a year, during which the brothers heard nothing, remained ignorant of the reasons for the delay, and had no idea whether their appeals would ever actually be heard.

In the meantime, Alfredo was combating his own depression and pessimism by finally doing something on his own. As he slowly lost faith in the sincerity and goodwill of people outside the prison, he began, like many another long-term prisoner, to study law, plowing through basic textbooks on arrest, trial procedure, and constitutional rights in the prison library and in his cell, discussing cases with a handful of like-minded prisoners during his free hours in the prison yard, and filling notebooks with details and citations that seemed useful. Carlos, after his own appeal had been denied, tried to do the same thing, but, having less native ability and determination, contented himself with reading desultorily and calling to Alfredo's attention anything he came across that he thought might be useful; Alfredo, if he deemed it so, would make note of it for future use for both of them.

A few months after the failure of Alfredo's appeal, while Mrs. Lowe was still trying to get permission to take his case on up to the Court of Appeals, he wrote her the first of several letters proffering his advice and help, and offering her material he felt would be of great help in presenting his case to the Court of Appeals. From textbooks, and from journals in which higher-court decisions were printed, he copied out statements of constitutional principles and their application to arrest, evidence, and other matters that he wanted to make sure she knew about, and faithfully included clusters of references in proper legal style, as she herself had done in her brief. But she made no reply and sent him no further news; he heard not another word about his appeal as the long, bitter upstate winter dragged on, and as spring slowly and uncertainly returned. Finally, word did arrive that in June 1969, more than three years after he and Carlos had been found guilty, their appeals would be heard together in the Court of Appeals in Albany.

Briefs filed with the Court of Appeals are usually similar, in the points they raise, to those heard in the Appellate Division, though often longer and more detailed. In this case, however, Mrs. Lowe not only expanded her brief but revised it considerably, to make the most of *Bruton*. She argued that *Bruton* applied; the use of co-defendant confessions, not redacted, was error—and not harmless error, as Sullivan had maintained and as the Appellate Division had decided. For good measure, she also developed once again her previous complaint that the arrest had been illegal and that Alfredo's confession should therefore have been ruled inadmissible. Popolizio, in his brief on behalf of Carlos, likewise laid heavy stress on the *Bruton* question; in addition, he threw in three other lesser complaints in the hope that one of them might work.

Once again Sullivan studied these briefs, thumbed through the latest law journals and reported decisions, and then updated his own rebuttal. He argued against each and every point at fifty-four pages' length, but paid most careful attention to the constitutional question involved in *Bruton*. He handled it much as he had in his answer to Carlos' previous appeal, but added the very latest Court of Appeals decisions involving *Bruton* and defining its limits:

> Cases decided . . . as late as last week have shed additional light on the problem under discussion. . . . *Bruton*—according to this Court in a decision wherein the majority voiced its agreement with the holding of the Appellate Division in Carlos Ortiz' case—is inapplicable "***where each of the defendants has himself made a full and voluntary confession which is almost identical to the confessions of his co-defendants" [*People* v. *McNeil, et al.*, —— N.Y. 2d —— (decided April 23, 1969); *People* v. *Galloway*, ——N.Y. 2d, —— (May, 1969)].

Therefore, he said once again, even if the use of all three unredacted confessions in the joint trial had been error, it was harmless error.

On June 5th, 1969, Mrs. Lowe, Popolizio, and Sullivan all appeared in Albany to offer oral argument before the Court of Appeals.

The courtroom was awe-inspiring—hushed and splendid, the floor carpeted in rich red, the walls, bench, and deeply beamed ceiling all made of intricately hand-carved teak, a great onyx fireplace to one side, and, ranged all around, portraits of former judges looking down upon the proceedings. Unlike the shirt-sleeved clerk of the court in the Bronx, the clerk and other officials of this court wore striped pants and morning coats, and a court crier formally announced the judges, and called out "Hear ye, hear ye, hear ye" and invited all persons having business before the court to draw near. Seated at the bench, the six judges were a formidable phalanx of black-robed seriousness (normally there were seven of them, but one was absent), concentrating their collective attention upon Mrs. Lowe, Popolizio, and Sullivan as they presented their arguments, and often breaking in to "inquire" about some subtle and complex point. It was an intensely stressful hour for the three lawyers—a dignified and soft-spoken dialogue, but intellectually the equivalent of hand-to-hand combat—and each one, at the end of the allotted twenty minutes, was as exhausted as if at the end of a day of trial work.

At the end of the hour, they left, knowing that there would be no final word for weeks; the judges of the Court of Appeals customarily hear cases for about two weeks at a time and then for the next three weeks make their decisions and, where necessary, write their opinions. It was nearly four weeks later, on July 2nd, that the decision came down: the judgments against both Alfredo and Carlos were affirmed without opinion, all six judges concurring.

Sullivan, when the news reached him, felt deeply gratified that the law, as he had argued it, had been upheld. Popolizio, of course, was disappointed, while Mrs. Lowe was outraged and heartsick, and considered the decision all but incomprehensible. As for the Ortiz brothers, they were dejected, bitter, even more suspicious than they had previously been of Mrs. Lowe and the Legal Aid Society, and more determined than ever to play a direct role in their continuing fight for freedom. It now seemed to Alfredo, with the spurious wisdom of hindsight, that he had always really known that he and Mrs. Lowe had had no rapport concerning his efforts to assist her in preparing his appeal, and that her failure to respond to his suggestions or answer his technical queries had played a part in its failure. Feeling almost (but not quite) ready to handle things on his own from now on, he assembled facts, quotations, and case references from his notes and law books, and began drafting his own petition for a writ of *certiorari,* to be addressed to the U.S. Supreme Court. But because he still felt a little unsure of himself, he wrote Mrs. Lowe a letter in which he bitterly criticized her for not having written to him about his ideas or replied to his questions, but then informed her that he was preparing a *certiorari* petition and would send it to her for her comments and criticisms; he had learned a great deal about the law, but he was not trying to outdo her—he was only shouldering part of the burden.

Mary Lowe, having given so much time and effort to his appeal without being remunerated—not even for her expenses—was something less than gratified by his tone. She had already given up much of her July 4th weekend to working on his petition to the Supreme Court, and meant to complete it, but at this point a death in the family badly upset her, and for some weeks she did scarcely any legal work and answered none of her correspondence. In early September she received a large, heavy envelope from Alfredo which contained a thirty-three-page handwritten manuscript of his petition, which, he felt sure, would win reconsideration of his case by the U.S. Supreme Court. With it was a frigidly formal letter in which he rebuked Mrs. Lowe again for not having replied to his letters about the legal points involved in his case; he also praised her for having laid down a sound basis for appeal during the trial, and asked her to go over the petition, and to submit it for him.

The painstakingly neat manuscript, carefully spaced and with all references neatly underlined, began with a section entitled "An Intrusion on a Constitutionally Protected Area." In numbered paragraphs, and with numerous titles, subtitles, references, quotations from decisions, and extracts from his own trial record, it made the familiar point that his arrest had been illegal and that his confession should therefore have been inadmissible. Much of what he wrote would look, to lay eyes, highly professional; only the trained lawyer could see at a glance that it was the work of a diligent amateur parroting (a little inaccurately) whatever seemed pertinent to him. In its more learned sections it read something like this.*

Where suspicion cannot substitute for probable cause, and there is no evidentiary proof of implication in any crime, there

---

* The original of the petition has been lost, and is described above from memory. The quotations given here, while close to the original, are actually taken from a *habeas corpus* petition that Alfredo wrote somewhat later and filed with the Federal District Court in Manhattan.

is lacking grounds for an arrest. Because, it is oft-quoted that probable cause must precede an arrest. (see: WONG SUN vs UNITED STATES, 371 U.S. 471) . . . The complaint herein is not merely premised on illegal arrest, but moreso on the deliberate illegal acts of Det. McCabe. (see: WONG SUN vs UNITED STATES, supra; TRAUB vs CONNECTICUT, 374 U.S. 493 (1963); KER vs CALIFORNIA, 374 U.S. 23. . . . Whereas, the illegal acts complained of hereunder, are so distinct, without being able to dissipate the harm done, that the circumstances subsequently involved, create an unavoidable question of Constitutionality.

A second section, entitled "Malicious and Unconstitutional Prosecution," accused Scheer of various irregularities, including his refusal to redact the confessions, and a third section attacked Justice Lyman's charge as prejudicial. A lengthy concluding section, based on the first three, asked the Supreme Court to find that his constitutional rights had been flagrantly violated.

No wonder Alfredo was proud of this piece of work; for someone who less than four years earlier had been a barely literate street-corner lounger and drug addict, it was a remarkable achievement. To Mrs. Lowe's trained eye, unfortunately, it was far from good enough to send on to the Supreme Court. But time to file a petition for Alfredo was running out and she was still unable to muster the psychic energy to write it up herself, particularly since she had earned something less than his unmixed appreciation for her efforts. She therefore wrote Alfredo as follows:

> I received your letter and papers and decided the best way to handle the matter is to request the Legal Aid Society to prosecute your appeal along with that of Carlos. I have had a very bad summer and find that I cannot do the job I would like to do on your appeal to the Supreme Court. I have not abandoned you because I believe in my heart that the foundation has been laid down for any success you may have in the future; it is all there in the record.

Alfredo bitterly told his friends, "She let me down. I had all my hopes on her before, but I see things somewhat different now. I'm more realistic. I couldn' never have believed she'd be droppin' off my case with only two days left to file! She *abandoned* me!" Carlos, shaking his head, agreed: "All them letters she sen' us, tellin' us she'll never be satisfied until justice be done an' that she'll never give up the case or nothin' like that—an' then she turn aroun' an' give up on it!"

Mrs. Lowe had not, however, abandoned either of them; Carlos, she knew, was already safely in the hands of Legal Aid, and she pleaded successfully with that organization to take on Alfredo, too. Nevertheless, she suffered keen guilt feelings. "Do you know what the boys wrote me?" she said to a friend a little later. "They said, 'You promised not to abandon us, and we believed in you.' It ate my heart out. *Aiye!*"

Down at the cramped, dingy offices of the Legal Aid Society's Appeals Bureau, at 19th Street and Fifth Avenue, both cases were assigned to Julia Heit, a young lawyer just three years out of law school, and filled with idealism and liberalism. Miss Heit, a tall, attractive, earnest young woman, knew the case well, having worked with Popolizio in preparing Carlos' brief for the Court of Appeals, and she felt strongly about it. Born in the Bronx and trained at Brooklyn Law School, she had worked on a special project in Criminal Court while in law school, helping indigent defendants obtain release without bail prior to trial. From that experience she had seen the justice system, through young suspects' eyes, as vast, impersonal, and terrifying, and as soon as she got her law degree, she went to work for the Legal Aid Society to defend the poor and the young. As it happens, she has not met any defendants face to face since then, but has been working in the Appeals Bureau, studying trial records and drafting closely reasoned appeals and petitions. But it has proven deeply satisfying to her; although the defendants she represents, including the Ortiz brothers, are only names on paper to her—as she is only a signature on a letter to them—she feels she is helping them individually and, at the same time, striving to correct defects in the entire system.

"I've never seen the Ortiz brothers," she said last year, "and I have no idea whether they were really innocent or guilty, but what I've read in the record of this trial is *wrong!* They were just two young kids with a whole huge system against them, and the system shouldn't take their liberty away from them except by means that are absolutely in accordance with the law. In fighting for them, all I'm really doing is saying to society: If you want to put a couple of teen-age kids behind bars for life, you have to do it fairly and squarely."

Miss Heit, with some help from her superior, William Hellerstein, spent much of her time, over a period of some weeks, drafting Carlos' petition to the U.S. Supreme Court for a writ of *certiorari,* and had already filed it when Alfredo was added to her caseload. With only days to go to file for Alfredo, she applied to the Court for a brief extension of time, rapidly adapted the basic text of Carlos' petition to fit Alfredo's case, and rushed down to Washington to submit it in person rather than trust the mails. In both petitions asking the Supreme Court to review the judgment of the New York Court of Appeals, she first briefly reviewed the evidence, then argued that to call the use of the unredacted confessions at a joint trial "harmless error" was to emasculate the Supreme Court's decision in the *Bruton* case. This was the sole issue, she and Hellerstein felt, that merited the Supreme Court's consideration, but they both felt that it was indeed a "substantial federal question," and that the Court was very likely to consider the case.

It was October 1969 when she handed in Alfredo's petition; there was nothing more she could do for the Ortiz brothers but wait patiently until word came down, for their petitions were only two of thousands that the Supreme Court receives each year, every one of which has to be read by the justices and rated either worthy or unworthy of the Court's attention. Before that could happen, however, her petitions had to be joined by Sullivan's rebuttal; as soon as he received copies of both, he revised his own previous briefs, and filed his Brief in Opposition in January 1970. In it he omitted the matters that were no longer raised by appellants' counsel, and concentrated on certain points he had already made: namely, that the defense had wanted the trial to be joint for tactical reasons, and that the Court of Appeals of New York, in affirming the judgments, had "properly applied the doctrine of harmless error" without contravening the meaning of *Bruton.*

In Auburn, Alfredo and Carlos heard nothing, worked and waited each day, sometimes wrote to Julia Heit and, occasionally, to Mrs. Lowe, received mail from no one except their mother, watched the weeks and months dragging by, and hoped for the best: the United States Supreme Court, after all, would surely recognize the truth of Julia Heit's argument (she had sent copies of the petitions to the Ortizes) and would certainly look at the trial record and see everything that was wrong; the Supreme Court, after all, was Supreme, and infallible.

In March 1970, five years after the first trial of the Ortiz brothers and nearly four years after their conviction, the justices of the Supreme Court read Julia Heit's petitions and Daniel Sullivan's Brief in Opposition to see if the case did indeed present a question of national import. Their opinion was shortly announced in two letters, each one sentence long, from John F. Davis, Clerk of the Supreme Court, to William Hellerstein. The one concerning Alfredo read:

RE: ALFREDO ORTIZ v. NEW YORK
*No. 1165 Misc., Oct. Term, 1969*
Dear Sir:
     The Court today denied the petition for a writ of certiorari in the above-entitled case.

The other one, identical except for the title, read:

RE: CARLOS ORTIZ v. NEW YORK
*No. 1034 Misc., Oct. Term, 1969*
Dear Sir:
     The Court today denied the petition for a writ of certiorari in the above-entitled case.

At the Legal Aid offices, the morning the letters arrived, Julia Heit and Hellerstein sat and stared at each other glumly for a while. "I just don't understand how they could *do* this," Julia Heit said, "I just don't understand it!" She looked as if she were about to cry; Hellerstein himself was deeply upset, but calmed her by saying they'd consider other courses of action—*habeas corpus* petitions to the Federal District Court, perhaps. With a deep sigh, she went back to her office, put the "Ortiz, Carlos" and "Ortiz, Alfredo" folders back in the file cabinet, and got to work on another case.

The Ortiz brothers were unaware for over a month, probably through oversight on Julia Heit's part, that their petitions had been denied; eventually they did hear about it, were newly depressed, and emerged from their depression more grimly determined than ever to continue the fight. Alfredo, having now become what is known in prison slang as a "jailhouse lawyer," felt that he could do better for himself—and eventually for Carlos—than either Mrs. Lowe or Julia Heit. Mrs. Lowe's appeals, he had decided, involved a cardinal error: "The way Miss Lowe wrote up my case," he has said, "she's hittin' them with the Fourth Amendment—illegal arrest; the Fifth Amendment—self-incrimination; the Sixth Amendment—right to counsel; an' the Fourteenth Amendment—due process of law. Now, if you hook up all these amendments, the courts would have to make a rule that any violation of one is a violation of all, an' they're never goin' to give up nothin' like that. An' as for Miss Heit's petition, I tol' her that it was *nice,* you know, but the way she wrote it was like she was tellin' the court our rights was violated but we *committed* the crime."

Alfredo, indeed, perhaps as a mental defense, had by now begun to sound quite paranoid about everyone who had tried to help him. He saw some mention in a law journal of a district attorney named Lowe, supposed that Mrs. Lowe had become a D.A. (she had not), and thought that it showed what her real bent had always been. In August 1970 he wrote Julia Heit a letter saying that he no longer wanted her to represent him, accusing her and Mrs. Lowe of obstructing his access to the courts, and informing her that he intended to appeal to the Federal District Court *pro se* (by himself). (Carlos, not having Alfredo's dedication or skill, decided to stick with Julia Heit and the Legal Aid Society; actually, he felt that he had practically reached the end of the line with them, but that Alfredo would eventually break out through his own efforts, and would then rescue him.) Alfredo laboriously prepared a petition asking for a hearing under the *habeas corpus* rule and sent it to the Federal District Court in Manhattan, and in due course received word that a Brief in Opposition would be forthcoming—advice which, far from discouraging him, filled him with pride and new hope. For he alone had written the brief, had it typed up by a fellow prisoner in the front office, and mailed it in—and the United States Federal District Court had paid attention to him, and had ordered an assistant attorney general to study his points and to reply to them. Sooner or later a judge of that court would read both his appeal and the Brief in Opposition, and, if Alfredo's argument had merit, would have him brought down to New York City and give him a hearing as to whether the State of New York had or had not been wrongfully depriving him of liberty.

With this kind of hope, he and Carlos were able to survive after all. The attorneys general and judges who decry the lack of finality in present-day criminal law ought to meet and talk to people like Alfredo and Carlos Ortiz, to learn what finality means to them: not just a legal nicety, and a convenience for courts and prosecutors, but a form of psychic execution, killing the spirit and letting the body live on.

# Epilogue

## 1  Two Stories Without Endings

*Seven and a half years have passed since Alexander Helmer lay dying on the floor of his kitchen in a puddle of his thin old blood, and nearly six years have passed since Alfredo Ortiz and Carlos Ortiz, having been convicted of participating in Helmer's murder, were sentenced to life imprisonment. And how does the story end?*

*It would be neater, more satisfying, and more artistic if the story had an ending, but it does not. Helmer has long since been forgotten, or at least is almost never thought of by those who knew him, but the ultimate outcome for the Ortiz brothers is still in doubt. Though they have now been imprisoned for nearly a third of their lives and cannot be paroled until 1992 at the very earliest, they are far from resigned to their living death; both of them are pursuing their legal fight for freedom, and will be actively appealing their convictions for years. The odds may be against them, but the ending of the story is far from certain.*

More than ten years have passed since the rapid rise in violent crime began to tear apart the fabric of American urban life, nearly five years have passed since the Crime Commission published its sweeping program for fighting crime, nearly four years since a bipartisan congressional majority, ignoring many of the Commission's progressive recommendations, enacted the conservative, police-oriented 1968 Omnibus Crime Control and Safe Streets Act, and over three years since Richard M. Nixon, blaming the Supreme Court, Attorney General Ramsey Clark, and liberals in general for being soft on criminals, promised to restore law and order to this nation, and won the Presidency. And how does the story end?

One cannot yet say, although daily we hear dire prophecies that the ending is imminent and catastrophic. Many Middle Americans and conservatives bitterly complain that criminals no longer fear the law, that the police are shackled by the courts, that the entire criminal justice system is about to collapse, and that our society is in desperate peril. Many liberals and radicals, too, say that the criminal justice system is collapsing and that American society is moribund, but blame the imbalance of privilege and power; they find the police more vicious and uncontrolled than ever, prosecutors, judges, and juries hopelessly prejudiced against the poor (especially the non-white poor), and prisons mere dumping-grounds in which a corrupt ruling class enslaves and torments those it has made criminals.

As far apart as the two views are, both foresee the early decline and fall of American society. Apocalyptic prophecies, however, have rarely been high in predictive accuracy, and perhaps will prove wrong in this instance, too, for there are some in this country who, though actively participating in the fight against crime, are at the same time deeply committed to preserving and even extending our classic freedoms—believing, indeed, that the two things are related rather than opposed. If they are correct, and if their courage does not fail, it is possible that they will prove the prophets of doom to be wrong.

## 2   The Growth of Crime and the Decline of American Cities

ALTHOUGH the ending is not certain, it seems quite clear that unless the growth of violent crime is arrested and reversed, life in large American cities will soon degenerate into something like that in the most ungoverned and lawless parts of medieval Paris or Visigothic Rome. The wealthy and the upper middle class will live in fortified enclaves protected by private guards, virtually never venturing out after dark or daring, even by day, to travel through many parts of the city. The rest of the middle class and most blue-collar workers, however, will abandon the residential areas of the cities to poor non-whites, who will live in festering slums, unemployed or unemployable, state-supported but only marginally surviving, preyed upon by uncontrollable bands of criminals, and growing ever more alienated from American culture and more inclined to listen to the revolutionary voices among them. Crime is only one of the massive problems besetting America today, but it alone, if it continues to increase at the rate it has in the last decade, will soon debilitate and distort our society beyond recognition.

It is reassuring, therefore, to keep hearing from our government of the swift and striking success of the Nixon Administration's fight against crime. In June 1970, only a year and a half after President Nixon was inaugurated, there came the following glad tidings from the Department of Justice:

> Attorney General John N. Mitchell announced today that the FBI's Uniform Crime Reports show that the rate of increase of violent crimes in the first three months of 1970 slowed down by 7 percent in the major cities of the nation. . . . In the 58 cities with populations of 250,000 persons or more, the rise in violent

crimes slowed down from 17 percent in the first three months of 1969 over 1968 to 10 percent for the first three months of 1970, as compared with the first three months of 1969—a 7 percent drop.

Again in January 1971 Mr. Mitchell indicated that the Nixon Administration was winning its war against crime, and in September he said with pride that "the decelerating rate of increase provided a basis for cautious optimism." In plain words, there had been no decrease in the total amount of crime, and not even in the crime rate; there had been only a decrease in the speed with which the rate was rising. Things were getting a lot worse, but a little more slowly; such was the achievement of which Mr. Mitchell was speaking.

The fact is that for the past several years the total amount of crime has increased substantially, and by roughly the same amount every year, despite the implementation of the 1968 Omnibus Crime Control Act and despite the law-and-order policies of the Nixon Administration. Total serious crimes known to the police, for instance, as compiled in the *Uniform Crime Reports* of the FBI, were as follows:

| Year | Total Serious Crimes Known to Police | Increase over Previous Year |
|------|-------------------------------------|------------------------------|
| 1967 | 3,802,300 | 538,100 |
| 1968 | 4,466,600 | 664,300 |
| 1969 | 4,989,700 | 523,100 |
| 1970 | 5,568,200 | 578,500 |

It is in order to obscure this inconvenient truth that Mr. Mitchell has concentrated upon the yearly rate of increase, for that rate is derived by dividing the year's actual increase into the previous year's total; if the actual increase each year is roughly constant, while the previous year's total is ever larger, the *rate* of increase will go down—an arithmetical victory, but hardly a real one.

Even more to the point, not only is crime continuing to increase rapidly, but the most feared kind of crime—robbery—is increasing more rapidly than most other kinds. While the total amount of crime increased 11 percent in 1970, robberies increased 17 percent; in the first half of 1971, although preliminary FBI data show only a 7 percent overall increase in crime—the first faintly hopeful sign—robberies increased by 14 percent. Whatever the Nixon Administration's fight against crime in general has achieved thus far, it has made relatively little headway against crimes of violence, and practically none against muggings and other robberies, the very type of crime most destructive of peaceful urban life.

The major emphasis of the 1968 Crime Control Act, and of the Nixon Administration's war on crime, has been on the strengthening of the nation's police forces through money grants for the acquisition of modern equipment, improved tactical training, higher pay scales, and through augmented powers to investigate and arrest suspects. Not only has this done little to slow down the rise in violent crime, but it has done virtually nothing to increase police effectiveness in solving crimes of all sorts; in 1968, throughout the nation, police cleared 21 percent of all serious crimes, in 1969, 20 percent and in 1970, 20 percent. In the larger cities, taken as a group, the crime clearance rate did rise very slightly in 1970, which was hopeful— but the rate of violent crimes rose substantially, which was not, for the net result was that more violent crimes than ever were being committed, and going unsolved and unpunished. In the majority of smaller cities, the situation actually worsened during 1970: the rate of violent crime rose considerably but the rate of clearance declined—often sharply—as small, unsophisticated police forces found themselves confronted by a phenomenon new and unfamiliar to them.*

The result of all this was that in most American cities the quality of everyday life continued to deteriorate. In New York, Buffalo, St. Louis, and a number of other cities, residents of various public housing projects were terrorized by endemic uncontrolled muggings, armed robberies, stabbings, and shootings. In Detroit, Newark, and Los Angeles, among others, plywood boarding and cinder block were becoming the prevalent styles of storefront architecture in poor and marginal districts, and on fashionable streets many merchants were keeping their front doors locked all day, opening them only when respectable-looking potential customers knocked. In Chicago, Philadelphia, and Washington, to name but a few cities, people were going downtown

---

* Preliminary data for the first half of 1971 showed no significant slowdown in the rate of increase of violent crime: although, unaccountably, cities between 500,000 and 1,000,000 had no overall increase, all other categories of cities, both larger and smaller, had increases ranging from 12 to 15 percent, far outstripping their rises in property crimes. (Data on crime clearance rates in 1971 were not available as of this writing.)

less and less often at night, and in many residential neighborhoods were venturing out as little as possible after dark. In September 1971 a commission set up by the National Urban Coalition, a private organization seeking to stem the decay of American cities, reported a general worsening in those "corrosive and degrading" conditions in urban slums that breed civil disorder and crime. The commission, headed by Mayor John Lindsay of New York and Democratic Senator Fred R. Harris of Oklahoma, visited a number of major cities and gathered information on many others; it found the rates of crime, unemployment, disease, and heroin addiction higher than in 1968, welfare rolls larger, housing still a "national scandal," schools more tedious and more turbulent, relations between the police and minority communities generally hostile, and the flight of the white middle class to the suburbs unchecked. If the trend continued, the commission concluded, "most cities by 1980 will be preponderantly black and brown, and totally bankrupt."

But who can blame the middle class for fleeing? Every day one hears of ever worsening levels of violence as the criminal norm. More robbers carry guns and more shoot their victims—not only if there is resistance, but sometimes even if the victim hesitates for a moment. Muggers bludgeon or stab their victims more often than before, and mere children of twelve, ten, and even eight operate in gangs, often armed with knives, mugging other children and even adults. As if to publicize the boldness of the enemy and the weakness of society's defenses in 1971, two New York prostitutes mugged West German Defense Minister Franz Josef Strauss late at night directly in front of the Plaza Hotel—in as safe a part of downtown Manhattan as there is—within a day of the fatal stabbing of an Italian industrialist by another prostitute and her pimp in front of the Hilton Hotel, also in a seemingly safe part of the city. And this was three years after the Congress of the nation passed a law designed to make the streets safe again, and two months after Attorney General Mitchell began to speak with pride of the Administration's initial successes in its war against crime.

*Visit Melrose, in the Bronx, if you would see it all in miniature. The streets are dirtier and more garbage-littered than ever, and more storefronts are boarded up or kept locked behind steel gates all day. Groups of indolent youths hang around on the front stoops, and on certain street-corners they congregate at regular times of the day, jittery and wild-eyed, waiting for the regular visit of the pusher; he comes, deals out his little packages in a doorway, and they disappear into cellars, burned-out buildings, and alleyways. People coming home in the late afternoon hurry along the streets, furtively glancing to one side or another, like medieval travelers in some dark wood infested by cutthroat bandits; at their own buildings, they duck inside, quickly unlock their doors and enter, slam them shut and bolt themselves in for the night with a sigh of relief. In 1964 there were 94 murders and some 700 muggings in the Bronx; in 1971 there were close to 300 murders and 7,000 muggings.*

*On Melrose Avenue near 155th Street a hardbitten white shopkeeper unburdens himself to a visitor: "The way the junkies infest this area, nobody can walk down the street at night. If it wasn't for the pushers, they'd be so strung out you couldn't walk the streets even by day. The cops bust a few of the junkies and the street sellers, but they leave the real dealers alone because they're all paid off. The politicians talk big about doing something about drugs, but they don't really give a shit; all they want is the publicity. The people around here get screwed every which way. But I got no sympathy for them either—they aren't worth pissing on. They wouldn't dream of working as long as they can get welfare, they throw the garbage out of their windows into their own backyards, they let their kids run around in the streets all hours of the night, they drink themselves stupid and get into knife fights—and then they tell everybody it's all the Man's fault, he's making them live this way. Around here, mankind's going down the drain. Dogs are more decent than what lives in Melrose and calls itself human."*

*A few blocks to the north, at 160th Street and Melrose Avenue, Mrs. Ambos' building looks much the same as always; it is a small rock of respectability, almost inundated by the high tide of decay. But a number of the tenants who were living there in 1964, including two of Helmer's neighbors on the third floor, have moved away, and others are trying to follow suit. Everyone who remains has either been mugged or knows someone who has been. Mrs. Ambos, frailer and drier than ever, was mugged three times in the past three years—once in her own lobby by a seventeen-year-old black girl who held a knife against her throat, and twice on the street by black boys no more than twelve years old. She is bitter about the lack of sympathy the city's political leaders seem to have for the problems of the victims. "No-body goes out at night," she says, "ve don't have a chance to live the right vay—unt the police is not allowed to do notting! This Mayor of ours, he stopped the police from doing anyt'ing to the Negroes unt the Spanish. The President, vot did he do yet to let the police go? I tell you somet'ing—if the cops vould take their sticks unt give a good beating to these lousy kids the first time they do somet'ing wrong, they vouldn't do it a second time. But nobody does notting for the vhite folks—only they do for the others."*

*Across Melrose Avenue, in the decrepit tenement at 406 East 160th Street, where Luisa Pomales and her three children used to live, almost no one remembers them now. Alfredo and Carlos last walked these streets in mid-October 1964 and have not been seen since. Luisa Pomales sent her daughter, Maria, back to Puerto Rico shortly after her sons were arrested, and moved away from the apartment a few weeks later; she lived in sleazy furnished rooms in Melrose for some time in order to be close to her sons, but after they were shipped off to Auburn she found life in the Bronx meaningless, and three years ago returned to Puerto Rico. She has never remarried, but lives a widow-like existence with her elderly mother in the village of Guayama, does odd jobs to earn a little money, visits her daughter and baby grandson often, occasionally writes to her convict sons, and last year, with money she had saved over a two-year period, traveled all night by plane and bus to visit them for a few hours. Though she is still in her forties, she says that since 1966, when her sons were convicted, her life has been no more than a slow dying.*

*Both of the Ortiz brothers' former friends and co-defendants have been hanging around Melrose these last years—except when they have been in jail, which has been fairly often. Doel Valencia successfully avoided entanglements with the law for a couple of years after his release, but in 1969 and 1970 he was arrested and booked at the 42nd Precinct on three different occasions for various drug offenses, including possession of drugs and works, and loitering for purposes of obtaining drugs; two of these arrests resulted in jail sentences of two months and three months respectively. In early 1971, he was arrested again in another Bronx precinct and charged with the criminal possession of stolen property; as of this writing, there had been no final disposition of the charge. Doel has not called upon his sister, Idalia, for help in these encounters with the law; indeed, he and she have hardly seen each other in recent years. She lives in Manhattan and would prefer to forget the past; occasionally, however, she talks to one of her other brothers or sisters, who tell her that Doel is married, has a child, is working, and is "doing just fine." With so many recent clashes with the law to worry about, it is unlikely that Doel has given much thought of late to the Helmer case, although he was never acquitted of that charge. Within the past year a young assistant D.A. in the Bronx looked into the matter of reopening the case, concluding that it was possible but not very promising, for legal reasons; in all likelihood, nothing more will ever be done about it.*

*Angel Walker has been in even more trouble than Valencia. After the dismissal of charges against him in the Helmer case, he was arrested and convicted on a drug charge and spent over half a year in jail, emerging in August 1966. In 1968 he was arrested again, this time in Manhattan, for possession of drugs and works, and later that year he was booked at the 42nd Precinct in the Bronx for grand larceny and possession of burglar's tools; both times, however, he escaped being sentenced. In 1969 he was not so lucky: he was arrested twice in the Bronx on drug charges, and was sentenced in May 1970 to an indefinite jail term. Released after a couple of months, he was arrested in September, again on narcotics charges, and sentenced to ninety days. There were no additions to his record in 1971, but it seems likely that he will come to the attention of the police again and again. One imagines that Alfredo and Carlos would make something very different of the liberty that Walker seems incapable of using to advantage; one supposes that they would make another kind of life for themselves, despite all obstacles, for each would think himself the happiest of men even in a ghetto slum, with black skin and only one arm, but free.*

# 3 Limited Successes of the Police Approach to Crime Control

As dark as the overall picture is, there are a few bright spots or at least gray ones; in 20 of the 154 American cities with populations of over 100,000, the number of serious crimes known to the police did not rise in 1970, and in some of the 20 showed perceptible decreases.* For the most part, however, decreases were minuscule, and in some cases they were due not to crime control but to population decline, a changed system of crime reporting, or a decrease in non-violent crime (such as auto thefts) that statistically offset the smaller but more serious increase in violent crime. Still, in a handful of the smaller, more manageable cities in the group there was an authentic, if modest, decrease in the volume and the rate of both non-violent and violent crimes, even though the volume and the rate of both had increased nearly everywhere else in the nation.†

The police-oriented approach to the war on crime embodied in the 1968 Omnibus Crime Control Act and in the legislative efforts of the Nixon Administration has been nationwide in application; one wonders why it has had some success in a handful of the larger cities but not in all the rest. *The New York Times* interviewed law-enforcement officers, elected officials, and other authorities in the cities that had shown significant decreases in crime, and correspondent John Herbers

---

* The 20: Berkeley, Cedar Rapids, Chicago, Cleveland, Columbia, S.C., Duluth, Flint, Fresno, Kansas City, Mo., Louisville, Oakland, Pittsburgh, Providence, Rockford, Ill., St. Louis, St. Paul, Savannah, Seattle, Washington, D.C., and Waterbury.

† Final data for 1971 were not available as of this writing, but preliminary reports indicate that a somewhat larger number of big cities showed marginal or modest decreases in reported crimes for the year. Again, however, population declines and other factors having nothing to do with crime control efforts appear to explain a number of these decreases.

reported that in most of these cities there had been not only substantial increases in the size of the police force, a new concentration of patrol activities in formerly shunned high-crime areas, and the modernization of police technology and equipment, but improved training and broadened education of the police, and new or expanded programs designed to improve relationships between the police and the residents of ghettos.

In Reading, Pennsylvania,* for instance, among other tactical advances were the assignment of special platoons to patrol high-crime areas at night, and the inauguration of a telephone police-watch system that would automatically alert the police to suspicious noises in empty houses. But of equal or perhaps greater importance were psychology courses and a program of sensitivity training given the members of the police force, and an expansion of community-relations activities to create close contacts between them and neighborhood groups.

In certain other cities, including Flint, Michigan, authorities told the *Times* that while federal grants to the police force had been helpful, social-service programs owing nothing to the 1968 Crime Control Act had been of equal or greater importance. In some instances where there had been a considerable expansion of the police force, a major increase in police salaries, and the large-scale acquisition of modern equipment, but no psychological retraining or community-relations programs, the crime reduction was trifling. In Chicago, for one, police pay is high, equipment plentiful, and manpower is 30 percent greater than a few years ago, but the decrease in crime in 1970 amounted to only three tenths of one percent. Nowhere did the *Times* find a significant decrease attributed primarily to tougher police behavior; the overall impression was that higher pay, more men, special patrols, and better equipment were all helpful, but particularly if combined with the development of a more cooperative relationship between police and the population of crime-ridden areas.

This concept has only begun to spread. In the great majority of American cities and towns, the police are still trained and still behave much as in recent years, but in a certain number of the larger cities, where the crime problem is most acute, mayors, city managers, and police chiefs are trying to develop rapport between their police forces

---

* Not one of the 20, its population being a little under 100,000; it did show a notable decrease in crime, however, and was included in the *Times* survey.

and the kinds of people who live in high-crime areas and hate the police, but are themselves severely victimized by the criminals in their midst. Some police academies are giving courses designed to broaden and humanize the police mentality, and to create an understanding of minority-group mores. A few police forces are now making college education a requirement for promotion, or even for appointment to the ranks. Some commanding officers are beginning to impose controls on patrolmen and detectives in the effort to stop illegal practices and summary punishments. A few police leaders are contacting ghetto organizations and offering better protection from criminals in return for cooperation and assistance in place of the traditional hostility toward the police. Some are making greater efforts to enlist Negroes, Mexican-Americans, and other minority-group members in their forces and to use them prominently in ghetto areas.

From the limited evidence available, one can reasonably conclude that new police technology, increased manpower, and better pay all help somewhat, and that programs designed to create good relationships between the police and minority groups may help as much, and eventually even more. And one can hope that liberalized education and training of the police, and the reshaping of the police mentality, will eventually help most of all.

But thus far the police-oriented approach to crime control has yielded only modest reductions of the crime rate, and only in a few of the smaller and more stable cities in the over-100,000 group. It seems indisputable that the police approach—particularly in its larger and more liberal sense—is an essential element of the fight against crime, but is only a minor part of what it will take to win that fight.

*It seems very likely, too, that in every police force the Old Guard will resent most efforts to educate them psychologically, socially, and legally, and will stubbornly resist every move to regulate their power over suspects, troublemakers, minority-group members, and anyone they happen to dislike. At least it is so in New York City, where the relatively new Police Commissioner, Patrick V. Murphy, a liberal and an intellectual, has rapidly won the enmity of a considerable part of his huge police force because of his socially progressive reforms, his all-out drive against corruption, and his efforts to make the Police Department a more nearly open and public institution. Many detectives of the old school, for instance, are angered by Commissioner Mur-*

*phy's restructuring of the detective division: the all-purpose, semi-independent detective squads in the station houses were abolished on January 1st, 1972, and nearly all detective personnel were reassigned to expert squads, each of which specializes in one category of serious crime and within which the men work under close supervision by their commanding officers. Meanwhile, precinct patrolmen have been given the responsibility of investigating many of the lesser crimes that were formerly the exclusive province of the detectives. This system, which began to go into effect during the latter half of 1971, has pleased some of the younger and more gifted detectives, but created fierce resentment in others, who find in it a serious threat to their autonomy and their élite status.*

*Detective Salvatore Russo is one of those who have been troubled by both the changing nature of the police role in society and by the specific organizational changes within the New York Police Department. "I can't think of anything I would rather do than be a detective," he said to an acquaintance not long ago, "but the conditions that prevail today are getting hard to take. The pay and fringe benefits are fine, but the policeman has become a target for abuse such as I never saw before. Politicians make us out to be the bad guys, because the balance of political power in New York today is Negro and Puerto Rican and it's easy to please them by attacking the cops. You go to a demonstration and people spit on you and throw things at you, and you have to take it. You go to court and get all sorts of verbal abuse, and the judges tell you that it's just one of your occupational hazards. You go to a party, and as soon as people hear that you're a cop, they jump all over you. You continually have to justify yourself and explain yourself, even to old friends. People just don't seem to have respect for the police any more."*

*Besides these general reasons for disaffection with his work, Russo had for some time felt painfully handicapped by recent developments in criminal law. "You have a homicide, say, and there's no evidence, but you're lucky enough to find some guys the murderer talked to about it, so you go out and track him down, and bring him in and sit him down. And then you have to give him* Miranda—*and after he's heard that, you think he's going to tell you anything? Or maybe he says he'll talk, but only if a lawyer is present—but once a lawyer gets there, forget it! They say it's necessary because there used to be many abuses in the past, but in the long run I don't think it's protecting the good people; it's only protecting the bad ones." And with a doleful shake of the head, he concluded, "I still love doing my job, and doing it to the best of my ability, but if I were a young guy contemplating coming on the Force today, I would never do it. It just isn't what it used to be."*

*Indeed, for a while he halfheartedly thought of looking for another job—he was well beyond the minimum time needed for a half-pay pension—and told friends that if the right thing came along, he would quit the Force and take it. But if the right thing had come along, leaving the Force would not have been easy: it would have meant saying good-by to everything that has given him his identity and his sense of achievement. Fortunately for him, he was spared that trauma: in December 1971 he accepted an invitation to become a member of the Bronx District Attorney's Office Squad. There, although still a detective and still a member of the Police Department, he has a considerable amount of freedom in his investigations of crimes about which citizens have made complaints directly to the District Attorney rather than the police; for the time being, this has made him content to remain on the Force.*

*His old friend and colleague, Stephen McCabe, has had to take more drastic steps to adapt to the changing situation. More than a year ago McCabe confidentially told a friend that he was not going to stay on past his twentieth year on the Force. "It's a jungle, it's worse than ever," he said. "The Force is going downhill, the detective division is finished. My main desire was always to make a good collar, to be a hero, and I didn't give a damn how hard I had to work to do it, but the younger guys coming in now want to put in their eight hours and go home. And the reorganization of the detective division is going to ruin the old camaraderie between the boss and his men. He always let you do a lot on your own, you were your own man, you had responsibility. But now it will all be different, you'll have somebody on your back all the time, you won't have the independence, you won't be respected and looked up to. I've always taken pride in what I do, but not any more. I'm getting out."*

*He did; he found himself a job as Supervising Investigator in the Hudson County Prosecutor's Office, and resigned from the New York Police Department in March 1971. In his new job McCabe does not investigate crimes himself, but supervises the detectives of fourteen small police forces in a dozen New Jersey communities. He has been teaching them something about up-to-date laboratory techniques and sophisticated investigative procedures, and making sure that their cases are complete and watertight before they go to court. "It's not a bad job," he says, striving to muster some show of enthusiasm. "It's okay, it's challenging in its way. Of course, there's not too much action—they only run around sixty homicides a year in all of Hudson County. And I guess I miss the Force—I miss the guys, the contacts, the fellowship. And, of course, the excitement of investigating cases myself. . . . Still, the job was going down the drain, and I had to get out, because to be a detective you have to love your work, you have to feel you're really* doing *something—and if they take that away from you, it isn't worth it."*

---

## 4  The Fear of Crime and the State of American Democracy

---

BY the late 1960s the mounting fear of crime had, as we saw earlier, led to a widespread resentment of the recent Supreme Court decisions in the field of criminal law, and to a mood of vigilantism that encouraged attacks upon the constitutional rights the Warren Court had sought to make the states respect. Many of the attacks were no more than verbal fireworks shot off by persons in public office to please their constituents, but others, including a number of the bills merged in the 1968 Omnibus Crime Control and Safe Streets Act, were serious attempts to counteract the Supreme Court decisions and to weaken and create exceptions to constitutional guarantees that had been sacrosanct since the ratification of the Bill of Rights in 1791.

Although it should have been clear by 1970 that the 1968 Crime Control Act, focusing upon financial aid to police forces and seeking to undercut *Miranda* and the Fifth Amendment, had not halted the growth of violent crime throughout the nation, the general public was more terrified and angry than ever, and more eager for tougher assaults upon the civil rights of criminals. Members of Congress in that election year knew which way the wind was blowing, and bent with it: not only the Nixon Republicans but less conservative members of that party and most Democrats, including many well-known liberals, talked about the need for law-and-order legislation during the campaign and made good their talk by voting—some eagerly, some reluctantly—in favor of two thoroughly repressive, police-oriented, prosecution-favoring bills before Congress.

One was the bill, proposed by the Nixon Administration, that sought to combat crime in the District of Columbia by various means, including a number of daring infringements upon due process and other constitutional guarantees. The District of Columbia is governed directly by Congress, and the D.C. Crime Bill therefore exposed to public view the stance of every Senator and Representative on the issue of crime control versus civil rights; it was impossible for anyone to duck it, especially since the Administration touted the bill as a model of crime-control legislation that could be copied by every major city in the nation. Among the extraordinary provisions of the bill was the first preventive-detention statute in the nation—a direct attack on the right to bail—and a "no knock" proviso under which police could, without warning, forcibly enter places where they suspected crimes were being committed—an attack on the right to be secure in one's person and house; in addition, the bill deprived many juvenile delinquents of the right to jury trial, broadened the power of the police to use wiretaps, and made life sentences mandatory upon conviction of a third felony. A handful of stalwart liberals fought the bill doggedly, but under election pressures most of the liberal contingent joined conservatives in backing it, and in July, with the election only a little over three months away, bipartisan coalitions in both the House and the Senate passed the bill by solid majorities.

By fall, in fact, almost everyone running for office was making law-and-order pronouncements of some kind and even those who had always talked of attacking the deep-lying social causes of crime were assuring voters that they were willing to crack down on offenders. Few of them dared to offer more than token opposition to the Nixon Administration's big crime proposal of the year—an omnibus bill aimed at combating organized crime and including many useful features, but also incorporating numerous provisos which, while primarily aimed at the *Mafiosi,* infringed seriously upon the constitutional rights of all Americans. One such proviso invaded the Fifth Amendment by limiting a witness' immunity from prosecution, even if he had been granted immunity and thus compelled to testify, under threat of contempt of court; another established a five-year statute of limitations on a defendant's right to challenge certain kinds of illegally acquired evidence, thereby undercutting the Fourth Amendment; and another authorized federal judges to impose additional sentences of up to twenty-five years on "dangerous special offenders" on the basis of a special hearing rather than a jury trial, thereby sidestepping due process and the protections of adversarial procedure.

For a while the bill was stalled in the House Judiciary Committee, whose chairman, Representative Emanuel Celler, and other liberal members felt that it incorporated clearly unconstitutional and repressive features. But as law-and-order pressure mounted during the campaign season, the bill was finally forced out and brought to the House floor, where it was passed overwhelmingly by a 341–to–26 vote. The Senate, not to be outdone, accepted it by voice vote, and it was shortly signed into law by a jubilant President Nixon three weeks before the election.

Of perhaps greater significance in the long run than his legislative achievements was the President's great good luck in having two vacancies to fill on the Supreme Court early in his Administration, one created by the retirement of Earl Warren, the other by the resignation, under fire, of Abe Fortas. Mr. Nixon, who had made a campaign pledge to change the liberal doctrines of the Supreme Court by appointing "strict constructionists" to any available seats, did indeed fill both vacancies with men of distinctly conservative leanings—Warren E. Burger, the new Chief Justice, and Harry Blackmun, a new Associate Justice, both of whom, where criminal law was concerned, were basically prosecution-oriented. Blackmun did not join the Court until some time after Burger became Chief Justice, but as soon as he did, it became clear that a narrow conservative majority now existed on the Court that would produce decisions consonant with the Administration's philosophy of crime control, and would not be loath to unravel the work of the previous dozen years.

In the first year with two Nixon appointees on the bench, that five-to-four majority held that co-conspirator testimony was admissible under certain conditions, even when the co-conspirator could not be cross-examined; this partly eroded the protection granted by *Bruton*. Later that year the same majority held that a statement obtained by the police without first giving the *Miranda* warning could be used in court if the defendant decided to take the stand, a decision which, Justice Brennan wrote in his dissent, "goes far toward undoing much of the progress made in conforming police methods to the Constitution." Other decisions in the same year narrowed the protection against double jeopardy, weakened the right to challenge one's own guilty plea as having been fear-induced, and limited the immunity of Grand Jury witnesses.

The Court was clearly leaning in the conservative direction, and sounding far more prosecution-oriented and far less inclined to stress constitutional rights than had been the case for a dozen years. And then in September 1971 came a startling development: the retirement —and death, a week later—of Justice Hugo L. Black, a notably liberal member of the Court, and the retirement of Justice John M. Harlan, generally (though not invariably) a conservative. From the first moment, White House hints made it clear that the President would seek to fill the vacancies with two more judicial conservatives. Very shortly President Nixon named his choices: Lewis F. Powell, a prominent lawyer and Southern conservative, and U.S. Assistant Attorney General William Rehnquist, a right-wing Republican who on every civil-liberties issue—wiretapping, electronic surveillance, no-knock entry, preventive detention, the rights of witnesses before congressional committees, mass arrests, and the rights of the accused—had already shown himself to be a militant conservative with little patience or respect for the niceties of the Bill of Rights. President Nixon, making these nominations, said, "As a judicial conservative, I believe some Court decisions have gone too far in the past in weakening the peace forces as against the criminal forces in our society." The implicit equating of police and prosecutorial power with peace, and of civil rights and due process with crime, was skillful demagoguery; by enlisting the fears and desires that block intelligent thought, Mr. Nixon had his way. There was no liberal resistance to Powell, only faint-hearted opposition to Rehnquist, and by January 1972 the Supreme Court had four Nixonian appointees (only four presidents since Washington have filled as many or more seats); Mr. Nixon would for long years to come be leaving his imprint upon, and wielding a continuing influence over, the entire criminal justice system and the American conception of justice.

*It is too soon, however, for the assistant district attorneys, the defense lawyers, and the judges working at the trial level in the Bronx (or elsewhere) to be much affected by these new influences. A dozen years' worth of evolution toward the Due Process Model of justice is not swiftly undone by legal methods, even with a law-and-order coalition in Congress and a conservative majority in the Supreme Court. Thus far the two omnibus crime laws and the decisions of the Burger Court have made relatively little difference in the day-to-day practices of the lawyers who prosecute and defend persons accused of crime, and the judges who govern the proceedings. The major difference, at this juncture, consists not so much of concrete procedural changes as of a subtle new attitude filtering down from above, making judges and juries somewhat more prosecution-minded and somewhat less inclined to lean over backward to observe every nicety of due process.*

*Prosecutors themselves, being the beneficiaries of the new attitude, are apt to consider it no more than their due; indeed, many of them feel that the balance is still far too much against them and too much in favor of the defendants. Alexander Scheer, for instance, still talks as if the prosecution were under continuing attack by recent developments in the law. As he puts it, "The burdens on the shoulders of the People in presenting their cases are much heavier than years ago, much heavier. Every one of my cases takes far longer than it used to—there are line-up hearings, and Miranda hearings, and Huntley hearings, and disclosure proceedings before you even get to trial, and any number of other obstacles to the presentation of the People's case that didn't use to exist. I've been a trial man all my life, and in all modesty I can say I think I've been doing an excellent job, but it's far harder to do an excellent job these days than it used to be." He even talks about retiring and going into private practice, but in truth not so much because the burdens of the prosecution are weighing heavily upon him as because he has been on the staff long enough to retire on pension. Besides, the atmosphere around him is no longer as congenial as it once was: there are more than twice as many assistant D.A.s in the office now as there were in 1964, and many of them are young men and women appointed by Bronx D.A. Burton Roberts on the basis of merit rather than political service; most of them are idealistic and somewhat civil-rights-minded, and have little in common with Scheer or he with them. But finding the right spot in a law firm after trying murder cases for many years is not easy, and for the time being he is still in the same office and still busily trying murder cases; woe betide the unlucky defendant whom he prosecutes, for he is, as always, a dogged, relentless, and formidable representative of the People of Bronx County.*

*James Hanrahan, still operating out of his seedy storefront office in Spanish Harlem, is keeping busy with his small-time, Spanish-speaking clientele, and maintains that thus far he has felt no impact of the events in far-off Washington. But perhaps he is being less than candid, for other defense lawyers tell a somewhat different story. Kenneth Kase, for one, says, "There is definitely a different feeling in the courts these days. It's not anything directly connected with the specific decisions of the Burger Court, it's the fact that the lower courts, anticipating that the higher courts are going to be stricter with defendants in their rulings, are getting a bit tighter themselves. It's nothing you can really put your finger on—it's just a general attitude you can sense." But he admits that even while things are tightening up in some ways, in other ways they are still getting easier: these days, for instance, he can get almost any client out on bail or released on recognizance pending hearings and trial, and in general, he says, "The defense has a far better shake than it did seven or eight years ago, when I was defending Doel Valencia." But the liberal trend has had an adverse affect on Kase's practice: although he now has handsome offices at 56th Street and Madison Avenue in Manhattan, the volume of criminal work available to him has decreased considerably (he has taken up the slack with divorce cases), because the city has increasingly provided defendants with free counsel through the Legal Aid Society. "I still get my share of assignments and private cases," he says, "but a big shift has taken place over the past five years, and especially over the last two or three. The typical criminal defendant has learned that all he has to do is say he can't pay and he gets Legal Aid right away. As far as I can see, the private practice of criminal law will never again be what it was."*

*Or at least not at the middle and lower levels. But for those lawyers able to attract high-paying clients, the nature of criminal practice has not changed. Herbert Siegal, at any rate, continues to carry a heavy load of active cases, most of them involving murder, robbery, or the large-scale packaging and wholesaling of drugs, and says he has had no loss of business: "Legal Aid takes the lower-strata cases and some of the lower end of the middle, but if you handle only the top, it doesn't affect you." As for the balance of power between the People and the defendant, he feels there has not yet been any notable change.*

*Quite recently, in fact, he won a reversal in a heroin-packaging case on the ground that an illegal use of wiretapping was involved, and another, in a case involving the private exchange of obscene films through the mails, on the ground that such an exchange is protected by the First Amendment. "But now that Nixon has four of his people on the Court," says Siegal, "there's going to be quite a change in what comes down to us. In a few years there may not be very much protection left against search and seizure, or self-incrimination, or the use of illegally acquired evidence. It won't be nice to see."*

*One who will not have to see it is Justice William Lyman: he died a couple of years after sentencing the Ortiz brothers to life imprisonment. Justice Irwin Davidson, however, who presided over their Huntley hearing and their first trial, is still on the bench and as brisk and firm-handed as ever. He may have his own opinions as to what is happening to the balance between the rights of society and those of the defendant, but declines to state them publicly. "It would be highly improper for me," he says, "to comment as to whether the appellate courts are, or are not, getting less solicitous about the defendant's rights. I am guided and controlled in my decisions by the appellate courts, and it is for them to tell me what they expect, not for me to comment on them." But from other remarks of his, it seems that he sees no particular cause for alarm about the state of criminal justice. "I can tell you this," he says sententiously, "—the administration of justice has become very enlightened, as compared to twenty-two years ago when I first sat on the bench. The care with which criminal justice is administered is definitely far greater than it used to be." But what of the future? He is unworried: "I would say that many of the enlightened approaches that have come about in the last decade or so in the criminal law are here to stay." Many; not all. And whether this is reason to be worried or unworried depends upon which side of the bench one is seated on.*

# 5   *The Growing Fairness of the American Criminal Justice System*

WHILE right-wing conservatives and Middle Americans regard our criminal justice system as too soft on criminals and as protective of the bad people at the expense of the good ones, many liberals and nearly all radicals consider it repressive and unfair to the poor, to minorities, and to political dissenters, especially those of the left. Indeed, some liberals and many radicals consider our criminal justice system a police-state mechanism cynically used by the ruling élite to dominate the lower classes and ethnic and racial minorities.

But even if one grants that the system is frequently repressive and unfair, the real question is to what extent this is intentional and was designed into the system, and to what extent it is the unplanned by-product of the huge increase in crime and of the simultaneous eruption of the poor and the non-white minorities into self-aware political activity.

A strong case could be made that the latter factors are far more to blame, and, moreover, that they have made us painfully aware of the system's defects but forgetful of the very considerable progress made in recent years toward the equal treatment of all classes and races. In principle, our criminal justice system has long been the most deeply committed, among those of the civilized nations, to the ideal of due process, and in recent years we have gone far toward embodying that principle in practice. Thus far, the Nixon Administration has not yet brought about a significant retreat either in principle or practice. Here, for instance, are but a few of the solid gains of recent years:

—The imposition of much of the Bill of Rights upon the states by the Supreme Court remains very largely intact. *Mapp, Gideon, Escobedo, Miranda, Jackson, Bruton,* and other foundation stones of the newly erected edifice of criminal justice still stand, only slightly chipped away, here and there, by the would-be demolishers.

—*Gideon* in particular has made a vast difference in the way state courts deal with indigent criminal defendants. In every state, every indigent person accused of a felony is now defended by a lawyer provided by the court at no cost to him. The same principle has been filtering down to the far broader substratum of misdemeanors: by 1971, the courts in at least 29 states were regularly appointing counsel for indigent misdemeanants. Granted all the well-known shortcomings of public-defender agencies and of Legal Aid societies, the poor are nevertheless getting a much fairer chance to defend themselves or to work out favorable pleas than ever before in our history or in the history of most other nations.

—The right to pre-trial disclosure—the right of the defendant to know ahead of time what evidence the prosecution intends to present against him—was considerably expanded by certain Supreme Court decisions of the late 1960s. Today, in every state, the defense has a right to know some categories of the prosecution's evidence beforehand, and in a few states, including New York, the right has been extended by state law to include nearly all of it.

—In a 1956 landmark decision (*Griffin* v. *Illinois*), the Supreme Court ruled that indigent persons convicted of felonies had to be given free trial transcripts if they chose to appeal their convictions. In December 1971 the Court extended this ruling to misdemeanor convictions, even in cases involving only fines.

—Despite the example of the District of Columbia Crime Bill and the urging of the Administration, no state legislature has yet adopted a preventive-detention statute. Even in crime-plagued New York where one was proposed, it was defeated; indeed, the new Criminal Procedure Law, which went into effect in New York in 1971, provides a number of significant additional protections for accused persons.

—Although convicted prisoners have long been deprived of nearly all their civil rights by custom and by statute, federal and state courts are beginning to reappraise the concept. In 1971 the Federal Court of Appeals, Second Circuit, held that prisoners could not be punished by state prison officials for expressing undesirable political views, and that prisoners could sue prison officials for violating their constitutional rights. In October 1971, Attorney General J. Shane Creamer of Pennsylvania announced that a "prisoners' Bill of Rights" had just been put into effect in that state: it consisted of a set of rules that assured virtually all the civil rights and living conditions for which prison reformers—and, recently, rebellious prisoners—have been fighting. Even inmates who have rioted are beginning to be treated more like citizens than formerly: at New York's Attica, after the historic riot in September 1971, prisoners were notified by officials that they had the right to have a lawyer present before answering state investigators' questions about the riot, and that the court would appoint one if they had no money. Also in late 1971 the U.S. Supreme Court ruled that a limited list of basic law books, in a California prison library, was not sufficient, in the case of indigent prisoners; the Court left it up to the state, however, to decide how to expand such prisoners' access to legal information.

—In 1971 the first significant moves were made to restore civil rights to parolees and ex-convicts. The American Bar Association established a Commission on Correctional Facilities and Services, a principal function of which was to spearhead a fight to repeal state and federal laws barring such persons from holding various kinds of jobs or obtaining certain kinds of licenses, security clearances, and other work prerequisites. In New York State, the Court of Appeals ruled that parolees had a constitutional right to have their lawyers present at hearings at which revocation of their parole was being considered. In the same year, a federal district court ruled that a federal parole board had violated the constitutional rights of former Soviet spy Morton Sobell when it forbade him, as a parolee, to participate in demonstrations of political dissent.

In a recent review of Artur London's memoir, *The Confession,* the distinguished legal scholar Professor Alan Dershowitz of the Harvard University Law School contrasted Communist-style justice with that of the United States and eloquently pleaded for a balanced view of American democracy and its criminal justice system. "We are undergoing a contraction of our civil liberties (or at least an end to the expansion accomplished in the middle sixties)," he wrote, but

> those of us who believe that the recently enacted "law and order" legislation trenches on important civil liberties must also acknowledge . . . that we are among the freest and least repressive societies in the world today and throughout history.

. . . We do need—and quite urgently in my view—more freedom, more liberty and more protection from governmental intrusion. But we must retain a sense of perspective about where we
are; we must not deceive ourselves—or permit others to deceive
us—into believing that we live under a totalitarian regime.

Saul Alinsky, the radical organizer of migrant workers, Chicanos,
blacks, and other underprivileged people, made the same point with
acerb simplicity not long ago: "Here's [Huey] Newton saying he
can't get justice in an American court," he snapped, "and all the time
he's saying that, he's out on reversal by a superior court."

*Mary Johnson Lowe frequently burns with indignation when she
considers the workings of the American criminal justice system as she
has experienced them. Only recently, for instance, she said that it was
the conviction of the Ortiz brothers that convinced her that the system
was basically unfair to the poor and the deprived. "That case was a
turning point in my thinking," she added. "I still believe those boys
were innocent—they'll be on my conscience all my life—but whether
they were or not, there was no proof whatever of robbery in Alfredo's
testimony, and it was absolutely wrong for him to be convicted of a
felony murder. And it was outrageously unfair to him and to Carlos to
try all three defendants together so that each one's confessions would
reinforce the others' in the minds of the jurors. I felt that if such a
thing could happen to them, it could happen to anybody; it was their
conviction that made me lose my belief that the system works for its
people." Nonetheless, until the end of 1971 she continued to defend
her clients—with more success than ever—often by methods that have
nothing to do with factual guilt or innocence but only with the requirements of due process; she continued to work within the system she
claimed she did not believe in, and to obtain justice, at least part of
the time, by adhering to its rules. "Sure I do," she said a trifle defen-
sively, some months ago. "I think the system's horrible, but if people
like me who have been trained in law don't try to do what they can
with their training, they're no good at all." If using her training succeeded in winning acquittals for her clients, didn't that mean that the
system works? "Once in a while," she admitted grudgingly, "but I'm
just sticking my finger in the dike."*

*Nevertheless, at some deeper level of thought and feeling she had enough regard for the system to be willing to become officially identi-fied with it. In late 1971 she narrowly missed being endorsed by the Democratic Party in the Bronx for a Supreme Court judgeship (an elective position), but a little later she was offered a spot on the Crim-inal Court (an appointive position) and eagerly accepted it. Mayor John Lindsay swore her in on December 31st, 1971, since when she has been not Mary Johnson Lowe, Esq., but the Honorable Mary Johnson Lowe, Judge of the Criminal Court, New York City.*

*Alfredo and Carlos Ortiz, whom she has not seen since June 1966, feel much the same disillusionment and bitterness that Mary Lowe has expressed—and much the same grudging belief in the capacity of the system to dispense justice. They are now young men—Carlos is twenty-five and Alfredo twenty-six—both of them still tiny, slim, and youthful-looking. They wear clean shirts, their pants are faultlessly creased, and their shoes are shined to a mirror-like finish. They pre-occupy themselves with such details by a way of self-administered therapy, but what keeps them truly alive in spirit is their belief that the machinery of the courts, if hand-cranked long enough, will even-tually follow its own built-in rules and set them free.*

*Carlos, despite his misgivings about the Legal Aid Society, has con-tinued to have it represent him. After the U.S. Supreme Court denied his petition for a writ of* certiorari, *he wrote to Julia Heit and begged her to continue to handle his case. For a long while she put off answer-ing him while she struggled with her conscience and with a dishearten-ing backlog of other cases on hand. ("Sometimes we don' get no mail for two-three months at a time," Carlos says, "an' that get us a little bit messed up in the head.") But after a year of indecision and several exchanges of letters with Carlos, she decided that his case had so much merit and his sentence was so severe that she had to fight it out to the absolute end. In July 1971 she filed a* habeas corpus *petition on his behalf in the Federal District Court, Southern District, asserting that the use of accomplice testimony in his trial had not been harmless error, and that, in consequence, it was illegal for the State of New York to continue to deprive him of his freedom.*

*The petition could—but almost certainly will not—result in an out-right reversal of his conviction; what is a little more likely is that it might result in a hearing before the judge (this in itself would be something of an achievement); and what is by far most probable, it could result in an affirmance of the conviction, which would be another—but not a final—defeat. But even if, after a hearing, the judge chose to grant a new trial, Carlos would not go free; instead, he would be returned to the Bronx to appear again in the County Courthouse, possibly facing Alexander Scheer once more. This time, however, he would be on trial by himself, with only his own confession available to the jury—and this, Julia Heit feels, would not be enough to convict him.*

*If, however, the judge affirmed Carlos' conviction after the hearing, Miss Heit would go on to appeal to the Second Circuit (the appellate level of the federal courts in the New York area), and if that, too, failed, she would then switch to a petition for a writ of certiorari. If that failed, she might at last feel that she had exhausted all reasonable avenues of relief and give up.*

*Meanwhile, Carlos still has faith—or at least hope—that these legal maneuvers will eventually free him, although he somewhat naïvely supposes that in order for Julia Heit to make the system operate for him, she must be convinced of something more important than the existence of prejudicial error in his trial; he has remarked that if she believes him to be actually innocent, she will fight harder for him. If her best efforts all fail, however, he trusts that his brother Alfredo will eventually gain freedom through legal action, and will then be able to get him out.*

*Alfredo, because of his pervasive suspicions about everyone who has ever sought to help him, is now relying upon his own ability to use the law to gain his freedom. Every lawyer he had ever had, he recently remarked, had made him empty promises—at least, none of their promises to see him freed had been made good. Now he had given up hoping for help from other people; he was relying on what he could do for himself by studying the law and using his knowledge to approach the courts on his own. In October 1970 he filed with the Federal District Court, Second District, an eleven-page habeas corpus petition he had written, which asked the court to grant him a hearing as to the legality of his arrest by Detective McCabe. The petition, and an Affidavit in Opposition written by an assistant attorney general of the state of New York, lay on the desk of Judge Constance Baker Motley for over a year, while Alfredo suffered endless agonies of waiting. But at last, in December 1971, Judge Motley read the petition and the affidavit, and decided that the matter did indeed deserve a hearing; Alfredo, alone and without help, had made the wheels of the federal courts move an inch. From then on, however, he would need technical help, and Judge Motley appointed a lawyer to represent him at the hearing. On December 30th, Alfredo—having been brought down to New York City from Auburn for the purpose—testified before Judge Motley, in a hearing room in the U.S. Courthouse, about the circumstances of his being taken to the Precinct by McCabe seven years earlier. McCabe and Russo were there, too, looking much as he had remembered them all these years but both of them a bit fleshier; they told their version of the story as smoothly and unhesitatingly as if it had all happened only weeks ago. Judge Motley reserved decision, and asked counsel for both sides to submit briefs before she came to any conclusions about the matter. Such was the state of affairs at the end of January 1972. Alfredo was still a long way from retrial and a longer way from freedom: even if Judge Motley were to order a retrial—which was by no means certain or even probable—Alfredo could expect the state to appeal her order and would have to fight that appeal. Yet it had become a trifle more possible that he might some day win retrial—and if he did, according to some of Scheer's colleagues, he might well be acquitted or even escape trial altogether. For if his trip to the Precinct were ruled an illegal arrest, his confession might well become inadmissible—and since, under the Criminal Procedure Law, the confessions of his co-defendants were insufficient to convict him, the People might have no case against him.*

*Whatever happens, Alfredo believes that the law will eventually work in his favor. Recently in a private interview at Auburn he explained the basis of this faith: "The system ain' bad, in itself. What makes things bad is the lower courts—they make plenty of errors, because the D.A. an' the police, sometimes they have nothin' to go in with, but the D.A. he don' want to cut nobody loose, so he more or less depends on trickery an' semantics, an' he's only doin' this to get another conviction. But if you have a legitimate beef an' it's a constitutional matter, you got a ninety percent chance to get into the federal courts an' get it corrected. An' in the United States Supreme Court, in ninety-nine percent of the cases where there is illegal arrest an' confession, they have corrected the errors of the lower courts." After a thoughtful pause, he concluded, "Like I say, the system ain' all bad, if you know how to make it work."*

# 6   *The Declining Efficiency of the American Criminal Justice System*

AND yet, even if the ethical heart of the system is beating strongly, all its other parts seem to be moribund. For, over and above the many criticisms of the philosophy and goals of the criminal justice system, from all sides there now comes a hailfire of complaints to the effect that the very machinery of the system is faltering and failing. Conservatives and Middle Americans, aiming their fire more at the courts and prisons than at the police, denounce the system for not preventing the commission of crimes, for not catching most of those who commit them, and, above all, for letting an unreasonable punctiliousness about the rights of criminals stand in the way of efficient crime-control. Many liberals and most radicals likewise criticize the system as being woefully inefficient and on the brink of collapse, but ascribe this to the class and racial prejudice of the police and their indifference to the crimes committed against the poor, the bureaucratic inefficiency of the courts and the callousness of prosecutors and judges toward poor defendants, and the vengeful correctional methods which further criminalize all prisoners—but especially the non-whites and the poor among them.

There is a mote of truth and a beam of untruth in the eyes on either side. The legal proprieties recently forced upon the police, prosecutors, and judges have undoubtedly made the job of arresting and convicting criminals more difficult; yet even in the past only a small percentage of all crimes were ever cleared by arrest and only a fraction of these ever resulted in conviction. And on the other hand, it is true that the criminal justice system is serving the ghetto people ill—neither protecting them from criminals, nor, when they themselves are charged with crime, giving them speedy trials; yet this is not the case everywhere, but is so chiefly in large cities, where the poor and non-whites exist in greatest numbers and where the rise in crime has been the greatest.

In other words, the inefficiency of the system is primarily due neither to an excessive concern for due process, as many conservatives say, nor to a lack of concern for the rights of the poor and of non-whites, as many liberals and radicals say. In far larger part, it is due to the immense and rapid increase in crime which has overloaded the existing machinery and caused it to function less efficiently than before, to the harm of everyone involved. There is, moreover, a perceptual distortion at work that makes the system seem to be in even worse condition than it actually is: The revolution of rising expectations among the underprivileged has made the workings of the criminal justice system, which they always took for granted, suddenly seem outrageously unfair. At the very time when the system is actually becoming somewhat more fair—but simultaneously slowing down under its increased burdens—slum peoples and many middle-class liberals see nothing but its inefficiency and interpret this as an expression of its built-in bias against the underprivileged.

But the police, to begin at the beginning of the system, are not notably, if at all, lazier, less conscientious, or more cynical than in recent years. They often seem so to the middle-class citizen, however, because the overwhelming increase in major crimes in large cities keeps them from investigating—or caring about—many lesser ones, and because the proliferation of paperwork and legalities causes them to spend more time in courthouses and less on the street. Nor is there any good evidence that they have become more brutal toward members of minority groups or more indifferent toward the victimization of ghetto people by criminals than they long have been. But it often seems so to minority people because they no longer accept police contempt and mistreatment as inevitable and normal, and because the overt hostility and threats of attack that police now often experience in ghetto areas have made them cautious about pursuing and arresting suspects in such areas.

For many of the shortcomings of the police, remedies have recently been devised or suggested by experts in police operations, by sociologists, and by specialists in administration. The more creative and complicated correctives, which involve a reeducation of the police as to their purposes, rights, and relationship to the community, have been ignored by most police chiefs in favor of increased manpower, newer equipment, and modernized patrol techniques. These, as we have seen, have done little to slow the rate at which crime is increasing, least of all of violent crime. Only a few of our mayors and police chiefs have sought not just to enlarge their forces and modernize their technology, but to make their police less authoritarian, more understanding of minority-group feelings and attitudes, and more aware of the need to create an image of themselves as law-abiding.

Nonetheless, while police inefficiency owes something to the causes advanced by either side, it owes a great deal more to the explosive growth of crime and to the changing attitudes of the underprivileged about themselves. We are doing something to increase police efficiency in both technical and fundamental ways—something, but surely not enough; in any case, however, increased police efficiency is only a small part of the total answer, for an effective police force achieves nothing if the criminals it catches cannot be tried and corrected by the rest of the criminal justice system.

The criminal courts of many large cities are undoubtedly in crisis, as critics on both sides say, but again not so much from the causes each side names as from the phenomenon of overload. For it has been the huge increase in the volume of criminal cases—exacerbated, to be sure, by the increased protections of the accused—which has produced long delays, the protracted imprisonment of persons awaiting trial, the dominance of plea-bargaining, and the attrition and collapse of many valid and deserved prosecutions. The rise in arrests and prosecutions, ironically, has harmed the victims of crime by making it harder for the criminal justice system adequately to try and punish the predators; the increased protections of the accused have hurt many of the accused themselves by increasing delays, keeping them longer in ever more crowded jails, and putting ever greater pressure on them to plead guilty and get it over with. By 1970 and 1971 the situation had become critical: many city courts were falling hopelessly behind, city jails were suffering epidemic rioting, the middle-class public was losing all confidence in the ability of the system to protect it, and minority groups were losing any belief they had that the system would treat them fairly.

Desperate situations call for desperate measures: in January 1971 the United States Court of Appeals ordered the federal district courts in New York, Connecticut, and Vermont to try defendants within six months or to drop charges against them. A few months later the state courts in New York got similar orders, effective as of May 1972, from their Chief Judge, Stanley Fuld; California, Illinois, and the District of Columbia had put such rules into effect even earlier; and a number of other jurisdictions began seriously to consider similar steps.

Such orders do not, of course, create the manpower or facilities to handle more cases; they merely put immense pressure on prosecutors and judges either to settle cases for almost any kind of plea or else to drop them, and thus indirectly put pressure on legislatures to allocate money to expand the court system. Chief Judge Fuld, in trying to reduce the critical backlog of cases during 1971, demonstrated what would happen when the six-month limit went into effect unless the legislature acted: civil judges in New York City were assigned to criminal cases for a good part of the year, at the cost of letting civil actions fall further behind; some courts were ordered into overtime and weekend sessions; judges took over the *voir dire* questioning of jurors for half a year; and judges were ordered to dismiss cases if prosecutors made too many tactical delays, and to order cases to trial if defense lawyers did so. More important, the city's courts dismissed an even higher proportion of weak or old cases than ever, granted bail or pre-trial parole to well over four fifths of arraigned defendants despite a growing "jump" rate, and offered more generous deals than ever to anyone who would save the court time by pleading guilty to a lesser crime than he was charged with.

In seven months of heroic effort, the backlog of cases pending in New York's Criminal Court was cut by more than half—from 59,000 in January 1971 to less than 28,000 in July—and detention time for those awaiting trial had been trimmed from forty to thirty-one days for Criminal Court cases, and from six months to five and a half for Supreme Court cases. But it was less than a triumph for the criminal justice system, for, as critics of the all-out drive complained, "They're giving away the courthouse to get disposition." Or, in the more formal words of the Mayor's Criminal Justice Coordinating Council:

> It is the citizens of this City who are paying the real price. They now have a system for the administration of justice that is nei-
> ther efficient enough to create a credible fear of punishment nor

fair enough to command sincere respect for its values. The resulting inability to deter crime has left New York in fear.

Indeed, almost no one was pleased with the ways in which court efficiency was being stepped up—not the victims of crimes who saw their attackers going unpunished; not the police who saw their work being thrown away; not the prosecutors and judges who knew what they were being forced to do in the name of justice; and not even the defense lawyers, or the defendants themselves, who felt that the pressure upon them in court all but forced them to cop pleas even when there was a good chance of acquittal in a trial. Yet, paradoxically, in some ways both society and the suspects were being benefited: society, in that its courts were being saved from total collapse, and made to function in at least a small proportion of cases; and the suspects, in that they were being granted bail so readily or spending less time in jail awaiting trial, and being sentenced very leniently in return for guilty pleas.

But such emergency measures are like saving a sinking boat by furious bailing. To make the courts function properly, a major overhaul is needed: this would necessitate generous allocations for additional personnel, additional courtrooms, and various technical modernizations that have been devised by judicial conferences, bar groups, and court administrators. Here and there, state legislatures have made modest increases in appropriations for the courts—a gesture in the right direction, but no more than that. As for Congress, in 1970 it amended the 1968 Crime Control Act, greatly increasing future authorizations for grants to the states (the 1972 budgeted total of block grants and discretionary grants comes to $487 million), and shifting the emphasis somewhat away from the police toward other components of the criminal justice system. But the courts are apparently going to get only about 10 to 15 percent of this, or some $50 million to $75 million; this will add only about 4 to 6 percent to the total amount being spent on the courts by state and local governments. We are, in sum, doing something at both the state and federal levels to salvage our courts—something, but not much. And very late; possibly too late.

By far the most disheartening area of criminal justice is that which is euphemistically called "corrections"—our jails, prisons, and probation and parole services. Disheartening, not only because most American prisons are shameful, but because there has actually been some significant reform in recent years which is in danger of being wiped out by the presently erupting conflict between law-and-order conservatives and the militant underprivileged.

In a number of major cities there have been some efforts to ameliorate the worst conditions in city jails; in many states there have been some efforts to make prison regulations less crushing and to increase privileges and rehabilitative opportunities. But the reforms have proceeded slowly and in niggardly fashion, while the dissatisfactions and expectations of the prisoners have expanded with great speed. As a result, explosions have occurred with increasing frequency—not necessarily where conditions were worst, but often where they were best. The phenomenon is familiar enough: with prisoners, as with oppressed or underprivileged people in evolving societies, the reforms that make their lives less wretched please them briefly and then, having given them a new vision of themselves and of their potential, make them increasingly discontented and revolutionary. This does not justify keeping them poor, ignorant, and powerless, but it does suggest that slow and cautious social reforms may, at some point, be far more dangerous than swift and daring ones.

California, for instance, has long had one of the most liberal prison systems in the United States—even according to so harsh a critic of prisons as Dr. Karl Menninger—yet it was there, in the past two years, that the new style of prisoner rebellion first gained national prominence. It was there that the "Soledad Brothers"—three black prisoners accused of beating a white guard to death—became a *cause célèbre* of radicals both inside and outside the prisons. It was there that George Jackson first became the hero not only of radicals but of many liberals for refusing to cease his political agitation inside prison —the reason, they believed, that he was refused parole year after year, although it was also true that as a prisoner he had committed numerous violent acts for which any parole board would have denied any convict his liberty. It was there, at San Quentin—which for a generation had been widely considered a model prison, pioneering in academic education, vocational training, group counseling, and even, in 1971, conjugal visiting outside the walls—that Jackson and twenty-five other prisoners rioted in August and cut the throat of three guards and two fellow prisoners, and that Jackson himself was slain, instantly becoming a martyr of the movement.

It was where prisoners had the greatest freedom to talk, to read, and to behave and feel like men rather than captured animals, that they dared to be outraged at their imprisonment. And in that spirit of rebellion, the more revolutionary spirits among them saw themselves as oppressed people fighting for their freedom, rather than as common criminals upon whom society, with due process, had imposed suitable sanctions. At the very moment in history when many American prisons were beginning to abandon most of their severe and brutal forms of discipline, inmates in those prisons were growing ever more restless, discontented, and troublesome. A national survey by *The New York Times,* published in May 1971, was headed, "Prisons Curb Brutal Discipline; Find Relaxed Controls Effective," but another one, only four months later, was headed, "Mood of Protest, Often Highly Political and Radical, Emerges in Nation's Prisons." Lawsuits, sit-downs, work stoppages, mass refusals to obey orders, assaults upon guards, mass demonstrations and destruction of prison property, and actual riots occurred during 1970 at prisons in New York, California, Georgia, and Michigan, and in 1971 spread to Massachusetts, Vermont, Texas, Illinois, and New Jersey. Increasing numbers of prisoners—especially blacks—were reading Eldridge Cleaver's *Soul on Ice* and Jackson's *Soledad Brother* (ironically, it was only in liberally run prisons that they could get such radical literature), and beginning to consider themselves political prisoners. The Black Panthers, the Black Muslims, the Young Lords (a Puerto Rican group), the Weathermen, and other radicals instigated prisoner rebelliousness, but they were only mobilizing feelings that had been growing spontaneously among non-radical and non-political prisoners as the criminal justice system itself became more fair to the underprivileged and as prisons inched toward more liberal and rehabilitative treatment.

The unhappiest result was the polarization of opinion and the drawing-up of battle lines. By the end of 1971, fermenting discontent and radicalism were widespread among prisoners and their outside sympathizers, and angry, punitive neo-conservatism was equally widespread among prison officials and the middle-class public. Huey Newton, paying tribute to George Jackson for having tried to shoot his way out of San Quentin, called him "a hero who died in a significant way" and "who showed us how to act"; the Atlanta *Constitution,* in a savage editorial on the rioters at Attica, called them "animals" and said they deserved to be executed; and between these two extremes there lay only a no-man's-land of liberalism.

*Inevitably it came to Auburn Prison—an institution whose inmates had long considered themselves lucky to be there rather than anywhere else in the New York State system. In 1969 and early 1970, Warden John Deegan used to walk through the cell blocks and the yard unescorted by guards and unafraid, cheerfully greeting prisoners as he passed among them, proud of the school and the workshops, and pleased at the sight of prisoners playing ball in the yard, reading law books in the library, painting or playing the piano in various studios, passing out through the front gate on work release or wandering freely in and out of the mess hall in the late afternoon, and chatting easily with guards.*

*But by that summer the revolutionary tide was lapping around the walls of Auburn Prison and seeping under them. Even Warden Deegan had to admit that the Black Panthers being shipped into his domain were stirring up rebelliousness, and that many of his guards were getting tense and resentful of his "laxity" and "softness." Incidents began to occur: during the summer a guard openly called several black prisoners "niggers" and "black bastards"; a day or two later, in the yard, he was silently "crowded" and swiftly beaten, suffering a serious spine injury; other guards retaliated later, beating some of the offenders; and in the next several weeks there were more attacks on guards, clubbings and Macings of inmates, brawls and knifings. A handful of the troublesome prisoners were put in solitary confinement, but the tension only grew. Warden Deegan tried to handle the situation gingerly, but found himself losing rapport with the prisoners and in open conflict with his guards. "The employees actually complained to a Grand Jury about my lenient policies," he said later, "and the inmates were working up to some kind of real protest of their own. It was getting harder and harder to be progressive." Feeling disheartened, and having become eligible for retirement, he left; Harry Fritz, a somewhat more traditionalist warden, took his place; and less than two months later Auburn had a full-scale riot.*

*Warden Deegan used to read* The New York Times *every day, and would have known that November 2nd, 1970, was Black Solidarity Day, when blacks were staying away from their jobs; Superintendent Fritz (the title had just been changed) did not read the* Times *and knew nothing about it. Some of the black prisoners refused to work that day, and Fritz, regarding this as insurrectionary, ordered them put in confinement. Two days later, at line-up time after break-fast, a couple hundred black prisoners, by secret prearrangement, refused to go to work and milled about in the yard, shouting slogans and trying to persuade or threaten other prisoners into joining them. The guards gave up ordering them to take their places and waited to see what would happen. After some time the rebels—who by now had armed themselves with sticks and pipes—suddenly seized the several dozen guards among them in the yard, forced them to sit in the center, and poured gasoline around them and on them, threatening to burn them alive if force were used to end the revolt. Some stood guard over the hostages, with matches ready; others rampaged through the part of the prison they controlled, shouting and screaming, making speeches over the public-address system, gang-raping some of the smaller prisoners, wrecking the kitchen and storage rooms, smashing locks, and improvising hand weapons of many sorts. Leaders of the riot drew up a list of demands and sent it to Superintendent Fritz; it asked for the immediate release of the prisoners who had been con-fined two days earlier, a more generous allotment of money with which to make purchases at the commissary, a better law library, the inclusion of Spanish-speaking interpreters on the staff, better food, more group therapy, and the assurance that there would be no re-prisals of any sort.*

*Superintendent Fritz conferred with a delegation of the rioters, but refused to agree to their terms as long as hostages were being held; meanwhile, he had called the state and the local police for help, and several hundred policemen and troopers had rushed to the scene, some of them guarding the exterior of the prison and others entering it and occupying the areas not controlled by the rebels. For hours the situation hung in delicate balance: at any moment a false move could have resulted in the beginning of shooting and in the immolation of the hostages. At its height, the rebellion involved some 400 of the 1,700 inmates; the rest were either caught in their cells when it began or stayed out of it, even though they were in the yard at the time. Carlos Ortiz later described the fragmentation of the prison popula-tion: "The ones that were doin' all the runnin' aroun' an' beatin' up the polices, they were the Brothers," he said. "The Spanish guys grabbed pipes to protect themselves an' stayed off in one corner, an' the white boys were on another side. We di'n' want no part of that.*

*The Brothers been makin' talk about a riot for months, an' some kids, they eat up all this talk about revolution, but we di'n' want no part of that, because it jus' mess up things for everybody."*

*Sometime in mid-afternoon Deputy Commissioner of Corrections Harold Butler made it clear to the negotiating team of the prisoners that the large, armed contingent of state troopers and local police was ready to use force, and that no demands would be negotiated until the hostages were released. After what seemed an endless delay, word came back from the yard that the hostages would be released, and in a while they started coming in one or two at a time. By 5:00 p.m. they had all been freed, the prisoners were returning to their cells, and the riot was over.*

*Parts of the prison were in ruins, but what had been wrecked most completely was the atmosphere which had formerly existed, and of which Warden Deegan had been so proud. Nearly all the prisoners were locked in their cells for many weeks and were marched in small groups to the mess hall and the showers; recreation, industry, classes, and counseling were all suspended; some 120 of the active rioters were segregated and, according to their friends and lawyers, and their own testimony in court, kept in filthy strip cells, deprived of exercise, showers, and mail, and threatened, cursed, savagely beaten, tear-gassed, and Maced.*

*"Auburn is dead" a dejected guidance counselor said a month after the riot. "I don't know to this day what was so bad about it that they had to do this. But now it is bad, now it's like it used to be a century ago." A hard-line deputy superintendent, talking to a reporter, took a smug, almost pleased attitude about it: "You've seen the beginning of the end of prison reform," he said. "It's been tried—and this is what happens." Meanwhile, the segregated rioters were doing whatever they could to perpetuate the disturbance, resisting and fighting guards at every opportunity, and even having to be carried, kicking and screaming, to and from their court appearances. The new Commissioner of Correctional Services, Russell G. Oswald, wrote to them after they had been in segregation for two months and asked them to cease their "deliberately contrived harassment tactics" so that he could work with them and institute reforms, but they would have none of it; they considered themselves revolutionaries, and continued to be as resistant as they could, in the circumstances. As one of them, Charles Leon Hill, wrote in a letter which somehow got through the censors:*

*We are engaged in protracted struggle at Auburn Concentration
Camp. . . . Either we dare to fight, to resist, to demand human
treatment, or succumb to the wrath of tyranny and forsake the
cause of human dignity. . . . We maintain no illusions of su-
perhuman victory behind these walls; we but keep aflame the
spirit of the freedom fighter.*

*Half a year after the riot, seventy-two of the inmates were still in
segregation and—according to guards and prison officials—were still
so ungovernable and uncooperative that they could not be returned to
their own cells. Not until seven months after the riot was the state of
emergency officially declared over and many of the lost privileges
restored to the prison population. A year after the riot most of the old
privileges had been restored and an inmate advisory board, elected by
the prisoners themselves, was meeting regularly with a new superintendent to pass on grievances and offer suggestions; nonetheless, the
atmosphere was not what it had once been. "It used to be the most
progressive prison in the state," a Service Unit counselor says, "but
now the atmosphere is very different. The guards know that they
really can't control the inmates if there's a riot, and the inmates know
the guards fear them and even hate them. There's no sense of security,
no trust or rapport between the staff and the population. Most of the
inmates don't want it that way, and certainly none of us do, but no
one knows how to put things back together the way they were. It's a
damned shame. It's tragic."*

*Two who feel the same way are Alfredo and Carlos Ortiz. Actually,
they were hurt less by the riot than many others: having taken no part
in it, and being needed to help run the laundry, they were allowed out
of their cells within a matter of days, as were a limited number of
others who were both trusted and necessary to prison operations. But
even though the Ortiz brothers themselves were not deprived, the
atmosphere around them was greatly changed, and they missed the
way it had been. "This here penitentiary was all right," Carlos said
sadly, months later, "but they messed it up. This was the best prison
in the whole state, but it won' never be the same."*

And then Attica.

Attica is a New York State prison, but not much like Auburn—it is
sternly disciplinary, has almost no facilities for rehabilitative treat-

ment, offers few privileges, has long cell hours every day, and is staffed by guards with a local tradition of quasi-military toughness and hostility toward the inmates—three quarters of whom are blacks, mostly from New York City and anything but passive and docile. Attica was not worse in 1971 than it had been the year before or ten years before, and it was certainly not one of the worst prisons in the country, but the materials in it were combustible, the temperature was right, and the conflagration was inevitable.

Unless, of course, major steps were taken to prevent it. Commissioner Oswald, a genuinely progressive man with a background in parole work, had taken command of the Department of Correctional Services in January 1971, and had been making plans to institute a number of significant reforms in New York prisons, including more schooling, vocational training, and other rehabilitative measures, expanded work-release programs, home furloughs for those deemed to be safe, the ending of censorship of mail, and so on. He even made his first public announcement of all these plans in a taped speech broadcast at Attica over the public-address system on September 3rd, 1971, and concluded by asking for the inmates' patience, trust, and confidence.

But the State Legislature had not given him the money to bring his changes about swiftly, and the leaders of the incipient rebellion neither had patience, trust, and confidence, nor wanted such attitudes to prevail among the rest of the inmates. Less than a week later, on September 8th, 1971, a prisoner punched a guard in a trifling yard incident. When guards removed him from his cell later that day against his will to go to a disciplinary hearing, the word was spread around that he was being taken out for a beating; the rest is history.

In the morning, more than one thousand prisoners rioted, seized thirty-two guards as hostages, and took control of part of the prison. Threatening to execute the guards if action were taken against them, they made weapons, dug trenches, set fires, and issued a long list of demands that went beyond the reforms promised by Commissioner Oswald to include "freedom of worship" (this was a Black Muslim demand, signifying their objection to the pork in the prison diet), permission to hold political meetings, and the establishment of regular grievance procedures.

At first Oswald intended not to discuss the demands of the rebels until they had released the hostages, but their temper was so fierce and reckless that he changed his mind and entered into negotiations with a committee they named, and eventually agreed to twenty-eight of the prisoners' thirty demands, refusing only to fire the superintendent and to promise amnesty for all their acts. Legally, he had no power to grant amnesty, nor could he, in any case, have dared to set such a dangerous precedent; unfortunately, the rioters absolutely insisted on this demand because they knew that one of the guards, who had been badly mauled in the first hours of the riot, had died, making them all co-conspirators in a felony murder.

By the fourth day, negotiations had broken down, National Guardsmen and state troopers were massed around the prison, eager to attack, and leaders of the rioters had put eight of the hostages on display in the center of the yard with "executioners" stationed beside them, holding knives at their throats to be used the moment an assault began. Commissioner Oswald, his face a mask of tragedy, agreed with Governor Rockefeller to send in the attack forces: helicopters flew overhead, lobbing tear gas into the yard, and a thousand state troopers, National Guardsmen, and sheriff's deputies stormed the prison. In the hail of bullets and shotgun pellets, at least twenty-seven convicts died—as did all eight hostages displayed in the yard, not of cut throats but of bullet wounds inflicted by the wildly firing assault forces.

It was the worst prison riot, and the worst prison massacre, in many years. It shocked Americans of all shades of opinion—some because of the power that prisoners were able to wield and the violence they had threatened, others because of the violence used by the state to put the riot down, a violence that was all the more horrifying and senseless because an all-out assault was bound to be much more likely to cause the deaths of the hostages than were continued talks. All the dreadful predictable results ensued: retaliation by enraged and hate-filled guards (beatings, gassings, the smashing of inmates' eyeglasses and tearing-up of their legal papers), hostility so extreme on the part of the inmates that a number of guards resigned and others refused to risk letting the inmates into the yard for exercise; and worst of all the almost total polarization of the viewpoints of conservatives and of reformers, with prison officials and conservatives throughout the country backing the Commissioner for ordering the assault, and liberals and leftists everywhere regarding it as proof of the depravity of America and the degeneracy of its criminal justice system.

Attica was a disaster—but not without its lessons for everyone:

in a few other prisons outside New York since then, inmate resistance has remained non-violent or, even when it has not, prison officials have negotiated patiently rather than resort to force. The real lesson, however, has not yet been learned—that major reform of our prisons has been coming about much too slowly and too late, and that there is no time left for thrift or caution. It may take more Atticas to teach America that lesson; and by the time the lesson has been learned, it may have become impossible to apply it.

---

# 7  Three Alternative Attitudes Toward Crime Control and Democracy

AT this critical juncture, when crime threatens to destroy society as we know it, the American way of life is endangered not only by the acts of the criminals but by their effects on the attitudes of Americans toward the criminal justice system and toward certain fundamental tenets of our democracy. A deep and dangerous schism has appeared in America, separating two antithetical poles of opinion—a new conservatism on the one side, and a rebellious and often radical dissent on the other; and although the two are in violent opposition, both are antagonistic toward the ideal of due process, scornful of the ideal of fairness, and potentially destructive of our concept of justice and of the essence of democracy.

The conservative reaction is the product of fear, traditionalism, and prejudice; it seeks to roll back the civil-rights advances of the past fifteen years or more, and to weaken and limit some of the most important guarantees of individual rights embodied in the Constitution. Conservatives and many middle-of-the-road Americans favor crime-control methods that would greatly increase the power of the state and its representatives, and decrease the freedoms of the individual and his ability to defend himself against wrongful deprivation of his life, liberty, or property. The cure is not only worse than the disease, but in any case would probably prove unavailing; throughout history, nearly every reactionary effort to restore bygone serenity by damming up the movement toward greater equality has lasted only until the accumulated pressures have burst the dam and destroyed the social order.

The rebellious response, on the other hand, is compounded of disillusionment, bitterness, and self-interest; it seeks to sabotage and to wreck the criminal justice system and, indeed, the entire structure of American democracy, in order to give non-whites, the young, and underprivileged persons the power to run things in a way that will better their lives. But it seeks these goals at the expense of everyone else in society, for it offers no guarantees of freedom or fairness to whites, middle-class persons, or any who dissent from its populist methods and goals. As a cure for race prejudice, for the lopsided distribution of power in American society, and for the defects of the American justice system, it is worse than all these diseases combined; recent history has amply proven that the victory through violence of a people who are oppressed in an imperfect democracy leads not to a better form of democracy but to a new tyranny—first of the victorious oppressed, and later of their Party. In Europe, in the East, and in Latin America we have seen how the victory of "People's democracies" leads to the repudiation of liberal justice—including the fundamental concepts of due process, fairness, and adversarial trial—and to its replacement by People's Courts, public trials by voice vote of the spectators, and inquisitorial methods in more formal court settings, all these being justified on the grounds that the well-being of society is vastly more important than the rights of the individual, particularly if he has already been deemed an enemy of the People by virtue of his class, education, or profession.

Both the conservatives and the radicals have, for wholly different reasons, lost faith in the basic values of our system of laws and our democratic style of government. Both sides are willing to abandon its guarantees of individual liberty in return for other advantages: for security, in the case of the conservatives; and for equal opportunity and power, in the case of the radicals and rebellious minorities. But security so achieved deprives the middle-class people who seek it of the very freedom they would deny to those they fear; and equal opportunity and power so achieved lead the poor and the minorities into a new subjugation by the totalitarian government they think will end their enslavement.

There is, however, another alternative, another possible attitude toward crime and democracy—one that would make for a broader and deeper fight against crime than that of the conservatives, for a more constructive attack on social inequities than that of the radicals and minority militants, and for an unyielding defense of liberty and due process against extremists of both sides. Essentially, it would be a new liberalism, reborn out of the ashes of the old one—a bolder, more daring version than its predecessor, an activist liberalism that kept its faith but performed good works with revolutionary intensity.

Those who embraced this view would assert an unequivocal belief in the ethical and social ideals of constitutional democracy: among other things, they would insist that legal rights should be fully extended to all people, of whatever color or economic condition; they would cherish and strengthen the rights by means of which the individual can defend himself against the state; and they would maintain that even the seemingly dangerous mental patient and even the apparently incorrigible violent criminal should have every civil right except freedom, and every opportunity to prove himself neither dangerous nor deserving of confinement.

As the expression of these beliefs, they would energetically seek to accomplish sweeping change throughout the criminal justice system, and swiftly enough to save the system from destruction. They would strive to reshape, according to democratic concepts, the structure and the sociology of police forces. They would fight to radically expand and modernize the courts, spending as freely to multiply courtrooms, judges, prosecutors, assorted adjunctive personnel, and legal services to the poor as if the nation were at war, which it is, and as if all of our lives depended on winning that war, which they do. They would seek to make jury trials a reality and the rule, instead of an ideal and the exception. They would multiply probation and parole services many times over, create community-based rehabilitation centers and staff them thoroughly, open wide the secret world of the prisons and revolutionize life in them until they became at least reasonably rehabilitative. They would regretfully admit the need to segregate in special institutions those untreatable sociopaths for whom society can do nothing, but from whom it must protect not only the law-abiding but those treatable criminals it has to institutionalize.

This wholesale and revolutionary reconstruction of the criminal justice system would, at best, contain crime, but not eliminate it or even reduce it significantly at the source. Hand in hand, therefore, with a massive remodeling of the criminal justice system, there would be a far greater commitment than Americans have thus far shown to making our country a truly open society, to wiping out the economic and political disadvantages of being born black, Puerto Rican, or Mexican-American, to bringing all minorities into the mainstream of American life and giving them good reason to cherish democracy and to help preserve it. This would take place not by means of larger handouts, increased welfare payments, or ever larger gifts of buildings, money, and services, but by means of far more daring and difficult measures such as the strict enforcement of fair housing practices, massive efforts to provide equal educational opportunities, and other intensive programs designed to wipe out the borders of the ghetto, both physical and mental—anything and everything that would give all Americans an equal chance to make the most of their abilities, equal reason to respect themselves, equal capability to defend themselves against the might of the state, and equal cause to believe in, and to preserve, liberty.

Such might be the third alternative: a revolutionary liberalism that is neither gradual nor cautious (there being no time for gradualism or caution), but faithful to democratic ideals (there being a terrible price to pay in trading them for anything else). It would be liberal in philosophy, making no concessions that encroach upon individual civil rights; it would be revolutionary in action, moving swiftly and daringly to implement its beliefs before there is no more hope of doing so. The word "revolutionary" seems to imply the overthrow of democratic government, but once it did not: our own forebears in this country were revolutionaries—but liberal revolutionaries or, perhaps, revolutionary liberals, who dared to break with the King and the Empire, yet preserved what was best and most democratic in English law and government, expanded it, and built a new nation upon it. We, too, in our time, could be revolutionary in the speed and magnitude of our deeds, but liberal in our faith in democratic principles; we could deal with the crisis of crime, and yet preserve and perfect American liberty. We could, but will we?

*Acknowledgments*
*Notes on Sources*
*Bibliography*
*Index*

# Acknowledgments

I AM indebted to a number of organizations for providing me with essential, and often unpublished, data, and for other research assistance. They include the following agencies and departments of the New York City government: the Planning Commission, the Mayor's Criminal Justice Coordinating Council, the Police Department, and the Department of Correction. Outside the city government, they include the New York Legal Aid Society; the New York State Department of Correctional Services; the Law Enforcement Assistance Administration and the Federal Bureau of Investigation, both of the United States Department of Justice; the National District Attorneys Association; the National Legal Aid and Defender Association; and the National Council on Crime and Delinquency. To the many persons within these agencies and organizations who provided me with material and with guidance—but whom, this book being overlong, I shall not name individually—my thanks.

Particular thanks, however, go to Burton Roberts, District Attorney of Bronx County, and to Daniel J. Sullivan, Assistant District Attorney in charge of the Appeals Bureau under Mr. Roberts, for making available to me many of the materials I needed to re-create the story of the murder of Alexander Helmer and its sequelae. I am deeply grateful to the many persons who submitted to lengthy interviews, some of whom I need not name, since they are the major and minor figures in the narrative, and others of whom I may not name—detectives, jurors, assistant D.A.s, prison guards, and others who asked to remain anonymous. But I am grateful to them all, and I trust they know it.

Daniel Markewich and David Bernheim deserve my explicit thanks for having spoken freely to me, three years ago, after I had served as

447

a juror and they as the assistant D.A. and the defense lawyer, respectively, in a trial in New York Supreme Court; it was what I learned from them that started me upon this project. I gladly acknowledge, too, my indebtedness to my agent, Robert Lescher, who strengthened my resolve when it weakened; Violet Serwin, indefatigable amanuensis; Paul Hirschman, splendid copy editor; and to my wife, Bernice, who sustained and aided me in ways beyond counting and beyond recompense.

# Notes on Sources

I HAVE resisted the impulse to demonstrate scholarly diligence by amassing a vast heap of source notes; instead, I have sought merely to satisfy the average reader's curiosity by indicating the most important and accessible sources from which crucial data or controversial statements have been drawn. For that reason, too, as well as in the interests of brevity and simplicity, I have omitted page references except where the reader, pursuing the matter to the source, could not easily locate the item by means of an index or, in the case of newspaper articles, by simple scanning.

Articles in law journals and court publications are listed here in legal bibliographical style rather than the more conventional literary style.

Quotations by persons, whether named or unnamed, if not identified as to source in these notes, are from interviews conducted by myself.

The details, quotation, and dialogue of the narrative sections of the book (to which almost no notes are appended here) are drawn from extensive taped interviews, letters, personal observation, the minutes of the first trial, and the official Record on Appeal of the second trial. The case is officially listed as Indictment No. 1902/64, Supreme Court of the State of New York, County of the Bronx.

## Prologue
### (*pages vii–ix*)

Data on the growth of violent crime in America, and in its large cities, are from the Violence Commission Report and *Uniform Crime Reports*.

## Chapter 1
### II (*pp. 6–8*)

Three times as likely to be victimized: Schafer. Predisposing nature of age, parcels, dress: from interviews with New York City policemen and district attorneys. On the poor as victims of robberies: Wilson, p. 57; but for the shift, see *Crimes of Violence*, pp. 213 f. Racial aspects of criminals and victims: *ibid*. Role of solitariness: Schafer. Propinquity, and the high rate of mugging along interface between slums and middle-class neighborhoods: *Plan for New York City*, pp. 4, 18.

On the general theory of victimology: von Hentig; Mendelsohn; Schafer, chap. 2; chapter by LeRoy G. Schultz in Hartogs; Barnes and Teeters.

### III (*pp. 8–9*)

Violence is more common on weekdays: Schafer, p. 88.

### IV (*pp. 9–12*)

Details are from *The Melrose Report* and *Plan for New York City*, plus personal observation.

### VI (*pp. 16–23*)

Physical injury to the victim occurs in one out of every three cases: Crime Commission Report, p. 19.

23.4 percent which involve the use of a knife, club, or blunt weapon: *Uniform Crime Reports* for 1970 give the percentage of all robbery that is armed (63.3), and break this down by type of arms; my figure is an extraction, omitting guns. Total muggings in 1964 and 1970: my own figures, based on conservative estimate of muggings as constituting half of the robberies reported in *Uniform Crime Reports*. I derive the chance of being mugged in 1970 by dividing total muggings (half of total robberies) in each category of cities into total population of those cities, all figures coming from *Uniform Crime Reports*.

On distortions in crime data, see Schur (1969); Wilson; Crime Commission Report; Violence Commission Report. True rate of crime greater than reported rate: Crime Commission Report, Table 4.

The rate of violent crime had tripled since 1941: Violence Commission Report curves, extrapolated by means of data in *Uniform Crime Reports* for 1969 and 1970.

Sixty-five percent . . . are Negroes: *Uniform Crime Reports*, 1970. Crime rate among Germans, Irish, etc.: Crime Commission Report. Murder rate in African tribes: Paul Bohannan, ed., *African Homicide and Suicide* (New York: Atheneum, 1967), esp. Chap. 9. Crime among juveniles and males: *Uniform Crime Reports*, 1970. Training in violence, in slum childhood: Schur (1969); Toch.

Coles's quote is from his chapter in Hartogs; Rivers' is from a talk he regularly gives; Brown's is from House Select Committee Hearings, "Improvement and Reform"; Kaufman's is from his paper, "Sources of Legal Psychiatric Confusion," delivered at Amer. Psychiatric Assn. meeting, May 1970.

The Philadelphia study: André Normandeau: *Trends and Patterns in Crimes of Robbery* [in Philadelphia] (Univ. of Penna. Ph.D. diss., sociol., 1968, Univ. Microfilms). Gratuitous violence by muggers: *Uniform Crime*

*Reports,* 1970; 1969 and 1970 *Annual Reports* of the Crime Victims Compensation Board, State of New York; and direct communications from various police officials, New York and other cities.

Sheriff Powell's quote: House Select Committee Hearings, "Response of a Midsouth Community."

### VIII (*pp. 27–35*)

Less than seven percent: multiplying percent reported (Crime Commission Report), by percent cleared, by percent prosecuted and convicted (*Uniform Crime Reports,* 1970). Comparable data on murders: *Uniform Crime Reports,* 1970. The survey made for the Crime Commission is summarized in its Report. *Life* survey: *Life,* July 11, 1969. Batten: " 'You Must Be Out of Your Mind to Be Out Alone After Dark in a Neighborhood Like This,' " *The New York Times Magazine,* March 22, 1970.

Ineffectiveness of police power: Crime Commission Report; Violence Commission Report; *Criminal Justice Plan for 1971;* Caleb Foote's chapter in Sowle.

Senator McClellan's statement: Senate Judiciary Committee, "Controlling Crime," p. 320.

The CBS News Poll is reported in *Time,* April 27, 1970, under "American Notes."

Rise in crime, and crime rate: *Uniform Crime Reports* for 1969, 1970, and preliminary releases from the FBI during 1971; see also Notes to Epilogue, 2, below.

### IX (*pp. 35–37*)

Shift to indoor mugging: by 1969 a majority of Bronx muggings were being committed indoors, according to a Police Department report cited in *The New York Times* of Dec. 24, 1969.

### Chapter 2
### II (*pp. 45–51*)

On the way police spend their time: *Science and Technology;* Wilson; *The New York Times,* Aug. 3, 1970; and *Criminal Justice Plan for 1971.*

The distinction between law enforcement and keeping the peace is discussed in Wilson, as is the policeman's feeling of hostility and suspicion towards citizens he deals with. See also chapter by David Dodd in Hartogs. The "Honeymooners": Thomas R. Crooks, "Necessary Force—Or Police Brutality?" *The New York Times Magazine,* Dec. 5, 1965.

Social origins and attitudes of police: H. Richard Lamb and Thurman McGinnis, "Police Professionalization and Mental Health" (paper read at Amer. Psychiatric Assn. meeting, 1970); Seymour Lipset, "Why Cops Hate Liberals—and Vice Versa," *Atlantic,* March 1969; *The Police.* Alienation of the police, and the Murphy quote: Lipset, *loc. cit.,* and Skolnick (1966).

The *Miranda* study at Yale: Wald *et al.*

*The Times*'s special report on convictions of muggers: May 20, 1968 (*see* Burnham).

Detectives' status, duties, attitudes: Skolnick (1966); Wilson; and Paul Wilkes, "Real-Life Detective Stories," *The New York Times Magazine,* April 19, 1970.

Clearance rates: *Uniform Crime Reports.*

The Rand Institute study: "An Analysis of the Apprehension Activities of the New York City Police Department," The New York City Rand Institute, September 1970.

Escobedo: *Escobedo* v. *Illinois,* 378 U.S. 478.

### IV (*pp. 61–68*)

Sociological and psychological theories of crime causation: *Crimes of Violence;* Radzinowicz and Wolfgang; Glaser; and many others.

Disrespect as a crime, and as grounds for rough treatment: Wilson; Chevigny; Albert J. Reiss, Jr., "Police Brutality—Answers to Key Questions," *Trans-action,* Nov./Dec. 1970. Police favoritism toward whites: research by Theodore N. Ferdinand and Elmer G. Luchterhand, summarized in *Trans-action,* Nov./Dec. 1970. Anti-Negro feeling among police: Donald Black and Albert J. Reiss, Jr., *Studies in Crime and Law Enforcement in Major Metropolitan Areas,* 1967 (for the Crime Commission); Skolnick (1966).

Field interrogations and invitations to the station house: Chevigny; Packer; Chaps. 4 and 5 in Hall *et al.* The Mississippi round-up case: *Davis* v. *Mississippi,* 394 U.S. 721. The use of vagrancy and other catch-all charges to effect round-ups: Packer; Hall *et al.*

On the use of informers: Leonard; Skolnick (1966); Richard Donnelly in 60 Yale L. J. 1091; *The New York Times,* article on heroin traffic, April 20, 1970. Mr. Hoover's quote is from the FBI *Law Enforcement Bulletin,* June 1955. Detectives' prejudging of the suspect: Skolnick (1966); Wilson; Chevigny; and David Dodd chapter in Hartogs.

### VI (*pp. 79–83*)

Police lying and other illegalities, in connection with collecting evidence: Packer; Skolnick (1966); Morris and Hawkins; Chevigny. The Rand study of police stealing, etc.: *The New York Times,* Nov. 20, 1970.

Conflict for policeman between work ethic and legal ethic: Skolnick (1966).

Use of the due process clause of the Fourteenth Amendment: *Criminal Law Revolution.* Mapp: *Mapp* v. *Ohio,* 367 U.S. 643. Gideon: *Gideon* v. *Wainwright,* 372 U.S. 335. Malloy: *Malloy* v. *Hogan,* 378 U.S. 1. Escobedo: *vide supra,* 2, II. Miranda: *Miranda* v. *Arizona,* 384 U.S. 436.

Search and seizure decisions of the 1960s: *Criminal Law Revolution.* Detention: Sowle; Caleb Foote in 52 N.W. Univ. Law Rev. 16; Hall *et al.* on the Vita, Seals, and Morales cases. Supreme Court definition of arrest: *Long* v. *Ansell,* 293 U.S. 76.

**VII** (*pp. 84–92*)

But many slum youths do not perceive it that way: the Ortiz brothers themselves do not; see also Thomas.

## Chapter 3
### II (*pp. 102–109*)

The history of torture is covered in standard encyclopedias, including the *Britannica;* see also my own book *The Natural History of Love* (New York: Knopf, 1959), and G. Rattray Taylor, *Sex in History* (New York: Vanguard, 1954).

Criminal investigation as a recent police function: see Note, 73 Yale L. J. 1000, 1034. Police use of torture, and the Wickersham Commission: Dodd chapter in Hartogs. *Brown* v. *Mississippi*, 297 U.S. 278, and see also *Malloy* v. *Hogan* for later interpretation of the significance of *Brown.* Progressive limiting of coercion, by the Supreme Court: Leonard; Shapiro.

The cases of police abuse in Brooklyn and the Bronx: Senate Judiciary Committee ("Controlling Crime"), pp. 26, 211; and Zimbardo.

Professor Inbau's comment on morality of investigative techniques: 52 NWU L. Rev. 80–83.

Whitmore: see *Miranda;* but the details are from Shapiro, except for the dropping of six other murder charges, for which see Chevigny.

### IV (*pp. 117–122*)

The development of the privilege against self-incrimination was reviewed by Chief Justice Warren in the *Miranda* opinion; on the expansion of fairness in confessions cases, see Karlen; Leonard; Shapiro; and *Brown* v. *Mississippi, Escobedo,* and Justice Douglas' concurring opinion in *Spano* v. *New York,* 360 U.S. 315.

Said the court in 1941: *Lisenba* v. *California,* 314 U.S. 219. And twenty years later: *Rogers* v. *Richmond,* 365 U.S. 368.

Bishop: "The Warren Court Is Not Likely to Be Overruled," *The New York Times Magazine,* Sept. 7, 1969.

D.A.s Specter, Koota, Hogan: Senate Judiciary Committee ("Controlling Crime").

Evading *Miranda:* 36 U. Chi. L. Rev. 413; Inbau and Reid quoted in the same, Note 41. New Haven study: Wald *et al.* Pittsburgh study: 29 U. Pgh. L. Rev. 1. For Richard Anderson's statement, see House Select Committee ("A Mid-American View"). Declining clearance rate: *Uniform Crime Reports,* 1964 through 1968. Ineffectiveness of *Miranda* and evasions of its requirements: 66 Mich. L. Rev. 1347; 1968 Duke L. J. 425.

### VI (*pp. 128–131*)

On guilty pleas as implicit confessions, see Note 5 in Justice White's dissent in *Miranda*. Mr. Koota is quoted in Klein; Mr. Hogan in *The New*

*York Times,* Dec. 2, 1965; Mr. Michael Murphy, address before 28th Annual Judicial Conference, Third Judicial District of the U.S., Sept. 8, 1965.

Clearance rates before and after *Escobedo* and *Miranda: Uniform Crime Reports,* 1964 through 1970. Justice Mosk's report: "The Anatomy of Violence," *Beverly Hills Bar J.,* Oct. 1968. Post-*Miranda* survey in Los Angeles: 35 Fordham L. Rev. 169, 259. Justice Sobel's study: N.Y.L.J., Nov. 22, 1965.

Years before . . . the police were unable to solve the majority of robberies: the 1955 *Uniform Crime Reports,* for instance, show a clearance rate of only 42.8 percent for robbery.

## Chapter 4
### II (*pp. 145–154*)

Historic origins of Sixth Amendment right to speedy trial are reviewed in *Klopfer* v. *North Carolina,* 386 U.S. 213, and further discussed in *Smith* v. *Hooey,* 393 U.S. 374. On the purposes of bail: *Stack* v. *Boyle,* 342 U.S. 1; Packer, in 113 U. Pa. L. Rev. 1; Foote, in 11 U. Pa. L. Rev. 960, 1125, 1180.

Time spent in jail awaiting trial: *Life,* Aug. 7, 1970; *The New York Times,* May 22 and Oct. 11, 1970, Feb. 14, 1971. The percent eventually found innocent: Morris and Hawkins.

The 1970 study on growing backlog in New York City: Clarke. Reasons for postponements: *The New York Times,* May 12, 1970 (statement by Justice Dudley); Dec. 6, 1970 (article by L. Oelsner); Feb. 21, 1971 (statement by Justice Ross); Hogan; Skolnick (1966); *Life,* Aug. 7, 1970.

Justice Jackson: concurring opinion in *Stack* v. *Boyle.*

Initial bail for most muggers: direct communication from Vera Institute, New York. Use of fixed bail schedules by most judges: Freed and Wald, in Hall *et al.* Census Bureau study on jails and jail populations: *see* United States Dept. of Justice, LEAA: *1970 National Jail Census.*

Unpublished data on bail-jumping: direct communication from Mayor's Criminal Justice Coordinating Council. Senator Goodman: *The New York Times,* Dec. 25, 1970, Jan. 6, 1971; corrections on this matter from New York Police Department and Criminal Justice Coordinating Council by direct communication.

Jail conditions; U.S. Dept. of Justice, LEAA: *1970 National Jail Census;* Menninger; *Corrections; Newsweek,* March 8, 1971; *Time,* Jan. 18, 1971; N.Y. State Senate Committee on Crime and Correction, *The Tombs Disturbances.* Homosexual rape: Alan J. Davis, "Sexual Assaults in the Philadelphia Prison System and in Sheriff's Vans," *Trans-action,* Dec. 1968. Guards: Glaser; see also sources named above on jail conditions.

Even in 1964: *Corrections.*

### IV (*pp. 162–169*)

Douglas anecdote: William O. Douglas, "West from the Khyber Pass," *National Geographic Mag.,* July 1958.

Nature of typical criminal law practice: Crime Commission Report; *Newsweek*, March 8, 1971. Shortage of criminal lawyers: *ibid.;* Hall *et al.* (p. 2); Karlen; *The Courts.* Typical fees of criminal lawyers: direct communications from lawyers; Karlen; Blumberg. Post-*Gideon* defenders: Crime Commission Report; *Karlen;* Mills (1971); *Criminal Justice Plan for 1971;* direct communication from National Legal Aid and Defender Assoc. Disillusionment and loss of idealism: *Newsweek*, March 8, 1971.

Hastings quote: Stryker. Jay Goldberg: *The New York Times*, May 24, 1969. Erdmann: Mills (1971). Carr: *Life*, April 2, 1971 (Letters to the Editor).

## VI (*pp. 178–184*)

Prosecutorial discretion and options: Davis; Karlen.

Part-time nature of most prosecutorial positions: *The Courts.* Prosecutorial salaries in 1965: *ibid.* Idealists and the ambitious: *ibid.; The Courts; Newsweek*, March 8, 1971.

Half a dozen states: direct communication from National District Attorneys Assoc.

20,000 to 25,000 prosecutors and assistant prosecutors: my own estimate, based on the admittedly imperfect data given mc by the National District Attorneys Assoc., and the National Legal Aid and Defender Assoc. (The Bureau of the Census, and the Law Enforcement Assistance Administration of the Dept. of Justice, have no data on prosecutors and assistant prosecutors as such, but only on total prosecutorial personnel.) Total prosecutions of felonies: *Uniform Crime Reports*, 1970. Total prosecutions of misdemeanors (between 4 and 5 million): based on estimate in *The Courts*, adjusted upward in accordance with *Uniform Crime Reports* increase ratios. Misdemeanors handled without prosecutors: *The Courts.*

5.6 percent of serious crimes: the computation uses factors drawn from *Uniform Crime Reports*, 1970; it comes very close to the Violence Commission's figure of 6, using data a couple years older.

Prosecutorial goal of invincibility: Skolnick (1967).

## VIII (*pp. 192–197*)

Percentage of conviction by guilty pleas: *The Courts.*

Skolnick's phrase is the title of his book.

Lightening of sentences for guilty pleaders: Oaks and Lehman; Burnham article in *The New York Times*, May 20, 1968; *The Courts;* Glaser. Chief Justice Burger: *Time*, Aug. 24, 1970.

The prisoner dutifully utters the right lies, etc.: *The Courts; Newsweek*, March 8, 1971. Legitimization of plea-bargaining: Crime Commission Report; A.B.A. quoted in Hall *et al.; Brady* v. *U.S.*, 397 U.S. 742; *Parker* v. *U.S.*, 433 F 2d 15, and cert. denied, 401 U.S. 925; *Alford* v. *North Carolina*, 400 U.S. 25.

Defendants' attitudes toward plea-bargaining: Blumberg, pp. 51–67. *Village Voice* article: June 12, 1969.

Cook County study: Oaks and Lehman chapter in Blumberg.

## Chapter 5
### II (*pp. 207–214*)

Purposes of jury trial: Justice White's opinion in *Duncan* v. *Louisiana*, 391 U.S. 145; John T. Noonan, Jr., in 64 Mich. L. Rev. 1485; and see Notes to Section VI of this chapter, below. Historical origins of jury trials: Botein; Kaplan chapter in Berman; Mayer; and Notes to Chapter 3, Section IV, above. Due process as a check upon police and others: Hall chapter in Berman.

A numerically insignificant proportion of criminal prosecutions: *The Courts;* Kalven and Zeisel; and Notes to Chapter 3, Section IV, above.

Total number of prosecutions: see the *Miranda* opinion. Number of jury trials: Kalven and Zeisel say 80,000, which I have extrapolated upward in accordance with *Uniform Crime Reports* rates of increase of clearances and prosecutions. Importance of jury trials: *The Courts.*

The mechanics and biases of jury selection: Note, in 52 Va. L. Rev. 1069; *Time,* April 6, 1970; Rothblatt, 2 Crim. L. Bull. 14; Steinberg & Paulsen, 7 Prac. Law 25; *Swain* v. *Alabama,* 380 U.S. 202; Hogan.

Hearsay, and evidence proving disposition toward criminality: Wigmore; *Drew* v. *United States,* 118 U.S. App. D.C. 11; Karlen. Introduction of criminal record to impeach credibility: Karlen.

Prosecutor's role-playing: Skolnick (1967). Defense attorney's role-playing: Blumberg, pp. 51–67; Karlen; and Monroe H. Freedman in 64 Mich. L. Rev. 1469.

Uses of cross-examination: Freedman, *loc. cit.;* Wellman; Stryker.

On judges, their limitations, and their political servitude: Blumberg in Glaser; *The Courts;* Crime Commission Report; Martin and Susan Tolchin, "How Judgeships Get Bought," *New York Magazine,* March 15, 1971 (the massive study referred to, cited here, is Wallace Sayre and Herbert Kaufman, *Governing New York City*). The noted jurist who always found a principle suited to his view was James Kent, quoted by Blumberg in Glaser. Packer's quote is from his *Ex-Communist Witnesses* (Stanford: Stanford U. Press, 1962).

### IV (*pp. 230–235*)

Techniques of attacking credibility: Wellman; Nizer.

Frequency of perjury formerly and today: Crime Commission Report.

California troopers' practices: Nicholas Pileggi, "From D.A. to Dope Lawyer," *The New York Times Magazine,* May 16, 1971. Justice Mosk's quote: *ibid.* Dropsy cases and Judge Younger: *The New York Times,* Sept. 19, 1970.

Defendants' perjury: Crime Commission Report; *Newsweek,* March 8, 1971.

Monroe Freedman: in 64 Mich. L. Rev. 1469.

Fear of criminal record being revealed, as reason for defendant silence: Karlen; Schaefer; and *Drew* v. *United States,* 118 U.S. App. D.C. 11. Jurors' interpretation of past record: Dorsey Ellis, in *Law and Order Reconsidered.* Griswold: 51 A.B.A.J. 1017.

### VI (*pp. 252–259*)

Sebille: 10 A.B.A.J. 53. Griswold: 1962–1963 *Harvard Law School Dean's Report.*

On Burger's views, see *The New York Times,* Sept. 8 and Nov. 13, 1970; for the quotation, *Life,* Aug. 7, 1970.

Jury selection in the trial of Seale and Huggins: *Time,* March 22, 1971. Dismissal of charges in the same case: *The New York Times,* May 26, 1971.

Arguments against jury trial: Hall *et al.,* Chap. 22; Schaefer; *Law and Order Reconsidered; The Courts;* Chief Justice Burger, in *Life,* Aug. 7, 1970; Barry Farrell, "The Manson Jury," *Life,* April 16, 1971.

The requirements are minuscule: In New York City, for instance, all prosecutions of offenders (not just in jury trials), plus all court-appointed defense of same, account for 1.5 percent of the criminal justice budget; police patrol and investigation account for nearly three quarters.

*Voir dire* handled by judges: Hogan. English handling of pre-trial publicity: Karlen.

### Chapter 6
### II (*pp. 281–287*)

Criminal trials without defense lawyers, pre-*Gideon:* Nagel, in Blumberg; *The Courts. Johnson* v. *Zerbst,* 304 U.S. 458. Supreme Court indecisiveness on the issue: Leonard; *Betts* v. *Brady,* 316 U.S. 455. Nagel: *loc. cit.* Crime Commission figures from *The Courts.* Volunteer and other defense, pre-*Gideon:* Silverstein.

Gideon's story: Lewis; *Gideon.* Definition of when the right to counsel begins: Chap. 8 of Hall *et al.; Criminal Law Revolution; The Courts.* And when it ends: the same (but in Hall *et al.,* Chap. 3).

Distribution of assigned-counsel and of defender systems: National Legal Aid and Defender Assoc. survey (mimeo.).

New York City's expenditures: *Criminal Justice Plan for 1971;* direct communication from Mayor's Criminal Justice Coordinating Council.

Graham's echo of Justice Holmes is the title of his book. Evelle Younger; House Select Committee ("Improvement and Reform").

**IV** (*pp. 306–311*)

Mr. Nixon's remarks: *The New York Times,* Aug. 4, 1970. Mr. Will Wilson's comment: address at the A.B.A. Convention in Dallas, Aug. 1969. (Ramsey Clark, in a direct communication, adds, "My impression is that representatives of the Nixon Administration have frequently referred to presumption of innocence as a mere rule of procedural evidence.")

General description of inquisitorial system: *Enc. Soc. Sci.,* "Criminal Law"; *Enc. Amer.,* "Criminal Law"; Feifer; and Mavis Gallant, "Annals of Justice," *The New Yorker,* June 26, 1971.

General description of adversarial system: *Enc. Soc. Sci.,* "Criminal Law"; *Enc. Brit.,* "Criminal Law." Development of the system: *ibid.;* also, *Enc. Brit.,* "Habeas Corpus"; and see Notes to Chapter 3, Sections II and IV, above.

Comments by prosecutors on silence of the defendant: Karlen; Schaefer; *Griffin* v. *California,* 380 U.S. 609. The Louisianian conviction and reversal: *Rideau* v. *Louisiana,* 373 U.S. 723.

Curtis quoted in Mayer.


**VI** (*pp. 321–324*)

Reasonable doubt as one of the great principles: Botein; *Enc. Brit.,* "Criminal Law." Its rootedness in common law: *Enc. Soc. Sci.,* "Criminal Law."

Efforts to elucidate meaning of reasonable doubt: *Black's Law Dictionary,* "Doubt"; *Enc. Brit.,* "Criminal Law"; *Egan* v. *U.S.,* 287 D.C. Cir. 958; *State* v. *Koski,* 100 W. Va. 98; *People* v. *Rogers,* 324 Ill. 224.


### Chapter 7
**II** (*pp. 343–350*)

Inconsistencies in the criminal justice system: Crime Commission Report; *Corrections.*

Retribution vs. prevention, as the purposes of punishment: Packer.

History of the criminal sanctions, from earliest times to the Enlightenment: Schafer; *Corrections.* Enlightenment and beyond, including the Auburn System: *Corrections.* Punishment vs. treatment, as the dilemma of the criminal sanctions: Packer; Menninger; Schafer.

Coexistence of punishment and treatment without our criminal justice system: Packer; *Criminal Offenders; Corrections.*

Research studies showing deterrent value of certain and swift punishment: *Law and Order Reconsidered,* Chap. 1.

Typical statement about the two-thirds recidivism rate: John Bartlow Martin and others, cited in Morris and Hawkins. Studies showing identical recidivism rates for the treated and the untreated: Morris and Hawkins; James Vorenberg in *The New York Times Magazine,* May 11, 1969.

Proper method of studying recidivism, and true rate: Crime Commission Report; Morris and Hawkins.

Treatment in non-punitive settings: Morris and Hawkins. Experiment of the California Youth Authority: *ibid.*

## IV (*pp. 360–368*)

About 1½ percent of serious crimes result in imprisonment: Violence Commission Report; see also Notes to Chapter 4, Section VI, above. As one convict writes: Griswold (p. 252).

Physical conditions of prisons: *Law and Order Reconsidered; Corrections.* On the incident at Raiford: *The New York Times,* Feb. 28, 1971.

On brutality: various studies cited in *Law and Order Reconsidered; Corrections; The New York Times,* May 15, 1971, and Feb. 7, 1971, I, p. 64. Prison guards: "A Time to Act"; *Corrections;* Griswold; *The New York Times,* May 15, 1971; and numerous newspaper pieces in the Auburn *Citizen-Advertiser,* fall 1970 and spring 1971, and *The New York Times,* fall 1971, under headings of Auburn and Attica respectively. Ken Jackson's quote: from a lecture he gives as representative of the Fortune Society. Soledad treatment of political activists: *The New York Times,* Feb. 7, 1971, I, p. 64.

Mistreatment by fellow prisoners: Crime Commission Report; *Corrections.* Moundsville: *The New York Times,* July 12, 1971. Consensual homosexuality: Clemmer; Griswold; *The New York Times,* April 25, 1971, I, p. 40; and interviews with various prison officials and ex-inmates.

Dependency of inmates, regimen of orders: many sources, but esp. *Corrections* and Crime Commission Report; Menninger; *Time,* Jan. 18, 1971; Griswold.

Less than 10 percent . . . do teaching, etc.: *Corrections; A Time to Act.* Employment problems of the ex-convict: *Time,* Jan. 18, 1971 (citing a Harris poll); Koch; *Corrections.* The role of unemployment in recidivism: Daniel Glaser: *The Effectiveness of a Prison and Parole System* (Indianapolis, Ind.: Bobbs Merrill, 1964). Parole boards and indeterminate sentences: *Corrections;* Griswold; *The New York Times,* Sept. 27, 1971. Probation: *Corrections;* Morris and Hawkins.

Worsening atmosphere in prisons today: interviews with prison officials; La Mott.

## VI (*pp. 378–383*)

Right to appeal not constitutionally guaranteed: Karlen; Hall *et al.,* p. 1245. Discretion of appellate courts: Karlen. What takes place in an appeal proceeding: Karlen. Prejudicial error, and the purposes of appellate review: Karlen; Packer; Wright. Karlen's quote: Karlen.

The Court accepted only three percent: *Time,* Oct. 26, 1970.

Poor odds on gaining freedom through appeal: Hall *et al.,* p. 12; *Law and Order Reconsidered,* p. 501; Justice Mosk's report cited in Notes to Chapter 3, Section VI, above.

Increased volume of appeals: *The New York Times,* Nov. 24, 1969 and Jan. 25, 1971. *Griffin* v. *Illinois,* 351 U.S. 12; *Douglas* v. *California,* 372 U.S. 353. Various others: *Brown* v. *Allen,* 344 U.S. 443; *Fay* v. *Noia,* 372 U.S. 391; *Townsend* v. *Sain,* 372 U.S. 293.

Court reporters as a bottleneck: *The New York Times,* Jan. 25, 1971. Loss of finality: Bator, in 76 Harv. L. Rev. 441.

Mr. Mitchell's speech in Alabama was reported in *The New York Times,* June 26, 1971. The London A.B.A. speech was reported in the *Times,* July 17, 1971. Brandeis: *Olmstead* v. *United States,* 277 U.S. 438.

# Epilogue
## 2 (*pp. 402–408*)

Department of Justice news releases of June 22, 1970, Jan. 19, 1971, and Sept. 29, 1971. All national data from *Uniform Crime Reports,* 1967 through 1970, and "Uniform Crime Reporting," preliminary data (from the FBI) for six and nine months of 1971. Effects on American cities: *The New York Times,* March 17 and July 19, 1971. National Urban Coalition report quoted in the *Times* of Sept. 24, 1971. Killings, use of guns, child muggers, and the attack on Strauss: *The New York Times,* Aug. 29, 1971, IV, p. 4, Sept. 11 and 22, 1971; *New York Magazine,* Jan. 12, 1970; the *Times,* March 17 and Oct. 4, 1971.

Data on Bronx muggings: my estimate, taking half of the robberies reported by the New York Police Department (direct communication).

## 3 (*pp. 409–414*)

Data on the 20 cities: *Uniform Crime Reports* for 1969 and 1970 (Attorney General Mitchell released preliminary and more optimistic figures, but I have drawn upon the final and official ones). The *Times*'s survey: article by John Herbers in *The New York Times,* April 12, 1971. Changing police role: various interviews, plus *The New York Times,* May 18, 1970, and Sept. 28, 1971.

## 4 (*pp. 414–420*)

Law-and-order talk, and voting, by members of Congress in 1970: Fred Graham in *The New York Times,* Jan. 4, 1970, and John Herbers in the *Times,* Oct. 12, 1970. Discussion and voting on the D.C. Crime Bill: the *Times,* July 24, 1970. Ditto on the 1970 Omnibus Crime Bill: the *Times,* Oct. 13 and 18, 1970, and July 1970. Bulletin No. 1, Vol. 9, of the Association of the Bar of the City of New York.

In the first year with two Nixon appointees: *Time,* Dec. 28, 1970, and June 12, 1971; *The New York Times,* Dec. 16, 1970, and Feb. 25, Sept. 18, and Sept. 24, 1971.

**5** (*pp. 421–427*)

Court-appointed counsel for misdemeanants in at least 29 states: data gathered in 1971 by National Legal Aid and Defender Assoc., and presented in Brief in re *Argersinger* v. *Hamlin* (No. 5798, U.S. Supreme Court, Oct. term 1970).

Pre-trial disclosure: *Criminal Law Revolution;* Hall *et al.,* Chap. 21. Rights of prisoners: the Sostre case, Federal Ct. of Appeals, Second Circuit (see *The New York Times,* Feb. 25, 1971). Right of convicted misdemeanants to free trial records: *The New York Times,* Dec. 14, 1971. Pennsylvania prisoners' Bill of Rights: the *Times,* Oct. 5, 1971. Attica prisoners' right to lawyer: the *Times,* Sept. 28, 1971. Indigent prisoners' right to legal information: the *Times,* Nov. 9, 1971.

Rights of parolees and ex-convicts: direct communication from A.B.A.; *The New York Times,* Jan. 14 and May 21, 1971. Prof. Dershowitz's review: *The New York Times Book Review,* Feb. 7, 1971. Alinsky quote: from interview with Israel Shenker in the *Times* of Jan. 6, 1971.

**6** (*pp. 428–441*)

On police behavior and changing police role, see Notes to Section 3 of Epilogue, above. Some recent suggestions for improvements and reforms are in Crime Commission Report. Recent reforms in New York City are detailed in the Mayor's Criminal Justice Coordinating Council, *Two-Year Report,* and *Criminal Justice Plan for 1971.* For problems and remedies being applied throughout the nation, see *LEAA 1970.*

The various speedy-trial orders: *The New York Times,* Jan. 6 and April 30, 1971. On the emergency procedures used in New York Criminal Court during 1971: *ibid.,* Oct. 18, 1970, and Jan. 7 and Aug. 4, 1971. Decreased detention time: direct communication from Department of Correction, City of New York. Quote from the Mayor's Criminal Justice Coordinating Council: *Criminal Justice Plan for 1971.* Suggested court reforms: Crime Commission Report; *The Courts; LEAA 1970.* 1972 assistance from the Law Enforcement Assistance Administration: *The New York Times,* Dec. 28, 1970; U.S. Dept. of Justice, Law Enforcement Assistance Administration, *Expenditure and Employment Data for the Criminal Justice System, 1968–1969;* and late data by direct communication from the Law Enforcement Assistance Administration.

Soledad: LaMott; *The New York Times,* Aug. 29, 1971, I, p. 4; *Life,* Aug. 13, 1971; *Time,* Sept. 6, 1971.

The two surveys by the *Times:* May 15 and Sept. 19, 1971. Huey Newton is quoted in the *Times* of Aug. 29, 1971, and the Atlanta *Constitution* in Attica article in *Time,* Sept. 27, 1971.

The Auburn riot: from interviews with guards, Service Unit personnel, Deegan, townspeople, and others; also, the Auburn *Citizen-Advertiser,* Nov. 5, 1970. Sequelae of the riot: divers issues of the *Citizen-Advertiser* throughout the spring of 1971; also, *The New York Times,* Feb. 6, 11, 20, and May 17, 1971 (the last date includes the Hill letter). Late 1971 conditions: by direct communication from the Superintendent; also, Auburn *Citizen-Advertiser,* Aug. 6, and Nov. 4, 1971.

The details of the Attica riot are drawn primarily from the very thorough account in *The New York Times* of Oct. 4, 1971, and from a similar account in *Time,* Sept. 27, 1971.

# Bibliography

WHAT FOLLOWS is in no sense a general bibliography of primary works in criminal law, nor even a complete listing of the sources I consulted; it is merely a reference guide to those sources directly named in the text or cited in the Notes on Sources. For those who wish to consult a comprehensive and relatively up-to-date bibliography in this field, I suggest the one contained in Hall *et al., q.v.* below.

American Bar Association. *Code of Professional Responsibility and Canons of Judicial Ethics.* 1970.

Association of the Bar of the City of New York. *Reports of Committees of The Association of the Bar Concerned with Federal Legislation:* Vol. 9, Bulletin No. 1 (July 1970), No. 2 (August 1970), No. 3 (September 1970).

Barnes, Harry Elmer, and Negley K. Teeters. *New Horizons in Criminology.* 3rd ed. Englewood Cliffs: Prentice-Hall, 1959.

Berman, Harold J., ed. *Talks on American Law: A series of broadcasts to foreign audiences by members of the Harvard Law School Faculty.* New York: Random House, 1961. Paper.

*Blacks' Law Dictionary.* 4th ed. St. Paul: West, 1968.

Blumberg, Abraham S., ed. *The Scales of Justice.* Chicago: Aldine, 1970. Paper.

Botein, Bernard, and Murray A. Gordon. *The Trial of the Future: Challenge to the Law.* New York: Cornerstone Library, 1963. Paper.

Burnham, David. "Fear of Muggers Looms Large in Public Concern over Crime," *The New York Times,* May 20, 1968. A special study of the prosecution and sentencing of muggers in early 1967.

Chevigny, Paul. *Police Power: Police Abuses in New York City.* New York: Vintage Books, 1969. Paper.

Clark, Ramsey. *Crime in America: Observations on Its Nature, Causes, Prevention and Control.* New York: Simon and Schuster, 1970.

Clarke, Stevens H. *The New York City Criminal Court: Case Flow and Congestion from 1959 to 1968* (Report to the Mayor's Criminal Justice Coordinating Council). April 1970. Mimeo.

Clemmer, Donald. *The Prison Community.* New York: Holt, Rinehart and Winston, 1968. Paper.

*Corrections. See* President's Commission on Law Enforcement and Administration of Justice.

*Courts, The. See* President's Commission on Law Enforcement and Administration of Justice.

Crime Commission Report. *See* President's Commission on Law Enforcement and Administration of Justice.

*Crimes of Violence. See* National Commission on the Causes and Prevention of Violence.

*Criminal Justice Plan for 1971. See* New York, City of: Mayor's Criminal Justice Coordinating Council.

*Criminal Law Revolution 1960–1969, The.* By the Editors of *The Criminal Law Reporter.* Washington, D.C.: The Bureau of National Affairs, 1969.

*Criminal Offenders. See* New York, State of: Governor's Special Committee on Criminal Offenders.

Davis, Kenneth Culp. *Discretionary Justice.* Baton Rouge: Louisiana State Univ. Press, 1969.

Deutsch, Albert. *The Trouble with Cops.* New York: Crown, 1955.

Feifer, George. *Justice in Moscow.* New York: Delta, 1965. Paper.

Glaser, Daniel, ed. *Crime in the City.* New York: Harper & Row, 1970. Paper.

Graham, Fred P. *The Self-Inflicted Wound.* New York: Macmillan, 1970.

Griswold, H. Jack, and Mike Misenheimer, Art Powers, and Ed Tromanhauser. *An Eye for an Eye.* New York: Holt, Rinehart and Winston, 1970.

Hall, Livingston, and Yale Kamisar, Wayne R. LaFave, and Jerold H. Israel. *Modern Criminal Procedure.* 3rd ed. St. Paul: West, 1969.

Harris, Richard. *The Fear of Crime.* New York: Praeger, 1969. Paper.

————. *Justice: The Crisis of Law, Order, and Freedom in America.* New York: E. P. Dutton, 1970.

Hartogs, Renatus, and Eric Artzt, eds. *Violence: Causes and Solutions.* New York: Dell, 1970. Paper.

[Hogan, Frank S.] *Statement of District Attorney of New York County: Proposals for Reducing Delays in Criminal Justice in New York City.* [Office of the District Attorney, 1971]

House Select Committee. *See* United States House of Representatives.

Inbau, Fred E., and John E. Reid. *Criminal Interrogation and Confession.* Baltimore: Williams & Wilkins, 1962.

Joint Commission on Correctional Manpower and Training. Final Report: *A Time to Act.* Washington, D.C.: 1969.

Kalven, Harry, Jr., and Hans Zeisel. *The American Jury.* Boston: Little, Brown, 1966.

Karlen, Delmar (in collaboration with Geoffrey Sawer and Edward M. Wise). *Anglo-American Criminal Justice.* Oxford: Clarendon Press, 1967.

Klein, Herbert T. *The Police: Damned If They Do—Damned If They Don't.* New York: Crown, 1968.

[Koch, Edward I.] *Conference on Correctional Institutions Sponsored by Congressman Edward I. Koch and a Committee of Community Sponsors.* New York, May 23, 1970. Transcript.

LaMott, Kenneth. "The San Quentin Story—The Prisons Are Getting A Tougher Class of Convicts," *The New York Times Magazine,* May 2, 1971.

*Law and Order Reconsidered. See* National Commission on the Causes and Prevention of Violence.

*LEAA 1970. See* United States Department of Justice, Law Enforcement Assistance Administration.

Lewis, Anthony. *Gideon's Trumpet.* New York: Vintage, 1964. Paper.

Leonard, V. A. *The Police, the Judiciary and the Criminal.* Springfield: Charles C Thomas, 1969.

Mayer, Martin. *The Lawyers.* New York: Dell, 1968. Paper.

*Melrose Report, The. See* New York, City of, City Planning Commission.

Mendelsohn, B. "The Victimology," *Études Internationales de Psycho-Sociologie Criminelle,* July–September 1956.

———. "The Origin of the Doctrine of Victimology," *Excerpta Criminologica,* Vol. 3, No. 3 (1963).

Menninger, Karl. *The Crime of Punishment.* New York: Viking, 1968.

Mills, James. "I Have Nothing To Do with Justice," *Life,* March 12, 1971. Biography of Martin Erdmann.

———. *The Prosecutor.* New York: Farrar, Straus and Giroux, 1968.

Morris, Norval, and Gordon Hawkins. *The Honest Politician's Guide to Crime Control.* Chicago: Univ. of Chicago Press, 1970.

National Commission on the Causes and Prevention of Violence. Final Report: *To Establish Justice, To Insure Domestic Tranquility.* Washington, D.C.: U.S. Govt. Printing Office, 1969.

——— Staff Report: James S. Campbell, Joseph R. Sahid, and David P. Stang: *Law and Order Reconsidered.* Washington, D.C.: U.S. Govt. Printing Office, n.d.

——— Staff Report: Hugh Davis Graham and Ted Robert Gurr: *Violence in America: Historical and Comparative Perspectives.* Washington, D.C.: U.S. Govt. Printing Office, 1969.

——— Staff Report: Donald J. Mulvihill and Melvin M. Tumin, with Lynn A. Curtis: *Crimes of Violence.* 3 vols. Washington, D.C.: U.S. Govt. Printing Office, 1969.

New York, City of, City Planning Commission. *The Melrose Report: A Neighborhood Plans for Change.* 1969.

———. *Plan for New York City: 2: The Bronx.* 1969.

New York, City of, Department of Correction. *Annual Report.* 1968, 1969.

———. *Progress Through Crisis, 1954–1965.* 1965.

New York, City of, Mayor's Criminal Justice Coordinating Council. *Two-Year Report,* April 1969.

————. *Criminal Justice Plan for 1971.* March 1971.

New York, City of, Police Department. *Annual Report,* 1967, 1968, 1969.

New York, State of. *The Code of Criminal Procedure.* Brooklyn: The Eagle Library, 1965 and 1969.

————. *The Penal Law of the State of New York.* Brooklyn: The Eagle Library, 1965 and 1969.

New York, State of, Governor's Special Committee on Criminal Offenders. *Preliminary Report.* New York: June 1968.

New York, State of, Joint Legislative Committee on Crime, Its Causes, Control & Effect on Society. *Report* (Legislative Document, 1969). 1969.

New York, State of, Senate Committee on Crime and Correction. *The Tombs Disturbances.* Oct. 5, 1970.

*Newsweek,* March 8, 1971. Special Report: "Justice on Trial," pp. 16–19; "How Justice Works: The People vs. Donald Payne," by Peter Goldman and Don Holt, pp. 20–37; and "The Public" and "What Can Be Done," pp. 39–46.

Nizer, Louis. *My Life in Court.* New York: Pyramid, 1963. Paper.

————. *The Jury Returns.* New York: Pocket Books, 1968. Paper.

Oaks, Dallin H., and Warren Lehman. *A Criminal Justice System and the Indigent.* Chicago: Univ. of Chicago Press, 1968.

O'Hara, Charles E. *Fundamentals of Criminal Investigation.* Springfield: Charles C Thomas, 1956.

Packer, Herbert. *The Limits of the Criminal Sanction.* Stanford: Stanford Univ. Press, 1968.

*Plan for New York City. See* New York, City of, City Planning Commission.

*Police, The. See* President's Commission on Law Enforcement and Administration of Justice.

President's Commission on Law Enforcement and Administration of Justice. Report: *The Challenge of Crime in a Free Society.* Washington, D.C.: U.S. Govt. Printing Office, 1967.

————, Task Force on Administration of Justice. Task Force Report: *The Courts.* Washington, D.C.: U.S. Govt. Printing Office, 1967.

————, Task Force on Corrections. Task Force Report: *Corrections.* Washington, D.C.: U.S. Govt. Printing Office, 1967.

————, Task Force on the Police. Task Force Report: *The Police.* Washington, D.C.: U.S. Govt. Printing Office, 1967.

————, Task Force on Science and Technology. Task Force Report: *Science and Technology.* Washington, D.C.: U.S. Govt. Printing Office, 1967.

Radzinowicz, Leon, and Marvin Wolfgang, eds. *Crime and Justice.* 3 vols. New York: Basic Books, 1971.

Schaefer, Walter V. *The Suspect and Society.* Evanston: Northwestern Univ. Press, 1967.

Schafer, Stephen. *The Victim and His Criminal: A Study in Functional Responsibility.* New York: Random House, 1968. Paper.

Schur, Edwin M. *Law and Society: A Sociological View.* New York: Random House, 1968. Paper.

————. *Our Criminal Society: The Social and Legal Sources of Crime in America.* Englewood Cliffs: Prentice-Hall, 1969.

*Science and Technology. See* President's Commission on Law Enforcement and Administration of Justice.

Senate Judiciary Committee. *See* United States Senate.

Shapiro, Fred C. *Whitmore.* New York: Pyramid, 1970. Paper.

Silverstein, Lee. *The Defense of the Poor in Criminal Cases in American State Courts.* Chicago: Amer. Bar Foundation, 1965.

Skolnick, Jerome H. *Justice Without Trial: Law Enforcement in Democratic Society.* New York: John Wiley, 1966. Paper.

————. "Social Control in the Adversary System," *J. of Conflict Resolution,* 1967.

Sowle, Claude R., ed. *Police Power and Individual Freedom.* Chicago: Aldine, 1962.

Stryker, Lloyd Paul. *The Art of Advocacy.* New York: Cornerstone Library, 1965. Paper.

Swados, Harvey. "The City's Island of the Damned," *The New York Times Magazine,* April 26, 1970.

Thomas, Piri. *Down These Mean Streets.* New York: New American Library, 1968. Paper.

*Time,* Jan. 18, 1971. Special Report: "The Shame of the Prisons," pp. 46–56.

*Time to Act, A. See* Joint Commission on Correctional Manpower and Training.

Toch, Hans H. *Violent Men: An Inquiry into the Psychology of Violence.* Chicago: Aldine, 1969.

Trevor-Roper, Hugh. *The Crisis of the Seventeenth Century.* New York: Harper & Row, 1966.

*Uniform Crime Reports. See* United States Department of Justice, Federal Bureau of Investigation.

United States Department of Justice, Federal Bureau of Investigation. *Uniform Crime Reports for the United States.* (Also titled, on spine and cover: *Crime in the United States.*) An annual; each year's issue deals with the previous year's data and includes that year after the title. Washington, D.C.: U.S. Govt. Printing Office, 1950–1970.

United States Department of Justice, Law Enforcement Assistance Administration. *Expenditure and Employment Data for the Criminal Justice System, 1968–1969.* Washington, D.C.: U.S. Govt. Printing Office, 1970.

————. *LEAA 1970: LEAA Activities, July 1, 1969 to June 30, 1970,* and *LEAA 1970: Grants and Contracts, Fiscal Year 1970.* Washington, D.C.: U.S. Govt. Printing Office, n.d.

————. *1970 National Jail Census.* LEAA–NCJISS Stat Center Publication SC–No. 1. Washington, D.C.: February 1971.

United States House of Representatives, Select Committee on Crime.

Hearings: *The Improvement and Reform of Law Enforcement and Criminal Justice in the United States*. Washington: U.S. Govt. Printing Office, 1969.

————. Hearings: *Crime in America—Aspects of Organized Crime, Court Delay, and Juvenile Justice*. Washington, D.C.: U.S. Govt. Printing Office, 1970.

————. Hearings: *Crime in America—A Mid-America View*. Washington, D.C.: U.S. Govt. Printing Office, 1969.

————. Hearings: *Crime in America—Response of a Midsouth Community*. Washington, D.C.: U.S. Govt. Printing Office, 1970.

————. Hearings: *Crime in America—In the Nation's Capital*. Washington, D.C.: U.S. Govt. Printing Office, 1970.

United States Senate, Committee on the District of Columbia. *Report of the Advisory Panel Against Armed Violence*. Washington, D.C.: U.S. Govt. Printing Office, 1969.

————. *Staff Study on Drug Abuse in the Washington Area*. Washington, D.C.: U.S. Govt. Printing Office, 1969.

United States Senate, Committee on the Judiciary, Subcommittee on Criminal Laws and Procedures. Hearings, March 7 through July 12, 1967: *Controlling Crime Through More Effective Law Enforcement*. Washington, D.C.: U.S. Government Printing Office, 1967.

Vera Institute of Justice. *Bail and Parole Jumping in Manhattan in 1967*. New York: August 1970.

*Violence in America*. *See* National Commission on the Causes and Prevention of Violence.

Violence Commission Report. *See* National Commission on the Causes and Prevention of Violence.

von Hentig, Hans. *The Criminal and His Victim*. New Haven: Yale Univ. Press, 1948.

Wald, Michael, *et al*. "Interrogations in New Haven: The Impact of Miranda," 76 Yale L. J. 1519–1648.

Wellman, Francis L. *The Art of Cross-Examination*. New York: Collier, 1962. Paper.

Westley, William A. *Violence and the Police*. Cambridge: The MIT Press, 1971.

Wigmore, John H. *Wigmore on Evidence*. Boston: Little, Brown, 1940.

Wilson, James Q. *Varieties of Police Behavior*. Cambridge: Harvard Univ. Press, 1968.

Wright, Charles Alan. *Federal Practice and Procedure*. St. Paul: West, 1969.

Zimbardo, Philip. "The Psychology of Police Confessions," *Psychology Today*, June 1967.

# Index

## A

Accomplice testimony: *see* Confessions; Error, prejudicial; *Bruton* v. *United States*
Adams, John, 164
Adversarial-accusatorial system of justice: *see* Justice, system of criminal
Alabama State Bar Assn., 283
Alinsky, Saul, 424
Ambos, Anna, 10, 25, 34, 38–39, 52, 54, 55–56, 59, 60, 132, 136, 189, 200, 230, 236–239, 262, 267, 288, 294–296, 303, 314, 315, 316, 326, 327, 331–32, 406–7
American Bar Assn., 149, 193, 195, 382; Commission on Correctional Facilities and Services of, 423; Fifth Canon of Ethics of, 167; *Journal* of, 253
*American Jury, The* (Kalven and Zeisel), 235, 258–59, 310, 323–24
Anacharsis, 253

Anderson, Richard, 121
Appeals, 378–83; in appellate court, 379, 388–89, 390; and *coram nobis* petitions, 381; delays in, 381, 383; and due-process mechanisms, 382–83; growing volume of, 380–83; and *habeas corpus* petitions, 381, 382; lack of finality in, 381–82, 399, 426; in N.Y. Court of Appeals, 391–93, 397; and prejudicial error, 379–80; and Supreme Court, 379; and writ of *certiorari,* 426
Aristotle, 102
Arrests, illegal: *see* Police
Arrow, Irving, 204, 269
Atlanta *Constitution,* 434
Attica State Correctional Facility, 438–40; riot at, 423, 434–435, 439–40
Auburn *Citizen-Advertiser,* 370
Auburn State Correctional Facility, 346, 358, 360, 368–78, 435–38; riot at, 435–38

# B

Baer, Harold, 274
Bail system, 181; bail-jumping,
    150; as an escape from jus-
    tice, 146, 148, 150; fixed
    schedules of, 150; as instru-
    ment of punishment, 149,
    150; and overcrowded jails
    and courts, 151, 431, 432;
    prisoners who can't afford,
    142, 144, 146, 150; right
    to, 145, 309; setting high,
    149
Baltimore, Md., 29
Batten, James K., 29
Bellamy, Conrad, 204
Bench trials, 209, 255, 256
Bennett, James V., 149
Bentham, Jeremy, 346
Bernstein, Samuel: as lawyer for
    C. Ortiz, 275, 279, 289,
    290, 300, 301, 304, 311,
    313, 315, 321, 327, 329–
    330, 333, 334, 339–40, 341
Bishop, Joseph W., 120
Black, Danetta, 204
Black, Hugo, 283, 417
Blackmun, Harry, 416
Blumberg, Abraham S., 196, 212
Boston, Mass., 30, 63
Brandeis, Louis, 185, 383
Brennan, William, Jr., 417
Breslin, Edward, 85, 90
Brooklyn House of Detention,
    89, 90, 109, 142–44, 154–
    159, 162, 172, 274, 352,
    358

Brown, Carl, 204
Brown, Claude, 21
Brown v. *Mississippi,* 105, 119
Brumley, Jayne, 30
*Bruton* v. *United States,* 385,
    389–90, 392, 397, 416, 421
Buffalo, N.Y., 404
Burger, Warren E., 193, 195,
    254, 416, 418, 419
Butler, Harold, 437


# C

California, 431; indeterminate
    sentence laws of, 366; pris-
    ons in, 362, 423, 433–34;
    Youth Authority of, 349
Carney, James, 140–41, 158,
    160, 244
Carr, Edward, 168 n
Casey, Thomas: as lawyer for
    C. Ortiz, 275, 304, 305,
    327, 329–30, 339, 341
CBS News, 34
Celler, Emanuel, 416
Census Bureau: survey of jails,
    150, 151
Center for the Study of Demo-
    cratic Institutions, 254
*Chapman* v. *California,* 391
Chevigny, Paul, 232
Chicago, Ill., 12, 63, 197, 404,
    410
Cities: crime decrease in, 409–
    411; crime rise in, viii, 17,
    22, 402–5, 430; decay in,

Cities (*continued*)
viii, ix, 12, 284, 402, 404–5, 429; flight from, vii, 10–11, 402, 405. *See also* Ghettoes; *individual cities*

Civil rights, 441–44; of defendants, 419–22, 428; of parolees and ex-convicts, 423; of prisoners, 415, 422. *See also* Confessions; Interrogations; Investigations; Jails and prisons; Supreme Court; *individual amendments*

Clark, Lt. Edward G., 52, 56–57

Clark, Ramsey, 130, 401

Clearance, crime, rate of: *see* Crime; Police

Cleaver, Eldridge, 434

Coles, Robert, 20–21

*Confession, The* (London), 423

Confessions: accomplice testimony and, 115, 117, 190, 222, 296–97, 321, 416, 424, 425, 427; arrests and indictments and, 129, 131; civil rights and, 50, 51, 102, 117, 128–31; convictions and, 128–29, 130–31; in muggings, 131; physical force and, 102–5, 118; psychological force and, 102, 106–109, 117, 118; repudiation of, 102, 107. *See also* Interrogations; Plea-bargaining; *individual suspects*

Connecticut, 431

Consolidated Millinery, 73, 75, 89, 113, 176–77, 239

Correction: *see* Criminal sanctions; Jails and prisons

Courts, 443; appeals in, 379–80, 388–89, 390, 391–93, 397; arraignment, 138–41; congestion in, ix, 144, 147, 181, 192, 193, 285, 286, 383, 429, 430–32; criminal, 141, 161; emergency measures for, 431–32; magistrates', 139, 181, 209; need for money in, 383, 431, 432, 443; police, 181; Supreme (state), 141, 161, 198; trial delays in, 147–48, 151, 181, 430–32. *See also* Judges; Supreme Court; Trial by jury

Credibility of witnesses, attacks on, 211, 212, 230–31, 234–235. *See also* Defense lawyers; Prosecution lawyers; Trial by jury

Creamer, J. Shane, 422–23

Crime: decrease in rate of, 409–411; evidence in, 50, 51; Nixon Administration and, 32–33, 34, 131, 154, 401, 402–4, 407, 409, 415–16, 422; organized, vii, 415; rise of, viii, 120, 146, 400, 402–405, 414, 421, 429–30; social causes of, x, 19, 31–32, 131, 415, 444; statistics on, viii, 17–19, 35, 120, 121, 183 n, 361, 402–4, 409; unreported, 27–28; white-collar, vii. *See also* Muggings; Police; *crime legislation*

Crime Commission (President's Commission on Law Enforcement and Administration of Justice), 18, 28, 31, 32, 35, 45, 63, 164, 180 n, 193, 195, 233, 278 n, 283, 363, 401

*Crime in America* (Clark), 130

*Crime of Punishment, The* (Menninger), 254

*Criminal Interrogation and Confessions* (Inbau and Reid), 106, 121

Criminal sanctions, 343, 344–50; against non-whites, 428; and deterrence, 344–47, 348–350, 361; and prison reform, 346; and recidivism, 348, 366, 367; and rehabilitation, 344, 346–50; and retribution, 344–47; and solitary imprisonment, 34, 435, 436; and young prisoners, 347. *See also* Jails and prisons

Cross, John C., 67

Cross-examination: *see* Credibility; Defense lawyers; Prosecution lawyers; Trial by jury

Curtis, Charles P., 309–10

Czolgosz, Leon, 370


**D**

Davidson, Irwin D., 199–207 *passim,* 214–29 *passim,* 235, 240–52 *passim,* 262, 263–264, 267–71 *passim,* 301, 320, 322 n, 420

Davis, John F., 398

Davis, Rennie, 254

Dayton, Ohio, 30

Deegan, John, 376, 435, 437

Defender system: *see* Defense lawyers—as public defenders

Defense lawyers, 163–69, 172, 178, 179, 182, 419–20; and appeals, 381; in assigned-counsel system, 284; attacks on credibility of witness, 230–231; and jury selection, 210, 233; from Legal Aid, 140, 146, 149, 166, 167, 168, 196, 283, 284, 285, 375, 376, 389, 393, 395, 396–398, 399, 419, 422, 425; and perjury, 212, 233–234; and plea-bargaining, 193–195, 196, 422, 432; as public defenders, 140, 165–166, 168, 169, 196–97, 283, 284, 422; summation of, 260; and trial delays, 148, 181, 287; in trials, 211–12, 308. *See also* Trial by jury

Demosthenes, 102

Denmark, 254–55

Dershowitz, Alan, 423–24

Detectives: *see* Police

Detroit, Mich., 12, 30, 404

Deutsch, Albert, 78 n

Devlin, Lord, 324

District attorneys: *see* Prosecution lawyers

District of Columbia Crime Bill (1970), 34, 149–50, 415–416, 418, 422

Dodd, David, 47
Dollinger, Isidore, 184–85
*Don Juan* (Byron), 323
Douglas, William O., 162–63
*Douglas* v. *California,* 380
Doyle, Sir Arthur Conan, 50
D'Rall, George, 280
Drugs, vii, 15, 21, 63, 67, 68, 69, 70, 87, 89, 405, 406
Due process, 105, 118, 119, 286–287, 421–24; and jury trials, 213–14; model of criminal justice, 80–83; recent advances in, 421–23 *passim;* recent attacks on, 32–35, 415–17. *See also* Fifth Amendment; Fourteenth Amendment; Trial by jury

**E**

Edelman, Stanley, 204
Eighth Amendment, 146
Elmira Reformatory, 351–53; Reception Center, 341, 353–60
England: criminal justice system in, 118, 208, 257, 309
Eppinger, Theodore, 188
Erdmann, Martin, 168
Erikson, Erik, 20
Ervin, Sam, 149
Error, prejudicial, 379–80
*Escobedo* decision, 51, 82, 119–120, 121, 129–30, 131, 206, 284, 421
Evert, Frederick, 204

Evidence, admissibility of: and police investigatory work, 48–50, 79–80, 104–5, 118–119, 130–31; and prejudicial error, 379–80; and violations of constitutional rights, 64–65, 81–82, 104–105. *See also* Appeals; Confessions; Error, prejudicial; Trial by jury

**F**

Fairness, doctrine of, 116–19; and defense lawyers, 162–163, 168–69; and *Gideon,* 281–82; and jury trials, 209, 213–14, 235; "preoccupation with" (J. Mitchell), 286; recent growth of, in American justice system, 421–23 *passim. See also* Due process; Fifth Amendment
Fear of crime, effects of, vii, 25, 28–31, 122, 256, 285; vigilante groups and, 30, 414. *See also* Law and order concept
Federal Bureau of Investigation, 18; *Uniform Crime Reports* of, 16, 17, 18–19, 22, 121, 402–3
Feifer, George, 310–11
Ferry, James, 280
Fifth Amendment, 34, 131, 255, 256, 399, 414, 415–16; confessions and, 102, 117–

Fifth Amendment (*continued*) 118, 128; Supreme Court and, 33, 120, 281, 309. *See also* Trial by jury—defendants on stand in

Flint, Mich., 410

Flynn, Patrolman John, 220

Foote, Caleb, 82–83

Fortas, Abe, 416

Fortune Society, 21, 363

Fourteenth Amendment, 282, 283, 399; confessions and, 128; Supreme Court and, 81

Fourth Amendment, 34, 64, 385, 399, 416; Supreme Court and, 64–65, 82, 281

Frankfurter, Felix, 286, 301

Freedman, Monroe, 233–34

Fritz, Harry, 435–36

Fuld, Stanley, 431

*Fundamentals of Criminal Investigation* (O'Hara), 106


**G**

Georgia, 434

Ghettoes, 405; police and, 61–63, 67–68, 405, 410–11, 428, 429–30; poor non-whites in, 402, 444; youths in, 14–15, 19–22, 62–63, 87–89, 158, 288, 405–6. *See also* Cities; Crime—social causes of; Drugs; Melrose section, Bronx

Gideon, Clarence E., 283

*Gideon* v. *Wainwright* decision, 82, 165, 169, 281–87, 421–422

Gilbert, Thomas V., 280

Gillette, Chester, 370

Giuliani, Arnold, 280

Gladwin, Walter, 91

Goffman, Erving, 155

Goldberg, Arthur, 51, 120

Goldberg, Jay, 168

Goldstein, Detective, 292

Goldstein, Irving, 239

Goldwater, Barry, 32

Goodman, Roy M., 150 n

Graham, Fred, 285

*Griffin* v. *Illinois* decision, 380, 422

Griswold, Erwin N., 235, 253

Gurven, Mildred, 204


**H**

*Habeas corpus: see* Appeals

Halpern, Dr. Milton, 293

Hand, Learned, 120

Hanrahan, James, 419; background of, 171; as lawyer for Ortiz brothers, 160, 161–62, 169–74, 177, 178, 199–200, 202–7, 215–20, 223–28, 229, 236, 246–52, 260–61, 262, 267–71 *passim*, 275, 330; offers plea-bargaining, 161, 190–91, 270. *See also* Helmer case, trials of

Harlan, John M., 120, 417

Harms, Inspector August, 57
Harney, Malachi L., 67
Harris, Fred R., 405
Harris, Richard, 33
Harris & Associates, Louis, 29, 33
Harvard Law School, 164
Hastings, Sir Patrick, 167
Hawaii, 366
Hawkins, Gordon, 18, 348
*Haynes* v. *Washington,* 51
Heit, Julia, 396–99, 425–26
Hellerstein, William, 397, 398
Helmer, Alexander, ix, 3–5, 8–9, 10, 12–16, 23–24, 26, 137–144, 159–62; burial of, 136; discovery of body, 38–44; investigation of murder, 43, 52–61, 68–78, 84–85, 90–101, 109–17, 122–23, 124–28, 132–36; mugging and murder of, 35–37, 400
Helmer, Emma, 4
Helmer, George, 5, 58–59
Helmer case, trials of, 137–44, 159–62, 169–78, 188–91, 199–200, 202–7, 214–30, 235–52, 260–71, 273–81, 287–305, 311–21, 322 n, 325–34, 408; accomplice testimony in, 115, 117, 190, 222, 296–97, 320, 384, 385, 387–88, 389–90, 392, 395, 397; defense case, 235–51; evidence in, 174, 176, 189, 220, 223, 225, 226, 236, 297, 301, 302–3, 314, 316, 318, 320, 340, 384, 387; Huntley hearing

Helmer case (*continued*)
for, 205–7, 301; juries on, 202–5, 207, 214, 215, 222, 247, 252, 260–72, 278–80, 294, 312, 313, 319–21, 325–34, 335; prosecution case, 215–29, 290–305; time discrepancy in, 113, 116, 132–33, 174, 176, 189–90, 227, 228, 261, 262, 263, 265, 298, 303, 304, 316, 319, 327, 328, 331, 339, 388
Hentig, Hans von, 7, 8
Herbers, John, 409–10
Hill, Charles Leon, 437–38
Hochman, Dr. Charles, 44, 136, 218–19, 292–94, 318, 326
Hogan, Frank, 49, 120, 129, 131, 210
Holland, 254–55
*Honest Politician's Guide to Crime Control, The* (Morris and Hawkins), 18
Hoover, J. Edgar, 66
Horowitz, Isidore, 279
House Select Committee on Crime, 23, 121, 285
Huggins, Ericka, 255–56
Hughes, Charles Evans, 285

## I

Illinois, 434
Inbau, Fred E., 106, 121
Indigent defendants: *see* Justice, system of criminal

*Informer in Law Enforcement, The* (Harney and Cross), 67

Informers: *see* Investigations

Inquisitorial system of justice, 118, 165, 167, 254–55, 307–8, 309, 310–11, 442

Interrogations: civil rights and, 33, 48, 50, 51, 113, 119–121, 131; differing versions of, 76, 84, 90, 93–96, 101, 113; field, 64, 65, 68–69, 82; station house, 64, 65, 69, 70–71, 82, 106, 118; techniques in, 77, 106–7. *See also* Confessions; *individual detectives and suspects*

Investigations, 50–51; civil rights and, 106, 121, 130; dragnets, 61, 63–66, 68, 70, 131; Fourth Amendment and, 64–65, 82; improper, 79–83; informers and, 61, 66–67, 70, 71, 131. *See also* Interrogations

Israel, Eve, 204


# J

Jackson, George, 433–34

Jackson, Ken, 363

Jackson, Robert, 149

Jacobi Hospital Morgue, 43–44, 218

Jails and prisons, 360–61, 432–441; abominable conditions

Jails and prisons (*continued*) in, 151–53, 181, 361–64, 433; boredom in, 142, 143, 155–56, 362; breed violence, 153, 361, 363, 364, 428; city and county, 151, 362, 433; civil rights in, 422–23; correction officers in, 147, 152–53, 361, 362, 363, 364, 370–71, 374, 435, 438, 439, 440; employment problems for released prisoners, 365–66, 423; hostages in, 436, 439; inability to make decisions in, 364–65; inmates as a sub-society, 155, 361; militants in, 153, 363, 367, 433–40; overcrowded, 144, 151, 153, 193, 362, 364; parole, 366–67, 423, 431, 433, 443; physical tortures in, 362; rape in, 152, 159, 159 n, 362, 364, 436; reform in, ix, 346, 368, 433–434, 437, 439, 441; rehabilitation in, 362, 365–68, 382, 383; riots in, viii, 151, 155, 423, 430, 434–40; segregation in, 437–38, 443; state, 151, 362; strip cells in, 362–63, 437; time prisoners in, 143, 151, 155; trial prisoners in, 143, 146, 148, 150, 151, 153, 155. *See also* Criminal sanctions; *individual jails and prisons*

Jay, Joseph, 200, 204, 215, 230, 279

Jiacobello, Detective Bartholomew, 137
Johnson, Lyndon, 33
*Johnson* v. *Zerbst,* 282 n
Judges, 418, 428, 432; arraignment, 139–40; bail and,
149, 150, 151; charges of,
260; and court congestion,
147; party politics and,
212–13, 258; and past record of defendant, 235, 344;
and plea-bargaining, 193–
195, 196, 431; prosecutors
and, 179; and reasonable
doubt, 322–24; and
sentencing, 336, 338, 339,
343–44, 416; setting aside
verdicts, 274; in trials,
212–13, 256, 308. *See also*
Courts; Justice, system of
criminal; Trial by jury
Julius, Johannes, 103
Juries and jurors: *see* Trial by
jury
Justice, system of criminal, x,
163, 184, 209, 286–87,
361; bail cases, 148–49;
conservatives on, 401, 415,
421, 428–29, 433, 434,
440, 441–42, 443; democ-
racy and, 423–24, 441–44;
Grand Jury and, 171–72,
188; inadequate, 146–47,
428–29; and indigent de-
fendants, 164, 165, 166–68,
196, 276, 281–87, 288–89,
428–29, 430, 434; jail cases,
148–49; liberals on, 401,
415, 416, 421, 428–29,

Justice (*continued*)
440, 443–44; no-knock
searches, 34–35, 415; and
presumption of innocence,
145, 146, 167, 169, 290,
306–11; and preventive detention, 34–35, 149–50,
307, 415, 422; and proba-
tion, 150, 336–38, 344,
349, 367, 423, 433, 443;
proposals for change, 153;
and protection of accused,
308–9; radicals on, 421–29,
433, 434, 441, 442–43; and
reasonable doubt, 313, 321–
325; sentencing, 338, 339,
343–44, 366, 415, 416;
and speedy trial guarantee,
144, 145, 146, 192, 195;
and wiretaps, 415. *See also*
Appeals; Bail system;
Courts; Criminal sanctions;
Jails and prisons; Plea-bargaining; Trial by jury
*Justice in Moscow* (Feifer),
310–11
*Justice Without Trial* (Skolnick),
81


**K**

Kacerosky, Patrolman Edward,
39, 40–41, 53, 219, 220,
290, 291–92
Kalven, Harry, Jr., 235, 258–59,
310, 323–24
Karlen, Delmar, 379–80

Kase, Kenneth, 419; background
    of, 175; as lawyer for A.
    Ortiz, 275, 294, 299–300,
    304, 311, 314–15, 327,
    329–30, 334, 339, 341; as
    lawyer for D. Valencia,
    161–62, 174, 176–78, 199–
    200, 202–7, 216–20, 224–
    225, 227–30, 236–43 *pas-
    sim,* 246, 251–52, 261–62,
    267–71 *passim,* 292; offers
    plea-bargaining, 161, 176,
    190–91, 270. *See also* Hel-
    mer case, trials of
Kaufman, Harold, 21–22
Koota, Aaron, 120, 129, 130
Kunstler, William, 165


**L**


Landy, Patrolman Joseph, 42–
    43, 219, 292
La Rocco, Detective Anthony, 72
Law and order concept, viii, 32–
    35, 122, 403, 415–17, 418,
    423; appeals and, 382; Su-
    preme Court and, 33, 34,
    120, 401, 414–15
Lawyers: *see* Defense lawyers;
    Prosecution lawyers
*Lawyers, The* (Mayer), 310
Leff, James, 148
*Life* magazine, 29, 33, 148, 168
*Limits of the Criminal Sanction,
    The* (Packer), 80, 282,
    382 n
Lindsay, John, 405, 407, 425

London, Artur, 423
Los Angeles, Calif., 404
Loughery, Leo, 233
Lowe, Mary Johnson, 424–25;
    appeals conviction of A.
    Ortiz, 374–76, 384–89,
    391–96, 397, 398–99; back-
    ground of, 275–76; as
    lawyer for A. Ortiz, 275,
    277, 278, 279, 288–305
    *passim,* 312, 313, 314, 320–
    321, 327, 329–30, 333,
    334–35, 339, 340, 341, 356
Lussen, Asst. Chief Inspector
    Frederick, 57
Lyman, William, 91–92, 162,
    174, 277–81 *passim,* 290–
    305 *passim,* 311, 313, 317,
    319–21, 322 n, 327–41
    *passim,* 384, 387, 389, 395,
    420


**M**


Maizel, Sergeant, 39, 40–41
*Malloy* decision, 82
*Manchild in the Promised Land*
    (Brown), 21
Manson case, Charles, 256–57,
    307, 344
*Mapp* v. *Ohio,* 80 n, 81, 421
Massachusetts, 434
Mayer, Martin, 310
Mayor's Criminal Justice Coor-
    dinating Council, N.Y.C.,
    147, 150, 431–32
Mazer, Eli, 280

McCabe, Detective Stephen, 42, 43, 76, 135–36, 140–41, 160–61, 162, 172, 188, 247, 265, 266, 268, 269, 271, 319, 329, 334, 335, 336, 358, 413–14; cross-examination of, 227–29, 302–4; interrogation of suspects, 74–75, 76–77, 94–96, 100–1, 110–17, 122–123, 125–28, 132–35, 173, 176, 189, 190, 205, 221–222, 226–28, 241–43, 246, 249, 250, 260, 263, 298, 302, 303–4, 316, 317; investigation of crime, 42–43, 44–45, 52–61, 68–74, 78, 84–85, 90–92, 225–26, 238–39, 262, 295, 302–3, 314, 316, 318, 340, 385, 387, 395, 426–27; testimony of, 200, 225–27, 301–2, 312, 315, 316, 325–326, 327
McClellan, John, 33–34, 109
McGuire, Detective, 292
McNeil, John, 204
Melrose section, Bronx, 3–4, 9–15, 23, 26, 405–8
Mendelsohn, Benjamin, 7–8
Menninger, Karl, 254, 433
Meridian, Miss., 64
Michigan, 434
*Michigan Law Review,* 234
Miranda, Ernesto, 130
*Miranda* v. *Arizona* decision, 49, 82, 106, 107, 109, 119, 120–21, 122, 129–31, 284, 342, 412, 414, 416–17,

*Miranda* v. *Arizona* decision (*continued*) 418, 421; New Haven study of results of, 49, 121, 130; Pittsburgh study of results of, 121, 130
Mississippi, 362
Mitchell, John N., 34, 286, 382, 402–3, 405
Montesquieu, Charles, Baron de, 346
Montreal, Canada, 31
Morris, Norval, 18, 348
Mosk, Stanley, 130, 232
Motley, Constance Baker, 426–427
Moundsville Penitentiary, 364
Mucelli, Hamlet, 280
Muggers, 15, 19–20, 63; choice of victims, 6–8; motives of, 19–23. *See also* Crime—social causes of; Ghettoes; Muggings; Negroes; Puerto Ricans
Muggings, vii–ix; bail in, 149; causes of, 19–22; confessions and, 131; courts and, 49; definitions of, 7, 16–17; evidence in, 43, 50, 52, 131; indoor, 26, 36; physical injury in, 22–23, 405; plea-bargaining and, 192–93; statistics on, 6, 17–19, 20, 22, 27, 403–4, 406; victims of, 6–8, 28, 432. *See also* Crime; Muggers
Murphy, Commissioner Michael J., 48, 129

Murphy, Commissioner Patrick
V., 411–12
Murray, Sir Gilbert, viii
*My Life in Court* (Nizer), 234

# N

Nagel, Stuart S., 283
National Bar Assn., 149
National Commission on the
Causes and Prevention of
Violence: *see* Violence
Commission
National District Attorneys'
Assn., 286
National Urban Coalition, 405
Negroes, 14, 412; Black Muslims,
434, 439; Black Panthers,
48, 150, 255, 434, 435; as
inmates, 355, 367, 370,
435–36, 439; as militants,
153, 254; muggings and,
6–7, 19–22, 27; police and,
62–63. *See also* Ghettoes
New Jersey, 434
New York City, N.Y., 12, 30,
146, 147, 150, 151, 213,
284 n, 367, 404, 405, 431–
432. *See also* Cities; Melrose section, Bronx
New York Police Dept., 36, 39,
411–12; Bronx Communica-
tions Bureau of, 39; brutality in, 105; corruption in,
79 n, detectives in, 412,
413, 414; duties of, 45–46;
Emergency Service of, 39–
41; Headquarters of, 137–
138; interrogation in, 106,

New York Police Dept. (*continued*)
107–9; perjury and, 232;
recruits in, 48. *See also*
Police
New York State, 431; Appellate
Division of, 388–89, 390–
391; Code of Criminal Procedure of, 115, 117, 422,
427; Court of Appeals of,
91 n, 380, 391–93, 397,
423; Criminal Court of,
138–40, 161, 431; inde-
terminate sentence laws of,
366; Penal Code of, 115,
338; prisons in, 362, 434,
439; Supreme Court of, 91
n, 141, 161, 198. *See also individual prisons*
*New York Times, The,* 22 n, 29,
49, 168, 192, 285, 409–10,
434, 435
Newark, N.J., 12, 404
Newhampton (reformatory), 88
*Newsweek,* 194
Newton, Huey, 424, 434
Nixon, Richard, 32–33, 34, 131,
154, 213, 286, 307, 401,
402–4, 407, 409, 415–16,
420, 421, 422
Nizer, Louis, 234
Norton, Lt. Howard, 52, 56–57
Norway, 254–55

# O

Odierno, Annette, 9, 59, 229,
305

O'Hara, Charles E., 106–7
Ohio, 362
Omnibus Crime Bill (1967), 33
Omnibus Crime Control and Safe
    Streets Bill (1968), 33, 34,
    401, 403–4, 405, 409, 410,
    414, 418, 432
Oquendo, Herbert, 123, 124
Ortiz, Alfredo, 72, 75, 85–92,
    93–101 passim, 112, 124,
    125, 127, 135, 137–38,
    242, 408, 424, 425, 426–
    427, 438; appeals of, 374–
    377, 383–89, 390, 391–99,
    400; arraignment of, 139–
    141; at Auburn, 368, 370–
    378, 384, 391, 397, 400,
    425; at Brooklyn House of
    Detention, 89, 90, 142–44,
    154, 155–59, 162, 172, 177,
    274; charges brutality, 111,
    125, 157, 172–73, 174,
    249, 358; claims illegal
    arrest, 91–92, 174, 301,
    304, 340, 385, 387, 392,
    394–95, 426–27; court ap-
    pearances of, 159–62, 177,
    190; cross-examination of,
    249–51; at Elmira, 351, 354,
    355–56, 358–60; habeas
    corpus petition of, 394 n,
    399, 426–27; heroin addic-
    tion of, 89–90, 110, 249–
    250, 337; indictment of,
    160, 188; interrogation and
    confession of, 110–17 pas-
    sim, 122, 132–33, 172–78
    passim, 189, 221–22, 223,
    226–28, 229, 236, 237,
    249–51, 289, 294, 296–97,

Ortiz, Alfredo (continued)
    299, 302, 305, 312–13,
    314, 316, 318, 325–26,
    328, 330, 331, 332, 340,
    387, 392, 394, 424, 427;
    and lawyer, 161–62, 172–
    173; past record of, 72, 89–
    90, 172–73, 249–50, 337;
    refuses plea-bargaining, 161,
    173, 190–91, 270, 279;
    repudiates confession, 110,
    172–73, 216; sentencing of,
    336–41; testimony of, 249;
    trials of, 199–200, 202–7,
    214–30, 235–52, 260–71,
    273–81, 287–305, 311–21,
    322 n, 325–35
Ortiz, Alfredo (father), 86
Ortiz, Carlos, 72, 75, 85–88, 90,
    111, 112, 114–15, 124,
    125, 127, 135, 137–38,
    242, 408, 424, 425–26,
    436, 438; appeals of, 374–
    377, 383, 389–91, 392–93,
    395–99, 400; arraignment
    of, 139–41; at Auburn, 368,
    370–78, 384, 390–91, 397,
    400, 425; at Brooklyn
    House of Detention, 142–
    144, 154, 155–59, 162,
    172, 177, 274, 352; charges
    brutality, 95, 99, 101, 109,
    125, 157, 172–73, 174,
    223, 246–47, 248, 356;
    claims illegal arrest, 90–91,
    174; court appearances of,
    159–62, 177, 190; cross-
    examination of, 247–49; at
    Elmira, 350–58, 360; ha-
    beas corpus petition of, 425;

Ortiz, Carlos (*continued*)
  indictment of, 160, 188;
  interrogation and confession
    of, 92–101, 109–17 *passim,*
    122, 132–33, 172–78 *pas-*
    *sim,* 189, 205–6, 221–22,
    223, 226–28, 229, 236,
    237, 246–49, 289, 294,
    296–97, 302, 305, 312–13,
    314, 316, 318, 325–26,
    328, 330, 331, 332, 424,
    426; and lawyer, 161–62,
    172–73; past record of, 72,
    87, 88, 172–73, 246, 261,
    337–38; refuses plea-
    bargaining, 161, 173, 190–
    191, 270, 279; repudiates
    confession, 93–96, 101,
    172–73, 216; sentencing of,
    336–41; testimony of, 246–
    247; trials of, 199–200,
    202–7, 214–30, 235–52,
    260–71, 273–81, 287–305,
    311–21, 322 n, 325–35
Ortiz, Luisa: *see* Pomales, Luisa
  Ortiz
Ortiz, Maria, 407
Oswald, Russell G., 437, 439–40


**P**

Packer, Herbert L., 65, 80, 213,
  282, 382 n
Paley, William, 346
Parker, Chief William, 48
Parole: *see* Jails and prisons
Patterson, Thaddeus, 204

Pavese, Rose, 200, 217, 290
Pawlowski, William, 280
Peltz, Philip: as lawyer for
  D. Valencia, 275, 296, 327,
  329–30, 334
Pennsylvania, 422–23
Perella, Sylvia, 204
Perjury, 231; by defendants, 212,
  233–34, 387; by defense
  lawyers, 212, 233–34; by
  police, 231–32, 233; prosecutions for, 233; by witnesses, 231. *See also* Trial
  by jury
Perrone, Patrolman, 219–20, 292
Philadelphia, Pa., 12, 152, 404
Pietrangeli, Rudolph, 289
Plea-bargaining, 128–29, 192–
  197, 209, 422; defendants
  and, 195–97, 430, 432;
  defense lawyers and, 193–
  195, 196, 432; judges and,
  193–95, 196, 431; prosecutors and, 148, 179, 182,
  190–91, 193–95, 196, 431;
  and Supreme Court, 195,
  197
Police, 443; ambivalence of public toward, 47–48, 412; bitterness of, 48–50; brutality
  and, 47–48, 79, 104–5, 288,
  358, 387; corruption and,
  vii, viii, 47, 79; courts and,
  49, 432; crime clearance
  rate and, 50, 51, 121, 129–
  130, 404, 428; detectives,
  49–51; detention and, 82–
  83; duties of, 45–46; education of, 410–11, 429–30;

Police (*continued*)
illegal arrests by, 78, 82;
loyalty to each other, 78,
78 n, 79; and minorities, 61–
63, 67–68, 405, 410–11,
428, 429–30; perjury and,
231–32, 233; power, 30–31,
32, 404, 409–10, 415, 430;
and prejudice against former
criminals, 63, 67–68, 69;
reaction of, to Supreme
Court decisions, 120–21,
401, 412–13, 428; recruits
in, 47–48; and value systems
of justice, 80–81. *See also*
Confessions; Interrogations;
Investigations

*Police Power* (Chevigny), 232

Pomales, Luisa Ortiz, 85–91
*passim,* 135, 140, 141, 157,
160, 162, 169–71, 173,
199–200, 247, 251, 267,
268, 273, 274, 275, 288,
313, 329, 334, 335, 337,
339, 341, 371, 373, 374,
375, 376, 397, 407

Pope, Alexander, 253

Popolizio, Emanuel P., 389–90,
391, 392–93, 396

Powell, Frank, 23

Powell, Lewis F., 417

President's Commission on Law
Enforcement and Adminis-
tration of Justice: *see* Crime
Commission

Presumption of innocence: *see*
Justice, system of criminal;
Trial by jury

Preventive detention: *see* Justice,
system of criminal

Prisons: *see* Jails and prisons

Probable cause (for arrest): *see*
Police—illegal arrests by

Probation: *see* Justice, system of
criminal

Prosecution lawyers, 147, 149,
163, 178–84, 207, 418,
428, 432; attacks on credibility of witness, 230–31; and
judges, 179; and jury selection, 210; and plea-bargaining, 148, 179, 182, 190–91,
193–95, 196, 431; summa-
tion of, 260; and trial delays,
148, 431; in trials, 211, 308.
*See also* Trial by jury

Prosecutors: *see* Prosecution lawyers

Pruzansky, Wallace, 90, 91

*Psychology Today,* 107

Public defenders: *see* Defense
lawyers

Puerto Ricans, 14–15, 24, 86–87,
412; as inmates, 355, 370,
372, 436; muggings and,
6–7, 22, 27; Young Lords,
434. *See also* Ghettoes

Punishment: *see* Criminal sanctions; Jails and prisons

Purcell, John, 280

Puvogel, Patrolman, 39–41, 217–
218, 290–91, 318

## Q

Quincy, Josiah, Jr., 164

# R

Rabin, Benjamin, 390
Radzinowicz, Leon, 19
Raiford, Fla., 362
Ramirez, Toro (pseud.), 71
Rand Institute, 50, 79 n
Reading, Pa., 410
Reasonable doubt: *see* Justice,
    system of criminal
Recidivism: *see* Criminal sanc-
    tions; Jails and prisons
Red Hook Houses, Brooklyn, 29
Rehabilitation: *see* Criminal
    sanctions; Jails and prisons;
    Justice, system of criminal—
    and probation
Rehnquist, William, 418
Reid, John E., 106, 121
Rivers, Melvin, 21
Roberts, Burton, 180, 279, 418
Robles, Richard, 108
Rockefeller, Nelson, 440
Rockefeller, Winthrop, 362
Russo, Detective Salvatore, 53,
    57–58, 135–36, 140–41,
    266, 268, 269, 271, 319,
    329, 334, 335, 412–13;
    cross-examination of, 223–
    225, 297–301; interrogation
    of suspects, 75, 77–78, 92–
    101, 110–17, 122, 125–28,
    132–35, 176, 189, 190,
    205–6, 221–22, 223, 242,
    243–45, 246, 248, 249,
    250–51, 260, 263, 298–99,
    302, 304; investigation of
    crime, 44, 53–61, 68–74,
    78, 85, 90–91, 220, 226,

Russo, Detective Salvatore
    (*continued*)
    297, 314, 427; testimony of,
    200, 220–23, 296–97, 312,
    315, 316, 325–26
Ryan, Thomas, 204


# S

Sackel, George, 204
St. Louis, Mo., 30, 404
San Quentin Prison, 433, 434
Savage, Patrolman, 39–41
Scandinavia, 349
Scheer, Alexander E., 260, 418–
    419, 426; background of,
    185–87; offers plea-bargain-
    ing, 190–91; prosecutes
    Helmer case, 187–91, 199–
    200, 202–5, 215–30, 235–
    241, 243–52, 262–71
    *passim,* 275, 278, 280–81,
    289–305 *passim,* 313, 316,
    318–19, 327–36 *passim,*
    339, 341–43, 395
Schur, Edwin, 20
Seale, Bobby, 254, 255–56
Sebille, Bruce G., 253
Senate Subcommittee on Criminal
    Laws and Procedures, 33,
    120
Sentencing: *see* Criminal sanc-
    tions; Judges; Justice, system
    of criminal
Siegal, Herbert, 419–20; back-
    ground of, 276–77; as law-

Siegal, Herbert (*continued*)
    yer for D. Valencia, 275,
    278–79, 280–81, 289–305
    *passim,* 312–13, 315–17,
    320, 326–34 *passim,* 341–
    343
Sirhan, Sirhan, 344
Sixth Amendment, 144, 145, 192,
    281, 282, 283–84, 390, 399
Skolnick, Jerome, 81, 183, 192
Slums: *see* Crime—social causes
    of; Ghettoes
Smith, Mrs. (tenant), 38–39
Sobel, Nathan, 131
Sobell, Morton, 423
*Society of Captives, The* (Sykes),
    365
*Soledad Brother* (Jackson), 434
Soledad Prison, 363, 433
*Soul on Ice* (Cleaver), 434
Specter, Arlen, 120
Steele, William, 204
Stowe, Peter, 270
Strauss, Franz Josef, 405
Sullivan, Daniel, 168, 385–90,
    392–93, 397–98
Supreme Court, 131, 282, 427;
    and accomplice testimony,
    222, 385, 389, 391, 416;
    and appeals, 379,
    380, 394–98; and civil rights
    decisions, 33, 34, 48–50,
    81–82, 129–30, 154, 255,
    281, 283, 285, 309, 401,
    414, 417, 421–23; and con-
    fession cases, 104–5, 106,
    107, 118–19; and Four-
    teenth Amendment, 81; and

Supreme Court (*continued*)
    Fourth Amendment, 64–65,
    82–83, 281; Nixon's nomi-
    nations to, 213, 416–17,
    418, 420; and plea-bargain-
    ing, 195, 197. *See also*
    Fifth Amendment; Sixth
    Amendment; *individual
    cases*
Swat, 162–63
Sweden, 254–55
Sykes, Gresham, 365

**T**

Tarcher, Mary, 167
Texas, 434
Tilzer, George, 390
Torture: history of, 102–4. *See
    also* Confessions, physical
    force and
Trenton, N.J., 30
Trial by jury, 201–2, 207–14,
    230–59, 443; accomplice
    testimony in, 115, 117, 190,
    222, 296–97, 321, 416, 424,
    425, 427; arguments against,
    252–57; credibility in 230–
    231, 235, 244, 319; cross-
    examination in, 212, 256;
    defendants on stand in, 211,
    234–35, 236, 310, 321;
    defense lawyers and, 211,
    256, 308; due-process prin-
    ciple and, 208, 213–14, 283,
    286, 385, 415, 416, 418,
    421, 424, 441; evidence in,

Trial by jury (*continued*)
208, 210, 321, 322, 323,
422; factual truth in, 207–8,
209, 213; history of, 208;
Huntley hearing in, 205,
418; judges and, 212–13,
255, 258–59, 308; jurors
and, 209–12, 230, 231, 234,
252, 255–59, 285, 306, 308,
309–10, 322–24, 344; juvenile delinquents and, 415;
legal truth in, 207–8, 213;
length of, 255, 285; mass
communication and, 255–
256, 257, 309; past record
of defendant in, 234–35,
236, 310, 321; presumption
of innocence in, 169, 202,
208, 264, 321; prosecutors
and, 207, 211, 255, 308;
selection of jurors in, 202–3,
210, 257, 278–79, 431;
sequestration of jury in,
256–57; Sixth Amendment
and, 144, 145, 192, 282,
283; theatricalism in, 256;
witnesses in, 212, 230–32
*See also* Bench trials; Defense lawyers; Helmer case,
trials of; Judges; Justice,
system of criminal; Perjury;
Prosecution lawyers
Trial delays: *see* Courts—congestion in; Defense lawyers;
Prosecution lawyers
*Trouble with Cops, The*
(Deutsch), 78 n
Tucker Farm, Ark., 362

U

University of Chicago Law Review, 121
Uviller, H. Richard, 231

V

Valencia, Doel, 71–73, 89, 93,
95, 96, 98, 99, 101, 111,
114–15, 124, 125, 127,
135, 137–38, 407–8, 419;
arraignment of, 139–41; at
Brooklyn House of Deten-
tion, 142–44, 154, 155–59,
162, 177, 274; charges brutality, 112, 125, 157, 176,
242, 244, 246, 289, 298–
299, 304, 327; claims illegal
arrest, 78, 84–85, 177, 224,
228, 236, 240, 262, 299–
300; court appearances of,
159–62, 177, 190; cross-
examination of, 243–46;
heroin addiction of, 73, 75,
158, 221, 244, 407; indictment of, 160, 188; interrogation and confession of, 73,
76–78, 84–85, 110, 111–15,
116, 117, 122, 132, 133–
134, 174, 177, 178, 189,
221–22, 226–28, 229, 236,
237, 241–45, 289, 294,
296–97, 298, 302, 303–4,
312–13, 316, 318, 325–26,
327, 328–29, 342, 390; and
lawyer, 161–62, 176; past
record of, 73, 236, 241,

Valencia, Doel (*continued*)
243; refuses plea-bargaining, 161, 176, 190–91, 270, 279; release of, 341–43; repudiates confession, 110, 176, 236, 239, 243, 246, 262, 267, 317, 327, 329; testimony of, 241–43; trials of, 199–200, 202–7, 214–230, 235–52, 260–71, 273–281, 287–305, 311–21, 322 n, 325–35

Valencia, Idalia, 73–74, 158, 161, 162, 174–75, 176, 236, 239–41, 274, 275, 407–8

Valencia, Josie, 73, 75, 158, 162, 268, 273, 274, 329, 342

Varela, Ena, 39, 55–56, 59, 200, 217, 237, 239, 290, 315

Vera Institute of Justice, 150

Verdicts, by juries as compared with verdicts by judges, 235, 258–59, 324

Vermont, 431, 434

Victimology, 6–8

*Village Voice,* 196

*Violence and the Police* (Westley), 79 n

Violence Commission (National Commission on the Causes and Prevention of Violence), 18–19, 20, 22, 30, 31–32, 35, 362

Vitale, Vincent, 132–34, 176, 205, 229, 236, 239, 243, 244, 248–49, 262, 267, 269, 305, 316, 317, 318, 331

*Voir dire,* 202–3, 210, 257, 278–279, 431. *See also* Trial by jury—selection of jurors in

Voluntariness: *see* Arrests, illegal; Confessions; Fifth Amendment; Interrogations

# W

Wainwright, Louis, 362

Walker, Angel "Negrito," 93, 96, 98, 101, 112, 114–15, 116, 123–28, 132, 134, 135, 137–38, 221, 242, 247, 248, 250, 266, 274–75, 317, 318, 321, 408; arraignment of, 139–41; at Bronx House of Detention, 142, 158; charges brutality, 125, 288, 312; court appearances of, 160; dismissal of charges against, 160, 161, 178, 188, 190, 215–16, 316; heroin addiction of, 123, 124, 408; interrogation of, 117, 122–23, 125, 132, 288, 304; past record of, 123

Walling, Capt. George, 47

Waltzer, Gilbert, 279

Warren, Earl, 48, 50, 106, 255, 285, 414, 416

Washington (state), 366

Washington, D.C., 12, 29–30, 63, 64, 146, 404, 431

Wasserman, Irwin, 132, 133, 134, 229, 305, 314, 316

Weathermen, 434
Westley, William A., 78 n
White, Byron, 120, 129
Whitmore, George, 107–8, 110,
  262, 358
Wickersham Commission, 104
Wigmore, John Henry, 212
Wilson, Will, 307
*Wong Sun* v. *United States,* 340,
  395
Wylie-Hoffert case, 107–8

**Y**

Younger, Evelle J., 285
Younger, Irving, 232

**Z**

Zeisel, Hans, 235, 258–59, 310,
  323–24
Zimbardo, Philip, 107
Zimmerman, Irving, 280

# Morton Hunt

MORTON HUNT, a native of Philadelphia, attended Temple University, where he received a B.A., and did graduate work at the University of Pennsylvania. During World War II, he was in the U.S. Air Force, and, as a pilot, flew twenty-seven combat missions over Europe. After three years as a magazine staff researcher and writer, he became a free-lance writer in 1949 and has been one ever since. His interests cover a wide range, but he has specialized in the behavioral sciences, and most particularly in psychology. Over 300 of his articles have been published in such major national magazines as *The New Yorker, Redbook, Ladies' Home Journal,* and *Playboy.* Mr. Hunt's best-known books include *The Natural History of Love, The World of the Formerly Married,* and *The Affair.*

Mr. Hunt is married to Bernice Kohn, a well-known author of children's books. They live in Manhattan and East Hampton, New York.